CRITICAL COMPANION TO

# Alice Walker

CRITICAL COMPANION TO

# Alice Walker

## A Literary Reference to Her Life and Work

CARMEN GILLESPIE

**Critical Companion to Alice Walker: A Literary Reference to Her Life and Work**



Facts On File, Inc.
An imprint of Infobase Learning
132 West 31st Street
New York NY 10001

**Library of Congress Cataloging-in-Publication Data**
Gillespie, Carmen.
Critical companion to Alice Walker / Carmen Gillespie.
p. cm.
Includes bibliographical references and index.
ISBN 978-0-8160-7530-0 (acid-free paper) 1. Walker, Alice, 1944–
Handbooks, manuals, etc. I. Title.
PS3573.A425Z66 2011
813'.54—dc22 2010018639

Facts On File books are available at special discounts when purchased in bulk quantities for businesses, associations, institutions, or sales promotions. Please call our Special Sales Department in New York at (212) 967-8800 or (800) 322-8755.

You can find Facts On File on the World Wide Web at http://www.infobaselearning.com

Text design by Erika K. Arroyo
Composition by Hermitage Publishing Services
Cover printed by Yurchak Printing, Inc., Landisville, Pa.
Book printed and bound by Yurchak Printing, Inc., Landisville, Pa.
Date printed: April 2011

Printed in the United States of America

10 9 8 7 6 5 4 3 2 1

This book is printed on acid-free paper.

# Contents

# Acknowledgments

Walking into the Alice Walker exhibition at Emory University in 2009 was a thrilling experience and a tremendous validation and acknowledgment of the work that black women artists and scholars have accomplished. For all of the work that went into the exhibition and continues with the archives, I wish to thank Rudolph P. Byrd, Sarah Quigley, and the staff of the Alice Walker Archives at the Special Collections of Robert W. Woodruff Library. I also thank them for their generous grant of access and permission for me to photograph and publish the pictures of archival materials displayed during the exhibition.

Thank you also to the Alice Walker Society, particularly to Professor Beverly Guy-Sheftall for her insights about Walker, Spelman College, and Ruby Doris Smith-Robinson, and for her invitation to attend the symposium. I was fortunate to have had Beverly as a professor in graduate school, and her mentorship, activism, and generous insights still inspire.

The details of Walker's life and works are complicated, and this volume would not have been completed without the assistance, research, and contributions of the independent scholars Harold Bakst and Vincent Stephens, as well as the Bucknell University graduate students who worked with me on this project, Cara Maria Cambardella, Hannah Choi, and Kate Parker.

These volumes take an enormous amount of time and energy to research, organize, and write. I apologize to my family for my absorption in this task over the course of the last 28 months and for my neglect of you three. Harry, your support, patience, and love in this, as in all things, makes it all possible.

# Introduction

In April 2009, Emory University opened the Alice Walker Archives. The archives derive from the collection of papers, photographs, and memorabilia that Walker had donated to the university in 2007. As the literary critic Cheryl Wall noted during the daylong conference that accompanied the unveiling of the archives, the establishment of this collection represents a landmark moment in the history of African-American women's literary study. These archives mark the success that African-American women writers have achieved in the struggle for scholarly recognition of the narrative traditions

Entrance to the Emory University Alice Walker Archives Exhibition *(Photograph by Carmen Gillespie, courtesy of the Emory University Alice Walker Archives Exhibition, April 24, 2009)*

they have preserved, expressed, and invented in their works.

The one-day symposium at Emory, *A Keeping of Records: The Art and Life of Alice Walker,* included presentations by various scholars and significant individuals in Walker's life. Among them were her former professor and noted historian HOWARD ZINN as well as longtime friends such as the feminist activist and publisher GLORIA STEINEM, SPELMAN COLLEGE professor Beverly Guy-Sheftall, and Emory professor Rudolph P. Byrd. Byrd also served as the curator for the exhibit accompanying the archive's opening.

At the end of the event, Walker gave a talk reflecting on the opening of the archives, the day's events, and her life as a writer and public figure, interspersed with occasional readings of her poetry. At the beginning of her remarks, Walker said something that seemed, in some ways, to contradict the intention of the archives to preserve her legacy. She said that as visitors experience the impressive and elegant exhibit—featuring life-size photographs of her, time lines, a quilt she made during the filming of *The Color Purple,* sample manuscripts, and other relevant documents from Walker's life and career—they should know that she herself is not there and cannot be found in the materials. As a member of the audience, having seen the archives and exhibition and heard the accolades and discussion of Walker's work during the symposium, it occurred to me that she was right—that all of the attempts to document and elucidate this life can only begin to outline the complex realities of the life of this woman, Alice Malsenior Walker.

After the symposium, I made the easy drive from Atlanta to EATONTON, GEORGIA, Alice Walker's familial home. Although Eatonton has changed in many ways since Alice Walker called it home, it still retains a southern small-town feel, one that would have been intimidating for an out-of-town African American not long ago. After passing the signs for the Uncle Remus Museum that is the town's primary claim to fame, I stopped at the Eatonton/Putnam County Chamber of Commerce to get the map for what is called the Alice Walker Driving Tour. The women who were working there

A chronology of Alice Walker's life and art as displayed on a wall of the exhibition *A Keeping of Records: The Art and Life of Alice Walker,* which was held in celebration of the public opening of Walker's archives at Emory University in Atlanta, Georgia, in April 2009 *(Photograph by Carmen Gillespie, courtesy of the Emory University Alice Walker Archives Exhibition, April 24, 2009)*

that day seemed a bit disconcerted about the interest that I had in Walker and tried to direct my attention to the Remus museum and also to nearby Milledgeville, Georgia, the site of Andalusia, the home of FLANNERY O'CONNOR. The women finally directed me to a dilapidated scrapbook that contained yellowing articles about Walker, none of which had been published in the new millennium.

I was taken aback by the seeming disregard of Walker in her hometown, until I perused some of the articles. Many of them had been clipped from the local paper and referred to what seemed to be a long-standing controversy—whether the town should emphasize JOEL CHANDLER HARRIS or Alice Walker as its primary hometown artist.

After leaving the Chamber of Commerce, I followed the directions for the self-guided Alice Walker tour, which included stops for her childhood home, the family and community cemetery, and other Eatonton locations. Stopping at the church to photograph the site and other locations for this publication, I walked across the street to a building identified as Walker's childhood home. As I walked across a green field, lush in a way that only Ray Charles's singing "Georgia on My Mind" can evoke, I was stunned to see Alice Walker herself coming toward me. In an inevitably uncomfortable way, I said to her that I had enjoyed her comments at the opening of the archives and then asked if the place had been her childhood home. Puzzled, she said to me that the rolling hill we stood by was where her parents were buried. I felt like an interloper trespassing on sacred ground. I tried to explain that the marking for the Alice Walker tour was hard to find and that I had been outraged that it was so difficult to find and correctly identify the locations. Walker replied that she did not want the identifying markers to be clearer. Our awkward exchange ended as she walked back to the documentarians who had been filming her at her family's resting place.

I have thought often about this encounter and the connection between my intentions on that day and what must have seemed a touristic violation. There also seem to be some parallels with the effort to create this book. The encounter made me think again about Walker's assertion that she could not be located in any scholarly archive (or for that matter in any biographical essay or critical volume). There is a distinction between a person's life and a biographical or scholarly account, no matter how thorough. Although the facts about her life and works are outlined in this volume, Alice Walker herself remains elusive. As with that sunny Georgia afternoon in April, I hope I have not in my efforts here encroached upon sacrosanct territory.

I can write about African-American women writers' struggle for recognition because writers like Alice Walker have given me that permission and voice, so much so that today it is hard to imagine that before the 1960s, narratives engaging black female subjectivity were rare or, at least, very hard to find. Like Walker, I grew up in a tradition where the women whom I knew and loved seemed to be able do everything and anything. The women I knew did not talk about how much they worked, how they felt about what they were doing, or whether they were tired or not, and never ever would they provide anything but a superficial positive response to the question, "How are you doing?"

I was lucky to be born around the time that Alice Walker started publishing. She and other African-American women provided a peek into the daily lives of women like those in my family. From the beginning, Walker's work was not conditioned by some older traditions within African-American literature, traditions that required that public articulations by black writers always be constructed in the service of lifting up the race.

Walker has always been unafraid to expose the reality that African-American women and men experience the same life complexities as everyone else. At the same time, she also shows how common human experiences—difficulties with money, interpersonal relationships, identity formation, etc.—are complicated by race and gender. Walker's writings allow for the possibility that crisp collars may have become that way not only because the woman who ironed them, either for herself or for someone else, was competent; her efficiency might have been a channel for unexpressed anger as well as artistry.

Walker's first published essay was about the Civil Rights movement. Her engagements in those efforts and her commitments to feminism are apparent in all of her work. In spite of, or perhaps because of, the many controversies that have always surrounded her work, it is hard to imagine the landscape of African-American women's literature without the contributions of and conversations generated by *The Color Purple,* WOMANISM, *Possessing the Secret of Joy,* Walker's rediscovery of ZORA NEALE HURSTON, and so many other artistic, scholarly, and theoretical engagements and productions over the course of the last 45 or so years. In addition, Alice Walker was the first African-American woman to win the Pulitzer Prize for fiction, awarded in 1983 for *The Color Purple.* She also won the National Book Award in the same year.

Walker's work unapologetically and audaciously grounds the concerns, experiences, and perceptions of black women and of others who have not always been considered worthy of serious consideration. Her works have been integral to the literary and cultural reconsideration of the black female. Walker links her focus on and reassessment of black womanhood to global issues concerning oppression, inclusion and exclusion, sexuality, dominance, and violence, as well as the general health and survival of humanity and the natural world. Her voice has been confrontational and challenging. As an author who has sold more than 10 million books, she has delivered her stories and their attendant questions to receptive audiences around the world. It is my hope that this volume will assist in the navigations of the complex worlds inhabited and created by Alice Walker.

## How to Use This Book

Part I of this volume offers an overview of Alice Walker's life and career. Part II provides detailed examinations of her work, with separate sections covering her novels, short stories, poetry, nonfiction, children's books, and audio recordings. Each entry on a major work of fiction contains subentries describing the individual characters in the work. Part III includes entries on people, places, and topics that are important to Walker's work. They cover biographical background and historic, literary, and intellectual influences. Throughout the text, references to entries in Part III are presented in SMALL CAPITAL LETTERS to denote the reference. Part IV contains a chronology of Walker's life and bibliographies of her works and of secondary sources. Critical information appears in two or more locations to ensure consistency and accessibility.

# PART I

# *Biography*

# *Alice Walker*

(1944– )

Alice Walker has said in interviews that she donated her papers to Emory University in Atlanta, Georgia, because the safety and comfort she felt there suggested to her that it was the right place to house her material legacy. Although Walker now has homes in California and Mexico and has visited and lived all over the world, it is impossible to understand any part of her persona or history without placing her in the context of Emory, Atlanta, and the South, and most particularly, perhaps, the small town of EATONTON, GEORGIA, the place Walker's family called home when she was born on February 9, 1944.

The central image of Alice Walker from the 2009 exhibition, *A Keeping of Records: The Art and Life of Alice Walker,* which was held in celebration of the public opening of her archives at Emory University in Atlanta, Georgia, in April 2009. The photograph comes from Walker's personal collection. The original photograph is by R. Nathans, taken in 1976. *(Photograph of exhibit by Carmen Gillespie, courtesy of the Emory University Alice Walker Archives Exhibition, April 24, 2009)*

Walker's parents, William (Willie) Lee Walker and her mother, Minnie Lou (Tallulah) Grant Walker, had deep roots in Eatonton, a small town about an hour and a half's drive from Atlanta. According to family lore, Walker's first relative in Eatonton, May Poole, arrived in Georgia in the early years of the 19th century by walking from Virginia in a slave coffle while carrying her two children. Walker has said that this story was one of the primary motivations for her retaining her family surname. Wards Chapel is the name of the black community located on the outskirts of Eatonton that is the more precise home of Walker's family. Her parents were members of black families who had been longtime Wards Chapel community residents. The stories Walker heard about both sides of her family, as well as her own early experiences in Wards Chapel, were the catalyst for many of her later short stories, poems, essays, and novels.

Born in the last years of World War II as a member of the baby-boom generation, Alice Walker was the last of her mother and father's eight children. By all accounts, she was much loved by her family and adored by the community. As a baby, Walker won a church contest as the most beautiful infant, an event that set the stage for her early sense of exceptionalism and self-confidence. Walker has defined her early childhood as a time of freedom and, most significantly, as a time when she felt beautiful and affirmed. Although the Walker parents had little money, they were doing better by the time their daughter Alice was born, especially compared to the earliest days of their marriage, when they sometimes found it a challenge to feed and provide basic necessities for their large family. Walker's father, Willie Lee Walker, was a farmer who made his living as a sharecropper. As with most African Americans who found themselves a part of the system of SHARECROPPING, Willie Lee Walker had difficulty escaping its inherently exploitative financial arrangements.

Like the majority of African-American women living in the American rural South in the early and mid-20th century, Walker's mother, Minnie Lou (Tallulah) Grant Walker, worked in a variety of jobs. Walker was particularly influenced by her

Wards Chapel African Methodist Episcopal Church, the church Alice Walker and her family attended when she was a child *(Photograph by Carmen Gillespie)*

mother's skill in creating a garden for the family. Minnie Walker's garden was a pragmatic and aesthetic terrain from which the family ate. They also were also able to benefit from the beauty of its legendary flowers. Walker would later reinterpret her mother's skills metaphorically when she penned perhaps her most important collection of essays, *In Search of Our Mothers' Gardens.* In the volume, she understands and reconceives the garden as one of the few spaces where African-American women could cultivate their artistic and aesthetic proclivities in a practical and non-threatening way.

The children in the Walker family, including Alice, consisted of three girls and five boys. Walker was particularly adored by her older brother and sister, Bill and Ruth. Nearly seven years older than her baby sister, Ruth functioned as a mother figure during the early years of Alice's life. Walker was always considered bright and vivacious as a young child, and her family and teachers encouraged her to pursue her creative impulses. Although they did not have a great deal of education themselves, Walker's parents valued learning and insisted that each of their children attend school even though there was pressure for them to have their children leave school early to work as laborers. Walker was particularly precocious, and at age four, earlier than most of her peers, she began a distinctive career as a student. She particularly loved to read and write. She remembers herself as an outgoing and engaging child, but her sense of well-being in the world was forever altered at age eight as a result of an accident.

While playing with her brothers Curtis and Robert, a unintentional shot from one of her brother's BB guns found its mark in Alice's eye, resulting in permanent blindness. Walker has maintained that the accident was a catalyst for her retreat into the world of books and to the less-conspicuous expressive venue of writing, particularly of composing poetry. She has written extensively about the trauma of the event and the transformative impact it had on her sense of self. Where she had felt lovely and enviable, she now perceived herself as ugly and as someone worthy of scorn and derision.

As Walker has written, the other major traumatic outcome originating with the accident was the fact that her brothers made her lie about it.

As children afraid of getting in trouble, Curtis and Robert made her tell their parents that the injury had been accidentally self-inflicted. Although her parents eventually learned the truth, this lie compounded the incident for Walker as she began to feel responsible for her impairment and pain. She also resented that she was the only one to suffer the consequences of her brothers' actions, since she felt punished by the great pain she experienced and also did not feel that her brothers had to bear any responsibility for the irreparable and permanent harm they had caused. By self-report, Walker began to feel alienated from her family and environs.

The rural world that had engaged Walker prior to the accident became a solitary place for the young woman. This isolation and the attendant psychological and emotional turn inward led her to become introspective and to use her intellect and creativity as solace and sanctuary. She also began to develop a writer's objective perspective, and her home became her first field of observation. This developing gaze also initiated a lifelong intimacy with the subtleties of the natural world.

A photograph of Alice Walker's parents, Minnie Lou (Tallulah) Grant Walker and Willie Lee Walker. The photograph was on display at the 2009 exhibition *A Keeping of Records: The Art and Life of Alice Walker,* which was held in celebration of the public opening of Walker's archives at Emory University in Atlanta, Georgia, in April 2009. The photograph is from Alice Walker's personal collection; the original photographer is unknown. *(Photograph of exhibit by Carmen Gillespie, courtesy of the Emory University Alice Walker Archives Exhibition, April 24, 2009)*

As previously mentioned, Walker named her mother as a source of inspiration for her creative life. Minnie Walker encouraged her daughter's pursuits and fostered creativity with the media available to her: sewing, cooking, storytelling, and gardening. Although Walker's family encouraged her as a child and young girl to pursue her interests, the family's home was frequently violent, mostly as a result of her father Willie Lee's explosive temper. Willie Lee's behavior affected and influenced Walker's brothers, who also expressed their emotions through violence. Walker has written about her discovery as she came of age of a sexual double standard in her family. She grew to understand that her brothers were encouraged to become sexual beings, whereas she and her sisters were led to believe that for them premarital sexuality was akin to death, at least a social death, which held the threat of excommunication from the family and community.

At a critical juncture in her development—the age of 14—one of Walker's brothers, Bill, arranged for her to have cataract surgery in Boston. Although the operation did not result in improvement to her eyesight, the cataract that had formed in Walker's eye as a consequence of scar tissue from the accident was removed, resulting in a dramatic improvement in her appearance and self-perception. With increased self-esteem, Walker began again to perform as a superlative and popular student, and she graduated from Butler-Baker High School as the valedictorian and the prom queen. As a result of her eye injury, which was considered by the college to be a disability, in 1961 Walker received a scholarship to attend SPELMAN COLLEGE in Atlanta.

While at Spelman, a historically black women's institution, Walker became involved in the heady and escalating CIVIL RIGHTS MOVEMENT, the activism of which had a particular resonance in Atlanta. As an attendee at the 1963 March on Washington and at other landmark events in the movement, she began to understand and to seek redress for some of the personal injustices she, her family, and her community had suffered. Her independent study and formal education began to reveal to her the ways in which racial oppression in the United

The dirt road in Eatonton, Georgia, that leads to Alice Walker's childhood home *(Photograph by Carmen Gillespie)*

States is connected to larger narratives and historical systems of exclusion and discrimination. Walker's classroom investigations and intellectual activities were amplified by experiential learning outside of the classroom.

In addition to her domestic activism, Walker traveled to Europe to attend the World Festival of Youth and Students in 1962. She also had as mentors the influential and noted scholars and activists HOWARD ZINN and STAUGHTON LYND. The mentorship of these intellectually radical and progressive men was a critical factor in Walker's decision to leave the South and Spelman and to transfer to SARAH LAWRENCE COLLEGE.

Lynd assisted Walker's transfer to Sarah Lawrence by persuading his mother, Helen Lynd, a professor at Sarah Lawrence, to encourage the institution to give Walker a scholarship. With this funding, Walker was able to transfer to Sarah Lawrence College and to relocate to New York in December 1963. According to her own assessments, Sarah Lawrence greatly expanded her creative and intellectual universe. During her time at the college, she again traveled overseas, this time to study in Uganda and Kenya. Walker also found writing mentors at Sarah Lawrence who would prove pivotal to her relatively seamless transition to professional writing. The poets MURIEL RUKEYSER and JANE COOPER encouraged her authorial aspirations and paved the way for her to access publishing venues.

Although the Sarah Lawrence years were intellectually productive and generative, Walker found herself contemplating suicide when she unintentionally became pregnant. The father of the child was a white Bowdoin student, David DeMoss. Walker terminated the pregnancy and found herself at an emotional nadir. In 1966, she completed her undergraduate studies and graduated from Sarah Lawrence. The work Walker had engaged in as a student led to her first publications. While still a student at Sarah Lawrence, with the assistance of Muriel Rukeyser, she wrote a short story entitled "To Hell with Dying," which, in 1967, became her first published story. It appeared in the collection *The Best Stories by Negro Writers,* edited by the legendary African-American writer and poet LANGSTON HUGHES.

After graduation, Walker went to work for a short time for the New York City welfare office, but less than a year later she received a grant to continue her activism with the Civil Rights movement by returning to the South to work for the Legal Defense Fund (LDF), an arm of the NATIONAL ASSOCIATION FOR THE ADVANCEMENT OF COLORED PEOPLE (NAACP) in Mississippi. Her supervisor in this position was the influential attorney and founder of the Children's Defense Fund, Marian Wright Edelman. While in Mississippi, in 1966, Walker met a young lawyer, MELVYN LEVENTHAL, who had also come to Mississippi as an activist to combat racism and discrimination through legal channels. The two married in New York in March 1967 before returning to Mississippi later that year.

Leventhal was born to a Jewish family in Brooklyn, New York, in 1943. His father abandoned the family when Mel was a boy, an experience Leventhal has described as defining. He sometimes felt like an abused outcast; he later connected this experience to his strong sense of empathy for the oppressed. This tendency to identify with the plight of others may have led him to become involved in the Civil Rights movement. While completing his studies in law at New York University, he periodically traveled south to work for various civil rights organizations.

After interning with the Student's Civil Rights Research Council during the summer of 1965, Leventhal interned in the summer of 1966 for the LDF. While on assignment he met Walker. The pair worked together to interview poor and disenfranchised black residents, and they both suffered overt and threatening harassment even before they became a couple. Walker has stated her belief that the two may have bonded as a result of their shared vulnerability.

While working as an activist, Walker continued writing. She had her first article published when she won an essay contest held by the *American Scholar Magazine*. The essay was published in a fall 1967 edition with the title "The Civil Rights Movement: What Good Was It." The following year, 1968, Walker published her first book, *Once,* a collection of poems. She also began working as a creative writing instructor at Jackson State College, replacing the well-known African-American poet Margaret Walker, who was on leave.

Walker and Leventhal struggled with the emotional and psychological difficulties of living in Mississippi as an activist and interracial couple. The risk that they took by living together at that time was potentially fatal. Leventhal worked long hours with passionate devotion to fighting against segregation, and Walker committed her time to writing and teaching. During the traumas of 1968, including the assassinations of MARTIN LUTHER KING, JR., and Robert Kennedy, Walker and Leventhal experienced a personal loss with the miscarriage of their first child. Shortly thereafter, Walker became pregnant again, and in 1969, she gave birth to the couple's only surviving child, REBECCA GRANT WALKER.

Throughout her career, Walker has written about her experiences as a wife and mother in ambivalent terms. The early years of Walker's marriage to Leventhal seem heady and infused with the kind of comradeship that comes from a relationship grounded in a mutual and deeply compatible vision of the world. The two appeared to grow closer as a result of the external threat that was a daily and tangible reality in the late 1960s American South, particularly in Mississippi. They cast themselves and their relationship as a direct counter to the racism and segregation that was the pervasive norm. The couple faced not only the ire of white southern racists but were also criticized by blacks who felt that Walker's marriage to a white man was somehow a betrayal—a naive disregard for the histories of violence that black men and women have experienced at the hands of white men.

Leventhal and Walker also experienced alienation from family and friends who did not approve of their union. A particularly vociferous antagonist was Leventhal's mother, Miriam Leventhal, who sat shivah (the Jewish mourning ceremony for the dead) for her son when the couple announced their marriage. In addition to the disapproval of family members on both sides, Walker and Leventhal lost some longtime friends as a result of their inability to accept the marriage.

Walker has also written about the complexities of her attempts to negotiate motherhood and her life as a writer. As a young mother to her daughter Rebecca, Walker has written that she often felt isolated and conflicted. The familiar dilemmas presented by parenting were complicated for her and for Leventhal both by the unrelenting nature of the work they were committed to and, more precariously, by the constant influx of threats from anonymous sources that amplified the normal pressures and tensions associated with the arrival of a new child. On the other hand, Walker has also noted the ways in which becoming a mother enriched and transformed her perspectives on the world. In the early years of their relationship, Rebecca's existence provided a new urgency to Walker's desire to improve the world and to address injustice. The ambiguity of the nature of the relationship between her and her daughter would later come to a head in Rebecca's adulthood and again when Rebecca herself became a mother.

When Rebecca was one year old, Walker published her first novel, *The Third Life of Grange Copeland* (1970). This appeared in the same year as a number of important debut works by other African-American women writers, including Toni Cade Bambara, Toni Morrison, and Maya Angelou.

Walker loosely based *The Third Life of Grange Copeland* on her understanding of and relationship with her father and her grandfathers. She learned from her older brothers and sisters that her father had been a different man when they were children. This notion of her father having transformed from a gentle, loving soul to a violent, distant enigma energized her desire to explore the threatening, sometimes fatal, dysfunctions of some relationships between the men and women who inhabited the communities of her childhood. Walker's novel explores these positive and negative male transformations. The titular protagonist, Grange Copeland, begins his adult life—his first life—as a man completely controlled by nonexistent and deficient examples of manhood and responsibility, and after his initial efforts to love and support a wife and child fail, he succumbs utterly to complete self-indulgence and abuse. Over the course of the novel, during his second life, Grange grows and comes to understand that his actions have consequences. He spends the last third of his life attempting to make amends for the consequences of his flaws and learns how to love in an authentic, nurturing, and selfless way. Grange tries to redeem himself by repairing the damage he has caused and, in the process, enriches and expands his own life and humanity. Fundamentally, the novel makes the assertion that circumstances, no matter how oppressive, do not have to be determinative.

*The Third Life of Grange Copeland* was instrumental in establishing Walker's reputation. It remains one of her most highly regarded works.

After the publication of her first novel, Walker decided to return to the North, which she was able to do as a result of a fellowship she received from Radcliffe University. The fellowship supported her as she wrote her second novel, *Meridian.* According to her biographer, Evelyn C. White, while at Wellesley College in 1972 Walker created and taught the first course on African-American women writers offered at a U.S. institution of higher education. While working on *Meridian,* she published her first collection of short stories, *In Love & Trouble: Stories of Black Women* (1973); another collection of poems, *Revolutionary Petunias & Other Poems* (1973); and a children's book, *Langston Hughes, American Poet* (1974). These publications expanded her reputation and readership. During this period, Walker's father, Willie Lee, died in 1973 after a long series of illnesses.

In the same year her father died, Walker discovered that when the African-American writer ZORA NEALE HURSTON died in 1960, she had gone unrecognized and was buried in an unmarked grave. Consequently, in 1973, Walker traveled to the field in Florida where Hurston was buried, found what she believed was her unmarked grave, and erected a tombstone on the site. Because of this posthumous recognition, as well as Walker's writings about the forgotten, prolific author, Hurston's work reentered the canon, and she has become one of the best-known American women writers.

*Meridian* appeared in 1976, the bicentennial year of the United States's founding and immediately after the years when Walker was most personally involved in the activism of the Civil Rights movement. As a consequence, the novel responds to the personal and interpersonal costs of the violence and unrelenting stress experienced by the workers in the movement. It engages the complexities of race within the movement, particularly the issue of interracial relationships between white women and black men. Through the preoccupations of its protagonist, Meridian Hill, the novel also reflects issues that were immediate concerns for Walker herself during the mid-1960s: the transition from a rural to an urban life as a young black woman; the tension

This grove in Eatonton, Georgia, is across the road from the church young Alice Walker and her family attended, Wards Chapel African Methodist Episcopal Church. Walker's mother and father, Minnie Lou (Tallulah) Grant Walker and Willie Lee Walker, and other family members are buried here. *(Photograph by Carmen Gillespie)*

between reproductive freedom and motherhood; the adult relationships between women and their mothers; and the conflicts between art and activism, self-sacrifice and autonomy. Walker has said that Meridian is also a partial portrait of a Spelman graduate and activist named RUBY DORIS SMITH-ROBINSON, who died at age 25 after devoting her energy to the movement and to her work with the STUDENT NON-VIOLENT COORDINATING COMMITTEE (SNCC).

The setting for *Meridian* is the segregated South and a black college campus called Saxon that closely resembles Atlanta's Spelman College, where Walker and Smith-Robinson met. The text traverses the culturally and ideologically fraught landscape of players in the Civil Rights movement through the lens of an idealistic protagonist who functions as a kind of allegorical figure for the determination and devotion of civil rights workers. The success of *Meridian* allowed Walker greater latitude as an artist.

Following her Radcliffe fellowship, and after a brief return to Mississippi, Walker told her husband that she wanted to relocate back to New York. The couple moved north in 1974, although there was increasing tension and unhappiness in the relationship. In 1976, Mel Leventhal and Alice Walker divorced. Subsequently, Rebecca lived alternately with her mother and then with her father, in two-year increments, until her adulthood.

In 1978, while in the middle of writing another novel that would become her most famous, acclaimed, and controversial—*The Color Purple* (1982)—Walker moved from New York to San Francisco. She also began a 13-year relationship with an old friend, ROBERT ALLEN, whom she had met at Spelman. Before the publication of *The Color Purple,* Walker had three other works appear in print: a book of poetry, *Good Night Willie Lee, I'll See You in the Morning* (1979); an edited collection of Zora Neale Hurston's writings, *I Love Myself When I am Laughing . . and Then Again When I Am Looking Mean and Impressive* (1979); and a collection of short stories, *You Can't Keep a Good Woman Down* (1981). Although the response to these publications was generally positive, nothing could have prepared Walker for the avalanche of critical attention and fame that came with the publication of *The Color Purple.*

*The Color Purple* is the story of the journey of Celie, the novel's central protagonist, as she progresses from a state of virtual invisibility and degradation to wholeness and graceful communion with herself and her community. The novel is epistolary in style, told through a series of letters that Celie writes, mostly to God, sometimes to her absent sister, Nettie, and, toward the end of the book, to the universe at large.

Through these letters, Celie is able to negotiate the horrors in her life, which include her impregnation twice at the hands of the man she believes is her father and an early marriage to a man who does not love her and treats her with abuse and neglect. Celie's husband, Albert, abuses her partly as a consequence of his unrequited love for another woman, his mistress Shug Avery. As a result of Albert's actions, Celie also endures the unexplained and unresolved absence of her beloved sister Nettie for most of her life.

An unexpected love for Shug Avery sets Celie on the path toward a greater understanding of herself and helps her to begin to forgive those who have wronged her and have tried to constrain her life. Walker's characterizations are particularly strong in *The Color Purple,* with figures like Nettie, Mr. ——, Harpo, Sophia, and Squeak surrounding Celie with a vibrant and complicated universe of compatriots and antagonists. The novel tackles issues of incest, domestic violence, lesbianism, religion, racism, poverty, and motherhood as manifested in a poor, black, southern community—a task that could not escape strong positive and negative responses from various constituencies.

The fervor surrounding *The Color Purple* was an unprecedented response to a work of African-American women's fiction. The book received critical acclaim and in 1983 won the Pulitzer Prize for fiction and the National Book Award for fiction. The novel also received scathing critiques, most of which centered on the charge that it presents black male characters in negative ways.

After winning the Pulitzer Prize, *The Color Purple* became an international best seller and catapulted Walker to an unexpected level of fame. In 1981, just before its publication, her mother, Minnie Grant Walker, suffered a stroke that kept her bedridden for the rest of her life.

In the same year that she won the Pulitzer Prize for *The Color Purple,* Walker published what is, arguably, her most important collection of essays. *In Search of Our Mothers' Gardens* is an anthology of her nonfiction writing, spanning the years 1967–82. Walker divides her collection into four parts, and the anthology features 36 essays, letters, speeches, reviews, and previously unpublished pieces. Most of the collected works were previously published in magazines such as MS. MAGAZINE and *Redbook,* as well as scholarly journals such as *The Black Scholar* prior to their collection in *In Search of Our Mothers' Gardens.* The wide-ranging collection is best known for its opening pages, wherein Walker provides various definitions of her term *womanist,* as "a black feminist or feminist of color," "a woman who loves other women, sexually and/or nonsexually," and a lover of music, dance, the moon, and self, among other open-ended possibilities. It concludes with the statement that "womanist is to feminist as purple to lavender" (xi–xii).

According to Walker's definition of WOMANISM, FEMINISM becomes a term that is inappropriately narrow for African-American women, as well as for others who embrace an inclusive and humanist vision of the world. Although womanism shares commonalities with feminism, it represents an expansion beyond the traditional feminist critical and activist agendas.

The introduction of the term *womanism* into the field of African-American women's writing has spawned a debate over its implications. Interdisciplinary critics who have embraced womanism as a foundational philosophy for their work include historians and theologians such as Darlene Clark Hines, Elsa Barkely Brown, and Katie Cannon. Womanism is an important literary critical movement that has influenced scholars of African-American women's literature, including Barbara Christian, Majorie Pryse, Hazel Carby, Valerie Smith, and others, to analyze literature in womanist terms (that is, by relying on analyses of SELF-AFFIRMATION, tradition, matrilineal inheritance, and so on). Walker's definition transformed the field of black women's literary criticism.

Throughout, *In Search of Our Mothers' Gardens* builds on Walker's definition of womanism. Walker is highly attuned to the intersections of race, class, gender, and sexuality and the relevance of these spheres to social and political constructions and activism. She also invokes international struggles against racial supremacy and imperialism in her discussions of domestic oppressions.

Several core themes recur in the collection, particularly Walker's personal quest to recover the overlooked history of black female artists. Centrally, she is concerned with the dearth of scholarly attention to black female authors such as Zora Neale Hurston, who Walker regards as a literary foremother. Hurston figures in many of Walker's discussions of the forgotten histories of African-American women. Walker champions her array of complex depictions of African-American female subjectivity in such essays as "Zora Neale Hurston: A Cautionary Tale and a Partisan View," "Looking for Zora," and "If the Present Looks Like the Past What Does the Future Look Like?" Walker employs the trope of searching in her explorations of her literary models and of other female artists. An additional focus of her essays is the important influence of a range of writers on the way she perceives literature and her craft of writing, including Hurston, Langston Hughes, FLANNERY O'CONNOR, BESSIE HEAD, LEO TOLSTOY, and VIRGINIA WOOLF.

In 1984, flush from her literary successes and the publication of another volume of poetry, *Horses Make a Landscape More Beautiful,* Walker, her colleague BELVIE ROOKS, and her then partner, the scholar, journalist, and writer Robert Allen, began a literary press called WILD TREES PRESS. Wild Trees focused on publishing works with a feminist perspective. Titles published by the press include J. California Cooper's 1984 short-story collection, *A Piece of Mine;* JoAnne Brasil's *Escape from Billy's Bar-B-Que* (1985); Cynthia Stokes Brown and Septima Poinsette Clark's 1986 autobiography of Clark, *Ready from Within: Septima Clark and the Civil Rights Movement,* which won an American Book Award; Charlotte Méndez's *Condor and Hummingbird* (1986); Henry Crowder's *As Wonderful as All That?: Henry Crowder's Memoir of His Affair with Nancy Cunard, 1928–1935* (1987); and Madi Kertonegoro's *The Spirit Journey: Stories and Paintings of Bali* (1988). The trio decided to end publishing operations in 1988, as the work had become overwhelming and had exceeded their original commitment to and conceptual vision of the project.

In 1985, the year following the founding of Wild Trees Press, Walker's trust in QUINCY JONES and STEVEN SPIELBERG was manifested in the release of the film version of *The Color Purple.* The film's screenplay was written by MENNO MEYJES, a Dutch-born screenwriter and director who had immigrated to the United States with his parents in 1972. His screenplay earned Meyjes an Academy Award nomination and launched his career as a screenwriter. Walker herself had written a screenplay for the novel, but Spielberg found it at odds with his vision of the film, whereupon she gave her approval to Meyjes's version. She was intimately involved in the film's production, a process she has written about extensively in her book *The Same River Twice: Honoring the Difficult, A Meditation on Life, Spirit, Art, and the Making of the Film* The Color Purple *Ten Years Later* (1996). In that book, Walker includes her own version of the screenplay, entitled *Watch for Me in the Sunset,* in order to reveal her original aspirations for the movie version of her story. She worked closely with Spielberg and Jones on the casting and the music, and she even insisted that at least half of those employed in making the film be African American or people of color.

There is no simple assessment that can be made about either the film itself or the responses it generated. According to Walker, some problematic distinctions between the novel and the film exist in the latter's emphasis on Mr. ——'s brutality without the counterbalance of the story of Nettie and Celie's real father, the recasting of Mr. —— and Harpo's incompetence as buffoonish and comic, and the reduction of the physical and emotional intimacy between Celie and Shug to a single kiss. Predictably, many of the same voices who had protested Walker's novel on the grounds that its depiction of black men is prejudicial and lacking nuance found the same flaws in the film.

The film's strengths lie in its performances and in Spielberg's ability to render a visually striking setting for these enactments to unfold. The film also generated stellar performances from cast members Danny Glover as Albert/Mr. ——, Margaret Avery as Shug Avery, Willard E. Pugh as Harpo Johnson, Akosua Busia as Nettie Harris, Adolph Caesar as Old Mister Johnson, and Rae Dawn Chong as Squeak. Particularly inspired are the debut performances of WHOOPI GOLDBERG as Celie and OPRAH WINFREY as Sofia. Although many aspects of the film have been criticized, there is almost universal praise for the performances of these two then newcomers. Goldberg was discovered by the director Mike Nichols, under whose mentorship she developed her one-woman act into the Broadway show *Whoopi Goldberg.* Spielberg saw Goldberg's Broadway performance while he was in the midst of casting the movie *The Color Purple.* After her inspired and convincing role as Celie in the film version of the novel, Goldberg was nominated for an Academy Award as best actress, and she won a Golden Globe for her performance. After her triumph in *The Color Purple,* she became a household name and a popular performer. The movie roles available to her as a black actress were limited; however, she has made a reputation of creating appealing and memorable characters from weak material.

*The Color Purple* also marked a pivotal transition for another burgeoning celebrity, Oprah Winfrey. After a stint as a television anchor in Baltimore, in 1984, Winfrey moved to Chicago, where she helped raise the ratings of a local television talk show. After her successful revitalization, the show was renamed *The Oprah Winfrey Show,* which was first broadcast in 1986.

Shortly before Winfrey began broadcasting nationally, as legend has it, Quincy Jones was in Chicago on business and was watching television in his hotel when he saw her then local talk show. He felt immediately that she would be the perfect person to cast as Sofia, one of the major characters in the novel. Although Winfrey says that she had wanted always to be an actress, she had little experience before being cast in the film.

She was a natural for the part. Having grown up in the rural South, Winfrey was able to identify with Walker's characters on a personal level, and she brought realism and authenticity to her portrayal of the long-suffering Sofia. Winfrey has said that her experiences making the film catapulted her to another level of understanding and awareness—one that allowed her to make her talk show the successful behemoth that it has become. As a result of her role as Sofia, Winfrey was nominated for both a Golden Globe and an Academy Award. She was also the producer of the Broadway production of the musical version of *The Color Purple* (2005).

Despite criticism, censorship, protests, and endless controversy, the cinematic version of *The Color Purple* proved a critical and commercial success. In addition to winning a Golden Globe for Goldberg, the film was nominated for 11 Academy Awards and five Golden Globe Awards, and it won an

This marker on the Eatonton and Putnam County Alice Walker Driving Tour identifies the house in which Walker grew up. *(Photograph by Carmen Gillespie)*

ASCAP Award, the Director's Guild of America Award, and a National Board of Review Award. Perhaps most notably for Walker's family, the film's premiere was held in her hometown of Eatonton, Georgia.

In *The Same River Twice,* Walker not only discusses the process of collaboration that resulted in the film version of *The Color Purple,* she also articulates what she experienced in terms of the film's personal costs. During the production, Walker's mother was ill. Walker's long-term relationship with Robert Allen began to suffer, and her daughter became pregnant and had an abortion. In spite of these personal challenges, she continued writing and in 1988 released her next collection of essays, entitled *Living By the Word: Selected Writings, 1973–1987,* as well as the children's book *To Hell with Dying.*

Walker's relationship with Robert Allen began to transition from a romantic involvement to a friendship. She also became more public about her bisexuality and her openness to having relationships with women. In 1989, Walker published her fourth novel, *The Temple of My Familiar,* a complex narrative that attempts no less than a rewriting of world history. The novel features an enormous array of characters whose lives intersect and overlap as the plot explores the intricacies of racism, nationalism, sexism, heterosexism, environmental desecration, economic exploitation, and a myriad of other concerns.

Although it introduces Walker's most voluminous fictional cast, *The Temple of My Familiar* focuses most of its storytelling energies on four main characters: Carlotta, Fanny, Suwelo, and Arveyda. The novel's title reveals its central metaphor, an exploration of the relationship between the inner and outer self, the spirit and the body, the FAMILIAR and the temple. Each of the central characters embarks on a journey of personal self-discovery in order to dislodge the detritus that is the external construction of the self and, by so doing, creates harmony and synchronization between the body and the spirit. In addition to the adventures of Walker's four protagonists, there is a matriarchal, shape-shifting goddess figure named Lissie Lyles, who becomes the voice of truth, the narrative's GRIOT.

The novel is also a reprise of sorts of *The Color Purple.* Although Walker has said that neither *The Temple of My Familiar* nor *Possessing the Secret of Joy* (1992) are sequels, several familiar characters from that novel revisit in *The Temple of My Familiar* including Celie, Shug Avery, Albert, Sofia, Olivia, and Nettie. Fanny, one of the central characters in *Temple,* is Celie's granddaughter. The characters progress through various moments of revelation until the cathartic end, where each of them finds sanctuary in self-love and mutual admiration. Although the novel's critical reception was mixed, *The Temple of My Familiar* was a best-seller and remains a book frequently taught in college classrooms.

In 1991, in addition to ending her long-term relationship with Robert Allen, Walker published her third children's book, *Finding the Green Stone,* and her fifth poetry collection, *Her Blue Body Everything We Know.* The next year, she released *Possessing the Secret of Joy,* the third in a loose trilogy of Walker novels, including *The Color Purple* and *The Temple of My Familiar,* with overlapping characters. The book's central character is Tashi, who came to the United States with Samuel, Nettie (Celie's sister), Olivia (Celie's daughter), and Adam (Celie's son) when the family left Africa after many years serving as missionaries to the Olinka people. Adam and Tashi are married by the time the family arrives in the United States and reunites with Celie. Tashi has also undergone the procedure of female genital mutilation.

Alice Walker in 2009 *(Photograph by Carmen Gillespie)*

*Possessing the Secret of Joy* spirals outward from that most pivotal moment in Tashi's life and moves in and out of time to trace the roots of the practice generally as well as to demonstrate the emotional, psychological, and physical impacts of this trauma on Tashi, on her friends and family, on other women who have had this procedure done to them, on communities that condone its practice, and on those cultures that refuse to acknowledge and intervene on behalf of those who unwillingly experience female genital mutilation.

The novel was controversial and provoked disparate reactions. Janet Turner Hospital's review in the *New York Times* asserted that, at its best, the novel resonates with the voice and impact of Greek drama. Other critics felt that Walker's background as a prominent western writer obscured the voices of the non-Western activists who had spoken out against the practice before her. She also was accused of writing without sufficient nuance regarding the different ways the procedure is practiced in different countries and about the relationships between the ritual and colonialism, racism, sexism, and violence. Nonetheless, the novel became a best-seller, and along with Walker's follow-up on the subject in the form of the documentary and companion book *Warrior Marks: Female Genital Mutilation and the Sexual Blinding of Women, Possessing the Secret of Joy* helped to bring worldwide awareness and attention to the subject of female genital mutilation.

In 1993, expanding her fictional treatment of this subject to documentary form, Walker, in partnership with the British filmmaker PRATIBHA PARMAR, created the film and companion book *Warrior Marks: Female Genital Mutilation and the Sexual Blinding of Women.* Parmar and Walker's film has as a thematic repeating image footage of a dancing African woman who seems to represent a counterpoint, a hope for liberation and freedom from the practice of female genital mutilation for the millions of women throughout the world who have been subjected to this practice.

The video mainly consists of interviews with various individuals whose stories relate either directly or tangentially to the topic of female genital mutilation. Included is an interview with Walker herself as she tells the story of the blinding of her eye and explains how that experience allowed her to understand and to empathize with the pain and trauma of mutilation. Walker's story also helps to illuminate the subtitle of the book and film, *The Sexual Blinding of Women.* Walker explains that the permanent damage retained by injured individuals should be understood as triumphant markers of their survival—warrior marks.

After a long illness, Minnie Lou (Tallulah) Walker Grant, Walker's mother, died from cardiac arrest in 1993.

In 1994, Walker collected all of her published short fiction into a compilation entitled *The Complete Stories.* She also changed her middle name to Tallulah-Kate in honor of her mother and maternal grandmother. Two years later, she published *The Same River Twice* to mark the 10-year anniversary of the release of the film version of *The Color Purple,* and in 1997, she released her collection of essays *Anything We Love Can Be Saved.* In this collection, Walker writes about nearly every aspect of her life and experiences. She frames these disparate pieces within her examination of the complex dynamics involved in constructing a life of activism. Walker asserts that writing is an essential strategy against oppression.

In 1998, Walker published her novel *By the Light of My Father's Smile.* This book received a mixed critical response. Some critics, including Francine Prose of the *New York Times,* found the book to consist largely of one-dimensional characterizations and new-age platitudes. Still others found the book to be a radical statement on the need to reevaluate and dismantle the dichotomy between sexuality and spirituality. Critics who praised the text for this accomplishment included Karen Schechner in the *Weekly Alibi.*

In spite of its mixed reviews, *By the Light of My Father's Smile* became another Walker best-selling novel. It traces the experiences of a family whose last name is Robinson. When their daughters, Susannah and Magdalena, are young, the Robinsons—Langley, the mother, and her husband, the family's patriarch (whose first name is not provided in the novel)—relocate their family to a remote location in Mexico. Robinson is dead for most of the text and spends his posthumous time watching his daughters and hoping to make amends for the wrongs he committed and for the consequent damage that he caused them through his behavior as their father. The novel concludes with the death of Susannah, who has become a writer.

The new millennium did not slow Walker's productivity. In 2000, she published a new collection entitled *The Way Forward Is with a Broken Heart,* which received generally strong reviews when it appeared. The collection is in part a fictionalization of the marriage between Walker and Mel Leventhal and Walker's insights and revelations about the intimacies and intricacies of relationships. The individual narratives deal with the pressure of external forces on relationships, the influence of personal and familial engagements, the impact of children on a marriage, and the effort to sustain cordiality when a relationship has ended. As the title implies, *The Way Forward* posits that relationships, even difficult and painful ones, can produce personal progress and growth.

Shortly after the publication of *The Way Forward Is with a Broken Heart,* the couple's daughter, Rebecca Walker, published her memoir, *Black White and Jewish* (2001); it was her intention that no commas appear in the title of her book. The memoir deals frankly with Rebecca Walker's sense of racial and cultural alienation and the complexities of the experiential distinctions between her parents' lives. The publication of *Black White and Jewish* marked the public beginning of a rift between Alice and Rebecca Walker. According to interviews, Rebecca has said that Walker was upset by the book's portrayal of her as a mother. In her memoir, Rebecca reflects upon her life from the perspective of her young adulthood. She repeats as a motif the idea that she felt obligated to function as a bridge between her mother and father's lives and contexts.

Alice Walker's examinations of the national and global impact of the terrorist attacks of September 11, 2001, appear in her short book *Sent by Earth: A Message from the Grandmother Spirit* (2001). In

Susan V. Booth serves as the artistic director of the Alliance Theater in Atlanta, Georgia, where the musical version of Alice Walker's novel *The Color Purple* premiered in September 2004. Booth was instrumental in many aspects of the creation of the musical and responsible for the musical's opening in Atlanta. *(Photograph by Carmen Gillespie)*

2003, she focused on her poetic craft and published two collections of new poems, *Absolute Trust in the Goodness of the Earth* and *A Poem Traveled Down My Arm.* The latter is a slim volume employing an experimental form that Walker uses to express very brief observations about human experience and relationships. The book's content varies between simple language and basic drawings that convey Walker's belief in the power of human connections to generate creativity and positivity.

*Now Is the Time to Open Your Heart,* published in 2004, was Walker's first novel of the new millennium—and it is, perhaps, her final novel. The narrative tells the story of Kate, a 57-year-old writer who is facing the physical and psychological realities of aging and, with those challenges, tries to rediscover the meanings of her existence. Disillusioned with her previous spiritual staple, BUDDHISM, Kate desires something more tangible to sustain her life experiences and to enter into a new way of understanding. She therefore leaves her lover, an artist named Yolo, and determines to travel to the Amazon to experience a drug called YAGE. This drug is used by the indigenous peoples of the Northern Amazon to induce a state of spiritual fluidity wherein an individual can access the spirit world as well as gain new knowledge about the world and the experience of living.

*Now Is the Time to Open Your Heart* received a scathing review from the *New York Times* book critic Michiko Kakutani. Other reviewers, such as Diane Evans of the *Times* (London), were more complimentary, but the book was generally not well-received by critics. In spite of the negative critical reception, this novel also became a best-seller.

Walker was at first resistant to the idea of creating a musical adaptation of *The Color Purple,* but after protracted negotiation and persuasion, the producer SCOTT SANDERS convinced her that it was good material for a musical. After attaining the blessing of both Walker and Steven Spielberg, Sanders spent several years developing the project, enlisting the assistance and expertise of various artists, including the Pulitzer Prize winner MARSHA NORMAN, who wrote the book for the musical, and the composers Brenda Russell, Allee Willis, and Stephen Bray, who wrote the music. Walker herself was not directly involved in its creation. The musical's story line is largely the same as the Spielberg film version of *The Color Purple,* except that the lesbian relationship between Celie and Shug is not hidden or subverted.

The third life of *The Color Purple* began in 2004 with the musical's premiere at the Alliance Theater in Atlanta. Staging the world premiere in Atlanta was the brainchild of Susan V. Booth, the artistic director of the Alliance Theatre. When Booth learned of Sanders's intention to turn Walker's book into a musical, she became convinced that, because of the location of the story and Walker's Georgia roots, it should first appear in Atlanta. The production was directed by the Chicago-based director Gary Griffin and featured LaChanze, who played Celie.

In December 2004, Walker's grandson, Tenzin, was born to Rebecca and her partner, Choyin Rangdrol. Alice Walker and Rebecca became estranged at the beginning of Rebecca's pregnancy. According to several interviews with Rebecca, and as chronicled in her 2007 book, *Baby Love: Choosing Motherhood after a Lifetime of Ambivalence,* the mother and daughter no longer communicate with each other.

The Broadway production of *The Color Purple: The Musical* premiered in 2005 at the Broadway Theater. The marquee producers of the show included Oprah Winfrey, Quincy Jones, and Scott Sanders. The original New York production was also directed by Gary Griffin and again starred LaChanze as Celie. The production was nominated for 11 Tony Awards, winning one for LaChanze, and ran on Broadway until 2008. The American Idol winner Fantasia Barrino played Celie for a part of the New York run and continues periodically in that role as a member of the touring company.

In 2005, Walker and an ordained Buddhist nun, PEMA CHÖDRÖN, coauthored the audiobook *Pema Chödrön and Alice Walker in Conversation: On the Meaning of Suffering and the Mystery of Joy.* In their conversation, the two expound on the Buddhist practice of TONGLEN and its role in their personal acceptance and negotiation of suffering.

In 2006, Walker published the essay collection *We Are the Ones We Have Been Waiting For,* which features tributes to revolutionaries of the past such as Dr. Martin Luther King, Jr., and FIDEL CASTRO. The pieces in the collection also suggest the need for new activist strategies more suited for contemporary civil rights struggles. Also published in 2006 was Walker's children's book *There Is a Flower at the End of My Nose Smelling Me.*

The touring company premiere of the musical *The Color Purple* was held at the Cadillac Theater in Chicago in 2007. As of 2010, the musical has continued its national tour. In the same year as the Chicago premiere, Walker published the children's book *Why War Is Never a Good Idea,* based on her poem of the same name. She also designated Emory University in Atlanta, Georgia, as the location for her official archives and as the repository of her personal papers.

Walker continued her formal experiments with writing when, in 2008, she began a Web site and blog entitled *Alice Walker's Garden.* In the introduction to her Web site, Walker says that she began it in response to her feelings upon turning 60. She further states that she no longer feels obligated to write for publication or to construct a public identity in ways that had occupied so much of her prior time; instead, she has taken to creating what she calls her living book, her blog on her travels through and observations of the world. After her 60th birthday, Walker had anticipated spending the rest of her life wandering and meditating, and although she did not expect to want to share those experiences publicly, she has been drawn to do so because of the awareness and understandings she has acquired through her travels. Her desire to have a public forum occurred also as a result of her excitement about the 2007 political campaign and the candidacy of Barack Obama, whom she publicly endorsed.

In addition to the home page, the Web site includes an official biography, photos, interviews, poems, bibliographic materials, public appearances, press releases, and her blog. Walker travels extensively to places in the world that are in particularly intense, often violent, conflict. She sees her role now as self-described witness and interpreter. The jazz musician Garrett Larson, Walker's life partner for the last several years, often accompanies her on what she calls her wanderings.

Alice Walker in 2009 *(Photograph by Carmen Gillespie)*

Alice Walker in 2009 *(Photograph by Carmen Gillespie)*

At the end of 2008, Walker's sister, Ruth Walker Hood, died after a long illness. Walker recorded her reaction to her sister's death in a blog entry entitled "Sister Loss."

On April 24, 2009, in celebration of the public opening of the Alice Walker Archives, the Alice Walker Literary Society cosponsored *A Keeping of Records: The Art and Life of Alice Walker* at Emory University. The event featured a symposium as well as an exhibition of Walker's writings and various personal archival materials in a display in the university's Robert W. Woodruff Library's Schatten Gallery.

As of 2010, there is talk of producing *The Color Purple: The Musical* as a movie. Fantasia Barrino has said in interviews that she has been asked to star in the film version. In addition, Walker published three new works in 2010, the short volume *Overcoming Speechlessness: A Poet Encounters the Horror in Rwanda, Eastern Congo, and Palestine/Israel;* a poetry collection, *Hard Times Require Furious Dancing;* and a series of interviews entitled *The World Has Changed: Conversations with Alice Walker;* edited by Rudolph P. Byrd. According to Walker's Web site, she is also in the process of writing another volume of poetry, *Turning Madness into Flowers,* excerpts of which appear on her Web site.

## BIBLIOGRAPHY

*Alice Walker's Garden* (Web site). Available online. URL: http://www.alicewalker.info/. Accessed October 17, 2009.

Banks, Erma Davis, and Keith Byerman. *Alice Walker: An Annotated Bibliography, 1968–1986.* New York: Garland, 1989.

Bloom, Harold, ed. *Alice Walker's "The Color Purple."* Modern Critical Interpretations Series. New York: Chelsea House, 2000.

Bobo, Jacqueline. "Sifting through the Controversy: Reading *The Color Purple.*" *Callaloo* 39 (Spring 1989): 332–342.

Dieke, Ikenna, ed. *Critical Essays on Alice Walker.* Westport, Conn.: Greenwood Press, 1999.

Gates, Henry Louis, and K. A. Appiah, eds. *Alice Walker: Critical Perspectives Past and Present.* New York: Amistad Press, 1993.

Lauret, Maria. *Alice Walker.* Modern Novelists Series. New York: St. Martin's Press, 2000.

Steinem, Gloria. "Do You Know This Woman? She Knows You: A Profile of Alice Walker." *Ms.* 35, no. 37 (June 1982): 89–94.

Walker, Alice. *The Same River Twice: Honoring the Difficult, A Meditation on Life, Spirit, Art, and the Making of the Film* The Color Purple *Ten Years Later.* New York: Scribner, 1996.

———. *The World Has Changed: Conversations with Alice Walker.* Edited by Rudolph P. Byrd. New York: The New Press, 2010.

Walker, Rebecca. "How My Mother's Fanatical Views Tore Us Apart." *Daily Mail Online.* Available online. URL: http://www.dailymail.co.uk/femail/article-1021293/How-mothers-fanatical-feminist-views-tore-apart-daughter-The-Color-Purple-author.html. Accessed January 12, 2010.

White, Evelyn C. *Alice Walker: A Life.* New York: W. W. Norton and Company, 2004.

Wiltz, Teresa. "Rebecca Walker; Measuring Out a Mother's Love." *Washington Post.* Available online. URL: http://www.washingtonpost.com/wp-dyn/content/article/2007/03/29/AR2007032902320.html. Accessed January 12, 2010.

Winchell, Donna Hasty. *Alice Walker.* New York: Twayne, 1992.

# Part II

# *Works A to Z*

# NOVELS

# *By the Light of My Father's Smile* (1998)

As with all of Walker's fiction since the publication of *The Color Purple*, *By the Light of My Father's Smile* received a mixed critical response. Francine Prose of the *New York Times* and other critics found the book to consist largely of one-dimensional characterizations and new-age platitudes. Still others found the book to be a radical statement on the need to reevaluate and dismantle the dichotomy between sexuality and spirituality. Critics who praised the text for this accomplishment included Karen Schechner in the *Weekly Alibi*. In spite of the mixed reviews, the book became a best-selling novel.

*By the Light of My Father's Smile* traces the experiences of a family whose last name is Robinson. When their daughters, Susannah and Magdalena, are young, the Robinsons—Langley, the mother, and her husband, the family's patriarch (whose first name is not provided in the novel)—relocate their family to a remote location in Mexico. Although Langley and Robinson are trained anthropologists, they cannot get funding to support their travel to Mexico to study a group of mixed African/Indian people called the Mundo. In order to do their work, Langley and Robinson pretend to be missionaries and do their work undercover and dishonestly. The girls grow up with the Mundo as their example. Magdalena (or Maggie) is particularly enamored of Mundo life and falls in love with their lifestyle as well as with a young man named Manuelito. When Robinson discovers the relationship between Maggie and Manuelito, he punishes his daughter by beating her with a belt. The reverberations from Robinson's act of violence against Maggie permanently affect his family. Magdalena becomes a self-destructive academic, while Susannah takes her sister's side against her father and loses the opportunity to have a relationship with him. Langley dies of a cancer caused by her inability to leave the man she loves even though she no longer respects him.

Robinson is dead for most of the text and spends his posthumous time watching his daughters and hoping to make amends for the wrongs he did and the damage that he caused them as a father. Manuelito (also called Manny), who dies in the middle of the novel, helps Robinson with his quest, and after performing his two required acts of penance, Robinson finds absolution in his daughters' forgiveness. The novel ends with the death of Susannah, the last remaining member of the Robinson family. After Susannah dies, her friends burn her house and her writings, signifying that she has reached epiphany and that there is no need for the written record of the four Robinsons to be preserved.

## SYNOPSIS

### Part 1: Angels

#### Angels

*By the Light of My Father's Smile* begins with the voice of Robinson, the dead father of the novel's protagonist, Susannah, reflecting on his daughter's life and his posthumous interactions with her. Although Susannah is unaware of her father's presence, he is a pervasive and constant force in her daily life. She reacts, almost always negatively, to his proximity. Robinson is aware of his daughter's ambivalent feelings about him and reflects on her lack of sorrow upon his death.

Robinson has access to all aspects of his daughter's life and watches Susannah and her Greek husband, Petros, make love. He also ponders his daughter's activities, including her obsession with angels and her trip to a place called Kalimasa. These observations lead him to the conclusion that he did not know his daughter while he was alive.

Kalimasa is a place that is, at least at the time of Susannah's first visit, full of spirituality, and it embraces creativity as an essential element of its citizenry. After her initial visit to Kalimasa with Petros, Susannah travels there with a woman who has become her lover and with whom she has a terrible time. On one of her ventures into the town to try to escape the woman, she finds a ring whose beauty and craft resonate deeply, and she buys it. When she returns home, her lover finds the ring objectionable because she wanted to purchase a ring for Susannah herself. Robinson describes this woman, whose name is Pauline, as childish and self-absorbed.

Although he can observe his daughter's actions and seems to be able to discern her feelings, Robinson does not have access to her thoughts and wonders about her musings. He wonders if she might be thinking of her husband and how he left her for another woman with whom he is no longer satisfied. In fact, Susannah reflects on the changes she has seen in Kalimasa, particularly in the young, who seem to be increasingly dissatisfied with what she sees as the inherent gifts and advantages of their lives as somewhat removed from the ravages of civilization.

Although on different emotional wavelengths, Pauline and Susannah engage in an intense and graphic sexual encounter, which Robinson describes in detail. The sex is fraught with power dynamics, and Pauline loves the moment when she feels she has Susannah in her control—the moment Susannah acquiesces and begs for fulfillment. This dynamic mirrors the one observed indirectly by Susannah in her parents' relationship, a partnership fraught with conflicts that seemed resolved or, at least, relieved by their sexual encounters.

### MacDoc

Pauline seems to Robinson to act in ways that are similar to his daughter Magdalena, who is also known throughout the story as Maggie, MacDoc, and June. Robinson recalls a time in the 1940s when Maggie was a little girl and he and his wife, Langley, were working as missionaries in Mexico among a group of indigenous people called the Mundo. The Mundo are a group of people whose descendants were both black and Indian. Although Robinson and Langley are supported financially by their work for the church, they are, by training, anthropologists committed to the work of recording the ways of the Mundo before they disappeared.

Robinson's recollections of Maggie are largely negative and colored by his perceptions of her as lazy and sexually provocative, even as a child. In his memories of that time, Robinson and his wife disagree about the nature of their child and whether her interest in sexuality is problematic. Robinson is deeply in love with his wife and recalls that she was always able to see the light side of things and to laugh. Langley's family belongs to a well-heeled African-American community, while Robinson comes from an economically compromised background.

Central to the Mundo's life are pots that the women craft with a round perfection. These pots—colored only in black, white/gray, and green—are both practical and artful, and Susannah and her mother learn how to create them while the family lives among them. The remoteness of the Mundo has enabled the unusually intact preservation of their traditions and cultures, and that lifestyle and way of being is increasingly threatened by encroaching technologies, particularly when the railroad arrives.

While Langley and Susannah are involved in learning the ways of the Mundo women, Maggie loves to run among the young boys and learns from them the skills traditionally attributed to the men of the group. Maggie's behavior disturbs her father and engenders negative feelings between the two. MacDoc is the name given to her by the Mundo; her adopted name originally was Mad Dog, a representation in the vocabulary of the Mundo synonymous with wild spirit, but Robinson insists that the name is inappropriate; therefore, Maggie is called MacDoc instead. Later, she is allowed to choose her own name, a Mundo tribe tradition. The name that she chooses is June.

As a child, Maggie is active and free-spirited, perhaps understanding the sexual-spiritual essence of life at an early age. Her father, pretending to be a missionary to the Mundo tribe and absorbed by his feigned role as minister, begins to try to control her and to prevent her from embodying his fear of wildness. Robinson sees Magdalena as oppositional to Mad Dog, and he refuses to abide his daughter's transformation into something and someone he cannot control.

By the time Maggie is 15, she has become a silent and solitary young woman whose greatest pleasure lies in books and in reading. Robinson imagines that the reading signifies some greater transformation in his daughter, a kind of settling down or conformity, but it does not. Robinson believes that her choice of the name June also signifies a deeper acquiescence in the girl. As the family prepares to leave the Mundo for good, June begins to sing a song she has learned from them about the unsullied embrace of creation and the human impulse to connect. Robinson is threatened by the song and by his daughter's singing of it because it seems to him to represent the exercise of a kind of authority outside of his purview.

### Twigs

This chapter is written from Maggie's perspective. She writes in retrospect about the punishment she received from Robinson, who beat his daughter with a belt that was given to her as a present from her lover. Maggie reveals the details of this sexual relationship with her lover, a young Indian boy, Manuelito. The two enjoy horseback riding and find a natural place in the Mundo lands in which to make love. They call this location their home. Manuelito has learned from the men of his tribe how to have sex without impregnating a woman, and so the two are free to make love without worrying about reproducing.

Maggie does not understand why her father is not happy for her and is completely alienated by the violence of his actions. The beating unsettles not only Maggie but the rest of the family. Langley says that she will leave Robinson, although she never does, and Susannah's relationship with her father is altered irreparably.

### Twins

In this one-paragraph chapter, Robinson comments about Susannah's writing, noting that she is composing a novel about her former marriage and is having a hard time writing about the sex. Although she does not get his message, Robinson encourages his daughter to write about sex. He feels responsible for what he sees as her repression because he believes that it derives from the incident when he beat Maggie.

### Ritual

Robinson also reflects on the damage to his marriage caused by his having responded to Maggie's sexuality with violence. In the afterlife, Robinson is able to understand his actions as problematic and believes that he was missing a strong sense of self while he was living. He says that he was a shadow among fully fleshed men and women. He recounts the process of reentering his wife's good graces, when he showed her how devoted he was to her by working to understand her needs and fulfilling them as best he could. Through their sexuality, Robinson found a way back to Langley's heart.

### Grace

Another opportunity to regain his wife's favor occurs when her younger brother, Jocko, dies. Robinson describes a curative sexual encounter where he is able to touch his wife's grief and to move her to celebrate rather than mourn her brother.

### Inches

In another one-paragraph chapter, Robinson remembers back to his girls' coming-of-age and the way in which they were suddenly taller than he and his wife. For him, this experience represents an unexpected shift in the power dynamics between parent and child.

### Twenty Kisses

Robinson discusses Susannah's former husband, Petros. As Petros navigates a boat across the Ionian Sea, he is thinking about how much Susannah taught him about his culture and how to appreciate it. He recalls that he was ashamed the first time he brought Susannah home to his mother and father, embarrassed by what he saw as their backwardness. She loved them and the environment of their home. The couple made love that night at his parent's home in a physically fulfilling way that, ironically, signaled the beginning of the end of their relationship.

### The Reason You Fell in Love

Susannah asks Petros's mother many questions that the older woman attempts to deflect by encouraging her son to take his lover sightseeing. Petros and Susannah visit an ancient cathedral where they see women kissing the feet of a statue of the Virgin Mary. There they also encounter a dwarf whose name is Irene.

### Eyes

Irene lives at the cathedral and is responsible for tending it. Susannah has a moment of connection with Irene when the woman gazes intently into her eyes. After the exchange, Susannah wishes to speak with the woman, but she seems to have vanished. Susannah seems smaller and shorter after the meeting.

### Paradise

The narration shifts to Susannah, who remembers that Petros asked her not to mention the encounter with Irene to his mother. He begins to tell Susannah what he knows of Irene's story. He tells Susannah that Irene's mother was raped as a young girl, and when she told her family what had happened, they did not believe her; in fact, she was punished by them and held accountable for the violence that had been perpetrated against her.

Irene's mother's family and community stopped speaking to her at that point. Irene's mother died giving birth to Irene, and from the time she was baby, Irene was forced to give her life in service to the church.

Susannah has empathy for Irene and wants to speak to her. Petros says that doing so would make her an "American busybody." Susannah is insulted by the characterization, and this exchange marks for her a moment when the couple begin to separate emotionally. Petros's home contains the contradictions of inequality and extraordinary beauty.

### Of Course

Susannah does get the opportunity to speak with Irene, who tells her that she not only speaks English but is fluent in at least four other languages. Irene tells Susannah that the people in the community used to stone women of whom they did not approve. The women discuss Irene's red curtains hanging in her room at the back of the church. Susannah also asks the woman why she does not leave. Irene tells her that when she was young, she was not allowed to leave, and now she is not able. Irene's experience of rejection causes Susannah to reflect on her own rejection of her father after his abuse of Maggie. She wonders how her rejection might have made him feel.

### Relatives

Susannah asks Petros to accompany her on a walk. She leads him to the place Irene identified as the location where the town's stoning of women used to occur. Petros did not know the history of the location and is angry at what he perceives as Susannah's obsession with the negative. Susannah continues to visit Irene, and the woman begins to read Susannah's life using tarot cards. Irene tells Susannah in an indirect way about the guiding presence of her father and that she is on a journey back home, a return to the self.

Invisible to the women, Robinson blows the cards, and both women are startled. When she eats dinner with Petros and his family later that evening, Susannah tries to dispel the rumors they all have heard about Irene that have no basis in fact.

### Wealth

Irene and Susannah continue to exchange narratives. Irene tells Susannah that her father was a rich man and that he had purchased the church in order for her to have a place to go after her mother's reputation had been ruined by her rape. Irene says that some of the rejection she experienced was because of her physical condition, her dwarfism, which caused her father to find her abhorrent. She speaks of her affinity for other dwarves and says that, in the past, they used to exist as a group, like the pygmies. She also feels a connection to the Gypsies, which she says comes from their ability to retain their sense of connection in spite of their geographical flux. She sees their movement as opposed to her stasis. She also admires their love of music. During their final meeting, Irene says that Susannah is one of the few tourists of whom she has grown fond.

### Doing Well

Robinson records that when Petros and Susannah left Greece, Petros felt that the visit had gone well, noting that his parents loved his wife and felt appreciated and respected by her. They also felt that Susannah was good for their son and that he seemed emotionally and physically well. Petros also notes that Susannah seemed remote and disconnected when the couple left the island, and he feels that his home has been a sad place for his wife.

### Piercings

June narrates this chapter. As an adult, she has grown physically heavy and works as a successful academic. Before his death, her father, Robinson, visits her, wanting to earn her forgiveness for his transgressions. Her father makes unannounced periodic visits to his daughter. June torments him by eating extraordinary amounts of food.

Robinson wonders whether he has caused this behavior in his daughter through his actions. June remembers a small change purse that her father gave her when she was a little girl. She recalls that the purse had a small, hidden gold zipper. Her father does not remember giving her the gift just before the family left for Mexico and life among the Mundo. For June, the trauma of the move was compounded by the loss of her purse with the secret compartment, the present from her father. She tells her father that the memory of its loss was the catalyst for her obsession with zippers.

June recalls one of her sister's novels in which there is a story of a Scandinavian family that returns to Africa, acknowledges their African ancestry, and expresses a desire to repair their fraught relationship with the darker members of their family. June explains that the move to Mexico was alienating for her in that her father seemed to be pretending to be what he was not and that his pretense frightened her to the extent that she no longer trusted him.

### Green

Susannah recounts that her conversations with June were always about her sister's physical sufferings. She remembers a remarkable exception, a conversation she had with June after June reconnected with her childhood lover, Manuelito, when she coincidentally encountered him on an airplane. The two were in the first-class section, Manuelito because he was the only member of his army platoon in Vietnam to survive an attack, and June because she was too large for a standard economy seat.

June takes over the narration. On the airplane, without knowing who each other are, the two begin a conversation. June learns that Manuelito, now called Mannie, spent years recovering from his injuries and is married with children. He tells her that he first came to the United States looking for a girl; it takes some time for June to realize that she was the girl he was searching for. He has also become an alcoholic.

The chapter continues with a letter from June to Manuelito in which she tells him who she is and what has happened to her since the two were together. She also accuses him of the murders he committed while working as a soldier. Mannie replies to her letter, telling her that he did recognize her on the airplane and that he is hurt that she chose to renew their contact by accusing him of murdering others. He explains that as a soldier, he had no choice about what to do to survive. He believes he had to kill others or he would have been killed himself. He ends by saying that he is coming to find her immediately.

June tells Susannah that when Mannie arrived, the two of them walked by the river. He explains to June that he told his wife where he was going and with whom and that the couple had agreed to accept infidelity to each other during the two years that he was in Vietnam. June says that the adult Mannie is somewhat disappointing to her and that she keeps dreaming of the boy she knew and once loved. Eventually, she comes to see in the man the boy of her childhood and learns to love him again.

### Apology

When Robinson observes June and Mannie's love, his posthumous regret about his actions is tremendous. He feels responsible for the situation they are in and believes that his behavior, his beating of June, changed the trajectory of their young lives and prevented them from coming together in a way that would have allowed them both to be more fulfilled and complete human beings. Robinson begins to do what he can to try to make amends to the couple.

### What Is Left

Manuelito and June make love and reconnect on a spiritual level. They decide that they must be lovers and agree to tell Mannie's wife, Maria, about everything. Through an unvoiced agreement, Mannie pledges to stop drinking, and June promises to lose weight. On the way out of the restaurant where the couple make these decisions, Manny is hit by a bus and dragged to his death.

### To Be a Sister

Susannah comes to her sister to provide comfort and compassion. When Susannah arrives, she finds that her sister is not bereft with grief. June seems to believe that her encounter with Mannie was supernatural, that he did not actually come to her as a living being. She says that she thinks that Mannie was killed in Vietnam and that her time with him was a visitation. June also tells Susannah that Mannie died singing the initiation song of his people, a song he taught to June—Mad Dog, MacDoc, Maggie—when they were young. June sings it for Susannah. The sisters also share memories of their parents; they feel that Langley and Robinson were liars who spied on and stole the Mundo culture.

### Why the Mad Dog Is Considered Wise

This chapter is told by Mannie, who recalls when Maggie asked him why the Mundo consider the mad dog to be wise. He answered that the dog is wise because "it has lost its mind." Maggie did not understand why that would be a good thing. Mannie told her that in the West too much emphasis is placed on thinking. The mad dog represents a lack of control and an ability to access visceral emotions. Mannie reveals that his people saw Maggie as a natural woman who had access to her own power. They called her a Changing Woman, one of the highest compliments bestowed upon women.

### Luck

Mannie recalls that he sang even as the bus rent his body and rendered him lifeless. He states that dying while singing is an extremely fortunate fate and that he will continue to sing in the new state he occupies. He sees his reunion with Maggie, temporary though it was, as a way of validating for her the power of their union and the shared understanding that their relationship was unique and transcendent. He believes that in Maggie he found the one soul to whom he was supposed to be attached.

### Meat

Pauline, Susannah's lover, recalls that her father worked in a meatpacking plant when she was a girl, a profession that brought Pauline much pain. Pauline often speaks with Susannah about her girlhood. She recounts her mother's crafty management of the limited resources that her family of 10 children had at their disposal. Pauline's father was an alcoholic, yet he had a side that also allowed for gentle interaction.

Pauline tells Susannah the story of her marriage at the age of 15 to a family friend, named Winston, who happened to come to dinner one evening. Winston raped Pauline while she was unconscious; he had the blessing of her family to behave in this way. She became pregnant from the encounter and married Winston.

### She Rode Horses

In spite of the pain and desperation of Pauline's tale, Susannah feels no great sympathy for the woman. In the present tense of the novel, Pauline is 55 years old and is unlike the victimized child she portrays in the tales.

Pauline tells Susannah about her early life as a married woman and young mother and her misery at every aspect of the experience. She says that she felt trapped, an experience Susannah finds hard to match with the reality of the woman she has come to call her lover. Eventually Pauline joined the navy to escape her life with Winston. She chose many different pursuits before meeting Susannah. She also was a restaurant owner. Susannah believes that Pauline fundamentally does not like her. The differences in the women's class statuses seem to interfere with their ability to negotiate their sexual power dynamics.

In spite of her difficulties with her marriage, Pauline has a great relationship with her son and feels that he is an amazing human being. He went to MIT and seems happy and well-adjusted with his own family. Pauline does not like her son's wife, however.

Susannah feels that Pauline's bold bluntness creates a tension and vulnerability for her as the woman in her life. The sex between the two is so fulfilling for Susannah that she is willing to tolerate the aspects of Pauline that she does not like and that make her feel exposed.

### The First Thing That Happens When You Die

This chapter begins with the revelation that the first thing that happens to you when you die is the overwhelming physical desire to urinate. Mannie reveals that "spirituality resides in the groin," a fact he learned from the Mundo. He states that the time one feels close to the divine is either when having sex or when one is creating. Upon his physical demise, the second sensation Mannie has is a feeling of serenity. He had been prepared in life for the experience of death, and so nothing about it is surprising to him. Then he has an interaction with Robinson, Maggie's father, whom he finds utterly bereft. Robinson grieves Mannie's death in a way that Mannie himself does not.

Robinson is in the ironic position of receiving consolation from Mannie, who has just died. The two contemplate each other. Robinson expresses regret at not embracing the beliefs of the Mundo people, despite all the time he spent with them. Mannie reminds Robinson that he originally came to stay with the Mundo because they were a group of people derived from two races who had preserved many of their original customs. Mannie says that what bound his people together was the common denominator of their experiences as vanquished peoples who had to leave various homes and who suffered greatly as a result of these upheavals. He also states that it is this gift of reinvention that enabled his people to survive. Part of the Mundo strategy was to examine the enemy by living among them and, in that way, to be prepared for any potential onslaught. The chapter ends with Mannie's observation that when one dies, the soul knows everything.

### Ashes

The narrative returns to June and to the scene of Mannie's death from the perspective of the living. June finds herself singing the same Mundo initiation song, the song she had used as a child as a sign of defiance against her father, Robinson. Feeling confident that the authorities will contact Mannie's wife, Maria, June leaves the scene and returns to her home. She makes herself a drink and goes to bed.

Later, after her sister Susannah's arrival, June sits and observes Susannah from across a room. She notices that her sister is physically small in a way that June imagines must be endearing. She asks her sister about her current relationship. The two also discuss their relationship with their parents. June feels that her father did not trust her and that the absence of that element in their relationship led to an unfulfilled longing. She wanted to be understood in a way that she was not with her father. She believes that her father destroyed her life.

Susannah maintains that as a result of the beating her father gave to her sister, she always had to choose between them. Although she acknowledges that this is not her sister's fault, she maintains that June never let her forget the incident and move beyond it into some kind of forgiveness and healing.

June has a flashback to the moment when her father beat her and feels the connection between that memory and the incident that took Mannie's life. She has a nervous breakdown and has to be restrained by professionals. In the midst of her losing touch with reality, she bites Susannah and grabs her throat in an attempt, perhaps, to kill her. She only lets go of her sister when she receives a tranquilizer.

### Mad Dog Behavior

June comes back into consciousness in a bed in a mental hospital ward. She contemplates her professional life and feels that as a professor she has failed her students. From her perspective, the world is in decay, and she feels that she has nothing to provide them that will serve as a bolster against that reality. She remembers her mother's final illness. At the time of her mother's death, June no longer loved her because she felt her mother had abandoned her and taken her father's side over her daughter's. Langley had been physically ravaged by her cancer, and yet Robinson had selfishly continued to see her as a sexual object, even as the disease destroyed her.

The narrative returns to the present, and June finds herself being questioned by a doctor. He tells her that she nearly bit Susannah's arm to the bone. She remembers Mannie's death and begins, again, to lose control. A battered Susannah comes to visit her, and June is surprised to see her sister's black eye. Susannah does not seem to be angry with her sister and puts the incident in the context of a larger narrative of suffering. The sisters engage in conversation, and June concludes that some experiences in life are irreparable. Susannah asks June if she is sorry about attacking her, and June acknowledges that she is regretful. Susannah does this to present what might be possible for June if she were to allow herself to forgive her father for all of the damage that he did to her as a young girl.

### Memories Are So Heavy

The doctor returns to June's hospital room and informs her that it is a priority for her to lose weight. June tells him that the weight correlates with the burdens of her life. Susannah is there and offers to help her sister. June is repulsed by her sister's apparent saintliness. As soon as Susannah returns home, June begins to eat and drink in the ways that she used to before Mannie's reappearance in her life. She says she is afraid that if she becomes a smaller person, she will also lose her feelings of anger and hostility, which have become the defining features of her life. She acknowledges that she does not have enough forbearance to let go of those negative emotions.

### Bad Women Aren't the Only Women

This chapter begins with June and Pauline having a conversation about Susannah. June tells her sister's lover that Susannah sleeps with a large number of people. Pauline defends Susannah, saying that the woman is always faithful to the person she is with at any particular time. June counters that Robinson, the sisters' father, loved Susannah but not her. Pauline will not let her shift the conversation from the subject at hand. Her verbal deftness causes June to envy her sister even more. Pauline begins to tell June the story of her family and of their 10 children. She talks about the transformation that her father has undergone as an adult and of the improved dynamic in their relationship that has occurred as a result of her ability to move beyond the past and to allow her father to grow. Pauline stresses the need for compassion and understanding. June is entirely resistant to the lesson the woman tries to convey.

### Sticking Out to Here

Pauline tells Susannah of her mother's oppressive life and locates the source of her misery in her bearing so many children. She believes that her mother's death was brought about by her relentless production of children, which took its toll on her emotional, physical, and psychological life. Pauline's mother, according to her sisters' account, died blaming Pauline for her demise.

Pauline sees the saga differently. She counters that her mother was filled with self-hatred instigated by her fertility. Pauline believes that she came to hate the body that was so reproductive that her life, as a consequence of motherhood, became unmanageable. Pauline wonders about her mother's relationship with sex and sexuality and ponders whether the experience was ever pleasurable for her, or if she was perpetually filled with dread, thinking that the sex might lead to the creation of another child and thus a more complicated and burdensome life.

Pauline tells Susannah about a former lover that she had named Gena. Gena had given Pauline an abortion and then became her lover. From Pauline's account of the affair, Gena was not a very talented lover. Pauline speaks of her pregnancy with her son, Richard, a child she grew to love. She had been terrified to become a mother because she was afraid of being like her mother and having a life that was unmanageable and that had no space for her in it. She and Susannah speak of sexuality and of sexual liberation. They conclude that sexual freedom has historically been the province of men and that women's sexuality has always been threatening to the status quo.

Susannah's sexual energies were truncated by her parent's insistence that the only antidote to slavery is traditional spirituality. She sees the Christianity she experienced as a child as antithetical to what she calls the orgasmic freedom of men. Pauline agrees, stating that she experienced orgasmic freedom for the first time during her affair with Gena. For Pauline, this sexual experience was a "revelation," an entryway into another kind of being: another level of psychic experience and one that is generally rare. Through this revelation, Pauline found herself ready to escape the boundaries of her existence and to begin a new life. She began to sell pies in her neighborhood and gained some economic independence; she also joined the navy. As a result of this experience, Pauline concludes that her country, the United States, is doomed because those designated to protect the country have no love or respect for women. She says that she survived her military experience by finding suitable creative outlets that allowed her to channel her creativity. She also reveals that when she left her son to join the navy, the boy was told that she was not his mother but his sister.

### Lily Paul

Lily Paul is the name of a restaurant that Susannah visits at the suggestion of her husband, Petros, and where she met the restaurant owner, her current partner, Pauline. At the time of Susannah and Petros's visit to the restaurant, Pauline calls herself Lily Paul! The restaurant is organic and serves soul food, and thus it delights Susannah. There is also the same tablecloth on each table that Susannah observed at Petros's family home on his mother's table. Petros takes her to the restaurant as a way of reconnecting and salvaging the couple's endangered marriage. The attempt is unsuccessful. The issue that ruins the dinner is Petros's observation that the owner of the restaurant, Lily Paul, is attracted to his wife. His response upsets Susannah, who did not pick up on the woman's signals until Petros pointed them out to her.

The restaurant owner covertly gives Susannah her card when she gives her the bill, and Susannah contacts her. The two begin their first conversation with Lily Paul's complaints about menopause. She also tells Susannah that her girlfriend does not want to have sex as frequently as she does, which is another source of consternation for her. Lily Paul says she thought that Petros seemed inauthentic, and Susannah laughingly agrees. Lily Paul says to her, without any other preface, that she and Susannah will make love, and she goes on to describe the details of the imagined encounter.

### Myrrh

Susannah receives a letter from Irene, the woman who resides in the church in Petros's hometown. She says to Susannah that she appreciated her kindness and, as a result, wants to reach out to her to tell her about the tremendous change that has occurred in her life. Irene tells Susannah that she has finally walked out of her life as a prisoner within the church. She reveals that her father, when he died, left all of his money to her seven brothers and did not expect that she would outlive them. All of her brothers did die, and so Irene became a wealthy woman with her own means and with no need to remain imprisoned within the church.

After inheriting her family's wealth, Irene found herself with nothing to do, and when a group of Gypsies came through town, she left with them. She describes the ecstasy of meeting the people about whom she had dreamed for so long and is particularly effusive about the effect that the Gypsy music has on her. She finds herself on the other side of the tourist gaze in her travels. Eventually, Irene comes to question the group's wanderlust and to see the need to avoid permanency as a kind of disability. She becomes disillusioned, believing that the Gypsy need to travel is rooted in a kind of odd habituation, rather than in a true embrace of freedom.

Irene is despondent because she has lost her idealistic vision of the world. She finds that she needed to believe it was possible to escape the ordinary and to invent a kind of life that was truly improvisory. She makes connections between various oppressed groups of people, particularly between the Gypsies, Jews, and blacks. As Susannah reads the letter, she expands on Irene's thought and includes the Tasmanians and the Nunga in the group.

Susannah continues reading the letter, which is scented with myrrh. Irene writes about her journey and the travels she has undertaken since and as a result of her acquisition of wealth. Her most recent journey brought her to the Pygmies of Africa, where she is residing as she pens the letter to Susannah. Irene finds her life among them to be perfect, a kind of paradise. She believes, though, that the people's lives, customs, and traditions are endangered and cannot be maintained with the current state of their world. She sees the land's development and decimation carried out by people who care only about deriving personal wealth from its material resources. They commit violations against the people and their land, raping women and cutting down trees. She asks Susannah for advice. She notes that African Americans have suffered a similar plight and have survived, and she seeks to learn from Susannah the secret of their survival—the ways in which misery and exploitation can be endured.

Calling Susannah "Favorite Tourist," Irene concludes that the examples of the Gypsies and of African Americans present models for survival and for the use of artistry and beauty as talismans against despair. Irene adds that she often contemplates the possibility of coming to America to visit her Favorite Tourist. She has inherited her father's yacht, which, after leaving the Gypsies, she has been using to travel around the world. Perhaps she will sail off with Susannah.

## Part 2: A Kiss between the Dead Is a Breeze

### The Story You Were Telling Us

The opening chapter of this section resumes the narrative of Manuelito and Robinson after their departure from existence as commonly understood. Mannie tells Robinson that the ways of being that he tried to introduce to the tribe were seen as peculiar and at odds with what they understood of the world, its ways, and its meanings. Mannie says that the Mundo people were sun worshippers and that the essence of life seemed, to them, to be missing from the Christian narrative. They could not comprehend the concept of a father figure who resided in the sky.

On the other side of death, roles are reversed, and Mannie becomes the authority and teacher. He tells Robinson that he has work to do. He shares with Robinson that all who die are required to assist the earthly journey of a person whose path has become tangled because of the dead person's misdeeds. Additionally, all dead souls must create a ceremony of cleansing and release for those individuals wounded by the dead one's earthly actions and behaviors.

Robinson is stunned by this information and by his complete misconception of the afterworld. Mannie tells him that his mistake was in his unwillingness to have the experience of living with the Mundo to be mutual—to have embraced the notion that he could learn from them as well as instruct. He points specifically to Robinson's over-reliance on the Bible as a sole source of information.

Mannie tells Robinson that, in the Mundo vision of the world, there is no distinction between good and bad people. The central premise of their belief system comes in the understanding that it is a moral transgression to hurt another person, and when we disregard that fundamental aspect of humanity, inevitably we engage in hurtful and damaging behavior.

After the dead have performed their two rituals of penance, according to Mannie, they are forgiven. He says that the Mundo do not know what happens to an individual after he or she has been forgiven. He explains that part of the Mundo way of life and belief is an acceptance of the mystery of the unknown.

Robinson ponders Mannie's words and compares them to his experiences since dying. He understands that Susannah can sense his presence, although not on a conscious level. He asks Mannie if it is appropriate for him to have been watching Susannah have sex. Mannie states that this behavior is part of his mission, although such access might feel taboo and wrong to Robinson because of the beliefs he held in life.

When Robinson asks Mannie whether the Mundo believe in ghosts, Mannie replies that they do not define ghosts as distinct from other spiritual beings such as angels and spirits. In fact, the Mundo interpret Jesus as one of these bodies, one of the recent dead, who visit and commune with those alive and to reassure them.

Mannie says that he believes he is supposed to function as a guide for Robinson, and he sees Robinson's task as helping to heal the daughters whom he has damaged through the limitations of his earthly understandings and actions. He tells Robinson that he has been focusing his efforts on the wrong daughter: Susannah can take care of herself, but Maggie is the one who is languishing and most in need of his assistance.

The two suddenly obtain a clear vision of Maggie as she is in the present. The woman appears comatose and is being removed from her home by medical professionals who are unsympathetic and mock her as they proceed with their efforts. Mannie mentions Langley and the need Maggie has to interact with her mother. Robinson expresses surprise at his disconnection from his wife since his death. Mannie explains that the disconnect is a sign that the relationship between Langley and Robinson was a complete one that no longer requires work after their deaths. He also surprises Robinson by revealing to him that the only reason the Mundo tolerated his presence among them was because of his relationship with his wife—specifically, because of the obviously passionate nature of their sexual life. He also tells Robinson that the whole village learned of his abuse of Maggie. Finally, he says that it was Robinson's ability to love women completely that made his presence acceptable to the Mundo community. Robinson begins to see the extent of his errors and asks Mannie for his forgiveness. Mannie reassures Robinson that the two of them will enact the ceremony of forgiveness.

### Sucked into the Black Cloth

"Sucked into the black cloth" is the metaphor Mannie uses to illustrate the loss of personhood that happens when an individual becomes enamored of his own power and authority and uses the role of Christian spiritual guide, or priest, in order to validate their identity and existence.

After his "conversation" with Mannie, Robinson comes to accept that he has succumbed to this trap, and he begins to reflect on his own behavior and to see the problems that his belief system caused for others. Robinson comes to understand that his spiritual emptiness was the catalyst for his wife's cancer and early death. He knows that she could see the truth about him and could not bear to live with it. Neither could she live with him. Consequently, she died.

Mannie and Robinson resume their vigil over Maggie and see her removed to the hospital. They anticipate her reunion with her mother at "the river," where, Mannie says, all dead children reunite with their dead mothers.

### The River

Langley and Maggie do reunite by what seems to be the remains of a river. Maggie says to her mother that she wants to cross over, but that she does not know how. The narrator of the chapter is Maggie, who comes to understand her role in the encounter with her mother as that of a guide. She believes that her role is to teach her mother how to progress: in this case, how to cross the river.

Maggie is full of blame for her mother. Maggie says that her mother's failure to defend her is the source of all of her problems. She says that, nonetheless, she will help her to move on. Maggie begins the process of trying to persuade her mother to go to the other side of the river. Langley asks her daughter why she should cross. Finally, Maggie says that crossing itself is the objective, not what is gained on the other side.

Langley replies with a defense of Robinson. She tells Maggie that her father tried as hard as he could to be the best man he was capable of becoming. Maggie sees her mother's retention of her love for Robinson as a betrayal and holds that Langley should have left him in a show of solidarity for her daughter. Langley sees their deception of the Mundo people as the downfall of her relationship with Robinson.

The end of the chapter reveals that Maggie has died. The chapter ends with Langley giving her daughter a breezy kiss.

### Anyone Can See That the Sky Is Naked

Mannie and Robinson await Maggie's arrival, and while they are waiting, Mannie teaches Robinson the Mundo initiation song, or tries to. Robinson struggles mightily with the effort to master the tune and the words. The song sums up the Mundo's philosophy and states their emphasis on the inevitability of the journey. The two discuss the intricacies of these beliefs and their implications.

Robinson shares with Mannie his knowledge of Susannah's horror regarding the physical tortures women often endure in the effort to conform to the standards of beauty and the expectations of their cultures. He also talks about his wife and her ability to persist through an enduring faith in her own consciousness. She is able to study cultures that oppress women because she does not always seek simple answers. She understands the women's positions and actions, although she does not support the practices that produced them. Robinson broaches the topic of female genital mutilation, and Mannie is shocked to learn that such a practice exists. Mannie ends the chapter with the optimistic assertion that, since life has been so very difficult to comprehend, understanding death should be easier by comparison.

### Crossing

Susannah narrates this chapter and shares her sorrow at having to travel to her sister's apartment to gather, sort, and pack her life's possessions. She observes that she is the sole survivor from her family. While cleaning the refrigerator, Susannah finds a photograph of herself on which Maggie has written the words "suffering makes you thin." This discovery shocks Susannah, and she struggles to understand the meaning of her sister's message.

Susannah thinks back to the last time she was at her sister's home, right after Mannie's death, and remembers that the only consistent endeavor her sister was willing to engage in was singing—specifically, singing the song of the Mundo.

Susannah had been trying to get her sister to follow the doctor's advice and to lose some weight. When Maggie actually lost two pounds, Susannah celebrated. Maggie responded with the same phrase she later wrote on the photograph of Susannah, "suffering makes you thin." Susannah regrets that her sister died alone and wonders if she was singing at the time.

There is some sense of relief for Susannah now that Maggie has died. She has ambivalent feelings about her sister and is somewhat unburdened by her passing. Susannah receives a package from her sister, a note and photograph Maggie had assembled for her sister shortly before she died. The photograph is of Manuelito riding the horse Maggie had loved so much as a girl. The package also contains the belt Mannie gave Maggie when they were young, the same belt Robinson beat her with when he uncovered her sexuality. Maggie also leaves Susannah a letter, in which she includes the lyrics to the Mundo initiation song she loved so well. She acknowledges that she destroyed the relationship that they had shared as children, and she does not feel that they will meet again. She says that she did not love her sister and advises her to "get a life" rather than to distance herself from reality by only writing about it from a safe and remote place. The letter continues with such a negative characterization of Susannah that Susannah has to regroup and assess the potential truths of her sister's statements.

In the hateful dismissal of Maggie's letters, Susannah finds that she has betrayed her own instincts and impulses by denying her love of her father in defense of her sister. She feels that she destroyed an essential part of herself in an attempt to align herself with a sister, who in the end despised her and rejected her attempts at love and solidarity. Susannah understands her behavior to have caused her most fundamental loss, the loss of her father's love in her life and the ability to experience authentic emotion. She comes to understand that she never forgave her father. After this cathartic revelation, Susannah feels a profound peace that she personifies as a dancing black man bearing peacock feathers. It occurs to her that the image might have been that of her father before he was her father.

Susannah finishes reading Maggie's letter, determined not to let the missive affect her newfound awareness. After finishing it, she discovers that she has released her childhood burdens and has become a full-fledged adult. The chapter ends as she drops Maggie's letter to the floor.

### For Every Little Sickness . . .

Pauline, Irene, and Susannah share a joint as they discuss political complexities, such as the belief that the CIA deliberately decimated African-American communities at the end of the 1960s by distributing and allowing the flow of drugs into those communities. Pauline comments on the irony of such a conversation as they indulge in illegal drug use. The women defend the use of marijuana, calling it a gentle, woman-grown drug. The conversation continues as each drifts off into her individual thoughts.

As she stated she might, Irene has come to America to visit Susannah. Susannah has to adjust to the changes that wealth has brought to her friend's life. Irene travels in a limousine and with bodyguards. The three women get along well during Irene's visit.

### Getting the Picture

The chapter begins with a conversation between Irene and Susannah about the apostle Paul. The women examine his positions about women, and Irene says it is too bad that Lily Paul (Pauline) was named after the biblical apostle. This revelation alarms Susannah, who thought that her lover's name came from her father, who was also named Paul. She makes a play on her own name, Susannah, which is like the song "Oh! Susanna." Susannah says that her father used to sing her the song when she was a child.

The two continue with their conversation about Lily Paul's name, saying that the Lily derives from the biblical Lilith who was Adam's partner. They also discuss myths about a time in which women were self-impregnating. Then Susannah begins to discuss the difficulties of her life with Pauline, maintaining that the woman wishes to control her life in ways that are uncomfortable and unacceptable. She discusses Lily Paul's misconceptions about her—the notion that Susannah had a kind of perfect, charmed life. Susannah believes that Pauline is jealous and wants to have as an adult the experiences she was deprived of as a child.

Irene notes that Susannah wears black every day. Irene used to wear black all the time when she lived in Greece, but she has traded in that habit for a more colorful wardrobe. Irene also says that she misses Susannah's long hair, which Susannah cut off because she had grown tired of it.

### Church

Robinson reenters the narrative with an observation about his daughter. He thinks that his daughter is about to "be sucked into the black cloth." Robinson tries to visit his daughter through the conduit of her dreams. He envisions her riding with him in a truck eating watermelon. Susannah talks about the dream with Irene. She says that the two were very happy in the dream and that the experience and revelation that occurred when her sister died opened channels of communication between her and her father. Both Irene and Susannah lament the relative absences of their fathers in their lives.

Irene says that her father was too corrupt to have been a positive presence in her life and that the money she has is tainted by his actions. Irene provides an explanation for the exploitative actions of Europeans by saying that their negativity derives from the Ice Age and their feelings of betrayal at the loss of warmth and sun. Irene also believes that Europe lost its mother by abandoning GODDESS worship for male-centered Christianity. She references the witch burnings of the Middle Ages and asserts that they deprived Europe of some of its brightest and strongest citizens, a loss from which it has yet to recover.

### Living with the Wind

Susannah begins this chapter by stating that she uses her orgasms to find what is on the other side of that experience. She believes that for Lily Paul, what lies beyond the orgasm is another orgasm. Susannah tells Lily Paul that, in spite of this difference in perspectives, Lily Paul has been a remarkable lover to her and has moved her to new understandings about herself.

Lily Paul wants Susannah to marry her, but Susannah says that she does not want to be in a permanent partnership. In the course of their conversation, Lily Paul and Susannah come to the conclusion that men go to war because they do not have access to the mysteries of life that are embedded in the female experience of being able to give birth and to reproduce life.

Rather than be married, Susannah suggests that the two have a ceremony that somehow reflects the authentic essence of their relationship. She states that Pauline has been a teacher to her, and as such their relationship is fundamentally about education. Pauline says that she understands that she cannot have or be Susannah, and that her experiences and what she has to offer are valuable. Susannah affirms this observation, although she seems ambivalent about Pauline's request that the two attempt to have a committed life together.

## Part 3: Fathers

### The Cathedral of the Future

According to the first line of this chapter, "the cathedral of the future will be nature." This observation comes from Mannie as he converses with Robinson about the world and its close. He says that humanity will have to take refuge in the trees and to return to a more natural way of life. Robinson has come to admire Mannie and wonders about his foolish decision to dismantle the relationship between him and Maggie. He mourns the loss of the grandchildren who might have come from Maggie and Mannie's union and might have had a positive impact on the world.

Mannie tries to explain some of the reasons why Robinson was unable to think clearly while he was living. According to Mannie, the Mundo believe that the world cannot be comprehended, and so, rather than formulating theses about existence, the Mundo tell stories that do not make frank assertions but assert possibilities. He suggests that stories are pliable and therefore do not prohibit other possibilities and limit or close the conversation.

Mannie tells Robinson that he must leave him and that Robinson will be alone for a time. He says that Robinson must practice the initiation song in Mannie's absence. Mannie leaves Robinson in order to perform one of his two death tasks, which he states involve Maggie and Vietnam. Mannie must go and try to right the life of a Vietnamese prostitute who has AIDS. He has to intervene in her life because he killed her parents while fighting during the war, having followed orders to destroy the village in which her parents were living.

Mannie tells Robinson that the girl is on the brink of death and that he will go to her at that time to help her as she makes her transition. Although Mannie was responsible for killing the girl's parents, he saved her life because, as he explains to Robinson, she seemed like Maggie. As Mannie leaves Robinson, he laughs and states that his laughter is the other aspect of tears demonstrating the relationship between sorrow and joy and adding that during human existence, the two are always simultaneous.

### Bears

As this chapter begins, Susannah is on Irene's yacht and has in her hands a letter from Pauline. The letter speaks of what Pauline calls the fear that develops between women when they discover that they can be a couple. They find they become bears. Susannah processes this idea with amusement. Her thoughts reveal that which she feels the relationship with Pauline is over, but she continues to feel ambivalent toward the woman.

The letter continues with musings about relationships, whether same or different sex. Pauline wants Susannah to return to her and says that she misses her all the time. She asserts that the relationship between them was as complicated as all others inevitably become. After finishing the letter, Susannah decides that she will tell Pauline the truth—that she is afraid of committing to their relationship.

Irene and Susannah are on a journey to bury Irene's mother in a place other than at the church where Irene was imprisoned for so many years. The spot that Irene has chosen is beautiful, and Susannah tells her friend that she feels she has chosen well. Although Irene's mother will have a new resting place, the church where she lay in rest for so many years has also transformed. The church is no longer a conventionally religious institution and is now home to various nurturing establishments such as a nursery, hospital, school, and women's center. These new operations attempt to make syntheses between the spiritual and pragmatic. Irene is the architect of the new facility.

### Being Scared

Robinson once again accesses his daughter through her dreams and sees that she is controlled by her fear. Irene reads Susannah's tarot cards and tells her that she is fooling herself in many ways. Irene says that although she has never had a lover herself, she is able to read the relationships of others with exact accuracy. Irene tells Susannah that there is a strong relationship between her feelings about her sister and her feelings about her lover. She reveals that the two women whom Susannah has not seen as sharing any commonality are similar in their intersections in her life. Irene says that the relationship she has had with Pauline was an opportunity for Susannah to experience a second childhood that, as a consequence of Pauline's self-absorption, has been ruined. This destructive quality is what Pauline shares with Maggie.

Irene continues with her reading, informing Susannah that she has a broken spirit that is in need of healing. She also says to her that the women in her life have not only wanted to steal her childhood, but also to ensure that Susannah was not happy and that she had no peace. Irene's revelations make Susannah physically ill, and she retches over the side of the boat. Susannah says that she is perplexed by this revelation because she wanted both of these women in her life to have their own happiness. The delivery the next morning of a tin of jelly beans—the symbol of Susannah's relationship with her father that she denied herself in order to defend her sister—somewhat counters Irene's message and reading.

### Crossing Over

This chapter returns the reader to the spirit world and to the activities of Robinson and Mannie in the afterlife. Mannie returns to Robinson, who is practicing the Mundo initiation song as instructed. Robinson notices that Mannie looks particularly exuberant and is emanating a kind of internal light. Mannie describes his encounter with the Vietnamese girl whose parents he killed. Robinson expresses surprise that the girl has her own tasks to complete since she was victimized since birth. Mannie tells Robinson that, no matter the circumstances under which one dies, there is always the need to be forgiven. According to Mannie, there is mutuality to forgiveness.

The two travel back to Mannie's home, back to the land of the Mundo. There Mannie takes Robinson to the place that he and Maggie used to call home, a cave with a blanket for a bed and a dirt floor. The view from inside the cave exposes a drift of blue flowers so prolific that they appear to resemble the ocean. Mannie tells Robinson that this is where his ceremony will begin. He says that the Mundo have a tradition of bringing the father of their bride-to-be to the house that the couple will occupy prior to the marriage so that the father will have a chance to preview the happiness his child will experience with her husband. Mannie asks for Robinson's approval, and the older man grants it, understanding as he does so that the man he was in life could not have appreciated the beauty in the simplicity of the space. With Robinson's approval, the ceremony to achieve forgiveness can commence.

The men watch Magdalena approaching from the distance. Robinson's daughter and Mannie's love is no longer the caricature she had become. She has returned to this home as the woman she was before her family left the land of the Mundo. She is young and thin, and she rides the black horse she and Mannie loved so much when they were together. Maggie's arrival appears as an optical illusion. She seems to be riding very fast, but her approach is delayed, almost as if she were suspended. Robinson comes to the realization that the slow approach has been orchestrated by both Maggie and Mannie to extend their experience of pleasure in the moment.

Mannie corrects Robinson's misperception by telling him that he is the one slowing the process because he is not yet ready for her arrival. Mannie tells Robinson an involved tale about the relationship between women and men and the moon. When the moon is waning, there is no room for lovemaking, but when the moon returns, the men understand that the women are now receptive. The ability to read the moon and to utilize that information as a defining principle in their sexual relationships with their wives is man's connection to the moon.

Mannie says that when a couple is in love and decide to make love, the moon is like a father figure who oversees that endeavor and thus is the central reference in the titular allusion *by the light of my father's smile.* He says that the moon is "a smile in a dark face, in the sky."

Robinson seems to understand, to embrace even, what Mannie is telling him. He finally understands the significance of the initiation song and its nuances. He had not fulfilled his role as the smiling father moon, accepting of the essential, natural, and inevitable occurrence of his daughter's sexuality. By refusing to bless her passage, Robinson effectively damaged his daughter's life to the extent that it was not possible for her to live. When he fully apprehends his complicity, Robinson states that he wishes he were dead, to which Mannie replies that, with this admission and awareness, Robinson can now progress into the performance of his ceremony. Suddenly, Maggie arrives and dismounts from her horse.

### Fathers

Robinson narrates this short chapter and begins by stating, "My name is Father." He says to his daughter that he is fulfilling the role he had failed so utterly in life; he is now the smiling father gazing down on his daughter's sexual emergence with understanding and joy. Maggie is overjoyed with his assertion and looks at him with a gratitude that is palpable.

Mannie provides Robinson with the details of the ceremony, and he kisses Maggie in a ritual that affirms her and helps her to recover her own essence.

### Light

The narrative fast-forwards to Susannah's death. Unlike the other members of her family, she lives to be an elderly woman. She and Robinson watch the mourners who gather at her home, and he asks his daughter about the subject of the dream she had while she was dying. Susannah tells her father that she was dreaming of her lover, Anand, who is the brother of her former husband, Petros.

Susannah relays to Robinson the narrative of her relationship with Anand. She tells him that the two met on the day that she and Irene buried Irene's mother away from the church; Irene's mother was buried in the trunk that contained her trousseau.

Maggie and Susannah watch the gathering of mourners at her house. Among the grieved are Anand and Pauline. Susannah proceeds to tell Maggie her story. When Susannah first saw Anand, he looked so much like Petros that she thought he was her husband's brother. He was assisting with the entombment of Irene's mother. During the process, Irene asked to see her mother's body. When the corpse was unveiled, they found that she had been bound and that her face had been covered completely in black cloth. This revelation so injured Irene that she died a month after reburying her mother.

Maggie asks Susannah if she is curious about her family in the afterlife and why Maggie is there with her. Maggie thinks about the moment when her father blessed her relationship with Mannie. After looking at her with compassion and understanding, Robinson disappears. Mannie and Maggie begin to kiss. Soon, Maggie finds herself with Susannah. She knows in that moment that she and Mannie have been kissing for tens of years. She can now understand Mannie's statement to her explaining that, although after death there is some forgiveness and resolution, eternity only lasts for as long as it takes to accomplish these tasks.

All of Susannah's friends gather and begin to spread frankincense oil over all of her possessions. Maggie is horrified and says that her sister must preserve her legacy. Susannah replies that being remembered is dangerous and that all she desires is what has happened already with the gesture of reconciliation that is Maggie's presence.

Maggie and Susannah watch as Anand genuflects at Susannah's deathbed. Susannah's friends the house, with Susannah and her possessions in it, afire.

## CRITICAL COMMENTARY

At one point in *By the Light of My Father's Smile,* the central protagonist, Susannah Robinson, comments that the most important foundational component to the world is stories, not ideas. This statement and distinction help the reader to understand Alice Walker's methodology and thinking in the novel. In the text, Walker tries to establish a set of stories that will function as a counter and substitute for traditional narratives—Christian, Western, and historical—that are the bedrock of many contemporary cultures. Walker suggests that these formative narratives need to be destabilized and uprooted in order for an alternative, healthier, and truer set of tales to begin the process of restoring a more equitable order in the world. The alternative narratives that Walker suggests generally fit under the three topic areas of forgiveness, acceptance, and transcendence. The novel's controlling myth, the story of the smiling father, forms the core of each of these imperative substitute narratives.

All of the Robinsons, the family who constitute the main characters in the narrative, suffer under the burden of unforgiven wrongs. Each of them is weighed down by the past and by events that have occurred that prevent them from progressing. Although all of the members of the family are affected by the inability to forgive, the daughters of the family, Magdalena and Susannah are the most profoundly impacted.

The Robinsons are anthropologists who have disguised themselves as missionaries in order to have funding to do their work. They choose to study the Mundo, a group of African and Indian peoples whose location is so remote that their stories and rituals remain unadulterated by the encroachment of technology and development.

When Magdalena (or Maggie), the Robinsons' oldest daughter, is a young girl, she becomes involved in a relationship with a Mundo boy named Manuelito (or Mannie). Mannie and Maggie's relationship becomes a model in the novel for the way in which maturity should be achieved, particularly sexual maturity. Manuelito and Magdalena are perfectly compatible in their relationship. Maggie and Mannie's adventures in the environs surrounding the Mundo allow them to bond emotionally, physically, and psychologically. It is the physical aspect of their relationship that causes the problems. Robinson, Maggie's father, cannot accept his daughter's emerging sexuality and so he beats her with a belt.

This violation of what the novel posits is the natural order of Maggie's development causes a chain reaction of blame and rejection that affects the entire family and results in their dissolution. As a consequence of her father's violent response to her emerging womanhood, Magdalena, whose name suggests the biblical Mary Magdalene, is cast as the sexual transgressor and guilty woman. Robinson's disapproval results in Maggie's acting out her father's perceptions of her. She cannot forgive him for his inability to appreciate her joy at exploring all of the dimensions of her self and as a result sets about destroying her own life. As the "fallen woman," she becomes a self-caricature: She will not take care of her body and literally eats herself to death.

Susannah, the second daughter in the Robinson family, is equally affected by Robinson's condemnation of Maggie's burgeoning sexuality. Susannah witnesses Robinson's treatment of her sister, which causes her to feel that her love for her father indicates some disloyalty for her sister. Susannah believes she has to choose between her sister and her father.

Susannah has a dream that she is a small child and that her father offers her some green jelly beans. Although she wants to accept the gift that her father offers her, she feels that she cannot because she does not want to be disloyal to her sister. Susannah comes to believe that the dream represents the loss of a relationship with her father that could have provided her with pleasure and would have allowed her to develop into a more fully formed and healthy person. She also realizes that her sister Maggie was not worthy of her loyalty. As it turns out, Maggie had always been jealous of her sister and particular of Susannah's relationship with their father: Susannah had been Robinson's favorite. After Robinson responds to Maggie's sexuality with violence, Maggie uses her victimization in order to destroy the relationship between Susannah and Robinson.

When Maggie dies, she leaves Susannah a letter telling her sister the truth: that she never loved her sister. The letter engages in a character assassination of Susannah. Upon reading Maggie's letter, Susannah realizes that, because of her sister's lack of forgiveness of her father she herself was emotionally blackmailed into choosing her sister over her father and was harmed by this choice. When

Susannah remembers the dream of the green jelly beans, she realizes it represents the narrative truth she should have embraced rather than relying entirely on the brutality she witnessed between her father and her sister and believing that her perception was the only reality.

As a result of their failure to forgive their father, both Susannah and Maggie end up losing significant dimensions of their potential life experiences. Until they are able to shed their primary and erroneous narratives—Susannah upon Maggie's death and Maggie posthumously—and replace them with new understandings that are grounded in principles of forgiveness, both sisters are stymied in their efforts to become healthy and whole.

At the end of *By the Light of My Father's Smile,* the Mundo legend recounts the experience of coming-of-age. In the story, the light of the crescent moon becomes equated with the loving gaze of a father as he acknowledges and accepts his daughter's sexuality and subsequent emergence into adulthood and mature sexuality. This story has at its heart the principle of acceptance—acceptance of the inevitable passage of time and of the reality that the movement of days and years ensures that one's children will change and grow, and that part of that process means that, inevitably, they will become sexual beings.

Robinson is the character in the story who is most engaged in the process of acceptance. The novel begins with his observation of his daughter Susannah's life, including her various sexual relationships with men and women. Through his observation of his daughter in her totality, as her complete self, Robinson is forced to confront his desire to limit his daughters' experiential lives to what was palatable to him. In other words, Robinson has to accept that his daughter, as a mature woman, is a sexual creature. Through his posthumous acceptance of this reality, Robinson grows in understanding and begins to realize the damage that he has wrought in not accepting his daughters in their completeness. He must become the smiling light that guides his daughters' spiritual evolution.

Finally, the characters must experience transcendence. The novel suggests that Susannah, Maggie, and Robinson must enter an alternative narrative from the one that has controlled their lives in order to become fully actualized beings. For Robinson and Maggie, this transcendence occurs after they have died. In death, Robinson meets the recently deceased Mannie, Maggie's teenage lover. Through their conversations with each other, Mannie describes to Robinson the flaws with the narratives that controlled his life. He also reveals the ironies of Robinson's false posturing as a missionary and tells the older man that he has been collecting stories as a spectator that could have enriched his own experiences and liberated him to live a fuller and less oppressive life. Mannie informs Robinson that the Mundo people were not fooled by his disguise as a missionary and only tolerated him because of his passionate attachment to his wife. According to the Mundo, Robinson had been "sucked into the black cloth"—dominated by the lure of power and authority in ways that blinded him to the truth that surrounded him—the narrative truth of the Mundo people.

Mannie also explains to Robinson that, in order for him to move beyond his current location in a kind of limbo, he must make amends in a ceremony specifically designed to remedy the wrongs he has caused on earth. Before his instructive time with Mannie, Robinson has been obsessed with his daughter Susannah's activities and with improving her life. Mannie tells him that his energies need to be redirected to the situation of his other daughter, Maggie.

By the time that Robinson tunes into Maggie's life, she has managed to end it through her self-destructive behavior. As Robinson is too late to intervene in his daughter's life, Mannie shows him how to make reparations to her after she "crosses over." Mannie takes Robinson to the spot that he and Maggie called their home when they were adolescents, a simple, natural location that would have allowed them to live and thrive in harmony. When Robinson sees what he has destroyed with his shortsighted prejudices and sexism, he is mournful and wishes to make amends to his daughter and to Mannie. Mannie tells Robinson that he can repair the damage he has caused the couple by his acceptance of his dead daughter and of her union with Mannie. Robinson immediately agrees, and the two men watch Maggie approach on horseback from a distance. Once Robinson accepts his daughter as she appears as a mature woman and as a sexual being and receives her forgiveness for his interference in her life and the prohibition of her happiness and development, he transcends the boundaries and limitations of his human self and enters another realm of being. Robinson becomes like the moon smiling down on his daughters in their completeness. In the warmth of that light, both Susannah and Maggie are able to access the full potential of their beings and to forgive, accept, and transcend themselves.

## SIGNIFICANT THEMES, ISSUES, CONCERNS

### Dreams as Revelation

This work emphasizes the role that dreams play as a conduit to knowledge of the truth about the world. Through her dreams, Susannah begins to reconnect with her dead father. Robinson is able to interact with Susannah through dreams and to begin to convey to his daughter his sorrow at the divide that occurred in their relationship as a consequence of his behavior toward her sister. Through a series of dreams, Robinson demonstrates to Susannah the merits of their association and the loss that has resulted from her inability to forgive her father. Other characters in the novel are also affected by their dreams, including the mystic dwarf, Irene.

### Universality of Women's Oppression

One of Walker's consistent concerns is with the subjugation of women throughout the world. In this particular novel, she traces the life paths and experiences of several women and focuses on the situations that disable their autonomy and sense of self-worth. Susannah is the narrative's central focus, and she is disconnected from her fundamental experiences and impulses because of her father's poor behavior. As a result of Robinson's duplicity with the Mundo, representing himself as a missionary rather than as an anthropologist, in combination with his abuse of Maggie, Susannah grows up mistrustful of men and unable to feel comfortable with her own feelings of pleasure. The consequences of Robinson's behavior for Maggie are even more severe. As a result of his violence toward his daughter, she becomes self-destructive and ends up dying prematurely and alone.

This evisceration of the fundamental integrity of women by the men in their lives and communities is not isolated by geography. Another character in the novel, Irene, has her life confined and contained because of the rape of her mother, who becomes pregnant with Irene as a consequence of physical violation. The mother was beaten by Irene's father and brother owing to her pregnancy. When Irene is born, her mother dies in childbirth, and Irene is given to the church to spend her life there as a servant. This story supports the novel's thesis that women are victimized across the world because of their sexuality, even when they are the indirect victims of sexual exploitation and violence.

### Wisdom and Superiority of Indigenous Peoples

Throughout *By the Light of My Father's Smile*, Walker asserts directly that native or indigenous peoples have a more accurate perception, interpretation, and understanding of the world. The first group she presents in this way in the novel is the native people in the fictional Greek town of Kalimasa. In the narrative, Susannah sees the Kalimasa people in idealized, essentialist terms—as somehow innocent and in touch with ways of being that are more positive and that engender healthier relationships with one another and with the natural world. The first time Susannah goes to Kalimasa with her husband, Petros, the people there are, according to her, in a more original and pure state. When she returns years later with her lover Pauline, the people in Kalimasa seem less connected to Susannah's definition. They seem to her to be increasingly influenced by the outside world and, in her estimation, contaminated by these influences.

The narrative highlights the worldview of the Mundo. Although they are described as a historical combination of African and Indian peoples, the word *Mundo* means "world" in Spanish, and so the Mundo people come to represent all of the world's inhabitants. After Robinson dies, Manuelito, a Mundo man who also dies, becomes a spiritual guide for him. One of the first exchanges between Mannie and Robinson confirms the superiority of the Mundo worldview. Mannie tells Robinson that when he died, he was not at all surprised by what he discovered because the Mundo people, through their folklore and legends, had already conveyed to him the truth about what happens when human beings die. Mannie is not in the least surprised by anything that happens in the afterlife. By contrast, Robinson is utterly befuddled by his experiences in the afterworld, and the narratives that he has believed he discovers have no credibility. More significantly, he finds himself, after a lifetime of study and exploration as an anthropologist, bereft of any useful information that will help him to understand his present condition and to do something to help himself to transition to another state of being. This differential demonstrates the novel's advocacy of the superiority of indigenous cultures in their understanding of the truths about life and, perhaps more significantly, about death.

### Conflation of Sexuality and Spirituality

The most frequently noted characteristic of *By the Light of My Father's Smile* is Walker's graphic depiction of sexuality. The overt descriptions of both heterosexual and homosexual intimacy is part of her thesis in this novel. Through these scenes, she asserts that sexuality, particularly female sexuality, is not only natural in all of its forms, but that sexuality is a form of spirituality and communion with whatever divine or universal force exists. Part of the work that Robinson has to do after his death is to reconcile himself to his daughters' sexuality. He does so by observing Susannah as she is engaged in various sexual acts. By allowing Robinson this posthumous voyeuristic capability, Walker forces the audience to confront what she proclaims to be artificial polarities—the distinctions and divisions between sexuality and spirituality.

## CHARACTERS

**Anand** Anand is Petros's brother. Susannah meets him in Skidiza while disinterring Irene's mother's body to rebury her on a hillside. During the ceremony of reburial, Anand begins to weep and dance with the women. Susannah learns that he works with poor and battered women and children in refugee camps in Greece. He becomes one of Susannah's lovers; later, he is just a good friend. While he resembles Petros in appearance, they are markedly different in that Petros seems unable to understand women—and more importantly, Susannah—while Anand seems emotionally concerned with the welfare of women.

**Bratman** Bratman is mentioned briefly by Pauline. He is one of Pauline's grandsons; his father is Richard, Pauline's son.

**Father Robinson (Robinson)** The novel begins with the death of the Robinson patriarch. While his first name is never actually stated, he identifies himself as both husband and as father at various points of the novel. He narrates posthumously, often watching his daughters' love and sex lives and thinking about his relationship to his wife and daughters in a series of flashbacks. In life, he was an anthropologist. In an attempt to receive funding for his study of the Mexican Mundo tribe, he pretended to be a missionary.

Despite his atheism, Robinson's role as missionary within the Mundo community absorbed him. He became increasingly anxious about the sexual-spiritual nature of the Mundo tribe and the effects of exposure to these beliefs on his daughters. While Susannah was perhaps the more reserved and obedient of his two daughters, Maggie's "wild" nature and her tendency to play with the boys created a point of tension between him and his oldest daughter, which culminated when he discovered her making love to Mannie. Robinson beat Maggie to the point of drawing blood, an act Susannah witnessed through a keyhole. Robinson's relationship with his daughters changed permanently. Maggie's resentment toward him spread to Susannah, who distanced herself from him, despite her father's affection.

The novel is in part about Robinson's rediscovery of his place as father. In watching his daughters' sexual relationships, he eventually understands how to bless rather than repress their sexuality. He renames himself Father at the end of the novel, after the death of Maggie. By finally blessing the sexual union of his daughter and Mannie posthumously, he is able to undo the beating he had inflicted in his lifetime.

The reacquisition of Robinson's role seems inextricably linked to the process of crossing over. Mannie becomes his guide into his final passage.

**Gena** Gena was Pauline's first female lover. She helped Pauline realize that women can have sexual enjoyment. Their affair had a nurturing quality. She was a white woman, the daughter of Eastern European immigrants. She was married to Richard, after whom Pauline named her son.

**Irene** Irene is a dwarf woman Susannah meets in Skidiza. When they meet, she has lived her entire life up that point within the church, forbidden to leave. She was born illegitimate as the product of a rape, and her mother died giving birth to her.

Petros, Susannah's husband, seems to accept Irene's place within the society as an outcast, and he harbors the assumption that she is both uneducated and sheltered. However, Susannah is immediately drawn to her because of the red curtains hanging in her window. Susannah begins to visit Irene every day during her stay in Skidiza, and they develop a friendship. Irene is well educated, speaks several languages, and is knowledgeable of the outside world despite the fact that she has never left the church. She has access to a television and a computer through which she learns much of what she knows. She tends her mother's grave every day and reads tarot cards; she reads Susannah's fortune.

A few years after they part ways, Irene inherits a fortune from her father, who died and left her a yacht on which she travels the world. She has always felt close to Gypsies and their oppressed, nomadic existence. She travels with a caravan of Gypsies for awhile, but after learning that their nomadic existence is not voluntary but an anxious response to oppression, she leaves the group. At this point, she begins to travel around the world. Several years after Susannah's visit to Skidiza, Irene writes to her and visits her. Eventually Susannah travels with her on the yacht. Irene eventually reburies her mother on a hillside close to Skidiza. She dies shortly after burying her mother.

**Jocko** Jocko is Susannah and Magdalena's uncle and Langley's favorite little brother. As a young boy, he pretends he is Zorro, often using Langley as his damsel in distress. As a grown man, he works "behind the scenes" in Hollywood. He has visited the Robinsons in the mountains in Mexico one time. His appearance is described as tall, thin, with close-cropped hair and a beautiful nose. He is mentioned in the story in reference to his funeral, at which Langley grieves. Jocko's death is the point at which she is able to reconcile with her husband after his physical abuse toward Magdalena.

**June** *See* MAGDALENA ROBINSON.

**Langley Robinson** Langley Robinson is Susannah and Magdalena's mother. She is an anthropologist, studying the Mundo tribe in Mexico with her husband under the guise of being missionaries. She and her husband maintain a passionate sex life, and she enjoys being naked. After her husband beats Magdalena after discovering her making love with Manuelito, a Mundo boy, she shuts her husband out, feeling a fundamental divide between their worldviews. The incident initially has a profound effect on her, and she forces her husband to sleep separately from her, saying, "We were beaten in slavery!" The couple reconcile after her brother's funeral.

Throughout her life, Langley shares a passionate and deep love and sexual bond with her husband. She dies of cancer some years before her husband dies. When Magdalena dies, she meets

Langley posthumously at a river, and she teaches her mother to cross over.

**Lily Paul** *See* PAULINE.

**Magdalena Robinson (Maggie, MacDoc, June)** Magdalena has several names within the story. She is Magdalena, Maggie, MacDoc, and June. MacDoc is the name the Mundo people give to her. Her original Mundo name was Mad Dog, a representation of wild spirit, but her father insisted that it was inappropriate, and she was called MacDoc instead. Later, she was allowed to choose her own name, a Mundo tribe tradition, and she decided on the name June.

Maggie is an active, free-spirited girl as a child, perhaps understanding the sexual-spiritual essence of life at an early age. Her father, pretending to be a missionary to the Mundo tribe and absorbed by his role as minister, began to try to control her, trying to prohibit her from embodying wildness. When she is discovered making love with Mannie, her first and only love, her father beats her with a belt to the point of drawing blood. Her resentment and hatred toward her father at having robbed her of the moment when she felt most loved and whole stays with her throughout her life. She only becomes reconciled with her father after death, when he finally blesses her union with Mannie.

At a young age, following the incident with her father, Magdalena acted as an inhibitory figure between her sister Susannah and her father, blocking their relationship, never allowing Susannah to forget their father's transgression. As a result, Susannah never recovers the affectionate relationship with her father she once had. As Maggie gets older, she gains weight, becoming obese, using food as a manifestation of her continued resentment of her family. She is a college professor as an adult.

Maggie meets Mannie again years later by chance on a plane. She recognizes him despite his broken, war-torn appearance, and they are able to reconnect. Soon after their meeting, however, Mannie dies. In her grief, Maggie attacks her sister. Ignoring Susannah's efforts to help her live a healthier lifestyle, Maggie dies in bed with chocolate cake in one hand and a beer in the other. After death, she is reunited with her father and receives his blessing. She reunites with her sister in the afterlife when Susannah dies of old age.

**Manuelito (Mannie)** Manuelito is a Mundo and Magdalena's lover. As a character, he seems to be a voice of the Mundo people, as he leads the other characters, particularly Robinson, through the process of death. In life, while a young man, Mannie makes Maggie a belt with circular metal disks on them as a present. After their first sexual encounter, Maggie's father beats her with the same belt, and the Robinsons move away from the tribe soon afterward.

Mannie eventually moves to America in search of Maggie. He fights in the Vietnam War and comes home injured and scarred, with surgical wires holding together his body. By this time, he is known as Mannie and has a wife named Maria. At this point in adulthood, he meets Magdalena again. Even though both have changed in appearance, they recognize each other immediately. They write letters to each other, reunite, and share a passionate sexual encounter. Soon after, crossing the street, Mannie is hit by a bus, singing a Mundo song of passage as he dies. After his death, Mannie meets Robinson and teaches him the Mundo process of crossing over as well as the Mundo song. He also coaches Robinson in blessing the marriage between Maggie and Mannie, and the couple find posthumous bliss.

**Maria** Maria is Manuelito's wife. He meets her after he moves to America in search of Magdalena. She never physically appears in the story and is only mentioned by Mannie and Maggie.

**Pauline** Pauline is Susannah's lover. She and Susannah meet in a restaurant that Pauline owns, called Lily Paul. She is forward, animated, and honest and has short silver hair. When they meet, they are immediately interested in one another and shortly begin their affair while Susannah is still married to Petros. They travel to Kalimasa together, during which they often find themselves in contention. They resolve the irritations with their passionate sexual relationship. Pauline wants to settle down with Susannah and marry her, apparently in order to anchor her free spirit. Susannah decides to travel with Irene instead.

As a young woman, Pauline was tomboyish and enjoyed learning. At 16, she was impregnated by Winston, a charming but good-for-nothing 25-year-old, against her will and did not come to enjoy sex until she met Gena, her first female lover. She gave birth to a son, Richard. She has two grandsons, Will and Bratman.

**Petros** Petros is Susannah's Greek husband, whom she later divorces. He came over to America seemingly as a way to run away from his Greek heritage, which he regards with a certain amount of distaste. To Petros, Susannah is the realization of a kind of American dream, or fantasy—a distinctly "American" woman. When they visit his home, he likes to make love to her in his childhood bedroom. Following their visit to Greece, where Susannah meets Irene, she begins to feel a sense of distance between herself and Petros. Petros is petulant as a character. He also seems openly homophobic, at the very least toward lesbians. This characteristic pushes Susannah even further away.

**Richard** Richard is Pauline's son, named after Gena's husband. He never appears in the story and is only referenced by Pauline and Susannah.

**Robinson** *See* FATHER ROBINSON.

**Susannah Robinson** After Robinson dies at the start of the novel, he watches his daughter Susannah make love to her husband, Petros. He follows her (and sometimes her sister, Magdalena) after death, looking in on their sexual relationships and gaining a certain understanding about them.

As a little girl, Susannah was close with her father, calm and obedient. She was always more affectionate than Maggie during their stay with the Mundo tribe. When Susannah witnesses her father beating Maggie through a keyhole, their relationship changes for the rest of their lives. Susannah has a recurring dream about a time when her father presented her with green jelly beans, her favorite, and even though she wanted them, the presence of her sister prevented her from reaching out and taking them. Instead, she rejects them and, in turn, rejects her father. As an adult, she confronts her sister about their relationship with their father, questioning why Maggie did not let her just love her father. In a rage, Maggie attacks her, but the sisters reconcile. Susannah tries to help her sister become healthy, which Maggie rejects.

Susannah's adult life forms most of the novel's narrative. She is married to Petros, and together they travel to Greece, where Susannah is intrigued by the treatment of women in Skidiza and also with Irene, who eventually becomes her friend. Susannah feels her position as a woman in the world acutely and, therefore, finds a connection in Irene. She eventually splits with Petros and shares a love/sexual relationship with Pauline. In the process, she learns the healing force of a sexual relationship and a kind of feminine sexual enjoyment.

Susannah's insistence on continuing to explore the options of her life and be a free spirit lead her to leave Pauline (despite her lover's desire to settle down and get married) and to explore the world with Irene. Irene reads Susannah's dreams in which two women each prepare food. Irene interprets the first woman in Susannah's dream as her sister, Maggie, who slowly made Susannah into something that she was not, and the second woman as Pauline, who always believed that she was someone other than who she was.

Susannah stays with Irene until Irene dies. She meets Petros's brother, Anand, and is drawn to his appreciation of women. Susannah dies of old age. Magdalena comes to meet her at her death, to guide her in the process of crossing over.

**Will** Will is one of Pauline's grandsons. His father is Richard.

**Winston** Winston impregnated Pauline against her will. She and her family later realized that despite his charming personality, he was not able to support her. Their sexual relationship was entirely one-sided and usually for his satisfaction. Her pregnancy provided an excuse for him to continue to have sex with her. Pauline did not stay with him.

### FURTHER READING

Bernstein, Richard. "'By the Light of My Father's Smile': Limp New-Age Nonsense in Mexico." *New York Times.* Available online. URL: http://www.nytimes.com/books/98/10/04/daily/walker-book-review.html. Accessed January 12, 2010.

Pemberton, Gayle. "Fantasy Lives." *Women's Review of Books.* 16, no. 3 (December 1999): 20–21.

Prose, Francine. "Sexual Healing: Alice Walker Sings a Psalm to the Pleasures of the Flesh." *New York Times.* Available online. URL: http://www.nytimes.com/books/98/10/04/reviews/981004.04proset.html. Accessed December 27, 2009.

## *Color Purple, The* (1982)

*The Color Purple* is the story of a woman's journey from invisibility and degradation to wholeness and graceful communion with herself and her community. The novel is told through a series of letters that the protagonist, Celie, writes, mostly to God; sometimes to her absent sister, Nettie; and, toward the end of the book, to the universe at large. Through these letters, she is able to negotiate the horrors in her life, which include her impregnation twice at the hands of the man she believes is her father; an early marriage to a man who abuses and neglects her, partly as a consequence of his unrequited love for another woman, his mistress Shug Avery; and the loss of her beloved sister, Nettie, for most of her life. An unexpected love for her husband's mistress sets Celie on the path toward greater understanding of herself and helps her to begin to forgive those who have wronged her and have tried to limit her quest.

Walker's depictions of her characters are particularly strong in *The Color Purple,* with figures like Nettie, Mr. —— (also called Albert), Harpo, Sophia, and Squeak surrounding Celie with a vibrant and complicated universe of compatriots and antagonists. The novel tackles issues of incest, domestic violence, lesbianism, religion, racism, poverty, and motherhood as manifesting in a poor, black, southern community.

The fervor surrounding *The Color Purple* was immense. The book received intense critical acclaim, winning the 1983 Pulitzer Prize. It also received scathing critiques, most of which centered on the novel's presentation of male characters in negative ways. After winning the Pulitzer Prize, the novel became an international best-seller and catapulted Walker to a previously unimagined level of fame.

### SYNOPSIS

Note that the individual letters are not titled or numbered in the novel. They are numbered here in an attempt to reflect the novel's structure.

#### Letter 1

*The Color Purple* begins with lines spoken by Alphonso. Celie, the novel's protagonist, believes that Alphonso is her father. He says to her, "You better not never tell nobody but God. It'd kill your mammy." This line sets the tone for the novel. Celie is a much-abused character who is silent about her experiences for most of the novel, except for her letters, which constitute the body of the text and are often addressed to God. In these letters, Celie articulates all that she has been forbidden by Alphonso to speak. In the novel's initial letter, Celie reveals that she is 14 years old and that, although she believes that she has been a "good girl," many events have transpired in her recent history to make her doubt her own self-perceptions.

#### Letter 2

Celie's mother is absent from the home following her delivery of Celie's half brother, a baby named Lucious (whose name is revealed in the first letter). Celie reveals in her second letter that, in her mother's absence, she has been sexually molested and raped by Alphonso and is now pregnant from the encounter. Celie gives birth to a child. Although later she learns that the child has lived, she originally believes Alphonso murdered her daughter. After the birth of that first child, a girl whom Celie named Olivia, Celie becomes pregnant again through Alphonso's abuse. Soon after the birth of Celie's second child, Celie's mother dies, angry about her husband's betrayal and physically destroyed by the too-frequent births of her children. She dies, leaving Celie and her brothers and sisters alone with Alphonso.

### Letter 3

Although Alphonso also takes Celie's second child, a boy, Celie does not believe that Alphonso killed the infant.

### Letter 4

Alphonso marries a woman who is nearly the same age as Celie. Celie begins to worry about the possibility of Alphonso abusing her younger sister Nettie in the same way that he abused Celie. Nettie has a boyfriend, a man Celie calls Mr. ——, who resembles Alphonso and whose wife was killed by the man with whom she was having an affair. Celie warns Nettie against getting involved with someone who needs a woman to take care of his children and advises her little sister to continue to pursue her education.

### Letter 5

Celie writes that she is not interested in men because they frighten her, unlike women to whom she seems to have an early attraction. Mistakenly believing that she is flirting with a boy, Alphonso physically abuses Celie as punishment. Celie then changes her advice to Nettie, telling her to marry Mr. ——. Celie believes that Mr. —— is so in love with Nettie that he will be kind to her sister for at least a year and that a year is the best that Nettie can hope to enjoy. Celie also reveals that she cannot have any more children because she no longer menstruates.

### Letter 6

When Mr. —— finally comes to propose marriage to Nettie, Alphonso tells him that he cannot marry her, giving the excuse of knowing about Mr. ——'s long-term affair with a woman named Shug Avery. Celie sees a photograph of Shug Avery that Mr. —— inadvertently leaves behind. She becomes enamored of the woman, stating that Shug is the most beautiful woman she has ever seen. Celie even begins to dream about Shug.

### Letter 7

In an attempt to distract Alphonso from Nettie, Celie tries dressing up. Alphonso responds by beating and then raping Celie. Later, Mr. —— comes over and asks again to marry Nettie. Alphonso offers him Celie instead. As he makes the offer, Mr. —— insults Celie by denigrating her sexual purity and calling her ugly.

### Letter 8

After four months, Mr. —— decides to marry Celie. She writes of the urgent and desperate attempts she and Nettie make to improve her ability to read and write before she is taken away by Mr. ——. The sisters realize that writing may be the only way that they will be able to communicate.

### Letter 9

After Celie marries Mr. ——, her life consists of tending to his children, cooking for his family, and cleaning his house. One typical and horrific event occurs on Celie's wedding day when Mr. ——'s oldest son, Harpo, hits her in the head with a rock. Later that day, bleeding and injured, she spends the evening untangling the hair of her stepdaughters. The girls' hair has not been combed in months. After all of this debasement, she is subjected to thoughtless sex with Mr. ——.

### Letter 10

One day, while shopping in town with Mr. ——, Celie encounters a woman with a baby. Celie believes the baby might be her lost little girl. After speaking with the woman, she is convinced that the little girl is her lost child and is thrilled that she might be alive.

### Letter 11

Nettie comes to live with Mr. —— and Celie after Alfonso attempts to have sex with her. Mr. —— continues to flirt with Nettie, and the sisters realize that Nettie's stay will be short-lived. Mr. —— tells Nettie that she has to go. The sisters promise to write each other, but Celie does not receive the promised letters from Nettie and believes she never will.

### Letter 12

Mr. ——'s sisters, Kate and Carrie, come to visit. They tell Celie about Anna Julia, Mr. ——'s first wife. They also gossip about Mr. ——'s long-term girlfriend, Shug Avery. The women try to help Celie out by defending her to their brother and to their nephew, Harpo. They also buy her some material to make some clothes for herself. Although they try to help Celie develop some sense of self-esteem, their efforts are virtually fruitless at this point in Celie's development.

### Letter 13

Mr. ——'s behavior toward Celie becomes a model for his son Harpo, who believes, based on his father's actions, that women should be beaten in order for the man of the household to retain his authority and status. This miseducation negatively impacts Harpo's developing relationship with the love of his life, Sofia. Although the relationship does not have the approval of either's father, Harpo and Sofia are determined to marry. Celie describes Sofia as pretty and brown-skinned and notes that Harpo, because he is so dark, thinks that Sofia is light-skinned, which contributes to his adoration of the woman.

### Letter 14

Shug Avery arrives in town to sing at the Lucky Star. Celie helps Mr. —— get dressed for her arrival and wishes that she could attend the homecoming performance with him. Celie is racked with curiosity about her husband's mistress.

### Letter 15

Mr. —— returns distraught after being away with Shug for two days. Celie wants desperately to know what happened between him and Shug, but he does not tell her, and Celie is left where she began—with her imaginings of Shug.

### Letter 16

Harpo and his father fight about Harpo's relationship with Sofia.

### Letter 17

Because Harpo's mother, Anna Julia, was killed by her lover after an adulterous affair, Sofia's father tells Harpo that he is not fit to marry his daughter, even though Sofia is pregnant with Harpo's child. Sofia's father is not the only one who disapproves of the relationship between Harpo and Sofia. Mr. —— also reiterates his disapproval and forbids the two from marrying.

### Letter 18

Despite the censure of both of their fathers, Harpo and Sofia get married and start to live their lives together in a house located on land adjacent to Mr. ——'s house. Harpo builds what Celie calls a creek house out of a shed that Mr. —— no longer uses, and the couple take up residence.

### Letter 19

Although Harpo and Sofia are happy, Harpo says that he wants his new wife to do as he says—to be obedient. Sofia is independent and free-thinking. When he asks his father about his perceived problem, Mr. —— advises Harpo to beat Sofia. Celie tells Harpo the same thing. This shared suggestion inaugurates a new phase in Harpo and Sofia's relationship, one full of violence, as the two battle each other physically.

### Letter 20

Harpo and Sofia continue fighting. The fighting gets so extreme that Celie is afraid to enter their house during a visit. Harpo and Sofia go to visit her sister.

### Letter 21

Celie comes to regret her words to Harpo about Sofia. She explains to Sofia that she did not mean to harm her with what she said to Harpo, and she says that her experience comes from her life and from the inability to feel any anger. She also says that she thinks things will be better for them all in the next life. Sofia tells her that she should defend herself and try to enjoy her life here. After the talk, Celie feels that she has made amends to Sofia and stops feeling guilty about her advice to Harpo.

### Letter 22

Shug Avery falls ill and as a result comes to stay with Mr. —— and Celie. Ironically, Mr. —— and Celie are equally excited by the arrival of the woman with whom they are both infatuated. Shug is simultaneously Mr. ——'s long-term love and Celie's unseen idol. When Shug arrives, she is ill and immediately insults Celie, her lover's wife, by telling Celie that she is ugly.

### Letter 23

Despite this insult, Celie does her best to make Shug feel better and welcome in the house she shares with Mr. ——. Shug also insults Mr. ——, reminding him that he did not have the strength of character to stand up to his father and marry her.

### Letter 24

Celie learns that Shug and Mr. —— have had three children together. Shug tells Celie that her mother is raising the children she had with Mr. ——. Despite their shared history, Mr. —— feels uncomfortable giving the ill Shug a bath, and so the task falls to Celie.

### Letter 25

Under Celie's care, Shug begins to recover her health and stamina. Mr. —— is relieved to see Shug's recovery.

### Letter 26

In a pivotal scene, Celie cares for Shug by combing her hair. While she dresses the woman's hair and body, Shug, whose primary vocation is singing, begins to hum a tune, signaling a healing that is not only physical but also spiritual and psychological. Shug tells Celie that her gentle care has made her think of a song she wants to write.

### Letter 27

A visit to the house by Mr. ——'s father highlights the oddity of Shug's temporary residence there. Mr. ——'s father comments that not every woman would let the woman their husband is sleeping with live in her house. Interestingly, Celie takes Mr. ——'s side in this appraisal and defends Shug by secretly spitting in a glass of water before offering it to Mr. ——'s father.

### Letter 28

Celie and Sofia begin to quilt. As she recovers, Shug Avery joins the women, a sign that she is beginning to be healthy again, both physically and emotionally. While the women quilt, Sofia tells them that Harpo has begun to eat enormous quantities of food and that she does not know why.

### Letter 29

With great emotion, Harpo finally tells Celie that he is trying to get larger so that he can beat Sofia.

### Letter 30

Celie goes to tell Sofia what she has learned. Sofia says that she had a feeling that the reason Harpo had been eating so much was to be able to control her physically. She tells Celie that she is growing tired of Harpo and his need to have her become totally dependent. She says that she does not like the sex that they have any longer and that Harpo is selfish and self-absorbed. Sofia has grown so tired of Harpo's abuse and attempts to dominate her that she is thinking of leaving him, taking their children with her to her sister Odessa's house.

### Letter 31

No longer able to tolerate Harpo's abuse, Sofia goes to live with her sister. She takes their children with her when she leaves.

### Letter 32

After Sofia has been gone for six months, Harpo decides to turn their former home into a JUKE JOINT where BLUES and JAZZ musicians come to perform and people can drink and dance. He builds it away from the main part of the community so that whatever happens there does not draw the attention of the law.

### Letter 33

After he opens the juke joint, Harpo does not get much attendance until he invites Shug to sing there. Subsequently, his business becomes a success. The first time that Celie visits the juke joint, she is embarrassed by her clothes and by the sneers of the folks in the place. Shug transforms Celie's experience by singing a song for her. The song is one Shug says she started writing when she was unwell and Celie was taking care of her. Celie writes in her letter that this song was a gift to her and that it marks the first time anyone cared enough for her to make something for her alone.

### Letter 34

Shug gets ready to leave town and tells Celie that she will be gone before long. Celie tells Shug about Mr. ——'s physical abuse of her when Shug is not there. Shug promises to stay until she can be certain that Albert (Mr. ——) will not be abusive.

### Letter 35

Shug and Albert are sleeping together more often. Shug asks Celie if she minds that Albert sleeps with her, and the two women talk about sex. Shug reveals that she loves to have sex and, in particular, loves having sex with Albert. Celie is surprised to learn this and tells Shug that she has never enjoyed sex. Shug tells her that she is still a virgin and proceeds to teach her about sexuality. She gives Celie a mirror and tells her to look at her genitals. Shug tells Celie about what makes sexuality feel pleasurable, and Celie tells Shug that she does not mind if she wants to sleep with Albert. After she gives Shug this permission, Celie finds herself feeling sad and lonesome when she knows that the two are together.

### Letter 36

Celie writes about one night at Harpo's when Sofia returns to her former home. She is accompanied by her new boyfriend, a prizefighter named Henry Broadnax. Harpo is there with his new girlfriend, a woman he calls Squeak. Harpo confronts Sofia about her presence in a juke joint even though she has five children, and Sofia responds by saying that she needs to have a little fun once in a while and that she actually *is* at home. The two begin to laugh and then to dance together, angering Harpo's new girlfriend, who tries to break up their dance. Sofia does not interfere with the woman's attempts until Squeak slaps her, prompting Sofia to punch the woman in the face, knocking two of her teeth out. With that, Sofia leaves arm in arm with the prizefighter.

### Letter 37

Celie writes of Sofia's downfall. Noticing that Harpo is despondent, Squeak asks Celie if she knows what is wrong. Celie begins by advising Squeak to make Harpo call her by her actual name, Mary Agnes. She then proceeds to tell Squeak about what happened to Sofia. One day, Sofia, the prizefighter, and Sofia and Harpo's children travel into town. Just as they arrive, they encounter the mayor's wife, Miss Millie, who is condescending to the group and asks Sofia if she would like to be Miss Millie's maid. Sofia responds, "Hell no," repeating it several times. The mayor intervenes. Sofia repeats her refusal, and the mayor hits her in the face. Sofia responds by hitting the mayor back, and chaos ensues. Eventually, Sofia is beaten nearly to death and taken to jail. Mr. —— tries to intervene on Sofia's behalf as he has developed a relationship with the sheriff through the misdeeds of his son Bub. The sheriff allows the family to visit Sofia. Celie is shocked by Sofia's appearance and by the damage that she has suffered. Celie does her best in the dank prison to wash and dress Sofia's wounds.

### Letter 38

After her brutal encounter with the mayor and his wife, Sofia is sentenced to work in the prison laundry. The job is debilitating, and doing the work makes Sofia ill. She is forced to live in conditions that are inhumane: Her cell is infested with vermin, and she is silenced. The subservience needed to survive damages Sofia's spirit, and she finds herself transformed from a strong, self-reliant woman into a meek and devastated human being.

### Letter 39

Her family is worried that the situation will not only kill Sofia's psyche but will also destroy her physical self. They determine to do something to help her situation. Celie, Mr. ——, Harpo, and Sofia's extended family meet to brainstorm solutions about what to do to transform Sofia's plight into a more endurable situation.

During the meeting, Celie imagines God intervening on Sofia's behalf. This God is white, all white, with white eyes. She imagines this figure enacting Sofia's liberation. Mr. —— suggests something more practical when he asks the group about the warden's black family. In small southern communities, particularly during the novel's time frame, the family ties between blacks and whites were public and pervasive, due largely to the sexual exploitation of black women at the hands of white men. Squeak reveals during the family meeting that the prison warden, Bubber Hodges, is her uncle. She tells the group that Bubber's brother, Jimmy, had three children with her mother. The group decides that since she is related to Bubber, Squeak may have some influence over him, and so they decide to send her to deliver misleading information about Sofia.

### Letter 40

The family dress Squeak up in formal and unfamiliar clothing and tell her to tell the warden that Sofia is not being punished sufficiently and that the real punishment the woman dreads is the possibility of working for the mayor's wife. This clever lie is designed to resonate with the desire of Bubber Hodges and the mayor to punish Sofia as harshly as possible. Squeak's feigned motivation for telling Hodges that Sofia needs to be punished more is the fact that Squeak is living with Sofia's husband, Harpo.

Squeak is nervous and intimidated by her task. Harpo has given her the name Squeak because of her reluctance to talk and the sound of her voice, so the idea of approaching her unacknowledged uncle is a daunting prospect for her to consider. The others tell her that the key to her success is to make Hodges remember that they are related. They believe that if he remembers this, then Squeak's story will have some credibility for her uncle.

### Letter 41

When she returns, Squeak is disheveled. Her dress is torn, and it is obvious that her encounter with Hodges was violent. She had delivered her message as she was told to by the group. She tells them all that Hodges asked her who her family was and that she told him she remembered him coming by her house when she was a little girl with her mother's friend (her father) Mr. Jimmy. He tells her to take off her dress and then proceeds to rape her even though he is her uncle. After she tells the story of what happened to her, Squeak asks Harpo if her really loves her or simply wants to be with her because she is light-skinned. Harpo declares his genuine love for her. Then Squeak insists, as Celie has advised her earlier, that she be called by her real name, Mary Agnes.

### Letter 42

Mary Agnes's visit to Bubber Hodges and his rape of her prove to be transformative. Six months after the event, she begins to sing. Although the family does not appreciate her voice at first, eventually they come to enjoy it. Mary Agnes takes care of Harpo and Sofia's children, with help from Sofia's sisters. In her songs, she tries to deal with her feelings about her skin color and to assert herself as an equal member of the community, despite the circumstances of her birth.

### Letter 43

Celie writes that Mary Agnes's ruse has worked and that Sofia was reassigned to the mayor's house, where she is working as the mayor's maid. The situation is an improvement for Sofia, who, after three years of working for the mayor's family, begins to look something like her old self. One of Sofia's tasks is to take care of the mayor's children, a six-year-old boy named Billy and his younger sister, Eleanor

Jane. Eleanor Jane has a great deal of affection for Sofia, feelings that Sofia does not reciprocate.

### Letter 44

Although she tells her family that she is essentially a slave, Sofia survives the situation through humor and by telling stories about the mayor's family and their dysfunction. The car that Sofia and the prizefighter drove into town on the day that Sofia hit the mayor motivates the mayor to buy his wife a car. His wife, Miss Millie, does not know how to drive, and so it falls to Sofia to teach the woman. Miss Millie is not a good student, but Sofia teaches her the best that she can.

After she achieves some competence as a driver, Miss Millie offers to drive Sofia home to visit her children at Christmas time. Sofia has an emotional reunion with her children, who have not seen her in such a long time that they do not recognize her. Miss Millie tells Sofia that she can stay with her family until five o'clock and tries to leave. Miss Millie finds that she cannot put the car in reverse and so insists that Sofia come home with her and drive the car. Sofia is with her family for only 15 minutes.

### Letter 45

Celie reveals that Shug is coming back home and has written that she is bringing a surprise with her. Shug has been successful in her singing career, and both Mr. —— and Celie believe that she will bring something that they will enjoy. Shug arrives at Mr. ——'s house on Christmas day and genuinely surprises Celie and Mr. —— by bringing with her a recently acquired husband named Grady. Predictably, Celie does not like anything about the man. Shug tells Mr. —— and Celie that she and Grady have been driving all night in the new car that Shug has bought with the money that she has been earning. Shug says that the car is her wedding present to Grady. She seems pleased with her newfound status as a married lady.

### Letter 46

In response to Shug's news, Mr. —— remains intoxicated throughout the holiday. The two couples spend time celebrating and doing tasks around the house. Shug has become a celebrity, singing across the country with well-known performers such as Duke Ellington and Sophie Tucker. She has purchased her own home in Memphis, Tennessee. Celie reports that Shug spends a great deal of money on Grady, purchasing whatever he desires.

Shug tells Celie that she met Grady when her car needed repair, and he got it running again. Celie informs her that Mr. —— is hurt by her marriage to Grady. Shug tells her that once she learned that Albert had beaten Celie, she lost her desire for him and thinks of him only as family now. Celie tells her that Mr. —— does not abuse her as much since Shug confronted him about it. She also tells Shug that their sex life is somewhat improved, although she still does not have orgasms.

### Letter 47

One evening, Mr. —— and Grady go off together to drink, leaving Celie and Shug alone in the house. The two women lie in bed and talk about sex. Prompted by Shug's question about her children's father, Celie begins to describe the rape, defying Alphonso's warning never to talk about the violation she experienced. Celie tells Shug that she was in the process of cutting his hair when, without warning, he violently forced himself inside of her. Celie reveals how the incident shocked and hurt her as she had no knowledge of sex and had no one to tell what had happened. She adds that even after the rape, Alphonso was merciless, insisting that she finish cutting his hair.

Shug provides a sympathetic ear for Celie, and as a result, Celie finds telling her story to be a cathartic and healing experience. She talks about her mother and how she believed Alphonso's story about Celie having a boyfriend rather than having compassion for her own child. Celie talks of how Alphonso eventually turned his attentions to Nettie and of her mother's eventual death. She tells Shug about how that violation ruined one of the activities that she most loves, cutting hair. After the rape, cutting hair always reminded her of the trauma, yet she was still responsible for cutting Alphonso's hair.

Celie informs Shug about the ways in which the abuse she experienced at home continued after she married Mr. ——. She shares the story of her arrival in Mr. ——'s house and details Harpo's violent welcome—his act of throwing the rock at her head. Shug is distraught when she learns that Mr. —— demanded to have sex with Celie even though she was injured by Harpo's rock. After her revelation, Celie comes to the conclusion that she is unloved. Shug tells Celie that she loves her. The two begin to kiss and then to make love.

### Letter 48

Celie and Shug awaken when Mr. —— and Grady return, and they slip into their respective beds before the men discover what has happened. There are many things that Celie does not like about Grady, including his obvious attraction to Mary Agnes and his willingness to spend Shug's money. Despite these realities, Celie tries to like him because he is Shug's husband, and she loves Shug. Meanwhile, Shug encourages Mary Agnes's aspirations to sing. She tells Mary Agnes that she has an unusual voice that will make people think about having sex. Shug suggests that Harpo let Mary Agnes sing in the juke joint, telling him that the woman he has singing there now is too religious and that the crowd that comes to the joint would rather hear Mary Agnes. Shug also argues that Mary Agnes's appearance will help to attract people to Harpo's juke joint. As she shares these perceptions with Harpo, Shug looks to Grady for affirmation, signaling to him that she is aware of his attraction to Harpo's girlfriend.

### Letter 49

Celie finally is able to hold a letter from Nettie. Shug has discovered that Mr. —— has been hiding letters he takes out of the mailbox. Shug asks Celie to tell her all about Nettie, and she does. Celie is overwhelmed with the confirmation that Nettie and her children are alive and that she will be coming home.

### Letter 50

After finding one letter from Nettie among Albert's possessions and giving it to Celie, Shug reveals that she believes Albert still has all of the letters that Nettie has been sending since he made Nettie leave. Celie grabs a razor and goes to where Mr. —— is sitting, but Shug stops her from doing anything. Shug confesses to Celie the reasons why she is estranged from her family. She tells Celie that her mother could not tolerate her promiscuity and forced her to leave the house after she had three children with Albert without being married. Albert's father forbade him to marry Shug, and having little ability to confront his father, Albert did not defy the command. Shug tells Celie what a good dancer Albert used to be and says that she does not understand the kind of man he has become, particularly in light of his treatment of Celie.

### Letter 51

Celie knows that Albert keeps everything that is valuable to him in a trunk. Shug gets the key from Albert without his knowing, and Shug and Celie find all of Nettie's letters in his trunk. The two remove all of the letters they find and replace the envelopes so that Albert will not realize that they are missing.

### Letters 52–58

Nettie's letters are revelatory. As she reads them, Celie learns of Albert's attempted rape of Nettie and that her children are alive and living with Nettie in Africa. The subsequent letters continue to reveal the nuances of the life Nettie has been living since her escape from Mr. ——'s advances. She tells Celie of Samuel and Corrine's kindnesses, the ways that they make her feel welcome and a part of their family. Nettie learns that Samuel and Corrine are not only religious; they are missionaries, members of the American and African Missionary Society. Nettie travels to Africa with Corrine and Samuel in place of a missionary who is unable at the last minute to make the trip. Nettie works for Samuel and Corrine caring for and teaching their children. As she experiences Africa, Nettie loses her misconceptions about the continent as primitive and backward, ideas she inherited from common popular depictions. Nettie particularly describes her feelings of awe when she first sees the African coastline.

### Letter 59

After reading several of Nettie's letters, Celie wants to kill Mr. ——. Shug talks her out of it and arranges for Celie to sleep with her while she and Grady are visiting.

### Letter 60

The women do not have sex, though, because Celie is so angry that she is unresponsive. In order to distract her, Shug suggests that they make Celie some pants. In that way, Celie can channel her anger into a creative endeavor rather than harboring it. Sewing becomes an essential outlet for Celie.

### Letter 61

As Celie reads more of Nettie's letters, she learns of the family's arrival in the village of Olinka, where they will work as missionaries. Nettie tells of the village's recent history, the way it fell on hard times because of the greed of the chief who sold the village's staple product, roofleaf, to traders and almost destroyed the village.

### Letters 62–64

In Olinka, the girls are not educated. Nettie reveals that Olivia is the only girl in school. She tells Celie about Olivia's sense of injustice as a result of the exclusion of girls—particularly of her friend Tashi, whose father will not let her attend. In her letters, Nettie compares the sexism of the Olinka people with what she knows of sexism in the American rural South.

### Letter 65

After five years of life in Olinka, Nettie tells Celie of the approach of a road upon the village. The villagers originally believe that the road is to lead to Olinka, but in reality it is to go through the village. The road was built by a rubber manufacturer who purchased the territory that includes the village. The purchase forces the Olinka to have to pay rent for their land in addition to paying taxes. Also, Nettie writes that after her father's death, Tashi is allowed to attend school.

### Letters 66–67

As a consequence of Corrine's jealousy, Nettie learns the truth about her family history from Samuel and shares this information in a letter to Celie. Celie and Nettie's father was a prosperous land and store owner. Due to jealousy about the success of his store, whites burned it down and killed him and his two brothers who worked with him. Nettie and Celie's mother began to lose touch with reality as a result of these events and was taken advantage of by Alphonso, the man the sisters know as Pa. Alphonso married Celie and Nettie's mother and successively impregnated her until, bitter and weary, she dies.

### Letter 68

Celie is stunned to learn that Alphonso is not her father. Shug offers to take Celie with her when she leaves to return to Tennessee with Grady.

### Letter 69

After learning the truth about her parents from Nettie's letter, Celie goes with Shug to confront Pa (Alphonso). Celie also begins to address her letters to Nettie. Both Celie and Shug are surprised by the prosperous condition of the house and surrounding yard and land, as well as by Alphonso's 15-year-old wife. Celie asks Pa where her father is buried, and she and Shug go to the cemetery to try to find her parents' graves. They cannot find any trace of the graves at the cemetery.

### Letters 70–72

Nettie shares with Celie news of the death of Corrine and the troubles that affect Olinka as a result of the rubber plantation. She also tells of her expanded and developing relationship with Samuel.

### Letter 73

Celie now ends each of her letters with the word amen, as if they are a kind of prayer. In her writings, Celie shares the conversations that take place between her and Shug about God. After she learns about her family history, Celie rejects God. Shug argues against this rejection, telling Celie that she believes God is not an old white man, an idea Celie finds alienating, but that he is genderless and raceless. In fact, Shug thinks that God is formless—that God is a force in all living things. Celie begins to adopt this view and finds the God Shug describes in the natural world, particularly in trees.

### Letters 74–75

In spite of her newfound theology, Celie is still very angry, and when she tells Mr. —— that she is going to leave with Shug, she also finally confronts him about all of the abuse and mistreatment she has suffered at his hands. Squeak announces that she also is leaving and has plans to pursue a singing career in Memphis. She also repeats to the gathering that her name is Mary Agnes. After 11 years at the mercy of the mayor and his family, with Celie's pronouncements, Sofia also seems to regain her voice. She tells Harpo that their sixth child, Henrietta, his favorite, is not his. Before Celie leaves with Shug for Memphis, Tennessee, she curses Mr. —— and tells him that everything in his life will fail until he makes amends.

### Letters 76–77

In Tennessee, Celie and Shug set up house, creating a home that suits their aesthetic needs. Shug takes special pleasure in cooking, and the two eat, listen to music, and talk. Periodically, Shug goes on the road for singing tours to make money. Celie occupies her time sewing, making pants. After a time, encouraged by their popularity, Celie goes into business making pants and is able to contribute to the income of the house that she, Grady, Squeak, and Shug share.

### Letter 78

Celie travels back home for Sofia's mother's funeral. Sofia and her sisters make the unusual choice to serve as pallbearers with their brothers at the funeral despite objections from several quarters. While there, Celie shares marijuana with Harpo and Sofia, and they all seem to have a spiritual experience.

### Letter 79

Celie notices during the times that she sees Mr. —— that he appears uncharacteristically clean and well-kempt. Sofia tells her that he has become religious. Mr. —— speaks to Celie with deference and respect. Sofia tells Celie about Mr. ——'s decline, saying that Mr. —— had become a depressed recluse, with his house filthy and disordered. Harpo helped his father to recover and encouraged him to do right by Celie by sending her all of the letters Nettie had mailed. After Mr. —— returned the letters, he began to turn his life around and became a much better person than he had been previously.

### Letter 80

In Nettie's letter, she tells Celie of her marriage to Samuel and of the hardships of the Olinka. The roofleaf that had been the centerpiece of their culture and their literal and metaphorical protection was destroyed by the rubber manufacturers, and they are forced to top their houses with corrugated tin. This final blow, coupled with the takeover of the village by the rubber company as its headquarters, was a death knell to the village and its inhabitants. Nettie, Samuel, and the children travel to England to try to be of assistance to the Olinka.

Doris Baines is a woman Samuel and Nettie meet on the boat aboard which they travel to England. She is leaving Africa in advance of World War II after spending most of her life there. Doris was born to a wealthy family in England and left Europe after finding the life she inherited stilted and superficial. She became a missionary and author, publishing books under the pseudonym Jared Hunt. She spent her life among the Akwean tribe. When Nettie meets her, she is returning to England with her adopted grandson, Harold.

After their arrival in England, Nettie and Samuel present the Olinka's situation and dilemmas to the bishop of their church. The man disregards their concerns and their requests, instead focusing on the relationship between Nettie and Samuel and the impropriety of their living in close quarters without being married. Samuel is furious and shares with Nettie some of his and Corrine's history with the missionary movement. He tells Nettie that their involvement began as they listened to the stories of their aunts Theodosia and Althea, who had been missionaries when they were young women. The stories these women told inspired their niece and nephew also to pursue missionary work. During this exchange, Samuel gives into his grief about his and Corrine's thwarted dreams of helping to improve the Olinka's situation. As Nettie consoles Samuel, the exchange becomes sexual. Afterward, the two confess their love for each other, tell the children the whole story, and are married soon thereafter.

Nettie learns that Adam is in love with Tashi and that he is angry with her because she wants to engage in a SCARIFICATION ritual.

### Letter 81

When the family returns to Olinka, they discover that Tashi has undergone both scarification and a clitoridectomy (removal of the clitoris). Adam is eager to return home, yet Nettie states that she and Samuel are developing a happy and satisfied relationship.

### Letter 82

Celie writes to Nettie that Pa has died. She has learned from Pa's wife, Daisy, that the house and the land that Alphonso had occupied all these years belongs to Celie and Nettie. Celie inherits the house and begins to transform the location that had been her source of misery as a child and young girl into a home she can share with Shug and, eventually, she hopes, with Nettie and her children.

### Letters 83–84

Ironically, as Celie works to make this house into a home, Shug falls in love with someone else. Shug falls in love with a young boy of 19 named Germaine. When Shug tells Celie, Celie cannot even verbalize a response, she is so upset.

Henrietta grows ill with what seems like sickle-cell anemia, and the family rallies around her to help in any way they can. Celie comments on the changes in Mr. ——. He has become meticulously neat and devoted to helping his family. He even begins to collect seashells. He and Celie begin to be able to have conversations with each other. Celie discovers that she is only sexually attracted to women and tells Mr. —— that men look like frogs to her when they are undressed.

### Letter 85

Celie receives a telegram saying that the ship that Samuel, Nettie, and the children were on was sunk by German mines. Celie still addresses this letter to Nettie, yet she speaks of her despair and difficulty finding the will to live. Also, on the same day she receives the telegram, all of the letters she ever sent to Nettie are returned.

### Letter 86

In the next letter from Nettie, which indicates nothing of the family's fate since there is a lag time with the mail, she tells Celie about Tashi and Catherine's flight to live with the (*mbeles*), the secret people who live in the bush. She also tells Celie that Adam went to find Tashi and her mother.

### Letter 87

Celie shares with Nettie her hurt at Shug's relationship with Germaine. The two travel the United States and even go to Panama while Celie's heart breaks at home. She says she does not believe that Nettie and the rest of the family are dead even though the news about them seems so definitive. Mr. —— and Celie become friends of sorts, sharing their love for Shug and reminiscing about good times they had with her over the years. Mr. —— gains insight and awareness of his own life and the people in it. He even begins to learn how to sew and helps Celie sew pants in her shop, which she opened after inheriting her father's land. Celie learns from Shug's letters that she has been visiting with her son in Arizona and trying to make peace with her past.

### Letter 88

In the next letter Celie receives from Nettie, she learns that Adam and Tashi returned safely from the *mbeles*. Nettie writes about what she has learned from Tashi about life with the *mbeles*—that they have created a system of living that supports an entire community. Nettie also writes that Adam plans to marry Tashi even though Tashi does not think she can be accepted in the United States after her surgery. In order to reassure her, Adam undergoes the scarification ritual, and the two are married by Samuel. Celie believes that this is the last letter Nettie wrote before the boat was bombed.

### Letter 89

Celie continues to write to Nettie although she thinks that there is a possibility that her beloved sister and family were killed on the ship. Celie tells Nettie that Mr. —— has been in extensive conversation with Shug since they received the telegram about the ship. Shug travels to Washington to see if there is something she can do to ascertain the facts about what happened to Nettie and her family. Sofia begins to work for Celie in her store. She also tells Celie that Eleanor Jane has come back in her life. After finding out from her mother the truth about why Sofia had to work for them, Eleanor Jane returns to Sofia and helps her by preparing yam dishes that the ill Henrietta likes to eat. Sofia and Harpo are happily reunited in their relationship.

Mr. —— and Celie have become friends, and they talk honestly with each other. As Mr. —— reflects on his life, he observes that although he and Shug were not able to be together, she ended up in a better place than he did. Celie tells him that the difference is that Shug knows how to love people in a way that Mr. —— never has. Mr. —— becomes philosophical in his old age and comes to wonder about the fundamental questions of human existence and, although he does not have the answers to the questions he asks, the ability to question opens a new world of possibility for him. He tells Celie that the more he wonders, the more he realizes that to him, love is a fundamental necessity and a refuge from the terrible mystery and terror that comes from not knowing. Mr. —— even asks Celie to marry him again. She refuses, but the two continue to build a strong friendship.

Shug finally returns, but before she does, Celie has gained peace in her life without Shug. She is thrilled when Shug returns, but she does not need the other woman in order to be peaceful in her life. Shug loves the house and the home that Celie has created there. Shug tells Celie that Germaine has enrolled in college at the historically black institution Wilberforce, in Ohio. Celie explains to Shug the new relationship she has with Mr. ——, and Shug is surprised at the progress the two have made and is a bit jealous of the new relationship.

### Letter 90

The final letter of the book is written by Celie and addressed "Dear God. Dear stars, dear trees, dear sky, dear peoples. Dear Everything. Dear God." Celie writes about the return of her sister, Nettie, Samuel, and Celie's lost children, Adam and Olivia, as well as Adam's wife and Olivia's best friend, Tashi. Celie writes about her reunion with her sister and of her terror when she first lays eyes on the group. They all begin to cry and then say each other's names. They hold on to each other, and then Nettie begins to introduce Celie to the rest of her family.

The letter ends on the 4th of July, at an annual family celebration. Harpo tells Henrietta that what they are celebrating is each other rather than the traditional liberation from England. Mary Agnes has returned to get her daughter Suzie Q., and she now lives in Tennessee with her mother, who helps her to take care of the child while she is on the road. Mary Agnes has left Grady and no longer smokes marijuana.

The new members of the family are admired and welcomed. Adam and Tashi's scars are not an issue for them. They also find that they all share similar taste in food. Celie writes that her children give her a strange feeling. She believes that her children see everyone in the family as old. Celie finds this perception disconcerting because, with the return of her sister and her children, she proclaims that she has never felt younger. The book ends with the signature conclusion of the traditional Christian prayer, the word *Amen*.

## CRITICAL COMMENTARY

An epistolary novel is told in a series of documents, such as letters, journal entries, newspaper articles, and so on. The letters can be written by one or more characters and are effective at providing insight and a first-person perspective. The epistolary novel was most popular in the 18th century, but the form has never disappeared. It is often associated with female characters and writers; it also recalls the letters of the Bible and in a sense functions as a kind of contemporary gospel. Here, it teaches through parable and analogy the specific story of a black woman whose life has lessons and provides insights as universal as those of any major literary character.

By choosing the epistolary form for *The Color Purple,* Alice Walker is able to confront some of the conventions and assumptions made about women and class. In particular, Walker is able to emphasize the centrality of literacy to Western culture and to correlate Celie's increasing mastery of the form with her ability to more completely and compassionately perceive her role in the universe. Through her protagonist's increasing literacy, Walker both acknowledges the centrality of literacy to contemporary understandings of power, intelligence, and hierarchy and at the same time undermines it as a sole marker for competence. Walker is also able simultaneously to attack traditional presumptions about the lack of intelligence and creativity of African Americans. Celie acquires not only literacy but a concomitant wisdom that is grounded in alternative sources of knowledge, such as storytelling, physical and emotional intimacy, and an intuitive "reading" of the natural world. The inner world of someone like Celie was relatively unexplored literary terrain when Alice Walker wrote and published *The Color Purple.* Therefore, the character's interior point of view provides a nearly unprecedented literary perspective.

*The Color Purple* consists of some 90 letters. Many are addressed not to a particular person but to God, and they read more like diary entries than conventional letters. Later in the novel, Celie begins to write to her sister, Nettie, and to the universe generally. There are also letters from Nettie to Celie—letters that Celie does not for the most part discover until many years after they have been written and delivered (though intercepted by Mr. ——). Through the differentiation in the types and purposes of the letters that comprise the novel, Walker is able to trace Celie's development and ever-expanding horizon and perceptual universe. The letters and their intended recipients mark a progression in Celie's self: As her self-perception improves, she acquires increasing voice, and with that self-articulation she is able to claim greater authority. She seems to understand that she has something to say that others—indeed the whole universe—will find valuable.

The novel begins with Celie's writing frankly about the situation she finds herself in, though the first lines she writes are actually spoken by Alphonso. Celie believes that Alphonso is her father. He says to her, "You better not never tell nobody but God. It'd kill your mammy." This line sets the tone for the novel. Celie is a much-abused character who is silenced about her experiences for most of the novel, except for her letters. In these letters, Celie articulates all the horrific experiences and painful feelings she has been forbidden by Alphonso to speak. In the novel's initial letter, Celie reveals that she is 14 years old and that, although she believes that she has been a "good girl," many events have transpired in her recent history to make her doubt her own self-perceptions. Through her writing, Celie searches for answers. In the beginning, she does not have enough information to answer the various questions she has begun to pose about her own situation. Her power at this early point in the novel lies in her willingness to examine her situation in search of that information. Like prophets and secular philosophers alike, Celie appeals to what she understands as a higher authority—a benevolent and just source of wisdom and information. For Celie, the only such source available to her is the God in whom she has been taught to believe. Celie communes with that force using a voice, vision, and language that is uniquely hers and yet distinctly and appealingly familiar and primary.

It is Celie's use of common language and her matter-of-fact, tell-all delivery of the brutal realities of her life that both endeared readers to the novel and garnered fierce criticism. Some considered the voice of the central protagonist as exploitative, unrealistic, and prejudicial. Through the novel's first letters, the reader learns of the particulars of

Celie's situation and discovers that her only outlet for conveying the horrors of her experiences is these letters. As such, the reader is positioned as a kind of stand-in for God as he or she functions as a nearly voyeuristic presence in a private dialogue, discerning the particulars of Celie's situation and sitting in judgment of her situation and of her description of her reality. At the same time, the reader maintains a sympathy with that situation and functions as a kind of benign, yet supportive, sounding board that seems to energize Celie's transformation.

No matter the reader's position and assessment of Celie's voice, it is soon clear that Celie is not a passive heroine. She is one who demands, through her efforts at self-representation, a response and a reaction. These initial letters establish the context for Celie's victimization and also demonstrate that she is keenly aware that she is considered to be a bad girl. This self-perception is imposed by the words and actions of her rapist stepfather and leads Celie to believe that she is somehow responsible for the calamities that have befallen her. Alphonso's mischaracterizations of Celie also have the effect of cowing her into acquiescence. Alphonso tells Celie that the only way to preserve the remaining semblance of normalcy that remains in their family—and, most significantly, that the only way to not destroy her mother—is for her to remain silent about the abuse she has suffered. Alphonso's prohibition on truth telling is a kind of death. Celie might have been forced to martyr herself to a disavowal of the truth had she not mustered up the courage to challenge Alphonso's dominance. She does so by appealing to a greater authority—a force she understands at the novel's inception as God, but that the reader from the beginning recognizes as Celie herself. When understood in this context, Celie's act of writing becomes an assertion of her own power, discernment, and authority.

From the beginning of the novel, Celie's letters are a sly undermining of her stepfather's attempt to silence her and also to mischaracterize her. While her denial of Pa's authority is not overt—she does not, for instance, tell her mother what he did to her—Celie does find in her letters a validating outlet through which to express her anguish and also to assert her morality, innocence, and outrage at injustice. This ability resonates with the traditions of African-American SLAVE NARRATIVES and echoes the long and pervasive history in the African-American literary tradition of correlating the acquisition of literacy and voice with the attainment of freedom. Following in that tradition and with full awareness of its specificity, Walker sets her young protagonist on a journey down this well-worn path.

One of the worst traumas of slavery for women was the inability for most to have any real choice or authority over their bodies or their reproductive capacities. Most slave women were not able to exercise freedom about the most fundamental aspects of their selfhood, particularly with respect to their sexual experiences and the safety and well-being of their children. Like enslaved women, Celie also has no control over her sexuality or the lives of her children. Celie's mother is absent from the home following her delivery of Celie's half brother, a baby named Lucious. Celie reveals in her letter that, in her mother's absence, she has been sexually molested and raped by Alphonso and is now pregnant from the encounter. Celie gives birth to a child. Although later she learns that the child has lived, she originally believes Alphonso has murdered her daughter. After the birth of that first child, a girl whom Celie names Olivia, she becomes pregnant again through Alphonso's abuse. Soon after the birth of Celie's second child, Celie's mother dies, angry about her husband's betrayal and physically destroyed by the too-frequent births of her children. Celie and her brothers and sisters are left alone with Alphonso. Although Alphonso also takes Celie's second child, a boy, Celie does not believe that Alphonso kills the infant.

As happened with many children of enslaved women, Celie's babies are taken from her without her having any knowledge about what has happened to them. She does not even know whether her children are alive or dead. The information that she is given is false. However, like some historic slave women, Celie is able to use literacy to discover the truth. In time, she learns about her children; her actual relationship to Alfonso, the man she thinks is her father; and the details of her family history.

Celie's reading acumen is not limited to written texts. She is able to read between the lines of Alphonso's spoken text to discern intuitively from that information that her baby is not dead. By allowing Celie to read the circumstances of her life from multiple sources of information, Walker decentralizes and expands the trope that connects the acquisition of freedom with the ability to read and write. Unlike some other African-American first-person narrators, Celie does not privilege the written text as her primary or sole source of information. Throughout *The Color Purple,* Celie's behavior suggests and indeed valorizes other ways of reading and knowing.

One of the ways of knowing that provides substantial and critical information is contained within the context of creative artistry. Her ability to create provides Celie with an original and specific vocabulary. This language and ability to "read" emerges when Celie encounters Corrine in town one day while she is shopping. At the time, Celie has no idea of who Corrine is and of the enormous connection the two women share as a consequence of Albert's theft of Celie's children. It is Celie's creativity that makes the connection between these two women visible. Before the children are taken from her, Celie embroidered the name of her daughter, Olivia, on the baby's undergarments—almost like a castaway writing a message in a bottle. She hopes that whoever has her daughter will use the name for the child, and in that way, someday, Celie might be able to locate and reclaim her child.

During Celie's encounter with Corrine, the two women exchange polite conversation. Celie is curious about the baby who she thinks might be her child. The child's face resembles Celie's, and she is the age Celie's daughter would have been. Celie seeks confirmation of her feelings by the evidence of her creative gift to the child—a decorative embellishment of the practical. As with so many fairy tales and legends, the gift of a name is, perhaps, the most tangible transmission of creativity that occurs intergenerationally. In the particular case of slave mothers, a name was often the only potentially permanent influence they might have on their lost and stolen offspring. In her conversation with Corrine, Celie learns that Corrine calls the baby Pauline. Through this revelation, the novel presents the reader (and Celie) with a conflation of ways of reading and a choice. The choice is between accepting the literal inscription of meaning through letters—the apparent name, Pauline—and the intuitive affirmation that Celie has simply by experiencing her child's presence. As it turns out, Celie's sense that this child is her daughter is correct, and thus the novel affirms that such readings not only have validity but may fly in the face of the apparent rational "facts" of a given situation or narrative. Celie's gift of selfhood, bestowed upon her child in the form of a name for her daughter, proves the lasting gift.

The novel also demonstrates the significance of language and naming by drawing attention to their absence. In earlier forms of fiction, particularly in the 18th- and 19th-century novel, the convention of excluding the entirety of a character's name became commonplace. In these novels, the practice was supposed to imply either a character who was so well-known and prestigious that it became unnecessary for there to be an explicit reference to his or her (usually his) full name. Alternatively, the absence of names could also signify an attempt to signify anonymity, where the blank after the Mrs., Miss, or Mr. would entice the reader to participate in identifying the character or could indicate a kind of illicit, unspoken action between the characters that could not be overtly articulated without violating the mores of the time. Walker's invocation of this convention in her novel allows her both to employ and subvert these literary conventions.

### Mr. ——

When the character of Mr. —— appears as a reference in Celie's letters, the namelessness of the character functions in multiple ways. Mr. ——'s appellation becomes a reference to the conventions of the form, to the power of an individual who has a title, and to the universality and lack of specificity of the abusive and disregarding aspects of his character. With Mr. ——'s name, Walker makes a generalized statement about the power of patriarchy over time and for all women and situations, as well as about the behavior of this particular black man within that dominant structure.

Mr. —— is arguably the most controversial character in the novel. He enters into the narrative as a nearly generic villain who lacks the ability to see the world in other than self-interested terms. Mr. ——'s introduction in Celie's letters occurs as she describes Nettie's boyfriend, Albert; Celie calls him Mr. ——. For Celie, Mr. —— resembles her putative father, Alphonso. Through Celie's reflections, readers learn that Mr. ——'s wife was killed by the man with whom she was having an affair and that consequently he is looking to remarry, primarily to find someone to care for his young children.

Celie warns Nettie against getting involved with someone who needs a woman to take care of his children and advises her little sister to continue to pursue her education. Later, Celie changes her advice to Nettie, telling her to marry Mr. ——. Celie's change of heart is rooted in her hope that Mr. —— is so in love with Nettie that he will be kind to her sister for at least a year. As a consequence of her own experiences, Celie believes that a year is the best that Nettie can hope to enjoy in her life as a woman and wife.

When Mr. —— finally proposes marriage to Nettie, Alphonso tells him that he cannot marry her. Alphonso gives Mr. —— the excuse of knowing about his long-term affair with a woman named Shug Avery. Later, Mr. —— asks again to marry Nettie. Alphonso offers him Celie instead. As he makes the offer, Alphonso insults Celie by denigrating her sexual purity and calling her ugly. After four months, Mr. —— decides to marry Celie.

After Celie marries Mr. ——, her life consists of tending to his children, cooking for his family, and cleaning his house. One typical and horrific event occurs on Celie's wedding day when Mr. ——'s oldest son, Harpo, hits her in the head with a rock. Later that day, bleeding and injured, Celie spends the evening untangling the hair of her stepdaughters. The girls' hair has not been combed in months. After all of this debasement, she is subjected that night to thoughtless sex with Mr. ——.

Mr. —— is the product of a culture and of a larger society that has sanctioned this assignment of privilege as a right of gender. What complicates his situation is that his position as a black man differentiates him from other men, specifically from white men. Race trumps gender in America's social hierarchy. Although Mr. —— is not allowed to access the power of masculinity in the larger culture, he is still, within his community, a relatively well-off man with a measure of power that encourages and enables his sexist behavior. In light of her desire to illustrate these complexities, Walker may have used the signifier "Mr. ——" to indicate his compromised position as a man both empowered and disempowered, occupying both an authoritarian and a marginalized position.

Many critics of *The Color Purple* have failed to note the various and complicated transformations Mr. —— undergoes during the course of the novel. One of the signs of his changes is linked to Celie's references to him, and particularly to his name. When Shug Avery comes to stay with Mr. —— and Celie, Celie has to remind herself that her husband's name is Albert. Shug's casual, often irreverent use of Albert's name helps to move the character from open-ended caricature to some more complex characterizations and understanding. Through the knowledge that Celie acquires from Shug about her husband, Mr. —— moves closer to becoming Albert for both Celie and the reader.

Ironically, while Shug is living in Celie and Albert's house, she occasionally becomes a unifying force for the couple. An exchange with Mr. ——'s father highlights the oddity of Shug's temporary residence there and the function that her presence serves in Mr. ——'s transformation and in Celie's reassessment and forgiveness of him. One afternoon while Shug is still recovering in Mr. —— and Celie's house, Mr. ——'s father comes to visit. He comments to Celie that not every woman would allow the woman their husband is sleeping with to live in her house. Interestingly, Celie does not see the comment as personally insulting or as significant as an insult of her husband; rather, she views the remark as an insult directed at Shug. This disparagement of Shug infuriates Celie, who consequently begins to empathize with Mr. ——, at least in terms of his lifelong struggles against his father. It is Mr. ——'s father who forbade Albert from marrying Shug as he had wanted. Celie takes Mr. ——'s side against his father's appraisal of their situation and defends Shug by secretly spitting in a glass of water before offering it to Mr. ——'s father. With Shug's presence in the house, Mr. —— achieves a more complicated humanity and moves closer to becoming Albert.

Mr. —— has to come to recognize the inhumanity and anonymity with which society has treated *him* in order ultimately to reclaim his subjectivity and to find, in the very long run, his authentic identity—to find and reclaim Albert. Before Celie leaves with Shug for Memphis, Celie finally confronts Albert about all of the abuse and mistreatment she has suffered at his hands. She curses Mr. —— and tells him that everything in his life will fail until he makes amends. This curse is a marker of the transition in her self-perception, and it is a milestone and turning point in Mr. ——'s development as well. After Celie's departure, he becomes a depressed recluse, and his house becomes filthy and disordered. Harpo helps his father to recover and encourages him to do right by Celie by sending her all of the letters Nettie has mailed. After Mr. —— returns Nettie's letters to Celie, he begins to turn his life around and becomes a much better person than he had been previously.

Celie comments on the changes in Mr. ——. He has become meticulously neat and devoted to helping his family, and he begins to collect seashells. He and Celie are even able have conversations with each other. Through these conversations, Celie discovers that she is only sexually attracted to women and tells Mr. —— that men look like frogs to her when they are undressed. Like her relationship with Shug, the transition in her relationship with Mr. —— allows Celie to understand and read herself with greater clarity and wisdom. Mr. —— and Celie become friends of sorts, sharing their love for Shug and reminiscing about good times they had with her over the years. Mr. —— gains insight and awareness of his own life and the people in it. He even begins to learn how to sew and helps Celie sew pants in her shop. The two talk honestly with each other. As Mr. —— reflects on his life, he observes that although he and Shug were not able to be together, she ended up in a better place than he did. Celie tells him that the difference is that Shug knows how to love people in a way that Mr. —— never has. Mr. —— becomes philosophical in his old age and comes to wonder about the fundamental questions of human existence, and although he does not have the answers to the questions he asks, the very ability to question opens a new world of possibility. He tells Celie that the more he wonders, the more he realizes that for him love is a fundamental necessity and the refuge from the terrible mystery and terror that comes from not knowing. Mr. —— even asks Celie to marry him again. She refuses, but the two continue to build a strong friendship

Eventually, Mr. —— is motivated to access his humanity rather than to exercise his power. He is able to grow and mature into a full-fledged human being who is respectful of women and men and has enough self-assurance to have compassion. Mr. —— becomes Albert, a transformation that allows Celie to forgive the wrongs he has committed against her. By the end of the novel, neither the anonymity nor the titular and empty power signified by the name Mr. —— is necessary or applicable to name the character that the reader, along with Celie, has learned to regard as Albert.

Celie exudes a fundamental grace in her relationship with others as evidenced in her long-term dealings with Albert and in her faithfulness to her relationship with her sister. Nettie and Celie's relationship is another example of the combined pools of wisdom and information from which Celie draws during her journey. Celie and Nettie's relationship reveals the selflessness and compassion of Celie's character, and her early emphasis on Nettie's schooling reinforces the novel's reiteration of the importance of education to African-American liberation. Celie understands this imperative, internalizes it, and transmits it to Nettie in much the same way her slave ancestors did. Nettie reciprocates in her desire to share what she has learned with Celie. Celie's foresight is what allows her to have some access to Nettie after Nettie is forced to leave Mr. ——'s house. Of course, that connection, in the form of the letters Nettie writes to Celie from Africa, is withheld from Celie by Mr. —— for many years.

### Shug Avery

Besides Celie, Shug Avery is perhaps the novel's most important character. Over time, in the course of their long relationship, Shug functions for Celie as a way to reinterpret her world and the abuse Celie has suffered and as a channel for Celie to articulate her thoughts and feelings outside of the confines of private, written discourse. Shug and Celie's relationship privileges human connection as instructive and posits that the intimate bonds between human beings have the potential to create a discourse that fosters the acquisition of knowledge that is at least equivalent to that provided by the written word. Shug's occupation as a blues singer foregrounds the ways in which she fulfills this role in Celie's life. She provides for Celie the means, the vocabulary, and the methodology with which to find and sing her own song—her truth, her self-worth, and her desires.

### Sofia

Although Celie's story is in part a narrative that highlights the successful development of a subjective self, her environment seems completely opposed to her achieving her potential. The novel's time frame, the community's gender-based expectations, and the pervasive racial segregation of the time all combine to make such declarations of selfhood radical and dangerous. The hazards of public assertions of voice for African Americans in this context, and particularly for African-American women, become clear in *The Color Purple,* most particularly in the story of Sofia.

One day, Sofia, her post-Harpo boyfriend Henry Broadnax, and her children with Harpo travel into town. Just as they arrive, they encounter the mayor's wife, Miss Millie. Miss Millie condescendingly asks Sofia if she would like to be her maid. Sofia response to the mayor's wife is "Hell no." The mayor intervenes. Sofia repeats her refusal, and the mayor hits her in the face. Sofia responds by hitting the mayor back, and chaos ensues. Eventually, Sofia is beaten nearly to death and taken to jail. Mr. —— tries to intervene on Sofia's behalf as he has developed a relationship with the sheriff through the misdeeds of his son Bub. The sheriff allows the family to visit Sofia. Shocked by Sofia's appearance and by the damage that she has suffered, Celie does her best in the dank prison to wash and dress Sofia's wounds.

After Sofia's brutal encounter with the mayor and his wife, she is sentenced to work in the prison laundry. The job is debilitating, and doing the work causes Sofia to fall ill. She is forced to live in inhumane conditions. Her cell is infested with vermin. The subservience she needs to display in order to survive damages Sofia's spirit, and she finds herself transformed from a strong, self-reliant woman into someone meek and devastated.

Like many African-American freedom fighters, Sofia pays dearly for her refusal to mask her authentic voice and selfhood, and she loses at least her physical freedom for a good part of her adult life. Like Celie, she finds her circumstances not easily distinguished from those of enslaved women.

### The Letters from Nettie

A central turning point of the novel occurs when Celie recovers the letters that Mr. —— had withheld from her since he forced Nettie to leave their house. In an experience akin to the sudden acquisition of the ability to read, Celie has access to the truth about what happened to her sister as well as knowledge about her family history, and she is overwhelmed when she is able to confirm that her beloved Nettie is alive.

Nettie's letters are revelatory. As she reads them, Celie learns of Albert's attempted rape of her sister and that her children are alive and living with Nettie in Africa. The subsequent letters continue to detail the nuances of the life Nettie has been living since her escape from Mr. ——'s advances. She tells Celie of Samuel and Corrine's kindnesses, the ways that they make her feel welcome and a part of their family.

Nettie learns that Samuel and Corrine are not only religious; they are missionaries, members of the

American and African Missionary Society. Nettie travels to Africa with Corrine and Samuel in place of a missionary who is unable at the last minute to make the trip. Nettie works for Samuel and Corrine caring for and teaching their children. As she experiences Africa, Nettie loses her misconceptions about the continent as primitive and backward, ideas she inherited from common popular depictions. Nettie particularly describes her feelings of awe when she first sees the African coastline.

After reading several of Nettie's letters, Celie wants to kill Mr. ——, but Shug stops her and eventually encourages her to make pants. Artistry in the form of sewing provides for Celie an alternate outlet for her articulation. She expresses her destructive impulses through a different vocabulary, one that enables her simultaneously to create and to expiate. This alternate literacy derives from an expanded sense of possibility, enhanced by Nettie's location in Africa.

As Celie reads more of Nettie's letters, she learns of the family's arrival in the village of Olinka where they are working as missionaries. Nettie tells of the village's recent history, the way it fell on hard times because of the greed of the chief who sold the village's staple product, roofleaf, to traders and almost destroyed the village. In Olinka, the girls are not educated. Nettie reveals that Olivia is the only girl in school. She tells Celie about Olivia's sense of injustice as a result of the exclusion of girls—particularly of her friend Tashi, whose father will not let her attend. In her letters, Nettie compares the sexism of the Olinka with what she knows of sexism in the American rural South. Through the information contained in Nettie's letters and the model they present of the possibilities for growth and transformation through experience, Celie's mind is primed to embrace an alternative vision of the world and way of being. Central to that shift in perspective is her acquisition of knowledge and information about the children she felt were lost to her forever.

Unlike so many slave women, Celie is able to reclaim—through narrative and, ultimately in reality—her stolen, lost, sold children. Through Celie's knowledge about her children and ability to read about their lives, Walker addresses and tries to rewrite, even redress, the historical loss of black women's children. Celie's children are not only found, arguably they are thriving in a healthier environment than she could have provided for them had she been allowed to keep them.

Armed with new knowledge and insight, Celie prepares herself to confront Mr. ——, which she does. She begin her life anew by deciding to no longer live in oppression as his wife. Nettie's letters function as a more formal school for Celie than any she has ever attended, giving both her and Shug access to a new world of knowledge and information. Although Nettie has a much broader view of the world, in many respects, the problems of patriarchy, provincialism, and narrow-mindedness prove to be universal in their applicability. Through her letters, Nettie shares the complexities of life in Olinka and, as a consequence of the universality of those issues, the complications of living life.

## Sewing and Healing

As previously mentioned, Celie finds another creative vocabulary in the unisex pants that she begins to sew and to sell; at the same time, she gains some economic autonomy through her creations. Celie translates her reframing of the world into a tangible and rewarding endeavor that has unexpected benefits for those she loves. Perhaps most dramatically, Albert's acquisition of the ability and proclivity to sew transforms him and allows him to access aspects of himself that were previously unavailable.

The sewing motif fits nicely with the structure of the end of the novel, where all of the loose ends are neatly stitched together and each cuff is carefully hemmed. Celie writes about the return of her sister, Nettie; Samuel; and Celie's lost children, Adam and Olivia, as well as Adam's wife and Olivia's best friend, Tashi. She also describes how other characters have resolved their lives. The scars that Adam and Tashi bear do not bother Celie or the others who welcome the new members of the family. Those scars are a kind of suture—a representation of injury but, more importantly, of healing and closure—like the end of Celie's final letter.

## SIGNIFICANT THEMES, ISSUES, CONCERNS

### Double Consciousness

At the turn of the 20th century, the writer and educator W. E. B. DuBois introduced the term *double consciousness,* which refers to the dilemma of categorizing someone as both an African (a black person) and as an American. During much of the 20th century, being an African American meant constantly negotiating identities that were in conflict because of the virulence of racism, discrimination, and segregation. Being a black person meant living as a second-class person and experiencing indignity and even violence or death because of the color of one's skin. At the same time, the ideals and principles associated with life as an American remained elusive and unattainable.

In *The Color Purple,* Walker has her main characters negotiate the physical terrains of Africa and the United States to illustrate both objectively and subjectively the contradictions of double consciousness. As missionaries in Africa, Nettie, Corrine, and Samuel have a measure of autonomy and access that Celie does not. Although the realities of colonization and development compromise the relative freedom of the missionary family, their experiences show Celie a way toward the psychological transcendence of American apartheid. Ultimately, this insight helps her develop into a more self-sustaining and less oppressed person. At the end of the narrative, Celie is not a victim of her twin status as an African American and an American (or as a woman, for that matter); rather, she uses what she knows of her multiple identities to craft a self-defined life.

### Sexism within the African-American Community

One of the major controversies about Walker's *The Color Purple* concerns her unflinching portrayal of sexist behavior within the African-American community. In the novel, several male characters, including Alphonso, Albert, and Harpo, are guilty of brutalizing their wives and children. The damage that these men inflict is so intense that it often has dire, even fatal, consequences.

Walker is not, however, one-dimensional in her depiction of most of her male characters, including these most problematic figures, who—with the possible exception of Alphonso—are significantly transformed by the end of *The Color Purple.* Harpo and Sofia reunite happily, and Celie and Albert become friends. Most significantly, Albert plays a crucial role in the reunion of Nettie and Celie, as well as the other members of her family. Furthermore, there are other male characters in the novel who do not exhibit any violence or viciousness and who are nurturing and supportive. Most notable in this category is Samuel, the missionary, who adores his first wife, Corrine, and, after Corrine's death, is a loving and supportive husband to Nettie.

### Color Imagery as Theology

Any novel with a title like *The Color Purple* would have to make significant use of color imagery. Although there are many references to color throughout the novel, a conversation that Celie has with Shug is particularly significant and helps to expose several of the novel's central themes. It occurs when, one day, as Celie and Shug are walking in a field, Shug says to Celie that she thinks God gets angry if a person walks past the color purple in a field and does not notice the display.

The character of God in the novel is a fluid construction. In the book's opening scenes, just after Celie has given birth to her second child, conceived with the man she believes is her father, that man (Alphonso) warns her from talking about his abuse with anyone but God. This warning silences Celie, with the exception of the letters that she begins to write to God and through which she is able to express herself and her experiences. The God to whom Celie writes resembles the patriarchal authorities in her world. Celie describes him as white and old.

After Celie begins to convey the particulars of her experience to Shug, the other woman shares her alternative, more nature-based sense of divinity. These exchanges have the effect of dismantling Celie's traditional understandings of God. She begins to internalize a different theology—an understanding of God not as a punitive authoritarian but as a natural force who seeks to provide pleasure for humanity. It is this God who reigns in the second half of the novel and whose theology Celie affirms. In her cosmological reconstruction, she replaces all of the imagined authority and hierarchy of a patriarchal God with a vision of egalitarian exchange with a congenial and supportive universal spirit—one that embodies a regal, sensuous divinity. This final association transforms the Lenten connotations of the color purple from its roots in representation of sacrifice and martyrdom to associations with a blooming and pantheistic verdancy.

### The Correlation between Sexuality and Self-Awareness

*The Color Purple* deals explicitly with the topic of sexuality. There is a clear correlation in the narrative between the sexual openness of the characters and their psychological and emotional health. Same-sex relationships are an important part of the continuum of sexuality.

One of the novel's most overt confrontations with sexuality occurs when Shug inaugurates Celie into a world of sexual pleasure. When Celie reveals to Shug that she has never derived any enjoyment from sex, Shug responds with the healing rejoinder that, as a consequence, Celie is a virgin. In a world where women are evaluated on the basis of their sexual purity, Shug's statement provides for Celie the possibility of rebirth and for regaining control over her self-perception. Celie has been labeled a fallen woman and has been castigated for sexual behavior that was beyond her control—that was, in fact, rape. What Shug's declaration gives to Celie is an opportunity to reclaim her violated body and to reassess the evaluations that have been levied against her as a consequence of circumstances beyond her control.

One additional dynamic of this exchange is the opportunity for redefinition that it presents for Shug. Although she does not show it, Shug has internalized the evaluation of her own sexual behavior, which the community uses to castigate and exoticize her. As a consequence, she has tremendously low self-regard. Her behavior when she first comes to Albert's home represents her insecurity and hostility toward Celie, who occupies the sanctioned role as the married wife. When Shug learns to love Celie, she is also freed to redefine herself in terms other than those created and defined by her community, becoming able to reconsider and to take control of her own desires. Her exploration of the possibilities presented by that freedom becomes a challenge within the relationship between the two women. Ultimately, however, the freedom to make their own decisions, undeterred by the opinions of others, allows both Celie and Shug to claim and sustain a self-defined relationship.

## CHARACTERS

**Adam** Adam is Celie's second child. He is conceived in an abusive sexual relationship between Celie and Alphonso, Celie's stepfather, whom she believes at the time of Adam's conception is her father. After Adam's birth, Pa takes the child away from Celie, giving him (and Olivia, Celie's firstborn) to a minister and his wife, Samuel and Corinne, who eventually become missionaries and travel with the children to Africa.

**Addie Beasely** Addie Beasely is a teacher at the school Nettie and Celie attend before Celie is married to Mr. ——. Addie says that she thinks Celie is smart. Nettie is fond of Addie and enjoys attending school. Addie visits Nettie and Celie's home in order to persuade Pa to let Nettie go to school.

**Albert** *See* MR. ——.

**Albert's children** Albert and Anna Julia, the woman he was married to before he marries Celie, have four children, two boys and two girls, of whom Harpo is the oldest. The younger children eventually leave their father's house; the two girls both get pregnant and leave home at a relatively young age.

**Alphonso** *See* PA.

**Althea** Althea is Samuel's aunt. She is the best friend of Corrine's aunt Theodosia. The friendship between these two women was the catalyst for Corrine and Samuel meeting each other and, eventually, marrying. Althea and Theodosia tell tales of their adventures in Africa building schools and proselytizing. Although Samuel and Corrine gently mock their aunts, the stories the women tell them serve as a support not only for their relationship but also for their own travels as missionaries.

**Anna Julia** Anna Julia is Mr. ——'s first wife. Celie learns from Mr. ——'s sisters, Kate and Carrie, that Anna Julia had straight hair, was darkskinned, and was a terrible housekeeper. Later, after he transforms into a caring and compassionate man, Mr. —— tells Celie that he regrets the way that he and Shug treated Anna Julia. He says that Anna Julia's family abandoned her after she married him, that she had no support, and that they married only because his father wanted the marriage.

**Billy** Billy is the mayor's son. Sofia takes over care of Billy and his sister, Eleanor Jane, when she begins working for the mayor's wife. As a young man, he becomes troubled and is said to be a violent racist who drinks excessively, womanizes, and generally functions as a miscreant.

**Boo** Boo is an animal on Sofia and Harpo's farm.

**Bub** Bub is Mr. ——'s son and Harpo's brother. When Mr. —— is older and in his redemptive phase, he invites Bub to come stay with him. Bub stays for two weeks and steals his father's money. He becomes an alcoholic as an adult.

**Bubber Hodges** Bubber Hodges is a black relative of the town jail's warden. He is also Squeak's (Mary Agnes's) uncle. In order to get Sofia moved from the jail to the relatively easier service working as Miss Millie's maid, Sofia's friends and family send Squeak on a mission to tell Bubber that Sofia prefers jail to working for Miss Millie. She delivers the message, and the plan works to shift Sofia's sentence. But Squeak pays a price for delivering this helpful message when Bubber rapes her while she is there.

**Carrie** Carrie is Mr. ——'s sister. She comes to visit Celie and Albert with her sister Kate.

**Catherine** Catherine is a woman in Olinka who believes that Nettie is not worth much because she does not have children and works for Samuel and Corrine. Catherine tells Nettie her thoughts during a conversation about whether or not girls should be educated. Catherine's thinking evolves over time and with exposure to Nettie's ideas, and the two women become friends. Catherine is the mother of a little girl named Tashi, who becomes Olivia's best friend and, eventually, Adam's wife.

**Celie** Celie is the central character in *The Color Purple*. The novel is comprised of letters she writes in journal style, most of them addressed to God. The novel begins with Celie as a young teenager. She is abused sexually by the man she calls Pa and bears two children with him—a girl, Olivia, and a boy, Adam. Pa takes their children from Celie shortly after they are born and gives them to a religious missionary family, who then raise them as if they were their own. Celie stops menstruating after the births of her children.

Arguably, the great love of Celie's life is her sister Nettie. Inseparable as young girls, Celie tries to warn Nettie about the dangers of Pa's advances. Celie's marriage to Mr. —— separates the girls temporarily until Nettie comes to stay with her at Mr. ——'s house after Pa begins to approach Nettie sexually. When Mr. —— also makes sexual advances to Nettie, Nettie runs away and finds sanctuary with Corrine and Samuel, coincidentally, the same couple who adopted Celie's children. After Nettie's departure, with her promise to write to Celie, Celie believes that her sister is dead because Mr. —— hides Nettie's many letters to her.

Celie is good-hearted and long-suffering. She tolerates abuse from Mr. —— and his children while cooking for them, cleaning their house, and generally ordering their lives with no reward for her efforts. The arrival of Shug Avery, the love of Mr. ——'s life, transforms Celie's life. Despite Shug's cruel words and actions, Celie grows to adore the woman and eventually falls in love with her.

Through her relationship with Shug, Celie grows in self-awareness. She discovers her sexuality through a physical relationship with Shug, who also begins to repair the hurt of Nettie's absence when she helps Celie to find and read the many lost letters Nettie has written to Celie over the years.

Eventually, Celie leaves Mr. ——, going away with Shug and discovering a new life. She expresses her creative self through her construction of originally designed pants and forges a healthier life with Shug. Mr. ——'s regrets motivate him to repair the abuse he inflicted on Celie, and he facilitates Nettie's return from Africa and Celie's reunion with her sister and her long-lost children.

**Coco** Coco is an animal on Sofia and Harpo's farm.

**Cora Mae** Cora Mae is the wife of James, Mr. —— and Shug's son. James and Cora Mae live in Tucson, Arizona, on an Indian reservation where he works as a teacher. They have two children, Shug's grandchildren, Davis and Cantrell.

**Corrine** Corrine is Samuel's wife and the adoptive mother of Celie's children. Samuel says that Corrine's Indian ancestry is an unacknowledged but essential part of her character. Corrine travels to the African village of Olinka with Samuel, her husband; Olivia and Adam, the couple's adopted children; and Nettie. While in Olinka, where they work as missionaries, Corrine begins to feel insecure about her marriage because the villagers think of Nettie as Samuel's other wife. This characterization causes a rift to develop between the two women and, eventually, between Corrine and Adam and Olivia.

Corrine falls ill and confronts Nettie about her resemblance to Olivia and Adam. Nettie swears that the children are not hers. Corrine believes that the children might be Nettie's and Samuel's. Eventually, Nettie tells Corrine and Samuel that the children belong to her sister Celie, and Corrine dies believing Nettie.

**Corrine's mother** Corrine's mother is described as less adventurous than her sister, Theodosia, but supportive of the relationship between her daughter and her sister.

**Daisy** Daisy is the woman Pa marries after the death of Nettie and Celie's mother.

**Darlene** Darlene is a twin to Jerene. The girls live in Memphis and help Celie with her pants business. Darlene tries to help Celie lose her accent and to speak standard English.

**Dilsey** Dilsey is an animal on Sofia and Harpo's farm.

**Doris Baines** Doris Baines is a woman Samuel and Nettie meet on the boat they travel on to England in an attempt to secure some help for the Olinka. She is leaving Africa in advance of World War II after spending most of her life there. Doris was born to a wealthy family in England and left after finding her life there to be stilted and superficial. She became a missionary and author, publishing books under the pseudonym Jared Hunt. She spent her life among the Akwean tribe, nurturing the community and raising some young ones until they were like her children.

**Eleanor Jane** Eleanor Jane is the mayor's daughter. Sofia takes over the care of Eleanor Jane and her brother, Billy, when she begins working for the mayor's wife. Eleanor Jane has a special affection for Sofia. Even after Sofia is no longer working for the family and has returned home, Eleanor Jane visits with her and consults with Sofia about the problems she and her family face. Eleanor Jane and Sofia have a falling out when she asks Sofia if she loves Eleanor Jane's infant son. When Sofia tells her honestly that she does not, Eleanor Jane is hurt and insulted. Eventually, Eleanor Jane asks her mother how Sofia came to work for the family. When she learns that Sofia's service was part of a prison sentence, she forgives Sofia and even goes to work for her, helping with Sofia's sick daughter, Henrietta.

**Germaine** Germaine is the young man Shug Avery falls in love with in Memphis. He is a flutist in Shug's backup blues band. Shug finds him physically attractive. He has curly hair and is a good dancer. When the relationship ends, Germaine goes to Wilberforce to study the flute.

**God (G-O-D)** In the novel, God functions as a companion to Celie and serves as an ear for Celie's confessions and observations. Eventually, after she finds and begins to read Nettie's letters, she starts to write to Nettie instead of God, though her last letter is addressed "Dear God."

**Grady** Grady is Shug Avery's rather slick husband. Shug breaks Celie's and Albert's hearts when she returns to them as a married woman. Grady is a good-natured man who has a wandering eye with respect to other women. He becomes enamored of Squeak when they return to Memphis. He and Squeak develop a fondness for smoking marijuana, which Grady grows in the backyard. Eventually, the two head off together for Panama, although Squeak later leaves him.

**Harold Baines** Harold Baines is the African adopted grandson of Doris Baines, a woman Samuel and Nettie meet on the boat they travel on to England in an attempt to secure some help for the Olinka. She is leaving Africa in advance of World War II after spending most of her life there. Doris was born to a wealthy family in England and left after finding the life she inherited stilted and superficial. She became a missionary and author, publishing books under the pseudonym Jared Hunt. She spent her life among the Akwean tribe nurturing the community and raising some young ones, like Harold, until they are like her children.

**Harpo** Harpo is Mr. ——'s oldest child. He is 12 years old when Celie marries Mr. ——. An unnamed man who claims to be her lover killed Harpo's mother, Anna Julia, when she tried to return to her children after running away with the man. Mr. —— marries Celie to help take care of his children.

Because he misses his mother and is neglected by Mr. ——, Harpo hits Celie in the head with a rock the first time she comes to his father's house. When he is just 17, he falls in love with and marries a local girl named Sofia Butler. Harpo loves Sofia, but their relationship is undermined by his desire to control her and to curtail her spirit and independence by beating her physically. Celie reinforces Harpo's abuse of Sofia by advising him to beat her when he seeks Celie's advice about his marriage.

At one point in his marriage to Sofia, Harpo tries to eat enormous quantities of food in order to shift the power dynamic between them by becoming physically larger. This ploy does not work, and eventually, after 12 years of physical altercations, Sofia takes their children and leaves Harpo.

After recovering from Sofia's departure, Harpo takes up with a new girlfriend, Mary Agnes, better known as Squeak. He also opens a juke joint in the house that he formerly shared with Sofia and their children. In a little less than 12 years, Sofia is released from her service as the mayor's maid. Shortly after she returns home, Squeak leaves with Shug and Celie, and Sofia begins to regain her status as the matriarch in her own home.

**Henrietta** Henrietta is initially presumed to be Harpo and Sofia's child. After Sofia returns from service as Miss Millie's maid, she tells Harpo that Henrietta is not his child. Henrietta is a moody, surly girl who gives Sofia a hard time. She is sick with a disease that, in the description provided in the text, sounds like sickle-cell anemia.

**Henry Broadnax (Buster)** Henry Broadnax is Sofia's boyfriend, the man she keeps company with after she leaves Harpo and goes to live with her sister Odessa. He is a prizefighter.

**Hettie** Hettie is one of Nettie and Celie's stepsisters.

**Jack** Jack is Sofia's brother-in-law, Odessa's husband. Celie describes him as a sweet and gentle man. He is tall, supportive, and sensitive. In order to express her gratitude for the kind of man Jack is, Celie makes him a special pair of pants.

**James** James is the son of Mr. —— and Shug. He was raised with their other two children by Shug's mother. When they are grown, two of the children are doing well but do not want to have anything to do with their mother. The other one, James, lives in Tucson, Arizona, and works as a teacher on an Indian reservation. When Shug takes up with Germaine, the two of them stay with her son in his adobe house for a period of time. James is married to a woman named Cora Mae, with whom he has two children, Shug's grandchildren, Davis and Cantrell.

**Jerene** Jerene is a twin to Darlene. The girls live in Memphis and help Celie with her pants business.

**Jimmy Hodges** Jimmy Hodges is Bubber Hodges's brother and Squeak's father, having had three children with her mother. He is married to the Quinten girl whose daddy owns the hardware store.

**Joseph** Joseph is the man who meets Nettie, Corrine, Samuel, and the children at the ship when they arrive in Africa.

**Kate** Kate is Mr. ——'s sister. She comes to visit Celie and Albert with her sister Carrie. She is described as an old maid and, while she is visiting, she makes Celie a dress.

**Lucious** Nettie and Celie believe that Lucious is their brother. He is the baby their mother gives birth to shortly before she dies.

**Mama** Mama is Celie and Nettie's mother. She has six children by the man that the girls know as Pa. She dies bitter and unhappy while Nettie and Celie are young girls. Her death may be hastened by her knowledge that her husband is engaging in sexual relations with her daughters. Mama begins a slow mental decline after the death of her first husband, Celie and Nettie's father. The girls' father was a prosperous farmer and store owner whose store was burned and who was murdered as a result by envious whites. Unable to care for herself or her children as a result of her mental deterioration, Mama remarries the man Celie and Nettie know as Pa and has a succession of children whose births wear down her health.

**Marcia** Marcia is Sofia's sister.

**Margaret** Margaret is Mr. ——'s sister-in-law, Tobias's wife.

**Mary Agnes** *See* SQUEAK.

**May Ellen** May Ellen is Celie and Nettie's half sister. Celie sees the girl with Pa one day while she is in town with Mr. ——.

***mbeles*** The *mbeles* are a group of African guerrillas who live miles from the outskirts of the village of Olinka where Nettie, Samuel, Adam, and Olivia live.

**Miss Millie** Miss Millie is the mayor's wife. One day, while in town, she encounters Sofia, who is with her children. Miss Millie condescendingly comments on the neat appearance of Sofia's children and asks Sofia if she would like to work for her as a maid. Sofia replies, "Hell no." Her response provokes the mayor, who strikes her. She defends herself by hitting the mayor, and then she is placed in jail, where she is beaten and forced to perform backbreaking labor. Celie and the rest of Sofia's family devise a plan to help Sofia get into relatively improved circumstances. With B'rer Rabbit–like tactics, they ensure that the mayor will learn that the worst punishment Sofia could receive would be to work for him. In that way, they get Sofia's punishment changed from prison labor to working for the mayor's wife as her maid.

While Sofia serves out her punishment, she tries to teach Miss Millie to drive. One Christmas, Miss Millie offers to drive Sofia to her family so she can spend time with them. While there, Miss Millie discovers that she cannot drive home, and so Sofia does not spend the day with her family after all.

**Mr. —— (Albert)** Mr. —— is Celie's husband. Like his father, he is slender and short. He marries Celie after Pa refuses to let him marry Nettie. Mr. —— desires a wife so that someone will take care of his house and order his life, particularly the four children he has had with his first wife—Harpo, Bub, and two unnamed girls. Mr. ——'s first wife was killed by her lover when she tried to return from the relationship to him and her children.

Mr. —— is abusive, inconsiderate, and unkind to Celie. Some of his behavior may be explained by his unreconciled passion for Shug Avery, the love of his life. Mr. ——'s domineering father forbade his son from marrying Shug, and Mr. —— did not have the gumption to defy his father. He therefore lives in bitterness and regret about his lost love.

When he learns that Shug is ill, Mr. —— brings her to live in his house, even though he is married to Celie. Against his will, Shug and Celie eventually develop a close bond that results in Celie's psychological and emotional coming-of-age and her escape from their marriage. When Celie and Shug leave his house for Memphis, Mr. —— begins a decline into depression and isolation. With his son Harpo's help, he is able to recover and to become a better man than he was before. Sofia says that the turning point occurred for Mr. —— when Harpo made him send Celie all of the letters from Nettie that he had been hiding and hoarding for many years. Eventually, he and Celie reconcile and become friends. He spends a great deal of time as an older man staring off into space from her front porch.

**Nettie** Nettie is Celie's much beloved younger sister. She is thought of as attractive. Her physical appearance catalyses the inappropriate lust of her stepfather, known to her as Pa, and of Mr. ——, Celie's husband. Nettie is bright and learns quickly. Celie, the schoolteacher Addie Beardsley, and, later, Corrine all encourage Nettie's intellectual development.

After spurning Pa's advances, Nettie goes to Celie and lives for a while with her and Mr. ——. But Mr. —— interrupts this brief interlude when he also tries to violate Nettie, and she is forced to flee once again. She finds a home with a minister and his wife, Samuel and Corrine, who later become missionaries and travel with her and Celie's children, whom they have adopted, to Africa. During the entirety of her absence, Nettie writes letters to Celie about all that happens with her, faithfully maintaining her promise to keep in touch and demonstrating the loyalty and love that exists between the two sisters. Nettie's letters work in the novel as an important counterbalance to Celie's voice as articulated in Celie's letters to God.

While the family is in Africa, Corrine dies of a fever. Eventually, Nettie marries Samuel, and with Mr. ——'s assistance, they all return to the United States and to a joyous reunion with Celie.

**Odessa** Odessa is Sofia's sister. Sofia goes to stay with her when she leaves Harpo. Odessa is married, but her husband has been drafted to join the military.

**Old Mr. ——** Old Mr. —— is Mr. ——'s (Albert's) father. Old Mr. —— forbade Mr. —— from marrying Shug Avery and cast his son's life and emotional well-being out with the tide as a consequence. Old Mr. —— gives his son the land that Mr. —— works to support himself. Father and son also sell off parts of the land that they own in order to get occasional cash. After Celie leaves Mr. —— to go off to Memphis, Tennessee, with Squeak, Grady, and Shug, Old Mr. —— comes over to Mr. ——'s house and tries to help his son, whose life has fallen into disrepair. He advises Mr. —— that he should remarry in order to have someone to take care of the house, advice he originally gave his son after the death of his first wife, Anna Julia, which had resulted in Mr. ——'s marriage to Celie. Upon hearing his father's advice the second time, Mr. —— promptly escorts him out the door and begins to get his life together with his own resources and with Harpo's help.

**Olivia (Pauline)** Olivia is Celie's firstborn child. She is conceived in an abusive sexual relationship between Celie and Pa, whom Celie believes at the time of Olivia's conception to be her father. When Olivia is born, Pa takes the baby, and at first Celie believes Pa has killed her. Pa has given Olivia to a minister and his wife, Samuel and Corrine. When Olivia is seven years old, Celie sees her with Corrine in a store. Celie believes that she recognizes the child as her own. Corrine tells Celie that the little girl's name is Pauline but that she calls her Olivia. Eventually, Samuel and Corrine become missionaries and travel to Africa with Olivia and with Celie's son, Adam, whom they have also adopted.

**Pa (Alphonso)** Celie and Nettie are led to believe that Pa is their father. In reality, he is their stepfather. He has six children with Celie and Nettie's mother. Pa sexually abuses Celie, which leads to the birth of her two children, Olivia and Adam. Despite her pleas to the contrary, Pa gives her children away to a minister and his wife, Samuel and Corrine, who eventually become missionaries and travel to Africa with the children. Pa knew Samuel from years prior to the time that Samuel became religious.

Pa allows Celie to be married to Mr. ——. Pa also attempts to have sexual relations with Nettie, which prompts Nettie's flight to Celie and Mr. ——'s house. After the death of Celie and Nettie's mother and the departure of the girls, Pa remarries a woman named Daisy. He has four more children with his new wife. Upon his death, Celie learns that he was not her father, and she inherits the land where Pa had been living, which legally belonged to her father and was willed to her and to Nettie.

**Reverend Mr. ——** *See* SAMUEL.

**Reynolds Stanley Earl** Reynolds Stanley Earl is Eleanor Jane's son with her husband, Stanley Earl. The baby is the final straw in the relationship between Sofia and Eleanor Jane. Sofia tells Eleanor Jane the truth, that she does not love her son; Eleanor Jane is offended and, in the short-term, unforgiving.

**Samuel (Rev. Mr. ——)** Samuel is the husband of Corrine. He is originally from New York, where he spent his childhood and youth. His aunt is friends with Corrine's aunt Theodosia from their missionary work in Africa, and it was she who introduced Samuel to Corrine during a trip to Atlanta where Theodosia lives. Samuel and Corrine have a happy marriage except for their sadness about not being able to have children of their own.

When Alphonso (Pa), an old friend of Samuel's from the time before he was converted, brings one child and then, later, another to him, Samuel and Corrine are grateful and adopt the children as their own. Similarly, when Nettie arrives on their doorstep in dire circumstances, the couple welcome her into their lives as well. The family travels to Africa to engage in missionary work. Samuel tries to assist the Olinka as their way of life, even their existence, becomes increasingly threatened by the encroachment of development on their lands. Corrine dies while the family is in Africa, and after a time, Nettie and Samuel fall in love and marry. After exhausting their ability to be of assistance to the Olinka, Samuel and his family, along with Adam's wife, Tashi, return to the United States.

**Shug and Albert's children** Shug and Albert have three children together. They are raised by Shug's mother. When they are grown, two are doing well but do not want to have anything to do with their mother. The other one, James, lives in Tucson, Arizona, and works as a teacher on an Indian reservation. When Shug takes up with Germaine, the two of them stay with her son in his adobe house for a period of time.

**Shug Avery (Queen Honeybee)** Celie says that Shug Avery is the most beautiful woman she has ever seen. Before her marriage to Mr. ——, Celie finds a photograph of Shug that Mr. —— accidentally leaves behind during the time he visits the house to find out whether or not Pa will let him marry her sister, Nettie. Celie thinks that Shug looks sad in the photograph, which she carries with her continually.

Shug is the love of Mr. ——'s life. The two did not marry because Mr. ——'s father disapproved of the union, and Mr. —— was too impotent to oppose his father. As a result, Shug scorns him, although the two continue to see each other and to have a sexual relationship. She and Mr. —— have had three children together, but she abandoned her responsibilities, and Shug's mother cares for the children.

**Sofia Butler** Sofia is a physically strong and capable girl who marries Harpo. She comes from a family of 12 children, six boys and six girls. Sofia is a confident and competent woman who challenges Harpo's ingrained notions of gender roles. As a result of their conflicts, Sofia and Harpo engage in physical disputes that eventually, after 12 years of marriage, culminate in her departure with their children.

After leaving Harpo, Sofia goes to live with her sister Odessa and keeps company with a boxer named Henry Broadnax. While in town one day, Sofia, who is with her children, encounters the mayor's wife, Miss Millie. Miss Millie condescendingly comments on the neat appearance of Sofia's children and asks Sofia if she would like to work for her as a maid. Sofia replies, "Hell no." Her response provokes the mayor, who strikes her. Sofia defends herself by hitting the mayor; she is sent to jail, where she is beaten and forced to perform backbreaking labor. She is given a 12-year sentence. Celie and the rest of Sofia's family devise a plan to help Sofia get into relatively improved circumstances by ensuring that the mayor will learn the worst punishment she could receive would be to work for him. In that way, they get Sofia's punishment changed to working for the mayor's wife as her maid.

After 12 years, Sofia is allowed to go home to her family, but she feels alienated from her children. The children old enough to remember her have left home, and the younger ones call her sister and Squeak mother. After Squeak leaves, Sofia is reunited with Harpo.

**Sofia's father** Sofia's father is the patriarch of 12 children, six boys and six girls. Two of his daughters are Odessa and Sofia. He initially tells Harpo that he cannot marry Sofia because Harpo is not good enough for her. Sofia's father cites the death of Harpo's mother, Anna Julia, at the hands of her lover as evidence of Harpo's bad genetic inheritance.

**Sofia's mother** Sofia's mother has 12 children, six boys and six girls. According to Harpo, while Sofia was working for the mayor, her mother told him that Sofia's way of being was as good as anybody's and that, most importantly, it was her uniqueness. Sofia's sisters and brothers serve as pallbearers for their mother.

**Squeak (Mary Agnes)** Squeak is Harpo's live-in girlfriend after his marriage to Sofia deteriorates. Although he is with Squeak, Harpo still loves Sofia. When the family convenes to brainstorm about how to get Sofia out of jail, Squeak confesses that her father is related to the warden. The family conceives a B'rer Rabbit–like plan to tell the man that the worst punishment Sofia can have is to have to be a maid for a white woman. They believe that when the warden learns this false information, he will send Sofia to work for the mayor's wife, thinking that he has dispensed a harsher punishment. They send Squeak to give her uncle this information, knowing that, through him, the falsehood will get back to the mayor. While there, her uncle rapes her. When she returns from the incident, she exacts a promise from Harpo that he actually loves her and is not merely using her as a substitute for Sofia.

Later, Squeak discovers a talent for singing and moves to Memphis with Shug, Celie, and Grady. She and Grady develop a fondness for smoking marijuana, and eventually, the two head to Panama together. Grady runs a marijuana plantation there, and the two make an enormous amount of money, but Squeak returns home without him, having given up marijuana.

**Stanley Earl** Stanley Earl is Eleanor Jane's boyfriend and then husband.

**Suzie Q** Suzie Q is Harpo and Squeak's daughter. She takes a special liking to Sofia after Sofia returns from her sentence working as the mayor's maid. She is also especially fond of Sofia's daughter Henrietta. Suzie Q is smart and does well in school. After Suzie Q's mother, Squeak, goes to Memphis with Shug, Grady, and Celie to sing, Sofia takes care of the little girl.

**Swain** Swain is Harpo's friend.

**Tashi** Tashi is an Olinka girl who is the daughter of Catherine. Although Catherine does not believe that girls should be educated, Tashi receives an education through Olivia, who becomes her best friend. After her father's death, Tashi is allowed to attend school. Eventually, Tashi marries Adam before the family travels back to the United States. Before this happens, she undergoes a clitoridectomy and scarification ceremony.

**Theodosia** Theodosia is Corrine's aunt. In her youth, Theodosia was a missionary in the Belgian Congo. While there, she met a friend, Althea, who is Samuel's aunt. The friendship between Theodosia and Althea was the force behind Corrine and Samuel meeting each other and, eventually, marrying. These two women would tell tales of their adventures in Africa, building schools and proselytizing. Although Samuel and Corrine gently mock their aunts, the stories the women tell them serve as a catalyst not only for their relationship but also for their own travels as missionaries. As a young woman, Theodosia attended Spelman Seminary, and she encouraged Corrine to attend the school.

**Tobias** Tobias is Mr. ——'s brother. He is described as light-skinned, fat, and tall, unlike his father and brother, who are said to be short and slender. He comes to visit and see Shug Avery the first time she returns to Mr. —— and Celie's house. When he comes to visit Mr. —— and Celie, he is fascinated with Shug and even brings her a box of chocolates. Tobias says that he comes to see Shug because he has heard that she is dying.

**white man** Celie inherits the store that Alphonso ran on her father's land. She hires M. —— to work in the store for her. When she takes over the business, Celie keeps the white male employee that Alphonso hired previously but also hires Sofia to work in the store to ensure that her black customers get the respect they deserve from the man.

## THE FILM ADAPTATION

The film version of *The Color Purple,* directed by STEVEN SPIELBERG and with music by QUINCY JONES, was released in 1985. The Academy Award–nominated screenplay was written by MENNO MEYJES, a Dutch-born screenwriter and director who had immigrated to the United States with his parents in 1972. His screenplay earned Meyjes an Academy Award nomination and launched his career as a screenwriter. Walker herself had written a screenplay for the novel, but Spielberg, the director, found it at odds with his vision of the film. Walker gave her approval to Meyjes's version. She was intimately involved in the film's production, a process she has written about extensively in her book *The Same River Twice: Honoring the Difficult, A Meditation on Life, Spirit, Art, and the Making of the Film* The Color Purple *Ten Years Later* (1996). In that book, Walker includes her own original version of the screenplay, entitled *Watch for Me in the Sunset,* in order to reveal her original aspirations for the movie version of her story. She worked closely with Spielberg and Jones on the casting and the music, and she even insisted that at least half of those employed in making the film be African American or people of color.

There is no simple assessment that can be made about either the film itself or the responses it generated. According to Walker, some problematic distinctions between the novel and the film exist in the latter's emphasis on Mr. ——'s brutality without the counterbalance of the story of Nettie and Celie's real father, the recasting of Mr. —— and Harpo's incompetence as buffoonish and comic, and the reduction of the physical and emotional intimacy between Celie and Shug to a single kiss. Predictably, many of the same voices who had protested Walker's novel on the grounds that its depiction of black men is prejudicial and lacking nuance found the same flaws in the film.

The film's strengths lie in its performances and in Spielberg's ability to render a visually striking setting for these enactments to unfold. The movie displayed stellar performances from cast members Danny Glover as Albert/Mr. ——, Margaret Avery as Shug Avery, Willard E. Pugh as Harpo Johnson, Akosua Busia as Nettie Harris, Adolph Caesar as Old Mister Johnson, and Rae Dawn Chong as Squeak. Particularly inspired are the debut performances of WHOOPI GOLDBERG as Celie and OPRAH WINFREY as Sofia. Although many aspects of the film have been criticized, there is almost universal praise for the performances of these two then newcomers. Whoopi Goldberg was discovered by the director Mike Nichols, under whose mentorship she developed her one-woman act into the Broadway performance, *Whoopi Goldberg.* Spielberg saw Goldberg's Broadway performance while he was in the midst of casting the movie *The Color Purple.* After her inspired and convincing role as

Props from the film version of *The Color Purple,* directed by Steven Spielberg *(Photograph by Carmen Gillespie, courtesy of the Emory University Alice Walker Archives Exhibition, April 24, 2009)*

Celie in the film version of the novel, Goldberg was nominated for an Academy Award as best actress, and she won a Golden Globe for her performance. After her triumph in *The Color Purple,* she became a household name and a popular performer. The movie roles available to her as a black actress were limited; however, she has made a reputation of creating appealing and memorable characters from weak material.

*The Color Purple* also marked a pivotal transition for another burgeoning celebrity, Oprah Winfrey. After a stint as a television anchor in Baltimore, in 1984, Winfrey moved to Chicago, where she helped raise the ratings of a local television talk show. After her successful revitalization, the show was renamed *The Oprah Winfrey Show,* which was first broadcast nationally in 1986.

Shortly before Winfrey began broadcasting nationally, as legend has it, Quincy Jones was in Chicago on business and was watching television in his hotel when he saw her then local talk show. He felt immediately that she would be the perfect person to cast as Sofia, one of the major characters in the novel. Although Winfrey says that she had wanted always to be an actress, she had little experience before being cast in the film.

She was a natural for the part. Having grown up in the rural South, Winfrey was able to identify with Walker's characters on a personal level, and she brought realism and authenticity to her portrayal of the long-suffering Sofia. Winfrey has said that her experiences making the film catapulted her to another level of understanding and awareness—one that allowed her to make her talk show the successful behemoth that it has become. As a result of her role as Sofia, Winfrey was nominated for both a Golden Globe and an Academy Award. She is also the producer of the Broadway production of the musical version of *The Color Purple* (2005).

Despite criticism, censorship, protests, and endless controversy, the cinematic version of *The Color Purple* proved a critical and commercial success. In addition to winning a Golden Globe for Goldberg, the film was nominated for 11 Academy Awards and five Golden Globe Awards, and it won an ASCAP Award, the Director's Guild of America Award, and a National Board of Review Award.

Perhaps most notably for Walker's family, the film's premiere was held in her hometown of Eatonton, Georgia.

The film received new life and a new generation of viewers when its DVD version was released to the public in 2003. This special edition of *The Color Purple* featured new interviews as well as more information about the book and about the film's soundtrack.

## THE MUSICAL ADAPTATION

Alice Walker was at first resistant to the idea of creating a musical adaptation of *The Color Purple,* but after protracted persuasion and negotiation, the producer SCOTT SANDERS convinced her that her novel was good material for a musical. After attaining the blessing of both Walker and Steven Spielberg, Sanders spent several years developing the project, enlisting the assistance and expertise of various artists, including the Pulitzer Prize–winner MARSHA NORMAN, who wrote the book for the musical; and the composers Brenda Russell, Allee Willis, and Stephen Bray, who wrote the music. Walker herself was not directly involved in its creation. The musical's story line is largely the same as the Spielberg film version of *The Color Purple* except that the lesbian relationship between Celie and Shug is not hidden or subverted.

*The Color Purple* premiered in Atlanta in 2004 and opened on Broadway in 2005. The world premier of the musical in Atlanta was the brainchild of Susan V. Booth, the artistic director of the Alliance Theater. When Booth learned of Sanders's intention to turn Walker's book into a musical, she determined that the play, because of the location of the story and Walker's Georgia roots, should premiere in Atlanta. The Atlanta premiere featured performances by LaChanze, who played Celie; Felicia P. Fields as Sofia; Saycon Sengbloh as Nettie; Adriane Lenox as Shug; and Kingsley Leggs as Mister. Gary Griffin was the director of the Atlanta production.

The Broadway production of *The Color Purple: The Musical* premiered in 2005 at the Broadway Theater. The marquee producers of the show included Oprah Winfrey, Quincy Jones, and Scott Sanders. The production in New York again featured LaChanze as Celie, Brandon Victor Dixon as Harpo, Felicia P. Fields as Sofia, Renée Elise Goldsberry as Nettie, Kingsley Leggs as Mister, and Krisha Marcano as Squeak, and the director was again Gary Griffin. The production was nominated for 11 Tony Awards, winning one for LaChanze, and ran on Broadway until 2008. The American Idol winner Fantasia Barrino played Celie for a part of the New York run and continues periodically in that role as a member of the touring company. The touring company premiere was held at the Cadillac Theater in Chicago in 2007. In 2010, *The Color Purple* first national tour was ongoing. A second national tour began in March 2010 and international productions are scheduled for Vienna, Austria, and London, England.

Scott Sanders is a Broadway producer responsible for the musical stage version of *The Color Purple,* which premiered in fall 2004 at the Alliance Theater in Atlanta, Georgia, and in December 2005 on Broadway at the Broadway Theater in New York City. *(Photograph by Carmen Gillespie)*

As of 2010, there has been talk of producing *The Color Purple: The Musical* as a movie. Fantasia Barrino has said that she has been asked to star in the film version of the musical.

### Further Reading


Bobo, Jacqueline. "*The Color Purple:* Black Women as Cultural Readers." In *Female Spectators: Looking at Film and Television,* edited by Deidre Pribram, 90–109. London: Verso, 1988.

———. "Reading through the Text: The Black Woman as Audience." In *Black American Cinema,* edited by Manthia Diawara, 272–287. New York: Routledge, 1993.

———. "Sifting through the Controversy: Reading *The Color Purple.*" *Callaloo: A Journal of African-American and African Arts and Letters* 12, no. 2 (Spring 1989): 332–342.

Collins, Glenn. "*The Color Purple.*" *New York Times,* 15 December 1985, sec. H, p. 1.

Digby, Joan. "From Walker to Spielberg: Transformations of '*The Color Purple*'." In *Novel Images: Literature in Performance,* edited by Peter Reynolds, 157–174. London: Routledge, 1993.

Dole, Carol M. "The Return of the Father in Spielberg's 'The Color Purple.'" *Literature-Film Quarterly* 24, no. 1 (January 1996): 12–17.

Early, Gerald "*The Color Purple* as Everybody's Protest Art." *Antioch Review* 50 (Winter–Spring 1992): 399–412.

Elsley, Judy. "Laughter as Feminine Power in *The Color Purple* and *A Question of Silence.*'" In *New Perspectives on Women and Comedy,* edited by Regina Barreca, 193–199. Philadelphia: Gordon and Breach, 1992.

Feingold, Michael. "Prosaically 'Purple.'" *Village Voice,* 7 December 2005: 68.

Fitzsimmons, Kate. "Go Ask Alice: Alice Walker Talks about *The Color Purple* 10 Years Later." *San Francisco Review of Books* 21 (March–April 1996): 20–23.

Gilliam, Dorothy. "*The Color Purple* Not as Simple as Black or White." *Washington Post,* 23 December 1985, p. B3.

Harris, Trudier. "On *The Color Purple,* Stereotypes, and Silence." *Black American Literature Forum* 18, no. 4 (1984): 155–161.

Hernton, Calvin C. "Who's Afraid of Alice Walker." In *Sexual Mountain and Black Women Writers: Adventures in Sex, Literature, and Real Life.* New York: Anchor Press, 1987, 1–36.

Milloy, Courtland. "A 'Purple' Rage Over a Rip-off." *Washington Post,* 24 December 1985, sec. B, p. 3.

Peacock J. "When Folk Goes Pop—Consuming *The Color Purple.*" *Literature-Film Quarterly* (1991): 176–180.

Shattuc, Jane. "Having a Good Cry over *The Color Purple:* The Problem of Affect and Imperialism in Feminist Theory." In *Melodrama: Stage Picture Screen,* edited by Jacky Bratton, Jim Cook, and Christine Gledhill, 147–56. London: British Film Institute, 1994.

Shipp, E. R. "Blacks in Heated Debate over *The Color Purple.*" *New York Times,* 27 January 1986, p. A13.

Terry, Jill. "The Same River Twice: Signifying *The Color Purple.*" *Critical Survey* 12, no. 3 (2000): 59–76.

Washington, J. Charles. "Positive Black Male Images in Alice Walker's Fiction." *Obsidian* (Spring 1988): 23–48.


## *Meridian* (1976)

*Meridian,* Walker's second novel, appeared in 1976. Published during the bicentennial year of the United States's founding, immediately following the years when Walker was most personally involved in the activism of the CIVIL RIGHTS MOVEMENT, the novel responds to the personal and interpersonal costs of the movement's violence and the unrelenting stress of its work. The novel engages the complexities of race within the movement, particularly concerning the issue of interracial relationships between white women and black men. Through the preoccupations of its protagonist, Meridian Hill, the book also reflects issues that were immediate concerns for Walker herself during the mid-1960s: the transition from a rural to an urban life as a young black woman; the tension between reproductive freedom and motherhood; the adult relationships between women and their mothers; and the conflicts between art and activism, self-sacrifice and autonomy. Walker has said that *Meridian* is also a partial portrait of a SPELMAN COLLEGE graduate and activist named RUBY DORIS SMITH-ROBINSON, who died at age 25 after giving the majority of her energy to the movement and to her work with the STUDENT NONVIOLENT COORDINATING COMMITTEE (SNCC).

The setting for *Meridian* is the segregated south, specifically a black college campus called Saxon that resembles Atlanta's Spelman College, where Walker and Smith-Robinson met. The text traverses the culturally and ideologically fraught landscape of the players of the Civil Rights movement through the lens of an idealistic protagonist who functions as a kind of allegory for the determination and devotion of civil rights workers. Like Walker's first novel, *The Third Life of Grange Copeland, Meridian* received generally positive reviews, which allowed her greater latitude as an artist. Some literary critics consider the book to be among the best novels about the American Civil Rights movement.

## SYNOPSIS
## Meridian

### The Last Return

*Meridian* begins with the character Truman Held arriving in the small town of Chicokema after a car trip from New York City. He arrives in the town just as the novel's protagonist, Meridian Hill, confronts a tank in the town square in an act of protest. The town acquired the tank as a weapon of defense against the civil rights activist who frequented their town in the past. Truman follows news of the event, inquiring about what has happened. He learns that some of the town's children wanted to view a sideshow exhibit, the body of a mummified woman on a day other than that allotted to them under the segregated rules to which the town still adheres. This information about the town's discrimination toward blacks surprises him.

When Truman arrives at the scene, he finds Meridian there with a group of children she has rounded up and organized into a small protest. The town's authorities try to use the tank as a combative countermeasure. In spite of these drastic actions, Meridian and the children reach the door of the circus wagon and enter, undermining the tank's weight and intimidation and defying the men with rifles.

Truman approves of Meridian's actions. A man holding a broom tells Truman about the embalmed woman. He tells Truman that the woman's husband strangled her and her lover after discovering his wife's infidelity. According to the story, the man threw the bodies into a place called Salt Lake. He escaped punishment after he revealed to police the fact that his wife had been unfaithful. After some time, the woman's body washed up, and her husband reclaimed it and created a sideshow with his murdered wife as the main attraction.

Truman goes to Meridian's house, where he finds her walls covered with letters from various people in her life. The letters are critical of Meridian's choices. The house is so sparse that it looks to Truman like a jail cell. He finds her in the house thin and unwell. She tells him repeatedly that he looks like CHE GUEVARA. Truman points out to her that her actions are meaningless and that to get the children to see the mummified woman accomplished nothing. She counters, arguing that she was able to prove to the children that the display was a fraud and that they were able to achieve that end by using knowledge they already had about dead things washed up from the sea. They talk about the fact that after the protest, Meridian has to be carried home after falling into a catatonic state. Meridian and Truman speak of her tendency to fall into paralysis as the result of experiences they have shared in the past. Truman reveals that he, too, has his scars, but that his wounds manifest in his predisposition to run away from difficult situations and confrontations.

Meridian reflects on a time when she and Truman had been in the midst of the trauma that continues to haunt them. She remembers her membership in a group whose initiation required that everyone in the group pledge that they would be willing to die and also to kill for the revolution they believe is unfolding. Although she wants to make the pledge, Meridian has her reservations. Deep within her, intuitive convictions assert that to commit murder—even justifiable murder—will place the struggle she and her compatriots are waging in moral jeopardy. She believes that such actions run contrary to the ineffable truths of the southern black communities they are fighting to liberate.

Reflecting on this moral dilemma, Meridian remembers the differences between her parents: Her mother followed a more traditional religious belief system, while her father followed what he knows of the practices of some of his Native American ancestors. Meridian is inclined toward her father's beliefs. He has told his daughter what he knows about the lives of the native peoples who used to inhabit the land they now know as Georgia and as home. Her mother is unconvinced by the spirituality Meridian's father embraces, seeing the practices of Native Americans as too primitive. Meridian's mother makes prayer pillows, which, ironically, cannot fit both knees.

The difference between the way she and her mother see the world causes Meridian pain. Because Meridian refuses to be baptized in her mother's church, a permanent rift develops between mother and daughter.

As a result of the lessons about religion and spirituality she has learned from both her parents, Meridian is not able to say that she would be able to kill for the revolution. This inability results in her alienation from the radical group she is trying to join and in her realignment of her goals and objectives with respect to the attainment of equal rights for black people. She also decides to return to the people themselves and to do the work of the people with the people, which helps to explain her presence and objectives in the town where Truman finds her at the novel's beginning.

Truman tells Meridian that he is no longer in touch with his former wife and has not really seen her since the death of the child they had together, Camara. Truman says that although he knows that Meridian has let go of the relationship they had in the past, he has not. He also says that he is surprised that Anne-Marion continues to harass Meridian with critical letters. Meridian tells him that she keeps the letters to have her friend's handwriting.

The next section of the chapter begins with a list of people killed in the struggle for social justice during the 1960s: "Medgar Evers/John F. Kennedy/ Malcolm X/Martin Luther King/Robert Kennedy/Che Guevara/Patrice Lamumba [sic]/George Jackson/ Cythia Wesley/Addie Mae Collins/Denis McNair/ Carole Robertson/Viola Liuzzo." We learn that Meridian's friend, Anne-Marion Coles, first became aware of Meridian during the televised broadcast of John F. Kennedy's funeral. Anne-Marion was motivated to become Meridian's friend because she believed that the relationship would somehow be beneficial to her ambitions and goals. Although this self-interest characterized the beginning of the relationship between them, eventually Anne-Marion developed genuine affection for Meridian.

### The Wild Child

The next chapter of *Meridian* describes a young woman who lives around the campus where Meridian attends college. She is said to live without parents and is thought to be about 13 years old. She earns the name Wild Child from the people who live in the neighborhood around the college, a place Wild Child has occupied since she was about five or six years old. The people in the neighborhood see the girl occasionally as she raids their garbage for sustenance and clothing. After it becomes apparent that Wild Child is pregnant, the people in the neighborhood decide to try to catch and help her during her pregnancy and with her delivery. Their efforts are to no avail as Wild Child continues to elude them.

After Meridian sees Wild Child for the first time, she has one of her recurrent fits of paralysis and is unable to move for several days before recovering. Meridian tempts Wild Child with food, captures her, and brings her onto campus. After these failed efforts to find a home for the girl, Wild Child escapes and is killed by a car while running across a street.

### Sojourner

While in college, Meridian is an honor student and lives in the honors house. Anne-Marion is described in the third chapter of *Meridian* as rounder and more physically substantial than her friend. She is quick to anger and is unmoved by the spiritual rhetoric of the leaders of the Civil Rights movement. Anne-Marion is one of the first women at the college to wear her hair naturally and short. Meridian and Anne-Marion share rebelliousness against the college's attempts to inculcate the women who attend the school into traditional notions of womanhood.

This chapter begins with the funeral of Wild Child. As the women carry Wild Child's body, they come to the center of campus, where there is a tree called the Sojourner. According to legend, a slave named Louvinie buried her tongue at the foot of the magnolia tree on the original Saxon plantation where the campus is now located.

Louvinie was thought of as unattractive. She was not traditionally beautiful and was especially distasteful to some because of her jutting chin and because she did not smile. Louvinie came from a family in Africa whose task it was to ferret out guilty and undiscovered individuals who aspired to commit murder. A part of their strategy involved intricate storytelling. Louvinie brought her family's storytelling ability, but not their ability to discern crimes, to the United States when she arrived as a slave. She told frightening stories to the children on the Saxon plantation. In the process of telling one of these scary stories, Louvinie accidentally brought about the death of the youngest, who had a Saxon son, of a heart defect. In retaliation for his son's death, the master of the Saxon plantation removed Louvinie's tongue, rendering her unable to tell her stories or anything else ever again. A version of Louvinie's story was written down by one of the Saxon daughters and preserved in the college's library.

Many years later, while Meridian is a student at the college, the tree is threatened with removal. Meridian joins those who protest the tree's destruction. The Sojourner has been the site of other subversive activities, such as lovemaking. Students who use the tree for such a purpose maintain that they cannot be seen while in the Sojourner. The tree is also the site for May Day festivals and, secretly, the celebration commemorating the suicide of a woman named Fast Mary of the Tower, whose death was attributed to her murder of her child, born after an unplanned pregnancy.

The college's women insist upon having the Wild Child's funeral at the chapel on Saxon's campus. The women are unable to break into the chapel and so proceed to the Sojourner and hold Wild Child's funeral there. Wild Child is buried in a cemetery off-campus. The students are so furious at the treatment of the fallen woman that they instigate a riot. During the riot, the Sojourner is destroyed.

### "Have You Stolen Anything?"

This chapter begins with Meridian grappling with feelings of guilt she has had since she was a child. The title of this chapter comes from the question Meridian's mother would repeat when her child told her about her feelings of guilt. Meridian's mother only knew a brief period of freedom as a young woman when she was able to make her own decisions about her life without the encumbrance of a relationship or of children. Meridian's mother had worked as a teacher, and this occupation provided her with the means to support her brief period of independence, which was insufficiently long. Soon after she married another teacher, Meridian's father. Meridian's mother conceived her first child and came to feel that child-rearing was a terrible experience that drained her of her inner life, personality, and autonomy. As a result of her deep resentment of her status as a mother, Meridian's mother was unable to provide her daughter with the resources she needed to become a well-adjusted and happy woman. In her mother's question lies the source of Meridian's insecurity and self-doubt, which manifests in her adult life as her tendency to succumb to physical paralysis when faced with a difficult psychological situation.

### Gold

As a child, Meridian discovers a bar of gold. She only makes this discovery after removing the dirt from its surface. She takes her discovery to her mother, who pays no attention to her daughter's find and shows absolutely no interest in the object or her daughter's enthusiasm. In fact, no one in Meridian's family finds the brick interesting or shares her belief that the bar has value. Finding no one to share her treasure, Meridian buries the bar under a magnolia tree that grows in the family's yard. Periodically, she digs up the treasure in order to revere it. After some time, her interest in the gold abates, and she forgets to dig it up.

### Indians and Ecstasy

Meridian's father creates a private space for himself in the family's backyard. In this room, he reads over old maps and indulges his fascination with the Native Americans who used to inhabit the land on which the family's home is now located. One day, while watching her father read a map, Meridian notices that he is crying. This display of emotion frightens her, and she runs from the spot and from her father.

On another occasion, Meridian hears her parents arguing about an Indian burial mound that happens to be on their property. Meridian's father has given some of the land to a Native American who told him about the burial ground and its location. Meridian's mother is angry that her father gave it away.

Later, Meridian sees the man to whom her father gave the land. The man reminds her of her father in that he replicates her father's interest in maps and the movement of people in his own movement from place to place. She also believes that her father and the Indian, as she calls him, share feelings of perpetual grief. Yet, she cannot imagine the Indian crying as her father did. The Indian's name is Walter Longknife, and he describes his arrival in Georgia. He drove into the state from Oklahoma in a truck that broke down at the Confederate monument at Stone Mountain, causing him to walk the rest of the way to the land his people were forced to leave. The land that Meridian's father has given to Longknife is an ancient burial ground for his tribe. Before Longknife leaves Meridian's family's land, he returns the deed to the property back to Meridian's father.

After Longknife leaves, the government claims Meridian's family's land and turns the burial ground into a tourist attraction. Meridian's family receives only minor financial compensation for the appropriated land and, in a final insult, are not able to go to the park because it is segregated. The mound is known to Meridian as the Sacred Serpent, and its preservation had been an accomplishment of Meridian's great-grandmother, Feather Mae, who had fought with her husband to keep the burial ground intact.

Feather Mae was said to be a playful and dreamy girl who loved to lie on the mounds and feel the connection to the earth. Feather Mae discovered an entrance to the mound, and when inside the center of the Sacred Serpent, she had a kind of supernatural experience, which transformed her. From that point on, she only believed in religious practices that were connected to physical pleasure. She spent time at the end of her life worshipping the sun and walking about outside without clothing.

Meridian is intrigued with this story about her great-grandmother and tries to have the same experience that so changed her ancestor. After many attempts to replicate her great-grandmother's experience, Meridian has this ecstatic revelation herself. During her revelation, she feels as if she leaves her body and sees images of her family and elements of the natural world. Her father tells her that the Native Americans who built the pit intended for the experience people had within it to replicate the experience of death. Meridian does not share her father's interpretation. She believes that the mound is supposed to generate a more intense understanding of life. The father and daughter spend time debating their positions, time that draws them closer to each other and unites them in their interest in the perceptions of their Native American ancestors. The power of the Sacred Serpent's center is lost after the mound is turned into a public park.

### English Walnuts

As an adolescent, Meridian has little or no information about sex, and so she engages in it often with her boyfriends from the time she is a teenager until she is in college, although she experiences no pleasure from the act at all. Without any knowledge of the subject, Meridian finds herself pregnant and is surprised. Her boyfriend at the time of her pregnancy, Eddie, is a rather attractive, dark-skinned man who plays sports and has a developed physique. He dresses well and has money at his disposal.

As a result of the pregnancy, Meridian and Eddie marry, and Meridian is expelled from school. They move in together, and their mothers begin preparation for the baby's arrival. Eddie has aspirations for a nice house in a beautiful neighborhood, aspirations Meridian does not share. As her pregnancy progresses, she loses interest in sex, and Eddie begins an affair with someone else, a woman who loves sex.

For Meridian, sex is mysterious. She does not find it pleasurable and only enjoys the feeling of cuddling and the close proximity of another body. When she loses interest in sex, she remembers that she was molested as a child and an adolescent by the mixed-race owner of the local funeral home, George Daxter. She was also preyed upon by Daxter's assistant at the funeral home, a man known to her as the Assistant. After his repeated assaults, the Assistant claimed her as his girl. The Assistant equated his sexual prowess with his skill as a mortician. Meridian agreed to continue having sex with him if he would promise to hold her in his arms after the act. This sexual agreement continued until Meridian became involved with Eddie. The experiences Meridian had with Daxter and the Assistant are implicated in her feelings toward Eddie and contribute to her lack of desire to have sexual relations with her young husband. The chapter's title comes from her imaginings about Daxter's penis. She believes the myth she has heard that fat men have small penises and so imagines that Daxter's penis looks like an English walnut.

### The Happy Mother

Meridian gives birth to a son, but she has a difficult time with the child's delivery and with the demands of motherhood. She feels imprisoned by her life as a mother and resents her child, who everyone tells her looks like his father. Meridian is so overwhelmed that she even has thoughts of killing her child, thoughts she shifts to killing herself. As a young mother, it becomes clearer to Meridian that she does not love her husband. She finds him childlike and interested in the wrong things, like the state of his clothes. Eventually the marriage breaks up, and Meridian is left with her son. After Eddie leaves, she becomes aware of the local activities of civil rights activists, particularly of a house owned by local activists that is not far from her. Shortly after her awareness of the house, it is blown up in a bombing protesting its activities. The people in the house were not there at the time and therefore were not injured. The reporting about this incident opens up Meridian's understanding of the larger world around her at a time when it is filled with the chaos and turbulence of social revolution.

### Clouds

After Eddie's departure, Meridian gets help taking care of her son from her mother-in-law, who has a late-life child, a three-year-old, of her own. Meridian spends her days looking out of the window of the rental house she once shared with Eddie that her in-laws help her to pay for. She enters a meditation-like state, and while watching young girls walk home from school, she reflects on the realities of her own adolescence and on the way she was unduly influenced by the films that she and her friends watched rather than by encounters with other young people themselves. She reflects that the encounter with the worlds depicted in film left her and her friends looking for and believing in happy endings that were unrelated to life in the real worlds that they inhabit. As a 17-year-old woman without focus and unhappy about her circumstances, Meridian finds herself bitter about her expectations and uncertain and pessimistic about her future.

### The Attainment of Good

This chapter begins as a reflection on Meridian's mother's life, which is limited to her personal sphere of friends and family and, more particularly, to her church. Meridian's mother believes that the physical structure of her church contains some essential element of what she understands as holy, and, as such, the building itself becomes her refuge. The church she attends encourages its parishioners to try to act in ways that it defines as good. She has no investment in politics or in the world outside of the immediate concerns of her daily routine. She does not vote, and she does not impress upon her children the liberating possibilities that voting offers in a democracy. Mrs. Hill regards the professional class of African Americans, such as teachers, as infallible and does not question their influence on her or on her children. Her only complaints are to and about her husband. She spends more time and energy in keeping her children tidy and presentable than in loving them.

### Awakening

Meridian ends her meditative explorations by venturing into the world and volunteering to work with the people whose house has been destroyed in the bombing. When she goes to the house, she meets several of the volunteers who work there, including a man named Swinburn, one named Truman Held, and another named Chester Gray. The men do not pay her much attention but put her to work typing out a petition. While undertaking the task, Meridian learns how to type.

### Battle Fatigue

After working with the civil rights workers for some time, Meridian begins to develop feelings for Truman Held. She becomes clear about her affections when Truman is arrested after a demonstration and is beaten in jail. Meridian herself participates in a protest and is also beaten by police. While she is subjected to violence at the hands of the police, she realizes that she is screaming Truman's name in her head. This revelation indicates to her that the two share a circumstantial bond.

As the two continue with their activist endeavors, they begin to become numb from the perpetual and unceasing abuse that they experience while undertaking their protests. The two begin to suffer from a condition Meridian calls battle fatigue. Truman's symptoms manifest as a perpetual blankness in his expression, while Meridian finds herself constantly in tears, even when circumstances do not seem to warrant such an expression of emotion. She also imagines herself being shot.

The work that Meridian and her colleagues engage in has the support of the majority of black people in the community. Her mother, however, does not share their opinion. Her mother berates Meridian's involvement and, in fact, believes that segregation is a kind of natural order ordained by God that should not be tampered with by anyone.

Meridian has other difficult news to share with her mother. While she was still in high school, she was tested and found to have an unusually high IQ score. As a result of her score on the test, Mr. Yateson, the principal of the local high school, offers Meridian a scholarship to attend Saxon College. In spite of his offer, Mr. Yateson does not approve of Meridian's premarital sexuality, as evidenced by her pregnancy and subsequent marriage to Eddie, and tells her so even as he informs her of the scholarship.

Meridian is partially influenced to take the scholarship after Truman reveals that his college is located in close proximity to Saxon and that she will fit in with the women who attend the school. Truman makes this assessment of Meridian's compatibility with the school without knowing about her son.

As her friends Delores and Nelda walk with Meridian to her mother's house to give her the news that she will be leaving to attend college, the two girls encourage her, telling her that education is important and that opportunities, such as that provided by the scholarship, are uncommon. But Mrs. Hill maintains that her daughter is immoral and would be committing an even greater trespass by leaving her child to pursue her intellectual life. In the middle of the conversation, Nelda—who is an old playmate of Meridian's—realizes that Mrs. Hill could have helped her and Meridian to successfully navigate their adolescence and become women capable of pursuing their dreams and goals, but instead she had denied them information essential to doing this. The revelation leaves Nelda angry and bitter with Mrs. Hill. She is especially bitter because, except for one free day on Sunday, she has had to work as the primary caretaker for her five siblings while her mother worked, and then, at 15, Nelda became pregnant herself.

Mrs. Hill is convinced that the only respectable option for her daughter is for her to get a job, probably as a maid, and to move back home so that she can have her family's assistance with Eddie Jr. The conversation does not go well, and the girls leave without obtaining Mrs. Hill's approval of her daughter's decision.

In order to take advantage of her scholarship, Meridian gives Eddie Jr. away. Before she leaves him, she renames him Rundi, a name she thinks is unique. After her decision, which she makes with conviction and the certainty that what she is doing is the right thing, she is surprised when she has nightmares about her child and about his well-being. Even after Meridian begins her studies, her feelings of guilt about having given her son away haunt her. She begins to feel inadequate and unable to live up to the expectations of motherhood generated by those who preceded her. In spite of this burden, she is a successful student during her first year at Saxon College.

### The Driven Snow

During that first year at Saxon, Meridian becomes enamored of the place and particularly of its physical beauty. She has experiences at the tree, the Sojourner, that are similar to those she had as a child at the Indian mounds called the Sacred Serpent. She has friends and in particular is drawn to Anne-Marion. Like Meridian, Anne-Marion understands the irony of the Saxon song that names the women as pure as the driven snow. Meridian does not tell anyone at the school about her marriage, divorce, and maternity. She also does not share the message implicit in the Saxon doctrine that there is a traditional God. Living with the contradictions between her lived life and her belief system and the school's fundamental philosophy takes its toll. Meridian begins to suffer from terrible headaches. She joins the activities of the Civil Rights movement in Atlanta, an activity that allows her an outlet through which to express her true passions and desires.

Many events haunt Meridian during her time at Saxon. One trauma involves her feelings of responsibility for a young Atlanta girl named Anne, whom Meridian encourages to join the movement. After the group is arrested, Meridian cannot locate the girl and believes that she has been raped and beaten by prison guards.

The disapproval expressed by Mrs. Hill also tortures Meridian. She begins to imagine her mother as the embodiment of an idealized version of motherhood—a standard she cannot achieve. Following the death of Wild Child, Meridian moves into the community surrounding Saxon. In order to support herself, she begins work as a typist for a retired professor. Because of the stress of her experiences, she begins to lose her hair and also finds that her vision is deteriorating. This physical decline occurs around the same time that she discovers that her feelings for Truman have become increasingly intense and that she is now in love with him.

### The Conquering Prince

Truman loves French culture and often speaks French to Meridian. He spent a year in the country, and that experience convinced him that France and French culture were superior to all others. Although Meridian does not speak the language, Truman insists on speaking it when he is with her. In the beginning, Truman is a novelty for Meridian. He is not like the other black men she has known in her life, and this originality is part of his appeal.

About the time her relationship with Truman gets more serious, Meridian begins spending time on activist work with a young white woman named Lynne. Truman is also involved sexually with Lynne. Meridian discovers this fact when she sees the two driving while she is traveling to the doctor's to abort the child she has conceived with Truman. She is angry with Truman because he is completely unaware of what she is experiencing and does not have to suffer as a consequence of his sexuality. Truman never finds out about the pregnancy or the abortion, and as might be expected, Meridian no longer finds him interesting.

### The Recurring Dream

Meridian dreams that she is in a novel whose resolution requires her death. Her involvement with the work of the Civil Rights movement and her experiences with discrimination begin to take a psychological toll on her. Anne-Marion moves in with Meridian. The women learn about systems of social organization and try to articulate their own theories of what is possible without creating further injustice.

Meridian temporarily loses her sight and cannot afford to go to a physician to see what is wrong. She passes out in a comalike state and awakens to find herself being molested by the campus physician. Her sight returns, but she still feels ill. Her body periodically works and then does not work. Sometimes she can walk, and at other times, she cannot. In this state, she begins to have a kind of spiritual ecstasy.

Anne-Marion becomes distressed at Meridian's condition and worries that what her roommate is experiencing may be terminal. She gets angry with herself when she starts thinking of Meridian as a kind of saint.

Anne-Marion reaches out to Miss Winter, one of the teachers at Saxon, for help with Meridian. Although Miss Winter is pretentious, she does not conform to the school's rigid sense of propriety. She is one of three black teachers at the school when Meridian enrolls as a student. She often fights with the administration to change policies and practices she finds objectionable. She is from Meridian's hometown and knows Meridian's family and situation. Miss Winter and Meridian bond for the first time when Miss Winter attends a speech Meridian gives at the high school they both attended. Meridian is unable to complete the speech because she finds that its false patriotism rings hollow. Miss Winter consoles and identifies with Meridian, saying that she had to memorize the same speech when she attended the school. Miss Winter helps Meridian through her troubled period and acts as the surrogate mother Meridian needs in order to recover from the various traumas she has experienced, including her abortion.

During her illness, Meridian recounts the history of her mother's side of her family. Her mother's great-great-grandmother was a slave who retrieved her young children from slave traders three times. As a result of her persistence, she was able to keep her children, but only on the condition that she fed herself through her own means. Ironically, the woman died as a result of protracted starvation, and her children were sold anyway.

Meridian's mother's great-grandmother was an artist who, although enslaved, gained a reputation for painting. Through her artistry, she earned enough money to buy her freedom and that of her family. Meridian's grandmother entered into an unfortunate marriage with an industrious man who was also promiscuous and violent toward his family members. Her grandmother ended up with 12 children, overworked, and yet determined that her daughter, Meridian's mother, would have the education she desired.

Meridian's mother, Mrs. Hill, determined to escape both her father and the advances of white men in her community by becoming a schoolteacher. Thanks to her mother's profound sacrifices, she accomplished this task. Meridian feels guilty about having burdened her mother with maternity and inherits from this maternal line a clear commitment to justice and to the tireless pursuit of what she believes is right.

After Miss Winter's intervention and surrogate mothering, Meridian begins to heal. She starts to eat and to regain her strength. Anne-Marion cannot bear the taxing nature of their friendship and leaves, calling Meridian obsolete. Later, when Anne-Marion has relocated to the North and Meridian spends her time and energy fighting racism in the South, Anne-Marion is surprised when she finds herself compelled to write long letters to Meridian.

## Truman Held

### Truman and Lynne: Time in the South

This chapter begins with descriptions of Lynne and Truman's relationship as they work on civil rights issues in the South. Truman feels their racial differences, which seem highlighted in the environment in which they live. Lynne's romantic notion of the South and of the people she encounters reduces them to an aesthetic experience for her. Despite the conflicts in their perspectives and the real dangers of living as an interracial couple in such an environment, Truman decides to move to Mississippi.

### Of Bitches and Wives

Tommy Odds is a civil rights worker in Mississippi with Truman and Lynne. He is shot by a racist as he walks downtown with Truman and another worker named Trilling. Trilling is a worker from Oklahoma who flees and is never seen again after Tommy Odds is shot. Lynne and Truman's relationship is transformed by the shooting. Tommy Odds loses the lower half of his arm in the accident. After the accident, Tommy begins to hate all white people and will not count Lynne as a friend. His attitude affects Truman and makes him question the nature of his relationship with Lynne and whether any involvement with white people is inherently problematic.

Lamumba Katurim is an activist whose decision to leave his white wife affects Truman while he is having doubts about Lynne. Truman wonders whether it is possible for a white person to be free of racism and whether, by marrying a white woman, he has somehow compromised himself and his loyalty to the struggle for black liberation. There are others who are leaving their white wives for black women, such as a movie star Truman admires named Randolph Kay.

Another black friend, Tom Johnson, has a white lover named Margaret, but he admits he is with her only in order to disrupt the social order. He even offers to let Truman sleep with Margaret. Lynne also faces the growing hostility within the movement toward whites generally and begins to feel unwelcome in the struggle.

### *The New York Times*

Truman decides that he loves Meridian rather than Lynne and visits Meridian with the intention of getting together. Meridian refuses his advances, stating that she is not interested in Truman and that she could not betray Lynne in that way. She also mentions the couple's daughter, Camara, and Truman's obligation to her. Truman maintains that he owes more to the black children who are persecuted as a result of their race. Meridian reminds him that his daughter is one of those children. Truman maintains that he should have married Meridian. She replies that he should have loved her.

Truman reduces Lynne to an intellectual idealist and sees himself as a grand patriarch and protector. She has other perceptions of him and no longer loves his current incarnation. Meridian tells Truman that he married Lynne because he was seeking an ideal that Meridian herself, as a divorced woman with a child, could never have embodied. This ideal is embodied for Truman in his assertion that the women he was attracted to in the past read the *New York Times.*

### Visits

Meridian continues her work despite physical limitations that impede her progress. Both Truman and Lynne come to visit her in Chicokema, the small Mississippi town where she has taken up residence and works to promote racial and social justice. Meridian has the support of the local African-American community. They provide her with a house and with sustenance.

Lynne comes to visit Meridian to spew her anger and frustration about her failed marriage and aspirations. Lynne is bitter about the way that her life has unfolded and blames Meridian. She maintains that Truman was always and inevitably connected to Meridian, and as a result, her marriage to him could never have succeeded.

Truman returns to Meridian's house and discovers Lynne there. The two descend into a nasty, racially charged argument in the backyard, while Meridian tries to ignore their angry screams. Truman finds himself physically repulsed by Lynne's appearance and cruelly assesses her flaws, making a list of what he finds unappealing about her. The attributes he notices are particularly associated with whiteness.

The fight concludes, and Lynne enters Meridian's house through an open window and continues her diatribe about the failures of her life. She is trying to understand the contradictions between the sexual attraction black men expressed toward her and their rejection of her based on racial animosity. Lynne tells Meridian about her parents disowning her because she married a black man. Then she begins to tell Meridian about Truman and an incident where he let another man rape her.

### Lynne

This short chapter adds nuance to the story of Lynne's parents' abandonment of their daughter. Lynne ran away as a young adult. Her parents traced her disappearance to Truman's house. When her mother discovered that her daughter was in a black neighborhood and with a black family, she began screaming with horror. Lynne feels that the screams of her mother will never leave her and will continue to haunt her throughout her life.

### Tommy Odds

This brief chapter recounts Tommy Odd's attraction to Lynne. He fetishizes her and imagines scenarios rooted in violation and domination.

### Lynne

Lynne reveals to Meridian that, after his shooting accident, Tommy Odds raped her. The moment is complicated by Lynne's feeling of racial guilt that prevents her from acting forcefully in her own defense. She rationalizes the rape through a series of mental gymnastics that situate responsibility for the rape in a larger social context, one that does not allow black men recourse for any wrong they suffer. This rationale allows Lynne to feel that Tommy's rape of her was in some ways justified. When she tells Truman what happened to her, he tells her that he refuses to believe her story or to help her leave.

Although he does not tell her, Truman does believe Lynne and confronts Tommy Odds about his wife's violation. The two have a fight, and Tommy Odds shakes Truman's sense of masculinity when he tells him that Lynne wanted to have sex with him. Tommy Odds also tells Truman that at the root of his marriage to Lynne is guilt and pity. He says that Lynne feels guilty for being white and pities Truman for being black, and that is why the two are together. This utterance, more than the rape itself, is the catalyst for the unraveling of Truman and Lynne's relationship.

Truman stops talking to Lynne, and she seeks company with the men in the town. At first, she talks to the men only to assuage her loneliness; later, she has to fight off their advances and eventually decides to sleep with them, mostly out of fear and confusion. She then becomes a town pariah and loses the respect of the men and the women.

After a time, the men stop coming to sleep with her. Although she and Truman resume a sexual relationship and conceive a child, their marriage is over. Lynne goes back to New York and lives in public housing on public assistance. Truman heads south to be with Meridian.

### On Giving Him Back to His Own

Truman returns to New York but does not live with Lynne and Camara. He writes African-American novels in an attempt at greatness and celebrity. The chapter begins with Lynne running to his apartment to tell him that their daughter, Camara, has been attacked. Lynne's thoughts are not all on the child. Part of her motivation for telling Truman this information in person is the hope that it might prompt a reconciliation between them. When she arrives at Truman's door, there is a woman there she does not know. Despite her intentions and efforts to be cordial, even alluring, Lynne becomes combative and demeaning.

### Two Women

Scarlett O'Hara is the name that Lynne gives to the woman Truman is living with when she comes to tell him about the attack on their daughter, Camara. The woman disappears from their lives after Camara dies. Meridian travels to New York to console and care for them both.

After Camara's death, Lynne has a nervous breakdown and travels to the South in a desperate attempt to reclaim some of the happiness she had felt when she and Truman lived there originally. Lynne feels homeless and lost but is grateful for the support she receives from Meridian. She goes to sleep with the South on her mind.

### Lynne

Lynne returns to the South and takes up residence in her old house, even though it is in a nearly uninhabitable space. When she awakens from the most restful sleep she has had in years, she begins to remember all of the good times that happened in the house and her experiences with the people in her and Truman's lives. It is as if Lynne walks through the haunting of the community that formed around the Civil Rights movement, its structures and shapes. She comes to the conclusion that she cannot be a part of a group like her parents, who are unapologetically engaged in oppressive lives, and that, for better or worse, she is glad that she made the choices that she did about her life. She also admits that she still loves Truman and wants him back.

## Ending

### Free at Last: A Day in April, 1968

Meridian and Truman attend Martin Luther King, Jr.'s funeral. The event starts as a somber occasion, but Truman and Meridian are surprised and befuddled about how quickly it turns into a kind of celebration, complete with popcorn and laughter.

### Questions

Truman and Meridian discuss the extent of their commitments to the Civil Rights movement and to social justice as they ponder the question of whether they would be willing to kill for the revolution. Truman is certain that he can, while Meridian remains deeply ambivalent about the consequences, personal and collective, of taking someone's life for any reason.

Meridian works for justice for the people in the community where she lives. When a black child dies as a consequence of a poorly maintained sewer, she challenges and rebukes the town's leadership. She brings the corpse of a dead boy to the mayor's office and gives the local people an opportunity to express their frustrations about their problems going unattended. The members of the community appreciate her activism and show their gratitude by providing her with the means to live there indefinitely.

### Camara

Meridian begins to attend church and finds herself particularly moved by the music. The image of Christ in the church is of a black man. The church she attends has a stained-glass window called "B. B., With Sword." It is in this church, while contemplating the significances of the window, where Meridian finds her answer about whether she would kill for the revolution, for the causes she believes in most passionately—and the answer is yes.

### Travels

Meridian and Truman work together in the community. Not only do they ask the people they speak with to empower themselves by voting, they listen to the struggles of these individuals and do what they can to help them.

### Treasure

Miss Margaret Treasure is a woman Truman and Meridian meet while they are registering people to vote in rural Mississippi. She is very old and has an aging daughter named Lucille. In spite of her advanced age, Miss Treasure believes that she is pregnant. Truman and Meridian take her to a doctor, where, of course, she is delighted to discover that she is not pregnant.

### Pilgrimage

Meridian and Truman visit a young woman named Carrie Mae, who is in prison for killing her own child. At this visit, Meridian adopts a Christlike attitude toward all of the people in the world who are burdened by shame. She writes two poems in which she expresses a desire to forgive them all so that people can live their lives without shame. In the next section of the chapter, "Atonement: Later, in the Same Life," Truman and Lynne come to some resolution of their relationship. Truman tells her that he wants to take care of her and to make sure that she is alright, but that he does not desire her sexually. Lynne seems to accept this proposal and suggests that they both return to the South. Truman is unsure why.

### Settling Accounts

Truman tells Meridian that he wants her to love him. Meridian replies that she does, and Truman says that she pities rather than loves him. Meridian receives a letter from Anne-Marion telling her that the tree, the Sojourner, that they believed was dead might live still.

Meridian and Truman remember an incident that happened while they were working on voting registration. They remember a man who told his wife that their dog had better characteristics than she did. The woman left him but had to return because she could not afford to feed their five children by herself.

### Release

Without possessions, Meridian sets out on a journey alone. She leaves Truman behind to do the work that she had been doing, and he accepts her role as a kind of savior to the community. Meridian and her compatriots all accept and bear the burden of fighting for the cause they all believe in.

## CRITICAL COMMENTARY

In Walker's works, particularly *Meridian* and *The Temple of My Familiar,* several characters utilize SELF-AFFIRMATION to claim and access their inherent selfhood. Within these novels, each character's discovery of wholeness involves rejection and personal redefinition of traditional Western definitions of womanhood, race, sexuality, and spirituality. Walker's central and titular character in *Meridian* also functions as a potential messianic figure. If Meridian does not provide a vehicle for salvation in a traditional sense, she does represent a model for communal redemption through her example of individual sacrifice and affirmation.

Meridian's salvation begins internally and may or may not positively impact the larger community. In the preface to *Meridian,* Walker includes a quotation from the autobiography *Black Elk Speaks.*

> I did not know then how much was ended. When I look back now . . . I can still see the butchered women and children lying heaped and scattered all along the crooked gulch as plain as when I saw them with eyes still young. And I can see that something else died there in the bloody mud, and was buried in the blizzard. A people's dream died there. It was a beautiful dream . . . the nation's hoop is broken and shattered. There is no center any longer, and the sacred tree is dead.

BLACK ELK's autobiography, particularly this quotation, can serve as a guide to understanding the novel and to elucidating Walker's philosophy. Black Elk articulates a philosophy in which self-affirmation is necessarily connected to the well-being of the entire community. In his narrative, chaos is associated with disunity. Like African Americans, his people have experienced a deterioration of common meaning and purpose due to oppressive external circumstances.

Early in the narrative, Black Elk is given the power to restore harmony to his people through a mystical vision. Meridian functions in Walker's novel in much the same capacity. Self-affirmation as developed in *Meridian* takes place as a subjective experience of Walker's protagonist, but Walker suggests that her heroine's journey also has the potential to catalyze revolution and reunification, not only for African Americans, but for the human community.

As an early work of the AFRA-AMERICAN RENAISSANCE, *Meridian,* Walker's second novel, provided a prototype for the contemporary black GODDESS FIGURE. Although many critics label *Meridian* a civil rights or feminist novel, those categorizations are only partially accurate. Through the spiritual journey of her protagonist, Meridian Hill, Walker demonstrates how individual discovery of inherent divinity is connected to the survival and well-being of all. Specifically, Meridian's personal struggle manifests through rejection of traditional Western models of Christian womanhood, through reconnection with her racial heritage and with the natural world, and finally through her resolution of the question of justified murder.

Early in the novel, Walker reveals the ways in which the subtextual paradigm of American society, the Western/Christian narrative, restricts the holistic development of women, particularly African-American women. At the same time, she graphically illustrates how the objectification of women within the Western/Christian schema makes it nearly impossible for a woman to cultivate personal autonomy. As such, Meridian's attempt to develop a personal female spirituality begins with her rejection of traditional Christianity. In the novel, her journey to self-affirmation provides an alternative to the model of womanhood as framed by Christian parameters. Within the first few pages of the first chapter, Walker reveals the narrow confines of Christian womanhood and uses metaphors to illustrate the way in which these boundaries lead to imitation of a dead icon or ideal rather than encouraging development of a self-defined identity.

Meridian's dynamic spirituality provides a vivid contrast to the stagnation of the Western/Christian ideal woman. An early scene depicts Meridian's attempt to attain equal access to a carnival freak show–like exhibit for the African-American inhabitants of a small southern town. The exhibit consists of a murdered white woman's remains. Outside the "show," there is a sign reading: "Marilene O'Shay, One of the Twelve Human Wonders of the World: Dead for Twenty-Five Years Preserved in Life-Like Condition." The man who killed Marilene O'Shay, who also happens to be her husband, displays her for profit. With this macabre image, Walker metaphorizes the dilemma of women within the Western cultural framework. The conflation of the names Mary and Magdalene into Marilene highlights the polarized framework. In the Christian paradigm, women are either virgins, mothers, or whores. Within such boundaries, there is no room for individuality or salvation without submission to an inhuman ideal. Rather than succumb to the oppressive system that creates and reveres this dead iconography, Meridian attempts to define her own existence and to chart a way of being in the world that will sustain her.

Meridian stages the protest that is the focus of the scene to allow the town's black children to view Marilene on the segregated town's designated "white day." In order to obstruct Meridian's demonstration, several white men employ a tank. In this scene, she defies white male authority and clearly establishes her nonadherence to traditional definitions of either gender or race. The statement of an observer reveals the audacity of Meridian's claimed power. "She thinks she's God." In fact, Meridian has replaced the hierarchical presumptions of traditional constructions of God with an unwavering personal surety and authority and, as such, is able to exemplify for the community an alternative to the oppressive status quo.

*Meridian* opens with a scene that occurs near the chronological end of the story. Meridian is not always the confident, redemptive individual presented at the novel's dramatic opening. The novel's flashback structure details the process she must undergo to negate the power of various oppressions to control her existence. The opening scene provides a signpost to the journey Meridian takes to avoid becoming like Marilene—to continue affirming her humanity and her life rather than becoming a "lifelike" manifestation of an ideal.

The sign that advertises Marilene labels her an "Obedient Daughter . . . Devoted Wife . . . Adoring Mother . . . Gone Wrong." These designations represent the four options traditionally available to women within the Western/Christian tradition. They also outline the roles Meridian must reject in order to discover her own personally styled selfhood.

In order to create an individual philosophy that can serve as a model for her oppressed community, Meridian rejects traditional religion. She recognizes that self-affirmation is a process of becoming rather than a state of being, and she reflects this dynamic condition through her never-ending quest for spiritual, emotional, and psychic health.

After her dramatic confrontation with the white men in the tank, Meridian collapses and is carried back to her home by four men of her community, "hoisted across their shoulders exactly as they would carry a coffin, her eyes closed, barely breathing, arms folded across her chest, legs straight." Her death and rebirth ritual represents the cyclical nature of her quest for health and distinguishes her spirituality and activism from the Western view of death and life. When Truman asks Meridian if she is ill, she replies, "Of course I'm sick, . . . Why else would I spend all this time trying to get well!" She subsequently explains, "What you see before you is a woman in the process of changing her mind." For Meridian, growth occurs from a process of rebirth into a new state of consciousness, one free of the constraints she finds inherent in the Christian construction of women. Meridian's Christ-like crucifixions, deaths, and resurrections return the possibility of redemption to the individuals of the community. Unlike Christ, however, she offers herself not as a vehicle for, but as an example of, salvation. As such, Walker subverts and then employs biblical strategies as reference points in her effort to rewrite and transform these narratives in service of her protagonist's self-invention.

Meridian's rejection of traditional Christianity occurs early in her life. The beliefs expressed by her mother, Mrs. Hill, emphasize Walker's concerns about the prohibitions of some Christian conventions. Meridian's mother exemplifies the oppression experienced by women who attempt to live an ideal Christian life.

> Her mother's life was sacrifice. A blind, enduring, stumbling—though with dignity—through life. She did not appear to understand much beyond what happened in her own family, in the neighborhood and in her church. . . . She thought the church was literally God's house, and believed she felt his presence there when she entered the door; when she stepped back outside there was a different feeling, she believed.

Meridian's mother is only referred to as "her mother" or Mrs. Hill throughout the text, emphasizing the way in which her life is defined entirely by her roles—by external rather than by internal definitions. With all of her energy completely focused on maintaining her roles, Mrs. Hill is unable to find satisfaction in anything she does outside of attending church. The state of motherhood, so revered in Western religion (the Mary half of Marilene), becomes for Mrs. Hill a barrier to self-affirmation. Each birth causes her to feel like a "person who is being buried alive, walled away from her own life, brick by brick." Intuitively, Meridian recognizes the oppression in her mother's definition of female spirituality. For Mrs. Hill, Christian womanhood requires adherence to an ideal and an endless quest for perfection. She never explores the multiple possibilities of her life as a result of her rigid adherence to the roles of mother and wife. Meridian refuses to subject herself to her mother's oppression:

> "Say you believe in Him." Looking at her daughter's tears: "Don't go against your heart!" But she had sat mute, watching her friends walking past her bench, accepting Christ, acknowledging God as their Master, Jesus their Savior, and her heart fluttered like that of a small bird about to be stoned. It was her father's voice that moved her. That voice could come only from the life he lived.

Like her father, Meridian chooses not to live her life according to the dictates of an externally imposed narrative or to passively anticipate redemption by way of a transcendent savior. Instead, she follows her father's example and finds her own voice and way of walking in the world.

From her father, Meridian extracts the foundations for her emerging life. As a young child, Meridian discovers the secret of her father's understandings and at the same time begins to connect with her heritage. Meridian's father derives his spiritual sense of self from his grandmother, Feather Mae. According to family myth, Feather Mae rejected traditional religion after experiencing spiritual ecstasy at an ancient Indian burial mound on the family property. Subsequent to the experience, "Feather Mae renounced all religion that was not based on the experience of physical ecstasy—thereby shocking her Baptist church—and near the end of her life she loved walking nude about her yard and worshipped only the sun." The story of Feather Mae passes down through the Hill family. Meridian's father also experiences the secret of the Indian burial mound, and eventually, Meridian discovers the mound for herself but interprets the experience differently from her father.

> The body seemed to drop away, and only the spirit lived, set free in the world. But she was not convinced. It seemed to her that it was a way the living sought to expand the consciousness of being alive, there where the ground about them was filled with the dead. It was a possibility they discussed, alone in the fields. Their secret: that they both shared the peculiar madness of her great-grandmother. It sent them brooding at times over the meaning of this.

Meridian's interpretation of her experience at the Indian burial mound provides the basis for her development and eventual self-affirmation. Ultimately, her agency derives from her constant quest to "expand the consciousness of being alive."

Unfortunately, as Meridian matures, her consciousness contracts in conjunction with her circumstances, and she temporarily succumbs to the overriding and powerful societal dictates about what a young woman must do in order to come of age. She variously samples the roles deemed appropriate for women. As she experiences them, each iteration proves oppressive, and she rejects its confines. For example, Meridian finds that for her, sexuality is "not pleasure, but a sanctuary in which her mind is freed of any consideration for all the other males in the universe who might want anything of her. It was resting from pursuit." The roles of mother and wife prove even less fulfilling. Meridian's marriage, instigated by pregnancy, causes extreme emotional and spiritual stagnation, and motherhood leads to thoughts of infanticide. Both create in her "a kind of lethargy. She could not even move about her own house purposefully." Sexuality, marriage, and motherhood prohibit her growth, and so she abandons each of them in succession.

The end of Meridian's marriage reopens her to the possibilities of self-construction. Her self-affirmation is inextricably intertwined with her activism. The night Meridian's husband leaves her, she dreams about Indians. This dreaming signals the reawakening of her visceral experience with an ineffable knowledge gained through her experience at the Indian mound, and it marks one of many deaths and rebirths she experiences in the process of attaining self-affirmation. "And so it was that one day in the middle of April 1960 Meridian Hill became aware of the past and present of the larger world." On this day, Meridian begins to realign herself with the spiritual experiences of her childhood by venturing beyond the confines of mother and wife.

This transition from the microcosm to the macrocosm reflects a basic element in Meridian's journey. She ventures out of the safety (and death) of conformity in pursuit of meaning. Meridian becomes involved in the Civil Rights movement and, within that context, she is "at a time and a place in History that forced the trivial to fall away." Her activism allows her to begin distilling the essential from the extraneous. Provided with an opportunity to attend a prestigious black women's school, Saxon College, Meridian relinquishes her identities as a wife and a mother. Well aware of the historical realities of African-American women, she suffers overwhelming guilt for abandoning the model of womanhood and, as a black woman, rejecting her right to raise her son. "Meridian knew that enslaved women had been made miserable by the sale of their children. And what had Meridian Hill done with her precious child? She had given him away." Although she suffers both mentally and physically from her feelings of guilt, this period of turmoil eventually frees her for other possibilities.

At the climax of Meridian's suffering, she is bedridden with guilt and anxiety. During this period, she has a spiritual experience similar to those she had as a child at the Indian burial mound. In her state of physical decimation, she dreams of slave mothers and the choices they had to make, and in her identification with those choices, Meridian achieves release from her guilt. With her dream of escape from the fate of her ancestral mothers who experienced the middle passage, the journey from Africa to slavery, Meridian frees herself from the legacy of slave mothers and begins to heal herself.

The forgiveness Meridian receives from surrogate and imagined mothers reinforces her rejection of the ideal of motherhood and implies that her choice to leave her son does not separate her from her heritage. Until this point, she had suffered from her belief that she could not live up to the standards set by the black women from whom she is descended. With the symbolic forgiveness of slave mothers as represented in her dream, she is able to discard her burden of guilt and continue unencumbered toward self-definition.

The spirituality Meridian discovers on her journey is composed of various symbols Walker incorporates in her novel. She associates Meridian's progression with the cyclical elements of the natural world, primarily the sun, trees, and earth.

Through her use of regenerative symbols, Walker expands the notion of self-affirmation beyond the individual into a globally resonant possibility.

The association between Meridian and natural, particularly regenerative symbols begins early in the novel. As previously mentioned, Meridian's earliest spiritual experience takes place in the ancient Indian burial mound that is shaped like a serpent. In the early symbolic history of the snake, it was seen as the representation of the interconnectedness of the natural world. Meridian's early experience at the mound seems to predispose her to make connections with the natural world. Meridian's relationship to these organic images can be found in her reaction upon learning about the assassination of MEDGAR EVERS. She "planted a wild sweet shrub bush among the plants in the formal garden in front of the honors house." The inseparable nature of life and death as represented by Meridian's simple reproductive gesture reveals the ways in which she instinctively connects humanity to the natural world and foreshadows her emergent understandings. Meridian's unusual relationship with the natural world leads her to photograph "trees and rocks and tall hills and floating clouds, which she claimed she knew."

The novel's most important natural physical symbol is a magnolia tree named the Sojourner, which came into existence as the result of the actions of an African slave women named Louvinie. Upon having her tongue removed as a punishment, Louvinie buried the mutilated organ under a tree, which grew in magnitude and in legend and eventually became the focal point of the Saxon College grounds. When Meridian first arrives at the college, the tree becomes her sanctuary.

> It gave her a profound sense of peace (which was only possible when she could feel invisible) to know slaves had found shelter in its branches. When her spirits were low, as they were often enough that first year, she would sit underneath The Sojourner and draw comfort from her age, her endurance, the stories the years told of her, and her enormous size. When she sat beneath The Sojourner, she knew she was not alone.

Meridian's feelings at the feet of the Sojourner reconnect her with an ancestral narrative and foreshadow her ability to create her own story and to work to claim her own voice.

Meridian's spirituality is an active one. Once she relinquishes the burden of guilt for her nonconformity, she is free to work to assist others in the African-American community in their struggle to acquire liberty from the oppressive roles to which they have become accustomed. Intertwined with this quest is her attempt to reconcile the question of whether murder can be justified. Meridian finds an answer for the question "Would you kill for the revolution?" in the South among the most oppressed of her people. As she struggles with the question of justified murder and reestablishes herself in her community, she advances her own formative journey.

Ironically, Meridian's final steps toward clarity occur in a church. During her 10 years of work as an activist in the South, she periodically attends the local churches. One Sunday in a Baptist church, Meridian discovers the answer to her question regarding justified murder. While listening to the service, she finds the people affirming and, observing them, she discovers her role in the liberation of her people from oppression.

> I will come forward and sing from memory songs they will need once more to hear. For it is the song of the people, transformed by the experience of each generation, that holds them together, and if any part of it is lost the people suffer and are without soul. If I can only do that, my role will not have been a useless one after all.

Although Meridian rejects the precepts of Christianity, the songs within that tradition, and particularly within this church, contain the essence of her philosophy. It is this visceral, very human emotional expression that she uses as a foundation for discovery. Song functions in the novel as a primary symbol of genuine self-expression and as a reflection of truth. Song becomes a conduit through which Meridian reconnects with the essence of her heritage and, eventually, through which she learns to sing her own song. She recognizes the purpose of her life as the keeper of racial memory in the form of song. In the language of Black Elk, Meridian functions as the heart of the race and restores the center to the racial struggle to transcend oppression by reframing, reclaiming, and rewriting the narrative. Meridian serves from a position of belonging. She is not elevated above her people but functions as an individual example of the common possibility of redemption in the face of multifaceted oppression. From within her community, Meridian emerges from the nadir to strive for the meridian. In so doing, she provides a model for earthly salvation.

## SIGNIFICANT THEMES, ISSUES, CONCERNS

### The Relationship between Revolution and Violence

One of the central questions posed by Walker's *Meridian* is about the nature and role of violence in a social revolution. As the movements for racial equality in the 1960s in the United States began to shift from a commitment to the strategy of nonviolent civil disobedience toward a more complicated embrace of nationalism, self-defense, and revolution, the activists themselves had to determine how far they were willing to go to secure the objectives of their struggle. Walker parses the details of those moral quandaries through the ponderings of her characters. Each of the major characters in the novel confronts the philosophical question about his or her willingness to kill and also to die for the movement. Ultimately, the novel suggests that violence is not the answer and that the cost of change should not be the emotional and psychological health of those who devote their life energies to the fight for justice. However, Meridian is willing to die (and to kill, if necessary) in defense of what she believes.

### The Personal Costs of Activism

The character of Meridian is in part Walker's homage to Ruby Doris Smith-Robinson who was one of the founders of the student activist branch of the Civil Rights movement of the 1960s, the Student Non-Violent Coordinating Committee (SNCC). Ruby Smith-Robinson died when she was 25. According to many accounts, she gave her life to the movement.

The novel *Meridian* illustrates the personal costs of involvement in the struggle for civil rights through all of its central characters, but none is more traumatized physically, emotionally, and psychologically by her engagement than Meridian Hill. Meridian experiences an abortion, physical trauma, fainting spells, and catatonia, as well as emotional and psychological disorientation. Through her traumas and breakdowns, the novel provides insight into some of the responses and costs of activism for those who were involved in the struggle. Additionally, her character helps to memorialize those who suffered in the effort to achieve the objectives of the Civil Rights movement and who lost their lives as a consequence.

### The Subjective Power Dynamics of Race and Gender

Through the relationships of its characters, *Meridian* engages questions of the power dynamics between a couple whose racial histories are fraught with narratives of exploitation and denigration. Although they are both African American, the relationship between Truman and Meridian is one example of this complexity. In spite of their mutual investment in the struggle to end racial inequality, Truman does not seem to comprehend the extent to which his sexist behavior is oppressive to Meridian.

Tommy Odds's rape of Lynne is another example of the novel's examination of questions about the centrality and power of those histories and the extent to which they have a determinative impact on interactions, in this case between a white woman and a black man. The novel suggests that those histories can be exploited to the point that they interfere with personal responsibility and enable a dangerous entitlement.

Lynne and Truman's relationship explores the ability of interracial partners to remain together and to sustain a healthy and vital relationship. Their union and the birth of their daughter, Camara, demonstrates another tangible complexity of an interracial relationship, the offspring that result from such unions. Camara's death functions as a representation of the impact of racism and racial categorization on children. The cost that children pay when the ideological struggles represented by their parents' union fails is a possible interpretation of Camara's death.

## CHARACTERS

**Alonzo** Alonzo works at a scrap yard and is Altuna's brother. He sometimes keeps Lynne company by playing checkers with her.

**Altuna** Altuna is one of the men with Tommy Odds when he publicly humiliates Lynne the day after raping her.

**Anne** Anne is a young Atlanta girl Meridian encourages to join the movement. After the group is arrested, Meridian cannot locate the girl and believes that she has been raped and beaten by prison guards.

**Anne-Marion Coles** Anne-Marion Coles is Meridian's college roommate and friend. Anne-Marion is critical of Meridian's choices and sends her disapproving letters detailing her criticisms. The two women meet during the television broadcast of John F. Kennedy's funeral. Anne-Marion is motivated to become Meridian's friend because she believes that the relationship will somehow be beneficial to her ambitions and goals. Although this self-interest characterizes the beginning of her friendship with Meridian, eventually Anne-Marion develops genuine affection for the woman. Anne-Marion is described in *Meridian* as rounder and more physically substantial than her friend. She is quick to anger and is unmoved by the spiritual rhetoric of the leaders of the Civil Rights movement. Anne-Marion is one of the first women at the college to wear her hair naturally and short.

**Assistant, the** The Assistant works for George Daxter at Daxter's funeral home. He tries to molest Meridian and pursues her relentlessly until, eventually, she gives in and has sex with him. The two continue to have a sexual relationship until Meridian becomes involved with Eddie. This early sexuality colors her feelings about her husband Eddie and affects her desire to have sex.

**Camara** Camara is Truman and Lynne's daughter. At the beginning of the novel, the young girl is dead. Camara dies at six years old after she is attacked in New York City. Lynne and Truman name their child after the African novelist Camara Laye.

**Carrie Mae** Carrie Mae is a young girl who is in prison for killing her own child. Meridian and Truman visit Carrie Mae in prison, and as a consequence, Meridian adopts a Christlike attitude toward all of the people in the world who are burdened by shame.

**Chester Gray** Chester Gray is one of the young men in the group where Meridian begins her work with the Civil Rights movement.

**Delores Jones** Delores Jones is a worker in the Civil Rights movement. Meridian brings Delores and Nelda Henderson with her when she tells her mother that she is going to accept a scholarship to attend Saxon College, which is two hours away from their home. Continuation of her education means that Meridian will have to leave her son behind, an action she knows her mother will not like. She is afraid to tell her mother of her plans by herself. In the middle of the conversation with Meridian's mother, Delores responds to Mrs. Hill's comment that she sacrificed her needs to raise her six children by saying that she could have done the same thing in slavery. Meridian later disagrees with Delores's comment.

**Eddie** Eddie is a rather attractive, dark-skinned man who plays sports and has a developed physique. He dresses well and has money at his disposal. Eddie conceives a child with Meridian while they are dating, and as a result, the two marry. Meridian loses interest in sexual relations with Eddie, and the two grow apart. Eventually, they divorce.

**Eddie Jr. (Rundi)** When Meridian is in college, she becomes pregnant as a result of her sexual relationship with her boyfriend Eddie. Eddie agrees to marry her, and Meridian gives birth to a son, Eddie Jr. She dislikes motherhood and has thoughts of killing herself and her child. Eventually, her relationship with Eddie disintegrates, and the two divorce, leaving her alone with and fully responsible for her child. After Eddie leaves, Meridian spends time thinking about her life, what she wants to do, and who she has become. She becomes involved with the Civil Rights movement and receives an opportunity to attend college. She decides that, in order to take advantage of this opportunity, she must give her son away to people who can take care of him. She does so, but before she leaves him, she renames him Rundi, a name she thinks is unique.

**Fast Mary of the Tower** Fast Mary of the Tower was a Saxon student whose suicide was attributed to her emotional reaction after murdering her child, born after an unplanned pregnancy.

**Feather Mae** Feather Mae is Meridian's great-grandmother. The preservation of the mound known to Meridian as the Sacred Serpent had been an accomplishment of Feather Mae, who fought with her husband to keep the burial ground intact. She was said to be a playful and dreamy girl who loved to lie on the mounds and feel the connection to the earth. Feather Mae discovered an entrance to the mound, and when inside the center of the Serpent, she had a kind of supernatural experience, which transformed her. From that point on, Feather Mae only believed in religious practices that were connected to physical pleasure. She spent time at the end of her life worshipping the sun and walking about outside without clothing.

**George Daxter** George Daxter is the owner of a funeral home located between a church and an all-night café. Daxter is a mixed-race person around 50 years old who had a white mother and a black father. When his mother became pregnant, she was incarcerated by her family in a basement and fed animal food. At birth, Daxter was given to an older woman to raise, the boy poisoned her with spoiled tomatoes. Daxter has an interest in Meridian and molests the girl periodically throughout her adolescence.

**Hedge Phillips** Hedge Phillips is one of the men with Tommy Odds when he publicly humiliates Lynne the day after raping her.

**Lamumba Katurim** Lamumba Katurim is an activist whose decision to leave his white wife affects Truman when he is having doubts about Lynne.

**Louvinie** Louvinie was a slave on the Saxon plantation, the land on which Saxon College now stands. A version of Louvinie's story was written down by one of the Saxon daughters and preserved in the college's library. She was thought of as unattractive. Louvinie was not traditionally beautiful and was especially distasteful to some because of her jutting chin and because she did not smile. She came from a family in Africa whose task it was to ferret out guilty and undiscovered individuals who aspired to commit murder. A part of their strategy involved intricate storytelling. Louvinie brought her family's storytelling ability, but not their ability to discern crimes, to the United States when she arrived as a slave. She told frightening stories to the children on the Saxon plantation. In the process of telling one of these scary stories, she accidentally brought about the death of one of the Saxons, a boy with a heart defect. In retaliation for his son's death, the master of the Saxon plantation removed Louvinie's tongue, rendering her unable to tell her stories or anything else ever again. Louvinie was said to be the person who planted her tongue at the foot of the Sojourner, the biggest magnolia in the country.

**Lucille Treasure** Lucille is Miss Margaret Treasure's sister.

**Lynne Rabinowitz** Lynne Rabinowitz is a woman Meridian meets while she is at Saxon College. She is described as a slight woman with dark eyes. At the end of his relationship with Meridian, Truman becomes involved with Lynne. Lynne and Truman's relationship develops as they work together on civil rights issues in the South. Truman feels their racial differences, which seem highlighted in the environment in which they live. Lynne's romantic notion of the South and the people she encounters reduces them to an aesthetic experience for her. Despite the conflicts in their perspectives and the real dangers of living as an interracial couple in such a space, Lynne and Truman decide to move to Mississippi.

Tommy Odds is a civil rights worker in Mississippi with Truman and Lynne. He is shot by a racist as he walks downtown with Truman and another worker named Trilling. The shooting transforms Lynne and Truman's relationship. Tommy Odds loses the lower half of his arm in the accident. Tommy begins to hate all white people and will not count Lynne as a friend. His attitude affects Truman and makes him question the nature of his relationship with Lynne and whether any involvement with white people is inherently problematic. Lynne faces the growing hostility within the movement toward whites generally and begins to feel unwelcome in the struggle.

Truman decides that he loves Meridian rather than Lynne and visits Meridian with the intention of getting together. Meridian refuses his advances, stating that she is not interested in Truman and that she could not betray Lynne in that way. Truman reduces Lynne to an intellectual idealist and sees himself as a grand patriarch and protector. Lynne has other perceptions of him and no longer loves his current incarnation.

Both Truman and Lynne come to visit Meridian in the small Mississippi town called Chicokema. Lynne comes to visit Meridian to spew her anger and frustration about her failed marriage and aspirations. Lynne is bitter about the way that her life has unfolded and blames Meridian. She maintains that Truman was always and inevitably connected to Meridian, and as a result, her marriage to him could never have succeeded. The two have a child, Camara, who dies after an attack in New York City.

**Margaret** Margaret is the lover of Tom Johnson. Tom Johnson offers her to Truman and tells him that she is only a white woman.

**Marilene O'Shay** According to the sign that hangs over her body exhibited in Chicokema, Marilene O'Shay is a woman who has been embalmed and displayed. The sign states that she has been dead for 25 years and, in life, was a daughter, mother, and wife who transgressed the rules governing those roles by leaving home and her husband and child to pursue her own interests and pleasures.

**Meridian Hill** *Meridian* details the process Meridian Hill must undergo to negate the power of various oppressions to control her self-definition and her existence. The novel's opening scene provides a signpost to the journey Meridian takes to continue living and affirming her humanity and her life rather than becoming a "lifelike" manifestation of an ideal. The sign that advertises a traveling exhibit of an embalmed white woman named Marilene labels her an "Obedient Daughter . . . Devoted Wife . . . Adoring Mother . . . Gone Wrong." These designations represent the four options available to women traditionally. They also outline the roles Meridian rejects in order to create her own autonomous identity.

In order to discover a way of being in the world that is sync with her values, Meridian rejects traditional religion. She recognizes that self-affirmation is a process of becoming rather than a state of being, and she reflects this in her quest for spiritual, emotional, and psychic health. After a dramatic confrontation with white men aboard a tank, Meridian collapses and is carried back to her home by four men of her community. Her death and rebirth ritual represents the cyclical nature of her quest for health and distinguishes her spirituality/activism from the polarized Western view of death and life as oppositional.

Like her father, Meridian chooses not to live her life according to the dictates of an external master or to be redeemed by a transcendent savior. Instead, she follows her father's example and finds her voice, her spirituality, and her self from within the life she lives. In the final analysis, Meridian emerges as one of the people—not one elevated above but as one who serves as an individual example of the common possibility of redemption in the face of multifaceted oppression.

**Meridian's father (Mr. Hill)** Meridian's father is described as gentle, consistent, and reliable. Mr. Hill creates a private space for himself in the family's backyard. In this room, he reads over old maps and indulges his fascination with the Native Americans who used to inhabit the land on which the family's home is now located. One day, while watching her father read a map, Meridian notices that he is crying. This display of emotion frightens her, and she runs from the spot and from her father.

On another occasion, Meridian hears her parents arguing about an Indian burial mound that happens to be on their property. Meridian's father has given some of the land to a Native American who told him about the burial ground and its location. Meridian's mother is angry that Mr. Hill gave away the land. The Indian, Walter Longknife, eventually returns the land to Meridian's father after spending some time there.

Meridian's father begins to decline after the government claims the farmland and the Indian mounds. He also loses his job as a teacher when desegregation threatens the jobs of longtime black teachers.

**Meridian's mother (Mrs. Hill)** Meridian's mother does not approve of her daughter's life or actions and says so in letters that she sends to her daughter laced with Bible verses and criticism. Mrs. Hill only knew a brief period of freedom as a young woman when she was able to make her own decisions about her life without the encumbrance of a relationship or of children. She worked as a teacher, and this occupation provided her with the means to support her brief period of independence, which was insufficiently long. Soon she married another teacher, Meridian's father. She conceived her first child and came to feel that child-rearing was a terrible experience that drained her of her inner life, personality, and autonomy. As a result of her deep resentment of her status as a mother, Meridian's mother was unable to provide for her daughter the resources she needed to become a well-adjusted and happy woman.

Mrs. Hill's life is limited to her personal sphere of friends and family and, particularly, to her church. She has no investment in politics or the world outside of the immediate concerns of her daily routine. Meridian's mother does not vote and does not impress upon her children the liberating possibilities that voting offers in a democracy. She regards the professional class of African Americans, such as teachers, as infallible and does not question their influence on her or on her children. Her only complaints are to and about her husband. She spends more time and energy keeping her children tidy and presentable than in loving them. Mrs. Hill is unsupportive of Meridian's desire to accept a scholarship to attend Saxon College and leave her son behind.

**Miss Margaret Treasure** Miss Margaret Treasure is a woman Truman and Meridian meet while they are registering people to vote in rural Mississippi. She is very old and has an aging sister named Lucille. In spite of her advanced age, Miss Treasure believes that she is pregnant, but Truman and Meridian take her to a doctor, and she is happy to learn she is not pregnant.

**Miss Winter** Miss Winter is one of three black teachers at Saxon College. Although she is pretentious, she does not conform to the school's rigid sense of propriety. She often fights with the administration to change policies and practices she finds objectionable. She is from Meridian's hometown and knows Meridian's family and situation. Miss Winter and Meridian bond for the first time when Miss Winter attends a speech Meridian gives at the high school they both attended. Meridian is unable to complete the speech because she finds that its false patriotism rings hollow. Miss Winter consoles and identifies with Meridian, saying that she had to memorize the same speech when she attended the school. Miss Winter helps Meridian through her troubled period and acts like the surrogate mother Meridian needs in order to recover from the various traumas she has experienced, including her abortion.

**Mr. Hill** *See* MERIDIAN'S FATHER.

**Mrs. Hill** *See* MERIDIAN'S MOTHER.

**Mrs. Mabel Turner** Mrs. Mabel Turner is the woman Meridian and Lynne encounter together as they try to get people to vote.

**Mr. Yateson** Mr. Yateson is the principal of Meridian's high school. As a result of her unusually high score on an I.Q. test, Mr. Yateson offers Meridian a scholarship to attend Saxon College, an opportunity provided by funds donated by a white family in Connecticut. In spite of his offer, Mr. Yateson does not approve of Meridian's premarital sexuality, which resulted in her pregnancy and marriage to Eddie, and Yateson tells Meridian of his disapproval when he informs her of the scholarship.

**Nelda Henderson** Nelda Henderson is an old friend of Meridian's from childhood. Meridian brings Nelda Henderson and a friend from the movement, Delores Jones, with her when she tells her mother that she is going to accept a scholarship to attend Saxon College. Continuing her education means that Meridian will have to leave her son behind, which her mother will not approve of, and Meridian is afraid to tell her mother of her plans by herself. In the middle of the conversation, Nelda realizes that Mrs. Hill could have helped her and Meridian successfully navigate their adolescence and become women capable of pursuing their dreams and goals, but that she had denied them essential information. The revelation leaves Nelda angry and bitter with Mrs. Hill. She is especially bitter because, except for one free day on Sunday, she serves as the primary caretaker for her five siblings while her mother works. She became pregnant herself at the age of 15.

**Nelda's mother** Nelda's mother is described as a large woman who was a wonderful singer. The woman is bald because she lost more and more of her hair during each of her five pregnancies. Nelda's father was killed during World War II, and Nelda's mother has other children by different men.

**Randolph Kay** Randolph Kay is a man Truman admires. He is a movie star and leaves his white wife because of her race.

**Raymond** Raymond is one of the men with Tommy Odds when he publicly humiliates Lynne the day after raping her.

**"Scarlett O'Hara"** Scarlett O'Hara is the name that Lynne gives to the woman Truman is living with when she comes to tell him about the attack on their daughter, Camara. The woman disappears from their lives after Camara dies.

**Sojourner** In the center of the Saxon campus, there is a tree named the Sojourner. While Meridian is a student at the college, the tree is threatened with removal. Meridian joins those who protest the tree's destruction. The Sojourner has also been the site of other subversive activities, such as lovemaking. Students who use the tree for such a purpose maintain that they cannot be seen while in the Sojourner. The tree is also the site for May Day festivals and, secretly, the celebration commemorating the suicide of a woman named Fast Mary of the Tower.

The Sojourner figures in the funeral of the local woman, Wild Child, who was a neglected child in the neighborhood surrounding Saxon College. The women of the college want to hold the girl's funeral at the school's chapel. When they are refused, they have a makeshift funeral under the branches of the Sojourner. Later in the evening, enraged at the way the college treated the dead young woman, the students riot, and during the mayhem, the tree is destroyed.

**sweeper** The nameless sweeper is an older black gentleman in the town of Chicokema who explains to Truman what is happening when the young man arrives in town. The sweeper tells Truman about the town's segregation and that he used to work in the guano plant until he was laid off as a result of his age.

**Swinburn** Swinburn is a young man who works with civil rights activists near the house where Meridian lived with Eddie. Swinburn is described as stocky, and he wears glasses. He is kind to Meridian when she comes to volunteer at the house. Meridian thinks that he looks Ethiopian. He wears a jacket that is covered with buttons that bear slogans of the movement. He has a deep and resonant voice.

**Tom Johnson** A black friend of Truman's, Tom Johnson has a white lover named Margaret, whom he offers to Truman as a sexual partner.

**Tommy Odds** Tommy Odds is a civil rights worker in Mississippi with Truman and Lynne. He is shot by a racist as he walks downtown with Truman and another worker named Trilling. Tommy Odds loses the lower half of his arm in the accident, after which he begins to hate all white people and will not count Lynne as a friend. His attitude affects Truman and makes him question the nature of his relationship with Lynne and whether any involvement with white people is inherently problematic. As the narrative progresses, Lynne reveals that after his accident, Tommy Odds raped her.

**Trilling** Trilling is a worker from Oklahoma who flees and is never seen again after Tommy Odds is shot.

**Truman Held** Truman Held loves French culture and often speaks in French to Meridian. He spent a year in France and that experience convinces him that France and French culture are superior. Although Meridian does not speak the language, Truman insists on speaking it when he is with her.

In the beginning, Truman is, for Meridian, a novelty. He is not like the other black men she has known in her life, and this originality is part of his appeal. Truman loses his mystic allure for Meridian after she becomes pregnant with and aborts his child. Truman falls in love with a white civil rights activist named Lynne. Eventually, Lynne and Truman marry and move to Mississippi in the mid-1960s. They have a daughter named Camara, who dies. Truman and Lynne find over time that their histories and differences are too distinct to be bridged.

**Walter Longknife** A Native American, Walter Longknife is a veteran of World War II. He reminds Meridian of her father in that he replicates her father's interest in maps and in the movement of people from place to place. She also believes that her father and the Indian, as she calls him, share feelings of perpetual grief. However, she cannot imagine the Indian crying as her father once did. The Indian arrives in Georgia, driving into the state from Oklahoma in a truck that broke down at the Confederate monument at Stone Mountain, forcing him to walk the rest of the way to the land his people were forced to leave. The land that Meridian's father has given to Longknife is an ancient burial ground for his tribe. Before Longknife leaves Meridian's family's land, he returns the deed to the property to Meridian's father.

**Wild Child** Wild Child is said to live without parents and is thought to be about 13 years old. She earns the name Wild Child from the people who live in the neighborhood around the college, a place Wild Child has occupied since she was about five or six years old. The people in the neighborhood see the girl occasionally as she raids their garbage for sustenance and clothing. After it becomes apparent that Wild Child is pregnant, the people in the neighborhood decide to try to catch and help her during her pregnancy and with her delivery. Their efforts are to no avail as Wild Child continues to elude them. After Meridian sees Wild Child for the first time, she has one of her recurrent fits of paralysis and is unable to move for several days before recovering. Meridian tempts Wild Child with food, captures her, and brings her onto campus. After these failed efforts to find a home for the girl, Wild Child escapes and is killed while running across a street.

## FURTHER READING

Barker, Deborah E. "Visual Markers: Art and Mass Media in Alice Walker's *Meridian*." *African American Review* 31, no. 3 (1997): 463–480.

Christian, Barbara. *Black Feminist Criticism: Perspectives on Black Women Writers.* New York: Pergamon Press, 1985.

Erickson, Peter. "Identity in the Work of Alice Walker." *CLA Journal* 23 (1979): 71–94.

Hendrickson, Roberta M. "Remembering the Dream: Alice Walker, *Meridian* and the Civil Rights Movement." *MELUS* 24, no. 3 (Fall 1999): 111–128.

McDowell, Deborah E. "New Directions for Black Feminist Criticism." In *The New Feminist Criticism: Essays on Women, Literature and Theory,* edited by Elaine Showalter, 186–199. New York: Pantheon, 1985.

———. "The Self in Bloom: Alice Walker's *Meridian.*" *CLA Journal* 24 (1981): 262–275.

McGowen, Martha J. "Atonement and Release in Alice Walker's *Meridian.*" *Critique* 23 (1981): 25–36.

Parker-Smith, Bettye J. "Alice Walker's Women: In Search of Some Peace of Mind." In *Black Women Writers (1950–1980): A Critical Evaluation,* edited by Mari Evans, 478–493. Garden City, N.Y.: Anchor, 1984.

Pifer, Lynn. "Coming to Voice in Alice Walker's *Meridian:* Speaking Out for the Revolution." *African American Review* 26, no. 1 (Spring 1992): 77–88.

Stein, Karen F. "*Meridian:* Alice Walker's Critique of Revolution." *Black American Literature Forum* 20, nos. 1–2 (Spring–Summer 1986): 129–141.

## *Now Is the Time to Open Your Heart* (2004)

*Now Is the Time to Open Your Heart* is Alice Walker's eighth novel. The narrative tells the story of Kate, a 57-year-old writer who is facing the physical and psychological realities of aging and, with those challenges, tries to rediscover the meanings of her existence. Disillusioned with her previous spiritual staple, BUDDHISM, Kate desires to find something more tangible to sustain her experiences with life.

Spurred by dreams of dry riverbeds, Kate begins to suspect that the answers to her questions might be found in an actual encounter with the challenges of traversing a real river. In search of this confrontation, Kate begins a journey rafting down the Colorado River. This experience helps her to rid herself of the initial burdens of the past, but it does not move her to the place of enlightenment that she seeks.

Determined to enter into a new way of understanding, Kate temporarily leaves her lover, an artist named Yolo, and decides to travel to the Amazon to experience a drug called YAGE, which is used by the indigenous peoples of the Northern Amazon to induce a state of spiritual fluidity wherein an individual can access the spirit world as well as gain new knowledge about the world and the experience of living. Kate finds the knowledge she seeks as well as a like-minded community of other souls with whom she develops a kinship.

Yolo has a life-changing experience while Kate is away. He encounters his own weaknesses and sets forth on his own journey of healing and affirmation. When the two reunite, they find that their relationship is stronger, and they determine to continue their lives together and invite all of their new spiritual kin in their lives to join them for a ceremony celebrating their union.

*Now Is the Time to Open Your Heart* received a scathing review from *New York Times* book critic Michiko Kakutani, who called it unpalatable and inane. Other reviewers, such as Diane Evans of the *London Times,* were more complimentary, but the book was generally not well-received by critics. In spite of the negative critical reception, the novel went on to become a best-seller. After its publication, Alice Walker stated that she would not publish any more novels, and recently she has taken to creating what she calls her living book, her blog on her travels throughout and observations of the world.

### SYNOPSIS

The novel begins with a description of its protagonist, Kate Talkingtree. The woman is at a meditation center and has moved, with a group of fellow meditators, from an indoor, sitting meditation to a walking meditation. She feels that there is a connection between the walking and her pervasive sense of newness and growth. She has recently acquired a new name. She changed her name from Kate Nelson to Kate Talkingtree.

Attending a lecture by one of the teachers at the center, Kate finds herself disturbed. The man's talk characterizes the notion of revolution, but Kate feels that there is a contradiction between his words and his lifestyle. From her assessment of the man's appearance, he seems too comfortable to be expert on the topic of revolution. She also judges her fellow meditators, thinking that they share the teacher's level of economic comfort. These thoughts disturb and disrupt her peaceful meditation, and she begins to wonder whether Buddhism is a practice with which she can continue.

This pattern of disconnect continues, and Kate finds herself unable to meditate. While others are meditating, she gazes out of the window and spots redwood trees that seem to her to be the perfect locale for humans to occupy. Kate leaves the center.

### To Kill or to Thaw the Anaconda

Kate has a dream wherein a frozen anaconda occupies her refrigerator. She calls for help, but there is no one to come to her aid. This dream, for Kate, reflects the realities of the world, truths explained to her by a woman she calls Grandmother Yagé.

Kate remembers her days as a civil rights activist and a story about a snake that was told to her and other activists as they participated in a protest march. The story tells of a snake who asks a man to take pity on him and to pick him up because he is cold. The man eventually does so, and after the snake recovers from the cold, he bites the man on the face. The man asks the snake why he has dealt this fatal blow to the one who helped him to recover. The snake replies that the man knew that he was a snake.

The old woman told the activists this story because she refused to suffer the fate of the man in the story, and she would kill each and every snake she saw. She believed that the work the activists were engaged in would ultimately prove self-destructive. Then she asked the activists to consider the story and its implications. She said that the snake should not be blamed for its desire to protect itself and that the story engenders consideration of both the nature of interactions and of human nature. With that, the woman gave the activists some grapes from her yard and sent them on their way.

### Change

Kate believes that she is in the midst of a life change. She removes an altar she has kept in her home that is devoted to various talismanic deities and political revolutionaries. She also notices that her body is changing, her knees begin to creak. She believes that this creaking is the first sign that her body is beginning to decline. Concerned, she seeks out a medical professional who informs her that she needs to spend some time devoted to her body, doing stretches and purchasing orthotics. These solutions do not reassure her or solve the problem.

Kate spends time examining her dismantled altar, recognizing as she does so that her experience with it is no longer marred by feelings of bitterness. She has come to a place of forgiveness with the people in her life that allows her to see and to experience only the love she feels for those who are or were in her life. There is an overwhelming feeling of release in Kate as she perceives the things that were once paramount to her, like the repair of her home and maintenance of her altar, begin to slip away in significance. She no longer wants to collect and store even her own writings. Instead, she has the urge to destroy, particularly to burn them. She even begins to burn money in the form of hundred-dollar bills. Even her pens begin, inexplicably, to run dry.

A psychic advises her to find a real river upon which to journey, and Kate feels this is sound advice. She decides to take a trip down the Colorado River. With camping gear in hand, she proceeds on her journey, accompanied by an experienced rafter and nine other women. After a restless night in a motel at the rim of the Grand Canyon, she is terrified by the prospect of rapids. In the brief sleep of that night, Kate dreams of a successful swim through oil and water and wonders what her vision of these seemingly incompatible elements might mean.

Earlier, when Kate said good-bye to her lover, Yolo, she recognized that both of them think that the relationship is over. They share a different sensibility about the world, and Kate cannot understand that the world of dreams, which functions like a roadmap for her, does not exist in the same ways or at all for Yolo.

After she leaves, he begins to ponder their relationship. He knows that, in spite of their different visions, he will miss her while she is gone.

He decides to return to bed and longs for Kate's presence in it. Although he has maintained that dreams are not an important element of his life, Yolo begins to have a dream. In it, there is a creature he does not recognize who says to him that he is lost. Yolo cries out to the creature for the directions to the river. His anguished outburst is so real that he wakes himself up with the sound of his cry. Awake, he is jubilant, feeling that finally he understands the power of dreaming in the way that Kate does. He takes a shower that seems to continue the affirmation.

Yolo thinks back to the couple's meeting and the ways in which Kate was drawn to his paintings. Trying to help her understand their appeal, he told her that he had been trying to fill emptiness. He recalls that with her, he feels at home. He recalls that Kate used to say to friends that Yolo had helped her to access the birdlike aspects of herself, a statement that at first disturbed him profoundly.

### River Run

Kate has begun her journey on the boat, down the river. She is next to a friend whose name is Avoa. She feels that the life vest is uncomfortable, and she knows, somehow, that at the end of the journey, she will be a different person.

Kate thinks back to a session with her therapist in which the woman asked her why she wanted to go on the trip. She replied that she was being called and that her dream vision of a dry riverbed was connected to the need to travel down a real river.

Back on the river, Kate experiences the real tumult of her first rapids and begins to feel sick. Eventually, she develops a high temperature. She feels that the river roars within her so loudly that she cannot hear to reply. She vomits and feels a purging of unexpressed language. After the episode, Kate says that she feels much better and wants to continue the journey.

### He Wondered

The narrative returns to Yolo and his smaller ventures around Kate's house. He ponders his inability to get rid of things, a problem he understands as attached to experience and memory. He feels that keeping an object allows him to remain connected with the person or event with which it is associated. Yolo also has an obsession with watches and with the idea of time, although he has a markedly ambivalent relationship with actual time and its keepers, the watches and clocks he collects, and he forgets to put batteries in or to wind them.

Kate is on the boat and recalling her lack of appreciation of the gift of a serving platter given to her by her first husband and daughter. She somehow interprets the memory as a sign of her aging and movement toward the loss of eroticism. She believes that she has vomited all of the traps of domesticity that were represented by the gift from her husband and child.

Kate's friend Avoa asks her to share her thoughts, and Kate says that she is pondering the way in which human beings are inclined to deny the end of relationships because of the fear of change. She thinks back to the house she shared with her husband and imagines the possessions that they had, seeing them as burdensome.

Looking at the river, Kate feels an unexpected lightness and remembers Yolo's firm belief that she will be a different person when she returns. Although ill, she is determined not to give up the trip and will continue on her journey down the river. She thinks that the pace of humanity on the globe has led to a kind of dysfunction from which it is hard to make sense, yet there is continuity in the natural world that makes it possible to make connections. She notes that all of the water in the world is recycled and that, similarly, all moments are simultaneous as they, too, are recycled.

Kate sees a spike of a yellow flower in her sandal and, inexplicably, is driven to eat it. When she does, almost instantly she feels better physically. She recalls the time when she told her husband that she was leaving him and her husband's response. They were hiking; she remembers saying to him that she needed freedom and that his response was to push her in such a way that she had to struggle to avoid falling. She tried to explain her position to him, and he raised a hand to her to strike at her again. Her husband's anger was unabated by the nearness of another couple passing them, and she remembers that she has not known her husband to be as angry with her as he was at that moment. Instead, her husband turned from her and ran down the path. When she arrived at the parking lot, her husband had left with the car. She was left there without any means of transportation and was at least two hours away from home.

Kate hitched a ride home, and when she arrived, she saw that her husband's car was there. The home that they shared was dark. She broke into her house using a rock from her yard. Her husband was inside sleeping, and she soon fell asleep herself. She awakened to her husband on top of her, attempting to have sex with her against her will; eventually, she gave up fighting him. For her, this event marked a point of no return, a place from which the relationship could not recover. Her husband finally left her for his secretary.

Kate rejoins the group in much better physical condition. The journey makes a turn for her, and she is able to enjoy it in ways that she could not before. The women speak of their concerns about growing older and their sense of themselves as women who are no longer considered in their prime. They speak about whether they do or do not use hair dye and what those choices mean to them.

Kate dreams of her mother, whose body had been mangled when she died in a car crash. She imagines that her mother is still in the condition she was as a result of the accident. In spite of her injuries, her mother is showing Kate how to fish by the sea. This dream makes the entire trip to the river worthwhile to Kate. Inspired by her dream, she begins to write a story about her mother on a Post-It note. It is set at the time when Kate's mother (or Kate's character's mother) died. She tries to see into her mother's existence and to understand why her mother did not approve of her behavior and life. In the story, she interacts with her sisters and her father, and they begin to have a conversation about their father eating. Unlike her relationship with her mother, the protagonist's relationship with her father is unsullied and unconditional.

The story ends with the space on the Post-It note, so she stops writing and watches the birds and other wildlife that surround the women's campground. She also thinks about Yolo and her recurring dream about the dry riverbed.

She remembers the details of her parents' death in the car crash and their destroyed bodies. She was horrified by the condition of her parents' bodies. She remembers trying to warm her father's dead foot and, with her failure to do so, coming to a realization about what death is and about its finality. These memories cause Kate some sorrow, and in an attempt to work though her feelings, she begins to move and to do some yoga while on the boat. She observes that her friend Avoa joins her, and they begin a short session together.

The boat encounters some rough rapids, and the women on the other boat are flung into the water; they are able to swim safely back to the others. After the literally tumultuous day, the women begin to discuss their sex lives and what they prefer when engaged in sexual acts. They have a great time sharing their experiences and preferences, and they seem to grow closer. Kate seems ever more comfortable with her companions.

There is one woman in particular to whom Kate grows close. Her name is Sue, and she and Kate spend some time away from the other women exploring the environs surrounding the river. The two find a rock-formation artwork of a figure giving birth. Kate is struck by the similarity between the figure and ancient figures she has seen that are similar in form. The two discuss their love lives, and Sue discloses that she was never attracted to boys or to men. Kate is fascinated by this revelation.

As the two wander through the landscape, Kate feels overwhelmed by both the beauty of the place and the accessibility to time that it provides. Here, she feels she can fully experience the world and is able to understand the lives of people who lived hundreds, even thousands of years earlier. She feels a profound sense of gratitude, not only for this experience but for the earth itself, from which the experience derives.

The narrative returns to the women's conversation, and Sue reveals that initially she believed that the source of her attraction to women was the fact that she was not loved by her mother. Without that, she felt that her romantic life was a perpetual quest for the substitute for that maternal relationship.

Kate says she has found that, at this point in her life, she does not really have a preference between men and women as sexual partners. She thinks that having such a proclivity, an attraction to both sexes, is natural and mirrors the relationship that children have with their parents. She feels that she is making a turn from defining herself as a sexual person and may decide to turn her energies inward rather than directing them toward another.

When she returns home, she tells Yolo that she thinks she is ready to give up on sex, and he asks her if it might be possible to do so gradually, as he is not in the same place as she is with regard to their sexual intimacy. She happily agrees and seems to enjoy the sex more, knowing that it is not something that she will choose to continue. Her relationship with Sue demonstrates to her that she is capable of developing close relationships that are not sexual.

## And Sure Enough

The narrative flashes forward to a point in the future when Kate goes on another journey down a river and has an encounter with a shaman that affirms her decision to withdraw from her sexual life. In this chapter, the story begins with a trip that Kate takes to the Amazon in South America. During their visit, the group Kate is traveling with is under the care of a shaman, whose name is Armando. He tells them that there is a time for sexuality and a time to abstain from it—that without sexuality, one has more energy and time to focus on spirituality.

Kate is aware that human beings are destroying the planet and that there is not much time left. She became sure of this reality during the 1970s, and the revelation was unbearably sad to her. At the time, she had taken mushrooms to help her with her feelings, and they had made her quite ill. There is a commonality between that experience and the one she has with the shaman, as a part of the ceremony with the spiritual leader involves ingesting a substance that makes her vomit.

During the hours of her discomfort, Kate thinks about her existence and contemplates the unique variables that produced her ancestry, and she feels more centered. When she is recovered, she eats a meal in preparation for her travel down the river of the rain forest. The forest reminds her of New York because it is so dense and lush. It is also incredibly dynamic, a place always changing.

## Yolo

Yolo leaves for Hawaii the same day that Kate leaves for her trip to the Amazon. The first encounter he has is with a desk clerk in a hotel who cannot apprehend his name. He felt that, in Hawaii, he would be spared the perpetual negations that come with having a name that is not familiar to speakers whose only tongue is English.

Although Yolo and Kate have parted, Yolo misses her and wonders often what she is doing. As he settles into his new residence, he thinks about the complexities of the past, particularly as they manifest for him personally in the form of his racial identity. He goes to the beach and, after a time, drifts off to sleep. Yolo wakes up to the sound of a man's voice asking him to watch something he needs to leave on the beach while he travels home to get something else. He is a fisherman, and he takes Yolo to the local side of the beach. Yolo is somewhat reluctant, afraid that he might be walking into some kind of trap. Instead, the two men fall over a dead body lying on the beach.

## The Curious Thing

From Armando, the shaman, Kate learns to understand her withdrawal from sex as an attempt to connect with the Grandmother spirit. She is trying to tap into this energy as she sits in the midst of the rain forest trying to recover her energy and stamina for the trip. She still feels somewhat impaired from the purging that she experienced at the beginning of the trip.

As they experience another element of the ceremony that Armando has arranged, Kate and the others in her group enter a ritual space, and they sit to begin the ceremony. For Kate, the ceremony is a prayer for forgiveness of the planet's destruction. She asks for safety while she is in the process of learning these difficult lessons. The medicine that is a part of the ritual is the most foul she has ever experienced.

Each member of the group becomes ill upon taking the medicine. After Kate vomits and returns to the ceremony, she feels a difference in her perception of the light. Part of the ritual involves sitting for at least four hours. She engages in what she calls visiting Grandmother. A woman grabs her hand and says that she would like Kate to join her for a trip to the trees.

## Had He Been Shot?

The narrative returns to Yolo on the beach in Hawaii as he wonders about the dead boy and how he came to lose his life. His glance at the corpse does not immediately reveal the reason that the boy has lost his life.

Yolo feels compassion for the dead boy and sorrow at the loss of his life. He waits for the man who interrupted his nap to return. He is still concerned that he may be the victim of a scam until he sees the man, whose name is Jerry, returning with authorities. There is a man who arrives who appears to have a relationship with the deceased as he immediately grabs the boy and holds him in his arms. Yolo comes to understand that this is the deceased's brother, and again, he feels profound grief at the loss.

The body is removed from the beach and taken away in an ambulance, but Yolo finds himself riveted to the spot and unable to leave. The experience, purpose, and expectations he had developed for his trip had changed forever as a result of his experience with the dead boy.

## When Kate Had Visited

The woman who asks Kate to join her by the trees says that she wants to be able to help Kate on her journey. The woman's name is Anunu, and Kate tells her of her firm belief that human beings have already consigned themselves to destruction. She says that she is uncertain that her life has any additional purpose as Anunu listens intently to her speaking.

Finally, Anunu congratulates Kate on her success so far. Kate, a writer, is surprised that Anunu knows who she is and is familiar with her works. She tells Anunu that she has been wrestling with the question of sex and also of abstinence in term of the impact either might have on her spiritual life. The two walk and converse about these issues, and Kate feels remarkably comfortable with Anunu. The two speak the same language. Kate says that she has felt Grandmother calling her and that she thinks her perception of that calling is connected to her lifelong affinity for and love of plants.

Anunu and Kate go to another room to try to negotiate Grandmother's visitation that Kate seeks. Kate envisions a brick wall before her and does not feel that it is an impediment because she empowers herself with the knowledge that she can remove each brick in the wall if necessary. Another assistant, Enoba, helps with the preparation. She reassures Kate that either she or Anunu will be with her throughout her journey. She feels taken care of in ways that she believes she might have missed as a child.

## Yolo Had Read

Before embarking on his journey, Yolo had read about the land he had come to visit. He recalls the way he met a Hawaiian woman he had once called his girlfriend. The woman, a hula dancer whose name was Leilani, was in a bar and was being harassed by a white man, her boyfriend, in a club where Yolo happened to be. The man wanted her to dance. When the situation escalated, and Leilani defended herself against her boyfriend by hitting him in the head with a bottle, Yolo intervened. Leilani then drove off in the car that she and her boyfriend had arrived in together. Leilani's boyfriend, Saul, was left stranded at the bar where Yolo and the other customers laughed at him.

After some time passed, Yolo saw Leilani again. She was upset and seemed to be assaulting a parking meter. Having paid the meter, she discovered that it was broken and that she had spent her money but did not have the freedom to park in the space. One of the first things she told Yolo was that her real name was not Leilani but Alma. She told him that she had taken the name Leilani because, as a Hawaiian woman, it was representative of what was expected of her, and so it was easier to have a false name than to use her real name.

Alma asked Yolo about his name, and he told her that it was from the Poewin Indians. Like her, he revealed that he named himself, finding his original name out of sync with his life. The name *Yolo* refers to a spot in a river where the rapids are born. Yolo told Alma that her birth name was defined as "soul." He suggested some other possibilities to her as the two continued to converse.

## First of All, Abandon

This chapter is a message from Grandmother as Kate sits in the ceremony for the encounter. The message that Grandmother sends is firm: She will not be destroyed by humans. She asserts that human beings are her creation, and as such she has no fear of what they can do to harm her. She maintains that what will be destroyed, however, is humanity. The effort to consume and to engage in selfish and self-absorbed activities only endangers the survival of the species, not its creator. The responsibility for what happens lies in the hands of human beings. Grandmother says that people can save themselves if they are willing to think, work, and act collectively. There is some need to stop relying on speech and to intuit one another's thoughts and feelings. If this new communication method is implemented, the plan to save the world will become apparent. It is not possible, nor is it likely to happen if people continue to rely on the inefficient tool of speech.

The chapter ends with a treatise on and conclusion about fear. The narrative maintains that human behavior is controlled and misaligned largely due to fear and the damage that it does to authentic communication.

## Like Elizabeth Taylor

Kate has been married several times. Her longest marriage is the one in which she had children. As she wanders though the rain forest, she reflects on a relationship she had with a woman named Lolly. She recognizes now that the relationship derived entirely from her feelings of loss about a cousin who had died. She remembers the wedding she and the woman had and also the tensions in their relationship that, ultimately, proved its undoing. The women had very different traits, including their sleeping habits. Kate was an early riser, while Lolly liked to sleep in. Kate felt that Lolly was a lazy person, and her lack of engagement bothered Kate.

As a child, Lolly had been considered slow. In fact, the girl had her own abilities, ones that were not immediately apparent from an initial encounter or assessment. The proverbial last straw for Kate happened when Lolly asked Kate to sign over half of her house to her because they were in a common-law relationship. Kate felt threatened and taken advantage of and slowly withdrew from the relationship after Lolly found another woman to exploit.

## At the Waterfall

Kate encounters another woman who is on the South American journey. Her name is Lalika, and she is from Mississippi. Through this experience, Kate has grown to be the one of the individuals in the group who can be of use to everyone. She is no longer affected by the medicine and so is aware of what is happening with the others during their sessions with Armando.

Lalika and Kate are at the falls where the group take their baths, and Kate notices that the other woman is weeping. Lalika is having doubts that the ceremony can be useful to her and says so to Kate, who asks her questions about what she wishes to get from the experiment. After a long pause, Lalika says that she wants to feel in sync with herself in ways that she has lost. Lalika weeps, and Kate allows the woman to grieve. She then tries to see if there is anything she can do to provide some psychological consolation to the distraught woman. As Kate holds Lalika's head against her shoulder, the two begin to feel that there is another presence in the vicinity.

Lalika seems much recovered after having someone listen to her concerns. Kate notices that the woman is very attractive and seems, somehow, physically in sync with the environment in which the two find themselves. Soon the women find themselves ravaged by mosquitoes, and they run back to camp.

Kate and her colleagues are participating in a ceremony that is central to some indigenous groups in the Amazon. Through the ingestion of a particular substance called yage, the participants are able to access information and knowledge that, it is believed, can help them to progress more effectively and healthily on their life journey. Kate and the others have personified this experience as an encounter with Grandmother.

Kate remembers her first session with Grandmother. She is able to remove the brick wall, the barrier between her consciousness and that of the other side, and is able to access information she has been craving and that has been missing in her life. Lalika is able to journey to Grandmother as well and appears to Kate as if she is aboard a train. The others in the group are similarly affected. Armando and his helper shaman, Cosmi, are available to assist should any of the participants need help. Kate wonders about the incursion of outsiders like herself on ceremonies that at one time would have been considered sacred and exclusive to the indigenous people from whom it derives. She feels that the generosity of the shamans is indicative of their greater humanity and evidence of their ability to forgive long-standing historical and continuing contemporary wrongs.

Kate still feels the desire to try to rectify the wrongs perpetuated against her ancestors and speaks to Armando about the source of his forgiving spirit. Armando asks her about her experiences with Grandmother, and she tells him that Grandmother has been told a story that Kate did not want to know and that Kate must bring back with her. Kate has learned about the life of an enslaved ancestor who, while living, was obsessed with his own appearance. The man's good looks got him noticed, and he became involved sexually with his mistress. The master, the mistress's husband, discovered the affair and removed the slave's teeth with a crude implement.

Kate begins to feel ill while telling this tale and allows Armando to comfort her. The man's presence is a balm. He also sings to her, and the song seems to help her to move to a place of understanding with her experiences and allows her to accept the inhumanity of the story she has learned. Kate falls into a deep and peaceful sleep after making some important connections between the story she has learned and her experiences in life as an intellectual and activist.

Shortly after the conclusion of Armando's song, Kate falls into a deep and restorative sleep. Armando gives her a medicine to take that he calls Bobinsana. The medicine is supposed to have the effect of helping her to clarify and access her dreams in a way that will contribute to the process of acquiring knowledge and lucidity about her life. Armando tells her that the medicine removes unnecessary negative emotions that might prevent her access to truth. She will be able to communicate with the ancestor figure who lost his teeth without the pain that initially impeded their connections.

Kate interacts with her ancestor, who tells her that dying is a long process. She meets him in a dream about a country where there is a road upon which she stands and her ancestor-figure floats. Even in death, the ghost has bloody gums that are horrifyingly visible to Kate. This individual has lived and died several times and so is able to share with Kate the intimate details of each situation. The common denominator is his realization of what he could have done to have had a better, more productive existence.

Kate's ancestor also tells her that, like trees, human work does not end with death and that work continues even after one has passed on. He says the tree has the work of decomposing and of fertilizing the spaces that they have left behind. He also says that ancestral figures are supposed to warn the living of the ways that they should walk in order to bring forth knowledge that will allow the living to access the reality of themselves. He warns her that this knowledge, if truly understood, cannot lead to revenge.

The ancestor reveals that his name is Remus, and Kate finds this fact amusing, thinking about the character UNCLE REMUS, made famous by southern white author JOEL CHANDLER HARRIS. He tells her that many slaves had that name and were so called because the name was a kind of joke to the slave owners, who thought that naming a slave after one of the original founders of the great city of Rome, Remus of Romulus and Remus renown, was absurd.

As the two walk, the ancestor continues to bleed from his mouth and from his foot. Kate catches a glimpse of her own reflection and continues her journey with this dead member of her family. He continues telling her of his experiences of life and of his labors. She shares with him her insights, thoughts that lead him to express his pleasant surprise that she has things to teach him as well—that the path of communication is mutual. Following up on this insight, Kate tells Remus to bite into the corn she has been husking. She does so in order to help him to heal part of his own past painful experience. Remus is reluctant and has to be persuaded by Kate to take the chance of hurting himself by attempting to bite into the ear without teeth. After a bit of back and forth, Remus braves the corn.

Miraculously, biting into the corn restores Remus's teeth. He wishes for a mirror; instead, Kate tells him to look into her eyes so that he can see himself. He is delighted to see himself so restored, and the experience sends him and Kate into an inexplicable forward fall. When she comes to rest, Kate finds herself in her own bed at the settlement in the rain forest.

## The Longer Yolo Kicked Back

After his involvement with the discovery of the dead boy on the beach, Yolo is unable to participate in his escape to the island in the ways he had planned. The hotel in which he is staying seems too unreal to be tolerated, and he finds himself searching for something more substantial. Even as he tries to read, he finds his thoughts wandering to the incident on the beach. His thoughts make him aware of the reality that he knows very little about Hawaii and that he has the opportunity to experience the place in a more complete way if he travels outside of the resort.

Yolo uses his rental car to escape the artificial barriers of the hotel and begins to experience parts of Hawaii that are not akin to a picture postcard. Wandering around for a bit, he arrives near a green church and slowly becomes aware that he is witnessing a funeral. As he drives, he sees that some of the people in the procession are familiar to him. He recognizes Jerry, the man from the beach who asked him to help by waiting with the dead body. Yolo pulls his car to the side of the road.

## What Is Missing from the World

Kate is conversing with Anunu, who cautions her not to give up on life and humanity as easily as she has in the past. Anunu says that things are always less predictable than they seem to be. She also tells Kate that in every woman's life there comes a time when she senses the absence of Grandmother and that the absence can come in many forms. The appearance and reoccurrence of the unexpected is one of the signs of this need. Kate tells Anunu of her recurring dream of a dry riverbed, the same dream that prompted her trip down the Colorado.

When asked if the journey down the Colorado had led to discovery of Grandmother, Kate pauses and recalls the experience. She says that she has come to understand that trip as a venture toward expiation, of ridding herself of the unnecessary in order to move forward on the journey toward Grandmother. She tells Anunu that the journey led her to restore and reestablish her life. She has a vision of Anunu. In it, the woman wears a feather headdress. Kate has the feeling that they had been engaged at some point in the distant past on the same kind of journey on which they find themselves in the present moment.

Kate finds herself having a different experience from her colleagues since she is no longer affected by the yage. She still drinks the Bobinsana, which allows her to have clarity about her dreams. She travels each day to the waterfall to take her baths and begins to find a profound experience of calm and resolution. Although intimidated by the animals in the waterfall, she faces them, feeling that attainment of her new feelings of peace will allow her to face any creature with the resources she needs to handle the situation.

Kate also has become a kind of assistant to Armando, who consults her about the state of the other members of the group. When he asks, she tells him that the problem with Lalika is that she has murdered a man and that she feels responsible for his life. Armando did not have that information and asks Kate for the details about Lalika's story. Kate tells Armando that the man whom Lalika killed had raped her and was in the process of raping her friend when she killed him. After Lalika and her friend were apprehended for the murder, they experienced more abuse at the hands of the police, who also raped them repeatedly.

Kate, Armando, and Cosmi perform a ritual over Lalika that has to do with forgiveness. After the ceremony, Lalika is able to share with the group the story of what happened to her. She says that she feels she had no choice about killing the man because he was so much larger than she was. She tells Kate that if she makes it through her encounters with yage, she will shave her head and wear the cap that she has been crocheting during her visit to the Amazon. Kate cries into Lalika's hat and says to her that they will always be together now as they share sorrow.

## The Mourners Outside the Church

The narrative returns to Yolo and his experience with the funeral procession of the boy who died on the beach. While he observes the procession, he notices someone approaching on a motorcycle. He sees after a time that the woman on the bike is his old girlfriend, Alma. She carries the ashes of the dead boy, and when she arrives, the others follow her into the church. As he observes Alma's reception by the church members, he begins to wonder if the boy who died on the beach is her son.

Later, the two have a conversation, and Yolo's suspicions are confirmed. Alma tells him that her son was a drug addict and that his death was caused by an overdose. Yolo comments on the coincidence both of running into Alma and to be the last one with her son when his body was discovered. Alma tells Yolo that her father wanted to be like James Dean and ended up, like his hero, dying in a traffic accident. She wears his motorcycle jacket in homage. She tells Yolo about the problems and exploitation experienced by the indigenous Hawaiians at the hands of various interlopers over time. She also tells him the story of her father, who was not Hawaiian but German and Portuguese. His parents had wanted him to travel back to the eastern United States and to the mainland to go to school, but he decided that he wanted to stay on the island and marry a native Hawaiian woman, Alma's mother.

Yolo switches the conversation back to Alma's dead son and asks her what she thinks was the specific cause of her son's death. Alma tells him that she believes that her son was addicted to crystal meth because the drug is so popular with young people and so readily available. Alma says that her son, Marshall, did not want to be addicted. She also says that the drug arrives on the island from the outside and on boats.

## Naturally

Lalika continues telling Kate about the abuse she suffered at the hands of the police after she murdered her rapist. The other woman who was with her during this ordeal and who suffered a parallel fate was named Saartjie. The two women conversed, and it was Saartjie's presence that sustained Lalika. The two women met originally in their occupation as migrant workers. While they were imprisoned, they happened upon a copy of *Jet* magazine in which there was a story about a South African woman named Saartjie (SARA) BAARTMAN. During the 19th century, Baartman was put on display in Europe because her body was seen as freakish and only worthy of display and spectacle.

Saartjie—whose name was Gloria before the women discovered the story of Baartman—and Lalika began to dream about Baartman. They thought about her body being dissected and parts of her being put on display after her death. The women began to have visitations from Baartman when their situations were at their nadir. Baartman came to them to offer comfort and relief from the pain that they were experiencing. By channeling their energy toward Baartman's loving gaze and embrace, the women were able to endure the abuse and pain that they experienced as captives. When they conjured Baartman, they found a new level of peace they would not have imagined possible in the circumstance in which they found themselves.

Baartman became a kind of divine mother for the women, and they saw her as a savior who helped them to endure their situation and to feel that the torture they were suffering had a parallel with a real person who had experienced the same or worse. In addition to the spiritual support that the vision of the woman provided, Lalika and Gloria also began to call each other Saartjie and to pray to Baartman, seeing her as a saint.

As Lalika and Kate talk, a storm begins in the Amazon, rain pelting the two woman as they shelter each other.

### I Am Peace

Grandmother says, simply, that she is peace and that she has existed before and without human beings. She says that yage is the way to find her.

### James Dean Was the Only

This chapter begins with the assertion that James Dean is the only American man with whom most Hawaiian men can find some commonality. Alma tries to educate Yolo about some of the details of recent Hawaiian history. She tells him about Queen Liliuokalani and the way that she was placed under arrest by men representing U.S. interests. Alma also tells Yolo that, in addition to her political abilities, the queen was an artist.

The picture that Alma shows Yolo of the queen reminds him of his grandmother. Alma tells him that Liliuokalani gave up the monarchy and her sovereignty over the Hawaiian people so that there would not be a war in which her people would be killed. The "peaceful" surrender was called annexation, and Hawaii became a playground for the rest of the country.

### We Mahus Believe

The narrative continues with Yolo's unfolding discovery of the world in which Alma resides and the individuals who people it. The scene includes a narrative about a particular group of people who roam the world and, although scattered, hold its secrets. They are the Mahus, who live all over the world, but only some of them know who they are and what they are supposed to be doing on the planet. A woman named Aunty Pearlua delivers this information to a group of men who are gathered around a fire on a beach in the Hawaiian moonlight. Although Alma has told Yolo about the Mahus, he remains incredulous about their existence. Aunty Pearlua tells Yolo that the Mahus are the ones who taught the Hawaiians the hula. She reveals that the Mahus are not particularly gendered in one direction or another but generally choose one sex as dominant. The Mahus work helping out the needy and neglected people of the world.

### It Was the Bones

The group in the Amazon has grown closer. Kate has befriended another person, a man named Hugh Brentforth. Hugh has been talking to Kate about dry riverbeds and the ways that they are not always what they seem. He says that even when a dry riverbed appears to be completely without water, sometimes the water has retreated underground, and if one has that information, all the water one needs can be found.

Hugh tells Kate about the enormous amount of land his family owns and of the indigenous older men who occasionally appear and ask for water. The Indians tell Hugh and his family that the water they request is for the bones. Hugh or one of his family members drives the men to a certain sacred spot, where they perform a ritual in memory of their dead ancestors. The ceremony ends with one of the men putting some of the water into the plastic jug he always brings with him and then leaving.

One time the Indian showed up with his son, with whom Hugh had a conflict. Hugh, although unhappy about the sons's presence, drove out to the spring to let the two perform the ritual. Upon his next visit, the older man brought his grandson with him. The boy seemed gentler and more receptive than his father. During that visit, Hugh told the older Indian that the energy company would be digging down by the spring and that he had no control over their actions. When the two returned, the spring had become a lake. When they arrived at the lake, the boy and his grandfather had a long conversation in their native language. Several months after the boy and his grandfather left, the lake disappeared, an occurrence that pleased the energy company because it made their job easier. After the drilling began, the Indians stopped coming to Hugh's property. In the course of the drilling, the energy company discovered thousand of years' worth of bones that belonged to the Indian's people.

Hugh tells this story and lets Kate know how transformative it has been in his life as an example of devotion, loyalty, and love. He comes to have questions about the bones of his own ancestors and to wonder where they might be located. He hopes also that someday the grandson might return to care for the bones once again in his grandfather's absence.

Hugh's story gets Kate to ponder the role of devotion in her own life. She wonders to what and to whom she is devoted. The first thing that come to mind is her children. Her sons, Charles and Henry, are central in her life. Henry works with the space program, and Charles is a musician. She also thinks of her lover, Yolo, and about the ways in which he enhanced her lived experiences.

She again speaks with Hugh about his story and wonders with him what the old Indian man did with the water he took from the site with the bones. She has had a dream about the situation that makes her think the man used the water in a healing ritual.

## In the Circle

In the group that Yolo has joined on the beach, there are two aborigines. The men are striking, particularly one of them, who has very dark skin and blonde hair. The men are there at the gathering as the guests of Aunty Pearlua. They have come because they are concerned with the problems that the youth in their country face. Like Alma's son, too many of them are dying at a young age for preventable reasons. They tell the group that they were also addicted to the local form of drug abuse, petrol sniffing. The men feel that what is missing from their lives is the connection with the land and with their ancestry. They speculate that the drug use is motivated by the desire to escape the fear and pain that comes with not understanding where one comes from and the history of one's people. They explain that the drugs are a form of escape that allows the young to cope with their sense of disconnection. One of the men concludes by thanking Aunty Pearlua for having the council and for including them.

Other than Yolo, the council also includes Jerry, the man on the beach, and Alma's other son. Others are also present, but they remain unnamed. The aboriginal man says that going to live with his sister saved him. Through her example, he is able to hold on to a kind of love and stability that had not been available to him before the relocation to her home in the city.

## Toward the Middle of Their Stay

The group in the Amazon have dinner with the shaman, Armando, and his assistant, Cosmi. During the dinner, several other members of the group are introduced to the narrative. Missy and Rick are sharing with the rest of the group their encounters with the various lizards and geckos that inhabit their living quarters during this excursion. Hugh says that he has been visited by a family of bats. Armando tells the group that they should notice who and what comes to visit because there is significance in the nature of these visitations. He also asks them if they have heard the call of the jaguar at night. Armando tells them that the jaguar is sometimes the disguised spirit of a sorcerer. He also tells them to try to focus on the reasons they are in the jungle and what they hope to accomplish. He cautions them against thinking too much about the outside world and about the narratives that are associated with popular culture. He says that paying attention to these narratives is akin to the experience of living in a world that is not your own. He thinks that these inane stories are the reason that so many people are lost in the contemporary world. People are distracted from the creation of their own narratives and experiences, and they should retreat as much as possible into silence so that they can begin to access the parts of themselves with which they have lost touch.

Kate speaks to Armando one-on-one and shares with him her fear that she is speaking too much, that she is spending too much of her energy interacting with the other members of the group. Armando brings Kate a container of water that she washes herself with in order to reorient her thoughts and to return to the centeredness that will allow her to connect with her inner self. Armando also reassures her that the conversations she is having with the others in the group are not problematic; rather, they are enhancing both her experience and those of the others who have gathered at the river in search of a new way of being. He reassures her that she is hearing the story of the people.

### His Streaked Reddish Hair

This chapter concerns one of the other characters in the book, Rick. Although he dyes his hair red, Rick has black roots that are beginning to grow in as he spends time away from such accoutrements in the jungles of the Amazon. He jogs through the jungle each morning, and Kate has an opportunity to have a conversation with him. Armando is scornful of the man, calling him "Mr. Young Man Let Me Stay." He speaks of the superficiality of an individual who fights against his age and will not accept the aging process. Armando is confident that Rick will, in spite of his limitations, learn his lesson.

Rick begins a first-person narrative as he reflects upon the source of his family's wealth, which comes largely from the sale of drugs to black communities. He admits this embarrassing reality to Kate and Lalika during an afternoon when the three are resting. The woman like Rick. He tells them of the complexities of his Italian immigrant family and of their desire to assimilate to American culture by differentiating themselves from the least respected of the American people, African Americans.

During the session with Grandmother, Rick acts out and is at odds with the rest of the group, who are quiet and introspective. While under the influence of the yage, Rick seems almost out of control. Armando and Cosmi try to help the man while he is traveling, and because of his seeming lack of cooperation, they become disturbed with Rick and are on the verge of abandoning him. Kate intervenes by telling Rick that she sees him. Hearing these words said has a profound effect on Rick, who immediately stops his infantile behavior and transforms. He leaves the circle and the group for an entire day.

When he returns, Rick has grown in awareness. He remembers his father and recalls the fact that his father is the one who decided to change the family name from its original Italian to an English name. During the conversation about Rick's drug-dealing father, Lalika mentions that her cell mate, Gloria (who renamed herself Saartjie), died from a heart attack after taking cocaine. Lalika shares that she tried to get Gloria to hold on to the comfort of their vision of Saartjie Baartman, but that she was unable to understand that what they witnessed was in fact a representation.

Rick shares more of his story and tells the women of his childhood in an all-white town and of the time when his black college roommate came to his home to visit. His parents were kind to the man in a superficial way. Rick discovered how thin the veneer of their acceptance was when he began to date a black woman. His parents did not approve and began to disparage not only her as an individual but the entire race.

Rick met up with an uncle who felt that he was, in some ways, estranged from the family. The uncle had not changed his name and was not involved in the family business. He revealed to Rick the involvement of the family in the destruction of African-American communities.

### After the Last Circle

Nearing the end of their stay in the Amazon, the group completes its last gathering in the circle, and it is after this meeting that a woman in the group named Missy finally has her breakthrough. Missy has been afraid of attaining wellness, and she resists recovery. During the last circle, Armando and Cosmi make music; Armando sings, and Cosmi plays the flute. The music is so beautiful that it causes Kate to cry and lose her defenses. Armando tells them all that they must lose their fear of letting go of what ails them. They must become aware of what the nature of their illness is and to master the problem so that they can free themselves of it.

Armando personifies their illnesses and says that they often behave like small children who are willful and do not wish to be eliminated. The child likes to play games with the body and the mind, does not want these pleasures to end, and will play them at the expense of the body, mind, and spirit the illness inhabits.

While at the center one afternoon, Missy's physical self seems to replicate the symptoms of death. When she awakens after the traumatic event, she tells those gathered around her that she has lost something. She also tells them that she has been on a journey. Kate says to her that she caused them alarm and welcomes her back. Missy says to the group that she experienced incest at the hands of her grandfather and that he was employed as a clown. Missy and her mother lived with her grandfather when she was a young girl. Missy did not know or have any relationship with her father, so her grandfather, her mother's father, was a kind of father figure for her.

Missy's grandfather was named Timmy Wimmins, and he called Missy by the affectionate pet name of Squiggly Wiggly. After Missy's mother learned about the abuse her daughter had suffered at her father's hands, the mother and child moved out of Wimmins's house but by that time, the damage had been done. The problem was that Missy had become attached to her grandfather in such an unhealthy way that, even when they left the man's house, she found that she missed his attention and abuse.

Missy says that she does not think that her mother was abused by Wimmins, but the two never talk about it so she does not know for certain whether her mother was also a victim. Wimmins was a small man; in fact, Missy was taller than him even as a girl. Missy's incestuous relationship damaged her as an adult. She has been unable to enjoy sex because she feels so guilty about the inappropriate physical pleasure she experienced with her grandfather.

After Missy and her mother left his house, Missy's grandfather died. Missy believes that his demise occurred as a result of his feelings of loss about Missy and her mother.

Missy has had many problems as a result of her grandfather's abuse. She began to use drugs in an attempt to escape from the pain that she feels. She begins to tell the group about the experience she had earlier that afternoon after taking the yage. She says that she had a vision of Grandmother, and the older woman came and sat with her. During the visit, Missy looked at the rushing water, and in it she saw the continuity of life. With this realization, she was able to allow the medicine to heal her pain and to let go of her dysfunction.

Missy tells the group who have gathered that they are the only ones she has told about what happened to her. She says that, during her journey, she actually saw dragons. Rick is relieved with this news as he, too, saw dragons during his journey with Grandmother. Hugh also affirms that dragons were a huge part of his experience. Armando explains that the animals and creatures that they have seen are an indication of their connection to an ancient past where such animals actually walked the earth and were a large part of the lived experience of early humanity.

## A Person Is Visible

Rick begins this chapter with a discussion between him and Armando. Armando notices that the man is thin and attributes his size to a lack of substance. Rick explains that once he found out about the source of his parents' money, he felt that he needed to purge and to rid himself of what was excessive in his life. Rick and Armando discuss power dynamics and the relationship between race and power in what is called the first and the third worlds. Rick speaks of the dilemmas of those who are in power as well as those who have large amounts of money in their possession. As one of the latter, he feels that he has a responsibility to make sure that his money goes to support endeavors in the world that help avoid the sort of inequities that do not allow each human being to reach his or her full potential. Rick says that he has a great number of possessions but that he lives humbly. Armando asks him if this humble abode does not sit on the waterfront, and Rick, chastised, admits that his small, one-room apartment does indeed face the water. Armando reminds him that he needs to become more engaged in his empathy and then his life will become more fulfilling.

### You Must Live: A Future Consequence

The message that Kate receives from Grandmother is that she must live in space for two years. The message confuses her, and she is not sure what is meant by the cryptic admonition. Later, when she returns home from her adventures in the jungle, she finds that her house has been painted blue. Yolo reminds her that the color is what initially attracted her to him and to his paintings. He suggests that perhaps the house is the space that Grandmother meant.

### Kate Awoke the Last Day

On the last day of the voyage to the Amazon, Kate is in the process of preparing to leave. She remembers a dream that she had the previous night. The dream is another visitation, this time from a woman who comes into Kate's temporary room and changes it into a verdant natural scene. This experience teaches Kate that aging is about creating transformations for other people, making the world that others inhabit more livable.

When she tells Armando about her dream, he responds with surprise, telling her that he was not aware of her concerns about aging. She says that she did not realize that she had been worried about aging either. The members of the group realize that they have grown close and that the experience has been rich and life-changing. They travel away from the locale that they have called home, and as they leave, they see the ways in which the rain forest communities have been ravaged by development. The people seem oppressed and downtrodden. It occurs to Kate that it would make sense for the people to grow vegetables so that they could have the proper nutrients to support their needs. Armando seems dubious about the possibility.

The group exchange contact information at the airport and make plans to stay in touch with each other. Kate has her doubts that any of them will ever see each other again in this life.

### Yolo Woke

The narrative returns to Yolo's trip to Hawaii and to some time that he spent with Alma. He finds himself thinking of the health of his former love and of her weight and habit of drinking and smoking without restraint. While he is at her house, he tries to model healthy behavior for her by eating and drinking well himself. Yolo shares with Alma the details of the council with Aunty Pearlua. He tells her that the woman she was named after, Aunty Alma, was in attendance and that she is involved in the session that was designed to educate the men present about the ways in which they can most effectively live in the world.

Aunty Pearlua told the men about the steps that they could take in order to proceed with their lives in the most effective way possible. She told the men that they must stop indulging in any addictive behaviors, including drugs, alcohol, cigarettes, and even coffee and black tea. Yolo reports that the men were reluctant to make even that promise because it was clear that it would be extraordinarily difficult. In fact, one of the men maintained that such a transformation was, in fact, impossible.

Aunt Pearlua returned to her narrative about the Mahus and her belief that the people who function in that role should not only be women, but that men should also work in this capacity as the healers of humanity. She told the men that their bodies were one aspect of their lives over which they could ensure some measure of control and through which they could acquire some freedom from the influence of hostile forces in the world.

The brother of the dead boy on the beach—Alma's other son, whose name is Poi—was a member of the group. He cried as he hears Aunty Pearlua's words because they reminded him of the loss of his brother. Aunty Alma arrived in the circle and reiterated what Aunty Pearlua said. The men were surprised by the circle and impressed by the things they learned.

### When I Come Back Here

Alma talks about her reasons for leaving New England and returning to her home in Hawaii. She says that after attending and graduating from college at one of the finest institutions in the world, she had thought that Hawaii would be like a paradise. She imagined that the house she would like to create could be managed by wind and solar power, energy sources readily available in Hawaii but underutilized by its population. The reality of what she found on the island did not match her expectations, and she had been disappointed.

Yolo is not happy with the direction in which Alma is moving. He listens to her reflections on what she anticipated finding in Hawaii and asks her what happened to her dreams and expectations. Alma replies that she tried to build the kind of house that she imagined but was told that it was illegal to utilize natural energy in Hawaii.

Alma tells Yolo that after her disillusionment with creating the home of her dreams, she decided to get married and become a real estate broker. This work was not satisfying for her because she felt that the land was betrayed by her decision to buy and sell it. She tells Yolo that her sons understood her decisions and shared her sorrows when she experienced disappointments.

Yolo asks Alma why she named her son Poi, and Alma tells him that as an infant, the boy would not drink prepackaged milk and would only eat poi. As a result, his childhood nickname was Poi, and it became a permanent appellation.

At the conclusion of the conversation, Yolo reminds Alma that one of the aunts who ran the council circle for the men, Aunty Alma, was the same woman that Alma was named for and who, Yolo believes, could help Alma out of the rut within which she seems to find herself stuck.

## On the Plane Home

While traveling back to her home after the end of her Amazon journey, Kate thinks that she would like to spend time chewing gum. While searching for the gum in her backpack, she discovers a written-on Post-It note that contains the beginning of the story she had started to write when she took her ride down the Colorado River several years before her trip to the Amazon.

Kate recalls the story that she began but never completed. The narrative is about a father and his daughter who are trying, in the best ways that they can, to cope with the death of the family's mother. The character who is most like Kate in the story is named Roberta. At the conclusion of the brief tale, Roberta has successfully persuaded the family father to eat something. Her ability to do so creates a problem for her sisters, who see her as a favorite of their father's and resent her closeness to the man.

Kate looks at the small scrap of paper and wonders to herself why she wrote such a thing, questioning her motivations for creating such a situation. She then remembers that the story was generated by her accessing her dream life; in particular, she recalls that the story derived from a dream she had about her mother.

She recalls that in the dream, her mother only had one hand and yet was able to fish with a net at the side of the ocean. During the dream, her mother had regrown her hand and had said to her daughter that the kind of fishing she was engaged in did not require the use of a boat.

As the plane nears its destination and Kate approaches her home, she begins to discern information from her memory of the dream. She begins to believe that her father was not the man with whom her mother conceived her—that he was not, in actuality, her father. Kate begins to understand that the reasons her mother was never pleased with her come from her mother's feelings of shame and fear about the fact that Kate does not belong, biologically speaking, to her husband.

Kate's "discovery" helps her to puzzle the other pieces of her life that she has never been able to understand, like the reason she does not look like her father or any of the rest of her siblings. She speculates that her conception was the consequence of a troubled period in her parents' relationship that had resulted in a brief affair and had concluded in the married couple's reunion. Kate thinks that this new awareness has its origins in her recent trip and in her visits to Grandmother. She feels free and is reassured that her relationships with her sisters will improve now that she has this new awareness.

## They Bombed

When Yolo and Kate reunite, he reminds her that that the world has still been engaged in its usual violence and that bad things have occurred since they parted. Kate responds with a sigh of resignation but also with some feeling of relief that the two are back together. Kate ponders what might be possible if the energy, time, effort, and money that was now directed toward war and fighting were shifted to creating joy and engendering peace. Yolo dismisses her hopes as unrealistic fantasy. As a counter, Kate brings up the example of South Africa and the Mandelas as she points out that surely their dreams of equality must have, at some points, seemed equally unrealistic.

During their voyages, both Kate and Yolo have lost weight. Kate notes that her partner seems more serious and that his hair has grown long. She also observes that he has acquired a new tattoo. Yolo tells Kate that he received it the night before his return. Kate feels that she has truly returned home and that her relationship with Yolo is in a better place as a result of their travels.

Yolo tells Kate about Alma and her life story. He conveys to Kate Alma's deep sorrow at having lost her mother when she was three years old. He also tells her about the untimely deaths of Alma's father and her son Marshall. Yolo says that Marshall's name derives from the Marshall Islands, the place where Alma's husband had traveled to try to stop the U.S. government's bombing of the island chain.

The two continue to share stories of their adventures into the next day when Kate suddenly realizes that Yolo has stopped smoking. He tells her about the council circle with Aunty Pearlua and of his vow to give up his addictions. Kate has a dream that night about the Hopi people and their origin story about their emergence from under the earth. She tells Yolo the story of her dream the next day.

Several days later, Kate catches Yolo smoking outside. He is tearful as he speaks of what he understands as his failure. Kate supports him in his efforts and tells him that he does not have to hide his smoking or go outside to do it. The two decide to stay together as a couple. At Kate's suggestion, they decide to have a ceremony celebrating their union and immediately think of inviting their new friends. The two contact their friends, and most of them agree to join the couple for the three-day celebration that they are planning. Yolo and Kate decide that everything must happen by a river, and they go in search of one beside which to marry.

Kate tries to remember all that Grandmother said to her during her experiences in the Amazon. She has had some resolution of the concerns she expressed in the beginning of the novel as well as of her anxieties about aging, acceptance of which she discovered while on her journey. Kate's grand revelation about Grandmother is that she herself is Grandmother and that the questions that she has about life and living can only be answered from knowledge she has within.

### Don't Go Anywhere

This chapter begins with an admonition from Grandmother that the people of the earth must remain on this planet rather than trying to escape to another place. She relays an origin myth that concerns the presence of other beings from other worlds on the planet. She says that the secret of that journey lies in the snake and acceptance of the creature that has generated so much revulsion.

### One Day, Standing in Her Garden

Armando surprises Kate with a visit. He brings with him a large group of people. They are shamans traveling to Washington, D.C., for a gathering. Armando affirms the color of her house, saying that it is in sync with the earth and is a color for healing in the Buddhist system of belief. Armando tells her that they are traveling to Washington to protest a drug company's intention to patent and own yage. They have come to ask her for a letter of support endorsing the shamans' efforts to preserve the sacred substance for the people to whom it belonged. She writes the letter for them and invites them to return for her ceremony with Yolo. Armando says he will come or will send a spirit in his place.

### It Will Be a Long Time

Kate has another dream that has some significance to her life. She sees, in the dream, ants that she is trying to kill with insecticide. She says that the dream is about fear and the need to confront it directly rather than trying to elude it.

## It Was a Warm Sunny Day

Kate and Yolo prepare for their ceremony by the river in autumn. Their friends are coming to join them, and they are looking forward to the ceremony. Kate reenters the altar room she disassembled and finds that all is as she left it. Yolo enters the room, and Kate begins to light candles. She sets up the altar again with the yage at the center.

## CRITICAL COMMENTARY

*Now Is the Time to Open Your Heart* is structured on the traditional literary trope of the journey. Walker employs this framework to explore the multiple voyages upon which she takes her protagonist, Kate Talkingtree. The point of embarkation for Kate's journeys is one that is common to contemporary American novels: the critical juncture between youth and maturity that often catalyzes a reassessment of self-definition, particularly in terms of purpose, interpersonal relationships, and belief.

*Now Is the Time to Open Your Heart* begins with the manifestation of Kate's disillusionment. Although not directly stated in the novel, presumably Kate has found in the early years of her life some sense of direction and purpose in her study of BUDDHISM; however, at the start of the novel, the precepts—or, perhaps more accurately, Kate's access to the fundamentals of Buddhism—have been limited by her new perceptions. She leaves a Buddhist retreat and, when she returns home, dismantles her altar. The altar is a mix of secular and religious icons, ranging from the political revolutionary CHE GUEVARA to the Mexican GODDESS FIGURE the Virgin of Guadeloupe. Up to this point in her life, Kate has managed to assemble these disparate representations into a coherent and accessible source of spiritual sustenance, but these images no longer have that sustaining effect. Kate seems to have lost focus and so embarks upon a quest to bring new purpose her life.

The initial realization of the journey emerges from Kate's interpretation of one of her dreams. She has a recurring dream about dry riverbeds and senses that the dream's message is to travel to an actual river in order to distill from it what answers may be there. She therefore joins a rafting trip down the Colorado River. In the same way that the river has etched a canyon through a rocky mountain, this segment of Kate's journey opens her up to the interior parts of her life. During this experience, she remembers her marriage and the difficulties of trying to conform to the domestic ideals and expectations that are placed on women and mothers. She becomes violently ill, and her vomiting becomes a metaphor for ridding herself of the oppressive weight of her attempts to conform and to withhold her words and feelings. The need to expel these toxins from her inner self constitutes the first phase of her journey to find a new purpose.

The second phase of her journey occurs as Kate decides that the trip down the Colorado was only the beginning of a larger experience of self-discovery. She learns about the experimental drug yage that is a part of the spiritual rituals of the people who reside along the North Amazon river. Kate joins a group of seekers who, like her, are on a quest to reinvent their lives. While in the Amazon, with the assistance of the yage and a shaman named Armando, she encounters her inner self and comes to the awareness that there is no source of meaning beyond that which she can access within. Having come to this understanding, Kate, like the traditional hero in the quest narrative, can return home and embrace life at middle age with a new sense of purpose.

The second thematic journey that Kate makes in the novel has to do with her personal relationships. One of the iconographic images that hangs in her home altar is a picture of her parents. Although most of Kate's personal relationships are not explored in the novel, there are many suggestions that these primary relationships are in need of some repair. Kate alludes to the potential problems in these relationships as she reveals a dream she has while on the voyage down the Colorado. She dreams of her mother and then spends some time writing down that narrative as the beginning of a short story. In the story, Kate writes the tale of three sisters who are trying to get their father to eat during the repast following his wife's death. When the character in the story, Roberta (who is Kate's corollary), is able to get her father to eat some food, her sisters are upset and jealous of her and of her ability to get her father to act. The novel suggests that there are similar tensions between Kate and her sisters.

After Kate comes home from the Amazon, as the plane is landing, she has an epiphany about her family that she feels derives from her experience with the shaman, Armando, and with the spirituality enhancing drug, yage. Kate feels that from this experience, she has learned that the man she thought was her biological father is not actually her father. This realization, an intuition that Kate processes as fact, makes her feel that she understands her family dynamic in ways that she did not expect, which will liberate her to develop healthier relationships with her sisters. As a result of this particular psychological journey, Kate is also able to reconcile and to understand more completely her relationship with her mother, a woman whom she feels did not approve of her and from whom she did not experience the kind of warm, loving affection that she needed from a maternal figure.

Kate also confronts, however briefly, the relationships she has developed as an adult. When she leaves for her initial voyage, the trip down the Colorado on the rafting trip, she leaves her lover Yolo at home and feels along with him that there is a need for their relationship to come to an end. The two both realize that, although they care for one another, the love that they share may not be enough rationale for them to continue to have a romantic partnership.

As Kate travels down the Colorado, one of the revelations she has that becomes a kind of turning point in her psychological journey is her growing awareness that she needs to distance herself from physical intimacy in order to become more spiritually energized. With this message, she begins to redirect some of her energy from her sexual relationship with Yolo to her self-development. While she is in the Amazon, she begins to think of herself in multiple ways. In the past, one of her ways of feeling strong and in control derived from her physical connections with the various others in her life, but now she begins to understand her ability to be generative as having dimensionality beyond its physical expression.

Kate has been a woman who has been able to be attracted to both men and women, and yet, while she is in the Amazon, although she is attracted to some of the people in the group, she does not feel the need for those relationships to become sexual. When Kate and Yolo reunite, the couple find that, rather than their relationship coming to an end, they are at the beginning of a new phase. At Kate's suggestion, the two choose to embrace a new, committed dimension of their relationship and enter a self-defined marriage. Kate has been able to move from her feeling that a committed relationship is inherently oppressive to a reliance on a relationship as a fundamentally healthy and progressive element of her life.

The second aspect of Kate's journey in *Now Is the Time to Open Your Heart* takes her from confusion about the nature of her relationships to clarity. By the end of the novel, she recognizes that there is a reason for the tumultuous relationships in her family, and she also embraces the possibilities of having an intimate relationship with a partner that can serve as a foundation for personal health.

The third component in Kate's journey from doubt to surety involves her belief system. As previously mentioned, at the beginning of the novel Kate is attending a Buddhist retreat and has found that the teachings there, and particularly the teachers and the practitioners, have become unreliable sources of information. As a result, she no longer has faith in the beliefs that she has access to, and so she physically leaves the retreat but, more significantly, spiritually begins the process of abandoning the need for teachers, healers, and intercessors.

Although she has guides on the various journeys chronicled in *Now Is the Time to Open Your Heart,* what Kate's experiences teach her is that she can only rely on herself to interpret the spiritual truths of her life. When Kate "goes to Grandmother" (experiences the yage), what she discovers is that the divine source of knowledge she has been seeking in her various spiritual quests does not exist and that the only way that she can access the divine is to look within—that she has the only spiritual information that she can discover and, more importantly, that she needs.

The quest narrative is one of the most common genres in literature. In this novel, Walker borrows from this tradition in order to trace Kate's progression, but she subverts some of the quest narrative's conventions by creating a nonlinear plot that weaves in and out of Kate's experiential universe. Furthermore, unlike the traditional quest narrative, the battles that Kate has to wage are against internal rather than external forces. Walker metaphorizes the success of Kate's voyage at the end of the novel when she returns to her altar room and places her clock, which is in the shape of a snake, in the lap of her Buddha. This coupling represents Kate's reconciliation of the central conundrums of her life through the reality of suffering represented by Buddha, the real effect and impacts of time as symbolized by the clock, and the universal truth of continuity as represented by the snake. All can sit together on Kate's altar as they now do in the spiritual and psychological world she has attained as a result of her quests.

## SIGNIFICANT THEMES, ISSUES, CONCERNS

### Dreams

Dreams figure prominently in *Now Is the Time to Open Your Heart.* Kate comes to believe that her dream life is not only more real to her experientially but that her dreams are more important to her understanding of the world and of her subjectivity than is any other source of information. Dreams play a critical role in Kate's assessment of her relationship with Yolo. Because Yolo does not dream at the beginning of the novel, both he and Kate feel that the disparity between them may be too great to bridge. Once Yolo begins to dream and to read his dreams as signs of the future, only then can he begin to believe that he and Kate are compatible enough to continue their relationship.

While rafting down the Colorado River, Kate has a dream about her mother. This dream leads to her revelation about her relationship with everyone in her family and ultimately to the conclusion that, as a consequence of her mother's infidelity, she is not completely related to her family; as a result, she is somewhat alienated from each of them in different ways.

Perhaps the most profound and central dream in the novel is the cumulative effect of the yage and of the various experiences Kate has with Grandmother while she is in the Amazon. The encounters Kate has while under the influence of the drug can all be characterized as dreamlike experiences, and they have the effect of transforming her entire perspective on the world.

### Rivers

Throughout African-American literature, rivers are central. The phrase *crossing the river* or *crossing over* is used in some forms of African-American vernacular as a synonym for death. The notion of crossing over has historical resonance in the crossing of the Atlantic Ocean in the Middle Passage; crossing myriad rivers while escaping from slavery into freedom; and, later, migrating north to escape the confines of JIM CROW oppression.

Walker employs rivers as important symbols throughout her canon. In *Now Is the Time to Open Your Heart,* she is transparent in her exercise of this important trope. Catalyzed by dreams of the disappearance of water from the rivers of her imagination, Kate is compelled to travel to two of the most geographically transformative rivers in the world, the Colorado and the Amazon. At these dynamic and metamorphic locales, she is able to actualize the psychological and spiritual transformations she seeks.

### Interface between the Spirit and Material Worlds

In the later works of Walker's canon, she privileges the connections between the spiritual and material worlds as primary conduits through which her characters can assess "the truth." *Now Is the Time to Open Your Heart* is one of her most overt creations in terms of her emphasis on these connections. In one of the most effective and important scenes in the novel, Kate Talkingtree is able to have an extended conversation with one of her ancestors, whose name is Remus. Through this exchange, she is able to redeem the humanity of the many slaves who were made anonymous by the generic and mocking names they received, and she also is able to process and individualize the horrors that they experienced by retelling Remus's story. Walker is also able to present tangible evidence for the power of narrative in healing historic wrongs by having Kate assist her ancestor's reclamation of the dignity lost to him because of his lack of power as an enslaved man.

## Interconnectedness of Natural and Human Worlds

Throughout her work, Walker emphasizes the familial relationship between humanity and the natural world. One of Kate's major concerns in *Now Is the Time to Open Your Heart* is the question of the earth's health and of Kate's feelings of impotence to act in ways that will preserve and save the planet. While she is in the rain forest, Kate comes to believe that humanity does not threaten the planet with its presence or behavior but that it does jeopardize its own existence through its careless misuse and abuse of the planet and its resources.

The novel ends with a reference to ownership of those resources as a group of shamans stop at Kate's house on their way to Washington, D.C., to protest the appropriation and regulation of yage, an indigenous ceremonial tool, by the world's pharmaceutical companies and governments.

## CHARACTERS

**Alma (Leilani)** Alma, whose name means "soul," is an ex-lover of Yolo. Although her birth name is Alma, she changed it to Leilani when she left Hawaii, feeling that people would be more receptive to a Hawaiian dancer who has a more stereotypical name.

At one point in her life, Alma lived in the east of the United States. While there, she felt exploited as a consequence of the stereotypes made about Hawaiians. One example of such an occurrence happened when Alma was made to dance a stereotypical hula in front of a room full of American men at a party. It was during this event that she and Yolo met for the first time. Although they had a relationship, it did not last, and the two lost touch.

By the time Yolo meets her again in Hawaii, Alma has experienced much loss in her life. One of the most difficult events happens just before the two reunite in Hawaii. Alma has just lost her son Marshall, who died after overdosing on drugs. Coincidentally, Yolo happens to be among those who discover Marshall's body when it washes up on the beach near where Yolo is staying when he first arrives in Hawaii.

Yolo stays with Alma while he is in Hawaii. He notices that she has put on weight in the years since they have separated, and that she smokes and drinks heavily. Yolo tries to model healthy behavior for her and to help her to regain her equilibrium. At the end of the novel, Alma is one of Yolo and Kate's friends who have agreed to witness their commitment ceremony.

**Annie** Annie is one of the women on the boat with Kate during the rafting trip on the Colorado River.

**Anunu** Anunu is an African-Amerindian woman who studied with the shaman Armando before Kate's journey to the Amazon. Anunu is a wise grandmother-like figure whom Kate describes as "ageless." She is a supportive figure for Kate, and she helps to guide Kate on her spiritual exploration.

**Armando** Armando is a shaman from the northern part of the Amazon. He is the leader of Kate's spiritual group on the trip she makes to meet the yage. Armando is young, in his 40s, and has a beautiful singing voice. He preaches the benefits of Grandmother (yage) and helps Kate and the others in her group to interpret and make sense of their experiences.

After the retreat, Armando comes to visit Kate to ask her to write a letter to the American government in opposition to the patenting of yage, the plant he uses in his spiritual work to help individuals connect with the lost parts of themselves. He brings Rela, Lila, Charlie, and six other male shamans to Kate and Yolo's house when he visits on his way to a protest in Washington, D.C., against the regulation of yage. He leaves telling Kate and Yolo that he will try to attend their commitment ceremony or will send a spiritual presence in his stead.

**Aunty Alma** Aunty Alma is the woman after whom Yolo's former girlfriend, Alma, is named. When Alma was a baby, her mother was in touch with Aunty Alma, and the older woman assisted with Alma. Aunty Alma and Aunty Pearlua are wise old women who lead the gathering on the beach that Yolo attends while in Hawaii. The group of men who gather under the tutelage of the two aunts learn from the women how to nurture their health and also begin to understand that health is a part of their culture.

**Aunty Pearlua** Aunty Pearlua is an older woman who teaches hula. She is a *mahu*—a man who lives his life as a woman. She and Aunty Alma are the two women who lead the council of men on the beach who learn from the women how to heal their lives.

**Australian aborigines (two)** The novel refers to two unnamed Australian aboriginal characters who are in their 30s. One of the aborigines is blonde, and both of them are drug addicts. Yolo meets them in the council circle with Aunty Pearlua and Aunty Alma on the beach in Hawaii. The Australians function in the group as spiritual leaders to the other men. Along with the other men, they accept the challenge that the aunts pose to them to transform their lives.

**Charlie** Charlie is one of Kate's two sons and the brother of Henry. Charlie works for the aeronautical industry and is interested in the development of space colonies.

**Cheryl** Cheryl is one of the women on the boat during the rafting trip that Kate takes down the Colorado River.

**Cosmi** Cosmi is Armando the shaman's apprentice. He is a musician and accompanies Armando when he sings. Cosmi also works with the members of Kate's group who travel to the Amazon in search of answers to their life struggles.

**Gloria (Saartjie)** Gloria is a friend of Lalika, who enters the novel through a story that Lalika tells to Kate. Lalika confides to Kate that she killed a man as he was about to rape her best friend, Gloria. Following the murder, Gloria and Lalika were imprisoned, raped, and tortured by the authorities who imprisoned them. While incarcerated, the two were held in a dark cell, gang-raped, and beaten repeatedly over the course of months. Lalika believes the rapists taped the crimes and sold them all over the world. In order to survive, the two women depended on one another and began to rely on the visitation of the spirit of Saartjie Baartman, the historical South African woman who was displayed and exploited in Victorian England and France. The image of Baartman sustained the women, and they trained their thoughts on her to survive their experiences; they even began to call each other Saartjie. Gloria died after the two women left the prison.

**Grandmother (Grandmother Yagé)** *Grandmother* is a term that Kate and the others who travel with her to the Amazon use to represent the union of things and the source of ultimate knowledge. This access is unavailable to them except through the use of a certain plant called yage, which catalyzes their psychedelic experiences through meditation and guidance by a shaman named Armando. In the novel, Grandmother is the personification of a drug-induced trip, as well as an experience and a symbol.

**Henry** Henry is one of Kate's two sons. When she talks about Henry, Kate describes him as smoking marijuana and notes that he makes a living playing jazz music.

**Hugh** Hugh is a white man who is very wealthy and owns a tremendous amount of land that has been passed down to him through his family. Some of the land that his family owns used to be a part of an indigenous territory and sacred burial ground.

Hugh is a member of Kate's circle in the jungle who travel to visit Armando and to experience yage. He tells the group a story about an old Indian man with red-ribboned braids who periodically visited his land and took from the site a plastic bottle half filled with water. In an ancient ceremony, this old Indian man came to honor the bones from thousands of years ago that remained buried beneath a stream on Hugh's property. Hugh was most touched by this old man's devotion to his roots. Observation of the Indian's behavior causes Hugh to wonder about the role of devotion in his own life.

Hugh has some kind of illness, and although it is unnamed, there is some suggestion that he has HIV/AIDS. After the end of the retreat, Hugh says that he will visit Kate when she has her commitment ceremony with Yolo.

**Jerry** Jerry is a Hawaiian man whom Yolo encounters on the beach just after Yolo's arrival in Hawaii. After Jerry discovers the body of a dead boy, Jerry asks Yolo to stay with the body until he can get in touch with the authorities. Yolo later discovers that the corpse is the son of his ex-girlfriend, Alma. Jerry turns out to also be on a spiritual journey. Later in the novel, Jerry invites Yolo to attend the men's circle council led by Aunty Alma and Aunty Pearlua.

**Kate** Kate is the novel's central protagonist. Her parents were killed in a car accident when their car was hit by a train. In the beginning of the book, she notices and is concerned about her aging body, in which she is starting to feel uncomfortable. Simultaneously, Kate is losing her faith in Buddhism, and a number of factors in her life lead her to the conclusion that she is searching for some new awareness or sense of meaning that has thus far eluded her comprehension.

Catalyzed by a series of dreams about dry riverbeds, Kate tries to renew her faith and understanding by undertaking a rafting trip down the Colorado River. She tells her therapist that she is feeling a compelling pull toward something. In the novel, Walker creates an image of Kate standing next to the river, emptied of harmful feelings, pent-up words, and fluids as the canyon mirrors and metaphorizes the new spaces that are created by this hollowing-out.

One of the issues that Kate has to resolve and leave behind is the residual negativity from her first and longest marriage. Kate's first husband was abusive. While hiking, she told him she was planning to leave him, and he pushed her toward the edge of the cliff. After the precarious shove, he abandoned her on the hiking trail and took their truck home, though she had no ride herself and no money. After she arrived home to find him there asleep, he awoke and raped her on their couch.

In the novel's present time, Kate lives with Yolo, an artist who is her partner. Before their journeys begin, both members of the couple feel the need to separate in order to find their identities. One of the issues that divides them is Kate's reliance on her dreams as a source of information. Kate pays attention to her dreams and tries to understand them. She often sees figures representing her mother in her dreams, as well as symbols of nature such as rivers, mountains, and animals. She dreams of Hopi Indians. Snakes also frequent her dreams.

Another central aspect of the narrative involves the exploration of Kate's sexuality. She is openly bisexual, but in spite of her ambivalences about her sexuality and her relationship with Yolo, in the end, she decides to stay with Yolo. She also concludes her spiritual quest with the reassuring knowledge that she has all of the answers that she needs to adapt to aging and to cope with difficult personal and communal issues.

**Lalika** Lalika is a black woman from Mississippi whom Kate meets in the Amazon while on her retreat using yage to find the answer to the problems in her life. Lalika confides to Kate that she killed a man as he was about to rape her best friend, Gloria. Following the murder, Gloria and Lalika were imprisoned, raped, and tortured by the authorities who imprisoned them. While incarcerated, the two were held in a dark cell, gang-raped, and beaten repeatedly over the course of months. Lalika believes the rapists taped the crimes and sold them all over the world. In order to survive, the two women depended on one another and begin to rely on the visitation of the spirit of Saartjie Baartman, the historical South African woman who was displayed and exploited in Victorian England and France. The image of Baartman sustained the women, and they trained their thoughts on her to survive their experiences; they even began to call each other Saartjie. Gloria died after the two women left the prison.

These experiences and the memory of them haunt Lalika. She has come to the Amazon to heal from her multiple traumas, and part of that process involves opening up to Kate. Kate listens to Lalika, and they became friends. After they leave the Amazon, Kate invites Lalika to come to the commitment ceremony that she and Yolo hold.

**Leilani** *See* ALMA.

**Lolly** Lolly is a woman Kate married. Lolly took advantage of Kate's financial and material prosperity by trying to claim some of Kate's wealth as her own. Kate ended the relationship with Lolly because she felt exploited.

**Margery** Margery is one of the women on the boat during the rafting trip that Kate takes down the Colorado River.

**Missy** Missy is one of the women who is a member of the party who venture to the Amazon to work with the shaman Armando and use the hallucinogenic drug yage in search of answers to their most pressing life questions. Missy's problems derive from her experiences with incest perpetrated by her grandfather.

**Remus** Remus is one of Kate's ancestors. She has an extended interaction with him while on a drug given to her by the Amazonian shaman Armando. Remus presents himself to Kate as a toothless ex-slave. He comes to her in what she perceives as a dream. He tells her that the purpose of encounters with and remembrance of ancestors is to show the living the traps of particular kinds of behavior. Remus's tale cautions against vanity by demonstrating its negative consequences. The exchange between Kate and Remus also demonstrates that the relationship between the living and their ancestors does not only benefit the living but that the living have the ability to help to restore the dignity and relieve the suffering of those who are dead. Kate helps Remus to see that the pain he endured during life does not have to be eternal. She sets him free by showing him that he has all that he believes has been taken away from him.

**Rick** Rick is a member of the party who venture to the Amazon to work with Armando, the shaman, in order to use the hallucinogenic drug yage in search of answers to their most pressing life questions. Rick has a hard time submitting to Grandmother. He is a wealthy man who is conflicted by the sources of his family's money. His family was in the drug business, growing rich by selling drugs to black people and, consequently, destroying the neighborhoods in which their customers lived. Rick did not know this about his family until he discovered it for himself. When he discovered the truth about his family's complicity, his world shatters. Rick tells Kate and the others that he feels invisible. Kate watches Rick during the group's meditations one day. During the session, she says to him that she "sees him." This simple acknowledgment has a profound effect on Rick, and he seems to become immediately more grounded.

After the group leaves the Amazon, Rick decides that he will join the group reunion at Kate and Yolo's commitment ceremony.

**Saartjie** *See* GLORIA.

**Saartjie Baartman** Saartjie Baartman (1789–1815) was an African woman who was brought to Europe in the early 19th century to be displayed in sideshows because of the physical traits she possessed that Europeans considered to be unnaturally sexual, particularly her large breasts and buttocks and prominent labia. She was labeled the Hottentot Venus because the Koikhoi tribe—of which Baartman was a member—were called Hottentots by colonial whites. A slave to an Afrikaner farmer in what is now South Africa, Baartman was brought in 1810 to London, where she began touring throughout Britain in shows that required her to dance in ways to show off her buttocks. She was then sold to a French animal trainer, who forced her into further sideshow tours, this time through France. She was later treated as the subject of anthropological studies, especially by the renowned French naturalist Georges Cuvier. These studies often involved Baartman posing in the nude so that her image could be painted. When her novelty wore off in France, Baartman lost her source of income, and she spent her last years as a prostitute. She died at the age of 26.

In *Now Is the Time to Open Your Heart,* Walker uses Baartman as a goddess figure who appears in spirit form to two women who are undergoing torture. Baartman's presence is a balm to the women. They find solace in her story and conjure her image and presence when they are in the most dire of circumstances. The women even begin to call each other Saartjie.

**Sally** Sally is one of the women on the boat during the rafting trip that Kate takes down the Colorado River.

**Saul** Saul was Kate's "too-white" boyfriend at the time she met Yolo.

**Sue** Sue is Kate's favorite woman on the boat during the rafting trip down the Colorado River.

**Yolo** Yolo is Kate's lover. In the beginning of the novel, he seems to be more logically centered than Kate. He does not dream, and he does not understand the needs of Kate's body. Yolo is an artist, a painter. He misses Kate when she leaves to go on the Colorado River and then, later, to the Amazon.

When Kate leaves for the Amazon, Yolo travels on his own spiritual journey to Hawaii, where he meets an ex-lover, Alma, and makes friends with a group of men who teach him about abstinence from addictive substances. He swears off smoking but cannot do it for long. Kate supports him and, in the end, decides that the best course is for the two of them to continue to journey together. After Kate and Yolo separate to affirm and strengthen their individual spirits, their relationship is revitalized, and they decide to hold a commitment ceremony for themselves and their friends.

### Further Reading


Evans, Diana. "*Now Is the Time to Open Your Heart* by Alice Walker: Healing for a Hurting World." *Independent,* 5 November 2004, 12.

Kakutani, Michiko. "If the River Is Dry, Can You Be All Wet?" *New York Times,* 20 April 2004, p. B7.

Lobodziec, Agnieszka. "Alice Walker's *Now Is the Time to Open Your Heart* as a Womanist Novel." *Indian Review of World Literature in English* 5 (January 2009): 38–44.

McHenry, Susan. "The Gifts of the Grandmother Spirit: Alice Walker's Seventh Novel Examines the Questing Soul." *Black Issues Book Review* 6 (May/June 2004): 44–46.

———. "*Now Is the Time to Open Your Heart:* A Novel." *Black Issues Book Review* 6, no. 3 (May/June 2004): 44–45.

Simcikova, Karla. "Life and Its Survival: Walker's New Religion in *Now Is the Time to Open Your Heart.*" *Cuadernos de Literatura Inglesa y Norteamericana* 9 (May–November 2006): 37–46.

Walker, Alice. "*Now Is the Time to Open Your Heart.*" *Ms.* 14, no. 1 (Spring 2004): 74–78.


## *Possessing the Secret of Joy* (1992)

In this novel, Alice Walker directly confronts the issue of female genital mutilation. This is the third in a loose trilogy of Walker novels that include *The Color Purple* (1982) and *The Temple of My Familiar* (1989), although Walker has said that the novels are not sequels to each other. Characters from both previous novels appear in *Possessing the Secret of Joy.* The book's central character is Tashi, who came to the United States with Samuel, Nettie (Celie's sister), Olivia (Celie's daughter), and Adam (Celie's son) when the family left Africa after many years serving as missionaries to the Olinka people. Adam and Tashi are married by the time the family arrives in the United States and reunites with Celie. Tashi has also undergone the procedure of female genital mutilation.

*Possessing the Secret of Joy* spirals outward from that most pivotal moment in Tashi's life and moves in and out of time to trace the roots of the practice of female genital mutilation as well as to demonstrate the emotional, psychological, and physical impacts of this trauma on Tashi, her friends and family, other women who have had this done to them, communities who condone its practice, and those cultures that refuse to acknowledge and intervene on behalf of those women who unwillingly experience genital mutilation.

The novel was controversial and provoked disparate reactions. Janet Turner Hospital's review in the *New York Times* asserted that, at its best, the novel resonates with the voice and impact of Greek drama. Other critics felt that Walker's background as a prominent Western writer obscured the voices of the non-Western activists who had spoken out against the practice before her. She also was accused of writing without sufficient nuance regarding the different ways the procedure is practiced in different countries and the about the relationships between the ritual and colonialism, racism, sexism, and violence. Nonetheless, the novel became a best-seller, and along with Walker's follow-up on the subject in the form of the documentary and companion book *Warrior Marks: Female Genital Mutilation and the Sexual Blinding of Women,* it helped to bring worldwide awareness and attention to the subject of female genital mutilation.

## SYNOPSIS

*Possessing the Secret of Joy* begins with several epigraphs, one of which comes from *The Color Purple.* The action launches with an extract from the earlier book about the small, simple wedding of Nettie and Samuel. Nettie is the sister of Celie, the central character from *The Color Purple.* She is marrying Samuel, with whom she has been living with since she came to Africa with him; Corrine, his first wife; and his adopted children, Olivia and Adam, whose birth mother is Celie. Nettie went to Africa with Samuel and Corrine to help them with the children, though she did not know at first that the children under her care were actually her sister Celie's lost children. After some time in the African village of Olinka, Corrine died of a fever. Many years later, Samuel and Nettie fell in love and talked of marrying, but they would not do this without the children's consent. When the children gave their blessing, Nettie and Samuel were married in London, where the family had traveled to seek assistance for the Olinka.

The action of *Possessing the Secret of Joy* begins with this wedding, as described by Nettie in *The Color Purple,* and with Olivia's report to Nettie and Samuel about what has been affecting Adam's behavior so negatively during the entirety of their trip. She tells them that the problem is Tashi.

Tashi is a childhood friend of Olivia and Adam's. Over the years, she has become more like a sister to them, and Adam has fallen in love with his childhood friend, whom he wants to marry. Olivia tells Nettie that what concerns Adam is that, in his absence, Tashi plans to get the traditional markings of her tribe, permanently scarring her face. She also will undergo a clitoridectomy—the removal of her clitoris. According to Olivia, Tashi has decided that she should receive the traditional markings in support of her people, who suffer under the evergrowing encroachment of whites into their land, resources, and cultures. The ceremony she will undergo is supposed to be performed on younger women who are approximately 11 years old. Tashi is substantially older, and therefore the healing process will be more extensive, slow, and difficult.

### Part 1

#### Tashi

The body of the novel begins with the line "I did not realize for a long time that I was dead." This intriguing opening leads to the narrator's reminiscences about a story. The story is about a handsome panther named Lara who has a "co-wife and a husband." Lara is in the midst of a difficult time as a result of the affection between her husband and co-wife. She is an appendage to their relationship, a position that is intolerable to her. The co-wife,

Lala, is jealous of the little attention Lara gets from her husband, whose name is Baba. The situation is causing such conflict that Baba and Lala have begun to fight with each other physically.

Baba tries to explain to Lala that he has to copulate with their co-wife, Lara. It is his duty according to the rules of their community. He feels he has no choice in the situation. Lala tells Baba that she understands this rule to be the case, but the reality of their group's customs do not help her to ease the pain she feels over the situation.

Lara is particularly miserable as she is the castaway. She happens also to be pregnant. In this profound isolation and introspection, Lara generates an internal voice to assuage her loneliness. Eventually, the voice really begins to speak, and Lara finds herself listening to her most inner secret self. This voice protects her from dangers and gets her to once again love and appreciate herself. She sees her own reflection in a stream and begins to love her inner self.

When Baba sees Lara with her new self, he grows attracted to her and makes love to her. Lala is grief-stricken and becomes as jealous as Lara was about her. She cannot stand the happiness of Lara and Baba, and Baba and Lala fight all the time. Lara is no longer jealous or possessive. She falls in love with herself and spends her time admiring her reflection and enjoying her life.

### Olivia

Olivia reflects on the way that Tashi communicates and finds that she is not a person who confronts a topic head-on but circumvents the heart of the matter. Catherine is Tashi's mother, and she remembers her child always speaking in fables rather than in linear and clear trajectories. Tashi's storytelling gets her labeled as a troublemaker and difficult child in the village where she lives.

Olivia recalls the time that she and Tashi met. In this reminiscence, they are about six or seven years old, almost exactly the same age, and Tashi is crying. The meeting takes place shortly after the arrival of the missionaries Samuel and Corrine, who are accompanied by Olivia and Adam, and by Nettie, who will help Corrine and lend a hand with the children.

During the arrival ceremony, Olivia and Adam spot Tashi and are curious about why she weeps. Before too long, they lose track of the little girl, but they do not forget their inquisitiveness about her sorrow. They see many children but do not see Tashi, and they begin to wonder if the little girl has disappeared.

Adam and Olivia finally get a chance to meet their new friend several weeks later, when Catherine brings Tashi back to the village. She is dressed in a pink dress that seems out of place in a village in Africa. Tashi addresses Corrine and Samuel, calling Corrine "Mama Pastor." Later, Olivia and Adam learn about the reason Tashi cried so much during the arrival ceremony and then disappeared for weeks. It turns out that Tashi's sister died on the very same day that Olivia and Adam arrived. The child's name was Dura, and she died from blood loss, because there were no facilities to adequately address her bleeding. The details and circumstances of Tashi's sister's death have not been told to her, so Dura's passing remains a mystery to her sister. As a result of the secrecy, Tashi grows up terrified of the possibility that she might hurt herself and begin to bleed. Later, as an adult, Tashi remembers that the time leading up to her sister's death had been full of celebration and presents for the older girl. Tashi says that Dura had been her favorite sister.

### Tashi

Tashi remembers that there had been a scar at the corner of Dura's mouth from an accident that had happened around a fire when she was a baby. The infant had stuck a burning twig in her mouth, and the burn had caused it to stick to her lip. The older people who were watching the child did not remove the stick and help the child who reached out to them.

As an adult in therapy, Tashi tries to remember the story. What she recalls is the sound of the older people laughing at the child. She cannot remember her sister being helped. She wants to remember the child's rescue and soothing. Tashi resents the therapist who listens to her story. She feels that he is using what she tells him as evidence of a systemic problem in African culture and as support for what she assumes are his racist beliefs. Olivia has asked that Tashi go to therapy as she is concerned for her well-being.

### Olivia

Olivia notes that it is easy for most Americans to forget about Africa because they have never been there.

### Adam

Adams says that, unlike Olivia, he does not remember meeting Tashi as a child. He does remember the day that the family arrived in Olinka and seeing small boys who seemed to be around his age. The boys seemed nearly naked from his perspective, and he saw the women's breasts and the babies they carried on their back. As a child, he had stared until he had to be reminded that it was impolite to do so. In spite of having all of these memories of the day, he cannot recall Tashi and the tears that Olivia says were streaming down the little girl's face. Rather, he remembers her as a laughing little child with endless energy, happily engaged in the tasks at hand. Adam is puzzled by the differences in his and Olivia's memories and is uncertain about the ramifications of his not being accurate.

### Tashi

Tashi remembers being told not to cry. Even when her sister died, she was supposed to put on a public face to welcome the strangers who were coming to live in their village. Tashi felt alienated from the women who gave her these admonitions. She could not understand their lack of emotion at the loss of her sister. She did not understand why everyone did not share her feelings and, if they did, why they did not express their emotions about her young sister's death.

Eventually she asked her mother if they could leave the celebration and return home, and they did. They went back home under the ruse of tending the crops, but they stayed much longer, allowing Tashi time to grieve the loss of her sister. She recalls that she never knew anyone who worked as hard as her mother or had more grace when doing so. She had told her daughter that she worked so hard in order to fill empty spaces within. Like Tashi, Catherine was also profoundly affected by the death of her older daughter but did not show it in overt ways, only in the subtle nuances of sorrow that her daughter Tashi could see.

### Tashi

As Tashi sits in therapy, she reflects on the psychiatrist's assertion that "Negro" women are the most difficult patients. The therapist is surprised that Tashi only has one child. This reaction prevents Tashi from bring entirely honest with the man about her other "lost" children. He continues saying that the reason that "Negro women" are not good patients is because they refuse to blame their mothers for their problems. Tashi does not understand and thinks again about the contours of her mother's life and suffering, the way that, after carrying a basket on her head for many miles, the mark from where the basket rested would remain on her mother's head. For some women, Tashi remembers, the mark remains permanent.

Tashi remembers that her mother told her that her delivery was premature because her mother had been frightened by a leopard that had crossed her path while she was walking. Tashi begins to imagine the life of the leopard and the details of its existence. She knows that the leopard's mate and children were killed and skinned, and she can conjure the pain of that experience for the cat and feel connected to it as a result. When she has these reflections, she goes into a kind of trance that used to cause children to tease her when she was a girl.

### Tashi

Tashi recalls when she went off to the Mbeles to receive the ceremonial scarring. In her memory, Olivia desperately attempts to stop her with any argument that she thinks might change her best friend's mind. But Olivia's pleas do not change Tashi's mind, and she rides off into the forest on the back of a donkey the Mbeles have sent for her journey. Before she leaves, she insults Olivia and tells her that although she is black, she is not an African. She also says that Olivia has been arrogant in her sense of superiority. After the conversation, Olivia thinks that Tashi hates her and lets her go. Tashi goes to participate in the scarification ceremony as a gesture of solidarity with her people, who she feels are disappearing and losing the core of who they have been for centuries. She does regret that her actions are so hurtful to Olivia.

### Tashi

Tashi is in the middle of another therapy session when the psychiatrist asks her about her dreams. She lies and tells him that she does not have dreams because she does not want to reveal her recurring nightmare.

### Adam

The therapist tells Adam that Tashi, whom he knows by her American name, Evelyn, will not tell him about her dreams. Adam is uncomfortable in the therapist's presence and feels mistrustful of both the man and his questions. He thinks of the panic that overcame Tashi during the night and what she told him of her dream. Tashi said that in the dream she is in a narrow structure that has many levels and is dark and cold inside. She feels as if she has wings and that they are broken by her presence in the structure. She is also being operated on, with things being inserted and removed from her.

Adam says that he did not anticipate marrying Tashi but feels that they have ended up together because they are so used to each other from childhood. They broke Olinka tradition by making love in the fields and as a result remained undiscovered.

Adam tries to focus on the doctor's words and tells the man that Tashi dreams of having her wings broken by someone. Who the violator is, Adam does not know. He remembers the pleasure of their first sexual encounters, when he performed oral sex on her and they both derived satisfaction from the act while avoiding the specter of possible pregnancy.

### Adam

Adam remembers not being happy for Samuel and Nettie when they married. He reflects on his misery about Tashi and his inability to share with anyone his feelings of concern for the childhood playmate he has come to love as a woman. He left London after the wedding to get his mind off of Tashi and traveled to Paris to visit his old friend Lisette.

Lisette had visited Olinka when she was young, and she and Adam became fast friends. Adam found her with little trouble in Paris and discovered that as an adult, she has been working as a teacher. Lisette told Adam that she has lost faith in the religion that brought her family to Olinka when she was a child. She is now disillusioned with the church's gendered hierarchies. Adam reflects on his relationship with Tashi and feels that it is a relationship of equals and is drenched in mutual pleasure.

## Part 2

### Tashi

This chapter begins with Tashi in court and undergoing questioning about her purchase of a razor. She has a hard time answering questions in a straightforward manner and thinks that to do so is antithetical to her nature.

Tashi tries in her circuitous way to explain the reasons why she is on trial. She reflects on a trip she made with Adam to Sweden and how orderly the landscape was there. The trip and the memory of it is an association for her with the trial because she recalls seeing a beautiful razor while on the trip. She thinks of other trips she and Adam have made, like the trip to America for the first time, and of their different responses to racism. Adam finds himself defensive and hostile, while Tashi sees racism and racist behavior not as an affront to her but as a reflection on the lives of the people perpetrating the hostility.

### Adam

When the family returns from Samuel and Nettie's wedding and their mission of getting some help for the Olinkas, Adam sets off to find Tashi. When he finds her, he is alarmed at the change in her. Tashi's expression is lifeless and without her characteristic animation. In order to recover his love, Adam has had to traverse difficult and inhospitable terrain. He has had a terrible time trying to communicate as there are many languages spoken by the various tribes he has encountered. He is finally able to communicate with the Mbeles when they find a common word, the word for water. The Mbeles bring an Olinkan to him, and he learns from the young man that Tashi is indeed in the camp and is ill. When he sees her, she has the scarification marks and is busy weaving baskets. She tells Adam that he should not have come. He asks her, "Where else should I be?" His response destroys her reserve, and she accepts his presence and love.

### Tashi

When Adam arrives, despite her harsh demeanor, Tashi is profoundly relieved. She had been hoping for Adam's rescue.

## Part 3

### Evelyn

Tashi is in the care of a spiritual advisor she calls the Old Man. He tells her that her pain is in some ways self-inflicted. She trusts him and seems to feel that he will soon die.

### Adam

Adam is alarmed to discover that Tashi has been cutting herself. One morning he awakens to find the bottom half of the couple's bed soaked with blood. Without being conscious of her actions, Tashi has sliced circles, like chains, around her ankles.

### Evelyn

Tashi thinks again of her trip to Switzerland and of the place where she and Adam stayed. The older man who owned the house was kind, and he fed Tashi and Adam well. Tashi called him their last hope, and he corrected her, saying that they are their own last hope.

### Evelyn

The Old Man encourages Tashi to draw. She recalls on paper the meeting between her mother and the leopard that was the catalyst for her early arrival in the world. She creates a leopard with two legs and depicts her mother with four. She tells the Old Man that she did not know why she did this.

### Evelyn

Tashi learns from Benny that there is a legal controversy about whether she can be put on trial by the Olinka government as she is now a U.S. citizen. Tashi thinks fondly about the United States, and she remembers feeling safe there. In Olinka, she feels the echoes of the fears and deprivations of her childhood. Although she will probably stand trial if extradited to the United States, the chances are that the charges would be dismissed.

### Evelyn-Tashi

Benny is Tashi and Adam's child. He was a large baby, and it took several surgical instruments to extract him from Tashi's womb. Adam was so embarrassed when the obstetrician pointed out this fact that he could not speak or touch Tashi's hand.

### Tashi-Evelyn

The birth of Tashi and Adam's son, Benny, causes a rift between Tashi and Adam that feels to her like the wave of a sonic boom, which is alternately silent and deafening.

### Tashi-Evelyn

Tashi describes the attempts she and Adam make to have sexual intercourse. He is unable to penetrate her, and she bleeds each time he tries. Nonetheless, she becomes pregnant. The pregnancy is traumatic for the couple as they understand that the birth will be extremely difficult for Tashi. She becomes a kind of medical curiosity for the Western doctors and nurses who have never seen genitals that have undergone a clitoridectomy. Adam stops the spectacle soon after Benny's birth, and Tashi is allowed to rest and to concentrate on becoming a mother to her newborn son.

The medical repairs performed on Tashi after the birth allow her to have more normal functioning than she did prior to the birth. Benny's brain is damaged by the birth, and the child is mentally challenged, a reality Tashi does not comprehend until many years later.

### Adam

The narrative flashes back in time to Tashi's clitoridectomy. When he arrives at the Mbele camp, Adam finds the Olinka midwife, M'Lissa, attending to Tashi as best she can. M'Lissa speaks of the kind of care Tashi would have received in the past, when the old ways were still enforced, but that day has passed, and M'Lissa has to tend to Tashi alone and to the best of her ability as an older woman. She is so old that Adam cannot imagine how she even managed to arrive at such an isolated location. She cares for Tashi as best she can and speaks of the girl's healing rather than her injury. M'Lissa has been working in the capacity of a doctor in the rebel camp.

M'Lissa tells Adam that there is a proper age for the clitoridectomy, which is right after birth or at five or six years old. Tashi had the operation of her own volition, when she is too old to heal from it. Adam says he still wants to marry Tashi, even though she has had this operation.

Tashi has the operation so that she can bind herself to the traditions of her people. The price of her act of solidarity is terrible. She walks bent over like an older woman and takes more than 15 minutes to urinate. She is permanently damaged.

### Olivia

Like Adam, Olivia notes that Tashi is a different person upon her return to Olinka, one who has lost her lightness of spirit, energy, and fresh hopefulness. She is no longer sprightly and seems to be devoid of joy, a joy that had permeated her very being prior to the operation. Adam returns Tashi to Olinka just before the family is set to return to America. He is determined to marry her, and, so that she will not be embarrassed by her scars, he has scarification marks inscribed on his face so they will both experience the same response from the world. Tashi also has an awful odor that comes from the complete closing of her vaginal opening and the backing up of all of her excretions. When the family arrives in the United States, doctors are able to help her to clean out the backed-up fluid more effectively.

## Part 4

### Tashi

Tashi again remembers the trip to Switzerland. The Old Man takes her and Adam sailing, and he becomes ageless behind the wheel of the boat. As she rides over the waters, Tashi seems to come alive, a transformation noted by both Adam and The Old Man.

### Tashi-Evelyn

In Switzerland, The Old Man plays music for Adam and Tashi. His record collection spans the globe, and they also see films of his various trips to the places from which the music comes. While watching the film, Tashi faints. The room in which she recovers has a picture of a fighting cock. The picture inspires her to do a series of paintings of fighting cocks. In one of the paintings, Tashi depicts a foot that holds within its grasp something small that the cock wants. Creating the painting makes her physically ill. The Old Man asks her whether the foot belongs to a man or a woman. She cannot answer his question.

Tashi also creates other paintings, one of which is called "Crazy Road" and is based on a pattern she learned when she was a child. This time, the foot that she creates in the painting is a woman's foot. She also paints a row of children, all of whom are approximately the age her sister Dura was when she died. Tashi recognizes that Dura is not depicted in the group. She imagines that the foot in the painting belongs to M'Lissa, and she envisions the foot tossing up its bounty and eating the crumbs. Tashi imagines the healing woman throwing vulvas from between her toes.

### Adam

Adam writes to Lisette about his hunger for her. He writes to Lisette from Switzerland, where he and Tashi visit with The Old Man, who happens to be Lisette's uncle. Adam tells Lisette that her advice to take Evelyn (Tashi) to the house was wise and that Evelyn seems more comfortable and at ease than he has seen her in some time. He also tells her about her uncle's films and Evelyn's fainting episode, during which he and The Old Man initially thought that Evelyn has died. Later, they are happy to find that she is all right and has fully recovered.

Adam continues with his letter, telling Lisette about Evelyn's paintings and particularly of the final painting that is on The Old Man's walls.

He also tells Lisette that Evelyn has begun to fling herself at the wall, and he becomes concerned that the woman he loves is truly in a battle against evil. Thinking about what he has seen prompts his letter to Lisette and his sleeplessness. He closes the letter with gratitude for her support and friendship.

### Tashi

Tashi calls her painting "The Beast," and she falls into a profound sleep. Creating the painting is a kind of exorcism for Tashi. After it is completed, she feels that she has somehow brought forth a representation of her anxieties that makes everything more tangible. When she realizes that the foot of the beast belongs to M'Lissa, she understands that it represents the harm that the woman perpetrated on Tashi.

As Tashi contemplates the painting, Adam walks in with food. They discuss the meal he has prepared for her, and she apologizes for the mess she has made of the walls of their host's house. Through her frenetic production of the painting, Tashi is able to recall the trauma of her sister Dura's death.

Tashi was there and witnessed what she now calls the murder of her sister. She says that the people performing the ceremony did not know that Tashi was hiding in the grass out of curiosity and concern for her sister. The film she saw earlier that belonged to The Old Man, also known as Mzee, had reminded her of the place where her sister's initiation ceremony had taken place. Tashi feels that she will never be free of the sound of her sister's screams. She feels comforted by the knowledge and memory of the truth.

### Mzee

Mzee writes to Lisette about the recovery of a name he has not been called since before he was an old man. The name is Mzee, which means "the old man" in a Kenyan dialect. The Old Man, whose actual name is Carl, tells his niece that having Adam and Tashi with him is a revelation to him and has made him understand his life and work in new ways that feel connected to a larger reality and truth.

## Part 5

### Olivia

In the novel's present, Tashi is in a prison that is quite old and is Victorian in style and sensibility. The town that the prison is located in is layered with the past and even has a street called White Ladies Lane. Olivia notes all of these details as she goes to see Tashi in prison. Part of the prison is now used to house AIDS patients who seem to increase exponentially in number. She kids with Adam as the two enter this fortress of misery that she wants to go home. Adam agrees as the two continue their progress toward Tashi's cell.

### Bentu Moraga (Benny)

Benny says to his mother that money is the only force that actually creates change. She tells him not to feel that way and that his thinking is not rooted in the truth of what Africa once was. Tashi recognizes that Benny is right from her observations about the hierarchies in the prison.

Benny acknowledges that there are some activities in which he will not be able to participate. He cannot drive and was not particularly successful in school because he is not skilled at remembering details. He has to have lists so that he can keep track of what he is doing. He cannot really keep information in his head.

One thing he does not forget is the smell of his mother. He is happiest when he is by her side. He does not tell his mother how much he loves the way that she smells because he is able to perceive that such a statement might be misperceived by her; she might get the wrong impression and think, perhaps, that he is referring to a bad smell. Even as a middle-aged man, Benny likes to cuddle with his mother, but she does not allow him to do so anymore.

Benny also says that if he wants to have a conversation with his parents, he has to prepare notes as if he were taking an exam.

### Adam

In a past summertime, Lisette and Adam are at Lisette's house and relaxing in her garden. Lisette is knitting with wool, and Adam comments that it is too warm to be working with wool. Lisette replies that she is knitting a pair of socks for a very small pair of feet, and thus she tells Adam about her pregnancy with his child. The two have been friends and sporadic lovers for many years, and Adam was always careful to ensure that she did not become pregnant by almost always avoiding sexual contact with her, with the exception of a few moments of weakness. During one such moment, their child was conceived.

Adam erroneously assumes that Lisette will abort the child—a presumption that enrages Lisette. She tells him that his child was conceived the previous April when he had come to visit her after Tashi had run away.

### Lisette

Lisette gives birth to Adam's son at her family's house. The birth is a wonderful and spiritual experience for Lisette and for her parents, who after some disagreement and disapproval come to accept her decision to have Adam's child. Adam is not there, and Lisette misses him, but his absence does not diminish her pleasure. Later, he says he did not come to the birth because he did not want to hurt Tashi, who knew when the birth was supposed to occur.

## Part 6

### Tashi-Evelyn

Part 6 begins with Tashi's trial. She sees her family in the courtroom; they are there to support her. On this hot morning the testimony is about Tashi's journey on the day she commits the crime for which she is on trial. There were witnesses who saw her buying razors, fruit, and paper for printing signs. She chose paper in the national colors of the country to make the signs because she wanted to make a point about the problem she was trying to expose being an internal one rather than one stemming from colonialism. Tashi is distracted during the trial and has a hard time focusing on the details of the proceedings.

The trial reveals that Tashi wrote a series of cryptic signs that warn against self-deception. A young woman who testifies says that she saw Tashi making the signs and was intrigued by their messages. She tells Tashi to be careful. Although the woman does not acknowledge it in court, she is afraid of the consequences of speaking out against the current government.

Tashi remembers writing the signs and feeling very happy about their honesty and about the courage it took for her to commit such a public act of defiance. She sees her act of writing as a counterweight to the commercialization of the place and the intrusion of the messages she reads on billboards, which have become the people's primary texts.

At the end of the trial, Olivia hands her a small paper bag. Tashi opens it when she returns to her cell and finds a small figurine that is identical to one she once found in M'Lissa's hut. The figurine depicts a woman masturbating. As a child, Tashi was told that the figurine was obscene. She now understands it to be a sign of resistance.

## Part 7

### Evelyn

The action returns to the past. After the Old Man dies, Tashi goes to an African-American therapist whose name is Raye. The Old Man had met Raye and felt that she would be a good person for Tashi to continue working with after he passed away. Tashi is prepared to not like the woman because she is not her beloved Mzee. She also resents the woman's relative wellness.

Tashi speaks to Raye about the man she calls Our Leader. She thinks of this figure as someone who was like Nelson Mandela and was exiled but managed to get his messages back home to his people, for whom he became a much-loved and respected figure. Eventually, he was imprisoned and then killed on the eve of the nation's independence. Tashi tells the therapist that Our Leader was a kind of Christ figure to her and her people. It was the admonitions of Our Leader that in part convince Tashi that undergoing the female initiation ritual was a good idea. He told the people that it was essential to maintain the old ways of being, and she believed that she was doing so by succumbing to the initiation procedures.

She talks through the trauma with Raye and tells her all of the details. She says that there are a number of myths that convince women the procedure is a good one. One in particular says that if a woman does not have the operation, she will not be able to have sex with her husband. Women are kept from honest knowledge about their bodies and so cannot refute the myths that they learn as facts from childhood. Tashi explains that she did not go through this ritual in childhood and was made to feel ashamed of her body and her emerging womanhood. She was ridiculed, as if something was terribly wrong with her.

Tashi also remembers that she felt pleasure in her genitals before the operation, and that when Adam performed oral sex on her, she always had an orgasm. She tells Raye that she was willing to forego all that she knew of pleasure to become what she understood to be an authentic Olinkan woman. She also felt that as a result of her close ties with Corrine, Samuel, Nettie, and Adam, many of the Olinka viewed her with suspicion. She returns to the influential absence/presence of Our Leader and his constant admonitions that the actions of individuals were critical to the survival of the whole, and that all Olinkans must conform to the old ways in order to save the nation. He told women that great warriors would never marry a woman who was not circumcised.

Tashi says that Adam was not her choice for a husband and that she married him because he was sweet, good, and familiar. She feels that she never had a choice in the matter of who would become her husband. She also feels that the boulder she has carried since witnessing her sister's initiation/murder has not only loosened from her spirit but has begun to roll away all together. She says that she fell in love with the ideal Olinkan man Our Leader, who to her youthful, romantic soul was akin to Jesus Christ.

### Adam

Adam has a different take on Our Leader. He remembers him as a kind of superhero to whom the people turned instead of working together to outline realistic strategies and goals that might bring more effective change in their lives. Even the absence of a real name increased his mysticism. The name "Our Leader" came about after the white regime made it a crime to say his name out loud. Adam remembers that fervent belief in Our Leader had made their missionary work somewhat futile and dangerous as the Olinkans had a near-religious devotion to their martyred leader.

## Part 8

### Lisette

Pierre, Lisette and Adam's child, is now 17 and has finished his primary schooling. His only desire is to travel to the United States and be with his father. Pierre is a beautiful child whose racial identity easily passes as Algerian in France. Lisette sends her son to Harvard to ensure that he gets the best education and that he can fulfill his dreams of being closer to his father.

Evelyn, as Lisette calls Tashi, was furious when she learned of her pregnancy and the birth of her son with Adam. The news of the child's existence was the catalyst for Tashi's suicide attempt; she even talked about murdering Benny. Lisette tells the other side of the story of colonialism, of her family having to leave their lives in Algeria, which had become home, and also of the guilt of the violence and exploitation that was associated with the French occupation and departure.

As a child, the return to France had been painful for Lisette, who loved her life in Algeria. She believes that her father found in his grandson Pierre a similarity to the Algerian boys who had been his parishioners in Algeria, and thus he found an immediate and healing connection with the boy, whom he was able to understand. Pierre reminded the family of their experiences in Algeria and of their fond and genuine memories and interactions with people there. Lisette's mother was particularly fond of Pierre, and she started to grow away from the racist assumptions that had controlled her life prior to the birth of her grandson.

### Evelyn

In a therapy session, Tashi tells Raye about her tendency to live in a world of stories. She says that without them, she would not have been able to understand her life with any accuracy. She says that she believes that perhaps storytelling has functioned for people as a way of masking the truth to make it bearable. The sessions with Raye are more productive as Tashi grows to trust the therapist.

Once, after she has had gum surgery, Raye says to Tashi that she cannot begin to imagine what the pain of her surgeries must have been like. Tashi begins to believe that Raye will help guide her on her journey to wholeness and that they are compatriots in the struggle, and she silently thanks The Old Man.

### Pierre

Pierre receives a sweater from his mother on each of his birthdays. He loves to see what she makes for him, and he loves that she has made each one with her own hands. Pierre is an avid reader and reads widely from the African-American canon. He reads authors from James Baldwin to Richard Wright. He thinks of these authors as family members, uncles who will help him to navigate the American world he is about to enter.

Lisette comments on how fast the time has gone. Pierre loves his life and his happy existence with his mother. He knows that he can depend on her. Lisette tells her son that "men don't remember things that don't happen to them." Pierre does know Adam, who comes to visit his son twice a year, in the fall and in the spring, for two weeks each time. Pierre is a bit distressed that his father is never there for his birthdays, as visits during that time cause problems for his father's wife, Tashi. He knows also about his half brother, Benny, and has seen pictures of Benny as well as Tashi, whom Pierre knows as Evelyn.

When Pierre sees photographs of his brother, he wonders if he will ever have a relationship with him. Adam tells Pierre about Benny's limitations, and Pierre is gratified to know that his father thinks of him as intelligent.

Lisette tells Pierre about the way that she and his father, Adam, met. She shares with him the details of her visit to Africa and about the young man she found so compelling. She tells him the story of Old Torabe, a dying man whom Adam cared for at the request of his father. Adam was not happy about having to care for the man and so was grateful for the company and distraction that Lisette provided.

Lisette tells the story of Torabe's life—that he had many wives and a history of negative interactions with them, including the fact that several of them died under mysterious circumstances. One wife ran away to her parents after marrying Torabe. She told her parents that the man cut her genitalia and would not let her mend from the injury. The father acquiesced to patriarchal notions of responsibility and told his wife that his daughter had to return to her husband no matter the circumstance.

Torabe was cast out of the village because he was no longer the voice of authority over his wife's behavior. The girl killed herself, and the villagers refused to bury her body. Lisette tells Pierre that Adam does not remember what the two of them talked about while he was tending the dying man. She remembers that she shared with him the story of a woman whom she knew when her family lived in Algeria and who was in a situation similar to Torabe's wife. The woman's name was Ayisha, and she sought the assistance of Lisette's family one evening when she understood fully what marriage would entail in terms of the mutilation of her body. Lisette was horrified about the circumstances women find themselves in around the world. She understands the dangerous ends to which cultures go to ensure that female sexuality is completely policed.

Lisette tells her son that her involvement with Ayisha and her knowledge of the woman's story and suffering are enough for her to never marry and subject herself to any control or oppression resulting from inherent gender inequity. She also tells him that her family returned Ayisha to her parents, and none of them ever found out what happened to the woman.

A quip her son makes about the marquis de Sade reminds Lisette that although violent mutilation of women's genitals is not a common occurrence in France, it certainly is not without precedent. Lisette reflects on her son's observations.

## Part 9

### Evelyn

Tashi confesses that she finds no problem in opening and reading the letters that Lisette and Adam send to each other. After reading their correspondence for years, Tashi finds Lisette to be autonomous and secure in her personhood and walks in the world in ways that Tashi can only imagine.

Even though he lies and tells her that he is going to a conference, Tashi knows that Adam is going to see Pierre in Massachusetts. She does not feel that the boy is a threat, since she and Adam live in California. Then Tashi learns that Lisette is terminally ill and has requested that Pierre transfer to Berkeley to be close to his father. Tashi's rage takes on new manifestations as she begins slapping strangers and abusing Benny by hitting the boy about the ears.

One day Tashi is looking outside when she sees Pierre get out of a taxi and share a congenial moment with the driver. Tashi approaches the young man and begins to pelt him with stones she says she has collected since the day she first found out that he was conceived. The cab driver rescues Pierre from the attack. Tashi's response to the violence she has perpetrated is to laugh. Pierre's suitcases remain behind as a witness to their owner's quick visit and unanticipated reception. Tashi makes certain that her stepson's luggage winds up in the street.

## Part 10

### Evelyn

The action returns to Olinka and to a bus ride Tashi is on while traveling to visit M'Lissa. M'Lissa has become a national hero for her work assisting the overthrow of the past government. M'Lissa appears to have stopped aging and is considered to be a good omen for the state of the nation. After a period of paralysis, she has begun to walk again, and she cooks and tends her own garden. Tashi does not view M'Lissa's longevity and vigor as a sign of holiness. Rather, she interprets it as a sign of the woman's evil and dangerous influence and practices.

### Tashi-Evelyn

At the house where M'Lissa lives, there is a national flag that towers above the roof. Tour buses frequent the location, but peering tourists must keep moving as no walking around the site is allowed. In spite of these precautions, Tashi manages to circumvent the security forces and make it to M'Lissa's porch. On the porch, a woman greets her and asks why she is there. Tashi tells the truth—that she has known M'Lissa for all of her life, that the woman was a central figure in every aspect of life in the village she grew up in, and that she had a profound effect on her personal life. She gives her mother's name in order for the woman to gain permission from M'Lissa for Tashi to enter the house and to see her face-to-face. By the way the woman walks, Tashi can tell that she also has undergone the initiation ceremony for women.

Tashi gains permission to see M'Lissa and to visit with her alone. Before entering M'Lissa's house, Tashi asks the gatekeeper, Mbati, what people want when they come to visit M'Lissa. The young girl tells her that mostly women come to visit M'Lissa. She is for them a real connection with the past that they feel is lost and that they mourn.

When M'Lissa sees Tashi, although she is gracious, the old woman is also suspicious and alert to the possibility that the visit may not be entirely reverential.

## Part 11

### Evelyn

The young woman Tashi speaks with when she enters M'Lissa's house, Mbati, is called to the witness stand during Tashi's trial. The young woman appears to Tashi as a long-lost daughter. Tashi has a moment of fantasy in which she tells the young woman that she is her mother, and Mbati responds with delight and instant adoration and love.

In reality, Mbati is telling the people in the courtroom about Tashi's arrival at M'Lissa's house and that she had no reason to believe that the woman had anything but sincere intentions. She shares her recollections, saying that M'Lissa had validated the relationship with Tashi and had agreed to have the visitor come to her side. M'Lissa also told Mbati that the two women needed time alone to speak together about the past.

Mbati acknowledges that not only had she left the women alone, she left the house altogether. Mbati says that she received M'Lissa's encouragement to leave and that she felt that she had been leaving M'Lissa in safe and secure hands. Mbati and Tashi share a glance. Tashi perceives that the other woman does not look at her with hatred or judgment.

### Evelyn

Tashi expresses compassion for her husband and feels for all of the suffering she caused him through the years and at this moment. Adam tells the court about Tashi's history and explains that all that had been done to her is the foundation for her crime. The people gathered in the courtroom are angry when Adam begins to speak about the mutilation Tashi experienced. They shout that he is an American and has no right to comment on the sacred practices of the people from whom Tashi comes.

Adam appears to be close to breaking down emotionally. The crowd continues to yell that Tashi has killed an invaluable representative of the best of Olinkan culture and that there is no defense for her actions. It takes some time for the judges to be able to enforce calm and quiet in the courtroom. When it is finally silent again, Tashi is once again in a reverie about the past.

She thinks that it is curious that she never met Lisette before she died. She remembers Lisette's many attempts over the course of years to communicate with Tashi. She also thinks that if Lisette really understood her, she would never have sent her precious son to Tashi.

The pattern of reaching out to Tashi that had been established by Lisette was continued by her son. Pierre wrote Tashi letters while he was at Berkeley, even after she pelted him with stones asking her to contemplate the possibility of their establishing a cordial and functional relationship. He expressed compassion for her and for her recurring nightmare of imprisonment in a tower. He said that he thought he understood the representational nuances of the tower, although not its precise meaning. He sincerely tried to reach out to her.

### Adam

In the courtroom, while he is undergoing the spectators' verbal abuse, Adam recognizes the fear that manifests in people's inability to hear the truth about their lives. He feels that they do not want to see that the practices they regard as sacred are in fact devastating their women and, in a more general sense, their entire culture.

Adam recalls his father, Samuel, and the thoughtful consideration that he would require his son to give to such complex issues. He recognizes that there is a need to see the pain and suffering of each individual, particularly those who consider you to be an enemy, and to see the child that exists inside them. He thinks of Torabe—of his misery as he was dying and of his misapprehensions of love, of women, and ultimately of himself.

Adam thinks of the men in the room and wonders if they might understand the problem with the ritual if they were threatened with having their penises excised. He feels like a father to all of the women who have experienced this kind of mutilation and yet do not feel that they have the authority to speak out against it or to make public their private anguish.

Adam faces the question of whether his wife is sane. He says yes, but Tashi's erratic laughter at that moment undermines the validity of his assertion.

### Evelyn-Tashi

Tashi is certain that her persecutors are attempting to take away her access to the United States. She says that she will not let that happen—that the way to ensure that something can be prevented is to believe in its impossibility and therefore to negate its existence.

### Adam

When Adam meets with Raye, she tells him that women who come to see her often talk about the fact that their male partners are sexually involved with someone else. She says that most women who seek her services with this complaint end up developing some type of sexual dysfunction. Raye wonders if it is not some kind of mental circumcision.

Adam replies that he does not have any useful knowledge about what she asks. He says he has never thought of what happened to Tashi to be one example of a larger and much more enveloping cascade of pain.

## Part 12

### Tashi-Evelyn

Part 12 begins with a story from a French anthropologist, Marcel Griaule, told to him by an African man. In this story, a god named Amma takes a lump of clay and throws it, and, as a consequence, the clay begins to cover the earth. The god of the tale, Amma, attempts to initiate sexual relations with the earth. This interaction is a major and primary transgression against the rules of the universe. The earth rebels against the attempted penetration, and Amma has to destroy the earth's sex organ in order to have intercourse.

This story is read by Pierre from Griaule's book: Pierre sits in Tashi's living room reading to her and to Benny. Tashi feels drugged and is confused about Pierre's presence and her lack of hatred toward him. She tries to piece together what is happening and gets a bit lost in the feeling of being out of touch with reality. The explanation that Pierre reads from the book about the removal of the earth's sexual organ justifies circumcision because it maintains that the operation helps to avoid gender confusion and allows for men and women to identify more closely with their true maleness or femaleness.

Pierre and Benny leave the house, and Pierre takes Benny to a basketball game. While the two are out, Tashi picks up the book and reads additional historical justifications of the violence of sexual mutilation.

### Adam

Adam regrets that Pierre has never married and seems perfectly content to spend his time with Benny. Pierre has graduated from college and graduate school and has become an anthropologist. Adam says that he can find the essence of Lisette in their son. He misses her but can bear her absence when he thinks of their son. His admonitions to Pierre about getting married fall on deaf ears. Pierre tells his father that his work is his top priority and that there is no need for him to marry because he is happy the way that he is. He even claims that his work, rather than producing actual children, will make the lives of children more bearable. He wants to get to the heart of the fears of children and attempt to understand them.

Adam and Pierre go on a hike where they have an extended talk about Pierre's life and work as well as his emotional and love life. Pierre tries to explain to his father that he believes that he is pansexual and does not need to categorize his attractions. He also says that clitoridectomy is about male insecurity and arrogance. He believes that the men who insist upon having the women in their communities circumcised do it because they need to reassure themselves that any pleasure the women experience is generated by the penetration of the vagina by the penis, not through the relative agency and independence of the clitoris.

## Part 13

### Evelyn

Tashi remembers a television show she used to watch called *Riverside.* The show was about a psychiatric hospital. Amy reminds Tashi of a character who was on that show.

Tashi does not know why Amy, whom she has just met, has been included in one of her sessions with Raye. Raye tells Tashi that she particularly wants her to meet Amy. Tashi, as usual, is distracted and cannot focus on what is being said. She does discern that Amy has a son named Josh.

Amy tells Tashi a story about Josh, who was a dancer and who committed suicide when he was in his 30s. She also talks about how her perpetual jolliness drove her husband away. She gets her personality honestly. Her mother had the same kind of unrelenting, unbearable false cheer.

Tashi notices that the woman's age cannot be determined by looking at her and that she seems surprisingly fit. Amy shares that the depression that killed her son may well have come from her. She tells Tashi that her parents were so disturbed about her masturbatory behavior as a young child that they had her clitoris excised surgically.

Tashi does not believe Amy's story and is angry at what she perceives as Raye's duplicity. She gets up to leave the therapy session, and Raye and Amy try to stop her. Amy tells Tashi about African-American women and white American women who have experienced the same procedure that she had. Amy also shares more of her own story and tells Tashi and Raye how her mother added insult to injury by telling her daughter while she was recovering that the injury she experienced and the pain she was feeling came from having her tonsils removed.

Amy says that she went through adolescence, young adulthood, and middle age pretending that everything was all right. This moving story does not have Raye's intended effect on Tashi. Tashi leaves the office and remembers only the parts of the story that do not challenge her and make her think about her own recovery in different terms.

## Part 14

### Evelyn-Tashi

There are demonstrations in the prison where Tashi is held. She can look out of her window and view the protesters below. Olivia attributes the protests to a limited group of ideologically immobile individuals who cannot bear the thought of a challenge to their ideas, particularly if that challenge comes from an American woman. She tells Tashi that there are women from all over the country who have come to celebrate her courage in challenging mutilation. They create a kind of shrine to her in celebration of her willingness to fight for what she believes, bringing flowers, seeds, and food and singing her praises. Those who do not support Tashi have been attacking the women and threatening them with physical violence. When they attack, Tashi can see that the women who support her do not hold their ground but are dispersed by their fear and lack of solidarity.

Tashi is sentenced to die for her crime, and Olivia tells her that, for some reason, on that day the men do not attack the women but leave them to their contemplation and sorrow. According to Olivia, the women do not speak a word or sing. They are dejected and defeated by Tashi's fall and punishment. After the initial shock of the news, the next day, the women return to their vigil and active engagement supporting her.

### Benny

Benny is incredulous at the sentence that is handed down in his mother's case and cannot comprehend that she is to be killed. In an attempt to process this overwhelming information, Benny berates Pierre with endless questions about death. Pierre tells his brother that when people die, they return to nothingness. He also tells Benny that he believes that everyone is reconstituted as another being. He provides his brother with a simplistic version of the more scientific view he holds himself. Even though Pierre tries to make Benny understand, his examples often elude his brother's comprehension.

### Adam

Adam tries to process the news of his wife's fate in his matter-of-fact way. He obsesses over the news in the country, trying to figure some way out of the nightmare in which he finds himself and his family.

Those members of the press who are not entirely under the government's control have been run out of the country, so traditional methods of protest are not available. The president has become exalted in the way that Our Leader had been in earlier times. He personally advocated for Tashi to receive a death sentence. In such an environment, there is almost nothing Adam can imagine that would make a difference in Tashi's situation. The president refuses even to visit with a group of women who try to visit him to plead for Tashi's life.

Adam's nights are colored with visions of Tashi's youth and of her exuberance and lust for life. Then his dream shifts, and the same child Tashi was is now on the verge of death on the gallows. As she is about to be hanged, Tashi does not know the danger she is in and is killed without comprehension.

### Tashi-Evelyn

Since the trial is over, Tashi is allowed to bring into her cell nearly any visitor that she desires. The women artists who make the masturbating figurines are her first guests. Tashi is pleased to have their company as they explain that their statues are goddess figures and represent the life force. The figures are modeled on various representations, some found on cave walls, rock formations, and earth etchings, and pictures painted on the interiors and exteriors of huts and small houses.

The women tell Tashi something of the history of these figurines. Children were given these statues and instructed about sexuality. The various statues combine and complement to form a narrative about a culture that loves the freedom and the joy of sexuality but is afraid of indulging fully in pleasure. Tashi feels that it is enough to have evidence of the powerful need for human beings to have pleasure. Although sexuality for her has had no association with pleasure, Tashi remembers and treasures her knowledge of the capacity of human beings, and her people specifically, to enjoy life, particularly a sexual life.

### Olivia

Olivia notes that the woman who is both her oldest friend and her sister-in-law faces her fate with bravery and aplomb. Tashi tells Olivia that she would like to appear before the firing squad in a red dress. Olivia has not yet given up hope and reminds her sister-in-law that the sentence and the verdict are still in legal limbo, working their way through the appeals process. Tashi does not respond to Olivia's reminder that the decision about what will happen to her is not yet final. Instead, she repeats her desire to wear red no matter what happens. She says that she is tired of dressing herself in bleak colors, mostly in blacks and whites. She says that she will wear red because it is the color of the substance that flows though women's veins. Olivia and Tashi spend time together sewing to create the new, vibrant wardrobe Tashi craves.

## Part 15

### Tashi-Evelyn

Tashi recalls the final moments she spent with M'Lissa. She thinks of sitting on the bed with the older woman and brushing her hair. M'Lissa had disputed Tashi's positions and told her that she was thinking too much of the past, rather than studying and apprehending the complexities of the present and reflecting on how those losses affect the way that people manage to live now. M'Lissa told Tashi that in the deep past of the Olinkan people, the blood of women was not considered to be evil; rather, women's blood was a sacred manifestation of the power of the life force.

In that time, she continued, both women and men were considered capable of functioning as spiritual leaders. Both used women's blood as a conduit through which they could return to a state of transition from the previous to their current lives, through bloody recreation of their appearance at birth. The ceremony came to invoke a kind of spiritual rebirth.

M'Lissa told Tashi that she was baptized by Adam's father, Samuel, and that she knew even at that time that the water used in various rituals was merely a substitute for the blood that used to be associated with such holy rites. She added that she knew the practitioners of the Christian Church and the missionaries did not realize that the water they used was merely a replacement for a more powerful organic fluid.

Tashi recalls that she spent much time before going to M'Lissa's house trying to identify precisely what it was that she wanted to do to the woman. She had purchased razors and spent some part of each evening feeling the weapons she had hidden in the interior of her pillows. She dreamed about killing the woman. She had vowed to deface M'Lissa's frame to the point that she would not be able to be identified by any person, spirit, or deity. Tashi was jubilant and peaceful when she imagined the mess of flesh she would make of the old woman's body; however, as she repeatedly imagined her planned encounter with M'Lissa, her goals continued to shift as, with each fantasy session, M'Lissa provided Tashi with another version of the story.

Tashi became lost in a sea of desire for something only the older woman could provide.

This memory of Tashi's is not precisely identified. It is unclear whether her next reflections are from an actual exchange between the two women or is merely one of her hopeful imaginings about the encounter. In this exchange, Tashi cared for the woman's feet while M'Lissa told her of an ironic myth held by the Olinkan people. She told Tashi that the true value of the circumcision cannot be ascertained until she is murdered by one of the people on whom she has practiced this operation. After this violent end occurs, then her worth becomes apparent, and she becomes a near deity to those she has left behind. M'Lissa told Tashi that her death by such means had already been foretold.

At this point in the narrative, it is clear from the way that Tashi speaks that the story comes from an imagined conversation between her and M'Lissa, and that the powerful potential of what she had imagined actually kept Tashi from committing M'Lissa's murder. She had been troubled that killing the woman might backfire and would give the woman even more power, authority, and weight than she ever had while living.

### M'Lissa

This chapter begins with M'Lissa reflecting on what she perceives as knowledge that is superior to that of the young people she encounters. She also knows that after one has lived long and seen and experienced a great deal, there comes a time when it is good to die.

M'Lissa says that she is able to see Tashi's intentions from the time that the two lay eyes on each other. She has had enough experience with murder and insanity to know when she is facing another person with violent and hungry intentions.

M'Lissa recalls her own childhood and the custom her village sustained of leaving all of those who were considered to be insane isolated in a space separated from the rest of the community. The dwellings of those who were out of touch with reality were decrepit and unclean. The insane people wore clothing that was falling apart, and they were unkempt.

Like the rest of the villagers, M'Lissa found that although these individuals were potentially dangerous, they and their behavior could be managed. The key to this kind of control lay in the ability to distract the focus of the potential perpetrator. M'Lissa says that these people were distracted by the most minute pleasures. When confronted with a potentially dangerous situation, all one had to do was to shift their focus from their desired action to something benign. By offering food, singing, or a story, these individuals could forget entirely what it was that they had intended to do. Such a strategy, according to M'Lissa, could bring the insane to tears or make them laugh as if there was something they were experiencing that was unimaginably funny. When a crazy person was in this mode, then the potential victim could easily make his or her escape.

M'Lissa tells of her history as a preface to a question that she has asked of Tashi, who, according to M'Lissa, has not responded properly to the question. M'Lissa gives Tashi a kind of riddle to answer. She says that she recognizes Tashi's devotion to her new country, the United States, but that she would like for Tashi to describe the appearance of an American.

### Evelyn-Tashi

Tashi thinks about M'Lissa's question. Immediately, the first person who comes to Tashi's mind is Raye, and she begins telling M'Lissa about the woman. Tashi talks about Raye's complexion and her hair. She speaks of the racial mixtures that are specific to the United States and are also embodied in Raye's physicality. M'Lissa considers Tashi's response and asks her if, in fact, Americans are not white.

Upon hearing this second question, Tashi begins describing Amy, the woman she met in Raye's office, and gives M'Lissa another portrait of an American. The older woman is unsatisfied with the second response as much as she was with the first, and so Tashi continues trying to come up with an answer that is satisfactory. She describes Asian-American people, and M'Lissa dismisses that answer as well. She poses the question to Tashi again, "Can you describe a real American?"

Tashi continues with her attempt. She outlines the features of white men she has seen on television as well as Asian Indians and Native Americans. She talks about people with mixed racial heritages and describes people who live in the country but who speak another language. All the while Tashi makes this effort, M'Lissa sits quietly and listens to what she is trying to say.

Tashi seems to have fallen in a hole of her own making from which there is no emergence. She is engaged in a fast and furious chase for a response M'Lissa knows does not exist. Tashi does not realize this and assumes that she has the upper hand and continues, futilely attempting to construct the right, perfect response. She says that unlike Africa, where you can specifically describe someone who is, say, Massai, Americans are too diverse and divergent to fit within a single descriptive definition. Tashi also realizes that she is part of an old game that she cannot win, although she is unsure why.

Finally, after several imaginary conversations with M'Lissa about this topic, and after Tashi endlessly tries to answer the question that is, in actuality, her own, she comes up with another response. She comes to the conclusion that an American is a person who is injured, either physically or emotionally, and whose wounds cannot be seen by others and, often, by the sufferer him- or herself. She concludes that she is what an American looks like.

## Part 16

### Tashi

Tashi finally begins to recount her actual exchange with M'Lissa. She tells of washing the old woman after Mbati leaves. She also sees that the woman has had a radical removal of her genitals and also has had an alteration done to a major tendon in her inner thigh. This surgery is the source of her limp. When Tashi touches the leg, she finds that the tissue is solid and unlike flesh. M'Lissa says to Tashi that the infirmity is "the mark, on my body, of my own mother's disobedience."

Tashi listens reluctantly to M'Lissa's story, which presents a conflict for her, as she knows that she wants and plans to kill the woman. Yet she has already begun to give M'Lissa a bath. Although uncertain, Tashi decides to listen to the woman's tale before killing her. She will hear the tale of M'Lissa's life when she was a child, "before she murdered Dura," as Tashi puts it. In spite of her intentions, Tashi also feels obligated to finish the bath.

### M'Lissa

M'Lissa remembers her mother as a sad woman who tells her daughter about a time when the people were defined by their relationship to their mothers. She notes that her mother tells her that the time when this reality was manifest was considered an evil period, although her mother is unsure why that should be the case.

One day, M'Lissa follows her mother as she furtively leaves the village and travels on foot through a decaying forest. She sees her mother reach into a decimated tree, take out a bundle, kiss it, return the bundle to its place, and then leave. M'Lissa is brimming with curiosity and goes to the tree to see what it is that her mother so worships and adores. She finds that it is a bundle of her mother's discarded genitalia, which she recovered following her surgical mutilation. M'Lissa has not yet undergone the operation that produces the fleshy items that her mother has privately enshrined, so she does not fully appreciate the significance of her mother's actions.

M'Lissa also finds a statue in the tree. The small figurine is posed with her hands on her intact genitals. M'Lissa models the behavior of the statue and is surprised to discover the responsive pleasure she feels. Her delight frightens her, so she quickly replaces the statue in its hiding place in the tree and runs back to the village after her mother.

After the discovery of her mother's secret, M'Lissa makes a regular habit of visiting the tree and examining its contents. She plays with the figurine but does not ever touch herself in the way that the positioning of the figure would suggest.

M'Lissa seems to regret that she did not touch herself more before her circumcision. She wishes that she understood what was so threatening about the feelings she was able to produce that the *tsunga,* or circumcisers, spent their lives trying to prevent it from occurring.

M'Lissa's grandmother is a circumciser called "I Am Belly" because her bloody work does not prevent her from demanding a large plate of food to eat immediately after she performs surgery on the young women who are given to her to mutilate. M'Lissa's mother is also a *tsunga,* but unlike her mother, she hates the work and would love to find a way to prevent it from occurring.

M'Lissa tells the story of what happens when her mother is called to circumcise the girls who are M'Lissa's age. As she performs the operation on her own child, M'Lissa's mother tries to do it in a way that will not completely mutilate her child. Other women observe her actions, and as a result of what they see as M'Lissa's transgression, they ensure that the operation on the little girl is finished by someone else. The punishment her mother receives for trying to spare her child and salvage some pleasure for her is to have to watch as her daughter receives an even more brutal excision of her womanhood.

M'Lissa takes three months to recover from the procedure. She says to Tashi that she was never the same child.

### Tashi

M'Lissa's story moves Tashi, but she works on hardening herself emotionally so that the tale does not prevent her from carrying out what she has come to see as her mission, killing the old woman. M'Lissa says that when she had the surgery, she lost her faith in any deity who could possibly care about women or children, and that the only God that women can know or should worship is independence and freedom.

Tashi encourages the woman to weep and to release the pain of her history. What Tashi discovers is that, like her flesh wounds, M'Lissa's emotional scars are too deep and calcified to generate deeply held feelings. Tashi learns that the older woman, in spite of her work performing this ceremony on countless young women and children, does not believe in the ceremony and feels that the ritual is empty and without significance. Tashi asks the older woman why, then, she performs the operation and lies to those who have the rite inflicted upon them.

Tashi recites to M'Lissa the words that she told her about the dangers of not performing the ceremony. She reminds the woman of her admonitions that she would not be an acceptable or attractive woman, that she would be unclean, and that she would be unable to give her husband pleasure. She also reminds M'Lissa that she was not told that she would not be able to experience pleasure or to give birth normally. Tashi begins to weep for all of the loss that was caused by her decision to have this ceremony performed on herself. She thinks of the pain and injury done to Adam, Benny, and the child that she aborted because she did not want her to have to endure the suffering that Benny went through at birth.

Tashi feels that M'Lissa is responsible for all of the suffering of her life, beginning with the death of her sister. The urge to kill M'Lissa returns. Tashi's physical impairment prevents her from responding in the way that she would like.

She thinks that M'Lissa has fallen into a deep sleep as she watches. M'Lissa's physical slightness is shocking to Tashi, who always imagines the woman to be large and imposing in stature. M'Lissa is not, in fact, sleeping; rather, she is contemplating the lost part of herself, the part that she left in the initiation hut when she was injured by her mother. She says that she can see the lost part of herself and that the little girl she was is crying and has been crying since she left her behind on the floor of that hut so many years ago. M'Lissa tells Tashi that her child-self has been weeping for all of them.

### M'Lissa

M'Lissa begins this short section with a simple statement about her strength. She tells all of the women and all of the people about her strength because that is what they want and need to hear. She feels that she has been working to support customs that torture children.

## Part 17

### Tashi

There is a small white chapel in the prison where Tashi has been kept where a group of her friends and family have gathered with her. Assembled for this meeting are Adam, Olivia, Benny, Pierre, Raye, and Mbati. Tashi says that Raye has flown in to witness her execution, but Raye reminds her that she is "not dead yet!"

Tashi agrees with that assessment but feels as if she is not fully alive either. The chapel where the family gathers is in good condition compared to the rest of the place, which is badly deteriorated. While the trial and appeal have been going on, Olivia has been working as a volunteer on the floor of the prison that is reserved for AIDS patients. Pierre, Benny, and Adam have been driving around the countryside exploring the region where Adam spent so much of his youth. While they are on their adventure, they take pictures and movies. They decide to show the film to Tashi and are concerned about her reaction.

Pierre introduces the film he has made by saying he believes that early humans imitated termites in their activities and made houses from the materials that they had before them, earth and clay. Tashi looks at Pierre gratefully and recognizes that Adam's son has been a great help to her life and that, finally, she appreciates his presence and persistence. She feels that his education has been so helpful to her that she sees the schools he attended, Harvard and Berkeley, as nearly holy spots.

Pierre continues with his lesson about the termite and the relationship between the termite and human beings. He tries to explain to Tashi that the tower within which she has dreamt her whole life of being imprisoned is actually a replication of a termite colony. Tashi, with her imaginative recreation of the insect civilization, has dreamt that she is the queen within this dark tower. The worker bees feed the queen, and as Tashi is the queen in the scenario, she is the one being fed. She has imagined also that there are things being taken from her. Pierre interprets that removal as akin to the eggs being removed from the body of the termite queen. She is the conduit for the life of the community and is in the end destroyed by those whom she has created.

Olivia interprets this reading of Tashi and the termites to mean that the woman functions as a kind of Christ figure who sacrifices her life for the good of the whole. Tashi wonders how it is that she could have imagined these details when she did not know anything about the lives of termites. Raye says she feels that knowledge of the life of the termite is intuitive to Tashi, and she likens knowledge about the termite queen to the processes through which the infliction of circumcision is inherited but never spoken about.

Tashi is fascinated and flabbergasted by what she has been told. She tries to comprehend that circumcision is related to mythologies that connect the termite mound to the reproductive function of the earth. In Dogon mythologies, the sky God cuts off the termite mound, Earth's clitoris, so that he can have sexual relations with the land. Pierre has read this myth as the foundation for the justification of female circumcision and has used it as a way to interpret and explain Tashi's recurring dream.

Tashi recalls an incident that occurred when she was very young. She brought food to the village men that her mother had prepared. While she was there, she overheard the men talking about the nature of men and women. They said that men were in control of women and that, through circumcision, they were able to control the passage and fruition of their seed. Tashi is able to discern that this conversation is the origin of her recurring nightmare about imprisonment within a dark tower. The men made an assertion that women were queens, and they affirmed as a unit that in order to control the women, to keep them in place and to disallow freedom, their wings must be cut. Hearing this exchange encouraged the development of Tashi's fear. As a result, her traumas became embedded in the key elements of the story. Like the queen termite in the myth whose wings are cut, the women, like Tashi, succumb to having their genitals—their wings, so to speak—removed.

Tashi is struck by her memory of the arrogance of the men, who did not expect that the young girl would hear their pronouncements about her life and the lives of women generally. They did not think enough of her little girl self to wait until she had left their presence to discuss, indirectly, her fate and that of the women in their lives.

As Tashi contemplates these realities, she discerns that what a person hears and experiences can have a profound impact on the outcome of his or her life. Adam holds Tashi's hand throughout this experience and revelation. She remembers the power and assurance of her childhood self.

## Part 18

### Evelyn-Tashi

The narrative shifts back in time to the moment when Tashi encounters and confronts M'Lissa. She asks the older woman about her thoughts when Tashi came to the camp where M'Lissa was working with the Mbeles. The older woman bluntly tells Tashi that she thought the girl was extraordinarily deluded and misguided in her decision to go through with the mutilation, a pain and anguish that she had avoided at the time the ceremony was normally performed. M'Lissa tells Tashi that the camp of outlaw rebels was not in any way different from the rest of Olinkan culture when it came to sexism, and that the Mbeles desperately wanted women in their encampments so that the women could do all of the hard domestic work the men did not want to perform.

Like Tashi, M'Lissa also arrived on a donkey that the Mbeles had sent to her. In retrospect, she realizes that she, too, was foolish to have been honored by such an invitation. The rebels saw female circumcision as a metaphor for the struggle they were fighting to live in a way that honored their patriarchal traditions. The Mbeles needed M'Lissa and Tashi to be in the camp and to perform the female circumcision ceremony there as a sanction of their activities and purposes.

Tashi and M'Lissa continue their conversation and try to identify who is culpable for Tashi's circumcision specifically and for enacting the practice generally. M'Lissa reveals the hypocrisy of Our Leader by stating that he was able to keep his genitalia intact and that he fathered 11 children by three different wives.

Their conversation continues circling around the complexities of women's pleasure and the role of circumcision in preventing—nearly destroying—the physical joy women might derive from sexual relations.

## Part 19

### Olivia

Tashi's legal appeal fails, and as the United States does not intervene in her behalf, an execution date is set. Tashi enjoys near celebrity status. While awaiting the execution, she receives visits from local and international dignitaries and activists. She also works on the AIDS floor with Olivia, assisting patients in any way she can.

She and Olivia are especially saddened by the condition of the children with AIDS who do not understand their illness and its fatal consequences. All of Tashi's friends and family ponder the relationship between geopolitics and the emergence and specificities of the AIDS pandemic in Africa. Tashi sees a connection between the practice of genital mutilation and the spread of AIDS among African women and girls.

### Olivia

Olivia asks Tashi why she confessed to killing M'Lissa. Olivia is convinced that Tashi did not commit the crime of which she has been accused and for which she has been sentenced to die. Tashi laughs and replies that she has no desire to live any longer and is curious about death.

### Tashi

Olivia pleads with Tashi to defend herself and not to go forward with her plans. Tashi reminds her of the other time in their lives when Olivia begged her not to go forward with a decision, just before she left for the Mbeles to have the circumcision. Tashi says to Olivia that she is right. Tashi did not kill M'Lissa, but that she was still culpable for her death. She also tells Olivia that she does not want it to be known that she is not guilty of the woman's murder. Tashi feels that she should have been.

### M'Lissa

M'Lissa begins reflecting on the death of Tashi's sister, Dura, and blames the child's untimely demise on her mother. She remembers that before the girl's ceremony, the chief had decided to stop the ritual. His order was motivated not by sympathy for the women involved but from a desire to please the white missionaries. In spite of the chief's orders, Tashi's mother had believed that the arrival of Nettie, Samuel, and Corrine, black missionaries, would mean a mandatory return to circumcision, and so she insisted that her daughter undergo the ceremony.

Although Tashi says that she does not want to know, M'Lissa tells her that her sister, who was prone to bleeding, probably had some type of clotting disorder and that it was this inability to stop bleeding that killed her during the ceremony.

## Part 20

### Adam

Adam is speaking with an AIDS patient who is on the verge of death and thinks of Adam as a priest to whom he can make confession. The young man, who has told Adam that he is a medical student, is named Hartford. As he and Adam speak, Hartford reveals that he is not in fact a medical student but an employee of a pharmaceutical company. He and others from his community were offered jobs hunting monkeys in the forest. They were only to capture the females and the babies for the company. The monkeys were captured and then raised so that their kidneys could be harvested. Hartford's job was to kill the monkeys by cutting off their heads. He describes to Adam the horrible sound the creatures made when they were killed.

Hartford tells Adam that the factory was so large that it was nearly incomprehensible to his imagination. The kidneys were used by men in white coats to make cultures. Hartford's confession to Adam implies that the spread of the AIDS virus occurred as a consequence of using the monkey kidneys to produce a vaccine for humans.

### Tashi-Evelyn–Mrs. Johnson

Tashi states that the reason she confessed at her trial to killing M'Lissa is that she had grown bored. Her boredom and frustration at the lawyers' insensitivity and grandiosity led her to say that she was guilty simply in an effort to end the spectacle.

## Part 21

### Tashi-Evelyn

Tashi is convinced that Mbati is her daughter. The two grow close as Tashi awaits her execution. They discuss a passage from Mirella Ricciardi's *African Saga,* from which the title of the novel is taken. Ricciardi wrote that black people "possess the secret of joy, which is why they can survive the suffering and humiliation inflicted upon them." Mbati and Tashi puzzle over the racist statement and consider what it could mean and if there is any possible truth in it.

On their parting, Tashi gives Mbati the figurine given to her by Olivia during her trial. Tashi has named the small statue Nyanda and tells Mbati to give it to her daughter when she is born. She hopes for the child to have more love, confidence, and self-assurance than either she or Mbati was able to muster.

### Tashi-Evelyn–Mrs. Johnson

This chapter takes the form of a letter Tashi writes to Lisette, Adam's mistress, who has been dead for years. She says to the dead woman that she writes in hope of making a friend in the land of the dead.

She feels kinship with Lisette because she believes that the woman made a genuine effort to understand her, unlike Tashi's mother, who Tashi believes did not have the emotional or psychological resources to do so. She writes to Lisette that she felt alienated from Adam's progressive ministry in San Francisco because of its focus on a Christian narrative, and therefore on the particular suffering of Jesus, it excluded the suffering of women from consideration and serious contemplation.

Tashi asked Adam to write one such sermon, and he told her that such a work would shame the congregation. After Adam's refusal, Tashi began to spend her time at the church outside rather than listening to the sermons in the sanctuary.

Tashi also clarifies her role in M'Lissa's death. She writes that she told Olivia that she did not kill M'Lissa because that is what Olivia needed to believe about Tashi. She says that she killed the older woman by covering her face with a pillow and laying on it. She had wanted to slash the woman to bits, but she lost her enthusiasm for committing a brutal murder after hearing the deeply painful stories from M'Lissa's life and understanding the context of her experience. She says that she merely did what M'Lissa wanted and carried out her wishes to be murdered and then burnt in order to fulfill the prophesy of what would happen to a well-loved *tsunga.*

Tashi tells Lisette that Pierre has grown up to be a wonderful man and that she especially appreciates the relationship between him and Benny. She also writes about and gives examples of all the information Pierre has given her regarding the history and context of the practice of mutilation that has helped her to understand the larger picture and to begin to piece out why the practice emerged and flourished. Pierre spends his personal and professional energies trying to root out and eradicate oppression against women.

Tashi writes to Lisette that she is certain the two will meet in the afterlife. She also regrets not appreciating and getting to know Lisette before her death so many years earlier. She writes that she has no fear of her impending death and that she wants to see the bullets as they come toward her body. She says that she will spend those moments gazing at the distant hills that surround the soccer field that the government uses to execute the condemned.

### Tashi-Evelyn–Johnson Soul

There are women at Tashi's execution who enact a silent protest, having been warned not to sing. The women take diapers off their children and hold up the naked babies in a sign of solidarity. The protest goes unnoticed by the soldiers. The people in Tashi's life who love her—Adam, Olivia, Benny, Pierre, Raye, and Mbati—hold up a sign that reads "<u>RESISTANCE</u> IS THE SECRET OF JOY!" It is the last thing Tashi sees as she is shot. She dies with contentment and peace.

The novel ends with a note to the reader about the realities of female genital mutilation and references to other works that help to illuminate the topic. Walker also includes at the end of the novel a page of acknowledgments that she titles "Thanks."

## CRITICAL COMMENTARY

While Walker's fifth novel, *Possessing the Secret of Joy,* seems to be about the life and traumatic experiences of its central protagonist, Tashi, the narrative is actually a commentary on many issues confronting the contemporary world. Of particular focus are questions of the relationship between the developing and industrialized world, the survival of the individual in the context of past suffering, the role of tradition in cultural practice, the exploitation and domination of women, the deification of political and cultural leaders, the often divided consciousnesses of those who are members of a global community, and the limitations of personal choice within the context of overwhelming cultural currents. This last concern emerges as primary to Walker's mission in crafting *Possessing the Secret of Joy.* The narrative ponders three central conflicts having to do with autonomy and choice. These conflicts emerge as questions about the nature of self-construction and identity, about individual and collective perceptions of reality, and about the ability to transcend the past in order to experience, even transform the present.

*Possessing the Secret of Joy* begins with an epigraph from a book entitled *African Saga* (published 1981) in which the author Mirella Ricciardi writes: "Black people are natural, they possess the secret of joy, which is why they can survive the suffering and humiliation inflicted upon them. They are alive physically and emotionally, which makes them easy to live with. What I had not yet learned to deal with was their cunning and their natural instinct for self-preservation" (11). Ricciardi is a white European woman who was born in Kenya and spent much of her early life there. Although *African Saga* is a novel, Ricciardi's primary occupation and the subject of most of her published work involves photography and the reproduction of images of Africa and its people. As such, her quotation with its misinterpretation and egregiously oversimplified characterization of black people is extraordinarily problematic, particularly as it seems to derive from a person who, as a consequence of her birth and long-term residence in Africa, would be considered an authority on the subject.

By employing this quotation from Ricciardi, Walker attempts to establish the novel's first interrogation, the question of representation contrasted with authentic selfhood. Throughout the novel, Tashi has to determine and authenticate her sense of selfhood. She has distinct and evolving perceptions of herself and of her ability to define her identity. The novel moves back and forth in time and allows the reader to encounter Tashi's self-perceptions at various points in her life. Unlike many other women who undergo female genital mutilation, when Tashi has the procedure, it seems that she does so because she is making a choice of her own free will. As the narrative unfolds, however, the extent to which Tashi actually has the ability to make a choice becomes less and less certain.

When Tashi is a young girl and makes the decision to undergo the initiation ceremony, even though she is older than most girls are when they undergo the ceremony, Tashi is not pressured into the circumcision. She decides that she wants to have the operation as a sign of defiance against colonial oppressors and as a marker of solidarity with the customs and traditions of her people.

Additionally, as a young woman, Tashi wants and needs to affirm her status as an African woman, partly as a consequence of her long childhood relationship with Nettie, Samuel, best friend Olivia, and lover and eventual husband Adam. Tashi's seeming choice to undergo the procedure is also influenced by a heroic figure and imprisoned political leader called Our Leader. Our Leader adheres to the traditions of the Olinka and suggests that political loyalty and patriotism relies on remaining true to the people's ancient customs and ensuring that the act of clitoridectomy remain in practice. These factors are major motivators for Tashi's decision to undergo the procedure. Over time, she begins to question the extent to which these factors predetermined her actions and caused her to act.

As an adult, Tashi discovers in therapy that she witnessed her sister Dura's clitoridectomy as a child. This event, the associated trauma of seeing her sister in such pain, and the feelings of loss that occurred with Dura's death may have instigated in Tashi feelings of guilt and responsibility for not having had the operation and also for being alive. As her recall of the experience improves, Tashi wonders if she had the operation as a gesture of solidarity with her dead sister.

Although Tashi volunteers for the operation against the advice and counsel of the people who are closest to her, as a young woman she engages in the ritual as a way of aligning her identity politically and possibly as a means to relieve her subconscious but overwhelming feelings of culpability for her sister's violent death. One of the questions that Tashi seems unable to resolve and that becomes a major factor in her decline into madness is the extent to which the choices she makes are her own or are catalyzed by factors beyond her control. This lack of resolution about her autonomy leads Tashi down a path of declining certainty. Even her act of retaliation when she begins to feel that the choice was not her own—her murder of M'Lissa—may not ultimately have been her own. The old woman seems to want Tashi to kill her, and therefore Tashi cannot even claim that act as one entirely of her own volition.

The various names that Tashi has throughout the novel also speak to the tension between her self-invention and the illusion of autonomy. Although Tashi chooses her Western name, Evelyn, this appellation is, in many ways, dictated by the language and conventions of the land in which she finds herself. The evocation of Eve in the name is also indicative of the tenuousness of personal choice. Just as it is unclear whether the biblical Eve has the choice to defy the suggestion of the snake to eat the forbidden fruit, the extent to which Tashi's choices are unconstrained is similarly ambiguous.

By focusing on the questions of Tashi's self-determination and identity, Walker asks a more general question. For women who support the practice of clitoridectomy, is their choice truly their own? Even more generally, are any of the decisions that we make the consequence of free will, or is everything that we think we decide predetermined for us by circumstance and situation?

These questions lead to the novel's second major category of inquiry: the attempt to determine the relationship between collective and individual perceptions of reality. The novel begins with a narrative told by Tashi, who ambiguously reveals that she is dead while telling the story. It is unclear whether Tashi's death is a physical one, and she is addressing the reader from the afterworld, or if she is referring to a state of emotional and psychological death. In either case, the story that Tashi tells has significance for the novel's investigation of the relationship between subjective and collective perception.

The story is about a panther family that consists of two co-wives, Lala and Lara, and their husband, Baba. Lara is in the midst of a difficult time as a result of the affection between her husband and co-wife. She is an appendage to their relationship, a position that is intolerable to her. The co-wife, Lala, is jealous of the little attention Lara gets from her husband, whose name is Baba. The situation is causing such conflict that Baba and Lala have begun to fight with each other physically.

Baba tries to explain to Lala that he has to copulate with their co-wife, Lara. It is his duty according to the rules of their community. He feels he has no choice in the situation. Lala tells Baba that she understands this rule to be the case, but that the reality of the customs of their group do not help her to ease the pain she feels regarding the state of affairs.

Lara is particularly miserable as she is the cast away. She also happens to be pregnant. In this profound isolation and introspection, Lara generates an internal voice to assuage her loneliness. Eventually, the voice really begins to speak, and Lara finds herself listening to her most inner secret self. This voice protects her from the dangers and gets her to once again love and appreciate herself. She sees her own reflection in a stream and begins to love herself.

Baba sees Lara with her new self, grows attracted to her, and makes love to her. Lala is grief-stricken and becomes as jealous as Lara was about her. She cannot stand the happiness of Lara and Baba, and Baba and Lala fight all the time. Lara is no longer jealous or possessive. She falls in love with herself and spends her time admiring her reflection and enjoying her life.

When this introduction is read in light of its function as a kind of segue between *The Temple of My Familiar* and *Possessing the Secret of Joy,* the function of the narrative and its role in illuminating the questions of collective and individual experiences of reality becomes clearer. In *The Temple of My Familiar,* Miss Lissie tells Suwelo about the history of human beings and reveals that reincarnation happened across different species. She reveals that she used to be a lion in a former life. In this context, particularly in light of Tashi's assertion that she is dead, the first story in *Possessing the Secret of Joy* is probably about a former life of Tashi's, one that has universal relevance for all of the characters in the novel. The narrative's fundamental lesson is that possessiveness is not an element of genuine adoration and love of another. The only authentic possession one can have is of one's self. The story informs us that self-love must be transcendent and balanced between deep self-knowledge and intuition, as demonstrated by Lara's reflected kiss, and a luminous embrace of the natural divine, as demonstrated by the lovemaking that occurs between Lala and the moon. The subjective and narratized way in which Tashi reads the world suggests that her perception of reality is grounded in an intuitive access to the collective. When she is most lucid, Tashi is able to translate her individual experiences into an archetypal story that has significance for all people.

Walker's embrace of this idea is substantiated by her inclusion of Mzee in the novel, a figure who she has said is an homage to and reinvention of CARL JUNG. Many critics have written about the novel's use of Jungian psychology. Walker employs Jung's use of a concept he named the *collective unconscious,* a concept in analytic psychology that refers to the shared built-in response to the world of every person (or every member of a given species). The collective unconscious is distinguished from the personal unconscious, which refers to the experiences and responses of a given individual. Jung believed that this collective unconscious can be explored through cultural expressions in the forms of myths, religion, and philosophy, and through individual expressions in the form of dreams.

Jung's theories resonate particularly with Walker's construction of Tashi's psyche. Just as Tashi's perceptions of reality access a universal truth with relevance for all life, Jung believed that the central goal for psychological well-being rested with the individual's need to balance his or her individual nature with the collective unconscious. This congruency leads to harmony and autonomy for the individual. By the novel's end, when Tashi is able to connect her perceptions of reality with a larger truth, accessible to others, she achieves, albeit in death, an acceptance of the conjunction between individual and collective reality. This resolution is most graphic in the banner that Tashi's family holds up as they watch her execution, "RESISTANCE IS THE SECRET OF JOY!" The sign acknowledges Tashi's lifelong refusal to accept reality as it is distorted by the ill intentions of others and to work to access, through her understandings, a collective experience of reality. The disparate assemblage of Tashi's family and friends at her execution acknowledge her efforts and their mutual understanding with their sign, and Tashi dies at peace.

Much of the peace that Tashi is able to achieve by the end of her life derives from her reconciliation of past events. The major traumas of Tashi's life haunt her present and prevent her from moving toward new interpretations of the present until she is able to release herself from their dominance and control. Two significant events that Tashi has to wrestle with and resolve are the death of her sister, Dura, following the girl's clitoridectomy and her husband Adam's relationship with Lisette.

Tashi comes to terms with her sister's death in two phases. Her experience with The Old Man, whom she calls Mzee, is restorative. Mzee is the therapist who leads her first to remember the event and then to use art to help her come to terms with the revelation that M'Lissa is responsible for the event. While watching a film with Mzee, Tashi faints. The room that she recovers in has a picture of a fighting cock, and this inspires her to do a series of paintings of fighting cocks.

In one of the paintings, Tashi depicts a foot that holds within its grasp something small that the cock wants. Creating the painting makes Tashi physically ill. The Old Man asks her whether the foot belongs to a man or a woman. She cannot answer his question. Tashi also creates other paintings, one of which is called "Crazy Road" and is based on a pattern she learned when she was a small child. This time, the foot that she creates in the painting is a woman's foot. She also paints a row of children, all of whom are approximately the age her sister, Dura, was when she died. Tashi recognizes that Dura is not depicted in the group. She imagines that the foot in the painting belongs to M'Lissa, and she imagines the foot tossing up its bounty and eating the crumbs. Tashi's memory of M'Lissa forges her determination to murder the woman.

Tashi's extended planning and prolonged murder of M'Lissa is the second phase of her acceptance of her sister's death as well as of the injury that has been done to her. When Tashi visits M'Lissa with the intention of murdering her, she comes to sympathize with the woman's own conflicted history and only kills the woman to fulfill M'Lissa's desire to die in the way that was prophesied to be her fate if she was a well-loved *tsunga.* It is not the act of murdering M'Lissa that heals Tashi, it is her willingness to hear and to empathize with the woman's story that allows her to forgive M'Lissa and to resolve her long-held conflicts about the source of the pain in her life.

Like the panther in the novel's opening narrative, Tashi is deeply jealous of her husband Adam's love for another woman, Lisette. Like Lara the panther, Tashi has to learn to shift her focus from the love that Lisette and Adam share to her love of her self. Curiously, it is Lisette and Adam's son, Pierre, who is the catalyst for Tashi's understanding of the fundamental meaning of her life. Consequently, Tashi is able not only to forgive Adam for loving Lisette but to feel grateful for their union and for their conception of Pierre. Toward the end of her life, Tashi anticipates meeting Lisette in the afterworld and having meaningful exchanges with her.

*Possessing the Secret of Joy* is a complicated and multilayered work that has as an objective the interrogation of universal philosophical questions about the interaction and nature of humanity. Through Tashi's journey, the novel ponders the nature of free will in the formation of identity, the relationship between individual and collective perceptions of reality, and the extent to which it is possible to reconcile existence in the present with the omnipresent specter of the past. Although critics have wide-ranging evaluations of the success, intentions, and positionality of Walker's ambitions, *Possessing the Secret of Joy* is an important and unique contribution to the canon of 20th-century literature.

## SIGNIFICANT THEMES, ISSUES, CONCERNS

### Female Genital Mutilation

*Possessing the Secret of Joy* examines the issues that surround the practice of female genital mutilation, sometimes referred to as female circumcision or clitoridectomy, in Africa, the Far East, and the Middle East. Although there are locally specific variations of the procedure, in general, it involves the excision of the clitoris and other parts of the female genitalia.

The procedure has become a subject of concern and activism for various writers, intellectuals, and public figures. Some of the protest against it derives from within the cultures that practice this tradition. Additional attention about the issue has come from voices that are not indigenous to the locales where clitoridectomies are performed. Critics of the practice generally share concern about the impact of the ritual on female sexual agency and health.

The Egyptian writer, physician, and activist Nawal El Saadawi and the Ghanaian writer Ama Ata Aidoo are among those who have questioned the politics and cultural issues and concerns that surround African female sexuality and the practice of clitoridectomy. Among the health risks associated with the procedure are hemorrhage, HIV transmission, increased vulnerability to infection, and emotional and psychological trauma.

### The Danger of Deification

*Possessing the Secret of Joy* exposes and critiques the human impulse to deify and consequently to follow blindly the leadership of others. There are several examples within the novel that demonstrate this. For example, when Tashi first seeks the assistance of Mzee, she says to him that she believes he is her last hope. Mzee quickly disabuses her of this idea and tells her that the process of gaining health is always mutual.

The novel's critique of the habit of deification is most pronounced in the novel's development of the character called only Our Leader, who becomes so idealized to his followers that anything and everything he says is believed to be the right course of action. Blind devotion to Our Leader causes those few who do not concur with his positions and strategies to be ostracized and considered enemies of the people.

### The Complexities of Independence

*Possessing the Secret of Joy* complicates the concept of freedom for both individuals and communities. One can understand Tashi's journey as a kind of quest for autonomy and freedom, yet each of the choices that she makes in the novel serve to constrain her in ways that are unexpected when she makes the choice. When Tashi decides to kill M'Lissa, for example, she imagines that killing the woman will allow some release from her past experiences and will avenge the death of her sister, Dura. However, Tashi's murder of M'Lissa leads to the loss of physical freedom and, ultimately, to the loss of Tashi's life. There is a parallel situation with the country of the Olinka, which has acquired independence from its colonial powers but finds that the internal struggles it faces replicate some of the conditions of colonization and introduce new internal difficulties and conflicts.

### The Centrality of Dreams

The references to Jungian psychology and repeated recitations of Tashi's dreams throughout *Possessing the Secret of Joy* signal a common assertion of almost all of Walker's works—the belief that dreams are a primary method for accessing the truth about experience and also for solving the conflicts and dilemmas of life.

The primary and recurring dream in *Possessing the Secret of Joy* is Tashi's dream of the tower and what she later understands to be a termite colony. Fairly early in the novel, Tashi reveals to her therapist that in her recurring dream, she is in a narrow structure that has many levels and is dark and cold inside. She feels as if she had wings but they were broken by her presence in the structure. She is also being operated on, with things being inserted into and removed from her.

Much later in the novel, Pierre, Adam's son with Lisette, tries to explain to Tashi that the tower of her dreams, within which she is imprisoned, is actually a replication of a termite colony. Pierre states that Tashi's dream is her imaginative recreation of the insect civilization and that she is a queen within this dark tower. The worker bees feed the queen, and since Tashi is the queen in the scenario, she is the one being fed. Tashi imagines also that there are things being taken from her. Pierre interprets that removal as akin to the eggs being removed from the body of the termite queen. Tashi, like the queen, is the conduit for the life of the community and is in the end destroyed by those whom she has created.

Olivia interprets this reading of Tashi and the termites to mean that Tashi functions as a kind of Christ figure who sacrifices her life for the good of the whole. Tashi wonders how it is that she could have imagined these details when she did not know anything about the lives of termites. Raye tells Tashi that she feels knowledge of the life of the termite is intuitive to her. Raye likens knowledge about the termite queen to the processes through which information and infliction of circumcision is inherited but never spoken about.

Tashi is fascinated and flabbergasted by what she has been told. She tries to comprehend that circumcision is related to mythologies that connect the termite mound to the reproductive function of the earth. Through Pierre's interpretation of Tashi's nearly lifelong recurring dream, Pierre reveals the truth to her about her understanding of the world and of her particular role in it. Tashi has known but not understood or recognized the truth all along. With Pierre's revelation and interpretation of her dream, Tashi seems able to face her death with some peace and resolution.

## CHARACTERS

**Adam Johnson** Adam Johnson is the son of Samuel Johnson, missionary pastor of an Olinka tribe in Africa. His stepmother is Mama Nettie Johnson, his sister is Olivia Johnson, and his wife is Tashi. When he was young, his family came to an Olinka tribe in Africa, where he first met Tashi. At a young age, they were lovers, having intercourse in the harvest fields, despite tribal legends that doing so curses the land. He performed cunnilingus on her, which is also considered a taboo in Olinka tradition.

After returning to Africa from a trip to England, Adam found Tashi had disappeared. He went looking for her, and when they met again, she had been circumcised, and it was as though a light had gone out from within her. He married her and brought her to America. When they had intercourse after they were married, it caused physical pain for both Adam and Tashi (who was renamed Evelyn when she moved to America).

Adam has an ongoing affair with a French white woman named Lisette, whom he met in Africa when he was younger, while he was assigned to take care of a dying man named Torabe. He fathers a son with Lisette named Pierre. He speaks of Tashi to Lisette only on occasion.

As a grown man, Adam becomes pastor of a church in San Francisco. When Evelyn asks him to speak of female circumcision to the congregation, he refuses, saying that such a personal matter would be embarrassing. At a certain point, he leaves the priesthood. Later, just a day before his wife is executed, he hears the confession of an African man named Hartford, who is dying of AIDS.

Adam is deeply sensitive to his wife's pain, often torn between his devotion to her while she is driven mad from the trauma of her circumcision and love for his lover and friend Lisette, with whom he corresponds through letters and visits twice a year. Despite being sensitive to Tashi's pain, he comes to a realization that he has regarded it as a singular event rather than a continuous trauma. He stays with Tashi throughout her life and testifies in support of her when she is put on trial for murdering M'Lissa.

**Amy Maxwell** Amy Maxwell is a white woman from New Orleans, Louisiana, who is introduced to Tashi by Raye. Her son, Josh, who was a dancer, and described as depressed almost from birth, killed himself around age 30. Amy has a perpetual smile, as though it is wired. Tashi learns that Amy's cheerful disposition seems to result from her experiences as a young girl. Even though she was the daughter of a wealthy white family, Amy suffered the trauma of female circumcision after her mother caught her touching her genitals. She attributes this trauma as the source of her lack of depression. Instead, as her mother told her, she continually rose above things. After Josh killed himself, she realized that her son internalized what was supposed to be his mother's depression, and he killed himself. While Tashi reacts negatively toward Amy's story, she does so because Amy shatters her illusion that America is a safe space away from the brutal practice of female circumcision.

**Benny (Bentu Moraga)** Benny is Tashi and Adam's son, who received head trauma during his difficult birth because of Tashi's mutilated genitals. As a result, he is cognitively impaired, lacking the ability to remember things, and this dysfunction affects his ability to learn. He loves his mother's smell and finds a best friend in his half brother, Pierre. He understands things only in simple terms. He does not fully understand the meaning of death when confronted with his mother's execution.

**Carl** *See* MZEE.

**Catherine (Nafa)** Catherine (whose African name is Nafa) was Tashi and Dura's mother, who converted to Christianity. Following Dura's death, Tashi believed that she and her mother shared the same pain, and Tashi related to her through the unity of their shared pain. M'Lissa later tells Tashi that Catherine, believing her daughter, Dura, would be unable to marry, had become complicit in her daughter Dura's circumcision, which ultimately led to Dura's death. Whether this information is actually true is never revealed, but Tashi believes M'Lissa's story.

**Dura** Dura was Tashi's sister. As a young girl, Tashi secretly witnessed her sister's death and heard her cries as she underwent genital mutilation. She apparently had some form of hemophilia, which contributed to her bleeding to death during the process. The trauma of Dura's death, in addition to her own genital mutilation, haunts Tashi and thrusts her into varying degrees of insanity throughout her life.

**Evelyn Johnson** *See* TASHI.

**Hartford** Hartford is a young man who is dying in the AIDS ward in the building where Tashi is kept prisoner during the final days of her life. As he is about to die, Hartford asks Adam to listen to his confession. At first, he states that he is a medical student, but later he says that this is a lie; to be a doctor was only a dream that he never achieved. In reality, he worked at a pharmaceutical company that performs animal testing on monkeys, collecting monkeys for the company and breeding them in cages. After a while, he was assigned to kill the monkeys by decapitating them. The kidneys of the dead monkeys were used in cultures to test certain drugs. Hartford's narrative suggests that this testing is how AIDS initially spread in Africa. He dies as he closes his confession. His story breaks through Adam's numbness toward the AIDS patients.

**Lisette** Lisette is a white French woman who is Adam's lover and Pierre's mother. She met Adam in Africa while he was tending to a dying man named Torabe. They developed a friendship and love relationship after Adam married Tashi. Her grandmother, Beatrice, was a French suffragette.

When Lisette became pregnant with little Pierre (named after her own father), her parents reacted with outrage, but over time they learned to accept their daughter's choice and eventually grew to love Pierre. Lisette gave birth to Pierre in her grandmother's bed, where her mother was conceived and born and where she herself was born.

Despite the fact that Adam only speaks of Tashi on occasion, Lisette becomes fascinated by Tashi, particularly with her nightmare of the dark tower.

Lisette passes the story of the nightmare down to Pierre, who later makes it his life's work to understand the origins of Tashi's pain. As she is dying of stomach cancer, Lisette writes a letter to Tashi, expressing the hope that Tashi will someday accept Pierre and allow him to be near her and Adam. At first, Tashi reacts with rage, but eventually she learns to love and accept Pierre as one of her own sons. Tashi and Lisette never meet in life.

As Tashi nears her death, she writes a letter to the already dead Lisette, detailing the connection she feels toward Lisette through Pierre. She believes that they will meet in heaven the way that they were able to meet through Pierre on earth.

**Mama Lissa** *See* M'LISSA.

**Mama Nettie Johnson (Nettie)** Mama Nettie Johnson is the same character as Nettie, Celie's sister in Walker's novel *The Color Purple.* She is the pastor Samuel Johnson's wife, stepmother and aunt to Olivia and Adam Johnson. The people of the Olinka tribe referred to her as Mama Nettie Johnson.

**Mbati (Martha)** Mbati is a house servant in M'Lissa's household. Tashi meets Mbati when she goes to kill M'Lissa. She feels an affinity toward the younger woman, as if Mbati is the daughter that Tashi should have had, the daughter that she had aborted because of the pain of birth. Mbati testifies in favor of Tashi, and their relationship strengthens as Tashi approaches the date of her execution. They discuss the myth of Africans and the secret of joy. Tashi asks Mbati to find the secret of joy and tell it to her before her death. As Tashi faces the firing squad, Mbati unfurls a banner that says, "RESISTANCE IS THE SECRET OF JOY!"

**M'Lissa (Mama Lissa)** M'Lissa is the *tsunga*—circumciser—of the Olinka tribe where Tashi grew up. Tashi's sister Dura died under M'Lissa's hand. M'Lissa circumcised Tashi in a Mbele camp. She later gained status and wealth, and she is living in relative comfort in her old age, the government having recognized her as an icon of Olinkan life and society, and as someone who upholds tradition.

When M'Lissa (sometimes called Mama Lissa) became a *tsunga,* she was following in the footsteps of her mother, who followed M'Lissa's grandmother before her in a kind of succession. While M'Lissa's grandmother was said to have performed her duty well and with enjoyment, for M'Lissa's mother, it was torture. Her mother hid a statue of a female doll in a rotten tree in the forest. The doll was of a woman, touching her genitals with a serene look of joy on her face. When M'Lissa was a young girl, her mother circumcised her and attempted to leave the clitoris. To punish her mother's efforts, another *tsunga* finished the process instead, severing a tendon on one of her legs, which gave M'Lissa a permanent limp.

When Tashi comes to see her late in her life, M'Lissa recognizes right away that Tashi has come to kill her. She tells Tashi that if one of the women she has circumcised kills her, it proves her worth to the tribe. Tashi spends time with M'Lissa before her death, hearing the stories she has to tell. After learning about M'Lissa's circumcision experience, Tashi decides instead to smother her with a pillow and set her house on fire. Tashi is subsequently executed for murdering M'Lissa.

**Mzee (Carl, The Old Man, Old Father)** Mzee is Lisette's uncle and serves as Tashi's therapist. Under his guidance, Tashi rediscovers the source of the trauma at the heart of her emotional problems. Through Mzee's techniques, Tashi remembers that she was present at her sister's clitoridectomy and that she had blocked the memory of that trauma from her consciousness. She also recognizes that M'Lissa is the source of both her sister's and her own mutilation, and later she resolves to kill the woman.

Mzee is a representation of the ideas, philosophies, and techniques of the noted psychoanalytical therapist Carl Jung. Tashi has a sense that Mzee is dying. Mzee feels that he has learned enormously from his encounters with Adam and Tashi and feels gratified for the experiences he has had with them. Tashi's life story seems to have a profound effect on him. He feels his strong connection to her and her pain as an important event in his own life. He sends Tashi to Raye, her new therapist, shortly before his own death.

**Nafa** *See* CATHERINE.

**Old Father** *See* MZEE.

**Old Man, The** *See* MZEE.

**Olivia Johnson** Olivia is Adam's sister; she is the daughter of Pastor Samuel Johnson and stepdaughter/niece of Mama Nettie Johnson. In addition, she is Tashi's best friend. She is kindhearted and sensitive to suffering. Even into adulthood, Olivia recalls the first time she encountered Tashi in the Olinka village, and she remembers Tashi's weeping face. She maintains a belief in the best of people, particularly Tashi, and does not believe that Tashi killed M'Lissa. She takes care of the patients on the AIDS ward during the interim period between Tashi's sentencing and execution. She has a potter make a replica of the fertility doll touching her genitals, a replica of M'Lissa's doll, which she gives to Tashi during the trial.

**Our Leader** Our Leader is the Olinkan political leader who was incarcerated by "white conquerors" in a similar vein to Nelson Mandela and other African civil rights activists. It became illegal to say his name, and therefore the Olinka referred to him as Our Leader. Unlike Nelson Mandela, he was never released from jail, and he died just before the country's independence. Despite his isolation, recorded messages reached the outside and became distributed among the Olinka, who regard him as a savior, a Christ figure who advocated for the continuation of tribal tradition, including female genital mutilation.

**Pierre Johnson** Pierre Johnson is Lisette and Adam's biracial son. When he was a boy in France, many people assumed that he was Algerian. Growing up, he saw his father only twice a year.

Pierre has his mother's eyes. With Lisette's encouragement, he decided to move to America and attend Harvard University in Boston to be closer to his father, but because his father lived in San Francisco, Pierre was not able to spend more time with him until after his mother's death. His mother died before his last year in college, and Pierre transferred to Berkeley. Before her death, Lisette wrote a letter to Adam and Tashi, with the hope that Tashi would accept Pierre and allow him to be near her and his father.

Pierre learned of Tashi's state from his mother, particularly her nightmare of the dark tower. This story becomes a kind of life obsession and leads him to study the myth that was the origin of female genital mutilation. During Pierre's first attempt to visit, Tashi pelts him with stones and jagged rocks. After some time, they meet again. Tashi behaves more civilly, and before her execution, he shows her a video he has made of termite behavior as a possible origin for the practices of containment and brutalization of women and helps to solve the puzzle of Tashi's dream. Tashi comes to accept Pierre as though he is her own son. She ultimately feels as though she is able to know Lisette through Pierre despite the fact that she never met Lisette.

Pierre fosters a strong friendship with his half brother Benny and continues his anthropological study of female circumcision. His work enlightens Tashi and others in his family.

**Queen Anne** Queen Anne was a former lover of Pierre. Born in Hawaii to pagan parents, she was named after the wildflower Queen Anne's Lace. Queen Anne was raised to enjoy and embrace the sexual element of all things and beings. More than hetero-, homo-, or bisexual, Queen Anne is described as pansexual. It was through her that Pierre realized his own bisexuality.

**Raye** Raye is Tashi's therapist, who was introduced to her through Mzee. At first, Tashi resents her because of her confident embrace of her identity as a black woman. Tashi begins to trust her when Raye has a procedure done on her gums that allows her to empathize with the pain Tashi has experienced. Raye introduces Tashi to Amy, who is a white victim of female circumcision from New Orleans, Louisiana. Raye is with Tashi's family to witness her execution.

**Tashi (Evelyn Johnson, Mrs. Johnson)** Tashi, whose American name is Evelyn Johnson, begins the novel as a young girl weeping over her sister Dura's death, after Dura died during a botched circumcision. As a young woman, she and Adam Johnson became lovers. They made love in the harvest fields despite the fact that tribal myths said it cursed the lands to do so. Adam performed cunnilingus on her, which is another taboo in the Olinka tribe. Adam traveled to rescue Tashi when she decided as a grown woman to submit herself to being circumcised, as well as to having her face mutilated with tribal markings. Tashi believed that without adhering to tribal tradition, she would never be desirable. But the process seems to have destroyed Tashi's light and carefree personality. The experience of her own mutilation and the memory of her sister's death haunt her throughout the rest of her life.

Adam married Tashi, but their lovemaking was always painful. When she gave birth, her vagina had to be surgically torn open, and the difficult birthing process left her son mentally impaired. The novel tracks her emotional and psychological damage as a result of these two events. In her fragile state, she is both attached to her husband and repulsed by him, and she often pushes him away.

At Lisette's suggestion, Adam introduces Mzee to Tashi. She trusts his age and his wispy hair, and they grow to care for and respect each other. When Mzee shows Tashi a video from one of his visits to Africa depicting children lined up on a straw mat and a clucking cock, she faints. The image triggers the traumatic recollection of her sister's "murder," as she calls it. She paints the cock bigger and bigger, eventually painting it on the wall of one of Mzee's rooms. Tashi accompanies the image with a foot, presumably M'Lissa's gnarled foot, and in between its toes, it contains a piece of the circumcised female genitalia. In addition to this episode, Tashi continually has a nightmare of a dark, rising tower.

Before he dies, Mzee introduces Tashi to Raye, an African-American therapist. Tashi regards Raye's strong confidence and bluntness with resentment at first, but then the two women develop a friendship and connection.

Tashi is aware of Adam's connection to and eventual affair with Lisette, a white French woman, whom he visits periodically. Tashi also knows about Lisette and Adam's son, Pierre. She devolves into neurotic and psychotic breakdowns on occasion when confronted with the realities of Adam's affair. Tashi never meets Lisette personally in life, but Lisette becomes fascinated with Tashi when Adam tells her of her recurring nightmare of the dark tower. She passes this story on to Pierre, who makes it his life work to understand this nightmare in addition to the origin of the practice of female circumcision. When Pierre comes to California, Tashi hurls heavy stones at his face, but later she accepts and comes to appreciate him.

Later, Tashi learns that M'Lissa, the *tsunga* of her tribe who murdered her sister and circumcised her, is still alive. She decides to kill the woman, but before she does so, she hears M'Lissa's stories and perspectives about the traditional ideas and duties of a *tsunga*, as well as her personal history. Tashi smothers the woman with a pillow and burns the house down. She is later convicted of murder by the Olinka and sentenced to death. Facing the firing squad, she does not let herself be blindfolded. She sees Mbati unfurl a banner that reads "<u>RESISTANCE</u> IS THE SECRET OF JOY!" and she is executed.

### Further Reading

Banks, Erma, and Keith Byerman. *Alice Walker: An Annotated Bibliography.* New York: Garland Press, 1989.

Barker-Benfield, G. J. *The Horrors of the Half-Known Life: Male Attitudes toward Women and Sexuality in Nineteenth-Century America.* New York: Harper and Row, 1976.

Benn, Melissa. Review of *Possessing the Secret of Joy,* by Alice Walker. *New Statesman and Society* 5 (October 9, 1992): 36–37.

Bloom, Harold, ed. *Alice Walker.* New York: Chelsea House, 1989.

Buckman, Alyson R. "The Body as a Site of Colonization: Alice Walker's *Possessing the Secret of Joy.*" *Journal of American Culture* 18 (Summer 1995): 89–94.

El Dareer, Asma. *Woman, Why Do You Weep?* London: Zed Press, 1982.

Gates, Henry Louis, Jr., ed. *Reading Black, Reading Feminist: A Critical Anthology.* New York: Meridian, 1990.

Hospital, Janette Turner. Review of *Possessing the Secret of Joy* by Alice Walker. *New York Times Book Review,* 28 June 1992, p. 11.

Kemp, Yakini. Review of *Warrior Marks* by Alice Walker and Pratibha Parmar. *Belles Lettres* 8 (Fall 1992): 57.

Lightfoot-Klein, Hanny. *Prisoners of Ritual: An Odyssey into Female Genital Circumcision in Africa.* New York: Haworth Press, 1989.

Ricciardi, Mirella. *African Saga.* London: William Collins and Sons Inc., 1981.

Souris, Stephen. "Multiperspectival Consensus: Alice Walker's *Possessing the Secret of Joy,* the Multiple Narrator Novel, and the Practice of 'Female Circumcision.'" CLA *Journal* 40 (June 1997): 405–431.

Wall, Cheryl A., ed. *Changing Our Own Words: Essays on Criticism, Theory, and Writing by Black Women.* New Brunswick, N.J.: Rutgers University Press, 1989.

Watkins, Mel. Review of *Possessing the Secret of Joy* by Alice Walker. *New York Times,* 24 July 1992, p. B4.

Willis, Susan. *Specifying: Black Women Writing the American Experience.* Madison: University of Wisconsin Press, 1987.

# *The Temple of My Familiar* (1989)

*The Temple of My Familiar* is a complex narrative that attempts no less than a rewriting of world history. The novel features an enormous array of characters whose lives intersect and overlap as the plot explores the intricacies of racism, nationalism sexism, heterosexism, environmental desecration, economic exploitation, and a myriad of other concerns.

Although it introduces Walker's most voluminous fictional cast, the novel focuses most of its storytelling energies on four main characters: Carlotta, Fanny, Suwelo, and Arveyda. Its title reveals its central metaphor: an exploration of the relationship between the inner and outer self, the spirit and the body, the FAMILIAR and the temple. Each of the central characters embarks on a journey of personal self-discovery in order to dislodge the detritus that is the external construction of the self and, by so doing, to create harmony and synchronization between the body and the spirit. In addition to the adventures of the Walker's four protagonists, the novel features a matriarchal, shape-shifting GODDESS FIGURE named Lissie Lyles, who becomes the voice of truth, the GRIOT of the narrative.

The novel is also related to Walker's previous novel, *The Color Purple,* although she has said that this novel is not a sequel. Several familiar characters from that novel revisit in *The Temple of My Familiar,* including Celie, Shug Avery, Albert, Sofia, Olivia and Nettie. Fanny, one of the central characters in *Temple,* is Celie's granddaughter. The characters each progress through various moments of revelation until the cathartic end, where each of them finds sanctuary in self-love and mutual admiration.

With several notable exceptions, critics generally did not find *The Temple of My Familiar* to be a convincing or satisfying novel and accused Walker of sacrificing artistry for polemics.

## SYNOPSIS

### Part 1

*The Temple of My Familiar* begins with the narrative of the Zedés—Zedé the grandmother and Zedé the mother of one of the novel's central protagonists, Carlotta. Little Zedé, as Carlotta's mother is called, learns the skills of sewing from her mother, but she is a bright student and so attends college. While working as a teacher in a progressive school, Little Zedé is arrested and imprisoned under suspicion that she is a communist; while imprisoned, she becomes pregnant. The narrative does not divulge the circumstances of the pregnancy and the identity of Zedé's lover, the father of her baby, until later in the novel.

Eventually, Little Zedé escapes from the prison with her baby, Carlotta, and the two settle in San Francisco. Zedé works at a sweatshop, where she steals feathers for her real work, creating costumes and capes for rock stars. During one of these deliveries, Carlotta meets the man she falls in love with, Arveyda, an African-American/Native American rock star. Arveyda influences Carlotta to eat well and exercise, and he generally expands her perspectives. He shares with Carlotta the intricacies of his personal history. When he finally meets Zedé, he is able to see her struggle and the deep wounds that have defined her life.

Arveyda is from Terre Haute, Indiana. The product of a lost father and disengaged mother, he has a sense of absence rooted in his childhood experiences. Mr. Isaac, the greengrocer in Terre Haute, was an important figure in his youth who showed him the way that music functions as a way to communicate and to transcend difference.

Carlotta reminds Arveyda of his mother. This resonance is significant because it is indicative of Arveyda's general hunger for maternal love and thus foreshadows his attraction to and later love for and sexual involvement with Carlotta's mother, Zedé. After her first meeting with Arveyda, Zedé tells Carlotta that Arveyda looks exactly like the father her daughter never knew.

Carlotta and Arveyda marry and have two children. The marriage falls apart after three years or so when Zedé and Arveyda finally acknowledge and act on the passionate feelings they have held for each other since their first meeting. After Arveyda and Zedé tell Carlotta about their affair, the two leave California and travel to Mexico and Central and South America.

Carlotta is emotionally devastated by what she perceives as the betrayal of her husband and mother. She becomes a teacher of women's literature and lives bitterly with her two children while her mother and Arveyda travel the world.

The narrative shifts to another story and set of characters. Suwelo is a young African-American man who has had a relationship with Carlotta and another of the novel's central characters, Fanny. When introduced in the novel, he is residing in his recently deceased uncle's home. His uncle, Rafe, has left the house to Suwelo, who spends his time in the house wondering about his uncle's life. In the house, he finds photographs of his uncle's friends and relatives. Almost involuntarily, he extends the time he planned to spend closing and selling his uncle's home as his curiosity about the man and his life develops.

Suwelo has had a relationship with Carlotta and is married to Fanny, although the two are in the midst of marital difficulties and are considering divorce. Suwelo is compared to an owl in appearance and is emotionally disconnected as a result of his impaired and prematurely terminated relationship with his parents, Marcia and Louis, who died in a car accident, leaving Suwelo orphaned at a young age.

As Suwelo explores his uncle's life, he discovers that Rafe used to work as a sleeping-car porter. This work was one of the few well-paying and stable occupations available to African-American men of his generation.

Suwelo explores the aspects of his uncle's life and meets two of Rafe's oldest friends, Hal Jenkins and Miss Lissie Lyles. Although the older couple knew Suwelo as a boy, he does not remember them. They take him into their care and, through stories, begin to nurture his spirit by connecting him with a personal, communal, and collective past.

Hal tells Suwelo about his relationship with Lissie. Lissie and Hal were friends from the time of their births in the same African-American community outside of Charleston Bay. Their relationship began when they were babies and continued through school. Hal confesses to Suwelo that he was always a bit intimidated by Lissie, and he suggests that his awe of her is warranted because of her past and origins.

The narrative shifts back to the story of Carlotta, Zedé, and Arveyda. Carlotta imagines her husband and mother on their travels through exotic and yet familiar landscapes. Zedé tells Arveyda of her life and of the rituals that defined her life before she became a political prisoner and the mother of Carlotta. She describes a place where women were valued as a powerful component of the community. She tells him of her mother and of her particular talents as a seamstress. She remembers that her mother resided in a separate space and was valued for her skill, even magical abilities, not only for her role as the mother and wife of her family.

Zedé tells Arveyda the reason priests are celibate. It is an origin story that begins with the tale of a woman who gives birth to a boy who, after a time, goes off to find other men. The men reside separately from women. In the tale, they are newcomers to the world and inexperienced; thus, they are jealous of the women. They feel abandoned and envious of the women, and the two groups remain separated by gender. The men try to acquire power by imitating the women's ability to give birth. Through misguided efforts, they often castrate themselves. Their failure to replicate the women's ability to give birth makes the men furious and vengeful toward the women. According to Zedé, this is the root of the bitterness and sexual deprivation of priests.

Lissie also tells Suwelo stories. She tells him of her multiple lives and her memories of her various incarnations throughout human history, including one of having been enslaved and having died after attempting to escape. Suwelo feels a kinship with her and is fascinated by her stories. There are certain continuities to her reincarnations. In all of her manifestations, she is always a courageous yet tender person as well as an individual consumed with the possibility of achieving fairness, equality, and individual and collective justice. She also tells Suwelo about her history in this lifetime. She says she was assaulted by her parents' ineptitude. Her mother was unintelligent, and her father was incompetent. She was not well-nurtured in any way, physically, psychologically, or spiritually. As she grew older, she insisted on having better food for herself and her peers, and eventually she helped her mother to become a healthier person.

Lissie tells Suwelo about her relationship with Hal. She says that Hal is the only person from this lifetime whom she feels she has known in prior lives, although she is not sure exactly which life she knew him in or the circumstances of their previous encounters. Hal's father objected to his son's desire to create art, and when Hal abandoned his passion, he lost part of his fundamental self. The abandonment of such an essential part of his constitution has physical ramifications. Hal lost part of his sight at the same time that he gave up his art. As a child, Lissie tried to help Hal to be able to continue in secret with his art, and she tells Suwelo that Hal was able to conjure memory with his painting.

The narrative shifts back to Zedé and Arveyda, who continue their travels though South America. Zedé tells Arveyda of the circumstances of Carlotta's conception, a story about Carlotta's father, Jesus, that she has never shared with Carlotta. Jesus had another name and was only called Jesus because his name was unpronounceable to his captors. He was imprisoned in the same facility as Zedé and was known as the keeper of his village's sacred stones. When the stones were disturbed in any way, Jesus would appear to reposition them. The stones marked the home of human beings, and their placement was essential to the survival of the species. Zedé fell in love with him, and during the one time they made love, they conceived Carlotta. The guards tortured Jesus after he was discovered with Zedé. They cut off his hair, mutilated, and murdered him. His people rescued Zedé, who was pregnant, and took Jesus's body. They gave Zedé the sacred stones to give to Carlotta, Jesus's child.

The tale of Zedé and Carlotta's escape from imprisonment with the help of Jesus's people continues. She found a job cleaning at a school called La Escuela de Jungla, where the children of rich North Americans were sent for various reasons. Some of the residents had mental problems, while others simply refused to conform to their parent's expectations and were sent away to ensure that they did not embarrass their families. Zedé befriended one such person, named Mary Ann Haverstock. Mary Ann was the daughter of extremely wealthy parents who were disturbed by their daughter's political views and drug abuse and sent her to La Escuela de Jungla. At the facility, Mary Ann met Zedé and Carlotta. Zedé pitied the young woman and saw that she was being exploited in the facility. She wrote to Mary Ann's parents to tell them the truth about the facility where they had sent their daughter. As a result of the letters, Mary Ann's parents rescued her from the school. Eventually, Mary Ann returned to the facility to rescue Carlotta and Zedé. She had had a transformation in her life and wished to dedicate it to rectifying injustice. The boat in which the rescue took place capsized, and Zedé believes that Mary Ann was killed in the accident, although she and Carlotta were rescued by the Coast Guard.

The novel returns to Suwelo and Miss Lissie and to her tales of her various lives. She tells Suwelo of a time when she remembered peace. It was an early time when human beings were very small and coexisted with animals who were more like family than a different species. Another group of humans destroyed the equilibrium and trust that bonded the animals and the humans. In that lifetime, Lissie's sexuality and gender caused her to be cast out, and she died as a prostitute from an infection.

These conversations with Miss Lissie influence Suwelo and make him reassess his understanding of the world. He notices that the photographs of Miss Lissie that hang at his Uncle Rafe's house appear to be of different women, even though he has been told that they are all photographs of Miss Lissie. Each of the photographs represents a distinct dimension in Miss Lissie's multifaceted self and her previous lives.

Suwelo becomes absorbed with the alternative realities Miss Lissie's narratives suggest to him, so much so that he loses the urgency to return to his previous life and its complications. He wishes that he could share his experiences with his wife, Fanny, who already had an appreciation for the past and for older people as its guardians.

Mr. Hal tells Suwelo about his life with Lissie. He says that in spite of his bad vision, he fought in World War I and that he and Lissie married. Hal soon returned from the war because his bad vision made him an inept soldier. Lissie was pregnant with their child, and the two spent a happy and healthy time during her pregnancy. The blissful happiness they shared ended with the birth of their daughter, Lulu. Hal was so guilt-ridden as a result of the pain Lissie went through when she delivered the child that he became unable to make love to her, and the marriage dissolved. Lulu's name comes from a previous life of Lissie's when she was an inhabitant of a harem in North Africa.

Hal continues his tales of his life and Lissie's. He tells Suwelo that Lissie had four other children after Lulu. Three of the children died while infants. Only one son, Anatole, fathered by Suwelo's Uncle Rafe, grew to adulthood. Anatole died while serving in the navy. Hal then tells Suwelo about Lissie's relationship with a man called the picture taker. Lissie left Hal for the picture taker after their marriage fell apart. The picture taker was married and already had many children by the time he became involved with Lissie, so their relationship was not a happy one or satisfying for Lissie. Eventually, Rafe and Lissie became involved and the three—Hal, Lissie, and Rafe—shared a household, love, and the responsibility for raising Lulu.

The narrative continues in Miss Lissie's voice as she reveals the story that contains the novel's controlling metaphor—the story of the temple and its familiar. Miss Lissie tells the story as a dream. She speaks of the familiar as a favorite animal, a kind of pet who, in Lissie's dream, keeps interrupting her conversation with Suwelo. As a result, Miss Lissie confines him in increasingly oppressive restraints in order to quell the interruptions the creature causes in the conversation. After he makes several escapes from the restraints Lissie places him in, the familiar glances sadly in her direction and flies away.

The narrative resumes with a reunion between Carlotta and Arveyda. Arveyda has returned from his travels with Zedé and tries to explain to Carlotta what happened between them and to clarify the status of their relationship. Rather audaciously, he asserts that he has been the conduit through which Zedé has been able to access her past and the truth of who she is. As a result, Carlotta can also experience fullness and clarity if she is able to forgive her mother and husband for loving each other. Carlotta is not yet ready to forgive and harbors bitterness that poisons her spirit and body. Arveyda persists and tells Carlotta about the stones her father had under his care. He sings to Carlotta of their deeper meanings, and she begins to understand and be receptive to the greater truths contained in the stones and in the story he has to tell of her mother and of the human race generally. Through his song, Arveyda is able to help Carlotta to begin to heal.

Suwelo hears one of Arveyda's records in the background of one of his calls to Fanny and remembers when he bought a ticket for her to attend one of Arveyda's concerts. He was resentful at the time because Fanny had been too overwhelmed to attend the concert because she did not think she could bear to see Arveyda in person.

Suwelo also remembers the first time that he met Carlotta. He had compared her to Coretta Scott King and felt that she looked like a Latina version of the Civil Rights widow. Now that he has new insights about human experience and human suffering, he feels that part of what attracted him to Carlotta was his sense of her suffering.

Mr. Hal tells Suwelo about his parents. He tells Suwelo that his mother was a joyous person, always laughing, but his father was grim, perhaps overshadowed by his inability to express his homosexuality in a time and community where it was not possible. As a result, Hal's father, David, espoused a bitter homophobia. David was named after the biblical David who slew Goliath.

Heath was a childhood friend of David, Hal's father. David felt resentment toward Heath because, as a result of racial privilege, Heath had greater liberty in the relationship than David. Although they were best friends as children, Heath grew up to be a racist, yet the men continued their tenuous relationship as adults. The two had a sexual attraction to each other that, under other circumstances, might have been a real relationship. The tension and power dynamic between them turned both into alcoholics. David's complete intolerance of his son's artistic nature and proclivities stemmed from his own self-hatred and truncated desires.

After hearing Lissie and Hal's voices telling stories, Suwelo begins to find his own voice and finally shares with them some of his own experience. He tells Lissie and Hal about Fanny. He recalls the day that she told him she no longer wanted to be married. She said that she loved Suwelo but wanted to change the contours of the relationship so that she could have more autonomy and not be bound to him through rules and regulations she found artificial and constricting. She loved Suwelo but did not want to be married to him. At the time of the confrontation, Suwelo was unable to hear her and to understand where she was coming from.

## Part 2

With the beginning of Part 2, *The Temple of My Familiar* shifts to Fanny's story. Olivia, Fanny's mother, tells her fiancé, Lance, the story of Celie, her mother, and Nettie, her aunt (from *The Color Purple*) and of her experiences in Africa. In these experiences and through the impressions of the world gathered from her mother and her aunt, Olivia gained insights that led her to become a minister. In recounting her experiences of Africa, she recalls when her brother, Adam, fell in love with her best friend, Tashi, leaving her feeling isolated and left out. She kissed a white man, Ralston Flood, while attention was focused on Tashi and Adam. Dahvid saw the kiss and insisted on sleeping with Olivia. The result of their sexual union was Olivia's pregnancy with Fanny. She returned to the United States, pregnant, after having spent her entire childhood and young adulthood in Africa, and there she soon gave birth to her daughter, Fanny Nzingha.

Fanny tells Suwelo that she is going to Africa with her mother to meet and visit her father and sister for the first time. When Fanny and Olivia arrive in Africa, they find that her father, a playwright and the minister of culture, has been arrested for writing plays that the government considers subversive. In his home, Dahvid is called Ola, a shortened form of his African name, Abajeralasezeola. Fanny and her father have an awkward meeting but seem to have a promising connection.

Suwelo remembers the contours of his relationship with Fanny and begins to understand that his reliance on traditional gender roles is at the heart of the failure of their relationship.

Fanny and her mother grow closer as they share stories during their travels in Africa. Olivia talks about the disconcerted feelings she experienced upon her return to the United States from Africa and to the congenial environment of Celie and Shug's home. Fanny's co-grandmothers developed a shared philosophy and theology that influenced both Fanny and her mother. Olivia tells Fanny about her need to leave such a free-flowing environment for the structure she found in college. She attended SPELMAN COLLEGE in Atlanta and, after graduation, worked at the black hospital where she met her first husband, Fanny's stepfather, Lance (otherwise known as Lancelot) a doctor. Olivia also recalls with Fanny the happiness of her marriage to Lance and their success at establishing a family with Fanny. Unfortunately, Lance died as a young man.

Fanny is delighted to discover Bessie Head in person during her travels. She writes to Suwelo about her encounters with the South African writer, and he experiences guilt as he remembers that Fanny tried to get him to read Head's books and he refused. Ola, Fanny's biological father, knows Head personally and tells Fanny that the author had suffered a nervous breakdown. Ola tells Fanny about his trials and tribulations, which have resulted from the government's responses to his writings. She listens to the conversations Ola has with his friends and learns about some of the complexities of his life and the relationship between artists in his country and their efforts at political activism.

Suwelo consults a therapist, though he is concerned about saying anything regarding Fanny's connection to the spirit world and her interactions and relationship with the spirits. Nonetheless, Suwelo tries talking to the man, named Bernie Kesselbaum, about his marriage and how to resolve his conflicts about it. Suwelo tells Kesselbaum about Fanny's ability to slip into discourses with those who are not living and to develop relationships with them. She describes the relationships as a kind of possession that feels to her akin to being in love.

Ola tells Fanny that he wants to write a play about Elvis Presley. He sees in Elvis a synthesis of Native American, African American, and white, and he locates this hybridity as central to Elvis's appeal. He tells Fanny that if he is exiled because of his writings, he would be interested in trying to write the play with her.

Miss Lissie shares with Suwelo more of her understanding about life and death. She tells him that no one ever leaves the earth and their primary incarnation in this space. Each person is reincarnated in a perpetual cycle. She also conveys to him her fear that after she dies this time, she is afraid of the condition the earth will be in and that it will, perhaps, be unlivable as a result of the destructive energy of human beings.

Suwelo takes a train back to California. Before leaving, he discovers that Miss Lissie and Mr. Hal still live together. He also learns about the fates of their daughter, Lulu, and Miss Lissie's son, Anatole. As an adult, Lulu became a performer and went to Paris to work. When the city fell to the Nazis, she disappeared and was never heard from again. Suwelo also discovers that before Anatole's death, he attended Fisk University and became a professor. As a parting gift, Lissie and Hal give Suwelo paintings they have created of each other.

Suwelo also finds a letter from Miss Lissie in which she details for him the intricacies of yet another of her lives. She recalls being burned at the stake as a witch. Miss Lissie has written the letter in a particular type of ink that disappears as it is read. As Suwelo reads the pages, he finds he cannot reread them since the words are gone when he returns to them.

Carlotta continues on her journey of healing. She takes the stones that belonged to her father out of their confines in her home and places them outside in a park in their original configuration and thus continues her father's mission. Carlotta has a dream that outlines the dynamics of her healing journey. In the dream, she is with an ancient and iconographic mother figure with whom she expresses her creativity. In the dream, the two are in a cave, and she sees open thresholds within the cave.

## Part 3

Part 3 of *The Temple of My Familiar* continues Mary Ann's story. After her rescue of Carlotta and Zedé from La Escuela de Jungla, Mary Ann Haverstock becomes Mary Jane Briden and lives her life in exile from all she had known before. She lives on part of her inheritance; gives her money away to people and causes she deems worthy; moves to Africa; and, eventually, becomes a playwright.

In the immediate wake of her feigned death, Mary Ann travels to London and spends time with her great-aunt Eleanora; in the process, she learns about the older woman's life. Eleanora had a twin sister named Eleandra to whom Mary bears a physical resemblance. From her great-aunt, she learns about another relative also named Eleandra, with whom she shares a spiritual kinship. The older Eleandra Burnham was an adventurer in Africa, and Eleanora's twin was named after this relative.

Mary Ann explores Eleanora's papers and uncovers the fascinating story of her great-aunt's life. Eleanora eschewed the privilege and prison of her life in England and traveled to Africa. She kept a diary, which has been preserved along with other donations to a college archive. Mary Ann reads the diary and thus learns the specific details of her great-aunt's narrative.

When Mary Ann travels to London, Eleanora is 100 years old. In the process of trying to identify some of her great-aunt's photographs, Mary Ann is given access to the diary of the older Eleandra and learns of the older woman's travels and particularly of Eleandra's encounters with an African woman named M'Sukta. Eleandra and her cousin Theodore, known as T, found M'Sukta in the Museum of Natural History. The woman had created artwork that Eleandra and her cousin admired. When they came upon her, she was spinning cloth. Eleandra's encounter with M'Sukta was what sparked and nurtured her interest in Africa and her eventual travels there. Indirectly, the story of M'Sukta also prompts Mary Ann's journey there.

As Mary Ann discovers through her diary, Eleandra was a woman who refused to conform to the expectations of someone of her class at the time in which she lived. She had been educated at home, and as her diary reveals, she became informed about and obsessed by inequity and injustice through her encounters with M'Sukta.

Although the diary is somewhat illegible as a result of age and abuse, Mary Ann is able to learn that after several years, Eleandra and M'Sukta were eventually able to communicate. Sir Henry Rowanbotham, a commander in the British Army, derived an alphabet so that the language M'Sutka spoke could be written down. He was also the one who made provisions for her in the Museum of Natural History in the wake of the complete destruction of her tribe. Mary Ann finishes reading what she can of Eleandra's diary, and after her great-aunt Eleanora dies, she leaves for Africa, armed with a year's supply of paints.

## Part 4

Part 4 of *The Temple of My Familiar* begins with Suwelo talking about his relationship with Carlotta, a relationship that began when he and Fanny separated. This reflection occurs before he sells his uncle's house and goes back to San Francisco on the train. He tells Hal and Lissie about the history of his relationship with Fanny, how they came to live in the Bay Area, and of his insecurities about their relationship. He was always afraid that Fanny would leave him for another man or woman. The relationship between Carlotta and Suwelo occurred during one of Fanny's trips to Africa. Suwelo was attracted to Carlotta's neediness and her oppressive femininity. He also took advantage of her disconnectedness. He did not care about her profound sorrow and even reveled Carlotta's refusal to reveal any information about herself. He felt he could have sex with her without obligation.

Suwelo talks about Fanny's evolution. She gave up materialism and pretension. Suwelo also tells Hal and Lissie of her grief when her father, Ola, died.

In a letter to Suwelo, Fanny talks about the details of her father's funeral. She also tells him about her meeting with her sister, Nzingha Anne. They had been introduced by their father. Nzingha told Fanny the story of her mother, whose code name was Harriet. Harriet was a guerrilla fighter who had little education but an intuitive and psychic ability that made her extremely dexterous as a fugitive fighter. Ola abandoned her and later returned to take their children, Nzingha and Hildegarde, to live with him. Harriet died, a shadow of her former vibrant and creative self, when Nzingha was 16. Nzingha told Fanny about her efforts to get their father Ola's attention and love without success. She felt as though she could not gain his love because she was always competing with Fanny, the American sister she had never met until their father introduced them.

Fanny and her sister bond through the commonalities they find in the overlapping edges of their shared narratives. Nzingha fills Fanny in about the details of their father's life that she does not know. She also tells Fanny about her time studying in France and the discomfort she felt as a result of the racism and sexism she experienced there. She reinterprets the MEDUSA story from an African perspective. In the tale, Medusa is not a horror whose appearance has the power to petrify. Rather, she becomes a goddess who is the representative of African culture and civilization, a history that has been erased and forgotten. Nzingha asserts that it is African history that forms the roots of Western culture and civilization. She left France because she refused to accept the false information that she felt she was getting in her studies.

Through their conversations and connections, Nzingha stops seeing Fanny as competition and also begins to value herself as an individual.

Before he leaves for San Francisco, Hal and Lissie have a farewell dinner for Suwelo, who continues his discussion of his revelations about Fanny. He discloses to them her uncanny ability to find information that she needs through mysterious means. She is in tune to the natural world and its energies, and they seem to respond to her. Suwelo feels that his quest for answers about life's most profound questions takes much more energy and effort on his part.

He speaks about his infidelity to Fanny and about his regret that he betrayed her trust. He speaks of his and Fanny's divorce as a loosening of the obligations that held them together, freeing them to bond with ties based in true connection and admiration rather than finances or other socially constructed ties. Fanny and Suwelo found that they were happy when their relationship was defined organically rather than by some preconceived agenda.

## Part 5

Part 5 begins with a set of beatitudes called *The Gospel According to Shug,* composed by Shug Avery over the course of her relationship with Celie. It expresses a kind of pantheistic, humanist creed with a kind of inner, intuitive knowledge that is accessible to all who genuinely seek to find it.

Arveyda gets a copy of the pamphlet and is moved by its contents. Carlotta and Arveyda have reached a peaceful reconciliation. They are able to spend time together without argument and share the responsibility for parenting their children. Carlotta tells Arveyda about her relationship with Suwelo and about her going to Fanny for massages. She picks up the copy of *The Gospel According to Shug* during one of her massage sessions. The pamphlet and his conversations with Carlotta find Arveyda wondering about his own mother, Katherine Degos; the church she founded; and her life in general. Carlotta also tells Arveyda about Fanny's terror that she will murder someone.

Robin Ramirez is Fanny's therapist. Fanny seeks out her help with the issues she is having when she feels that she wants to kill or injure all the people in the world who have blond hair. Fanny confesses that the hair color has come to represent oppression and domination generally, but Robin gets her to recognize that the anger she is experiencing has deeper and more personal roots. During her childhood, Fanny had a white friend named Tanya with whom she spent a great deal of time. The friendship was marred by the racial context that surrounded the girls in the rural South. As a child, Fanny was not allowed inside Tanya's house as a result of her race. Through her explorations with Robin about her first encounters with racism, Fanny is able to come to terms with her feelings and to access both forgiveness and compassion for those who practice racism. This problem precedes Fanny's trip to Africa to meet her father. When she learns of her daughter's troubles, Olivia decides to invite her daughter to join her as she reconnects with Fanny's father.

During her visit to Africa with her mother, Fanny discusses the issues surrounding race and violence. Olivia tries to help Fanny with her stories about the Santamarias. Abel Santamaria was a Cuban revolutionary who was killed as a result of his activism. His sister, Haydee, committed suicide in despair 20 years after the incident. Haydee has special resonance for Olivia, who uses her story as an example of the transcendent power of forgiveness. She also tells Fanny a story about her grandmother, Celie. The abuse Celie experienced as a young women she visited on her dog. Through her interactions with the dog, Celie eventually learned to be tender and to value everyone's feelings, even those of animals and insects.

The narrative shifts back to Fanny and Robin's therapy sessions. Robin shares with Fanny some of her own story, saying that her mother gave her the name Robin because it did not sound Spanish. She suggests that Fanny undergo hypnosis. Under this procedure, Fanny comes to understand her own culpability in the cycle of oppression and faces the self-destructive nature of her feelings. This epiphany sets her on the road to recovery.

Going back in time, Ola and Fanny have a conversation in which he imparts his understandings of issues of oppression. He states that language is primary and that there must be a common language for people to begin to understand each other fully. Ultimately, he agrees with what she has discovered—that hatred is ultimately self-destructive.

Both Fanny and Suwelo return to the Bay Area and meet to talk about their experiences and growth. Fanny decides that the roots of racism lie in a terrible misunderstanding between people with light skin and dark skin and the resentment of whites about the adaptability of blacks in a hot, sunny climate. The two continue conversing, and Suwelo apologizes for his infidelity. Fanny explains to him that she did not feel betrayed by the affairs but by Suwelo's casual lack of concern for the women with whom he had sex. Suwelo tells Fanny that he was hurt when she left him without an explanation. Fanny replies that she was tired of having to be the one to explain everything to everyone. The two agree to have a mutually shared and defined relationship.

Fanny gets in touch with her childhood friend Tanya, and through that reconnection she is able to come to terms with her rage and violent frustration. Tanya recalls for Fanny an incident in which Fanny innocently kissed her friend when they were little girls. Tanya's racist grandmother saw the kiss and hit Fanny so hard that she saw stars. This violence has plagued Fanny as an adult, although she has no conscious memory of the incident, but when Tanya tells her the story of what happened, Fanny is able to recover from her own desire to commit violence against white people.

### Part 6

Part 6 is the novel's concluding section. It begins with a letter from Hal to Suwelo in which he tells Suwelo of Lissie's death. Along with news of Lissie's passing, Hal sends Suwelo her last paintings and reflects on losing the love of his life. He tells Suwelo that he has discovered that Lissie lives inside him and that he can never fully lose her.

The narrative flashes back to a conversation between Fanny and Ola before his death. In response to her questions about his relationships with white women, Ola tells Fanny about his marriage to Mary Jane, also known as Mary Ann. He married her, he says, to cause trouble. He also tells Fanny of his relationship with a Swedish woman named Margrit. He says that he lived with the woman for two years and that, while they were together, they conceived a child.

Ola continues with his story about his interactions with Mary Jane. He met her and learned of the school she had established called the M'Sukta during a period in the history of his country when white people were being expelled. Ola married Mary Jane to allow her to remain in the country and to continue her work with the school she had founded and supported. Through the marriage, Mary Jane gained citizenship and the right to become a permanent resident.

After Ola's death, Fanny meets Mary Jane, or Miss B, as she has come to be known. Mary Jane tells Fanny that Ola died at her house. Mary Jane and Fanny talk for a while about their personal lives, their concerns about the status of Africa, and their shared desire to do something that will make a difference. The two part with Fanny's promise to return to Africa to write plays with her sister Nzingha. Mary Jane promises to allow the women to produce the plays at her school and contemplates writing one of her own about the adventures she has had and what she has learned as a result of her experiences.

Suwelo listens to a tape of Miss Lissie that she instructed Hal to send to him in the event of her death. Lissie tells Suwelo that she regrets not helping Suwelo work through his issues with his parents and that he must remember them in their entirety so that he can heal himself, progress in his life, and mend his relationship with Fanny. She tells him that his father returned from fighting in World War II a broken man. He lost his arm as well as a vital piece of his soul in the violence of his experience, and Suwelo has to fully understand that conflict before he can comprehend himself or his own issues.

Lissie also shares with Suwelo a story about one of her previous lives that was an obstacle to her during this life: her inability to accept that during one of her lives she was a white person. She had always maintained that in all of her previous incarnations, she was a black woman. She tells Suwelo of a time when humans were on a relational basis with animals now considered as dangerous, animals like lions.

Lissie tells the story of a particular lion named Husa. Husa is a lion with whom Lissie's mother was deeply connected in a previous life. In this life, Lissie is the only white person in her group. The rest of the members of the community do not know of her difference because her mother hides it with a paste that she makes out of berries. When Lissie discovers what she believes to be a deficiency, she kills the familiar of her best friend. After that act of violence and betrayal, the young white man Lissie is in that lifetime is bitter and alienated and spends much of his time alone in the company of a dog he domesticates.

Miss Lissie also remembers herself as a lion. The gender-based conflicts between men and women lead to the end of the lion's familial relationships with humans. On the tape, Lissie tells Suwelo that she never shared these facts about herself with Hal because the two things that he hated most in the world were cats of all sorts, including lions, and white men. Lissie believes that telling Hal the complete truth about herself will alienate her from him permanently, and that Hal would not be able to accept the complex truths she embodies. Lissie shares with Hal that it was Rafe's love that allowed her to accept all of the truths about herself.

The narrative continues with Suwelo, Carlotta, and Arveyda. Carlotta has become a musician and has moved back in with Arveyda, who, between concerts and composing, takes care of their children. Carlotta resides in a small cottage at the back of the property so that she can have the isolation she needs in order to be creative. Suwelo comes to the house to apologize to Carlotta for the way he treated her during the time that they were involved. He is surprised to discover that Carlotta's former husband is the famous musician Arveyda.

Arveyda makes bread in the kitchen while Carlotta and Suwelo talk. Suwelo is attracted to the energy and healthful attitudes Arveyda and Carlotta exude. Arveyda shares with Suwelo some of the complexities he has experienced as a famous musician. He is troubled by people's expectations and refusal to allow an artist's energies and products to change, transform, or evolve.

The four—Arveyda, Carlotta, Suwelo, and Fanny—become friends and then interchangeable lovers. They spend nurturing and compatible time with each other.

Arveyda tells Fanny the story of his mother and father. Through his discoveries about the truth of his parents' relationship, he begins to forgive them for failing to meet his needs.

Carlotta and Suwelo talk about Carlotta's mother. She tells him that at one point, she and Arveyda feared that she had been killed. During this time, she makes Arveyda tell her everything that he knows about her mother. Through these stories, she is able to understand Zedé as a person and to forgive and love her. When Arveyda tells Carlotta about her grandmother, Zedé the Elder, it sparks her own creativity and leads to her endeavors as a bell chimist. During the conversations Suwelo has with Carlotta about her mother and grandmother, he feels the need to reconnect with his own family, mother and father. Carlotta concludes her story by telling Suwelo that her mother is in fact not dead.

Suwelo begins to tell Carlotta about his mother and father. They died in an automobile accident when Suwelo was a young man. He remembers looking carefully at his mother's body after the accident and realizing that her hands were bloody and her nails were broken. He realizes that his father was deliberately trying to kill himself and his mother and had succeeded. Through his recollection of the truth, Suwelo is able to forgive his father and to envision and love him as a whole person.

Arveyda tells Fanny about Carlotta and Zedé and the whole family, including Carlotta's grandmother, Zedé the Elder. He discusses his epiphany about his wife's family, and the couple makes love after Fanny gives Arveyda one of her famous massages. The lovemaking is more than sexual and seems to join these two in a spiritual bond.

Suwelo goes to Baltimore to visit Mr. Hal, who is living in a nursing home and has married a woman named Miss Rose, who became his companion in the nursing home he moved to after Miss Lissie's death. The two married because the people in the nursing home would not allow them to live together if they were not married. Hal has stopped painting because he says he cannot bear to do it with Miss Lissie gone. Suwelo tells Hal what Miss Lissie revealed to him in the tape that she left—that in previous lives she had been a white man and a lion. During his attempt to tell Hal the truth, Suwelo recognizes that part of the reason the man cannot see the truth about Lissie results from Hal's limited imagination. He cannot accept the idea of Lissie having an incarnation so foreign to him. Even thinking about it makes Hal feel as if Lissie has abandoned him.

Since Hal cannot hear what Suwelo has to say, Suwelo plays the tape for him, hoping that hearing the truth from Miss Lissie herself will enable him to accept the truth about her encompassing every facet of humanity, not just those Hal finds most sympathetic. Mr. Pete, another resident of the nursing home, interrupts their conversation. Hal tells Suwelo that Pete has become his best friend. Hal's awareness that such a relationship is possible helps him to accept that Miss Lissie was a white man in a former life. Although he begins to accept Suwelo's story, Hal is not completely able to internalize the truth about Lissie. His gradually opening perceptions are still only partially receptive to the truth as signified by his inability to discern fully a red, high-heeled slipper on the foot of a lion in one of Miss Lissie's last paintings. Suwelo does not tell Hal about the shoe but trusts that Hal's vision and insights will expand to include the entirety of the truth about Miss Lissie and about the reality of the world. The painting of the lion is a painting of Lissie.

## CRITICAL COMMENTARY

Because the specific oppression of African Americans emanates from the historical reality of slavery, it follows that in order to reach SELF-AFFIRMATION, the novel's central characters must attain some peaceful connection and resolution with the effects of systemic oppression. As articulated in the novel, the healing of the past goes well beyond the specificities of slavery in the United States. Self-affirmation as it manifests in *The Temple of My Familiar* requires reclamation of a personal and communal heritage. With this novel, Walker expands the notion of a racial past to that of a collective human past. Her central characters overcome oppression and become self-affirming to the same extent that they are able to remember and to accept the truth regarding the common past of all humanity.

Within *The Temple of My Familiar,* the characters are at varying stages of self-affirmation. They all are seemingly disparate individuals; however, as the novel unfolds, their fundamental interconnectedness becomes apparent. Through her construction of the novel's philosophical premises, Walker centers individual psychological health as a starting point for the acquisition of well-being for the human community. Racial categorizations become meaningless in the face of the recall of collective memory and of authentic personal and communal affirmation.

In the novel, the path to awareness involves three major steps: A character must reconnect with a personal, racial, and universal historical past; he or she must release the hatred and bitterness of the oppression in that past through forgiveness; and finally, he or she must find a positive outlet for his or her creative energies. As in several of Walker's other novels, there is a character who is already self-affirming and functions as a spiritual guide for the other characters. In *The Temple of My Familiar,*

Lissie Lyles functions as the direct and sometimes the indirect guide for the spiritual journeys of the major characters. The novel's central controlling metaphor derives from a dream of Lissie's. As she narrates the details of her dream, Lissie provides an allegory that demonstrates how attention to one's temple (external self) as opposed to one's familiar (spirit) is destructive and leads to imbalance and desolation.

> "Last night I dreamed I was showing you my temple," said Miss Lissie. ". . . It wasn't made of stone but of painted mud. . . . My little familiar, no bigger than my hand, slithered and skidded here and there in the place outside the temple where we sat. . . . I put this white bowl on top of it. . . . It looked at me with pity as it passed. Then, . . . it flew away. And I was left with only you and the rest of your people. . . ."

Miss Lissie is connected to a larger personal/ancestral past and is able to remember much about the course of human history and development. Her repeated attempts to disregard and to repress her spirit in her dream represent a betrayal of self common to each of the characters in the novel.

Although *The Temple of My Familiar* is a vast book that documents the spiritual journeys of many characters, the narrative's central energies are exposed through examination of the particular trajectories of its two central female characters, Fanny and Carlotta, who have repressed and betrayed their spirits. It is not until they reconnect their physical selves with their spiritual selves that they can become fully alive and, through creative self-expression, expiate the bitterness caused by the oppression they have experienced. Although these characters are distinct and lead individual lives for most of the novel, their coming together and aiding in each other's spiritual development becomes a metaphor for the interdependence of all humanity.

Both Fanny and Carlotta are conceived under trying circumstances, and as a result, both women are alienated from their fathers and from knowledge of their heritage. Carlotta is the child of Zedé and Jesus. At the time of her conception, both of her parents were political prisoners. The brutal oppressors of Carlotta's parents murdered her father, Jesus, immediately after her conception. Although Zedé eventually escaped from her captors, she never shared the story of Jesus with Carlotta. Consequently, Carlotta's healing journey begins with her willingness to hear the truth about her history.

Carlotta has help in her reclamation of the past. She is deeply influenced by a musician named Arveyda, whose name is a conflation of the Sanskrit words *ayus* (life) and *veda* (knowledge). Arveyda can be understood to represent life knowledge. To those who hear his music or who interact with him, he provides access to critical information about themselves. Arveyda is Carlotta's husband and the father of her children. In time, he also becomes Zedé's lover.

Although Zedé and Arveyda have a sexual affair, their relationship is not fundamentally about physical attraction. Rather, it is about spiritual recognition and compatibility. With each other, Zedé and Arveyda open the doors of each other's past. "'It is as if you went out,' Carlotta's mother sobbed after that first meeting, 'and brought your father home.' . . . 'Arveyda loves you,' said Zedé. 'You must believe this. But also, he and I loved each other from the start.'" Carlotta copes with this difficult situation by taking herself and her children away from her mother and husband. This vengeful act becomes self-destructive for Carlotta. "She could not know at the time how much she was hurting herself." In order to be open to the truth and to understand her life, Carlotta must be able to access her past, and the only way she can do this is through her mother and Arveyda.

Arveyda is able to open people up to themselves through that music. "Arveyda and his music were medicine, and, seeing or hearing him, people knew it. They flocked to him as once they might have to a priest. He did not disappoint them. Each time he played, he did so with his heart and soul." When Carlotta allows Arveyda to reenter her life after his affair with her mother, she is open to his gift of revelation. He becomes a conduit between Carlotta and her mother and, more significantly, between Carlotta and her past. When Arveyda is with Zedé and away from Carlotta and his children, Zedé tells him about Carlotta's father.

Before Carlotta's father, Jesus, became imprisoned with Zedé, he served as sentinel for a triangular shaped set of stones. The stones were important enough to Jesus to risk his life to protect them; he died as a result of his efforts to protect these seemingly innocuous smooth brown stones. Later, Zedé reveals to Arveyda more about their meaning: "I only know that they gave me the last remaining symbols of who they were in the world—feathers from the red African parrot for my ears, this parrot that had been brought to their village so many hundreds of years ago by the men with rough hair, from a continent they called Zuma, or Sun, and they gave me, for Carlotta, the three pigeon-egg-size stones."

The significance of the stones lies in their symbolism. The stones in the novel represent the role of historical narrative in a culture. They are a tangible reminder of the ancient past of Carlotta's people and, as the novel discloses, ultimately of all people. To have the stones and to know their story is to never forget the lessons of humankind.

Carlotta has possession of her father's stones but does not understand their significance. Zedé managed to save the stones and the feather through their escape from captivity, but she has never told Carlotta their history. Without knowing what the stones represent, Carlotta is unable to reconnect with her own past and complete the narrative of her own development.

When Arveyda returns from his journey with Zedé, Carlotta agrees to see him and to let him spend time with their children. By opening the door to Arveyda, she gains knowledge about herself because Arveyda now knows the story of her family and her larger ancestral narrative. Betrayed by the actions and relationship of her husband and mother, Carlotta is not able to accept their love until she fully understands herself. As an artist and healer, Arveyda's powerful message not only brings a sorrowful awareness, but also has the effect of transforming the listener. Despite the pain he has caused Carlotta through his affair with her mother, he brings her truth and thereby enables her to reconnect with her personal and ancestral history. Proof that Arveyda's task has been successfully completed lies in the narrator's revelation that "Carlotta had not dreamed her numbed heart could be broken still more, or that breaking the heart opens it." At last, through an understanding of her past, Carlotta can begin to affirm herself and progress to the next stage of her journey—forgiveness.

Like Carlotta, Fanny's self-affirmation begins with her need to reconnect with her past. What initiates Fanny's need for transformation is a feeling of being trapped. She says to her husband, Suwelo, "I have never felt free, never in my life. And I want to." In order to find this freedom, Fanny, like Carlotta, must uncover the mystery of her past. Fanny already has access to the larger human communal past through her intricate and intimate dreamlife. During her marriage to Suwelo, she has spiritual encounters or affairs with various figures from the past. This ability of Fanny's to develop meaningful connections with the dead causes great strain with and resentment in her husband.

> "What do you love about these people," he'd asked her once.
>
> "I dunno," she said. "They open doors inside me. It's as if they're keys. To rooms inside myself, I find a door inside . . . It becomes a light, and the light enters me, by osmosis, and a part of me that was not clear before is clarified. I radiate this expanded light. Happiness."
>
> And *that,* Suwelo knew, was called "being in love."

This connection with the past catalyzes a sense of acceptance in Fanny, but within the context of her marriage, true development of her whole self is not possible. For Fanny to connect with her past, she must liberate herself from the restraining influence of her husband, who is unable to see women as anything other than sexual playthings. She must also explore her more personal and immediate history with her parents.

The reader learns Fanny's history through the recollections of her mother, Olivia, who is the daughter of Miss Celie of *The Color Purple.* Ironically, Miss Celie is the one who gave Fanny her name because, for her, it signified freedom. Olivia recalls of Fanny's birth, "Just as my baby's head emerged, my mother shouted, 'Little Fanny!' . . . 'Fanny,' a name that apparently represented freedom to her was a name she'd always wanted for herself. . . . Even so, just as she was sucking in her breath to continue the naming I shouted out a very tired and weak 'Nzingha!'" In order to find the freedoms signified by both her American and her African names, it is essential for Fanny to connect with her history.

Fanny was conceived under difficult circumstances. She is the product of a liaison between her mother, the adopted child of black American missionaries, and her father, Dahvid, also known as Ola, a native African. She grows up in a happy household with her grandmother, Miss Celie; Miss Shug, Celie's lover; and Olivia, Fanny's mother. Not knowing her father, however, creates an impasse to her psychological freedom and well-being.

In order to begin to address her problems, Fanny ends her marriage to Suwelo and returns to Africa to get to know her father. Ola is a writer, playwright, and revolutionary. Fanny finds that she is "taller than *he* is—and [he] stuck a ring on my thumb. It was his ring; I'd noticed it on his finger. I understood the gesture, too. It was something I myself might have done". Upon their first meeting, Ola gives Fanny something tangible, a ring, which, like Carlotta's stones, functions as a reminder of the connection between father and daughter, and it prepares Fanny for the discovery of her history.

Meeting her father for the first time reveals hidden aspects of Fanny. By listening to her father, she is able to gain a self-awareness that would otherwise have been inaccessible to her: "I laughed with him. What can I tell you, Suwelo? It was like hearing my own self laugh. I knew exactly the region of the soul from which his laughter came. They were breaking my father's heart." As happens with Carlotta, the heartbreak of Fanny and her father is revealing and transformative. Through her reacquaintance with her father, Fanny is able to become more aware of her own life, and with that knowledge she can begin to free her own familiar.

Olivia accompanies her daughter Fanny on her journey to Africa. Olivia is able to understand more about herself from her mother's stories. She tells Fanny of her family history, particularly of her grandfather, Simon, who was Celie's real father. Simon "was lynched when she (Celie) was a baby. He was industrious, an entrepreneur. And very successful; which is why the whites killed him. . . . Both my mother and I take after him." From this and other stories, Fanny sees that her own determination to find freedom, to take care of herself, is not her unique gift; it is, in fact, an ancestral legacy.

Another significant factor in Fanny's return to Africa is that her father's country has recently been liberated. While visiting this place, Fanny grows to understand that freedom is a very complicated state of being for a country and for an individual. Freedom has brought this small African country to an imitation of white, imperialistic ways. "Why is it that after curfew every night the only people one sees are in army uniform? Among other things, you would think we are an all-male country. And you know what the rest of the world would think of that." Ola teaches, and Fanny learns, that self-knowledge and freedom are one and the same. By accessing and understanding the complex lessons of her parent's lives, Fanny can connect with the past in a way that has personal significance. Through this knowledge, she covers the roots of her feelings of entrapment and can begin to change her behavior.

In addition to fleshing out the intricacies of her parent's narratives, while in Africa Fanny discovers that she has a half sister. During her first meeting with her sister, Nzingha, Fanny feels as if she is seeing another version of herself, and "my hand clung to Nzingha's, as hers did to mine. I felt I was looking into a mirror that was reflecting only the African." Nzingha's story of the oppression of women in Africa deromanticizes Fanny's return to Africa. For Fanny, the overwhelming nature of racial oppression in the United States makes the act of leaving the country synonymous with the transcendence of oppression generally. What becomes clear to Fanny through Nzingha's story is that the oppression of women is universal, crossing geographic and racial boundaries. One story Nzingha shares with Fanny is about her mother, who was an active fighter in the revolution that gave their father, Ola, his power and prominence. After the revolution, Ola abandoned Nzingha's mother because her parochialism and "village ways" embarrassed him. He eventually took Nzingha from her and left her to die alone. This story of classism and sexism among black Africans, particularly within her family, causes Fanny to recognize that the freedom she seeks is not to be attained by escape to another land but through internal work and exploration. Consequently, she returns to America.

After acquiring expanded awareness through their discovery of their personal pasts, Fanny and Carlotta must begin the process of forgiveness. The interconnectedness of these two characters emerges as they both attempt to attain the psychological freedom that occurs with forgiveness. In order to forgive the wrongs they have suffered, each woman will have to undergo a fundamental change in perspective. After her visit to Africa, Fanny recognizes that she must rid herself of hatred for others, particularly for whites, in order to progress. In this context, forgiveness implies release.

One of the chapters of *The Temple of My Familiar* is a set of beatitude-like dictums composed by Miss Shug and "translated" by Fanny's mother, Olivia. One of these sayings asserts that "Helped are those who forgive; their reward shall be forgetfulness of every evil done to them. It will be in their power to envision the new Earth." For Fanny, forgiveness means contextualizing and coming to terms with race-based oppression. If she can forgive the wrongs inflicted upon women and minorities, then she will be able to accept the interconnectedness of all humanity and to envision a new way of being. Fanny's quest to forgive requires her to develop an empathetic connectedness with all people.

Because of her experiences, Fanny has grown to hate all white people. As a result of her hate, she has gruesome fantasies about murdering whites. She imagines chopping off the heads of all the blond people she sees on the street. As a consequence, Fanny begins to wonder if the murder of whites is not, in fact, the solution to the oppression that people of color experience. In her pursuit of an answer to this question, she confides in Suwelo, who, although no longer her husband, is still a close friend and lover—closer, in fact, than before they were divorced. Eventually, Fanny comes to realize that there is no such thing as justifiable murder for, like Meridian in another Walker novel, she recognizes that the freedom she seeks for herself is connected to the survival and well-being of all humanity.

Despite Fanny's rejection of murder as a solution, she continues to have fantasies of decapitating blonds. These fantasies are evidence of her deep-rooted inability to forgive wrongs done to her in the past. This inability stands firmly in the way of her self-affirmation. Fanny understands this truth about herself because she says that the murderous visions make her feel "as if [her] very self is leaving." Miss Lissie affirms Fanny's assessment in another section of the novel as she states "all killing is an expression of self-hate." Wholeness is dependant on forgiveness. In quest of an answer, Fanny turns to therapy. While in therapy, she uncovers one of the sources of her hate for whites. Fanny discovers the roots of her racism in the trauma of a childhood experience. Although she is not responsible for creating her feelings of racism, she does recognize that to act upon those negative emotions could mean her own self-destruction.

The incident Fanny and her therapist uncover as the source of Fanny's bitterness involves a childhood white friend named Tanya. Tanya is a little blonde-haired girl with whom Fanny used to play as a child. As a black child in the South, Fanny was not allowed to go inside Tanya's house. One day when playing, Fanny innocently kissed Tanya, and Tanya's grandmother, seeing the kiss, violently slapped the girl. Although this information forms a specific and personal source of Fanny's racism, under hypnosis she finds that her true problem lies within herself. She sees in herself the gluttony of the oppressor, and it is that self that she projects on whites. Fanny begins to realize that without forgiveness, it will indeed be her own teeth on her leg. She cannot be whole until she acknowledges the unity of humanity by forgiving and letting go of her hatred.

In order to expiate her anger and pain over the oppressive acts she has experienced at the hands of white people, and to truly forgive and let go of her pain, Fanny seeks Tanya out. After getting the woman's address from Olivia, Fanny finds that the years have brought great changes to this childhood friend. Tanya has married a black man and borne children by him. Tanya recalls in detail the incident when her grandmother slapped Fanny. Through Tanya's validation and recollection of the event, Fanny is able to begin the process of forgiveness and to progress toward self-affirmation.

Although Fanny is convinced that forgiveness is the only way to bring about reconciliation and health, she nonetheless inquires of her parents what they think she should do. In keeping with her training as a minister, Olivia's reply to her daughter's question most closely resembles a sermon: "Forgiveness is the true foundation of health and happiness, just as it is for any lasting progress. Without forgiveness there is no forgetfulness of evil; without forgiveness there still remains the threat of violence. And violence does not solve anything. It only prolongs itself." Although not as carefully worded, Fanny's father responds with nearly the same advice. "You must harmonize your own heart. . . . Then harmonize as much as possible with your surroundings. . . . Make peace with those you love and that love you or with those you wish to love." Convinced, Fanny begins the process of forgiveness. In order for her to recognize her need to forgive, she has to uncover and reconnect with the past. Through her trip to Africa, her therapy, and her parental stories, Fanny learns to be open to forgiveness.

Similarly, Carlotta's growth requires knowledge of the past as a prerequisite to forgiveness. Carlotta learns the tale of her father and mother from her husband, Arveyda, but simply hearing that history does not allow her to immediately forgive the affair between her mother and Arveyda. True forgiveness, like that which Fanny eventually attains, must be actively sought. Carlotta becomes self-destructive before she begins to truly forgive the wrong that has been done to her.

Although much less attention is given in the text to Carlotta's process of forgiveness than Fanny's, this process is as essential to her self-affirmation as it is to Fanny's. In order to progress, Carlotta must let go of her anger and hatred over the affair between her husband and mother. After she finds out about the affair, Carlotta becomes a martyr of sorts. Rather than moving forward with her own life or forgiving her mother and husband, Carlotta turns her anger inward and becomes self-destructive. She begins to act in ways that cause her pain both physically and mentally. Some of her destructive actions include having an affair with a married man she neither loves nor respects. The man Carlotta has an affair with, Suwelo, remembers that the first time that he saw Carlotta, "she seemed like one afflicted with great loss and sorrow." Although Suwelo is aware of Carlotta's pain, he does nothing to try and lessen it. Involved in a meaningless sexual affair with a man who cannot possibly help her to get past her pain, Carlotta relies on her physical attractiveness in order to feel good about herself.

Carlotta becomes a reflection of the sexualized construction of womanhood. In her quest for acceptance and love she becomes an image with "no substance." Suwelo says of Carlotta that despite their long-term affair, to him she "was just a body." Contrary to what she wants, the attention Carlotta gets from men as a result of the way she looks does not bring her relief; rather, it increases her suffering. In order to remove herself from her pain, she objectifies herself by becoming an embodiment of oppressive femininity. To regain her subjectivity, Carlotta learns to relinquish her anger and reunite with Arveyda and her mother. Prior to that reconciliation, she describes herself as being in one "clenched knot of pain." One of the things that helps her to release some of her pain is massage therapy. Significantly, Fanny becomes Carlotta's massage therapist. Under Fanny's healing touch, Carlotta is able to release some of her hurting, which helps her to recognize her need for her family.

When Carlotta finally reconnects with Arveyda, she begins her healing. At first, her forgiveness of him and her mother is tentative and reluctant. Her gradual forgiveness takes place largely in the novel's subtext, but her transformation by its conclusion provides substantial evidence that healing has occurred and that she has come to understand and forgive Arveyda and Zedé's love for each other.

Through acquisition and understanding of a personal, racial/cultural, and human past, both Fanny and Carlotta release their pain through forgiveness and channel that newly unbound energy into creative production. Reconnecting with the past, these characters are able to unleash their spirits and to become true artists. As the novel ends, both Carlotta and Fanny have found engaging outlets for their energy and have, through their pursuits, become self-affirming.

Carlotta channels her creativity into music, becoming a self-proclaimed bell chimist. In the process of creating her music, Carlotta has reclaimed her body and allows it to reflect her subjective truth. Carlotta appears totally transformed as her tight skirts and heels have been replaced by "hair, cut nearly to my skull and standing out like a concentration-camp victim's . . . [and] my tight black running suit with teal Reeboks." Carlotta's contentment is obvious as she plays her bells. The first time she sees Suwelo after her transformation, she is disinterested in his presence and genuinely wants to be alone with her artistry. Her craft brings her to herself and creates within her great happiness and peace. Carlotta has let go of her pain and is no longer constrained by the burdens of the past.

Fanny has also come to embrace herself more completely. She recovers from the oppression she experienced as a result of her race and gender and has become her own woman. At the novel's end, Fanny plans to return to Africa to write plays with her sister Nzingha. She demonstrates her ability to channel her energy outward and toward a collaborative endeavor. The ultimate confirmation of Fanny's self-affirmation occurs at the end of the novel as she makes love with Arveyda. As established, Arveyda functions in the novel as a conduit of self-knowledge, and as a multiracial person, he also becomes the symbolic representative of the interconnectedness of all humanity. In him "the African and the European and the Mexican and the Indian and the Filipino and the Chinese" meet. As such, when Fanny makes love with him at the end of the novel, she symbolically relinquishes her racism and opens herself up to the joy of health and wholeness.

> . . . Weeping, they begin to kiss.
>
> Fanny feels as if the glow of a candle that warms but could never burn has melted her, and she drips onto Arveyda.
>
> Arveyda feels as if he has rushed to meet all the ancestors and they have welcomed him with joy.

Fanny and Arveyda's lovemaking session provides a vision of the shared history of humanity that is only possible with deep self-knowledge.

As the novel closes, neither Fanny nor Carlotta continues to be defined by her pain and oppression. They both have transcended their developmental inertia as they increase their knowledge of the past, forgive the transgressions of others, and become self-affirming and empowered. Although the circumstances that created their oppression still exist, they are equipped to survive intact. With their partners Arveyda (life knowledge) and Suwelo (wholeness), Fanny and Carlotta are no longer victims. They are in possession of a self-crafted authority, wisdom, and productive creativity.

## SIGNIFICANT THEMES, ISSUES, CONCERNS

### The Constancy of the Self

Miss Lissie is the best representative of *The Temple of My Familiar's* emphasis on the premise that there is a constant self that persists through time and that transcends and survives death. This self might look different and have distinct bodies, but the fundamental person remains intact. The photographs taken of Miss Lissie over the course of the years of her present life document this conundrum. In each of the photographs, she looks like a fundamentally different person, although the pictures are always of her. She comes to understand that each of these photographs reveals the way she looked during a particular past life.

Miss Lissie can remember many different lives that she has lived over generations of human experience. Although she has various physical characteristics in each of these unique manifestations, her essential self remains the same. She is able to remember her experiences as distinct episodes, but benefits from the cumulative lessons of the collective lives she has lived.

Through Miss Lissie, the reader learns that all of humanity descended from a common ancestor and is unified by a common shared reality. Miss Lissie's knowledge of the past allows other characters in the novel to access this information and to live more fully in the present as a result.

### The Relationship between the Body and the Spirit

Throughout *The Temple of My Familiar,* Walker makes it clear that in the universe she creates for her characters, there exists a clear distinction between the physical and spiritual selves, but that the two entities must coexist in a harmonious and equalitarian fashion if the human being to whom they belong is to have a happy and actualized existence. The body is the temple, and the spirit is the familiar. For each of the central characters in the novel, the defining feature of his or her earthly quest is the endeavor to reconcile the body's needs and demands in equilibrium with the spirit's requirements.

### The Wisdom of Elders

Each of the novel's central characters shares the quality of missing fundamental information about themselves. In order to reach his or her human potential, each of them must learn about the absent pieces of his or her narrative self-construction. All the characters have an ancestral or older figure to whom they turn in order to discover the information about their personal and communal histories that they did not know before. To a greater or lesser degree, each of the novel's elder figures—including Lissie, Zedé, Dahvid, Olivia, and Hal—help Carlotta, Arveyda, Fanny, and Suwelo move to a new level of personal awareness and development. The novel's message is that each person needs an elder wise individual from whom they can learn about themselves and about the mysteries of human experience.

### The Familial Relationship between Humans and Animals

One of the primary relationships that develops in the novel occurs in the stories that Miss Lissie shares with Suwelo. Miss Lissie is a storyteller, and through her, Suwelo and the reader learn about the earliest times of human experience. In one of these tales, Miss Lissie reveals that animals in ancient times were not perceived as distinct from human beings but were accepted and treated as members of a larger family consisting of all living beings. In Miss Lissie's various incarnations, not only has she experienced this intimate relationship with animals, but she even remembers having lived a life as an animal. It is this reality that she feels she cannot share with Hal because she knows that he cannot accept her truth. After her death, Suwelo tells Hal what Lissie could not. Miss Lissie's sense of Hal's limitations are confirmed in his inability to accept fully what Suwelo is telling him. Her narratives help the reader to understand the mythologies that Walker creates in the novel and to access her fundamental premise that all living entities are more alike than they are different.

## CHARACTERS

**Abajeralasezeola** *See* DAHVID.

**Abel Santamaria** Abel Santamaria is a Cuban revolutionary who is killed as a result of his activism. His sister, Haydee, commits suicide in despair 20 years after the incident. Haydee has special resonance for Olivia, and Olivia uses her story as an example of the transcendent power of forgiveness.

**Adam** Adam is Celie's first-born child. He is conceived of an abusive sexual relationship between Celie and Pa, her stepfather, who she believes to be her father at the time of Adam's conception. After Adam's birth, Pa forces Celie to give the child away. She does not know where Pa takes her child or if the child is still alive. Pa gives Adam and later Celie's second child with him, Olivia, to a minister and his wife, Samuel and Corrine, who eventually become missionaries and travel with the children to Africa.

**Anatole** Anatole was the son of Rafe and Lissie. He is one of five of Lissie's children, but only he survived to adulthood. Anatole dies while serving in the navy. Before his death, he attended Fisk University and became a professor.

**Arveyda** Arveyda is a rock star who meets Carlotta while she is delivering a cape to him that her mother has sewn by hand. Arveyda seems to see Carlotta in a way that others have not. Like Carlotta, he does not know his father. The novel suggests that he is Carlotta's soul mate or spiritual twin. The two fall in love and marry. Arveyda is originally from Terre Haute, Indiana, and has the ability to use his music to help others to access their inner realities. He has a relationship with Carlotta's mother while he and Carlotta are married. He and Carlotta have two children.

**Ba** Ba is the name of the familiar of Miss Lissie's friend when, in a former life, Lissie's body took the shape of a white man. In this past life, Miss Lissie killed Ba in a fit of anger when she discovered she was white and radically different from the people who inhabited her community.

**Benny** Benny is Adam and Tashi's child. He is raised almost as a brother to his cousin, Fanny, Olivia and Dahvid's daughter.

**Bernie Kesselbaum** Bernie Kesselbaum is a therapist whom Suwelo consults. Suwelo frets over telling the therapist about Fanny's connection to the spirit world and her intimate relationship with the dead. Nonetheless, he tries talking to Kesselbaum about his marriage to Fanny and how to resolve his conflicts.

**Bessie Head** BESSIE HEAD (1937–86) was a real-life South African writer whose work Walker has praised for her use of fantasy, myth, and mystery. Walker dedicated the poem "Having Eaten Two Pillows," published in *Goodnight Willie Lee, I'll See You in the Morning* to Head, who appears in *Temple* as a figure Olivia and Fanny meet on their travels through Africa.

**Carlotta** Carlotta is Little Zedé's daughter. Carlotta does not know at the beginning of the novel who her father is or the circumstances of her birth. Little Zedé, her mother, is from a rural village in South America and learned the skills of sewing from her mother. A bright student, she attended college. While working as a teacher in a progressive school, she was arrested and imprisoned under suspicion that she was a communist. While imprisoned, Zedé became pregnant. When Carlotta was born, Zedé escaped from the prison, and the two settled in northern California.

Zedé works at a sweatshop where she steals feathers for her real work, creating costumes and capes for rock stars. During a delivery of one of these capes, Carlotta meets the man she falls in love with, Arveyda, an African-American/Native American rock star. Arveyda and Carlotta marry and have two children. But Arveyda has an affair with Zedé, and much of the work that Carlotta has to do in the novel involves the process of forgiving her mother and husband for their relationship.

**Cedrico** Cedrico is the oldest child of Carlotta and Arveyda.

**Celie (Grandma Celie, Big Mama)** Celie is the central character in *The Color Purple;* she is the natural mother of Olivia and Adam and the grandmother of Fanny. She lives with Shug Avery.

**Chief John Horse** Chief John Horse is one of the spirits Fanny has communication with; he tells her of his life as a black Indian chief of the Seminole.

**Dahvid (Abajeralasezeola, Ola, the Quipper)** Dahvid is the man with whom Olivia became sexually involved when she was feeling left out of the union of her brother, Adam, and best friend, Tashi. Dahvid saw her kiss Ralston Flood, a white man, and insisted on sleeping with Olivia. The result of their sexual union was Olivia's pregnancy with Fanny.

Dahvid does not see his daughter until Fanny and Olivia travel to Africa. At the time of their visit, he has been arrested as a result of having written political plays that the government considers subversive. Dahvid has several children. When Fanny travels to Africa, she becomes quite close with her sister Nzingha Anne. Dahvid dies during the course of the novel.

**David** David is Hal's father. Hal describes David as grim, perhaps overburdened by his inability to express his homosexuality in a time and community where such a reality was not possible. As a result, David expresses a bitter homophobia. He feels resentment toward Heath, a childhood friend, because, as a result of racial privilege, Heath had greater liberty in their relationship than David. Although they were best friends as children, Heath grew up to be a racist, yet as adults the men continue their tenuous relationship. The two have a sexual attraction to each other that, under other circumstances, might have been a real relationship. The tension and power dynamic between the two turns them both into alcoholics. David's complete intolerance of his son Hal's artistic nature and proclivities stems from his own self-hatred and truncated desires.

**Eleandra Burnham** Eleandra Burnham is Eleanora's twin sister. Eleanora is disdainful of her twin because of her choice to marry and remain unchallenged in her life.

**Eleandra Burnham Peacock** Eleandra Burnham Peacock, an aunt to the twins Eleandra and Eleanora Burnham, was a woman who refused to conform to the expectations dictated for someone of her class at the time in which she lived. She was educated at home, and as her diary reveals to her niece, Mary Ann, Eleandra became informed about and obsessed by inequity and injustice through her encounters with M'Sukta.

**Eleanora Burnham** Eleanora Burnham is Mary Ann Haverstock's great-aunt. After arranging her own disappearance, Mary Ann travels to London and spends time with her great-aunt, and in the process, she learns about the older woman's life. Eleanora had a twin sister named Eleandra to whom Mary Ann bears a physical resemblance. From her great-aunt, she learns about another relative also named Eleandra with whom she shares a spiritual kinship. The older Eleandra Burnham was an adventurer in Africa, and Eleanora's twin is named after this relative.

**Eula Mae** Eula Mae was Lissie Lyles's mother and Dorcy Hoghead's daughter. She began mothering Lissie as an ignorant and neglectful caretaker, but she learned from her daughter to eat well and to be more conscientious about her life.

**Fadpa** Fadpa was one of Lissie Lyles's lovers while she was in a harem in North Africa in one of her previous incarnations as Lulu.

**Fanny Nzingha** Fanny Nzingha, one of the four central characters in *The Temple of My Familiar,* is Olivia's daughter. At her introduction in the novel, she is married to Suwelo, and the two are undergoing a separation. Olivia is a character who makes her first appearance in *The Color Purple.* Fanny travels with her mother to Africa to meet her biological father, Dahvid, and her sister, who is also named Nzingha. Fanny's husband, Suwelo, talks to a therapist about her intimate relationships with spirits. Fanny has an ability to slip into discourses with those who are not living and to develop relationships with them. Her major task in the novel is to overcome her murderous anger toward white people. At the end, she is in an open relationship with Suwelo and Arveyda.

**Frudier** Frudier is Arveyda's aunt, Katherine Degos's sister.

**Granny Dorcy (Dorcy Hogshead)** Granny Dorcy is Eula Mae's mother and Lissie's grandmother. She is described as a devilish woman. Unpleasant and disagreeable, she is also a brilliant midwife, responsible for many of the births on the island Lissie and Hal call home. She smokes a pipe that she believes helps with the birth process. Lissie learns much of her knowledge about the world and how to live in it from Granny Dorcy.

**Habisu** Habisu was one of Lissie Lyles's lovers in a former life. Miss Lissie met Habisu while she was in a harem in North Africa; at the time, her name was Lulu. Habisu was a eunuch who was responsible for ensuring that none of the women left the harem.

**Hal (Harold Davenport Jenkins)** Hal is Miss Lissie's husband and a lifelong friend of Rafe.

Suwelo comes to Baltimore when Rafe dies, and Hal and Lissie aid his journey of self-discovery. Hal is physically a small man with an intuitive understanding of people and a fear of cats. His blind spot lies in his inability to recognize the truth about his wife, Lissie, the woman he shared with his friend, Rafe.

**Harriet** Harriet was the code name for Nzingha Anne's mother. Harriet was a guerrilla fighter who had little education but an intuitive and psychic ability that made her extremely dexterous as a fugitive fighter. Ola (Dahvid) abandoned her and later returned to take their children, Nzingha and Hildegarde, with him. Harriet died when Nzingha was 16, and at the time of her death, she was a shadow of her former vibrant and creative self.

**Haydee Santamaria** Haydee Santamaria was a Cuban political prisoner who nobly suffered the deaths of her brother, Abel, and her lover. She committed suicide 20 years later.

**Heath** Heath was a childhood friend of David, Hal's father. David feels resentment toward Heath because, as a result of racial privilege, Heath had greater liberty in their relationship than David. Although they were best friends as children, Heath grew up to be a racist, and yet the men have continued their tenuous relationship as adults. The two have a sexual attraction to each other that, under other circumstances, might have been a real relationship. The tension and power dynamic between the two turns them both into alcoholics.

**Henry Bates** Henry Bates is a colleague of Dahvid's and one of the originators of the local writers' guild.

**Hidae** Hidae was a friend of Zedé from Guatuzocan, the place where she was imprisoned. Although she was the same age as Zedé, Hidae was hired to play an extra in a movie as an old woman.

**Husa** Husa was a lion with who was a companion to Lissie's mother in a previous life.

**Jack** Jack was Lissie Lyle's son with the picture taker. He died in infancy.

**Jesus** Jesus was Carlotta's father. He had another name and was only called Jesus because his name was unpronounceable to his captors. He was imprisoned in the same facility as Zedé and was known as the keeper of his village's sacred stones. When the stones were disturbed in any way, Jesus would appear to reposition them. The stones marked the home of human beings, and their placement was essential to the survival of the species.

Zedé fell in love with Jesus, and during the one time they made love, they conceived Carlotta. The guards tortured Jesus when he was discovered with Zedé. They cut off his hair, mutilated, and murdered him. His people rescued Zedé, who was pregnant, and took Jesus's body. They gave Zedé the sacred stones to give to Carlotta, Jesus's child.

**Katherine Degos** Katherine Degos was Arveyda's mother. She was one of three founders of a church in Terre Haute, Indiana, called the Church of Perpetual Involvement. Arveyda describes his mother as a busybody, obsessed with other people's lives. When he was 10, his mother mysteriously ceased her activity, and eventually she committed suicide. She asked that the phrase "Nothing, No Thing, Can Replace Love," be written on her tombstone, but her wish was not granted.

**Lady Hester Stanhope** Lady Hester Stanhope (1776–1839) was a woman who abandoned convention and went off to a so-called native land during the early part of the 19th century.

**Lady Jane Digby El-Mezrab** Lady Jane Digby El-Mezrab (1807–81) was a woman who abandoned convention and went off to a so-called native land during the Victorian era. Her behavior was considered scandalous because her last (of four) husband was an Arab man.

**Lance (Lancelot)** Lance is the man to whom Olivia is engaged when she first appears in this novel. The two meet after Olivia finishes Spelman College and begins working at a black hospital in

Atlanta—the same hospital where Lance is working as a physician. Lance's family is light-skinned and has issues with Olivia's darker skin color.

**Lissie Lyles (Miss Lissie Lyles)** Miss Lissie Lyles is described as little and black, a kind of condensation of blackness. She is self-affirming and functions as a spiritual guide for the other characters. The novel's central metaphor derives from one of her dreams. Lissie is connected to a larger personal/ancestral past and is able to remember much about the course of human history and development. Her dream provides an allegory that demonstrates how attention to one's temple (external self) as opposed to one's familiar (spirit) is destructive and leads to imbalance and desolation. Lissie's life and her tales about the history of humanity are a model for the novel's other characters and provide a thematic framework for the whole text.

**Louis** Louis was Suwelo's father. An arrogant and insensitive man, he lost an arm while fighting in World War II. The family he created with his wife, Marcia, and son, Suwelo, was an unhappy one. He died in an automobile accident when Suwelo was a young man. In photos, he appears brash and cocky. Suwelo comes to believe that his father killed himself in the car accident and murdered his mother at the same time. Suwelo has to learn to forgive his father for his actions.

**Louis Jr.** *See* SUWELO.

**Lulu** Lulu is Hal and Lissie's daughter. As a result of the pain Lissie experienced while giving birth to the child, Hal can no longer make love to her, and the marriage between the two dissolves after Lulu's birth. Lulu's name comes from a previous life of Lissie's when she was an inhabitant of a harem. As an adult, Lulu became a performer and went to Paris to work. When the city fell to the Nazis, she disappeared and was never heard from again.

**Marcia** Marcia was Suwelo's mother. She died in an automobile accident when Suwelo was a young man. In photos, she appears unhappy and resigned to her fate. Her relationship with Louis, Suwelo's father, was a tumultuous one. Suwelo believes that his father, Louis, killed, his mother in the car accident that also took Louis's life.

**Margrit** Margrit is a Swedish woman with whom Dahvid was involved. He tells Fanny that he lived with the woman for two years and that, while they were together, they conceived a child.

**Maria** Maria is the woman who lives with Tanya.

**Mary Ann Haverstock (Mary Jane Briden, Rowena Rollins, Miss B)** Mary Ann is the daughter of extremely wealthy parents who are disturbed by their daughter's political views and drug abuse and send her off to La Escuela de Jungla. At the facility, Mary Ann meets Zedé and Carlotta. Zedé has pity for the young woman and sees that she is being exploited in the facility. She writes to Mary Ann's parents to tell them the truth about the facility where they have sent their daughter, and as a result of the letters, Mary Ann's parents rescue her from the school. Eventually, Mary Ann returns to the facility to rescue Carlotta and Zedé. The boat in which the rescue takes place capsizes, and Zedé believes that Mary Ann is killed in the accident, although she and Carlotta are rescued by the Coast Guard.

After the rescue, Mary Ann Haverstock becomes Mary Jane Briden and lives her life in exile from all she had known before. She lives on part of her inheritance, gives her money away to people and causes she deems worthy, moves to Africa, and becomes a playwright. She also opens a school called the M'Sukta School, where she encourages the creative energies of young artists. In order to remain in the country when they begin to expel whites, Mary Jane marries Ola (Dahvid), Fanny's father. She dyes her hair the shade of blue delphiniums.

**Mary Ann's parents (Mr. and Mrs. Haverstock)** Mary Ann's parents are very wealthy individuals who have acquired their fortune by manufacturing a toxic product that is destructive to the environment. They love their daughter but cannot countenance her difference from them, so they send her to a facility called La Escuela de Jungla. When they receive a letter from Zedé telling them about the true conditions at the facility, they rescue their daughter from the place. Mary Ann returns to the school to rescue Zedé and Carlotta and leads her parents to believe that she has been killed in the effort. Her parents help Zedé and Carlotta to immigrate permanently after what they believe to be their daughter's death.

**Mbeles** The Mbeles are a fictional group of African guerrillas who live miles from the outskirts of the village of Olinka where Nettie, Samuel, Adam, and Olivia live. They are much rumored about but actually exist.

**Metudhi** Metudhi is Nzingha Anne's husband. He is politically active and not particularly engaged or helpful as a husband or father. He and Nzingha Anne have two male children.

**Miss Beaumont** Miss Beaumont set up the first school in the black community where Hal and Lissie grew up on one of the islands across from Charleston Bay.

**Miss Lissie** *See* LISSIE LYLES.

**Miss Rose** Miss Rose is Mr. Hal's companion in the nursing home he resides in after Miss Lissie's death. The two marry after Miss Lissie's death because the people in the nursing home will not allow them to live together if they are not married.

**Mose** Mose is Rena's husband and Suwelo's cousin by marriage. A picture of him hangs on the wall at Rafe's house. Suwelo sees it there when he briefly occupies the house following Rafe's death.

**Mr. Hal** *See* HAL.

**Mr. Pete** Mr. Pete is a resident of the nursing home where Hal and Miss Rose live. Hal tells Suwelo that Pete has become his best friend. His awareness that such a relationship is possible helps him to accept that Miss Lissie was a white man in a former life.

**M'Sukta** M'Sukta is an African woman Mary Ann discovers while reading through her great-great-aunt Eleandra's diary. Eleandra and her cousin, T, found M'Sukta in the Museum of Natural History; she came to reside there with the assistance of Sir Henry Rowanbotham, who arranged it after her entire tribe was killed. The woman had created artwork that Eleandra and her cousin admired. When they came upon M'Sukta in the museum for the first time, she was spinning cloth. Eleandra's encounter with M'Sukta sparked and nurtured her interest in Africa and her eventual travels there. Indirectly, the story of M'Sukta also prompts Mary Ann's journey there as well.

**Nettie** Nettie is Celie's younger sister and Olivia's aunt.

**Nzingha Anne** Nzingha Anne is the daughter of Ola (Dahvid) and Harriet, a guerrilla fighter. Ola abandoned Harriet but later returned to take her children, Nzingha and Hildegarde, with him. Harriet died when Nzingha was 16. Nzingha tells Fanny about her efforts to get their father Ola's attention and love. She felt as if she could not gain his love because she was always competing with Fanny, the American sister she had not yet met.

**Obenjomade** Obenjomade is the second son of Ola's father's third wife and thus a half brother to Fanny.

**Ola** *See* DAHVID.

**Olivia (Pauline)** Olivia is Celie's daughter. In *The Temple of My Familiar,* Olivia is the mother of Fanny Nzingha, whom she accompanies on a trip to Africa to meet Fanny's father and Olivia's onetime lover, Dahvid (Ola). Olivia also appears in *The Color Purple* and is an important character in Walker's 1992 novel *Possessing the Secret of Joy.*

**picture taker, the (Henry Laytrum)** The picture taker is the man who takes all of the photographs of Lissie through the years in which she looks like different women. The photographs hang in Rafe's house. Lissie leaves Hal for the picture taker after Hal will not make love to her following the birth of Lulu. He was married and already had many children by the time he became involved with Lissie.

**Rafe (Uncle Rafe)** Rafe was Suwelo's great-uncle and the love of Lissie Lyle's life. He lived in a Baltimore row house before his death. His home was left to his nephew, Suwelo. Rafe worked as a sleeping-car porter for 50 years. He was intellectually and politically engaged and used his job to acquire information from the places where he traveled and the people he encountered. Rafe was a compassionate man who took food from his job to feed a fatherless family in his neighborhood. Suwelo describes Rafe as tall and plump but not fat. Rafe was not married but had a nearly lifelong relationship with Lissie Lyles. Lissie and Rafe had four children; only one, Anatole, survived into adulthood.

**Ralston Flood** Ralston Flood was the white man whom Olivia kissed during a time when she was jealous of the attention focused on Tashi and Adam. Dahvid saw the kiss and, as a result, insisted on sleeping with Olivia.

**Rena** Rena is a cousin of Suwelo's whose picture hangs on the wall of his Uncle Rafe's Baltimore row house. Suwelo sees it there when he briefly occupies the house following Rafe's death.

**Robin Ramirez** Robin Ramirez is Fanny's therapist. Fanny seeks out her help with the issues she is having when she feels that she wants to kill or injure all the people in the world who have blond hair. Fanny confesses that the hair color has come to represent oppression and domination generally, but Robin gets her to recognize that the anger she is experiencing has deeper and more personal roots. Through her explorations with Robin about an early childhood encounter with racism, Fanny is able to come to terms with her feelings and to access both forgiveness and compassion for those who practice it.

**Rowena Rollins** *See* MARY ANN HAVERSTOCK.

**Shug Avery (Queen Honeybee, Mama Shug)** Shug Avery is the women with whom Celie lives. Celie says that Shug is the most beautiful woman she has ever seen. Shug is a grandmother figure to Fanny. She writes a series of beatitudes that figure heavily in *The Temple of My Familiar.*

**Simon** Simon was Olivia's grandfather, Celie's biological father, who died as a result of a LYNCHING when Celie was a baby. He was industrious and a successful businessman whose talents caused him to be a threat to the white community. He is interesting to Olivia as a role model.

**Simon Isaac (Uncle Isaac)** Simon Isaac was a Palestinian and a surrogate father for Arveyda, who thinks of the man as Uncle Isaac, but never called him by that name. Mr. Isaac, the name Arveyda used to address Simon, was the neighborhood greengrocer and played the violin, enchanting the children in the community. From him, Arveyda learned about the power of music to transcend difference. Eventually, Isaac left Indiana and returned to his home in the Middle East.

**Sir Henry Rowanbotham** Sir Henry Rowanbotham was a commander in the British army who derived an alphabet so that the language M'Sukta spoke could be written down. He was also the one who made provisions for her in the Museum of Natural History in the wake of the complete destruction of her tribe.

**Suwelo (Louis Jr.)** At the point of his introduction in the novel, Suwelo is living temporarily in Baltimore, Maryland, while he sorts though the possessions and the life of his recently deceased great-uncle, Rafe. Suwelo's name is the same as the RUNE for wholeness. The reference is ironic, though, since Suwelo finds that his life is fragmented. Suwelo has had a relationship with Carlotta and is married to Fanny, although the two are in the midst of marital difficulties and are considering divorce. Suwelo is compared to an owl in appearance and is emotionally disconnected as a result of his impaired and prematurely terminated relationship with his parents, Marcia and Louis, who died in a car accident, leaving Suwelo orphaned at a young age. He was befriended by Hal and Miss Lissie, and through their intervention and his acquisition of knowledge about the past, he becomes a less self-absorbed, more caring and sensitive person who is capable of loving another fully and without possession. Critical to his transformation are his acceptance of the truths contained within Miss Lissie's stories and discovery and reconciliation of the trauma of his parents' relationship and death.

**T (Theodore)** T was Eleandra Burnham Peacock's cousin, a confidante and a compatriot. He was one of the only people in Eleandra's life who understood her perspective. She and T discovered M'Sukta living in the Museum of Natural History.

**Tanya** Tanya was a childhood friend of Fanny's. The racial politics of the community and times in which they lived interfered with their relationship. Tanya's family would not allow Fanny to come into their house. Fanny innocently kissed her friend when they were little girls. Tanya's racist grandmother saw the kiss and hit Fanny so hard that she saw stars. This violence has plagued Fanny as an adult, although she has no conscious memory of the incident. As an adult, she reconnects with Tanya, who tells her this story, at which point Fanny is able to recover from her own desire to commit violence against those who perpetrate oppression.

**Tanya's grandmother** Tanya's grandmother is described as pathologically limited and unable to transcend the definitions of selfhood based in racial fixedness and hierarchy. She slapped Fanny after seeing her kiss Tanya, and this act of violence affected Fanny well into adulthood.

**Ulysses** Ulysses was the first black man that Mr. Isaac, Arveyda's father figure, ever encountered. Mr. Isaac met Ulysses on Ellis Island. Isaac was in quarantine in a barracks where Ulysses worked as a janitor. The two communicated about music as best they could in two different languages. When Isaac was released, Ulysses gave him an apple. The gifted fruit gave Isaac the idea to follow in his father's footsteps and become a grocer.

**Uncle Isaac** *See* SIMON ISAAC.

**Uncle Rafe** *See* RAFE.

**woman who specializes in found feathers** This woman resided in the Zedés' village in South America. Unlike the other women who collected peacock feathers, this woman collected the feathers that had fallen, refusing to cause the animals anguish by plucking their feathers.

**Zedé (Carlottas's grandmother, Zedé the Elder)** Zedé was a seamstress whose skills were so impressive that she was thought to employ supernatural talents. Her primary products were clothing. In particular, she made spectacular capes that were used in various ceremonies in the South American village where she lived. Eventually, circumstances forced Zedé to sell the items she made. Particularly difficult for her was selling her beautiful capes to tourists.

**Zedé (Carlotta's mother, Little Zedé, Consuelo, Connie)** Zedé is the daughter of the seamstress Zedé and the mother of Carlotta. As a result of a childhood experience with collecting peacock feathers, she has empathy for all creatures and an appreciation of beauty as a gift from the divine. Zedé attended college, and as a result of her work in a progressive school, she was arrested as a communist and spent years in prison. While in prison, she gave birth to Carlotta, who was conceived with Zedé's true love, Jesus, a mystical figure who was the bearer of his community's sacred stones. Jesus was killed when his and Zedé's lovemaking was discovered by a jealous guard. Eventually, Zedé escaped from the prison with her young daughter, and the two found a home in San Francisco.

In San Francisco, Zedé works sewing at a sweatshop until her work making capes for rock stars allows her to earn a living more creatively and exclusively. She has a major rift with her daughter,

Carlotta, when she falls in love with Carlotta's husband, Arveyda. Although Zedé is contrite about the situation, Arveyda and Zedé travel through South America together on a journey that helps to heal them both. Eventually, Zedé earns her daughter's forgiveness.

**Zedé's brothers** As men, Little Zedé's brothers were not allowed to enter the house where Little Zedé and her mother lived. They resided in a separate house with her father.

**Zedé's father** Described as a small and exhausted individual, Little Zedé's father died while she was a student in college. He was not allowed access to the house Little Zedé grew up in because he was a man. He lived in a separate house with her brothers.

### Further Reading

Castro Borrego, Silvia del Pilar. "There Is More to It Than Meets the Eye: Alice Walker's *The Temple of My Familiar,* a Narrative of the Diaspora." *Revista de Estudios Norteamericanos* 9 (2003): 9–22.

Durso, Patricia Keefe. "Private Narrative as Public (Ex)Change: 'Intimate Intervention' in Alice Walker's *The Temple of My Familiar.*" *In Process: A Journal of African American and African Diasporan Literature and Culture* 2 (Spring 2000): 137–154.

Jablon, Madelyn. "Rememory, Dream History, and Revision in Toni Morrison's *Beloved* and Alice Walker's *The Temple of My Familiar.*" *College Language Association Journal* 37, no. 2 (December 1993): 136–144.

Juncker, Clara. "Black Magic: Woman(ist) as Artist in Alice Walker's *The Temple of My Familiar.*" *American Studies in Scandinavia* 24, no. 1 (1992): 37–49.

Kuhne, Dave. "Alice Walker's African Connection." *Conference of College Teachers of English Studies* 63 (September 1998): 69–76.

Panda, Prasanta Kumar. "Strategies of Intertextuality in Alice Walker's *The Temple of My Familiar.*" *New Quest* 124 (July–August 1997): 226–230.

Reckley, Ralph, Sr. "His/tory: The Black Male in Alice Walker's *The Temple of My Familiar.*" *MAWA Review* 6, no. 2 (December 1991): 19–22.

Sol, Adam. "Questions of Mastery in Alice Walker's *The Temple of My Familiar.*" *Critique: Studies in Contemporary Fiction* 43, no. 4 (Summer 2002): 393–404.

Wisker, Gina. "'Disremembered and Unaccounted For': Reading Toni Morrison's *Beloved* and Alice Walker's *The Temple of My Familiar.*" In *Black Women's Writing,* edited by Gina Wisker, 78–95. New York: St. Martin's, 1993.

## *The Third Life of Grange Copeland* (1970)

Walker's first novel, *The Third Life of Grange Copeland,* is based loosely on her understanding of and relationships with her father and her grandfathers. Walker learned from her older brothers and sisters that their father had been a different man when they were young. This notion of her father transforming from a gentle, loving soul to a violent, distant enigma energized her desire to explore the sometimes fatal dysfunctions of relationships between the men and women in the black community of her childhood.

*The Third Life of Grange Copeland* explores male transformations, both toward and away from health. The titular protagonist, Grange Copeland, begins his adult life—his first life—as a man completely controlled by poor examples of manhood and responsibility. After his initial efforts to love and support a wife and child fail, he succumbs utterly to complete self-indulgence and abuse. Subsequently, during his "second life," Grange grows and comes to understand that his actions have consequences. He spends the last third of his life attempting to make amends for the result of his flaws and learns how to love in an authentic, nurturing, and selfless way. He tries to redeem himself by repairing the damage he has caused and, in the process, enriches and expands his own life and humanity. The novel makes the assertion that circumstances, no matter how oppressive, do not have to be determinative.

*The Third Life of Grange Copeland* received critical acclaim upon its publication and was instrumental in establishing Walker's reputation. The novel remains one of her most highly regarded works.

## SYNOPSIS

## Part 1

### Chapter 1

*The Third Life of Grange Copeland* begins with Brownfield, the son of the titular character, Grange Copeland, standing in the front yard of the family house, watching the departure of his Uncle Silas, Aunt Marilyn, and cousins in their 1920 Buick. Brownfield feels inferior to his cousins because they have knowledge of the city. Brownfield's aunt, uncle, and cousins live in Philadelphia, and Brownfield tells his father that he wishes his family lived there as well. Although Brownfield hates his mother's submissive attitude toward his father, generally he admires her and wishes that they could have another kind of life.

The family lives in south Georgia, in Greenfield County, and Brownfield thinks of the place as quiet, with nothing much ever happening. Brownfield's mother leaves him every day to work catching fishing baits. When he was a baby, Brownfield went with her to work, but after an incident at the job, his mother was ordered never to bring him back, forcing her to leave her child alone at home. He develops physical and emotional problems from the neglect.

Brownfield's father, Grange Copeland, works in a cotton field, and when he is old enough, Brownfield begins working with his father in the children's section of the field. Brownfield's father is a cold man who, despite their working together, does not develop a relationship with his son. Brownfield learns about the complex racial dynamics of the community in which he resides from observing his father's responses to the white men who come to the cotton field.

Brownfield often sees his father drinking. He is careful not to disturb the man while he drinks as he becomes volatile and violent. One day while he is drinking, his father says that he should throw his son down a well. This event and his father's general sullenness catalyze Brownfield's dreams of escaping to the North and living with, or at least like, his cousins and their family.

While his cousins are visiting, Brownfield learns from his cousin Angeline that his father, Grange, had tried to get his mother to prostitute herself, a concept that eludes Brownfield, who does not yet understand sexuality. Brownfield tries to put the information he gathers from his cousins in context. He remembers that his father was not always so remote and wonders if his changed behavior has to do with his failure to "sell" his wife. This new information only makes Brownfield more perplexed about his life and fuels his desire to have another kind of existence.

Brownfield describes the family's situation as entirely dependent on his father's mood. Grange's mood and drinking sets the family's barometer; as he feels, so the family functions. On Saturday afternoons, the family cleans up and awaits visitors who never arrive. Grange gets drunk in his despair and falls into a stupor, sleeping outside in the yard until Sunday morning. On Sunday, he awakens and heads to church, where he sings with sincere fervency, only to return home and fight with his wife.

Grange does not repair the family house or allow his son to attend school. He is stricken with hopelessness that in many ways paralyzes him and does not allow him to act in ways that might change his and his family's circumstances. Brownfield hears his parents talking about the possibility of him and his mother moving north. He learns that what his cousins told him is true, that the family had considered relocating to the North but that neither of his parents can imagine something different from what they already know.

### Chapter 2

Chapter 2 begins five years after the cousins' visit. Brownfield is again in his yard, this time watching a vehicle approach. The truck is gray and is driven by Johnny Johnson, a man who, like his father, works for Mr. Shipley, the owner of the cotton field. Brownfield watches his mother getting out of Johnny Johnson's truck and confronts her by saying good morning. In the intervening years, Margaret has had another son, named Star. She tells her son that she and Grange have had another fight about his girlfriend.

Margaret is no longer content to wait on Grange for her happiness. When he goes into town or leaves her alone, she goes off to find her own enjoyments and distractions. One of them is Johnny Johnson. Brownfield tells his mother that Grange told him that he was not coming back this time.

Brownfield still hungers for the life he imagined that his Uncle Silas and Aunt Marilyn have up north. His mother reminds him that their lives could not have been that wonderful as his Uncle Silas was killed trying to rob a liquor store and that his Aunt Marilyn has turned to drugs. This information convinces Margaret that the North is not a place for her.

Because of his parents' irresponsibility, caring for the baby largely falls to Brownfield. He dislikes caring for the infant and considers doing so a threat to his masculinity. Brownfield works at the bait factory with his mother and yearns to use the money he earns there to move north and to see finally the snow he longs for. He imagines that his life there would be full of riches and that he would reside in a mansion with servants and a perfectly content and beautiful family. In this fantasy, he mixes up the faces of the cook, who is black, and his wife, whom he describes as powdery white.

Brownfield's daydream becomes intensely real to him. He harbors ill feelings toward his mother for making him care for his brother and interrupting the time he has to dream and imagine his life up north. When the baby cries, Brownfield is lackadaisical about its care, taking his time in going to soothe the child. The child is light-skinned with gray eyes, and his paternity is undetermined.

Margaret transforms into someone Brownfield no longer loves or admires. She becomes distant and self-absorbed. Brownfield blames Grange and his abuse of his mother for the change in Margaret and is bitter toward them both for making him responsible for his brother and for so utterly neglecting him that they nearly forget that they have an older child. Brownfield has to fend for himself and try to make sense of his world.

One night, Brownfield wakes up and his mother is out of the house for the evening. His father is in the shadows, holding a gun, and the baby is asleep. Brownfield is terrified and pretends to be asleep. Grange reaches out to touch his son and withdraws his hand. When he leaves, he does not come back. Brownfield's mother commits suicide and kills the baby, Star, leaving Brownfield essentially orphaned.

### Chapter 3

Shipley, the owner of the local cotton plantation, says to Brownfield that he should continue working in the area and should take a job with him. He also advises Brownfield to get a wife. Brownfield is surprised that Shipley comes to Margaret's funeral. With his understanding that Shipley's invitation is a trap that will tie him to the place forever, Brownfield heads off with one box of possessions from the house.

## Part 2

### Chapter 4

Having no means of transportation, Brownfield walks away from his old life and home. He encounters a kindly woman named Mizes Mamie Lou Banks, who gives him something to eat. Mizes Banks tells Brownfield the story of her children and that her oldest ones have gone north.

### Chapter 5

Brownfield does not know where he is going or how to get there, so after frustrating attempts to figure out where north is, he decides to abandon his quest. He gets directions from a family who feeds him breakfast and heads him on his way after he asks them if they have seen Grange.

### Chapter 6

Brownfield arrives in the town the family has directed him to, and he is unnoticed there. He finds the town exciting after his relatively isolated rural life. He wanders into a juke joint and meets a woman who introduces herself to him as Fat Josie. She introduces Brownfield to her daughter, Lorene, whom he finds both repulsive and intriguing. Josie listens to his story and discovers that he is the son of her lover, Grange. Josie takes Brownfield in and allows him to live with her and Lorene. Josie and Brownfield become lovers. Brownfield does not know until later that he has become involved with his father's lover.

### Chapter 7

Josie is plagued by dreams in which she feels she has the weight of a spirit on top of her, riding her as she sleeps. She goes to a local spiritualist named Sister Madelaine, who has a son attending Morehouse College. Sister Madelaine tells her that there are physiological reasons for her symptoms and experiences, but Josie does not believe the woman. Eventually, Sister Madelaine acquiesces and tells Josie that if she can call the name of the witch, he or she will be forced to stop riding her sister. Madelaine sends the money Josie pays for her services to her son at college.

### Chapter 8

The spirit Josie believes is haunting her is her father. Josie remembers the story of her family and her relationship with her father. As a teenager, she became estranged from her family because they did not approve of her behavior. She became pregnant, and after she was cast out she worked as a prostitute to earn money. In her memories of these events, Josie recalls working hard to buy presents for the family to earn back their respect and to regain her place. She approached her family house on her father's birthday in the hope that she would be accepted and readmitted to the fold. She felt that she had been forgiven. During the party, Josie got drunk and fell down. Josie's father forbade anyone to help her up. Since that time, Josie has lived as a prosperous madam who owns her own establishment, called the Dew Drop Inn. With this change, Josie believes that she is in control of her life.

### Chapter 9

Josie wakes up from another nightmare to find Brownfield concerned about her dream. Brownfield sees her flaws and does not love her but cares about her welfare. Josie tells Brownfield about his father's involvement with her, and he is amused. Josie's feelings are hurt, and she uses her financial security as an emotional defense. She also lies and tells Brownfield that what she said about his father was not true. That night, Brownfield leaves Josie's bed for her daughter Lorene's.

### Chapter 10

Brownfield meets a woman named Mem, who is Josie's niece. Josie takes care of Mem as if she were her daughter. Mem has attended school in Atlanta. Her father conceived her out of wedlock and has another family whom he acknowledges. Like Josie, Mem's mother was put out of her father's house when she became pregnant. At the time he meets Mem, Brownfield is living with and sharing Lorene and Josie's affections. Lorene has a reputation as a rough and violent woman, a fact that makes Brownfield feel more empowered. He is happy in his situation with Josie and Lorene until he meets Mem.

Mem is pretty, sweet, and so quiet that she is not often noticed. She enjoys pleasures unknown to Brownfield, such as walking in the woods, and she is distinctly different from Lorene and Josie. Mem and Brownfield begin sleeping together. He is intrigued by her self-possession.

### Chapter 11

Mem makes Brownfield want to be more than he is and to prove himself to her. She becomes a kind of mother figure who begins to heal some of the wounds left by Margaret's absentee parenting. She encourages his newfound desire to learn to read and write, and under her tutelage, he learns the first skills of his life. He also learns to value the spoken word from Mem's graceful use of it.

Josie and Lorene become jealous of Brownfield's attentions to Mem, and he is almost afraid that they might hurt her to express their envy. Mem's guidance also reveals to Brownfield the connections between adulthood, maturity, and self-sufficiency. He feels terrible guilt about his involvement with Lorene and Josie.

### Chapter 12

Brownfield sees Mem with another man, a teacher, and he feels jealous and inferior. Seeing Mem with someone he believes is his better sparks his desire to marry her. Mem deliberately dates the teacher in order to bring the relationship with Brownfield to a head. In the course of the relationship, she discovers that she loves Brownfield. One night, when she is returning from a date with the teacher, Brownfield confronts her. The two declare their love for each other, and Brownfield decides to work as a sharecropper for two years until he can make enough money to take Mem to the North. Mem and Brownfield leave Josie's house for their new residence in the country. They are in love and full of hope for the future.

### Chapter 13

Things do not go as planned for Mem and Brownfield. Three years later, the two have one child, another on the way, and too much indebtedness to the farmer to think about their dream of relocation to the North. Although their dreams have not come to fruition, Mem and Brownfield are still in love. Mem is nurturing and loving to Brownfield and provides him with the emotional sustenance he needs to become a grown-up and a mature man. The two still make love, despite the complications and hardships of their lives. Brownfield's devotion to his wife leads him to accept his life as it is and to continue the backbreaking work of trying to make a living from the land.

## Part 3

### Chapter 14

When Brownfield sees his young daughter, Daphne, working in the cotton fields, mopping the cotton bushes with arsenic, the scene nearly breaks his heart. He comes to understand that he is trapped in the same cycle of oppression and exploitation that his father was, and he begins to contemplate suicide. He wants to be able to get out of the circumstances he and his family are in but cannot see a way to do so.

Brownfield is full of rage and frustration over what seems like impotence, and he turns it on Mem. He accuses her of infidelity and starts to abuse her. He also forces Mem to stop teaching school and begin working as a domestic at the houses of white people. In his anger, Brownfield blames Mem for all that is wrong with their lives. He sees her education as her complicit connection with the forces that have created their situation. He returns to Josie's house to have sex with her and to borrow money, and he works a variety of low-paying laboring jobs. Under such circumstances, Mem begins to wither and to look haggard and old.

Brownfield tries to destroy Mem by making her feel bad about the attributes he most loved about her in the beginning. He embarrasses and humiliates her in order to make himself feel superior. Consequently, Mem actually loses her way of speaking. By turning Mem into someone he does not respect or desire, Brownfield makes it easier for himself to treat her badly and to behave in the ways that he wants.

Brownfield spends the money Mem saves, first on a pig he thinks is a breeder, but it dies. Then he buys a fast, red sports car that eventually is repossessed when he cannot continue to pay the loan.

Three of Brownfield and Mem's children die and two live. The children are miserable and afraid of their father in the same way that Brownfield was afraid of his father. Brownfield becomes an alcoholic and beats Mem and the children. Mem thinks of leaving him but cannot imagine a place where she can go with her children to be safe. She tries to get assistance to get away from Brownfield and even writes to her father, whom she has never met. The man does not even respond to her letter. Mem loses weight, and her hair begins to fall out. She also loses the essence of who she is.

The family repeatedly moves from one house to another, undermining Mem's attempts to make a pleasant space, a home, for her family. After a time and under the pressure of all of the horrifying circumstances of her life, Mem begins to hate Brownfield. She fights him with the only weapons she has: words. Unlike his father, Brownfield feels no desire to escape his situation. He only wants to wallow in his misery and to bring everyone involved down with him.

### Chapter 15

Brownfield again becomes a regular customer at Josie's Dew Drop Inn. Lorene has left the South for a new life in the North. Josie and Brownfield become fast friends and spend a great deal of time rehashing the details of Brownfield's life, trying to piece together what happened and what went so terribly wrong.

They also talk about Brownfield's father. Josie tells Brownfield that Margaret was misguided in her attempts to try to hold onto Grange, and Brownfield tells her that she did the same thing. Josie disagrees and says that Margaret was trying to kill Brownfield. She tells Brownfield that she and Grange were planning to leave together and to go to Harlem. Instead, Grange left without telling Josie. Josie tells Brownfield that she has not seen Grange since he left.

Josie continues with her story, telling Brownfield that she knew Grange before he met Margaret and that she was the woman Margaret used to tell Brownfield about. She continues, explaining to Brownfield that Grange loved her and was forced into marriage with Margaret by his family. Even after the marriage, Grange continued to see Josie behind Margaret's back. Josie tells Brownfield how Grange would come to her every Saturday. Grange got the idea from Josie that Margaret should prostitute herself. Josie tells Brownfield that he should stop sleeping with her. She feels that his sexual interest in her is a way of getting revenge on his father. Josie says that if Brownfield really wants to make Grange pay, sleeping with her will not do it. He must go north to where his father lives and confront the man directly.

### Chapter 16

Time goes on, and Brownfield continues to obsess about his father. He is stung by the memory of Grange's single return to the South and of Josie's decision to abandon Brownfield. Brownfield knows that Josie prefers his father to him and would discard him in a second if given the choice. His feelings of guilt about Mem occasionally make him impotent when he tries to sleep with Josie. On those occasions, if he is able to imagine hurting or demeaning Mem, he can sometimes manage an erection and is able to make love to Josie.

The lovemaking between Brownfield and Josie is selfish and demanding, not nurturing like the honest and sustaining passion he experienced with Mem. His attraction to Josie is one grounded in a kind of pity and empathy rather than in mature sharing. One night, in the midst of such a sexual encounter, Grange appears. Brownfield's first impulse is to hit him, but instead he begins to cry at the sight of his father. Josie rejects Brownfield completely and chooses Grange.

Grange and Josie marry, leaving Brownfield even more bitter and angry.

## Part 4

### Chapter 17

Mem and Brownfield's youngest child, Ruth, is born in the midst of one of Brownfield's drunken stupors. Consequently, Mem has to endure the labor and delivery alone, and the child is born without a midwife. Brownfield is genuinely sorry for his neglect of his wife and new daughter and tries to make amends when he emerges from his drunken state.

In the midst of this tension-filled chaos, Grange walks into their home bearing food and goodies for the older children. Grange has become a regular benefactor for the family, yet his generosity makes Brownfield angry. The children have grown to adore their grandfather, who has made a practice of bringing them goodies.

Brownfield is perplexed by his father's behavior and even a bit jealous since he never received the same treatment from Grange when he was a child. He acts more like a child than a father in this situation.

Josie and Grange have purchased a farm and a house together, and the contrast between the place they live in and Brownfield's poorly warmed shack makes Brownfield feel angry and defensive. Grange has returned from his life in the North with enough money to create a secure life for him and Josie and to help out his son as much as he can.

Grange castigates Brownfield because there is no wood to light a fire to keep the house warm. Grange tries to explain to Brownfield the reasons why he left, how the sense of his life had become so small that he no longer could bear to try to fit into its confines.

Grange realizes what has happened, that Mem has given birth to his grandchild without assistance and in a freezing cold house. Mem tries to ensure the baby's life by rubbing its small and rather still shape. Grange pushes his son aside and tries to help his grandchild and daughter-in-law. He lights a fire.

Grange is fond of Mem, having known her when she was a child living at Josie's house. He feels particularly responsible for the state that he found her in when he returned from the North, and he tries to make amends to her by spending time with her and the children and by providing them with support. Brownfield acts like a child and constantly berates his father for the wrongs committed in the past.

### Chapter 18

Brownfield is a terrible father to his three daughters and is mostly concerned with perpetual intoxication. He does not have any affection for them and perceives them as burdensome. He speaks to them in ways that demeans them and does not show them any affection or warmth.

The oldest daughter, Daphne, does have some memory of the former Brownfield before he was so completely bereft and tells her sisters that their father used to be a different, better man. It seems to Brownfield that Daphne is trying to help her sisters to have some understanding of the core of the man they know as their father.

## Part 5

### Chapter 19

Mem returns home to Brownfield after spending the day looking for a home to buy. When she sees him, he humiliates her in front of their children. She thinks that she would like to kill him.

### Chapter 20

Captain Davis owns a dairy farm in Baker County where Brownfield works to pay off his debt. He is described as a gaunt, white man with sparse, white hair. Brownfield harbors hatred toward him but outwardly shows the appearance of obedient respect. Davis transfers Brownfield to his son J. L.'s dairy farm.

### Chapter 21

Daphne, her sisters, and Mem look at the Sears, Roebuck catalog, trying to plan out what will go in the home that they fantasize about. Brownfield returns, disrupting the scene and complaining about his dinner not being on the table when he arrives home. Ornette is appalled by her father's poor table manners and brutal eating style. Daphne swears never to marry anyone like her father. Brownfield tells his family that they will be moving to J. L.'s farm the following Monday, and Mem disagrees with him emphatically. She does not want her daughters to be vulnerable to the man's advances and to living with outhouses. Brownfield tells her that they are moving no matter what she thinks of the situation. He accosts her with his hands. Later, she wishes that she was a man so that she could beat up every man in sight.

### Chapter 22

When Brownfield arrives at home the following day, Mem is waiting for him. He greets her with an insult. She is unaffected by his attempted humiliation and is excited about something. He continues with his insults, but she responds by telling him that they have a new house in town. He says he will not move anywhere but J. L.'s place. Mem is so excited about the new house that she laughs and does not pay attention to any of Brownfield's negativity. She tells him that she has signed the lease. He is furious. His anger stems partly from the fact that, despite several attempts, he never learned how to read. He threatens her with violence. She asserts her newfound independence and says that they will move to town and he will work in a factory.

Brownfield persists with his insistence on moving to J. L.'s in spite of his own deep reluctance to go out to the man's place. The children watch their parent's conflict with increasing concern, especially in light of the volatile relationship between the two. Mem says that she is going to move into the house no matter what Brownfield wants. He grabs her, and finally she expresses all of the rage she has felt for him all of these years. Brownfield leaves, threatening that she better not defy him. His outburst does not deter Mem's objectives in the least. She determines that the family will move into the house on Monday.

### Chapter 23

Captain Davis asks Brownfield about Mem and how she feels about moving to his son J. L.'s farm. Brownfield replies enthusiastically that she is excited about the move and ready to go, but he can barely restrain his anger at the man who is partly responsible for his situation. Brownfield thinks that although it is 1944, Captain Davis acts as though he and his family are his slaves. He is frustrated and not sure what to do in this situation.

### Chapter 24

Mem tells Brownfield that she has obtained a job in town and that she can afford to pay for the rent herself. Brownfield is silent at her news. She asks him if he will be coming with the family when they move to town. He does not reply, and she and the children leave him there alone and still silent.

### Chapter 25

On Saturday, Brownfield is ready to fight with Mem after a night out drinking on the town. Mem feigns sleep as Brownfield enters the house. He gets violent with Mem and accuses her of thinking that she is superior to him. He insults her and their children and begins to cry. Mem does not say or do anything. Then she tells him that she is done with their fighting and arguments. Brownfield starts hitting her and tells her that she will do as he says. Even though Brownfield is beating her and yelling at her, she continues to insist that she is moving into town with their children.

Brownfield's insults grow more and more demeaning and his threats more frightening. He grabs his knife and Mem. She loses consciousness when Brownfield drops her on the floor and kicks her in the head.

The children are terrified and begin to cry. Daphne concocts a plan to kill him if he comes into their room. The girls are thinking of their plan when they fall asleep.

Brownfield loses consciousness, and when he awakes, he thinks of having sex with Mem, until he hears her voice telling him to open his eyes. She has a shotgun in her hands, and she tells him not to move. She tells him that if he does move, she will kill him.

Brownfield begins to throw up, and Mem orders him not to get it on the bed. She threatens to shoot off his balls, and Brownfield is stunned and ill. She gashes his head with the shotgun, and he begins to bleed. She tells him never to insult her again. She says that she and her children are moving to the city, that he had better not try to stop her, and that if he wants to come with them, there are some rules that she has decided will be the household's operating structure. He has to call her Mrs. Mem R. Copeland, Mrs. Copeland, or Mem. He also has to call their children by their real names. Mainly, she tells him that if he ever hits her again, she will kill him. She also tells him that he has to eat properly and with manners, that he cannot drink in her house or come home drunk, and that he must take responsibility for his actions and stop blaming everyone else for his life. Brownfield responds with silence and finally acquiesces to her demands. Mem, certain that he gets the point, puts the gun down.

## Part 6

### Chapter 26

The certainty with which Mem feels she has made her point is undermined in the beginning of this chapter when Brownfield awaits Mem's return to her submissive behavior. He hopes that aging will make her vulnerable in a way that will allow him to reassert control over their relationship.

### Chapter 27

The move to the new house becomes the stage for Brownfield's act. He pretend to be the submissive and obedient husband, while all the time planning his revenge on Mem who he now despises. He takes a job at a pie factory and finds the work frustrating. It is much easier than the work he used to do in the fields, but he is determined to find fault with every aspect of Mem's plans for improving their lives. Brownfield seems to enjoy the repetitive nature of the job and find solace from heat and labor of working in the fields.

The new house and life in town improves the life of the family. Brownfield even helps with the upkeep of the house, painting and tending to routine chores. The family enjoys the convenience of modern appliances. They own a refrigerator, stove, and heater and have indoor plumbing for the first time.

Because none of it is Brownfield's idea and because he was against the move, he cannot admit that any of the changes are good. He continues to resent Mem and to oppose, if silently, her goals and dreams for the family. He resents that she has proven herself a more effective leader of the family than he was and harbors thoughts of reordering the family's hierarchies. He is determined that he will reestablish his place as the head of the family.

The family establishes a kind of normalcy, and Mem and Brownfield nearly regain the type of relationship they had when they were first married. However, the depth of what they once shared is lacking now. Even when they make love, Brownfield envisions himself planting within her the seeds of her destruction. Because of his abuse of her and the years of poor health, Mem loses many of her teeth and no longer feels comfortable smiling. Brownfield does regret this loss, yet reflecting on it only makes him want to ensure her disappearance.

### Chapter 28

Mem falls ill after experiencing two additional pregnancies that do not produce live children but result in her own physical deterioration. Brownfield is pleased with her weakness and delights in her failure to maintain dominance in the relationship. Yet he also is somewhat sorrowful about her decline. Mem feels a kind of quiet triumph in the family's relative stability and the opportunities the move has provided for her children. She thinks that the personal sacrifices were worth it for what was accomplished.

Mem grows weaker and weaker, and she loses her confidence along with her health. As she loses strength, she begins to discern Brownfield's plan. She grows so weak that she can no longer work. Her final decline occurs in a tumultuous and long-lasting rainstorm. Mem begins to discern the danger she and her children are in as a result of Brownfield's long-harbored anger and resentment.

The first unraveling occurs when the heat is turned off because no one has paid the heating bill. When asked about the heat, Brownfield says that it is Mem's house and that she should pay the bill. Mem begins to realize that Brownfield has not changed but merely has been biding his time until she could no longer maintain the reins to the family's stability.

Brownfield tells Mem on her sickbed that he also has not paid the rent for nearly two months. He has an eviction notice that he shows her to rub in the insult and to make the failure of her efforts complete.

Brownfield begins packing. Mem asks him why he did not pay the rent even though he had the money. She makes a last effort to be strong and to save what is left of her dreams and aspirations for her family. Brownfield then tells Mem that the whole family is moving over to J. L.'s place. These words are Mem's worst nightmare. All that she has worked so hard for is unraveling, and this time she does not have the strength to fight Brownfield. In her weakness, Mem faints, and she is placed in the taxi that takes the family to J. L.'s. When they arrive, the house is still full of wet hay and half falling down. The windows have no glass, and rain pours in on the newly displaced family.

Mem faints again when she sees the house that Brownfield has brought them to, and she does not have the strength to enter the disheveled shack. When she awakes, she finds herself in the building's interior with her girls. Brownfield has returned to town. Her girls tell her that they had to fight with their father to make him leave the furniture Mem had so carefully acquired. He has tried to give it all away to the folks who helped him with the move.

### Chapter 29

When Brownfield returns to the house, he reveals to Mem that he has had this plan from the beginning of their relocation to town—a plan to bring her down and to regain control of the family and its destiny. He begins to insult her in the ways he used to do before the transformation. He tells her that he only wanted to make love to Josie and that she cannot compare sexually.

There is no electricity in the shack. In the near dawn, Mem can see Brownfield's insanity, which she had hoped had gone. Mem does not lose her dignity, even at this final insult by the man she once loved with all of her heart. She says that she will not die and leave her children with him, even though she now realizes that her death is precisely what Brownfield desires. She determines that she will regain her strength enough to leave him.

Brownfield continues to mock her and to ridicule her aspirations. He tells her that he will never let her leave him. He states that Mem's abandonment of him and the marriage would embarrass him in ways that he refuses to tolerate.

The children look on and are as horrified as their mother is by the specter of Brownfield. Like her, they had believed in the appearance of change that he had presented to them, and they cannot believe that the whole transformation was an act and that they really do not know their father at all. When Ruth says something to Brownfield, he begins to beat her for the first time in her life.

### Chapter 30

The family stays in the shack Brownfield brings them to for several years. Ruth is five and begins to attend school with her sisters. The living situation is horrifying. The children are exposed to the elements, insects, and animal waste. The house does not even have running water, and they have to go to a spring away from the house to get water.

The older children, Daphne and Ornette, are devastated by the return to the country and to primitive conditions. Ruth, the baby, is not as used to the town life as her sisters, and in a kind of childlike innocence, she finds the charms of the hovel in which they all find themselves.

When Ruth is four, Mem becomes pregnant again and gives birth to a son who has gray eyes that are reminiscent of Brownfield's brother, Star. Like Star, the infant dies very young and under mysterious circumstances. The baby is blue when it is discovered dead, and its older sisters believe that he has frozen to death.

After the baby dies, Mem takes a job that ensures she will not be at home during the day, working as a domestic for a white family in town.

Daphne is very aware of what is going on with the family and feels that she is the family's secret keeper. She still tells her sisters stories of what their father was like when she was a small child—that he had been sweet and had spent time playing with her and had taken her to buy candy. The girls internalize Daphne's memories, and the memories become part of their experience of their father even though they have never known their father to be anything except abusive and mean. The children play a game where they imagine involvements with the Brownfield/Daddy they imagine. One day, Brownfield overhears them and thinks, without concern, that his daughters might grow up to be liars.

As a result of her memories of her father, Daphne is more forgiving of his sins. Ornette is more angry with Brownfield. Daphne wants to love him and for him to be the father she remembers and imagines. Brownfield mocks Daphne and calls her crazy, which affects the girl's sense of self-esteem. This torment takes its toll. Daphne becomes jumpy and easily frightened. She understands that their current circumstances have resulted from Brownfield's attempt to punish Mem. Nonetheless, Daphne is able to distinguish her feelings about Brownfield from her resentments about the house and the family's living situation.

Unlike her sister, Ornette is basically a happy soul whose rebellion keeps her from internalizing her conflicts about the life that she and her mother and sisters are living. Brownfield is least fond of his daughter Ornette and tells the child that she will grow up to be used by men and will be fat. Whether Brownfield is right, or Ornette's behavior is determined by his judgments and proclamations about her, is unclear; she ends up somewhat as her fathers predicted, and she does not respect her mother.

Mem makes good on her promise to Brownfield to live. She recovers from the illness that precipitated the family's loss of the house in town. She makes sure that the house the family resides in is in decent shape but does not invest herself in its upkeep or beautification the way that she had in other houses.

## Part 7

### Chapter 31

Ruth awakens in the house of her grandfather, Grange Copeland. She went to her grandparents' home after Brownfield came home so drunk that Daphne, in her fear and desperation, hides herself and her sisters in the chicken house. The younger girls thought that being in the chicken coop was a kind of joke until Daphne slapped them hard when they began to laugh.

Brownfield's return home from his drunken binge was unusual in that he normally spent the nights that he drank out and away from home; or, if he did return home, he was usually so drunk as to be relatively harmless and passed out from the effects of the liquor rather quickly. This time, Mem tried to prevent Brownfield from beating the children, but she was unsuccessful in her efforts. Most often, he turned his ire and violence on her. By this time, he had lost his job, and Mem was the sole supporter for the family, who live in the property on J. L's farm as renters.

One day, Brownfield tried to learn how to read from one of Ruth's primers. When Ruth discovered her father attempting to learn her lesson, he was mortified and embarrassed and threw the book at the child. She then understood that her father's cruel words about her and her sister's education were grounded in jealousy. Since then, she has learned to value her education.

While the little girls hid in the chicken coop from their father, they realized that the situation was serious when they saw him with a gun and understood that he was waiting for their mother. Daphne left her sisters in the chicken coop in an attempt to tell her mother about her father's drunken rage and to prevent her from walking into a drunk and armed Brownfield.

Ruth saw her mother approach the house after having been dropped off by her employer. Daphne missed her mother, or her mother did not see the child in her attempt to protect her mother. Brownfield, drunk and angry, shot Mem in the face, killing her instantly as Ornette and Ruth watched from the hen house. It was Christmas time, and when the girls ran from their hiding place to their dead mother's side, all of the candy she had bought for them for the holiday lays scattered about on the cold ground. Daphne ran up to her mother and sisters and tried to warm her dead mother's legs.

At Grange's, the old man tries to soothe the children in the best way he can but recognizes that anything he might say to these girls about their dead mother would be ineffectual.

### Chapter 32

Grange as an old man is a striking figure with a lot of thick, silver hair and a tall, distinguished silhouette. He suffers from occasional bouts of illness and emotional distress. He sometimes lies on the floor, unable to move or to function. Ruth, his grandchild, brings new life and vision into his world. Ruth creates a division between Josie and Grange as Grange will not tolerate any disagreement with his view of how the child should be treated. He makes Josie learn how to care for Ruth's hair. Josie resents the little girl, and the two are at odds from the very beginning of Ruth's residence with her and Grange.

Ruth develops a strong bond with her grandfather, who lets her ride with him through his cotton fields but will not let the little girl ride atop the cotton while the truck travels into town, thinking that such behavior is beneath the little girl. When Ruth expresses concern about her safety from her father, Grange assures her that Brownfield is securely behind bars and cannot harm her or anyone else.

Ruth most misses her mother while she is in Josie's company and can feel the woman's resentment. She remembers working with her mother to pick and can the vegetables they had grown in their garden. With Grange, she can talk about her mother and father, and he wants to make sure that the little girl does not forget her mother. He tells her stories about her mother's strong qualities so that the child can retain some of the character her mother possessed. Grange rebukes Josie for not being more like Mem, a habit that distresses Josie and makes her feel bad about herself.

Grange is, in fact, somewhat abusive of his wife and does not treat Josie with respect. He takes out his frustrations on her and makes her feel bad about herself. There are times, however, that the old couple are happy with each other. As evidence of this fact, Ruth frequently has to sleep in her own bed rather than with them. Ruth does not understand the relationship between Josie and Grange, and on nights when she cannot sleep in her new circumstances, she feels her mother's presence come to her.

### Chapter 33

Ruth usurps Josie in her grandfather's affections and becomes the most important person in his life. Grange and Ruth spend a great deal of time together on the farm. He allows the child to help him with the various occupations he has around the farm and house, such as the ambrosia he makes at Christmas. Children are only allowed to visit Ruth at Christmas, and Grange makes a game of the occasion for Ruth's amusement. He tells Ruth stories as they all sit around preparing the ingredients for his concoction.

Grange talks about the events of his childhood and the stories he heard then. He tells Ruth that he feels Uncle Remus was foolish because he could have earned money by holding the little white boy he told stories to for ransom instead of spending his time at the child's mercy. Grange also tells Ruth about his youthful encounters with the supernatural world, the unexplained nature of the afterlife, and the spirits that dwell there. He tells Ruth about his spiritual belief and membership in the church.

Grange shares with the little girl that when he was about seven or eight years old he had attended a revival against his will. He felt that the preacher was a hypocrite because he beat his wife, who was Grange's aunt. Grange sat on the mourner's bench and, watching his much-despised uncle, who had fallen asleep, he struck a bargain with God. He prayed that if the fly that had landed on his uncle's lip went in the man's mouth and he swallowed it, Grange promised to join the church. The event happened just as he imagined, and he joined the church. Nonetheless, he tells Ruth that he does not believe in God.

When Grange takes Ruth to church, the two often sit in laughter, sharing his secret and other amusements that come from church culture, pointing out hypocrisy and self-righteousness.

### Chapter 34

Ruth and Grange dance together, and Josie sees them in Ruth's cabin, a structure Grange has built for the little girl's play. Josie castigates Grange, telling him to be careful of the holes in his heart. Ruth is unaware of her grandfather's health and loves to see him dance. Grange sings songs of his own invention, and Ruth loves to hear them. Grange and Ruth's dancing becomes a form of communication through which Grange transmits the lessons of life that he has internalized during his years.

Josie begins to spend her Sundays visiting Brownfield in prison. Ruth is daunted by the thought that Josie, or anyone for that matter, is brave enough to want to see her father and to spend time with him. After some time, Ruth becomes accustomed to Josie's Sunday visits to her father. Josie confronts Ruth with her built-up resentment and asks the child if she is aware of how she is indulged. Ruth does not understand what Josie is asking and cannot apprehend the older woman's feelings of jealousy.

### Chapter 35

Ruth and Grange make wine with the grapes they have grown on the farm. Ruth is allowed to drink the wine they make, and Grange is surprised by his granddaughter's ability to drink great quantities of the stuff.

Grange is an alcoholic, and both Ruth and Josie often help him home after a binge. Ruth responds to such episodes by withdrawing her affection from her grandfather, a technique that almost gets the old man to change his ways. For Ruth, Grange's drinking recalls Brownfield and the traumas of her young childhood at the mercy of her father's rages.

Grange and Josie become distanced from each other, and Ruth believes that this distance and the fate of his son are what lead Grange to drink. In her mind, the drinking her grandfather does is categorically different from the violent intoxication of her father. She absolves Grange of culpability in any transgression he has committed as a result of alcohol because she believes that his drinking is only self-destructive.

Ruth does not know about the history between Grange and her father and that their relationship is at the heart of her father's behavior.

### Chapter 36

After Ruth moves in with Josie and Grange, her horizons expand, and she begins to understand that the world is much bigger than the universe she had inhabited previously. Grange teaches her black history; he also teaches her how to shoot.

Grange's antipathy toward white people is a mystery to Ruth, whose encounters with whites has not been tainted with the deep prejudices and discriminations of Grange's experiences. He tries to explain to the girl about slavery and the subsequent system of SHARECROPPING and segregation he found himself bound up in as a young man. He also tells her about the violations that black women experienced under slavery and afterward. Grange tells his granddaughter that white people are evil. She feels that hatred should be personalized and tells her grandfather that she has never experienced any problem that was generated by her interaction with white people. Grange asserts that white people were responsible for the death of her mother. Ruth disagrees and does not understand what the old man means.

### Chapter 37

Grange feels that, with the murder of Mem, Brownfield is no longer living. He thinks that his son is so lost there is no point in trying to deal with him in the same way that one communicates with people who are alive.

Brownfield finds no redemption in prison. He continues to harbor bitterness and thinks constantly about what he imagines has been done to him and what he can do to get revenge. The person he shares his pathological vision with is Josie, his former lover and Grange's wife.

Grange is not unaware of the possible danger of Josie's bond with Brownfield. He believes that Josie is only trying to bother him, and he remains distracted by what he considers the mission of his older life, teaching Ruth what he knows of the ways of the world. He still keeps an eye on Josie and does not get jealous of his wife's preoccupation with his son.

Grange does worry about Ruth's curiosity about her father. He knows that the child finds it difficult to understand her father and what happened to him, as well as what he has done to others. Grange reflects that Ruth's sisters, Daphne and Ornette, were taken by Mem's father after her death. Mem's father and stepmother wanted to take all of the children with them, but Ruth clung to her grandfather and so was allowed to remain with him. Grange is surprised by his own response to the child and by his desire to care for her and to help her to mend from the dreadful mess of her parents' lives and her mother's death.

Grange thinks about his marriage to Josie. While he was in the North during his extended absence, he was confident that, although he knew Josie would have many lovers, she would always be his were he to return to her. When he actually returned, he found his predictions had been accurate. Josie was indeed drawn back to his side immediately, and the two married. Grange revealed that his return to the South was a deliberate attempt to gain autonomy from whites and to be able to live in an isolation of his own choosing. He realized that he needed to have access to Josie's money in order to bring his dreams to fruition, and that the easiest way to accomplish this was to marry her.

Josie does not share Grange's universal hatred of whites and argues with him that all life is important, that skin color is not a determinant of merit. Grange perceives Josie's attitude as rooted in ignorance and self-centeredness.

Grange wants to make certain that Ruth enters the world fully prepared for its realities as he understands them. He has traveled the world, and he tries to share his knowledge with his granddaughter. He tells her about his abandonment of his first wife, Margaret, and his son, Brownfield. Ruth asks if Margaret acted like Josie. Grange explains that Margaret did nothing to warrant his treatment of her and that her misbehavior occurred as a result of his mistreatment of her. Grange then excuses his own behavior, placing the blame for the whole situation on the shoulders of the white man he worked for when he was married to Margaret and Brownfield was a young man.

Ruth is angry at her grandfather's transference of his guilt and says to him that Brownfield is responsible for her mother's death, not white people. Grange states that he sees her point but that it does not take into consideration the whole situation. He wants her to understand that the circumstances of his life, as well as those of her father and mother, were, in fact, partially determined by the racial discrimination they all experienced.

Ruth asks him to share with her something he has done that she would consider bad. Grange is afraid to be honest with his granddaughter because he fears losing her love, a reality he could not bear. Ruth loves her grandfather so much that she cannot imagine he has ever done anything that is objectionable, much less truly damaging.

Although he has a powerful need to be honest with this child for whom he feels responsible, Grange knows that there are things about his past that he would not want her to learn. He thinks about an event in his life that happened right after he abandoned Margaret, Brownfield, and Star. He went at first to Josie, from whom he learned about Margaret's death from suicide. It did occur to him to be concerned about Brownfield, but not enough for him to act on it and to go to the boy in the wake of his mother's suicide. Instead, Grange focused on going north to find what he perceived as his freedom from the prison his life had become in his home in the South.

He traveled northward for several months, making money as he could along the way. He became involved in illicit activities that he could not have imagined before he left home. He was often so destitute that starvation became a distinct possibility. When he arrived in the North, he was disillusioned with the realities of the place. The world he discovered there was cold, not only in terms of climate but in connection and human energy. He felt ignored and insignificant in ways that he could not have imagined back home. While begging in Central Park and nearly mad from hunger, he robbed a woman with a small child. During his journey north, Grange had become quite skilled at robbery. His target in the park was a woman who was sitting, apparently waiting for someone to arrive. He saw that the woman was pregnant, and this reminded him of Margaret and the shape of her during her last pregnancy, when she was pregnant with another man's child.

The man the woman was awaiting arrived, and the two sat on the bench. The man was a soldier, and the two seemed delighted to be in each other's company. Hiding in the spaces behind them, Grange continued to observe the soon-to-be parents. The couple began to kiss each other, and the soldier put a ring on the woman's finger. The ring, and presumed proposal, sparked an argument between the two that Grange observed. The girl dropped the ring on the ground, and the soldier left. Before departing, however, the man gave the woman a large sum of money.

For Grange, the episode was a kind of revelation because he had never before witnessed any intimacy or true affection as shared and expressed by white people. He felt something for the woman and went to speak with her and to see if he could console her by saying or doing something to provide some comfort.

As the woman stood up, she dropped the dollars that the soldier had given her and left the scene. Grange approached the bench and picked up both the ring and the money she had left behind. The woman stood by the edge of a pond and stared into the water. For some reason, rather than leaving the park with the money, Grange decided to follow the young woman. Having lived on the road for several months, he looked unkempt and ragged. He did not think about his appearance or race when he decided that he had to see and speak with the woman. He took part of the money but planned to give the young woman some of it.

Grange came upon the woman, but she ignored him. He tried to give her the ring and some of the money. She demanded it from him when she learned his purpose, and when she discovered that all of the money was not there, she yelled to him that he had to give her all of the money that was left under the bench. She told him that before she would let him have the money, she would throw it into the pond. She proceeded to demonstrate her threat by throwing a $20 bill into the pond while demanding that Grange return the remainder of the money.

The woman called Grange a nigger and, again demanding the money, moved toward him and kicked him. Grange became enraged at the woman's response to what he saw as a genuine effort to reach out to another human being with compassion. The woman jumped toward him and landed on the pond's ice, which broke. She began to sink into the frozen pond, and although they had had a bitter and hateful encounter, Grange reached out to her and tried to pull her from the pond. The pregnant woman reached out but let his hand go as soon as she touched him. She went under the surface of the water saying "nigger." Grange left the park with the incident undiscovered.

Grange was haunted by the memory of that night and of the young woman. He knew that he could have saved her, and he remained astonished by the extent of her inability to see him in any way other than utterly repulsive and drenched in racial mythologies and stereotypes. Grange viewed the lesson as instructive and vowed never to let compassion mediate his belief in the fundamental evil of white people. He began to preach hatred for white people as he stood on a street corner in Harlem. He also began to fight with random white people on whom he vented his rage at the abuse he felt had been perpetrated by the entire race.

Later, he realized that he could not fight all whites, and he began a retreat back to the South, back home. Josie sold the Dew Drop Inn so that Grange could make his dream manifest. The farm that he purchased with the money became his sanctuary from the outside world and from the dangers of white violence and oppression. The sanctuary he finds in his farm is compromised by Josie's bitterness at having been exploited once more.

Grange resolves that Ruth will not hear stories like the one that he has just remembered. He asks her to remember him as someone who has only learned to love late in life and does not do it with the restraint and judgment necessary.

## Part 8

### Chapter 38

Even at Mem's funeral, Brownfield is sober but unrepentant. He rationalizes his behavior by saying to himself that Mem had grown too thin for his liking and thus he was justified in killing her. He does think of how she was when they first met, and he reflects on his fondness for the young woman he later destroyed. He has no capacity to reflect on the deeper significances of the situation or on the price of his actions for others, particularly for his dead wife. Mem is for him like the memory of pie or whiskey that he can no longer acquire, and his limited sorrow is confined to his own sense of truncated desire.

There is the possibility that had Mem not grown ill, not allowed herself to have any vulnerability, she might still be alive. Her trust in the possibility that Brownfield was capable of redemption and transformation had been her undoing. When she told him that she would eventually leave him, Mem had triggered in Brownfield the conviction that the only way to recover from the humiliation she had put him through when she took over as head of their household was to kill her—a belief that he could not back down from even in the face of her death. Her thinness was, in his mind, a marker of his failure to provide. He believes that he had to kill his wife in order to preserve his own fragile self-esteem. Even at her funeral, he believes that the responsibility for her death is her own, and he does not have a thought about the effects of his actions on the children that they produced together.

### Chapter 39

Brownfield has been sentenced to 10 years in prison for Mem's murder. He is paroled after seven years. While in prison, he learns that perhaps his only meaningful affection is for the South, the place in which he was born. He feels drawn to its randomness and refusal to acquiesce to uniformity.

When Josie visits Brownfield, she tells him about the relationship between Grange and Ruth. Brownfield is infuriated that his father is fathering his child when Grange did not take responsibility for him. He lets thoughts of the other children go, recognizing that he will never seek them out since they have disappeared into the unknown realm he understands as the North. Ruth, however, figures in his imagination as a perceived wrong. While he is in prison, he has time to think about Ruth and her luxurious upbringing in Grange's care, and he becomes more and more angry. He does not love his father but wishes that his father had some affection for him.

While in prison, Brownfield finally learns how to read and write. He recognizes that the skill comes relatively easily to him as a result of Mem's help in the beginning of their relationship. Although Brownfield weeps when he makes this discovery, he still has no epiphany about himself and the mistakes he has made in his life, nor about the damage he has caused.

Brownfield is not capable of looking within and reflecting upon his actions. He fears what he might discover if he should think too much about his life and behavior. He also cannot bear the prospect of isolation. In his newfound handwriting, he inscribes his plans or at least his desires to destroy his daughter Ruth and his father.

Brownfield befriends a man who killed several members of his family with a hatchet. The two share television time, and both men express in crude terms their sense of helplessness at the relative lack of power and control they have had in their lives. They both feel that the murders they committed were responses to their lack of autonomy.

### Chapter 40

Brownfield uses Josie in order to achieve his own ends. He pretends to be interested in her grievances about the relationship between Grange and Ruth so that she will begin to trust him. Josie shares with Brownfield her desire for Grange to return to his love for her alone and to forsake Ruth. Brownfield takes advantage of Josie's insecurities and inflames her complaints with the pretense of concern. He convinces her that he can take Ruth and that she and Grange will be free to rekindle their relationship. He assures her that such a thing is possible and that all will be the way it was before Ruth came to live with Josie and Grange. He says that he will wage a custody battle for his daughter so that legally Grange will have to relinquish the child into her father's care.

## Part 9

### Chapter 41

Ruth and Grange put up a fence. When the child pricks her finger on the barbed wire, it begins to bleed, and the sight of the blood reminds her of her mother's murder and of her body covered with blood after Brownfield's shooting. Grange distracts the girl by pricking his own finger and telling her about the Indians and the custom of becoming blood brothers. This diversion works, and the child returns to the task at hand.

Grange reflects on his life and the conflation of events of the past and the present. He thinks of his life in phases. His first life was the one where he worked as a sharecropper and was married to Margaret. He reflects on her youth and her energy and beauty. He also remembers the changes that occurred in the woman's appearance and demeanor as the couple's lives disintegrated. He understands his complicity in his first wife's death but is at a loss to understand how he could explain her suicide to her granddaughter Ruth, the real love of his life.

He knew when he married her that Margaret believed that marriage meant fidelity, but he continued to sleep with Josie anyway. Grange's refusal to give up his relationship with Josie made Margaret feel as if she was not attractive or desirable enough, and so she turned to other men for reassurance and companionship. When Margaret was most despairing and isolated, she was raped by Shipley, the man who owned the cotton farm and who Grange felt was responsible for his misfortune. This act was a transgression Grange felt he could not forgive, particularly because she became pregnant with Star as a result.

Grange also remembers Brownfield's birth and his and Margaret's despair that any good could come from the boy's birth. Margaret said that it did not matter what the child's name was; his fate would be the same. Through Grange's relationship with Ruth, he develops empathy and understands the loss and pain of Margaret's situation. He knows now that his wife killed herself out of despair and a feeling that she was such a sinner that she deserved to die.

Ruth and Grange spend the rest of the afternoon out in the sun building the fence and enjoying each other's company. The conversation between the two is lively and full of witty and loving banter. Grange takes her to look at the neighboring white family and tells her that all they do is to plot how to take his land.

## Chapter 42

At school, Ruth has her own experiences with race. Each morning, she and Grange walk to her school, and he leaves the child at the schoolhouse door. The pair love the walk through the woods as they both enjoy the sanctuary and quiet it provides. Mrs. Grayson is Ruth's teacher. She is very patriotic and teaches the children that their lessons are important as they will make them better citizens of the United States. Ruth spends much of her time in Mrs. Grayson's class daydreaming and trying to understand the relevance of what the woman tries to teach the extremely large class.

Ruth is a smart girl and has read the textbooks from her classes many times. During one of the times Mrs. Grayson is lecturing in a manner Ruth finds particularly incoherent, the young girl begins to flip through the history textbook. The book is new to the students, a hand-me-down from the local white school, which passes on its texts whenever its students get a new one. In the text, there are pictures that intrigue Ruth, and she sees many that are of interest to her. At one point, she flips to the page that has a diagram on it called "The Tree of the Family of Man." This "scientific" chart purports to map the hierarchy of the races that constitute humanity. When she discovers the chart, Ruth is horrified to find that blacks are characterized as the lowest primitives. Jacqueline Paine, the child who owned the book before Ruth, had written a note next to the figure of the black person that reads "nigger." Ruth is surprised and horrified to find this racial slur in her book.

While this incident occurs, Mrs. Grayson has called on her. Ruth had been paying attention to the book and had not heard the woman call her name. Mrs. Grayson begins beating the child with a strap she uses on her students. Ruth throws the book to the floor and walks out of the room, cursing the teacher. The woman insults her and tells her that she will not amount to anything. This lesson seems to support Grange's assertions and presumptions about white people.

During the summers, Ruth reads voraciously and plays freely on her grandfather's land. As a result of the general incompetence of the teachers and her traumatic experience, she begins to hate going to school. She is also stigmatized because of her parents' story. The fact that her father murdered her mother makes her status lower than the poorest student at the school. She also has no friends or relatives at the school since Daphne and Ornette live in the North and she does not hear from them.

Ruth is a social pariah at school, and as a result of the ridicule and meanness she experiences there, she walks around with her head down and tries not to speak with anyone. As soon as Brownfield gets out of prison, Josie goes to live with him and begins to spread rumors that Grange and Ruth have an unnatural relationship—another rumor that does not help Ruth's already established status as an outcast.

During the difficult years when Ruth attends school and is considered an outsider, Rossel, another girl at the school, treats Ruth with respect and befriends her. Rossel's mother has died, and her father is an alcoholic, and so she can identity to some extent with Ruth's situation. Rossel is also treated with suspicion and wariness by both the school's faculty and its student body. Rossel wants to marry Walt Terrell when she grows up. Walt Terrell, who is much older than Rossel, is a World War II veteran and the richest black man in the community. Ruth does not quite understand Rossel's strategy for using marriage to achieve economic and social security. Later, Rossel marries Walt and, from Ruth's vantage point, seems to accomplish her goals.

### Chapter 43

Ruth gets her period, and Grange helps her to acquire all of the supplies she needs. This awakening of her physical self prompts her to wonder what her adult self will be like. She tells Grange that she knows she will want to leave the farm eventually. She says that she will not leave as long as he is alive. She says that she is interested in going north and discovering what life is like there and if she can live in such a different place. She has a hard time imagining what she can do if she stays in the community where she now lives. She imagines her options are limited to teaching, and she knows that she does not want to do that. She has no respect for Mrs. Grayson and women like her after her experiences at school. When she examines the newspaper, all of the best and most desirable jobs specify that the person hired has to be white. She even jokes that Rossel's solution of marrying well has already been exhausted.

Grange speaks to her about racial progress and the possibility that things will change in time for her life to be different than his was and may not be defined entirely by a race-based caste system. Grange tells her that the farm will be hers when he dies and that she will be safe there as long as she knows how to use a gun.

Grange explains that love has defined the different lives he has experienced. He says that when he was married to Margaret, he was jealous of her capacity to love and that he could not love others in the way that she did, so he became jealous and fought with her. In the second life of Grange Copeland, he learned to hate white people and to love himself. Eventually, he recognized that hatred was a dead end and created an unending dichotomy. Therefore, in the third phase of his life, he became giving and sacrificing, allowing another to be the focus of his energy in a positive way for the first time when he began to love Ruth. He credits the child with allowing him to understand the complexities of his life and to understand its permutations. He says that he wants her to have lots of children so that that understanding and new way of being that is connected with him can continue into the future.

Ruth wisely points out that the kind of change Grange envisions cannot happen behind walls or fences and must involve whole communities of people. He asks how many people she knows who would be willing to participate in a fight for change. She replies that she only knows three black people who would be involved in such a struggle.

### Chapter 44

In the wake of Josie's departure, the house begins to resemble Grange and Ruth's cabin. It is more relaxed and homey and full of books and color. Ruth makes a quilt of yellow and white to adorn her bed. They grow tea to drink, and they offer it to their guests, who wonder what it is.

Grange becomes more confident and directed as he ages. He is certain that he is preparing Ruth for greatness. He teaches the young girl to be wary of others, particularly those who profess to be pious and to give spiritual counsel. Trying to imagine every possible contingency that might threaten his granddaughter, he even hires someone to teach Ruth how to swim so that she can avoid drowning. The community becomes convinced that Ruth Copeland is negatively influenced by her grandfather and is growing up on the wrong side of right.

## Part 10

### Chapter 45

After Josie begins living with Brownfield, Ruth sees them at her school trying to hide in the woods behind the building. The children at the school are terrified of her father and run away from him. After a time, there is an exchange between Brownfield and Grange, who picks Ruth up from school every day. As Grange and Ruth walk home, they nearly run into Brownfield and Josie on the path that they take back through the woods to Grange's farm. Josie greets them with a racial slur, a reference to the Gold Dust Twins, a racist symbol that appeared on laundry detergent at the time. Josie's naked jealousy frightens Ruth as she recognizes the extent of the woman's hatred of her. Ruth is deeply traumatized as she remembers Brownfield's voice and the violence and terror associated with that sound.

Grange asks Josie and Brownfield what they want as Ruth curls into Grange's coat. Brownfield tells Grange that he wants Ruth back, to which Grange replies with shock and anger. He tells his son that he no longer has any claim to the girl and that he must leave her alone.

Brownfield has his own surprise as a result of this meeting. He did not anticipate that Ruth, as an older child, would look so much like Mem. The resemblance alarms him and generates feelings of confusion and uncertainty. Grange tells Josie and Brownfield that he does not want Josie back and that he wishes they had never been involved. He also tells his son that he will never let Brownfield take Ruth from him. Brownfield says that he will take Ruth just to get back at Grange for not being a father to him.

Grange loses his voice for a second in horror at the shortsighted and self-interested goal of Josie and Brownfield. Then he turns to Ruth, the only person there he feels is worthy of address. He tells his grandchild that her father, Brownfield, has spent most of his life blaming Grange for abandoning him, and he has erroneously blamed every wrong event in his life on his father's actions. Grange says that even though he has major responsibility for his son's early failures and brokenness, once Brownfield had children of his own, he became responsible for his own actions and for the lives and emotional well-being of his children. Grange points out that Brownfield has never taken responsibility for what he has done and for the lives he has destroyed. He says that his son has wasted a lifetime blaming him and white folks for all of the misery he has caused himself.

Grange continues, telling Ruth that he himself has blamed white folks for some of what has happened to him, but he learned that, no matter what the circumstances, each person is accountable for his or her own soul. He tells his son that accountability is what makes for maturity, for manhood, in his estimation. He admits using Josie for her money, but he also says to his son that if it was white folks that led him to want to kill Mem, he should have turned the gun on himself. That, Grange maintains, is what it means to be a fully responsible human being. He also apologies to his son for the way that he treated Brownfield's mother, Margaret. He says that if he had to do it all over again, he would have died by her side, no matter the circumstances.

All of Grange's truth-telling does not move Brownfield in the least. He mocks his father and calls him demeaning names. Again, Grange takes responsibility for Margaret's death and says that Brownfield is likewise responsible for Mem's death and that they cannot begin to redeem themselves until they admit the wrongs that they have perpetrated. Again, Brownfield is unrepentant. He says that he will not admit anything and that the courts will support him in his efforts to regain custody of his daughter. Grange and Ruth return to the sanctuary of Grange's farm and feel defeated, imagining that their time together is threatened and limited by forces beyond their control. Ruth is terrified that once again she will be alone and defenseless, this time, at the mercy of her terrible and terrifying father.

That night, Grange reads Exodus to his granddaughter. He tells Ruth that sometimes leaving is the right and wise thing to do. He suggests to his granddaughter that the two of them leave the country. He knows that the limitations of the United States are not exactly the same in the rest of the world. He does not only mean that he and Ruth should escape from Brownfield and Josie's schemes, but that the two of them might be able to get away from the racial caste system that has taken such a toll on their lives. He says he is not sure that he can forgive white people; he still feels bitterness in his heart for all of the wrongs and sufferings he and his loved ones have experienced at their hands. Josie says she has her own feelings of anger toward whites now.

Grange castigates his granddaughter and tells her in no uncertain terms that she must work to temper her anger and hatred so that she can forgive. He wants her to work toward a kind of compassion that he wishes for himself. He knows that profound compassion is at the heart of the achievement of peace and solace. Grange worries that, with all of the oppression that the next generation faces, they will end up without the energy and optimism needed for real change and progress to occur.

Once, in the middle of the night, Grange awakens Ruth out of a sound sleep. He tells her he is fearful that Brownfield is up to some deviousness that might separate them, and so he gives her a bank book. The account contains $900, money Grange has made from his work bootlegging, and which he has been saving for his granddaughter to attend college. He also gives his granddaughter $400 in cash that he made playing poker. He cautions the girl to put the cash in to the bank the next day. The gifts make Ruth sad, grateful, and afraid. He also tells his granddaughter that several of his friends have signed over their life insurance policies to Ruth to pay off their gambling debts to Grange.

Because the sense of impending doom as a result of their encounter with Brownfield and their knowledge of his plans, Brownfield and Ruth begin to organize. Brownfield tells his granddaughter about the household bills and what needs to be paid when. He also begins to collect the money various people in the community owe him, and over time, Ruth begins to accumulate quite a sum of money in the account Grange has given to her.

Grange teaches the now 16-year-old how to drive, and she learns quickly, taking over the tasks that used to be Grange's. He also puts the car in her name. Grange begins to retreat into himself, sitting for hours thinking about life and smoking a pipe. He is still in full command of his granddaughter, though, ensuring that she remain feminine yet fully independent. He wants Ruth to do more than survive her life as he feels he has. He desires that the girl, his grandchild, should feel that her life is fully hers and that she does not have to make any splits or divisions to her spirit to live it.

### Chapter 46

One day, while on the way to school, Brownfield stops his daughter on her journey. He stands by the side of the road as she walks, and in her terror, she will not pass him. Her father appears different from the last time she saw him. To Ruth, the man seems smaller in stature and is graying. She is also surprised that he looks kempt and is not intoxicated. When she looks into Brownfield's eyes, she feels the old terror that is so familiar to her. She wants to get to school safely and asks Brownfield, her father, what he wants with her.

Brownfield senses his daughter's consternation and says to his child, to whom he has said so little during the course of her life, that she looks like her mother. Ruth still does not trust her father and asks him again why he has stopped her. The school bell rings in the distance.

Brownfield says that he only wanted to see his child and that he has brought her a present. Ruth is wary of her father and refuses to take it, kicking dirt on top of the package. This angry response does not seem to bother Brownfield, a reaction Ruth is unaccustomed to from her father. He asks his child whether she remembers her mother, and she replies that she does. He also asks why she does not seem to have any affection for her father. She says that she has had no reason to feel any fondness for him. It becomes clear to Ruth that Brownfield is desperate for some affection from her and that he seems to want her forgiveness. But she is not about to trust this man who has caused them all so much pain.

Brownfield sees himself in his daughter's refusal to accept his change and understands for the first time what that rejection feels like. Brownfield tells Ruth that he has tried to get her sisters to come back home but has been unsuccessful. Grange has discovered that Ruth's older sister, Daphne, ended up being committed to a facility for the psychologically disturbed and that Ornette became a prostitute. Brownfield is deeply disturbed about the fate of his daughters and is further upset when he learns that Josie is delighted about what has befallen Daphne and Ornette and that she laughs all day when they learn of their fate. Brownfield seeks comfort with Josie that evening, and she continues to be unsympathetic and mean, wanting to torture him with her sense of superiority in light of his children's downfall.

Brownfield is still unable to avoid expressing his anger as a primary means of communication. He tells Ruth that he loves her, her sisters, and her mother even though he acted in the ways that he did. Ruth does not understand the kind of love that is destructive and does not seem to have any positive manifestation. Brownfield also seems to see his daughter as a kind of possession. He says that he will have what is his, referring to his daughter.

Ruth replies to him that she is not his. She does not give Brownfield this reply out of anger or defiance, but out of genuine concern and confusion about her life and the many traumas that she has witnessed. At this point, Brownfield reaches out to touch his daughter, but the gesture is violent. He takes her arm and begins to pinch it hard between his forefingers. He says again that, like his livestock, Ruth is one of his possessions and that she cannot remain with her grandfather. He also says that if he is not successful, he will "see them both in hell."

Ruth's small feeling of hopefulness that her father may have actually changed is dashed with his violence toward her. She cries out in her despair that Brownfield has just told her that he loves her. He tells her that he cannot leave her with Grange because being a man means that you have to have something in your possession. Ruth disagrees loudly, telling him that a man does not possess but cares for and sustains his children. She tells him that he wants killing and that she does not like him, and she starts off to the school day that has already begun.

When Brownfield gets home to Josie, she is angry with him. She feels that her life is at its lowest point in light of Brownfield's obsession with regaining his family. Josie knows that Brownfield is not motivated by love or affection but merely cannot stand the lack of control of anything. This inability to lord over something or someone runs counter to Brownfield's definition of masculinity, and so he is motivated to "repossess" his daughter, the only one who remains within his possible reach.

Brownfield has a plan. He has an acquaintance who is a judge. When he was in prison, he worked for Judge Harry, whom he also knew when they were both boys. Brownfield says to Josie that Judge Harry and he have an understanding. He thinks that he will ask Judge Harry to help him to get custody of Ruth. Josie says to Brownfield that he should leave Ruth with Grange. She argues with him that she knows he does not really want his daughter back but is still hell-bent on getting revenge on Grange. Brownfield laughs and says to Josie that perhaps the stress of the situation will give Grange a heart attack and kill him. Josie feels more hopeless than she has since she was a young woman and her father kicked her out of the house for becoming pregnant after she was raped. She feels that she has never experienced real love in her entire life.

After feeling angry and frustrated all day, Brownfield tells Josie that one of Mem's children, the small boy with gray eyes who died, was white. What he means is that he and Mem had an albino child. Brownfield expresses his hatred for the child, who, he says, looked like a white version of Grange. Brownfield tells Josie that immediately after the child was delivered, he began beating Mem and accusing her of sleeping with white men even though he knew that she had not. He told Mem that the child had to get darker or he would kill it. One day, when he came home, he set the infant outside on the doorstep and went to sleep. He lied to Mem and told her that he was taking care of the baby and that she could sleep. Brownfield fell into a restful sleep with the child outside in the cold. He awakened to find Mem trying to revive the child, Brownfield's son, who had frozen to death.

Again, Brownfield tells Josie that he knows he was the father of the child he killed. After hearing this terrible and terrifying story, Josie feels real empathy for the first time for Mem and her situation. She also understands that there is no possible redemption for the man and that he is, in actuality, insane.

Brownfield can read Josie's response on her face and begins to defend himself. He says immediately that he is not crazy and that everything he has done is part of a larger plan. He tells her that he gets tired of the effort of being a father—or, as he puts it, "trying to be like a new person." Josie tells him that if he had been willing to make that effort, he would have a son now. He replies about his dead son, killed mercilessly at his own hands, that the child was a "little white bastard."

Josie sees that there is no hope for Brownfield. The sweet potential of who the man might have been is gone forever. She realizes that for Brownfield, his problems are located within, even though they are exacerbated by circumstances. Clearly, Brownfield is his own worst enemy.

Through the haze of his lost consciousness, Brownfield recognizes a hopefulness in his daughter Ruth that he does not understand. He knows that he cannot control this child, so he longs to break her spirit and her belief in possibility. Brownfield does not understand love. He thinks that he has loved but has no idea what the word means or entails. He almost feels sorry about the mess that everything in his life has become, but he has gone too far to back away from his primitive strategies, his ways of coping, and his rationalizations. Before falling asleep, he determines that he will continue with his battle to regain custody of his youngest child and thereby revenge the wrongs done to him by his father. He does not even think it necessary to plan for what he might do with Ruth when and if he regains custody.

## Part 11

### Chapter 47

Time passes as Ruth and Grange try to anticipate what Brownfield is planning and what he will do to accomplish the ends he is hell-bent on achieving. Ruth has a new understanding of and appreciation for the beauty of the world as her perceptions have become diminished by the shadow her father's threats have cast upon her life. There is a loss of pure pleasure from the unblemished joy she has experienced under Grange's loving protection and nurturance. She throws herself into the activities of the Civil Rights movement when she learns about it on the television show *The Huntley-Brinkley Report.* On the show, Chet Huntley and David Brinkley feature the activities of young blacks as they are involved with the movement. Ruth finds herself drawn to the concept of integration. Grange does not share her enthusiasm. Every night on the Report, the stories cover Dr. Martin Luther King, Jr., and the students and other grassroots folks who work with him to end the discrimination that African Americans have experienced in the United States since the days of slavery.

When Ruth asks Grange what he thinks about Dr. King, her grandfather replies that he would be happier and more content with the possibilities King and the movement represent if he believed that King could be elected president. The fact that Grange believes that such an opportunity does not exist for black men dims his sense of the movement's possibilities. He thinks that he can tell that King is a man who is tender with his whole family, and that helps Grange to be able to trust his intentions.

Ruth wonders aloud why there is so much singing associated with the movement's activities, and Grange says that the songs serve the same function as "whistling in a graveyard." Grange still does not believe that all of the movement's work and sacrifice can bring about fundamental change in race relations. He does not think that the strategy of nonviolent civil disobedience will work against such a persistent and unremitting racism as the southern United States has maintained.

When he sees pictures of white racists on the television screen, Grange recognizes the oppression and hatred he has fought against his whole life. He feels that the power of white hatred of African Americans is too long-standing and deep-rooted to ever change. Ruth maintains that the strength in the movement lies in the effort, not the result. She feels that taking a stand and fighting for what one believes in is worth the effort, energy, and lives, no matter the consequence. Grange allows himself to be persuaded by the hopefulness of his granddaughter's reading of the situation.

One evening, as Ruth watches *The Huntley-Brinkley Report,* Grange walks into the house looking stricken. He does not immediately reply to his granddaughter's questions and sits down facing her. Ruth believes that finally Brownfield has made a move to act on his plans and threats.

Grange begins to speak and tells her that his friend Fred Hill has been found in a ditch with half of his head blown off. Hill is a drinking and gambling friend of Grange's whose death is attributable to his involvement in the Civil Rights movement. Hill's death changes Grange's perspective on the movement and its effects.

Grange reflects on some of his experiences with the violence generated by southern racism. He recalls seeing a LYNCHING. The victim was a woman whose body had been entirely mutilated by her killers. The woman was hanged, cut, and burned. The official explanation of the woman's death was that she had killed herself.

Ruth remembers Hill and recalls her interactions with him as a little girl. Hill had been kind to her. He played marbles and taught her to shoot the round glass balls. His shooting probably happened not as a result of his direct actions but as a warning to his grandson, who was actively involved in trying to desegregate an all-white school. His grandson fails in his efforts as a result after his grandfather's murder.

Thus, the Civil Rights movement comes to Ruth and Grange's community. During the summer, there are protests in town against segregation. Seeing the marchers in person makes the whole movement more immediate and real for Ruth. The integration of the movement workers is striking to Ruth, who has really never seen blacks and whites working together as compatriots in a common cause.

Baker County, the home of Ruth and Grange, is startled and shaken up by the protesters' presence. The white women working to integrate the town receive the most virulent and aggressive negative responses from the town's residents. While watching the workers' activities, Ruth has an encounter with a young man that changes her forever. The young man tries to hand out flyers to passersby endorsing integration as a necessity for all Americans. When he hands Ruth a flyer, the two exchange a glance that Ruth finds unforgettable. She cannot concentrate as she drives home from town and puts the flyer the young man has given her into the mailbox of the white neighbors who live close to her and Grange. This gesture, small as it is, is Ruth's first activist effort.

Ruth and Grange sit on the porch of the house, reflecting on the notice they have received that Brownfield is, at last, going to take them to court to try to regain custody of Ruth. As they sit on the porch, a car approaches the house, prompting Grange to go for his shotgun. He sets the gun on the porch, and the two sit and watch the car's approach. When the car is close enough to observe, Ruth sees that one of the passengers is the young man who had given her the flyer while she was in town. He has been looking for Ruth, and Grange is deeply surprised to see the response his granddaughter has to the young man who approaches the porch. The young man comes up to the porch and extends a hand to Grange and introduces himself. He thinks, without saying it, that Grange looks like Bayard Rustin, a central organizer in the movement.

Grange realizes that he knows the young man. He is the son of Sister Madelaine, the community fortune-teller. He was a student at Morehouse before leaving to work in the movement. His father was a surgeon. The other riders in the car, some of whom are white, approach the house and also shake Grange's hand but do not try to come on to the porch.

The young workers ask Grange if he is a voter. Grange tells them that he is not, and they ask him why. Grange says that since everyone who runs for election is white, the results make no difference to him. A young worker named Helen tells Grange about the work they have been doing in Green County, where he is from. Grange listens to the tale of their efforts but still feels that they are wasting their time and putting themselves in needless danger. Grange wishes that he could protect the valiant young workers and Dr. King, but he knows that he cannot. As a result of his life experiences, he tells them that he does not want them to become bitter and to lose their lives in a fruitless struggle against an enemy he feels cannot be defeated.

Grange feels that the young people have the right motivation and are informed by their love of humanity. When they leave, Grange gives them a watermelon, and he waves to them all, black and white.

### Chapter 48

Ruth and Grange get ready in the morning as they prepare to face Brownfield in court. Grange is dressed in his finest, and Ruth thinks that her grandfather, when dressed up as he is, looks like her imaginings of God.

The town is mostly deserted as it is Saturday and many people do not come in early. Grange gives his granddaughter a kiss of reassurance before they walk into the courtroom. He tells her that she will always belong to him, no matter what happens.

The two enter the courthouse, and it becomes apparent before long that Judge Harry and Brownfield are in league with each other. Judge Harry does not allow Grange to speak in the courtroom, and before long, the hearing is over and Ruth has been given to Brownfield's custody. Brownfield approaches his child and father gloating. He tells Ruth that she must come with him. Ruth is reluctant and afraid for her grandfather. She does not want to leave him. Josie tells the girl that she will take care of Grange.

As Brownfield approaches Ruth, Grange takes out his gun and shoots his son dead in front of the judge, Josie, and Ruth. He then takes Ruth and returns to his home. He tells the judge as he passes him on the way out of the courtroom that he is not trying to escape. He also says that whoever comes on his property trying to take him to jail will get the same treatment his son received.

Grange and Ruth leave the courthouse with police in pursuit. Grange leaves his granddaughter unarmed in the house and heads to the cabin with all of the guns he can find. He is shot down in a hail of bullets. His last moments are a kind of prayer to himself. He consoles himself as he falls into the permanence of death, forgiven and embraced.

## CRITICAL COMMENTARY

*The Third Life of Grange Copeland* focuses on the process of self-actualization experienced by Grange Copeland as he confronts the complexities of life as a poor, black, southern, undereducated American. At the inception of his journey, Grange sees his condition and lack of awareness and opportunity for advancement as natural. As his life progresses, however, he is increasingly able to understand the factors that limit his circumstances, and he tries to make changes in his immediate circumstance and in his perception of the world. Through the journey of its protagonist, Grange Copeland, the novel demonstrates that with the acquisition of self-awareness, it is possible for individuals at any phase in their lives to undergo radical change and to become dramatically more functional and fully human.

As detailed in the title, there are three major phases of Grange Copeland's life experience, each one defined by a particular self-construction that he abandons at a critical juncture when his fundamental understanding of the world undergoes a transformation. Each of Copeland's three self-constructions derives from his experiences with and understanding of the oppressive circumstances of his life as a black man. His oppression is clear from the start of the novel, when he is a young man and has a small family consisting of his wife, Margaret, and his son, Brownfield. The family lives in a county called Greenfield, so Brownfield's name functions as an ironic commentary on the limitations that the young boy faces as a result of his race, in spite of the seeming verdancy of the physical world surrounding him.

Although involved with another woman at the time, Grange begins his relationship with his wife, Margaret, in hopefulness and with great expectations. The positive beginning of the relationship soon unravels, and the family disintegrates. The family is entirely dependent on Grange's mood; as the man feels, so the family functions. On Saturday afternoons, the family cleans up and awaits visitors who never arrive. Grange gets drunk in his despair and falls into a stupor, sleeping outside in the yard until Sunday morning. On Sunday, he awakes and heads to church, where he sings with sincere fervency, only to return home and fight with his wife.

Later on, Grange does not repair the family house or allow his son to attend school. He is stricken with hopelessness, which prevents him from trying to change his and his family's circumstances. Brownfield hears his parents talking about the possibility of moving north, but that neither of his parents can imagine something different from what they already know.

Copeland's family situation is the very definition of dysfunctional. The roots of his inability to effect a change in his family life can be found in his fundamental insecurity and self-doubt. There are no role models in his community that are accessible to him. He is not able to find any validation for either his masculinity or his human worth. He is particularly undone by his wife's perhaps involuntary affair with Shipley, the white man for whom Grange works.

Consequently, Copeland tries to find gratification in destructive ways. He becomes the bad man and revels in his reputation for disregard and abuse. In this way, he rescues his self-esteem but sacrifices the most important connections of his life. He constructs a self from a sense of dominance and control over his wife and child. His choices, his neglect of his responsibilities, and his ultimate abandonment of his wife and son cost his family dearly. Margaret kills herself after Grange leaves the family.

After a brief detour living with Josie and exploring life close to his hometown, Grange has the transitional experience that leads him to his second life—a life in the North, where he discovers that racism is not limited to the South. He travels northward for several months, making money as he can along the way. He gets involved in illicit activities that he could not have imagined before he left home. He is often so destitute that starvation becomes a distinct possibility. When he arrives in the North, he is disillusioned with the realities of the place. The world he discovers is cold, not only in terms of climate, but also in kindness and human energy. He feels ignored and insignificant in ways that he could not have imagined back home.

While in Central Park in New York, he has an encounter with a white woman whose hatred for and suspicion of blacks is so intense that she is willing to lose her life and the life of her unborn child rather than to consider the possibility that African Americans have the capacity to be giving and humanitarian. During his journey north, Grange has become quite skilled at robbery. He finds for a target a woman sitting in the park who, apparently, is waiting for someone to arrive. He sees that the woman is pregnant and seeing the woman reminds him of his dead wife, Margaret, and of her shape during her last pregnancy, when she was pregnant with another man's child.

The man the woman awaits arrives and the two sit on the bench. The man is a soldier and the two seem delighted to be in each other's company. Hiding in the spaces behind them, Grange observes the soon-to-be parents. The couple begin to kiss each other and the soldier puts a ring on the woman's finger. The ring and presumed proposal spark an argument between the two, an argument that Grange continues to observe. The girl drops the ring on the ground and the soldier leaves. Before departing, the man gives the woman a large sum of money.

For Grange, the episode is a kind of revelation because he has never been witness to any intimacy or true affection as shared and expressed by white people. He feels something for the woman and goes to speak with her and to see if he can console her by saying or doing something to provide some comfort.

As the woman stands up, she drops the dollars that the soldier has given her and leaves the scene. Grange approaches the bench and picks up both the ring and the money the woman has left behind. The woman stands by the edge of a pond and stares into the water. For some reason, rather than leaving the park with his windfall Grange decides to follow the young woman. Having lived on the road for several months, Grange looks unkempt and ragged. He does not think about his appearance or race when he decides that he must see and speak with this woman. Grange takes part of the money, but plans to give the young woman some of it.

He comes upon her and she ignores him. He tries to give her the ring and some of the money. She demands it from him when she learns his purpose and, when she discovers that he has not given her all of the money, she yells to him that he has to give her all of the money that was left under the bench. She tells him that before she will let him have the money, she will throw it into the pond. The woman proceeds to demonstrate her threat by throwing a $20 bill into the pond, at the same time, demanding that Grange return the remainder of the money.

She calls him a nigger and again demands the money and moves towards Grange and kicks him. Grange becomes enraged at the woman's response to what he sees as his genuine effort to reach out to another human being with compassion. The woman jumps down from the landing and lands on the pond, which breaks. She begins to sink into the frozen pond. Although they have had a bitter and hateful exchange and encounter, Grange reaches out to her and tries to pull the pregnant woman from the pond. The woman reaches out but lets his hand go as soon as she touches him. She goes under the surface of the water saying "nigger." Grange leaves the park with the incident undiscovered.

Grange is haunted by the memory of that night and of the young woman. He knows that he could have saved her, and he remains astonished by the extent of her inability to see him in any way other than as utterly repulsive and as drenched in racial mythologies and stereotypes.

The event in Central Park and Grange's interpretation of its significances leads him to enter the second phase of his life. As it begins, Grange is defined by his hatred of white people. After the incident in the park, he holds white people responsible for all of the problems that he has experienced in his life. By absolving himself of responsibility, he is free to live his life without any accountability for his actions and with no sense that his actions have consequences. Grange views the lesson as instructive and vows never to let compassion mediate his belief in the fundamental evil of white people. He begins to preach hatred for white people and also begins to randomly fight, venting his rage at the abuse he believes has been perpetrated by the entire race.

Later, Grange realizes that he cannot fight all whites, and he begins to retreat to the South—home. There he marries Josie and uses her money to purchase a farm, which becomes his sanctuary from the outside white world.

Grange finds himself responsible for the impact caused by his abandonment of his son, including Brownfield's complete inability to function in the role of an adult—particularly as a husband and father. Brownfield's marriage to Mem follows the same trajectory as Grange's relationship and marriage to Margaret. Mem is pretty, sweet, and so quiet that she is not often noticed. She enjoys pleasures unknown to Brownfield, such as walking in the woods, and she is distinctly different from the other women he has known. Brownfield is intrigued by Mem's self-possession; she is different from the other women he has known.

Mem makes Brownfield want to be more than he is and to prove his worth to her. She becomes a kind of mother figure who begins to heal some of the wounds left by Margaret's absentee parenting. She encourages his newfound desire to learn to read and write, and under her tutelage, he learns the first skills of his life. Mem's guidance reveals to Brownfield the connections between adulthood, maturity, and self-sufficiency He also learns to value the spoken word from Mem's graceful use of it. Mem and Brownfield begin their lives together in love and full of hope for the future.

Brownfield has learned from his father to be disrespecting, disregarding, and violent to women, and he cannot seem to perform any better than Grange did in his role as father. Things do not go as planned for Mem and Brownfield. Three years later, the two have one child, another on the way, and too much indebtedness to think about their dream of relocation to the North. Although their dreams have not come to fruition, Mem and Brownfield are still in love. Mem is nurturing and loving to Brownfield and provides him with the emotional sustenance he needs to become a grown-up and a mature man. The two still make love, despite the complications and hardships of their lives. Brownfield's devotion to his wife leads him to accept his life as it is and to continue the backbreaking work of trying to make a living from the land.

When Brownfield sees his young daughter, Daphne, working in the cotton fields, mopping the cotton bushes with arsenic, the scene nearly breaks his heart. He comes to understand that he is trapped in the same cycle of oppression and exploitation that his father was, and he begins to contemplate suicide. He wants to be able to get out of the circumstances he and his family find themselves in but cannot see a way to do so.

Brownfield is full of rage and frustration over what seems like impotence, and he turns it on Mem. He accuses her of infidelity and starts to abuse her. He also forces Mem to stop teaching school and to begin working as a domestic at the houses of white people. In his anger, Brownfield blames Mem for all that is wrong with their lives.

He sees her education as her complicit connection with the forces that have created their situation. He begins to be unfaithful to her, and he works a variety of low-paying laboring jobs. Under such circumstances, Mem begins to wither and to look haggard and old.

Brownfield tries to destroy Mem by making her feel bad about the attributes he most loved about her in the beginning of their relationship. He embarrasses and humiliates her in order to make himself feel superior. Mem actually loses her way of speaking. By turning Mem into someone he does not respect or desire, Brownfield makes it easier for him to treat her badly and to behave in the ways that he wants.

Three of Brownfield and Mem's children die, and two live. The children are miserable and afraid of their father in the same way that Brownfield was afraid of his father. Brownfield becomes an alcoholic and beats Mem and the children. Mem thinks of leaving him but cannot imagine a place where she can go with her children to be safe. She tries to get assistance to get away from Brownfield and even writes to her father, whom she has never met, but he does not respond to her letter. Mem loses weight, and her hair begins to fall out. She also loses the essence of who she is.

The family repeatedly moves from one house owned by a sharecropper to another, undermining Mem's attempts to make a home and a pleasant space, a home for her family. After a time and under the pressure of all of the horrifying circumstances of her life, Mem begins to hate Brownfield. She fights him with the only weapons she has: words. Unlike his father, Brownfield feels no desire to escape his situation. He only wants to wallow in their misery and to bring everyone involved down with him.

When Grange eventually returns to the South, he does so out of his own selfish needs. Grange only wants to return to the comfort of his relationship with Josie and to have access to her resources to create for himself the kind of life he has not had to date. Although he marries Josie and creates a life with her, he does not really love or respect her in her own right. In some ways, Grange's second life is an improvement on the first: He creates some stability for himself and begins to see that the way that he treated his son has had consequences. It is Grange who arrives at his son's home shortly after the birth of another of Brownfield and Mem's children—his granddaughter, Ruth.

Mem and Brownfield's youngest child, Ruth is born in the midst of one of Brownfield's drunken stupors. Consequently, Mem has to endure the labor and delivery alone, and the child is born without a midwife. Brownfield is genuinely sorry for his neglect of his wife and new daughter and tries to make amends when he emerges from his drunken state.

In the midst of this tension-filled chaos, Grange walks into their home bearing food and goodies for the older children. When he arrives, he discovers that his son has had no hand in the successful delivery of the baby. Brownfield has been drunk the entire time and has not helped his wife. The house is cold, and the baby and the rest of the family members are in danger of freezing to death. With this revelation, Grange comes to understand the impact of his neglect of his son and tries to make things better by showing him the way he should behave in the world. Grange becomes a regular benefactor for the family, yet his generosity makes Brownfield angry. The children grow to adore their grandfather, who makes a practice of bringing them goodies.

Even though his intervention in the lives of his grandchildren is key in Grange's developing self-awareness and ability to empathize, it takes him years to become the man he does in the third part of his life, the most complete and healthy Grange—a man who has the capacity to love and empathize and see beyond his own needs and perceptions.

The moment of transition to Grange's final transformation occurs with another echo of his own earlier behavior in his son's life. Although Grange did not directly murder his wife, Margaret, he was indirectly responsible for her death. Brownfield's experience of his parent's marriage sets the stage for his murder of his wife, Mem.

Brownfield comes home from one of his evening escapades so drunk that his daughter Daphne, in her fear and desperation, hides herself and her sisters in the chicken house. The little girls think that being in the chicken coop is a kind of joke until Daphne slaps them hard when they begin to laugh. While the girls hide in the chicken coop from their father, they realize that the situation is serious when they see their father with a gun and understand that he is waiting for their mother. Daphne leaves her sisters in the chicken coop in an attempt to tell her mother about her father's drunken rage and to prevent her from walking into Brownfield's violence.

Ruth sees her mother approach the house after having been dropped off by her employer. Daphne misses her mother, or her mother does not see the child. A drunken Brownfield shoots Mem in the face and kills her instantly while Ornette and Ruth watch from the hen house. It is Christmas time, and when the girls run from their hiding place to their dead mother's side, all of the candy she has bought for them for the holiday lays scattered about on the cold ground. Daphne runs up to her mother and sisters and tries to warm her dead mother's legs.

At Grange's, the old man tries to soothe the children in the best way he can but recognizes that anything he could say to these girls about their dead mother would be ineffectual. Once his son commits this terrible act, Grange Copeland finally understands the impact of his own past behavior. He is particularly moved by the effect the death of Mem has on Ruth. Josie and Grange take Ruth into their home, and that moment begins the third and best life of Grange Copeland.

In the third iteration of his adult experience, Grange is most fully human. Aware now of the consequences of his behavior, Grange is able to see that he cannot honestly blame larger forces for the experiences he has had. The responsibility for what has happened to others as a result of his actions lies with him. Grange works to make amends for his earlier incarnations by creating for his granddaughter Ruth a protected and secure environment in which to develop.

Ruth develops a strong bond with her grandfather. When Ruth expresses concern about her safety from the violence of her father, Grange assures her that Brownfield is securely behind bars and cannot harm her or anyone else. With Grange, Ruth can talk about her mother and father. He tells her stories about her mother's strong qualities so that the child can retain some of the character her mother possessed.

In this third life, Grange is not perfect. He exploits and ultimately discards his wife in favor of the more appealing and unknowing Ruth. He also does not make an attempt to save Ruth's sisters until it is too late for the girls to be rescued. Grange rebukes his wife, Josie, for not being more like Mem, a habit of his that distresses Josie and makes her feel bad about herself. Grange is in fact somewhat abusive of his wife and does not treat her with respect.

Through his relationship with Ruth, however, Grange learns to trust and, most significantly, to nurture and provide solace and sanctuary for another. Through giving, Grange gains humanity and awareness. Ironically, as a consequence of this new understanding, he feels that, rather than allowing the girl to be returned to her father's custody, he must kill his son, Brownfield, in order to rescue his granddaughter. By so doing, he becomes a martyr and willingly relinquishes his own existence to allow his granddaughter to flourish.

At the end of his third life, Grange becomes an example of the ultimate act of love—the willingness to surrender everything, even one's life, for the love of another. Through his death, Grange models the success of his third life. He has understood and has been able to make the ultimate sacrifice.

## SIGNIFICANT THEMES, ISSUES, CONCERNS

### The Oppressive Nature of Marriage

Throughout Walker's canon, there exists subtextual, often overt, criticism of the institution of marriage as a viable and healthy option for human relationships. Each of the marriages in *The Third Life of Grange Copeland* exemplifies the most oppressive and negating aspects of the institution. Significantly, each of the marriages depicted in the novel begins with hopefulness and a real affection between the woman and man who are getting married. In each of the marriages that are described in the novel there is an initial promise that goes unfulfilled. Each of these marriages—Grange and Margaret's, Brownfield and Mem's, and Grange and Josie's—signifies the limitations of marriage. Through its characterizations of those relationships, the novel conveys to its readers the sense that the power dynamics of traditional marriage do not allow for individual growth and development and suggest that, within those relationships, human potential is wasted. These relationships prove particularly destructive to women, for whom the unions are sometimes fatal. Ruth's romantic interests, which emerge but remain undeveloped at the novel's end, suggest that another kind of interaction between men and women might be possible with an alternative worldview and interpersonal framework.

### The Centrality of Personal Responsibility

One could argue that the fundamental lesson of *The Third Life of Grange Copeland* is that, no matter the circumstances an individual has to confront, he or she is still responsible for his or her actions. There are layers of economic, social, educational, racial, and gendered oppression that human beings face, and Walker uses her characters to demonstrate the impacts of these circumstances and the effects that they can have. She does not, however, suggest that, in spite of these odds, the oppressed individuals are somehow absolved of the need to confront their situation; they still must ensure that their actions do not perpetuate and exact further pain and hardship upon others. In other words, Walker's works in general, and *The Third Life of Grange Copeland* specifically, allow her characters the autonomy to act, irrespective of their condition. This freedom to exercise free will and to have some control over one's behavior imbues her characters with potential. They have the ability to transcend the lives that they have been born into and can find dignity and redemption. The women in the novel, particularly Mem and Ruth Copeland, exemplify this principle, but no one better demonstrates the centrality of personal responsibility than the life of the central character himself, Grange Copeland.

### The Necessity of Reinvention

A persistent task for the central protagonist of *The Third Life of Grange Copeland* is the work of reinvention. Grange Copeland faces extraordinary hardships in his life, circumstances that might have led a lesser individual (like his son, Brownfield) to harden his or her gaze upon the world and to tighten rather than expand the parameters of his or her experiential universe. In spite of his flaws, Walker's character does not ever become fixed to the point of inflexibility. When Grange is confronted with a reality that challenges the dominant experiences he has had, rather than giving into what he has known, Grange is willing to consider that the way he has previously understood and defined the world is incorrect. Although this leads him to some erroneous conclusions, like his belief following the incident in Central Park that white people are responsible for all of the wrongs of the world, he eventually proves willing to rewrite his narrative understandings in ways that are more compliant with the evidence that presents itself.

Brownfield serves as a direct contrast to his father. He is willing to ruin his life, kill his wife, and destroy his child rather than considering that the way he perceives the world might be flawed and engaging in reconsideration of his behavior. Brownfield's fixedness is a counterpoint to the growth demonstrated by Grange Copeland's ultimate willingness to reinvent himself and to move toward a more developed and actualized humanity.

## CHARACTERS

**Angeline** Angeline is Brownfield's cousin on his mother's side. She lives in Philadelphia with her brother, Lincoln, and her parents, Marilyn and Silas. When she visits the Copelands in Green County, Georgia, she eavesdrops and spies on the adults, gossiping to Brownfield. To Brownfield, she and Lincoln seem to know much more than he did, especially about urban life and the North.

**Aunt Marilyn** Aunt Marilyn is Margaret Copeland's sister. She lives in Philadelphia with her husband, Silas, and two children, Angeline and Lincoln. She is widowed when Silas dies, shot down while trying to rob a liquor store in Philadelphia. She keeps her husband's drug addiction a secret from her sister.

**Bill** Bill is a white man who is a part of an activist group advocating desegregation with Carol, Helen, and Quincy. Bill is described as dark and muscular.

**Brownfield Copeland** Much of the novel is told from Brownfield's close-third-person perspective, and the time line roughly follows his life from age 10 until his death. As a boy, he is quickly observant of his father Grange's attitude toward white people, particularly with Shipley, the owner of the cotton fields on which Grange works to pay off his debt. Brownfield has a desire to travel north, even as a young boy, enamored with his uncle's automobile and his cousins' knowledge.

Often neglected as a child, Brownfield grows up witnessing the cycle of his father's drunken abuse and his parents' frequent clashes. At 15, following Grange's abandonment and the death of his mother, Margaret, and his half brother, Star, Brownfield decides to leave Green County. He makes it to Baker County, where he meets Josie and Lorene, a mother-daughter pair who run the Dew Drop Inn, and he begins an affair with both women. At the Dew Drop Inn, he meets Mem, Josie's niece, and soon marries her, moving to a cotton farm in Baker County to begin his life.

After almost 10 years, Brownfield's anger and discontent toward the white farm owners begin to manifest itself as anger and violence toward his own wife and children in a cycle of abuse very similar to his own childhood, except that now he takes the role of the abuser. He continues his affair with Josie until his father, Grange, returns to Baker County. His anger toward his father and toward white people continues to grow, exacerbating his violence toward his wife and daughters until, finally, he murders his wife, Mem. He is sent to jail, only to be released on parole after serving seven years, during which his youngest daughter, Ruth, and father, Grange, have built a loving relationship. With Josie's help, he tries to take vengeance on his father by taking custody of Ruth. Following the custody hearing, he is shot by Grange when he attempts to take Ruth legally.

Throughout the novel, Brownfield degenerates, completely consumed by his anger and hatred toward white people and his own father, redirected mostly at his wife and daughters. He is mostly defined by his view of masculinity and by the idea that a man's strength derives from violence and from the ability to control the fate of his wife and daughters by inflicting misery without remorse. His character also relies on his own self-awareness as a black man in a society where white people are in power. His bitterness about working for white people and never for himself extends into his inability to take responsibility for his own wrongdoings. He ends up blaming his misfortunes on white people, his father, and his family—never himself. He finds justification for his violence and hatred in his own misery.

Brownfield's appearance also degenerates throughout the novel. He starts out as a handsome young man but quickly ages after he begins to work on farms. His hands are chapped, and his eyes become bloodshot and yellow. Ruth seems to notice the coiling chest hairs on his body toward the end of the novel. He bears a resemblance to his father, Grange.

**Captain Davis** Captain Davis owns a dairy farm in Baker County where Brownfield works to pay off his debt. He is described as a gaunt, white man with sparse, white hair. Brownfield harbors hatred toward him but outwardly shows the appearance of obedient respect. Davis transfers Brownfield to his son J. L.'s dairy farm.

**Carol** Carol is a white woman who is a part of an activist group advocating desegregation with Bill, Helen, and Quincy. Grange cannot bring himself to allow her under his roof or look her in the eye. Carol is described as small and freckly.

**Daphne Copeland** Daphne is Brownfield's oldest daughter. At five years old, she was already working on cotton fields, brushing arsenic on the cotton bolls. Of Brownfield's three daughters, she is the only one who remembers what her father was like before he became abusive, and she tells her younger siblings stories about when Brownfield was "good." Daphne develops a physical sickness from stress and nerves. She goes up north with her sister Ornette to live with her maternal grandfather when Mem is murdered. She does not appear again in the novel after her mother's death, but later Brownfield tells Ruth that she was placed in a "crazy house" in the North.

**Grange Copeland** As the title suggests, the novel presents Grange Copeland's life in three parts. In his first, or earlier, life, he works in a cotton field under Mr. Shipley to pay off a debt that will never be fully repaid. He both fears and hates Shipley. Grange is stony-faced and a man of few words. He treats his son Brownfield with detached disdain and lives in a seemingly perpetual cycle of working hard for no gain during the week. This makes him bitter, and on the weekends, he has an ongoing affair with Josie while also drinking and abusing his wife and son. Grange escapes to try to be "free" in the North. Shortly after he leaves, Margaret kills herself and her baby, Star.

In Grange's second life, he travels to New York and quickly learns that things are not any different in the North: Society is still run by white people, and there is not any more freedom. He sees a pregnant white woman whose lover leaves her in the park one day. In a moment of sympathy, he tries to reach out to her, but she only expresses vicious racism and hatred. After allowing her to die in a frozen lake in the park, he vows to never again feel any compassion for white people. He begins to fight any white person he can, letting out his pent-up anger and hatred. Eventually, he realizes the futility of his actions and returns to Georgia to isolate himself. He marries Josie in order to have enough money to buy his own farm. Regretful of how he treated his son, he tries to bring Brownfield food and be a part of his life. Brownfield rejects him.

Grange takes in Ruth the night that Mem is murdered, which initiates him into his third life. Through his relationship with Ruth, he learns the importance of compassion and love and the meaning of legacy. He understands what it means to be a black man in a markedly different way from Brownfield. In his third life, Grange is described as having a shock of white hair. He dances, drinks, tells stories, and shares nearly everything with his granddaughter. He finds a sense of freedom and peace in taking responsibility for his own actions. When Brownfield takes custody of Ruth through the courts, Grange shoots him and then dies protecting Ruth when the police come in pursuit. By the end of the novel, he is an old man, even to Ruth, who sees in him a sense of sweetness and life.

Grange's change in character is a direct inversion of his son's. While Grange begins the novel stuck in the seemingly perpetual cycle of hatred and abuse, he eventually learns to understand his mistakes as his own doing. Despite his abuse, Grange seeks redemption by treating his granddaughter with love.

**hatchet murderer** He is never named in the novel but is referred to as the hatchet murderer. He is in prison for murdering his wife, his mother-in-law, and his wife's aunt with a hatchet, and he is let out on parole after three years. Brownfield meets him during his own incarceration. They share similar views on life—that no matter how they have tried, "fate" seems to keep them in their place.

**Helen** Helen is from Green County and lives with her husband, Quincy, and her two white friends, Bill and Carol. They are part of an activist group advocating desegregation. She laughs easily and freely and is in love with her husband. She urges Grange to register to vote. She hopes to be "first lady of Green County" someday and dreams of Quincy becoming mayor. Grange is strangely drawn to her and feels protective toward her and her husband.

**J. L.** J. L. is the son of Captain Davis. He owns the dairy farm with a dilapidated house that Brownfield moves Mem and his daughters into as a form of revenge on Mem.

**Johnny Johnson** Johnny Johnson, a man who works for Mr. Shipley, is one of Margaret's lovers.

**Josie Copeland** At one point or other, Josie is mistress to both Brownfield and Grange. She becomes Grange's second wife. She is described as fat, freckly, and yellow-skinned. Having met Grange even before he married Margaret, they carried on their affair even after he was married. Margaret eventually knew about their affair, referring to her as "the yellow bitch."

At the age of 16, Josie was raped by her father's friends and impregnated. Her father behaved cruelly toward her, and she is continually haunted by the memory of him holding her down in front of all the men who had raped her and not letting her up even when she nearly choked on her own vomit. She calls the memory her demon. As a result of the rape, Josie gave birth to a daughter, Lorene. She became infertile following her first pregnancy.

When Brownfield arrives at the Dew Drop Inn in Baker County, Josie begins her relationship with him partially out of revenge against Grange and to become a wedge between them. She momentarily stops her love affair with Brownfield when Grange returns from the North and marries her. Despite her seemingly boisterous, sexually insatiable and brash exterior, Josie remains powerless against either Grange or Brownfield, who seem to control her existence. She pities others easily, which becomes a kind of weakness when confronting Brownfield. She loses her independence when she marries Grange and never regains it. After she marries him, she sells the Dew Drop Inn to help pay for Grange's farm. When Grange takes Ruth in after Mem's murder, Josie becomes jealous, eventually going off to visit Brownfield at the prison more frequently. Despite her continuous love for Grange, she eventually allows Brownfield to use her in an effort to exact his revenge on Grange and regain custody of Ruth.

**Judge Harry** Judge Harry is described as a white man with a benevolent face who allowed Brownfield to be assigned to garden work during his prison sentence because of their earlier friendship. Brownfield later uses his connection to Judge Harry to get legal custody of Ruth.

**Katie Brown** While Katie Brown never appears in the novel, readers learn that she has helped organize an activist group in Green County with her daughter, Helen; her son-in-law, Quincy; and their two white friends, Carol and Bill.

**Lincoln** Lincoln is Brownfield's cousin who lives in Philadelphia with his sister, Angeline, and his parents, Marilyn and Silas. He talks to Brownfield about his parents when he visits the Copelands in Georgia. He and his sister Angeline seem to know much about the North and of urban life.

**Lorene** Lorene is Josie's only daughter. She is described as dark, skinny, hairy, and sinewy as a man. She wears cheap perfume and keeps her hair reddish copper. While she is in Baker County, she maintains a reputation for being tough. She and Josie are sexually involved with Brownfield while he stays at the Dew Drop Inn. They use their relationship with Brownfield as a way to affirm their maternal-filial bonds. She eventually moves to the North.

**Margaret Copeland** Margaret Copeland is Grange's first wife and Brownfield's mother. At the beginning of the novel, she is submissive to Grange and kind. She works at the bait factory, canning worms to sell to fisherman. Eventually, Grange's affair, his cycle of drunken abuse, and their continuous fighting changes her. She sleeps with Shipley in an effort to help Grange get out of debt. She continues to have affairs with many men from the church and from the bait factory. Her second child, Star, is conceived from an affair. She is no longer kind and submissive but coarse and bold, and her appearance changes dramatically. She begins her marriage as a woman with a smooth, heart-shaped face; brown skin with a reddish sheen; straight, even teeth; and breath like clean, sweet milk. Just before her death, she becomes more unkempt, witchlike, and wild. Despite their dysfunctional relationship, Margaret still loves Grange. When he leaves them to go north, she commits suicide and poisons Star, leaving Brownfield mostly orphaned. At her funeral, no tears are shed except for Shipley's crocodile tears.

**Mem Copeland** Mem Copeland is Brownfield's wife. When Brownfield first meets her, she is plump and quiet, with cherry-brown skin and demure, slanted eyes. She is well-read and teaches younger children in school. Brownfield is immediately attracted to her, and she attempts to teach him how to read. They quickly marry and move out into the country onto a cotton farm until they can make ends meet enough to move to the North. They try to save up for a house and to get out of the debt. As that proves increasingly difficult, they are forced to move from place to place. Brownfield begins to drink and to abuse her, souring her good looks. She loses her plumpness, her hair goes white, and she loses her teeth. Her proper grammar becomes beaten down when Brownfield begins to accuse her of trying to talk white and embarrasses her in public. By the time Ruth is born, Mem has given birth to five children, only three of which survive.

When Brownfield tries to move them to J. L.'s farm, Mem refuses and instead finds a house in town to rent. After a harsh beating, she pulls a gun on Brownfield, scaring him into following her to the house in town. She enjoys a few short years, free from beatings, with Brownfield on supposed good behavior. After two lost pregnancies and a bout with the flu, in a weakened state, she loses her job and her house and is forced by a vengeful Brownfield to move to J. L.'s farm. She and her daughters have to deal with abuse once more. She later gives birth to an albino baby boy whom Brownfield murders. Brownfield shoots and kills her one night while she is coming home from work.

Mem is a passive, faithful, kind woman who shows a moment of strength against her husband when she pulls a gun on him and forces him to move to town. She slides back into passivity because "she was not a fighter, and rage had horrified her. . . . Instead of rage she had had an inner sovereignty, a core of self, a rock, which alas, her husband had not had. She had possessed an embedded strength that Brownfield could not match."

**Mizes Mamie Lou Banks** Mizes Mamie Lou Banks only appears for a short scene in the novel. While Brownfield is on the road before he arrives at Baker County, he stops for a drink of water and some food at Mamie Lou Banks's house. She is a washer with two children. She is kind to Brownfield.

**Ornette Copeland** Ornette is Brownfield's second daughter. She is described as "jolly most of the time. A loud, boisterous girl, sassy and full of darting rebellion. She was fat and glossy. Her skin had a luscious orange smoothness and felt like a waxed fruit." Her father often ridicules her, calling her a tramp, and she becomes familiar with sexual vocabulary at a young age. Of Mem and Brownfield's three daughters, Ornette has the least respect for her mother. She moves to the North with her maternal grandfather when Mem is killed. Readers learn that she eventually becomes a prostitute.

**Quincy** Quincy is the son of Sister Madelaine, the fortune-teller. Ruth is immediately attracted to him when she meets him and is disappointed to find out later that he is married. He is described as a thin young man, with brown skin and a beard that makes his lip stand out. A college graduate, he speaks with a degree of self-confidence and politeness. He is part of an activist group from Green County along with his wife, Helen, and his two white friends, Bill and Carol. He hopes to be mayor of Green County one day and urges Grange to register to vote.

**Rossel Pascal** Although she is older than Ruth, Rossel Pascal is the only girl at school that Ruth is interested in befriending. Because Rossel's father is an alcoholic and her mother is dead, she is disliked by the teachers at the school and is held in the same disdain as Ruth. For that reason, the two girls form a bond of friendship. Rossel plans to escape her marginalized fate by marrying well. Her target is the wealthiest man in the community, Walt Terrell. Ruth thinks that Rossel has the accent of a southern white woman. Rossel uses her beauty to achieve her aim and marries Terrel. Rossel's father dies from the heartbreak of having lost his wife. Ruth wants something different for herself than the presumptive refuge of marriage.

**Ruth Copeland** Ruth is perhaps the most outspoken, wide-eyed, and "pure" of Brownfield's three daughters. At a young age, she speaks out in defiance of her father when he begins to beat her mother. Ruth is seemingly untainted by the racial prejudices of either her father or her grandfather. When she is six years old, she is taken in by Grange when her mother is murdered and her father is sent to jail. She becomes a healing force in Grange's life and seems to possess an older kind of wisdom and self-awareness about her past. She and Grange dance together and laugh together in church. He tells her stories, and they make wine that they drink together. Her close relationship with her grandfather earns her the nickname Mrs. Grange at school.

At 16, after Brownfield is released from prison, Ruth refuses her father's attempts to get her to live with him and does not trust him or forgive him. While the end of the novel leaves her fate unknown, her grandfather ends up sacrificing his life for her sake. She is markedly different from her own mother. While Mem possessed an inner strength similar to her daughter's, she lacked the confidence and love her daughter has experienced from Grange. While Ruth relies on Grange, she does so out of mutual love, not dependence.

**Shipley** Shipley owns the cotton field where Grange and Brownfield work to pay off Grange's debt, he also owns the house where Brownfield grows up. Shipley is white, tall, has the "smooth brownish hair of an animal," and his breath smells of mint. Margaret sleeps with him in an effort to help pay off Grange's debt. Grange equally hates and is afraid of Shipley. Shipley is the only one who cries at Margaret's funeral.

**Sister Madelaine** Sister Madelaine is a fortuneteller in Baker County who consoles Josie when she has nightmares. She is acquainted with Grange Copeland. She believes in demons and has a son, named Quincy, who is in college at Morehouse in Atlanta.

**Star** Star is Brownfield's half brother from one of Margaret's affairs. They refer to him as "the baby." In his frustration at his mother, Brownfield retaliates against his brother, pinching him hard on the cheeks. Later, when Margaret commits suicide, she poisons the baby as well.

**Uncle Buster** Uncle Buster is Grange's uncle. He tells Grange that he will beat him if he does not join the church. During the church ceremony, Uncle Buster falls asleep with a fly buzzing around his mouth. Grange makes a bargain with God: If Buster swallows the fly, then Grange will join the church. Uncle Buster swallows the fly, and Grange joins the church, but he is never a religious man.

**Uncle Silas** Uncle Silas is Margaret's brother-in-law. He lives in Philadelphia with his wife, Marilyn, and his two children, Angeline and Lincoln. He drives a 1920 Buick, which Brownfield envies. His children describe him as having gone to the North to be "free." The novel later reveals that Uncle Silas has a drug addiction. He is killed robbing a liquor store sometime between his family's visit to Georgia and Margaret's death.

**Walt Terrel** Walt Terrel is the richest man in Ruth's community. Ruth's only friendly schoolmate, Rossel, determines to marry Walt as an escape from the dead-end options available to most African-American women in her community. Walt Terrel is a World War II veteran and decorated returning hero who owns land and garners respect from the community as a consequence of his exploits and wealth. Rossel, who is described as a beautiful woman, eventually achieves her aims.

### Further Reading

Butler, Robert. "Alice Walker's Vision of the South in *The Third Life of Grange Copeland*." *African American Review* 27, no. 2 (1993): 195–204.

———. "Visions of Southern Life and Religion in O'Connor's *Wise Blood* and Walker's *The Third Life of Grange Copeland.*" CLA *Journal* 36, no. 4 (1993): 349–370.

Harris, Trudier. "Violence in *The Third Life of Grange Copeland.*" CLA *Journal* 19 (1975): 238–247.

Mason, Theodore O., Jr. "Alice Walker's *The Third Life of Grange Copeland:* The Dynamics of Enclosure." *Callaloo* 12, no. 2 (1989): 297–309.

Walker, Alice. *In Search of Our Mothers' Gardens.* San Diego: Harcourt Brace and Company, 1983.

———. *Living by the Word.* New York: Harcourt Brace Jovanovich, 1988.

———. *The Third Life of Grange Copeland.* New York: Pocket Books, 1988.

Winchell, Donna Haisty. *Alice Walker.* New York: Twayne, 1992.

# SHORT FICTION

## *The Complete Stories* (2005)

Walker has written consistently about her belief that narrative is central to the human experience and a critical tool in the struggle to unmask oppressive institutions and replace those traditions with a more functional and healthy way of being. If there is a central thesis for Walker's collections of short stories, it would be that the world can be remade if it can be retold from the perspective of the those who are most often unheard.

Walker's 2005 publication of *The Complete Stories* is a compilation of her earlier short story collections *In Love & Trouble: Stories of Black Women* (1973) and *You Can't Keep a Good Woman Down* (1981). (For more information on specific stories, see the entries on those collections.) As can be discerned by their titles, the stories in these collections are usually about women who are in various predicaments and the creative, often unconventional solutions they employ in order to try to survive.

### Further Reading

Walker, Alice. "The Story of Why I am Here: or, A Woman Connects Oppressions." *Monthly Review* 46, no. 2 (June 1994): 38–43.

## *In Love & Trouble: Stories of Black Women* (1973)

*In Love & Trouble* is Alice Walker's first short story collection. The anthology of short narratives played an important part in her growing literary reputation. According to the Walker biographer Evelyn White, after the publication of *In Love & Trouble,* Walker received a letter of praise for the collection from writer Anaïs Nin. The collection, although not widely reviewed, was generally well-received.

### "Roselily"

The entire narrative of "Roselily" occurs as the titular character and protagonist is in the process of getting married. Roselily lives in Mississippi and is the mother of four children, three of whom live with her. Roselily has given her fourth child, a son, to his father, a Muslim who has relocated to the North. She feels confounded by what she perceives as the distinction between life in the North and life in the South, where she has spent her life and has worked as a seamstress.

As Roselily listens to the minister's words, she feels as if she is entering a trap and has visions of death and of being confined by chains. She tries to find some comfort and consolation but imagines herself being suffocated. Roselily's husband-to-be goes unnamed in the short story. Readers discover that the man has very traditional ideas about the role of women in a marriage and expects that his new wife will stay at home and that he will be the sole wage earner for his family. Though there are things about him that she loves, Roselily worries that the man is not Christian and that he is so unresponsive to her and to her needs.

#### COMMENTARY

The short story "Roselily" follows a somewhat experimental form, with each section of the story bounded by a particular line from the traditional marriage ceremony. Walker almost always writes ambivalently about marriage. In much of her writings, she suggests that marriage is fundamentally counter to human growth, autonomy, and health. Walker has written that she objects to the artificial confines and constraints that she believes are inherent in marriage—an institution that has its roots in economic agreements and in the control of resources.

In "Roselily," Walker explores her concerns about the limitations of marriage without directly announcing her intentions. Walker's protagonist embodies in her name the contradictory positions that women have occupied within the institution of marriage. The rose has associations with passion and sexuality, while the lily connotes purity and innocence. These readings of the name Roselily invoke the so-called whore/Madonna complex, an interpretation of gender roles asserting that women historically have been either defined as sexual beings and consequently labeled whores or alternatively understood as conforming and asexual nurturing mothers. The interior monologue that is the text of this story reveals Roselily's navigation of this difficult conundrum.

Roselily is a poor woman who has decided that, in order to support herself and her children, she must marry a man she does not love. From the free-ranging narrative flow of her thoughts, readers learn that she has lived as a relatively sexually autonomous woman, as evidenced by the fact that each of her children has a different father. What she relinquishes with her marriage is her freedom.

Walker provides the reader with access to Roselily's imagination—her impulse, for example, when she hears the distraction of car noise during the wedding to envision where the people in the cars might be going and to yearn to go with them. Roselily has to repress the urges that emanate from her imaginative self in order to be able to proceed with her wedding.

Roselily understands that when she marries her new husband, she will be trading her autonomy for what she perceives will be safety. During the ceremony, Roselily thinks of her children and of the burden that they place on her ability to live the life that she imagines for herself. She recognizes that her husband expects that she will no longer work outside of their home—and that she will stay at home. Roselily's role will be as caretaker of the children she already has as well as for children her husband alone anticipates and desires.

The tension in the story emerges from the reader's understanding of and access to Roselily's desires. That information is coupled with the sense that the life Roselily honestly wants for herself is at odds with the marriage in which she participates. The narrative's effectiveness lies in its limited point of view, which mirrors Roselily's narrowing horizons and impending confinement. Through Walker's employment of these techniques, she creates a story that enables access to the protagonist's subjectivity while simultaneously expanding the focus of the story to the larger issues of gender, motherhood, and relationship.

## "Really, *Doesn't* Crime Pay?"

This elliptical story follows the characters' actions chronologically from September to May of a year and then, through Myrna's journal, reverses time to proceed backward to September. The reader experiences Myrna's journal entries in reverse order.

Mordecai Rich is one of the central characters in the story. Physically, he is a thin man. Another character, Ruel, Myrna's husband, believes that Mordecai and his involvement with Myrna was the catalyst for her breakdown and attempt to murder her husband. Ruel is a veteran of the Korean War, and as a result of his experiences there, he wants to forget the past. Ruel does not support Myrna's writing aspirations. His central concern about their relationship is that Myrna should find a way to become pregnant and give him the child he wants.

At a time that precedes the story's present, Mordecai and Myrna are lovers. When Mordecai and Myrna are together, Mordecai tells Myrna that he is on a quest to discover "Truth and Beauty." After this revelation, Myrna feels that Mordecai is emotionally out of touch; she begins to think of his perspectives as calculating and says that he has a "cold eye."

Mordecai is fascinated by Myrna's writing. He steals one of Myrna's stories and then never talks to her again. As a writer, Myrna keeps a journal and writes in it faithfully. She has grown tired of her husband, Ruel. Before marrying Ruel, Myrna fell in love with Mordecai, but he disappeared. When Mordecai left, Myrna felt betrayed and abandoned. She felt particularly vulnerable after Mordecai's disappearance because she had shown him everything she had ever written.

Although Ruel wants a baby, Myrna feels particularly indifferent to the prospect. The story reveals that after her involvement with Mordecai, she had a mental breakdown and spent time in a mental hospital. After a year of hospitalization, Myrna was released from full-time psychological surveillance. Although she has promised Ruel that she will work with him to conceive a child, she takes birth control pills and does not tell him. At the end of the story, Myrna finds herself disillusioned and vengeful.

## "Her Sweet Jerome"

The central character in this story is an unnamed female character. The story depicts her actions as she rummages through her husband's clothes. Her husband is a man named Jerome Franklin Washington III. He is 10 years younger than the protagonist and works as a schoolteacher. Although he is guilty of beating women, including his wife, he is generally known in the community as a "gentleman." In spite of the many distractions he has to negotiate, Jerome spends most of his time lost in his books. He counts as his friends the principal of the school where he works, and also a few community women (both black and white) who are trying to go back to their African roots.

Physically, the narrative's protagonist is described is a big, awkward woman. She works as a hairdresser and has some money. One of the emotions that motivates her actions toward Jerome is her persistent jealousy about the women teachers with whom he works. As she works in the salon, she hears from the other women that Jerome is cheating on her. The protagonist is not a fully developed person and has many negative characteristics. She is materialistic and spends a significant portion of her money buying clothes for Jerome. She concentrates most of her energy and passion on appearances, and her jealousy causes her to become violent.

The protagonist's obsession with her husband's imagined affair causes her to become deranged, and her life begins to unravel. She stops caring about basic things and concentrates all of her energy on trying to find Jerome's lover.

As she rummages through Jerome's possessions, the protagonist learns that Jerome has been reading about the black revolution. This discovery makes her feels ignorant and causes her to become unduly enraged. She realizes that Jerome does not have another lover but is passionately engaged in intellectual questionings about the African-American situation. Acting on her feelings of rage, which are rooted in a fundamental ignorance and consequent insecurity, she stabs Jerome's books and lights his bed on fire. Foolishly careless of her own safety, she fails to leave herself an escape route from the burning room. She becomes entrapped in the burning room and dies with "pain and enlightenment."

## "The Child Who Favored Daughter"

As suggested by its title, this story revolves around the saga of an unnamed girl child. "Daughter" is the nickname of the protagonist's father's sister, and the young girl looks like her aunt. In fact, she so resembles her aunt that she is described as nearly a replica of the older woman.

The child is a thinker. She loves and finds beauty in simple phenomena and is extraordinarily close to her dad, a man she calls "Father." But conflict comes between the two when Father finds a love letter his daughter has written to a white man. One of the father's obsessions is his daughter's chastity. He is also conscious of the racial taboo she would be violating if, in fact, she were to have a relationship with this man.

After his discovery of the letter, Father waits for his daughter to come home. While he waits, he sits with a gun in his hand. Part of Father's problem and fixedness on his daughter's potential sexuality is rooted in his own history. His sister, the one who was called "Daughter" by the family, had been a sexually free woman in a sexually repressive time. She had intimate relationships with many men in the community and even slept with her brother's boss, but Father loved his sister fiercely anyway. Daughter became ill (there is a hint that she might have had syphilis). While she was ill, Daughter was restrained and punished by her family by being tied to her bed and treated like an animal. Father let his sister loose, but she then attacked him, knocked him out, and proceeded to kill herself. After this traumatic event, Father lives his life without trust. He particularly vows that he will never trust a woman.

All of this history surfaces for Father when he is confronted with the specter of his own child's sexuality. When his daughter arrives home, Father calls his daughter a white man's slut and then proceeds to beat her. He becomes so enraged and out of control that he cuts his daughter's breasts off and flings them to the dogs.

As a consequence of his rage and violence, Father ends up emotionally paralyzed and alone—slumped in a chair and staring at the road.

### COMMENTARY

Those who have written about this difficult and troubling tale often describe its raw emotionalism and its exploration of taboo subjects. The critic Neal A. Lester has even suggested that "The Child Who Favored Daughter" can best be understood as a slave narrative. The story is evocative, and although it suggests multiple readings, its subject matter and frank willingness to explore the transgression of boundaries has, perhaps, discouraged more critical investigation.

One of the narrative's primary assertions is that in some African-American southern communities, misogyny in some people is foundational and, significantly, embedded in racism. Father, one of the main characters in the narrative, enacts a scenario that seems deeply rooted in Freudian understandings of sexuality and relationships. Father's experiences with and treatment of his sister can be interpreted as protective gestures, while at the same time his actions are also destructive and seemingly layered with prohibited and incestuous sexual desires.

Father's stated motivation for his behavior toward his sister, a woman named Daughter, derives from his desire to save her from sexual exploitation, particularly from the sexual exploitation of white men. Through purported attempts to enact this protection, Father drives his sister to her death.

Rather than understanding his complicity in his sister's demise and using this information to proceed less recklessly into the future, Father amplifies his initial response to the impotence of his position in the racial hierarchy of his community and takes out his frustrations on those less powerful. Those at the bottom of the rung are the remaining women in his life, particularly his daughter.

Walker toys with the pervasive and dangerous implications of the whore/Madonna complex in her story. She demonstrates that the pathologies that result from racial hierarchy and segregation are linked explicitly to sexual presumptions and abuse. When Father discovers the letter that he believes reveals his daughter's betrayal of the strict boundaries he has placed on her behavior, it is not enough for him to punish his child; he believes that he must mutilate her and does so by eviscerating any signs of her sexuality before destroying and discarding her utterly by throwing her severed breasts to the dogs.

Through her use of graphic violence and anarchic authority, Walker makes an unmistakable assertion about the common roots from which racism and sexism derive. In so doing, she makes the claim that the two forces are both culpable in the destruction of the bodies and lives of African-American women.

## "Everyday Use"

"Everyday Use" is one of Walker's best-known and most widely anthologized stories. When the tale begins, the family around whom the central narrative revolves has relocated to a new residence because the family's old house burned down. The narrator of the story is the family's matriarch. One of the central characters in the story is Dee, the narrator's assertive, older daughter. Dee is described as having style. She has been educated and, as a result, has been away from her family. Although she has left her family, she comes back after a few years to visit her mother and sister.

In the years that she has been away from her family, Dee has attempted a transformation. Part of that transformation involves self-reinvention—for example, she renames herself Wangero. When Dee returns to visit her mother and her sister, she comes back with a man named Asalama Kim, who is uncomfortable and particularly awkward with Maggie, Dee's younger sister. Asalama Kim and Dee are a pretentious pair. Dee in particular is concerned with appearances and values them over the feelings of her mother and sister.

Unlike Dee, Maggie is timid and nervous. Part of her discomfort comes from an accident she had when she was burned in the fire that destroyed the family's home. Also, in contrast to her sister, Maggie is selfless and able to put the needs of others

A quilt made by Alice Walker in 1981. The quilt was on display at the 2009 exhibition *A Keeping of Records: The Art and Life of Alice Walker,* which was held in celebration of the public opening of Walker's archives at Emory University in Atlanta, Georgia, in April 2009. The quilt is from Alice Walker's personal collection and is now a part of the archives. *(Photograph by Carmen Gillespie, courtesy of the Emory University Alice Walker Archives Exhibition, April 24, 2009)*

above her own. Maggie bonds with her mother after Dee comes back home to visit them. The major distinction between Dee and her sister comes in their evaluation of and appreciation for their mother's, grandmother's, and great-grandmother's handmade quilts. Dee sees the quilts as art and wants to keep them. Unlike Dee, Maggie understands the more pragmatic as well as the emotional, familial, and personal significances of the quilts, which their mother has promised to her when she marries. She offers to give them up to Dee, but the mother tells Dee, "Take one or two of the others." The story ends as Dee leaves, and Maggie and her mother sit together, "just enjoying."

### COMMENTARY

"Everyday Use" is a family drama—a saga of two sisters with polarized values. Their mother is also a central character in the narrative. The sisters are completely different in terms of their orientation and their priorities. Dee has been away from home and, as the story begins, she has returned home for a visit. Unlike her sister and her mother, she is materialistic and attractive. She sees herself as socially sophisticated and upwardly mobile.

Unlike her sister, Maggie is shy and self-effacing. She appears to be contented to remain at home and to live out her days in her community of origin. Maggie and her mother share a set of values and an understanding of the world that are rooted in their experiences. Because Dee sees herself as having outgrown the life from which she came, she reads her sister and mother's belief systems as primitive and outmoded.

"Everyday Use" is often read as an examination of a cultural and intergenerational clash. Maggie is interpreted as the character representing the traditions of rural African-American communities and the aspects of African-American life associated with the South. On the other hand, Dee can be read as a symbol of the complexities of assimilation. The conflicts in the values of these two characters become manifest in their different readings of the family quilts.

Most interpretive readings of "Everyday Use" maintain that the quilts are a central feature of the narrative and essential to discerning the story's larger significance. African-American quilts are functional, artistic, and even textual. Theories about the aesthetics, traditions, and practices of African-American quilting are widely disputed and remain the subject of scholarly controversy. Some scholars maintain that traditional African quilting and textile production was a great influence on early African-American quilts. Many of these have noted patterns in early such quilts that are similar to African motifs, suggesting that these patterns survived the Middle Passage and thus provide a link from North American to African aesthetic traditions. Walker is able to use the quilt in her story to engage in a conversation about the transitions in African-American communities and the relationship between these shifts and assessments of material culture.

When Dee returns to her family, she wants to claim the quilts as art—*heritage* is the word she uses. Maggie values the quilts for their pragmatic and sentimental value. The distinctions between the two perspectives form the crux of the narrative drama. By the end of the story, the reader comes to understand and to sympathize with the perspectives of Maggie and her mother and to question the imposition of external values and judgments on communities that may have different but no less valid and valuable cultural understandings.

## "The Revenge of Hannah Kemhuff"

The central protagonist of this story is a woman named Hannah Kemhuff, an old woman who tells her story to another female character, Tante Rosie, a root worker, and her apprentice, the story's narrator. Hannah believes that she has been the victim of heartless discrimination.

As the story unfolds, the reader learns many details about Hannah. She is a woman who wears many skirts and shawls and who, during the Great Depression, developed an intimate understanding of what it means to nearly starve. During that time, Hannah's husband left her standing in the handout line. Later, after he abandoned her and their children, her husband drove his car off a bridge with his mistress in the car next to him.

Refusing to give up her dignity although destitute, Hannah stood in the food handout line and insisted that she and her children confront the humiliation of the occasion by dressing in their nicest clothes. According to those distributing the food, Hannah's actions could only be understood as pretentious, and so the individuals in charge refused to give Hannah and her family the much-needed food. One woman in particular, Sarah Marie Sadler, was responsible for turning Hannah and her family away. As a consequence of this misjudgment, all of Hannah's children died. After she lost her husband and children, Hannah became a prostitute. She also began to drink. The combination of these misfortunes caused her to grow old all at once.

In her bitterness, Hannah has focused her energies on finding a way to get revenge on the woman in the food handout line who turned her and her children away. Hannah Kemhuff calls this woman, Sarah Marie Sadler, "the moppet." Hannah wants nothing more than to be able to curse the moppet. Tante Rosie promises to help and instructs her apprentice to assist Hannah in reciting a "curse-prayer." Hannah realizes that she will not live long enough to see the result of the curse on the moppet, but she is nonetheless happy and leaves "bearing herself grandly out of the room."

Sarah Marie Sadler sees herself as the epitome of white womanhood and as somehow pure. Tante Rosie learns that Sarah Marie is now Mrs. Holley. Acting on Tante Rosie's instructions, the narrator goes to Mrs. Holley and makes it clear that Hannah Kemhuff has placed a curse on her. Mrs. Holley becomes terrified of the curse and goes into a decline. Shortly after Hannah's death, Mrs. Holley dies, worried into misery and eventual death about the potential power of Hannah's curse.

## "The Welcome Table"

"The Welcome Table" is a story about an older black woman who has had the humiliating experience of having been kicked out of an all-white church. In the story, the congregants feel that the woman does not belong among them.

After leaving the church, the old woman meets Jesus as she walks on the road outside. Following this encounter, she is later found dead on the highway where she had been "walking with Jesus." The people in the community who ponder her story come to believe that the old woman must have walked herself to death.

## "Strong Horse Tea"

The central character in the short story "Strong Horse Tea," Rannie Toomer, is described as physically unattractive and rather unappealing. She is not married but has had a baby boy whom she calls Snooks.

When Snooks becomes ill, Rannie wants to enlist the services of a real doctor to assist her son and to avoid the superstitious practices that those around her suggest. She is deceived and thwarted in her efforts by several people. Rannie tells the mailman that she wants to have a doctor come to see about her son, but the postman leads her on, telling her that he will send a doctor on the way. In spite of the postman's assurances, in reality there is no doctor coming.

Feeling that she has no recourse at her disposal, eventually Rannie gives in and hands the baby to Sarah, her neighbor. Sarah is an old woman who is a mystic and root worker. Sarah offers to help cure Snooks with her folk cures and tells Rannie to go get horse tea (urine) to give to the baby, who is dying of pneumonia and whooping cough. Rannie listens to Sarah and goes to get horse tea, but the baby dies while she is away.

## "Entertaining God"

Walker's short story "Entertaining God" is told in three parts. In the first part, the reader encounters John, a 15-year-old boy, interacting with a drugged gorilla who is housed at the Bronx Zoo. The second part of the story features a cyclone. In an attempt to avoid the violence and danger of the storm and to protect their family, John's father and his second wife throw their children into their emptied refrigerator in an effort to keep them safe. The children survive the storm. In the story's third part, readers encounter John's mother, John's father's first wife, and hear about what happened to John while he was with the gorilla in the zoo.

When John visits the zoo, he becomes enamored of the gorilla and sees him as a substitute god figure who can replace the unsatisfactory models of the divine that his mother has supplied for him. The gorilla is drugged and sleepy. After chasing him, John eventually falls asleep with the gorilla. He attempts to worship the gorilla with burnt offerings of bread, but the gorilla first throws him out of his artificial "jungle" (the zoo) and then, frustrated with hunger, kills John by hitting him on the head and proceeds to eat the bread offerings.

The second part of the narrative begins with John's father's dying thoughts. After saving their children by shutting them in the refrigerator, the father thinks about his other son and his first wife with some sorrow and regret. He realizes that part of what repelled him about his son was that he reminded him of the things that he liked least about himself, his dark skin and dismissive interactions with other. He dies during the storm in his second wife's arms with this new awareness.

The third section is about John's mother. The woman has become a poet in the years since her son's death. Through her voice in this section, the reader learns the details of the story. John's mother has visions of her dead son at her readings, and she has a ritual with him in which he escorts her from each of her readings.

## "The Diary of an African Nun"

"The Diary of an African Nun" is a story whose details come from reading a series of entries in a nun's diary. The narrator is a young Ugandan woman. Although her choice of profession indicates her dedication to Christ, the young nun is impatient to have the experience of being loved.

Outside her window, she can hear a ritual in which a young girl dances. During the ritual, a man comes from the watching crowd and "takes" the girl, after which the dance continues. The nun wants to have children of her own. She says that "barrenness is death." The nun ends her diary by cursing the dance and the cycle of life from which her religion has alienated her.

## "The Flowers"

This story's protagonist, Myop, is 10 years old. Myop is living a happy and contented life on a farm where she spends her time in childish joy, exploring the atmosphere of the graceful lands that surround her home and collecting flowers. One day, while playing she stumbles upon the decomposing head of a black man who had been lynched and steps into it. With this incident, "the summer was over."

## "We Drank the Wine in France"

Harriet, one of the two main characters in this story, is described as young and "brown-cheeked." She is the childish girl in her French class. The reader learns that Harriet is considered "dumb" but hungry for knowledge. Harriet has fantasies about the professor.

The professor is an older Polish man who chases beauty and travels in search of it in the world. The professor has a crush on Harriet. The reader learns that the professor lost his wife and daughter in a concentration camp during World War II. He dreams of leaving Mississippi for Mexico with Harriet but instead plans his resignation from his job.

## "To Hell with Dying"

Mr. Sweet, the main character in "To Hell with Dying," is a diabetic alcoholic as well as a fisherman and a guitar player. Mr. Sweet was ambitious when he was younger but became disillusioned because of racism. Periodically, Mr. Sweet would fall ill, near the brink of death. When he became ill, the kids in the neighborhood, particularly one little girl of whom he was particularly fond, would save him. This girl is the story's narrator. The love of Mr. Sweet allows the little girl to feel good and empowers her. Eventually, when Mr. Sweet is 90 years old and the little girl is an adult, Mr. Sweet dies and cannot be resurrected by the love of those around him. The little girl, now a woman, says that Mr. Sweet was her first love.

### Further Reading

Banks, Erma Davis, and Keith Byerman. *Alice Walker: An Annotated Bibliography, 1968–1986.* New York: Garland, 1989.

Estes, David C. "Alice Walker's 'Strong Horse Tea': Folk Cures for the Dispossessed." *Southern Folklore* 50 (1993): 213–229.

Hooker, Deborah Anne. "Reanimating the Trope of the Talking Book in Alice Walker's 'Strong Horse Tea.'" *Southern Literary Journal* 37, no. 2 (Spring 2005): 81–102.

Noe, Marcia. "Teaching Alice Walker's 'Everyday Use': Employing Race, Class, and Gender, with an

Annotated Bibliography." *Eureka Studies in Teaching Short Fiction* 5, no. 1 (Fall, 2004): 123–136.

Parker-Smith, Bettye J. "Alice Walker's Women: In Search of Some Peace of Mind." In *Black Women Writers (1950–1980): A Critical Evaluation,* edited by Mari Evans. Garden City, N.Y.: Anchor, 1984.

Walker, Alice. *In Love & Trouble: Stories of Black Woman.* New York: Harvest Books, 1973.

Whitsitt, Sam. "In Spite of It All: A Reading of Alice Walker's 'Everyday Use.'" *African American Review* 34, no. 3 (Autumn 2000): 443–459.

# *The Way Forward Is with a Broken Heart* (2000)

This work is a series of stories fictionalizing the marriage between Walker and MELVYN LEVENTHAL. It is a powerful expression of Walker's insights into her own relationship as well as relationships in general. The work deals with the intimacies, intricacies, and strains of external forces on relationships; the influence of personal and familial engagements; the impact of children on a marriage; and the effort to sustain cordiality when a relationship has ended. As the title implies, the book suggests that relationships, even difficult and painful ones, can produce personal progress and growth.

Although there were several negative reviews of *The Way Forward,* most reviewers commented favorably on Walker's strong and honest perceptions of the complexities involved in having a healthy relationship while also coping with the demands of life as an artist and activist in a country with a fraught racial history.

## SYNOPSIS

### To My Young Husband

#### *Memoir of a Marriage*

This chapter is written in the form of a letter by the narrator to her former husband. The narrator of the story reminisces about the house she and her former husband lived in while they resided in Mississippi. She writes that she saw the charming, small house as a kind of prison. She tells of her astonishment that the two, who used to be so in love, no longer speak, with the exception of the occasional necessary exchanges about their daughter. There is a sense of regret that all they had shared is no longer accessible to them in the present. A particular loss is the laughter with which they both greeted the world.

The narrator continues writing to her former husband, sharing with him that she visited their former home with her current lover, who is a woman. She says that the woman has never been to the South and that they drove from Memphis, stopping along the way to see various locations. At one place they see a quilt that reminds the narrator of one that she made in celebration of their wedding.

The house that the narrator revisits seems smaller than she remembered. She remembers a tree in the yard that the couple planted when their child was born. The tree is not in the yard where the narrator expects to find it, so she goes to the house next door to see if the woman she remembers living there is still present. The woman still lives there and confirms that the narrator has found the right location.

The woman who lives in the narrator's former home now does not open the door, so the narrator is not able to look inside and show her current lover the space. She wants to see the mirror where her younger face peered and to imagine how it felt to be that woman.

She writes that she has learned from their child that her former husband is writing plays and also that he left civil rights law for corporate law, and she ponders whether that work is entirely fulfilling. A former friend recalled that the couple were superlatively happy and in love with each other. The friend was astounded to discover that the couple have divorced and no longer speak to each other.

The narrator reflects that this supportive friend was an unwitting factor in the couple's breakup. She recalls that the friend had given her a copy of a novel by a forgotten African-American author and that she had become obsessed with the woman and sorrowful about her forgotten legacy. She recalls that she and her former husband shared a love of literature, but that he would not read that particular novel. The narrator sees this refusal as a root cause of their eventual separation. She concludes the letter with resignation and with her signature, Tatala.

### *Begging*

Tatala recalls a woman who used to come to the couple's home asking for money. The woman would only accept coins, not bills. She also refused to enter the home. Tatala ponders this woman's life, purpose, and significance. In her recollections, she is unsure of the woman's motivations and wonders if she was a spy. She shares her fear of having someday to beg for her sustenance like the woman seemed to have to do to survive.

Tatala also reflects on poverty and the ways that it can enrich one's life; there are lessons there that are difficult but satisfying. She wonders if her husband would recall this woman and if she ever came to the door while she was not at home when he had answered the door. She wonders if the begging woman also delivered the hateful warnings from the KU KLUX KLAN that the couple regularly received.

She notes that her husband has not yet responded to the letter that begins *The Way Forward Is with a Broken Heart,* although she knows that their daughter gave it to him. Tatala feels as if the man she knew and loved no longer exists. She says that she misses her former husband and regrets that the experiences they shared are not living for him. She says that their memories and time together deserve better homage.

### *Finding Langston*

Tatala tells the story of denying a ride to LANGSTON HUGHES, with whom she was friends. She says that she felt he was like a father to her. She talks of her longing for a father and remembers her brother telling her that her actual father, when he was younger, was much like the one for whom she wishes. She learns of her father's struggles that are, in some ways, akin to her own, and she is reminded of Sisyphus. She finds comfort in ALBERT CAMUS's analysis of Sisyphus and his conclusion that there is some dignity and satisfaction in accepting the unending nature of struggle.

Tatala recalls learning how to drive in the early hours of the morning in New York. The lovers would sometimes take the opportunity to go swimming in the university pool as it was empty at that time. During those occasions, her husband would teach her how to swim.

One evening, the young couple was at a literary event, and Langston Hughes was there as well. They all left the party at the same time. The couple did not offer the literary giant a ride because they had filled their backseat with a new painting and piece of furniture they had just purchased.

Hughes took the subway home. When the two married, Hughes wrote Tatala a note saying that she had guaranteed herself support by marrying her husband, who was white and well-connected. She later compares her situation to Hughes's and thinks of the compromises he was forced to make in order to have the life he wanted, and she wonders if he understood that, from her perspective, the marriage was not about money.

The couple attended Hughes's funeral together. Tatala remembers it as a joyful occasion, but she also remembers Hughes's words about her husband, and she thinks of her husband's unflagging support of her work. She hopes that Hughes had some experience of that kind of unfaltering loyalty.

### *Burned Bridges*

Tatala recalls an incident when she is riding with a friend who is pulled over by police. The officer refuses to answer questions about why the woman was pulled over and only asks the narrator's friend if she is the owner of her car. The police asks her to get out of the car and grills her about whether the car is hers or not. The incident brings up memories for Tatala of her time in the South with her white husband. As with the events in her past, she is uncertain about the best course of action to avoid escalating the situation and having someone get hurt. Eventually, the policeman calls in the registration on the vehicle and authenticates her friend's ownership and lets the women go. Both are humiliated and frightened by the incident.

The two continue with their evening and see the film *The Bridges of Madison County.* The movie reminds Tatala of what she was like and who she was when she met her husband. She says that although she had been hostile to the idea of whites' involvement in the Civil Rights movement, she felt a kinship immediately upon meeting the man who would become her husband. She says that upon arriving in Mississippi she was seduced by another lawyer who worked in the same office as the man who would become her husband, but that the affair meant nothing to her. She remembers an erotic moment between her and her future husband as they shared a chocolate ice cream cone. This moment she remembers as the one in which they fell in love.

Tatala says that it was obvious to everyone when the two of them fell in love. In the midst of the real threat of violence and the real threat of the South, her future husband promised to keep her safe, and she believed that he would do so.

The narrative switches voices, and the story proceeds in the voices of black people in the Mississippi town where the couple lived while they were married. The exchange is gossip about the two and "unnaturalness" of their relationship, particularly of the impending birth of their child. Their commentary about Tatala's husband's Jewishness is an explanation for what they see as entirely inexplicable behavior on his part.

One of the gossipers does not reveal her actual thoughts about the situation to her peers but reflects silently that the young Jewish man does not seem odd to her as he comes to the restaurant late at night to get his pregnant wife chitlins; rather, he seems happy. In fact, she thinks he may be the most contented person she has ever encountered.

### *Passion*

Because the couple face the threat of real violence, even death, they use lovemaking as a counterpoint to the possibility of destruction, spending hours in bed. In fact, they find themselves in the bed as much as is practical given the demands of their lives. She works writing a novel about the human costs of the movement, and he takes depositions about the legal realities of segregation for African-American sharecroppers. Although their relationship makes them vulnerable, the two feel as if their love insulates them from the possible dangers their relationship provokes.

In order to assuage both their fear and their vulnerability, they share the beauty of literary works, reading aloud to each other in bed. The two promise to return to New York together to embark on their interconnected journeys.

### *Handling It*

The narrative leaps forward to the couple's meeting after their divorce in the office of their daughter's therapist. Only as Tatala reaches the door of the therapist's office does she realize that she has put her dress on backwards. The couple greet each other and try to concede to their daughter's request that they meet together so that she can have some sense of who they are. Tatala recalls the man she married and his habits, his ways of being in the world, and the man before her seems unrecognizable to her.

The therapist asks what they want to accomplish from the session, and the couple's daughter says that she would like to understand the longing that she feels from both of her parents when they talk about, but not to, each other.

Tatala begins by saying that she remembers finding a wonderful partner in her husband and a fellow spirit in the movement. Then she talks of the struggle with an environment that was often both dull and potentially fatal and of their retreat into the work they were both committed to that required a kind of isolated persistence.

She says that her husband's work brought up memories of her conflict with her mother. The conflict was rooted in an understanding that separation was necessary to the economic health and sustenance of both her family of origin and the one she created with her husband, but that she resented the isolation and separation that was the inevitable outcome. She says that the circumstances of their lives depleted them and left them without the emotional and psychological resources to maintain their relationship with each other.

Tatala recalls boredom and frustration as she vacillates between her writing projects and a desire to escape. The couple's child knows that her parents were happy but remembers none of that pleasure herself. Tatala recalls the pleasure of her husband's evening homecomings and the infrequency with which such an occasion was possible. She asks her former husband why he works so hard and then begins to cry. She acknowledges how well they have done for themselves materially and wonders if it was the hard work or luck that brought them such economic fortunes.

Tatala weeps and wonders why the couple were not able to help to sustain each other. She also reflects on the fact that her family never accepted her former husband or were able to see him as an individual, outside of the dynamics of race and racism that had defined their lives.

The couple recounts for their daughter the story of her birth. Tatala speaks of the pain, but then recalls the wonder of her daughter's glance at both her mother and then her father when she entered the world and then retells the racial drama enacted by both the white and black staff members at the hospital.

Tatala also tells her daughter a story the girl's grandmother told Tatala about herself and about her sisters when they were young. She says that she and her brothers and sisters were walking together and had encountered white men. The brothers ran away and left their sisters to defend themselves. The girls were able to run fast enough to avoid being attacked by the young men.

Tatala continues her reflections, pondering about whether her ex-husband remembers that she used to develop sudden passions. She remembers loving arrowheads and that her love for them was connected to her discovery and embrace of her Native American heritage. She recalls that Mississippi was strangely absent of Native American people.

The narrative flashes back to an internal monologue by a Mississippi resident of the town where Tatala and her husband used to live. The woman speaker, whose name is Dianne, is also in an interracial relationship with a man named Harold. She says that she is constantly receiving stares because of the relationship she is in and, consequently, feels under scrutiny. She sees Tatala and her husband, the lawyer. She says that they are with their infant, to whom they speak as if she is a grown person—a fact that the observer finds peculiar and intriguing.

Dianne says that she thinks that Tatala does not care for her husband, Harold. She notices that the woman does not speak to him when the four of them meet; Tatala only speaks to her. The woman remembers her husband making a snide comment to the writer about her writing and Tatala's unequivocal response. Dianne feels that Tatala and her husband's attitude is a direct challenge to the racism of Mississippi.

### *The Ruin*

Although Tatala's ex-husband wants to discuss her role in their story, Tatala continues talking about Dianne and Harold. She wonders about the couple's relationship and then reflects on the fact that they have both died. She learns of the couple's fate from one of their children who meet her at a reading. After she recognizes their children, Ernesto and Rosa, the narrative returns to Dianne's first-person reflections on her relationship with Harold. These reflections are recorded in a diary of Dianne's that her children present to Tatala at the reading.

Dianne tells of the couple's meeting and of the ways that, initially, she had not been attracted to him but had grown to love him and to see him as a human being rather than as a white man. Tatala expresses her discomfort at reading the intimate details of the lives of Dianne and Harold, and the narrative switches from her reading of the diary to her response to her daughter's request for information about the past.

Tatala speaks about when the couple relocated from Mississippi to Brooklyn where they purchased and refurbished a brownstone. Tatala's mother-in-law does not approve of the choice of location and, with her influence, the couple chooses a house that needs an enormous amount of work and money, so much so that all of the energy and time that the couple has is devoted to caring for a home they have no opportunity to enjoy. Their daughter is happy in the space, and Tatala reflects on the fact that she did not know how much pain her mother and father were in at the time. Tatala thinks that perhaps the two did not spend enough time grieving all that was lost of their dreams, the lives of friends, colleagues, and leaders, their miscarried child, and the visions they had of making life better for humanity.

### Kindred Spirits

The narrative shifts to the story of African-American sisters Rosa and Barbara, who are traveling to visit their aunt in the wake of their grandfather's death. Rosa is in mourning for her lost marriage to a Jewish man. Barbara, who was fond of the man, comments on the fact that Rosa's ex-husband has completely abandoned his black family and will not respond to her attempts to be in touch by mail. Rosa tells Barbara that her ex has begun a new relationship with a Jewish woman and that the two are living together. The relationship with the new woman began only one week after Rosa had moved out of the house that she had shared with her ex-husband, Ivan. Rosa tells her sister that the whole family seems delighted with the change.

Barbara says to her sister that their mother finds Ivan's absence in their lives a sad reality. The two are surprised that Ivan does not engage with his mother-in-law, even after she becomes debilitated with a serious illness. Rosa is exhausted from travel and so does not enjoy the trip with the same enthusiasm as her sister. She falls into the familiar arms of the sister's Aunt Lily, who greets them at the airport at the end of the trip.

Aunt Lily and her husband have relocated to Florida, and there they have experienced the easing of racial segregation that has begun to change the South and the rest of the country. Raymyna Ann is a woman who lives with Aunt Lily to help her out as needed. Rosa has never felt particularly close to her Aunt Lily, who, she believes, does not like children.

As she tries to sleep in her aunt's house, Rosa ponders the many questions about her mother and aunt's relationship to which she does not have answers. She also thinks it is strange that her former husband should have completely withdrawn his love for her. She thinks about his not sending her a note when she had surgery shortly after their divorce. Rosa finds herself unable to be happy for Raymyna, who is soon to be married.

Rosa and Barbara go sightseeing in the coastal Florida town where her aunt lives. Rosa is silently critical. Later, Rosa tries to convey her feelings and the reasons why she did not attend her grandfather's funeral. She tries to explain her long-held plans to travel to Cyprus for work and writing. She goes on the trip with the hope it will have some effect on the political conflict that was happening at the time her grandfather died. Rosa regrets not attending the funeral, although she feels that she never really knew her grandfather, who was a quiet man who seldom spoke. She also has fallen out of touch with her sister, whose involvement in an abusive marriage has changed her so much that she has become nearly unrecognizable to Rosa.

Rosa reflects on her history with her sister and the ways that Barbara had became vulnerable to abuse. She remembers that Barbara was subjected to abuse as a child and that she defended her sister against their father by taking a butcher knife to him. Her attempted heroism had been ignored and had made no difference in the outcome of the situation.

Rosa also wanted to murder her brother-in-law when she discovered that he was beating her sister. She did not act on her impulse because she did not want to ruin her chances to succeed in her own life. She feels that Barbara and her grandfather developed the same resigned silence about life because they felt helpless to change the circumstances in which they found themselves.

Aunt Lily gives Barbara and Rosa some of their grandfather's possessions, and then Rosa asks her aunt to tell her what kind of boy her father was. Lily refuses to answer the question. She seems concerned about the possibility of finding her responses in her nieces' writings and cuts off the conversation. Barbara seems to concur with Lily about the dangers of speaking with Rosa. Rosa remembers her grandfather's silences and begins to see them as a form of observation akin to the tools she uses as a writer. She feels a profound loneliness upon leaving her aunt's home, and reflects further about her failed marriage. The narrative ends with Rosa's sister, Barbara, reaching out to hold her hand, quelling Rosa's fears that her sister dislikes and misunderstands her.

## Orelia and John

### Olive Oil

The narrative begins in the kitchen of Orelia and John, a couple who seem to love each other, although Orelia has a fundamental mistrust of men rooted in the childhood experiences and the lessons she garnered from her family's interactions. This mistrust undermines John's confidence in himself and in the relationship.

Orelia uses olive oil to overcome dry skin. John has a cold and cannot smell the oil. He loves the way that Orelia smells and the oils that she uses. When he begins to recover from his cold, he asks her what she is using on her skin. She replies that it is olive oil, afraid that he will not like the smell. Reassuringly, he does like the scent, and Orelia feels affirmed by John's love. After the conversation about the olive oil, Orelia uses some to try to help John with a dandruff problem he is having. The couple massage each other, make love, and fall into a blissful sleep, finding past pains healed by each other's acceptance.

### Cuddling (for Tall Moon)

This chapter begins with a man preparing a bath. Nearby, Orelia, his wife, is sad thinking about a man named Everett. She loves her husband, John, but is not in love with him. John has had an affair, and the couple have lost the spark that kept them excited about their relationship. Orelia does not feel that she can trust John any longer.

She reflects on the feelings she has for Everett. As the couple take their bath, and John washes her back, Orelia tells John that she is in love with Everett Jordan. John's reaction is a quiet, sighlike sound. He continues to bathe her, and she feels taken care of, even in the midst of giving her husband the news about her feelings for another man.

The man she has fallen in love with is a savvy politician and a generally unpleasant person. She says again to John that she does not want to change their lives. She loves him but is not in love with him. She begins to tell John about the evolution of her relationship with Everett. She says to John that she wants to treat her attraction to Everett like a sickness she must bear for a while until she recovers.

She falls into a deep sleep, relieved to have told John the truth. She proceeds to confide in him about her feelings and works to resist Everett. Three months after she tells John about her feelings for the other man, things begin to fall apart. Her feelings have intensified, although she continues to try to resist the man.

John takes her on a vacation to help her to work out her feelings. Her conflict lies in knowing that the relationship with Everett cannot be yet still wanting and needing to express her feelings. While on this vacation, Orelia begins to recover from her emotional malaise under John's patient and tender love. The couple make love and spend time cuddling in bed.

The story ends ambiguously as Orelia and John return home, and she runs eagerly up the stairs to a ringing phone.

### Charms

John doubts Orelia's love and is uncertain of where they stand as a couple. Orelia works as an interior designer, and she derives great pleasure from helping her clients to get a better view of nature from the interiors of their homes. Her houses are known for their ability to improve the lives of her clients.

The two meet when John is a law student at Columbia. She faints during their first meeting, and he takes her to his apartment. Later, they encounter each other in Brussels in a youth hostel where, coincidentally, they are both staying while traveling through Europe. John is getting ready to marry. Orelia tells him at the time that she will never marry, but later, John hears that she has married someone with money.

Although he is somewhat happy with the woman he marries, he continues through the years to think of Orelia. He and his wife, Leonie, have two children and seem relatively happy, but eventually he seeks out Orelia. She is in the midst of getting a divorce at the time he reconnects with her.

Although still married himself, John is delighted to discover her availability. In reality, the divorce takes a great deal more time to resolve, and Orelia moves to another city on the other side of the country. Shortly thereafter, John begins conversations with Leonie about divorcing. Even though she does not want to end the marriage, the couple finally separate, and John and Orelia begin to try to have a life together.

The couple do not have much money. John teaches college, and Orelia is just beginning her business, but they are extremely happy together. They are open and honest with each other. When Orelia becomes attracted to a woman, the couple share this occurrence with each other and with friends. John is her source of counsel when she is experiencing this deep confusion. His addiction problems are also open topics of conversation and discussion. John recovers when some Native American friends of the couple perform a sweat ceremony.

When Orelia leaves town for work, some women who know that she is gone attempt to hone in on the couple. In particular, a woman named Belinda spends some time with John, and the two begin an affair. They are together so much that they appear to be a married couple. The time that they spend together is complicated by the relationship he develops with her children. They begin to feel close to him, and John starts to understand the implications of the affair. When Orelia returns, he simply stops seeing the woman and her children. Belinda is terribly hurt and demands an explanation from him. He tells her that he also was sleeping with other women while Orelia was gone.

John eventually tells Orelia about the affair, and her response seems to indicate that she is hurt.

## There Was a River

### There Was a River

This story begins with a character named Marcella, who is gazing at a river with a companion named Angel. Ironically, in light of his name, she says that the man has lost his radiance. Another companion is with the couple, a woman named Sally, who is Marcella's best friend. The three are in turmoil because of Sally's attraction to and involvement with Angel.

### *Five Years Later*

The narrative continues five years later. Marcella is in her house preparing dinner for Sally and Sally's young grandson. Angel calls while the two are dancing with the baby. He shares with Marcella the details of his new relationship. Marcella is happy that her former love sounds so contented and that he seems to be with someone who is able to love him in the ways that he needs. Marcella reflects on the couple's former relationship and feels that they both were able to grow through each other's presence

After putting the baby to bed, Marcella and Sally indulge in smoking marijuana. They watch the moon rise and delight in the strength of their long-standing friendship.

## Big Sister, Little Sister

### Uncle Loaf and Auntie Putt-Putt

This narrative begins with the story of a young black girl's rape by an older, obese white man who is her master and owner. The story is written in italics and is attributed to Auntie Putt-Putt, who, apparently, had acquired it through gossip. In the tale, the man eventually dies, but not before his wife, the girl's mistress, discovers the truth about her husband (whom she hates) sleeping with the woman. After her husband's death, the woman becomes relatively friendly with the people she owns and particularly likes to spend time with the children. But their mother is reminded of her rape when she sees her children and so is distanced from them for their whole lives.

Big Sister is telling Little Sister this information in an imitation of Aunt Putt-Putt, who had been the raped woman's granddaughter as well as the family storyteller. Big Sister had been one of her primary audiences, and now she imitates Aunt Putt-Putt and repeats her stories.

As adults, the two women sit in the family cabin and exchange these family stories. Little

Sister is awaiting the arrival of her lover, who is visiting his family in a nearby town. She is reading Jean Rhys' *Wide Sargasso Sea,* but she also thinks of her married lover and his large family. He arrives and they make passionate love. The visit is so brief that, afterward, it does not seem to have happened.

On the following day, Big Sister and Little Sister set out on a quest to find their Uncle Loaf's house. Uncle Loaf was Aunt Putt-Putt's husband, and Big Sister wants to return to the house so that she can rid herself of the weight of her aunt's bitter stories. Little Sister cannot focus on the quest as her thoughts are preoccupied with her lover. She thinks of her relationship with her family and of her sister's resentment that she managed to escape. Little Sister thinks of her older sister's sense of obligation and her willingness to be at the center of the family's life. Little Sister feels that the difference in their lives was determined by her own unwillingness to love her family more than she relished herself and her own wellness.

The sisters come to a point in the trail where they cannot proceed. A tree has fallen over the path, and they cannot get over or around it without considerable risk. Little Sister sits down and waits to see what her sister will do. Big Sister is angry at her sister's refusal to take over the situation. She thinks of all the work she has done her whole life that her younger sister did not have to do. She also remembers her mother's lack of appreciation of the work that she did, the cooking and cleaning, and of her father and brother's indifference to the young girl's efforts. She gets upset remembering her youngest sister's difference from them. Little Sister appreciated her efforts but seemed to be disconnected from the reality in which Big Sister found herself immersed. Little Sister always seemed to be in a world of her own invention where none of them could reach or follow.

Deciding that her sister is determined to continue on the path they have begun, Little Sister tries to find a way for them to proceed to the house they seek. As they grope through the overgrowth, Little Sister thinks of how much her sister took care of her when she was small. The women make it through the tree-blocked passage to a clearing where Big Sister begins to recognize the landscape and the places where the buildings had stood. As a child, the place had been a sanctuary for her against the responsibilities and work of home. She also sees the connections between her aunt and herself—her aunt's state of virtual imprisonment and perpetual labor and the ways in which she became just like Aunt Putt-Putt. The sisters return home gleeful with the success of their quest, and they take a swim in the lake on the family property.

### Blaze

After the swim, Little Sister remembers a white childhood friend she had named Blaze. After a certain age, the two were not allowed to play with each other. Little Sister thinks about the relationship and tries to retrace its contours. She remembers that Blaze at some point would have become "Miss" Blaze, and the formal address that she would have had to have used would have enforced a hierarchy between the women, one based in race and privilege, which neither of them had designed but both would have been forced to adhere to, regardless of their genuine feelings of love and affection for each other.

This line of thinking connects for Little Sister with the response she has to the stories that are sent to her in her job as a magazine editor. Often, white women send in narratives about their childhood relationships with black women who had served as their caretakers when they were children. These narratives make Little Sister angry and resentful. They also force her to consider that these relationships may have actually consisted of circumstantial displays of emotion. She needs to believe that her mother did not love the little girls in the houses she cleaned. Periodically, she thinks of her lover as she watches her sister swimming.

Big Sister says that she feels she is always transformed during the times she spends with Little Sister. She thinks back to a time when she was a young adult and was about to leave her hometown to attend veterinary school. She remembers going to say good-bye to Aunt Putt-Putt and Uncle Loaf. When she got to the older couple's home, she sat next to her uncle instead of behind him as had been her custom. While sitting there, Uncle Loaf went into his room and changed into a hat, shorts, and a white cotton shirt, and he began to walk toward the garden. Uncle Loaf—who had never, in Big Sister's experience, done any work around the house—began to pick tomatoes alongside his wife. When she left, the couple sent her off with tomatoes, and her uncle gave her a handful of silver dollars.

This memory restores Big Sister. She realizes that she does not need to resent Little Sister and that she, too, had people who had loved and supported her efforts.

Although Little Sister awakens crying, before too long the sisters are smiling, reveling in each other's presence.

## Growing Out

### Growing Out

This story begins with Anne's discovery that she has outgrown her own self-perception. Her lover, Jason, is a perceptive and sensitive man whom she loves and whose love makes her feel fulfilled. The day is a celebration of Jason's birth, and the couple shares a delicious meal in celebration of the event. The couple then watches a television show that celebrates and acknowledges black performers. Anne is moved to tears several times during the show as she understands the complex lives of black performers in relationship to the power dynamics of the industries in which they tried to excel. She admires the talents of the various individuals who appear on the screen, such as Ben Vereen, Flip Wilson, Natalie Cole, Gladys Knight, the Mighty Clouds of Joy, and others. She and Jason have consumed magic mushrooms, and this intoxicant has an effect on her, making her cry and laugh more readily than she might have otherwise.

They try to find the right music for the mood they find themselves in, and BESSIE SMITH seems to be the right choice. She speaks to Jason of her love of a woman. She reassures him by saying that the love she feels for the woman is not as great as her feelings for him. Anne thinks of her lover and the way that they met when the woman, Jerri, and her then partner, Maude, arrived to help her fix her car when it was not starting. Jerri's ability to fix the car was attractive to Anne and led her to have a relationship with the woman.

### Conscious Birth

This section of the story begins with a statement delineating the reality that women of all races are subjected to fatal violence every day. It is a part of a letter written by Anne and sent by her to a woman's group who had asked her to write something supporting their efforts to end the violence against women in their home of Lexington, Kentucky. Anne wishes to make it clear that her understanding of violence against women transcends the immediacy of the women's concerns and is connected to the historical violence experienced by Native American and African-American women. She is concerned about the implications of her letter and the ways it might be misread in particular racialized contexts.

Anne has a psychological alter ego, Grandma, who serves a kind of truth-telling function in her life. Anne imagines her as she fights with herself about various moral and ethical complexities. She feels fortunate to have this presence in her head as she walks through life and is often confronted with these questions. Grandma is, in many ways, the voice of the planet.

Anne thinks about the problems of nuclear proliferation and of the damage the earth has experienced as a result of such methods of exploiting natural resources. She imagines a world before it was violated by the greedy inventions of humanity.

Grandma is more than a metaphor for Anne. She is a nurturing figure who holds her in her lap and cares for her emotionally, physically, psychologically, and spiritually. Anne avoids Grandma because she is overwhelmed by what she discovers with her. As a result of her interactions with Grandma, she believes that the world is ending. She begins to give in to feelings of overwhelming negativity and then remembers a saying by the author and activist Toni Cade Bambara: "Depression Is Collaboration with the Enemy."

Her lover comes in full of joy and making jokes. His enthusiasm reminds her of Grandma. During dinner, he reinforces her concerns about the earth, letting her know that he has heard about an attempt to mine on Native American lands that will expose the inhabitants to the dangers of uranium. Native lore about the spot on which they mine says that it is the heart of the earth and that mining there will cause the death of the planet.

Jason ponders the racial dimensions of the antinuclear movement and wonders about the lack of significant participation of many African Americans and women activist groups. Anne thinks about the ways in which the activism she and Jason participate in have changed.

She is friends with Jason's wife, a woman named Suni. They stayed in a house together to see if they could accept the polyamorous nature of their relationships. Each of them also had another lover who was not present at the house. Jason and Anne's lovemaking in the house did not seem to upset Suni, who said that the thought of the couple making love was sexually exciting to her.

With Anne, Suni is able to share her ambivalence about the racial dynamics of relationships, particularly of Jason's choice to be with her, a white woman. Suni points out the hypocrisy of this statement, reminding Anne that she was married to Phillip, a white man. All of this examination does not lead to a fulfilling relationship with Jason for either of them, and Suni admits she is attracted to Anne.

Twenty years later, Jason is married to someone else. Anne and Suni discuss the complexities of adult relationships and love. Suni speaks of her love for a guru, a woman named Gurumayi. Anne talks about her aborted child and the connections she feels between the man with whom she is involved platonically and the child she decided not to have. She says that she is so happy with Adam, her new love, that she does not know what to do.

## This Is How It Happened

### This Is How It Happened

This story begins with the speaker saying that, at the end of a happy 12-year relationship, she found herself and her partner having moments of what she calls "palpable deadness." These moments signal to her that the growth in the relationship has ended and that the two of them need to move in different directions. She says that in spite of this difficult transition, she still loves her partner and wishes him well. She asks herself how it would be possible to end the relationship in a way that is healthy for them both.

The narrator has a visit from an old friend named Marissa, a woman who is gorgeous as well as capable in a traditionally masculine way. The narrator says that at one time in her life, she had been attracted to Marissa. During the reunion, the two find that it is this aspect of their personalities that was repressed in other relationships that they were attracted to in each other.

The women try to understand why they have remained in abusive relationships. The narrator remembers her former husband, Tripper, wanted to make love with her the week that they were separating. This insensitivity indicates to Marissa the degree of unhealth in their relationship at its end.

Marissa and the narrator go out to a lesbian club, leaving the narrator's lover, Chung, happily at home. She wonders why she never had a relationship with Marissa, even though the two women have had more than once. The narrator watches Marissa from across the club and seems convinced that it would not be a good idea for them to be involved long-term. About the same time, a woman enters the club with what, at first, appears to the narrator to be an infant. Later, she sees that the child is about two years old. The woman enters the club to sell Guatemalan items, which she does efficiently and quickly while, unexpectedly, the narrator holds her child. After the woman completes her business, the mother and child are reunited and blissfully share a brief dance on the floor of the club.

### The Brotherhood of the Saved

The narrator returns home and finds her mother aging but well and familiar. She has come home to help her mother with an injury and takes her to a chiropractor. The older woman is surprised to find it helpful. The two exchange memories about the narrator's childhood and the ways that she was always hurting herself. Her mother remembers her falling out of a tree and breaking her arm. The two both observe that this injury did nothing to slow her down or to stop her from regularly climbing trees in spite of the pain it had caused her.

The narrator asks her mother about the Brotherhood of the Saved and what the group is saying about her. Her mother asks if the question is genuine and proceeds to tell her daughter that the group has determined that she is a sinner and is damned eternally. The group is particularly appalled with the narrator's disposition to have occasional relationships with women. She is indignant and replies that all human beings derive from within women and so there is nothing more natural than intimacy with a woman. She also replies that the very same men who are condemning her probably love to watch women sexually engaging with each other when it is presented in the form of pornography. She maintains that there are many other issues that warrant the men's attention and passions and that will have more of an effect on humanity in the long run. The mother and daughter resolve the issue peacefully and respectfully, although they do not agree.

The narrator is out with her mother, her Auntie Fanny, and an old family friend named Miss Mary. She comments on the fabulous and outlandish hats the other women are wearing. She herself wears a baseball cap turned the opposite direction from the way it was intended to be worn. The older women comment on her hair and her appearance. They are all going to a big mall in Atlanta and have dressed up for the occasion—they are going to see a porno film, the infamous *Deep Throat.* The women make note of the fact that they are the only women in attendance and that, to their surprise, there are white and black men in the line to get tickets for the film.

Although the women utter mild protests, it is clear that they are curious about the film. The narrator worries as the film begins and progresses because the women, who are loquacious, have become utterly silent. The silence continues through the ride home. The narrator begins to sing a song to herself, and her mother tells her to be quiet, saying that there is no reason to be singing after what they have just witnessed.

At that point, the women begin, in hushed tones to discuss the film. They ask about the name for an orgasm and say that the word does not derive from African-American culture. Then the conversation begins to focus on language and on the fact that the American language as it is used officially is not the same as African-American language. The women ponder what it would be like to have a language that is exclusively theirs. The narrator maintains that black Americans do have their own language. Then Aunt Fanny begins to discuss the words that describe sexual experiences and to make evaluations of them. The other older women in the car are shocked by her frankness. They also discuss a man who was sitting close to them and seemed to be struggling to have an orgasm. The narrator asks the women if they would like to see another film, and they all pretend to be disgusted but agree to go.

The narrator recounts a conversation with her father. The two have been able to talk frankly since she took him to Jamaica on a vacation and the two had the opportunity to experience each other as adults.

The narrator's father has never traveled anywhere, and she is surprised when she suggests the trip to Jamaica and he readily agrees to go with her. Her father cannot swim and is astonished when he finds himself on a beach where he can walk for miles in waist-high water. The two bathe in the beautiful water, and the narrator asks her father about marriage and how people can remain married for a lifetime. He reminds her that her attitude was different when he and her mother decided to divorce. She replies that she has grown with experience.

When her father returns with her from the trip to Jamaica, he is a changed man. He begins to wear his hair in locks. The narrator asks her father whether it is possible to rescue her mother from the sanctimonious community to which she belongs. She and her father decide to visit her mother's brother, who is called Uncle Brother, to see if he has any insights on the situation. The Brotherhood is an interdenominational congregation that is also interracial. The narrator's mother and Uncle Brother both belong to the church. The speaker—finally identified as Hannah—and her father discuss the rather amusing reality of white congregants gathered around Uncle Brother's bed and his terror of them although they only gather to pray for his well-being. They also discuss her cousin, Harry, who is gay and has left the family and the area because his family does not accept his sexuality and has kicked him out.

Following their unsuccessful inquiries with Uncle Brother, Hannah and her father enjoy a watermelon and a nap together.

## The Way Forward Is with a Broken Heart

### Epilogue: The Way Forward Is with a Broken Heart

Walker remembers the death of John F. Kennedy, Jr., in a plane crash in July 1999. She recalls that reporters had surmised that he had encountered what is known in aviation circles as hitting a square, a space wherein the pilot does not realize which direction is up and which is down. The metaphor appeals to Walker, and she thinks of her relationship with her former husband as a metaphorical form of hitting the square—a disorientation that is, in some ways, fatal, at least to the relationship and to communication between either of the members of the couple.

She thinks about John F. Kennedy, Jr., and feels that his death is a loss, although she does not understand exactly how. She thinks she may be mourning his young self, the boy who is associated in her mind with the Kennedy family and with the assassination and losses of the 1960s. She thinks back on all of the loss and sadness of her life and relationships and concludes with a hopeful sense for the spirit of the marriage that is, seemingly, to be left without a sufficient conclusion. She states that she and her former husband are part of the American race and that she still believes that Americans as a group of people are fundamentally good.

## CRITICAL COMMENTARY

In Walker's collection *The Way Forward Is with a Broken Heart,* she uses fiction to reflect on her experiences as a married person and in various relationships after that marriage failed. The picture on the cover of the book is a photograph of Alice Walker and Mel Leventhal, her former husband, looking young and happy and appearing very much in love. This emphasizes the autobiographical elements of Walker's life and sets up the text as a kind of conflation of fiction and memoir, leaving the reader to surmise which is which. The book's first story in its first narrative, "To My Young Husband," is often cited as the strongest of the collection. In this tale, the narrator recounts the bliss of finding a like-minded soul who is equally engaged in the effort to overcome racial inequality and discrimination. She recounts the optimism with which the two fell in love and the complexities that inevitably ensued, derailing the possibilities for the couple, which seemed so limitless when the relationship began. The essay provides a more personal outlook on the subjective realities of the CIVIL RIGHTS MOVEMENT than other more objective accounts of the history of the times and of the people who were involved in the struggle against racial oppression.

The other stories in the collection follow and detail the complexities of this original relationship and then branch out, using other characters and situations but always featuring a narrator or central character who is similar to Walker. The stories are not continuous but are related in theme, focus, and style. In the preface, Walker acknowledges the unilateral focus and perspectives of the pieces that constitute this collection. Some of the narratives' central concerns involve the issues of aging; recovery from loss; redefinition of self; the limitations of monogamy; the weight and influence of family history; and interconnections between personal, creative, and intellectual growth.

It is the struggle to grow that is at the center of this narrative and its primary question: What is the relationship between relationship and freedom, and how does one create a balance between the two that enables one to thrive? What also should be the response when one's efforts to create this balance and to love another are unsuccessful? Walker also addresses questions that are endemic to life as a literary artist and concern the relationship between fiction and fact as they pertain to family stories and the freedom to use that material as the basis for one's creativity.

The book concludes with Walker's feeling of connection to the airplane crash of John F. Kennedy, Jr. She describes the lack of orientation that may have caused his plane to crash as analogous to the feelings of loss and perplexity that come with the death of a set of expectations, hopes, and dreams. John F. Kennedy, Jr.'s death may have also been the last phase, an endpoint for the hopes represented by his father's time in the White House and the ambitions of the early 1960s—possibilities represented by Leventhal and Walker's interracial relationship and activism in Mississippi, which also met with an unforeseen and painful demise.

## SIGNIFICANT THEMES, ISSUES, CONCERNS

### The Complex Dynamics of Interracial Relationships

In the world Walker creates in her collection *The Way Forward Is with a Broken Heart,* she reveals and provides a close focus on the issues that interracial couples face as they try to create a life together. Several of the collection's stories engage the question of power dynamics between a couple whose racial histories are fraught with narratives of exploitation and denigration. Many of the stories ponder the question of the centrality and power of those histories and the extent to which they have a determinative impact on the ability of the partners to remain together and to sustain a healthy and vital relationship.

Another tangible complexity of an interracial relationship is the offspring that result from such unions. Several of the stories in *The Way Forward Is with a Broken Heart* question the impact of racism and racial categorization on children who, in their existence and histories, negate attempts at racial segregation and may serve as an affirmation of the parents' struggles to end race-based hierarchies. The cost that the children pay when the ideological struggles represented by their parents' union fail is another thematic issue for the collection. In "To My Young Husband," the desire of Our Child to understand her parent's relationship is an example of the effects of the long-term realities of racial strife on individuals, particularly on people whose personal commitments and relationships threaten the status quo in the way that an interracial marriage did in the 1960s—especially if that couple resided in the South.

### Sexuality as a Spectrum

*The Way Forward Is with a Broken Heart* deals explicitly with the topic of sexuality. There is a correlation in the narratives between the sexual openness and engagements of the main characters and their psychological and emotional health. There is also a presumption in the text that same-sex relationships exist as a part of the continuum of sexuality. One of the most overt confrontations with sexuality occurs in "The Brotherhood of the Saved," the second section of "This Is How It Happened." Through the narrator's determination to normalize the sexuality in pornography for her mother and her mother's friends, she also makes the point that all sexual behavior is an element of human experience and must be understood and examined as such.

### Generational Inheritance

In this collection, there is a subtextual assertion that the lessons learned by one generation are often the determinative factors for the behavior of the subsequent generation. In "Big Sister, Little Sister," Big Sister inherits the legacy of her Aunt Putt-Putt and spends her life sacrificing personal happiness for what she understands as the greater good: the happiness and contentment of the whole. Big Sister observes that Little Sister has made choices other than living her life with her family as its center and, consequently, has had different opportunities and avenues available to her.

## CHARACTERS

**Adam** Adam is the young man with whom Anne becomes infatuated platonically. She recognizes in him a similarity to the child that would have been her son. Anne aborted a child when she was a teenager. She would have named that child Adam. She feels that her son sent the boy in his place. Anne loves when he dances.

**Angel** Angel is referred to as a hollow man made of straw. He admits to being performative and never truly himself. Feeling the need and the pressure to please someone, he acts as he thinks others want him to act. Even a degree of being carefree, which Marcella had thought she had allowed him to be, was an act. His insubstantiality—his removal from self and reality—is something Marcella later realizes was a problem in their relationship.

**Anne Gray** Anne is a feminist as well as a civil rights and antinuclear activist. She is married to a white man, Phillip, but becomes involved with Jason, a sensual black man. She is friends with Jerri, a butch lesbian who helps show her a different definition of femininity that seems to have sparked her fervor toward FEMINISM (along with her progressive Grandma). She becomes friends with Jason's wife, Suni, in a kind of 1960s free-love relationship. They share a belief in mysticism and the karmic energy of the world. She is attracted to Suni but displaces that attraction to Jason, her lover and Suni's husband. Anne believes that the son that she aborted sent her a young man who would remind her of him.

**Ansel** Ansel is Belinda's son. He and his sister grow increasingly attached to John during his affair with their mother.

**Aunt BabySis** Aunt BabySis is Uncle Brother's wife. Quiet and passive, she is described as aged and nervous. She feeds Uncle Brother valerian and believes in homeopathic medicines and herbs, which the Brotherhood calls acting like a witch.

**Auntie Fanny Johnson** Auntie Fanny Johnson wears an ostentatious hat to the adult theater when she, Hannah, Hannah's mother, and Miss Mary go to watch *Deep Throat.* She later remarks that "come" is easier to say than "orgasm" and that "pussy" is hotter than "vagina." The four women feel equally trapped in what they call "white" language.

**Auntie Putt-Putt** Auntie Putt-Putt told stories of the women in slavery who were raped by their masters. She seemed to be named after her constant movement, puttering and doing the chores in the house. As much as she did the work and kept the house tidy, Uncle Loaf did precisely that—loaf.

**Aunt Lily** Aunt Lily is Rosa and Barbara's aunt. She lives in Florida, and has seven foster children. She is a strong, straight black woman who takes no nonsense from anyone. She sets up ground rules in her house that include no drinking, no smoking, and no complaining. She favors her niece Barbara, and she warns Rosa not to write about her or her father. She seems to be suspicious of Rosa and her writing.

**Barbara** Barbara is Rosa's sister; together, they travel to Florida to visit their Aunt Lily. Barbara is abused by her husband, and her grandfather paid for her trade-school education (which he did not do for Rosa). When she was younger, she was protective of her sister. As an adult, she gets along with her Aunt Lily better than Rosa does, and she shares Lily's opinion of Rosa—that she uses the family in her writing, twists the stories, and reveals something about them that she should not.

**beggar woman** While living in Mississippi, there is a beggar woman who regularly visits Tatala's house. She is dressed too nicely, it seems, to be a beggar and never accepts more than coins. She always regards Tatala coldly, and Tatala often wonders if perhaps she is a spy. Tatala is puzzled by the beggar women's occasional appearances on her porch.

**Belinda** Belinda is a mother of two children. She falls in love with John during their affair when Orelia is away in California on her consulting job. When John massages her feet, she states that no man has ever done that for her before, and she falls for his seeming tenderness. Soon John leaves her with no explanation. She sends a letter to Orelia that he mistakenly thinks is a confession of their affair, and so he confesses. The letter turns out to be a list of contacts for Orelia's design company.

**Belts, the** The Belts are Tatala and her husband's former neighbors in Mississippi. They recognize Tatala immediately when she brings her lover down to see her old house.

**Big Sister** As a child, Big Sister ran away from home to her Uncle Loaf and Auntie Putt-Putt's house. She hid behind Uncle Loaf's chair when her parents would find her and bring her home. She did not wish to be tied down to the home. She wanted to be relaxed and carefree like her Uncle Loaf seemed to be. She often resented Little Sister because Little Sister seemed to be constantly inside her own head, in her own world, beyond the reach of the needy family. She realized that while her Uncle was relaxed and carefree, her Auntie Putt-Putt was constantly working, doing chores, and moving to keep her uncle this way. What Big Sister wants is to be Uncle Loaf, but instead, she feels as though she is doing the duties of Auntie Putt-Putt. She and Little Sister set out to go to their aunt and uncle's old house. The journey for Big Sister is once again a search for liberation. Her resentment toward her sister slowly abates during their visit to their aunt and uncle's old home as she realizes that she was also perceived as someone who could be liberated and was allowed to do so.

**Blaze** Blaze is a white girl with whom Little Sister used to play when she was young. She is the daughter of the white family that Little Sister's mother worked for. One time, when Little Sister arrived at the house to play with Blaze, the girl's father told her that "Miss" Blaze was not available. To Little Sister, she represents the first realization of a difference between black and white.

**Carolyn** Carolyn is a blonde-haired white woman who worked as a secretary at the same law firm as Larry and Tatala's husband. She was attracted to Tatala's husband before they were married.

**Daniel** Daniel is Dianne's lover and father of her children. They see one another again the night she decides to move in with her white male lover, Harold. Daniel is about to go to prison for 20-plus years at this point; the crime is not mentioned.

**Dianne** Dianne is a black woman in Mississippi and friend of Tatala. She is involved with Harold, a white man who helps to raise her kids by a previous lover, Daniel, who is African American. The night that she decides to move in with Harold, she sees her Daniel. They make love, but it is at this point that she decides to end her relationship with Daniel. She writes this scenario in her journal, which her children later allow Tatala to read. She may have harbored secret desires to be a writer, which Harold never allowed.

**Ernesto** Ernesto is one of Harold and Dianne's children. He is named after CHE GUEVARA, and he hopes to be a television journalist. His mannerisms resemble his father, Harold, with a kind of masculine arrogance. He and Rosa bring their mother Dianne's journal to Tatala to read.

**Everett Jordan** Everett Jordan is an African-American politician who both intrigues and frustrates Orelia. She becomes attracted to his sense of humor and to his activism. He begins to call her regularly despite the fact that he has a wife and children and she is married. He is the kind of person who thinks that "a good woman" is someone who is submissive; loyal; soft-spoken; hardworking; long-suffering; and, above all, devoted. When Orelia falls in love with him, it causes her to suffer because she cannot understand her growing feeling, nor can she decide whether to have an affair.

**F.** F. is the African-American female author who sparked Tatala's passion for writing and who inspired her to write her own novels. Despite her love for her books and their constant literature and book sharing, Tatala's husband never read F.'s books.

**Grandma** Grandma is Anne's spirit guide. She is no-nonsense and assertive. She supports Anne's activism in both the antinuclear movement and as a feminist. Her support partially guides Anne in her activism, life, and writing.

**Hannah** Hannah is an African-American lesbian who speaks freely and without shame (which her mother's friends sometimes hush her for). She is also unashamed of her sexuality. Unlike her parents, she lives in a post-segregation world, not just politically but increasingly in attitude, as shown by her own demeanor. While she struggles with her relationship with her parents and still seems to love them, it is clear that she is unwilling to give up her own identity. She was briefly married to Tripper and is close friends with a lesbian named Marissa, to whom she is drawn through Marissa's fluid dancing, beauty, and sensuality. Hannah's section is narrated in the first person, a departure from the prevalent third-person narration throughout the collection.

**Hannah's father** Hannah's father accompanies her to Negril, Jamaica, on a vacation. They discuss Hannah's mother, with whom Hannah seems to have had a falling out over her sexuality and her mother's religious ties to the Brotherhood of the Saved. They go to see Uncle Brother and Aunt BabySis. Hannah's father seems to maintain that his daughter's sexuality does not change the person that she is and always was. He and his daughter seem to share a solid relationship, but he maintains that he is still not ready to hear about Hannah's lesbianism in any kind of detail.

**Hannah's mother** She is wrinkled in appearance, with grey hair. She calls her daughter Trane because as a young girl Hannah enjoyed John Coltrane's music. Hannah's mother is a member of the Brotherhood of the Saved, which is a Christian group that outwardly condemns homosexuals. While she herself loves her daughter (who is a lesbian), she does not defend her against the Brotherhood, which forces Hannah to move out. Hannah's mother accompanies her daughter to the adult film *Deep Throat* but is mortified by the experience. While she and her daughter seem to share a close relationship, they maintain a certain amount of distance and misunderstanding, about which Hannah later confides in her dad. Hannah's mother and father are divorced.

**Harold** Harold is a white man in Mississippi who is part of an interracial relationship with a black woman named Dianne. He helps raise her children from a previous lover. He looks down on female African-American writers like Tatala and refuses to allow Dianne to become one.

**Harry** Harry is Uncle Brother and Aunt BabySis's son and is gay. He leaves home when his father will not tolerate his sexuality.

**Husband** He is Tatala's husband. While his name is never revealed in the novel, the reader does gather that he is a white, Jewish civil rights lawyer from New York. After Tatala meets him in Mississippi, they marry during a time when interracial marriage is illegal, and their safety was often threatened. Despite this, they initially are and always appear to be in love and happy. He spends longer and longer evenings and nights at his law firm, working hard to fight civil rights cases. Their mutual political passion is initially how they are drawn together. When they are married, they read literature together, and when their daughter is born, he does not miss the birth, even though he is at a court case in New Orleans. Years after their divorce, he is balder, a bit more heavyset than when he was a young man. He smiles when he is defensive. At the therapy session, he does not say much, but he is present as they recollect the memory of their marriage. After their divorce, he marries a white Jewish woman. This character is perhaps based on Alice Walker's first husband, Melvyn Leventhal.

**Ivan** Ivan does not appear in text directly. We learn that he is a Jewish lawyer and that shortly after his divorce from Rosa, he married his second wife, Sheila, who is a white Jewish woman. Following their divorce, he does not write to any of Rosa's family members. Their divorce leaves Rosa heartbroken.

**Jason** Jason is a sensual black man who is Anne's lover and Suni's husband. He is also an activist invested in the antinuclear and Civil Rights movements.

**Jerri** Jerri is a butch lesbian who shows Anne that there is a different kind of beauty that does not involve dresses and heels and perfume. She has a lover, Maude, and she is a car mechanic.

**John** John is a white man and Orelia's lover. He was married to Leonie, a middle-class black woman who graduated from Vassar College, and he began his relationship with Orelia after his divorce from Leonie. He is highly attracted and attached to Orelia despite the fact that he is unfaithful to her. When Orelia falls in love with Everett Jordan,

John brings Orelia to an island off the coast of Baja, where he spends time rekindling her love for him. Eventually, she responds. When Orelia leaves for a six-month consulting job with her design company, John misses her, then fills the void she leaves with another woman, Belinda. He slowly realizes the mistake in his affair, in that Belinda (and her children) become too attached. One day, he leaves Belinda without a word or explanation, two weeks before Orelia returns. He confesses his affair, thinking that Belinda has revealed it in a letter that turns out to be a list of contacts for Orelia's company.

**Langston** Langston is a friend and perhaps a father figure to Tatala from the time when she lives in New York. She and her lover see him on the street and refuse him a ride. That is the last time they see him before he dies. When Tatala and her husband married, Langston said that she had married her subsidy. Tatala had high regard for his opinion; she and her husband attend his funeral. This character is probably based on Langston Hughes (1902–67), the African-American writer and intellectual.

**Larry** Tatala's husband works for Larry before he meets her. Larry is an arrogant, rich, white graduate from Yale. She is briefly his lover before she begins her relationship with her future husband. Larry is annoyed by Tatala's new relationship, and for a long time, he continues to send her husband on menial tasks like picking up dry cleaning.

**Leonie** A black woman who graduated from Vassar College, Leonie is John's first wife, whom he later divorces.

**Libby** Libby, Marissa's old lover, is domineering and bossy. They end their relationship just before Marissa becomes friends with Hannah.

**Little Sister** Little Sister has a lover who is married. They have a passionate physical and emotional relationship. She finds herself thinking about him all the time even when she is with Big Sister. She and Big Sister's relationship can be described as tense. Big Sister harbors a certain amount of resentment toward Little Sister for being "liberated" without ever having to run away or leave. Little Sister's good nature sometimes frustrates her older sister. Even so, she proves to be rather vulnerable. The resentment seems to go away as Big Sister comforts her.

When Little Sister was a little girl, her mother worked for a white family as their nurse and housekeeper. Little Sister used to play with the white family's daughter, Blaze. One day, when she arrived to play with her friend, she was informed that "Miss" Blaze was not available. She became aware of the stark difference between white "Miss" Blaze and her black self. She was seen as unfit to be Blaze's playmate. She looks back at this with resentment even later in life. She realizes that this moment is perhaps inevitable in any relationship with a white person.

**Little Sister's lover** Little Sister's lover is married with children. He visits Little Sister when he can. The meetings are always passionate, but he leaves almost immediately after they make love. Sometimes they steal some time together to get high and go swimming or lie in the grass. Little Sister thinks about him constantly when he is away.

**Louise** Louise is Belinda's daughter. She and her brother grow increasingly attached to John during his affair with their mother.

**Lover** Her name is never given, but she is Tatala's female lover, mentioned very briefly.

**Marcella** Marcella, Angel, and Sally sit on the edge of a canal, discussing Sally's dream in which Sally replaces Marcella in Angel's arms and Marcella disappears. Marcella is hurt by Sally's apparent disregard for her whereabouts in the dream. While she loves both Sally, her best friend, and Angel, her lover, she seems afraid of the feeling of being out of control. She begins to doubt Angel's substance and even her connection to him. Five years later, after she and Angel have split up, she meets Sally again and she realizes that Sally, perhaps, had helped her see that Angel's insubstantiality had been there all along.

**Marissa** Marissa is a beautiful black lesbian from Brooklyn who is described as shapely and brown, with dreadlocks to her knees. She has just gotten out of a relationship with Libby when she and Hannah become friends. She always clears the dance floor because she is such a good dancer. Hannah meets her after she and her husband, Tripper, divorce and has remained infatuated with her.

**Miss Mary** Hannah remarks that Miss Mary is fashionable. She accompanies Hannah, her mother, and Auntie Fanny Johnson to the adult theater to watch *Deep Throat*. She is unable to fathom how the woman in the pornographic film seemed to be enjoying it so much.

**Ned Bing** Ned Bing is a white activist minister whose house was firebombed and whose face was badly disfigured by members of the Klan. He is a friend of Tatala.

**Orelia Moonsun** Orelia is a black woman with dry, ashy skin; she rubs olive oil on it to keep it moisturized. Orelia worries that her lover, John, will not like the smell, but he ends up loving it. She owns her own company, called Genuine Illusions, which redecorates homes in order to create a certain illusion of nature within urban life. She is honest with John, even though she mistrusts men. She eventually comes to trust and fully love him. She later falls in love with Everett Jordan, a politician, but rekindles her love for John. They often cuddle, physical closeness being a healing component in their relationship. She is emotional and cries easily, and for a while, she becomes increasingly thin.

Orelia was married to but then divorced her husband. She and John began their relationship after John divorced his wife, Leonie. They are highly attached to one another. Despite having sometimes hurt each other, they stay together.

**Our Child** Tatala refers to her child as Our Child. The daughter is never named in the novel. As a child, and while growing up, she does not understand what happened between her parents. She is seven years old when they are divorced. She mediates between them, telling each other stories of their present lives with puzzles on both ends. When she is 25 years old, she arranges a therapy session between herself and her parents.

**Phillip** Phillip is Anne Gray's white husband, from whom she is separated. He is described as good-looking, warm, intelligent, and committed to the struggle for justice for black people.

**Raymond** Raymond is Orelia's loving and supportive brother. Orelia trusted and adored him until he, along with the rest of her brothers, made fun of her ashy skin. She considered it a betrayal and since then has lacked trust in men.

**Raymyna Ann** Raymyna Ann is a former foster child who was under Lily's care. She lives at the house and helps take care of the kids. She is marrying soon, something that Rosa cannot fathom as someone recently divorced.

**Rosa** Rosa is one of Harold and Dianne's children. She is named after Rosa Parks. She eventually becomes a writer, perhaps because of her mother's unfulfilled desires of doing the same, but mostly because she maintains an observant soul that she cannot seem to "switch off." She marries Ivan, a white Jewish lawyer, and later they are divorced. Shortly after their divorce, he marries a white Jewish woman. Rosa and her sister, Barbara, visit their Aunt Lily in Florida. Rosa remarks at the remnants of segregation, and she finds marriage unfathomable and heartbreaking in the wake of her own divorce.

Barbara has usually been a source of comfort to Rosa throughout most of her life. Her sister had been protective of her when she was little, and she of her sister. When their father had beaten Barbara, Rosa had tried to protect her with a butcher knife. As adults, when Barbara's husband beat her, Rosa did not try to protect her. While the sisters are visiting their Aunt Lily, Lily accuses Rosa of twisting the stories of their family around and manipulating what she sees for the purpose of writing. Rosa turns to her sister for support but realizes that Barbara offers none and, in fact, shares their aunt's opinion of her.

Rosa realizes that she has a kindred spirit in her dead grandfather. He had always been silent, seemingly tolerant, but increasingly detached as he lived with Lily. Rosa realizes that he, too, felt Lily's opposition to a kind of observant nature—that he, too, could not "switch off." He did not write his observations down; instead, Rosa suspects he may have replayed them in his head, thought things instead of actually writing. She takes one of his hats to wear, and she likes how she looks in it. She thinks that she resembles her grandfather.

**Sally** Sally dreams that her friend Marcella is hit by a white Peugeot and that she replaces Marcella's in Angel's arms as a lover. Sally tells the dream to her friend but fails to realize that it will hurt her. They are only able to repair their friendship five years later. At this point, Sally is a grandmother. She inadvertently allows Marcella to see that Angel was perhaps insubstantial as a person and lover.

**Sheila** Sheila is Ivan's second wife. Rosa believes that Sheila regards her relationship to Ivan as a triumph.

**Suni** Suni is a white woman with red hair and green eyes who is married to Jason, Anne's lover. The three of them rent a cabin near the coast down the road from Big Sur. The three of them are in perhaps a slightly polygamist, free-love situation. Suni and Anne are good friends and perhaps share similar beliefs in the mystical quality of the world. Suni is also attracted to Anne. She is committed to the struggle to change society and eradicate racism.

**Tatala** Tatala is the first-person narrator of the novel's first section. She is an African-American woman with a triracial heritage: African, Native American, and European. She looks back at her marriage to her husband, living in Mississippi when it was dangerous and illegal for an interracial couple. She describes their love as having "made them bulletproof" and says that despite their being surrounded by hatred, they felt impervious and happy. Their relationship becomes increasingly lonely and declines when they move to Brooklyn. They buy a dilapidated house in Brooklyn to renovate, and their savings from the books that she has written and the shares from his law firm go into paying for the renovations, and they are slowly worn thin. Eight years into their marriage, they divorce. They have a daughter who mediates between them after their divorce.

At the time that Tatala is recalling their marriage, she is in a relationship with a female lover who remains unnamed. Since their divorce, both she and her husband have experienced financial and professional success. She and her ex-husband are reunited years later in one of their daughter's therapy sessions. They discuss their relationship meaningfully for the first time since their split with a general lack of understanding as to why they divorced, despite their strong bonds of love.

Perhaps what is notable about this section is that it most closely resembles Alice Walker's marriage to Melvyn Leventhal, who was a civil rights lawyer in Mississippi when they met. Tatala can be considered an autobiographical figure.

**Tatala's husband** *See* HUSBAND.

**therapist** This character is Tatala's daughter's therapist. She is a middle-aged refugee from Latvia with a thoughtful face and a faint accent. Her body language immediately puts Tatala at ease, and she wonders if someone like this therapist would have benefited her past marriage to her husband.

**Tripper** Tripper is Hannah's ex-husband. He does not dance. Eventually, their sexual rhythm becomes dominated by Tripper's needs, and Hannah's desires for Tripper disappear.

**Uncle Brother** Uncle Brother is Hannah's uncle and her father's brother. He is a member of the Brotherhood of the Saved, and he is dying. The Brotherhood comes to pray at his house; this terrifies him. He has disowned his homosexual son, Harry, and presents a decidedly weary demeanor toward Hannah, who is bisexual.

**Uncle Loaf** Uncle Loaf did exactly that—he loafed around the house, chewing his tobacco, sitting in his chair, seemingly relaxed and carefree in contrast to Auntie Putt-Putt, who constantly did house chores and puttered around the house. Big Sister noticed the problematic nature of the dynamic between the couple. Most of her life, she has longed to be as relaxed and carefree as Uncle Loaf; she hid behind his chair, chewing on tobacco when she ran away. But she realizes that she was never like him.

### Further Reading

Billingley, Sarah. "'*The Way Forward Is with a Broken Heart*' by Alice Walker. Alice Walker's 'Way Forward' is A Step Backward." *Post-Gazette* 10 December 2000, E-11.

News-Horst, Adele S. "*The Way Forward Is with a Broken Heart.*" *World Literature Today* 75, no. 2 (Spring 2001): 335–336.

## *You Can't Keep a Good Woman Down* (1981)

Although the reviews for Walker's second collection of short stories were not as consistently positive as were those for her earlier collection, *In Love & Trouble* (1973), this book is generally considered to be excellent. The 14 stories in the collection reflect many of Walker's central concerns, engaging topics as wide-ranging as the relationship between black and white popular music and musicians, the memories and legacies of slavery, pornography, abortion, and the complexities of interracial friendships and romantic relationships.

### "Nineteen Fifty-Five"

"Nineteen Fifty-Five" begins with the reader's encounters with the characters Deacon and Traynor, who come to Gracie Mae Still's house looking to buy a song from her. Gracie is an African-American woman songwriter and singer. She is a family-oriented person who is not materialistic. Traynor is an Elvis-like character who performs Gracie's song after Deacon buys it. The song becomes a big hit and establishes Traynor as a major singing star. In spite of the song's success, Traynor does not understand its meaning.

As the story progresses, the reader encounters a very rich Traynor who, in spite of his success, does not seem to enjoy his life. Traynor makes a lot of money from singing Gracie's song, but he never understands its significance. He wants to understand it.

Traynor gives Gracie several material possessions, including a Cadillac and a new house. After he makes all of his money, he takes care of Gracie and her family from afar, sending them money. Traynor seems to feel guilty about getting famous from singing a song that was never his and that he never understood. He is responsible for getting Gracie on the *Tonight Show* to sing her song. Traynor dies never having figured out the complexities of his relationship with Gracie and the secret of his success.

#### COMMENTARY

"Nineteen Fifty-Five" is one of Alice Walker's most frequently anthologized and best-known stories. It derives in part from Walker's fascination with ELVIS PRESLEY, a figure she finds of interest as a result of his negotiation of American racial boundaries.

The story provides Walker with a vehicle to explore her interest in the multivalent currents that continue to surround Elvis and his legacy and times. Walker's intention with the invocation of 1955 in the story's title may have been to focus readers' attention on the racial turbulence that was a part of the history of that year.

In 1955, the racism that so defined the African-American experience came to the surface in dramatic and public ways. The post–World War II wave of consumerism, and the rise of popular culture presented a powerful and peculiarly American tension. In 1955, General Motors was the richest company in the world. Marian Anderson became the first black person to perform at the Metropolitan Opera. Rosa Parks was arrested. Emmett Till was murdered at the age of 14 in Money, Mississippi. Disneyland opened. The first McDonald's opened. The Montgomery Bus Boycott began, and Elvis Presley first appeared on film. These seemingly isolated events are not unrelated, but the relationships they reveal are not linear. They are rooted in the convoluted and disordered histories of American slavery, cultural production, and racial segregation and discrimination.

The relationship of Walker's central characters—the white popular cultural singer and icon, Traynor, and the African-American woman who is a source of his success, Gracie Mae Still—is the subject of her story. Through her exploration of the interactions between this unlikely pair, Walker is able to obliquely traverse the culture currents of 1955 and expose some of the tension that is fundamental to those occurrences.

Throughout their relationship, Traynor is unable to understand the song that Gracie Mae has given to him, although his raw talents allow him to be able to represent her artistry in a form that is palatable to the audiences who come to adore him. Although Traynor attempts to repay Gracie, he does not understand what she has given him and therefore does not feel satisfied with the inequity in their relationship.

Ironically, what Traynor most lacks is a voice. Although he has the gift of song, the song he sings literally does not belong to him; thus, what he sings is someone else's message. Walker uses this relationship to represent what she seems to suggest is typical of the historical realities of racial dynamics in the United States. At the risk of descending into essentialism, Walker implies that Gracie's song represents an ineffable entity that Traynor lack—soul.

Through her explorations of this relationship, Walker is able to demonstrate the interrelationship between seemingly unrelated aspects of American culture and to suggest that the birth of post–World War II American culture has its roots in the same kinds of exploitation and invisibility as was true during earlier periods of American history. Without knowing it, Gracie Mae's composition is the song that America sings.

## "How Did I Get Away with Killing One of the Biggest Lawyers in the State? It Was Easy"

In this story the central action concerns the relative freedom that white men have to violate black women sexually. One of the main characters in the short story is Bubba, a highly successful white lawyer who is married and has children. Bubba is responsible for raping the speaker when she is 14 years old and continues to abuse the girl for two more years. His father, the most prominent lawyer in town, supports segregation. Bubba tries to silence the girl by giving her money. In spite of her rape, the story's narrator seems rather complacent about her experience. When she is 17, she puts her mother in an insane asylum because her mother disapproves of her daughter's "relationship" with Bubba.

The narrator's mother is a nervous woman who works in white homes as a maid. The woman blames her daughter for seducing a white man. When she is incarcerated in the insane asylum, the mother receives shock treatment, and so she actually does lose her mind. She dies by the time her daughter recognizes that her mother is actually sane and was right about the exploitative nature of her daughter's relationship with Bubba.

After her mother dies, the narrator kills Bubba and never gets caught. She ends up babysitting for Bubba's children while his wife goes to his funeral.

## "Elethia"

"Elethia" is a complex commentary on slavery and the way in which the memory of the experience is commodified and exploited. Elethia is the story's central character, who carries about an apothecary jar of ashes. The reader learns how she comes to carry this odd item.

Elethia works in a restaurant that has in its window a figure that she thinks is a dummy until she discovers that it is really the stuffed body of Uncle Albert. The Old Timers who frequent the restaurant recount stories of the real Uncle Albert, who was born into slavery and kept ignorant of the law.

Old Man is the owner of the restaurant where Elethia works; he was also the owner of a plantation. When Old Man opens the restaurant, he places in the window the stuffed, preserved body of Uncle Albert, a caricature of a stereotypical old southern black man. Old Man does not allow black people to eat in the restaurant with the dummy of a black man in the window.

Elethia breaks into the restaurant with her best friends and steals the body, which they then burn in their school's incinerator. After this, Elethia becomes paranoid. Albert becomes an iconographic image of oppression in Elethia's mind. The reader discovers that the jar Elethia carries is full of Albert's ashes.

## "The Lover"

The short story "The Lover" is about a 31-year-old poet who leaves her husband to go to a poetry retreat. The poet, who remains nameless in the story, is tall, confident, and attractive. She is married to a man who works as a teacher and who is generally respectful of his wife. Although she has had a child with her husband, at the beginning of the story she feels no passion for either of them. The poet hates boastfulness and tries not to make her life her art.

Ellis is a man who attends the retreat, where he becomes the poet's lover. He is in his 40s, nearly 10 years older than the poet. She finds that Ellis talks a lot about himself. She also comes to believe that he does make his life his art. The poet has great sex with Ellis and just wants to feel in love, but she ends up fantasizing about her husband. Ellis wants to send the poet's child to boarding school. The encounter leaves the poet disappointed and largely unsatisfied.

## "Petunias"

In Walker's short story "Petunias," she uses the format of the diary to chronicle the experiences of the mother of a young man who has returned from fighting in Vietnam. During the story, she finds the bones of her great-grandmother, who was a slave, while gardening in her petunia bed.

## "Coming Apart"

The story "Coming Apart" features two main characters, a married couple who are not named. The two have a dispute about pornography. The husband is a black man who obsesses over porn magazines that contain photographs of white women. He takes his wife to 42nd Street in New York City and shows her prostitutes and plastic blow-up doll sex toys. He is aroused by the objects, while she finds herself disgusted. He thinks that consuming pornography is freedom.

The wife in the story is insulted by the pornography but remains largely oppressed and quiet. Although she fights with her husband about his addiction to pornography, she continues to sleep with him. The two come closer to each other's position on pornography after the husband has a revelation when she reads him an essay.

## "Fame"

The central character of this story is Andrea Clement White, who is married to William Litz White, a doctor. She is a famous older woman and is falsely humble. She has spent her life working as a writer, and she hates ignorance. When Andrea Clement White goes to speak as a guest at her alma mater, she encounters several sexist old men whom she has always hated. White does not want to speak until a young girl starts to sing an old slave song in the auditorium. The song inspires Andrea to speak and the audience to be silent.

## "The Abortion"

The central characters of "The Abortion" are the couple Clarence and Imani. Clarence works as a lawyer for, and is dedicated to, the mayor, with whose politics Imani disagrees. Clarence patronizes Imani and thinks she knows nothing about politics.

At the beginning of the story, Imani has already had one miscarriage, and she had one abortion in college. The couple have a child named Clarice. Imani is pregnant, and she and Clarence are not sure they want to have another child. Imani is unhappy in the marriage. She gets an abortion in New York for $1,000 but hemorrhages after the procedure and is ill from it for a year. She feels empty. Two years after Imani gets her second abortion, Clarence has a vasectomy, but their marriage falls apart anyway. Clarence resents Imani. By the end of the story, the marriage between Imani and Clarence is over.

## "Porn"

The main characters in "Porn" are not named. The story takes place in the 1970s and flips between scenes of pornographic sex and erotic sex. The male and female protagonists meet in Tanzania and have a great sexual connection. Both are divorced with kids. They find each other after years of not being with anyone.

He is characterized as abstract and scientistic. After sex one morning, he wants to show her his porn collection. She wants more than abstraction from the relationship and finds women more interesting than men. The story ends with the man fantasizing about the porn while the couple have sex, and neither of them enjoy the experience.

## "Advancing Luna—and Ida B. Wells"

In this story, the two central characters—the unnamed narrator and her friend Luna—work together in a highly segregated town in the South. Luna is described as white and passive. Physically, she has acne and is flat-chested. Luna comes from a very rich family. The narrator is black and grows up believing that black people are superior to all others. She is drawn to the idea of contrast. The narrator is writing the story, and she writes two endings.

The narrator and Luna work in the South to register people to vote. While they are there, they live with a middle-aged couple and their young, school-aged daughter. It is risky for the women to be living with the family because of segregation. The girls are working to advance the goals of the CIVIL RIGHTS MOVEMENT.

After their experience in the South, the two live together in Brooklyn and become good friends. In the interim between her experiences in the South and in the North, the narrator travels to Uganda. When she returns to the United States and to Brooklyn, she is evicted. Luna lives in a run-down, two-bedroom apartment in Brooklyn and allows the narrator to live with her when the narrator is evicted. During the time they live together, Luna tells the narrator that she was raped when they were in the South for a summer. When the narrator learns this, she is conflicted about whether or not to write about it. She starts to wonder if it really happened and thinks about the stereotypes about black men who rape white women.

In the story's first ending, Luna sleeps with Freddie, the man who raped her, before she leaves for Goa, and the girls split up. The second ending portrays Freddie as a pitiful representative of the movement and depicts him talking with Luna rather than having sex the night he stays over. In the postscript to the story, the narrator provides the perspective of an additional male character, a man the narrator calls "Our Muralist." This person suggests to the narrator that Freddie may have been paid to rape Luna.

### COMMENTARY

"Advancing Luna—and Ida B. Wells" has not received as much critical examination as some of Walker's other short stories. The narrative is structurally complex and does not have a definitive resolution. Although it is a short story, the tale contains elements of other literary genres, including the memoir and the nonfiction essay.

In addition to the complications of its structure and categorization, "Advancing Luna—and Ida B. Wells" has the additional historical and ideological weight of its subject matter, interracial relationships and rape. The story attempts to parse the "facts" of the rape through its central characters, young women who are friends. One of the women, the narrator, is African American and is from the South, while the other woman is white and is from the North. The two live together following time spent working as activists.

The story's drama derives from questions about the rape of the white woman, Luna. As with Walker's novel *Meridian*, "Advancing Luna—and Ida B. Wells" raises often unexamined questions about the racial and gender politics, dynamics, and internal divisions within the Civil Rights movement. Walker was in the process of composing *Meridian* when she wrote and published "Advancing Luna—and Ida B. Wells."

The multiple readings that are suggested throughout the story are often in conflict and contradict each other. As such, the structure of the narrative replicates the difficulties of communication within a group that consists of individuals, who, although hypothetically engaged in a common struggle, have unique perspectives, motivations, and values.

The story also reveals the complications of negotiating DOUBLE CONSCIOUSNESS. As a consequence of her engagement with the complexities of Luna's story, the black female narrator, who remains nameless throughout the story, is in a position of having to choose between loyalty to parts of her identity as either a woman or as a black person.

This complexity leads to an intertextual reference in the narrative. The narrator writes of her conundrum and shares it as a kind of confessional to the turn-of-the-century activist Ida B. Wells. She writes:

> Whenever inter-racial rape is mentioned, a black woman's first thought is to protect the lives of her brothers, her father, her sons, her lover. A history of lynching has bred this reflex in her. I feel it as strongly as anyone. While writing a fictional account of such a rape in a novel, I read Ida B. Wells's autobiography three times, as a means of praying to her.

Ida B. Wells (1862–1931) was known for her antilynching activism. By invoking her, the narrator demonstrates the stakes of her moral dilemma and substantiates her inability to casually or dispassionately assess Luna's claim. "Advancing Luna—and Ida B. Wells" is one of Walker's most structurally and thematically sophisticated works and does not allow for easy or reductive conclusions. With this short story, she provides the reader with a simultaneous glance into the heart of American racial solidarity and discord.

## "Laurel"

The central characters in "Laurel" are Annie and Laurel, who meet while working at *First Rebel,* a radical antiracism newspaper. They are immediately attracted to one another. Laurel is described as a dorky 22-year-old southern, sly, white guy with a bowl cut. Annie, the narrator, is a 20-year-old black female. When she meets Laurel, she is engaged. Annie goes to Africa and breaks up with her fiancé because he has slept with a 10-year-old while he has been there on an assignment with the Peace Corps. While she is away, Annie does not hear from Laurel. She becomes depressed.

Laurel's wife writes to Annie, telling her that Laurel has been in a car accident and is in a coma. She asks Annie to come see Laurel. When Annie gets the letter, she goes to see Laurel but fails to rouse him.

When Laurel wakes from his coma two years later, he writes to Annie. She is happily married by the time she hears from him. He becomes obsessed with her, writing to Annie repeatedly. Eventually, he goes to see her, although she tells him she is happily married with a daughter. Seven years later, Annie divorces her husband, and Laurel divorces his wife.

## "A Letter of the Times, or Should This Sado-Masochism Be Saved?"

This story is told through a letter written by the narrator, Susan Marie, to another character, named Lucy, who is the subject of the letter. Susan writes to Lucy about an event they both attended, the Elected Official's Ball. At the ball, Lucy was dressed as Scarlett O'Hara and consequently deeply upset Susan Marie. Susan Marie snubbed Lucy at the ball, and she is writing the letter to tell her why. She also tells Lucy about her belief in each person's innate ability to know God.

Susan Marie writes to Lucy that everything she taught her students about the true condition of enslavement was nullified by an image of a white woman and black woman enacting a master/slave fantasy. Susan Marie suggests the two of them get together to organize a ball to raise awareness about the topic.

## "A Sudden Trip Home in the Spring"

The story "A Sudden Trip Home in the Spring" features the central character Sarah Davis. Sarah has a white friend, Pam, who is described as very rich and "horsey." Sarah is an African-American native of Georgia. She is popular and tall. In addition to Pam, Sarah has lots of friends who admire her in superficial ways. Sarah paints, but only pictures of black women. She feels that she cannot paint black men because she sees the figure of a black man as defeated.

Sarah was very young when her mother died. Consequently, Sarah is close to the men in her family. She doubts that she has made the right choice about her education and feels out of place. She is the only black person enrolled at her college.

Sarah receives a telegram containing the news that her father is dead. She returns home for the funeral and is comforted by her grandfather. Sarah is very close to her grandfather. He is remarkably strong emotionally and does not cry at his son's funeral. After the funeral, she dedicates herself to "making her grandfather up in stone," as he has instructed. Sarah's brother reassures Sarah that she has made the right decisions about college and her life.

## "Source"

"Source" is about Anastasia Green, her friend Irene, and a character named Source. Anastasia and Irene attended an unnamed New York college, where they became friends. Anastasia transforms through various stages of appearance, falls in love a few times, moves a lot, and ends up living with a hippie couple whose names are Calm and Peace. Their baby is called Bliss. Anastasia has become a hippie as well. Calm and Peace give her Bliss, their baby. While living in San Francisco, Anastasia does not think change is possible in society, until she meets Source.

Source becomes a guru for Anastasia and the couple she lives with in San Francisco. She helps to get Anastasia back in touch with her parents, who are Jehovah's Witnesses. Source teaches that children do not belong to anyone in particular but to everyone. She has three daughters of her own. She does not work but is a "teacher."

In the years since college, Irene has worked teaching rural farm women to read and write. Her classroom is a trailer. She loses her position when the federal funding supporting her schooling ends. Irene goes to visit Anastasia in San Francisco. She resents Anastasia's lifestyle there and questions her friend's place in society and her impact on it. Irene is suspicious of the hippie lifestyle.

Anastasia thinks that Irene is too serious. She says that in San Francisco, Source teaches her that the good life requires embracing indifference. Anastasia asks Irene to leave because Irene does not approve of Anastasia's choices.

Years later, Anastasia and Irene reunite in Alaska and forgive one another. Anastasia still denies her race and struggles to find her identity between white and black. She is living with an Alaskan native. When the two reunite, Irene has been married and divorced. In the end, Anastasia and Irene reflect on the impact of race on their experiences and their relationship in college and beyond. They talk about their common goal of creating an egalitarian, multiracial community. The old friends hug good-bye and part on good terms.

### Further Reading

Johnson, Maria V. "'You Just Can't Keep a Good Woman Down': Alice Walker Sings the Blues." *African American Review* 30, no. 2 (Summer 1996): 221–237.

Mays, Jackie Douglas. "'Nineteen Fifty-Five': A Second Opinion." *Journal of College Writing* 4, no. 1 (2001): 103–106.

Mickelsen, David J. "'You Ain't Never Caught a Rabbit: Covering and Signifyin' in Alice Walker's 'Nineteen Fifty-Five.'" *Southern Quarterly: A Journal of the Arts in the South* 42, no. 3 (Spring) 2004: 5–20.

Petry, Alice Hall. "Alice Walker: The Achievement of the Short Fiction." *Modern Language Studies* 19, no. 1 (Winter 1989): 12–27.

Pollitt, Katha. "Stretching the Short Story: Review *You Can't Keep a Good Woman Down*" *New York Times*, 24 May 1981, A9.

# Poetry Collections and Selected Individual Poems

## *Absolute Trust in the Goodness of the Earth: New Poems* (2003)

In the introduction to her poetry collection *Absolute Trust in the Goodness of the Earth,* Alice Walker shares with readers the healing role that poetry plays in her life. She writes that she did not expect to continue writing and publishing but has found herself unrepentantly moved to compose the poems that comprise this volume. In the wake of 9/11, Walker's poems here attempt to divine some lessons for the country and the world through her efforts to examine the conflicts at the heart of the attack as well as other contemporary complications and calamities. The poems' truncated structure and brevity provide opportunities for a lay reader to contemplate the concerns and issues Walker addresses.

### Further Reading

Ellis, Kelly Norman. "*Absolute Trust in the Goodness of the Earth.*" *Black Issues Book Review* (March–April 2003): 38.

## "ballad of the brown girl" (1968)

This poem was published in the collection *Once.* Walker has written that she feels "ballad of the brown girl" is unsuccessful. The title of the poem alludes to another poem by the African-American Harlem Renaissance writer Countee Cullen (1903–46), who was a strong proponent of traditional poetic conventions. Through this allusion, Walker may have been making a statement about the ability of various genres of poetry with different structures to convey a similar message.

The title invokes the traditional ballad form. A ballad is generally a narrative and, in its earliest incarnations, was often set to music. Most often, ballads are written in quatrains. Walker's "ballad of the brown girl" is a narrative and has four stanzas. It tells of a young girl who seeks an abortion and is rebuked by the physician from whom she seeks the procedure. Written before abortion was legal in the United States, the poem takes as its subject many complicated, difficult, and then taboo subjects such as premarital sexuality, abortion, disparity of resources, suicide, intergenerational communication, and interracial sexuality.

The poem is written in free verse, and Walker sets certain key terms at a different margin in order to emphasize their significance. Particularly important in this regard is the word *question.* The poem hinges on certain questions that remain unresolved until the conclusion. The protagonist finds herself pregnant, and when she seeks an abortion, not only is she short of the necessary funds, she is also admonished by the doctor to talk to her parents to see if they might be persuade her to keep her unborn child.

The last stanza of the poem reveals the probable root of the woman's decision to commit suicide as the reader learns that the father of the baby is white, making the pregnancy impossible from the young black woman's perspective. The revelation of this information at the poem's conclusion helps to create narrative tension and to hold the reader's interest.

## "Be Nobody's Darling" (1973)

Although it is more structured than many other Walker poems, "Be Nobody's Darling" (published in the collection *Revolutionary Petunias*) has become a kind of signature for Walker. The poem is an instructive piece organized in four stanzas that examine self-awareness and self-discovery.

A theme that is a common feature throughout much of Walker's work is the struggle against conformity, particularly as that process occurs for women. Walker consistently urges women to assert their individuality outside the constraint of the traditional roles assigned them. The poem "Be Nobody's Darling" takes as its starting point the nickname *darling,* which, for the narrator, has connotations of submission, self-effacement, and infantilization.

From its opening lines, which repeat several times throughout the poem, the narrator affirms that there is a price to be paid for the refusal to acquiesce to the traditional stereotypes that outline what it means to be an adult woman. This assertion is made with the poem's opening lines: "Be nobody's darling: / Be an outcast." From the poem's beginning, the narrator establishes that the refusal to narrow one's horizons will probably result in ostracism.

Throughout the remainder of the poem, the primary images are evocative of that outsider position and also suggest strategies for surviving the attendant isolation. For example, in the first stanza, the narrator offers the possibility that the contradictions that she sees as inherent to the status of outcast can be employed as "a shawl, / To parry stones / To keep you warm."

Similarly, in the second stanza, the narrator outlines the pleasures that might be found in understanding one's outsider position as akin to lining "the crowded / River beds." The third stanza continues this theme by suggesting that this struggle carries with it a kind of nobility, even martyrdom.

In the refusal to "Be nobody's darling," the narrator claims that living an honest, uncompromised life is worth sacrifice, even death, as one tries to remain true to one's principles. The poem ends with the assertion that such an uncompromising life leads to reverence worthy of that earned by honorable ancestors: "Be an outcast. / Qualified to live / Among your dead."

## "Did This Happen to Your Mother? Did Your Sister Throw Up a Lot?" (1979)

This poem was published in the collection *Good Night, Willie Lee, I'll See You in the Morning: Poems.* It is about the price women pay when they love men who, to quote her opening line, are "not worth [their] love." The poem suggests that this situation is not only personal for the narrator but is epidemic among women of all generations.

Love is often the subject of poetry, but here Walker writes about it as a phenomenon that has potentially fatal consequences. She states overtly that "Love has made me sick." She extrapolates this pathology to her family and to other women as she asks, "Did your aunt always / seem to have something else / troubling her mind?"

The deleterious impacts of love are also represented by images of destructive weeds, the void of the Grand Canyon, and the impulse toward murder. The poem also equates this toxic love with the act of silencing. It ends with the lines "And I will never / unclench my teeth long enough / to tell him so."

## *Good Night, Willie Lee, I'll See You in the Morning: Poems* (1979)

Alice Walker has written that, at her father's funeral, she heard her mother whisper into her father's coffin the words "Good night, Willie Lee, I'll see you in the morning." From this line, which suggests a firm belief in the fluidity of experience and a dismissal of the permanence of the feelings of loss experienced when a loved one dies, Walker constructed her third volume of poetry. The collection addresses the inevitability of change and transformation in human experience—in matters of life and death, in one's experiential perceptions, and in interpersonal relationships.

The acceptance of change that her mother modeled for Walker at her father's funeral is the controlling stance of the narrator of the poems in *Good Night, Willie Lee, I'll See You in the Morning: Poems.* Walker reflects on the fundamental need for human connections and also demonstrates the potential hazards this need generates, particularly for women, who she posits are more vulnerable to abuse and exploitation. Walker also ponders the relationship between the personal and the societal, examining literary figures and characters who are significant to her, as well as iconographic political leaders and activists.

All of the questions that are raised by the poems in the volume seem to coalesce in a difficult but straightforward need for honest acceptance of the reality of what happens in one's life. They also endeavor to couple that acceptance with forgiveness toward the perpetrators of wrongs or transgressions.

### Further Reading

Griffin, Susan. "The Way of All Ideology." *Feminist Theory* 7, no. 3 (Spring 1982): 641–660.

Walker, Alice. "Good Night, Willie Lee, I'll See You in the Morning." *Iowa Review* 6, no. 2 (Spring 1975): 2–3.

## *Hard Times Require Furious Dancing* (2010)

In October of 2010, Walker released this new book of poems, some of which can be found on her Web site, www.alicewalkersgarden.com. *Publishers Weekly,* noting that Walker's "poetic goals are more inspirational than literary," declared that her "many fans won't be disappointed by this book." *Booklist* called the poems "powerful anthems of womanhood and age."

### Further Reading

Walker, Alice. *Alice Walker's Garden: Her Words.* Available online. URL: http://www.alicewalkersgarden.com/alicewalkerpoems.html. Accessed January 3, 2010.

## *Her Blue Body Everything We Know: Earthling Poems 1965–1990 Complete* (1991)

This collection of Walker's poems is a compilation of all of the published poems she wrote in the years between 1965 and 1990. The collection also includes 16 new, previously unpublished poems. With the poems collected in this comprehensive format, *Her Blue Body Everything We Know: Earthling Poems 1965–1990 Complete* presents a unique opportunity to review Walker's poetic voice and creative trajectory as a unit.

### Further Reading

Oktenberg, Adrian T. "Review: Revolutionary Contradictions. *Her Blue Body Everything We Know: Earthling Poems 1965–1990.*" *Women's Review of Books* 9, no. 3 (December 1991): 24–25.

## *Horses Make a Landscape Look More Beautiful* (1984)

This poetry collection expands on themes that are fundamental to Walker's artistic mission: the impact of racial and gender oppression, the ways in which the oppressive *and* joyous experiences of the individual also resonate with the problems of the collective, the consequences of inhumanity, and the destruction of the natural world. Structurally, her poems retain the distinctive, short phrasing that makes Walker's poetry recognizable. Her conversational approach allows the poems in this collection to serve as a kind of homage to the complexity of the Lakota quotation from which Walker extracted the title. The quotation acknowledges that, along with the near destruction Europeans brought with them to the New World, they also brought the horse, which was a gift and "made the landscape look more beautiful."

In *Horse Make a Landscape Look More Beautiful,* Walker uses the knowledge she has acquired through examination and experience to express her response to the bifurcation of the whole. As she reconciles her personal schisms in these brief narrative sketches, she attempts to present the reader with ways to bring together the divisions that, from her perspective, prevent wholeness.

### Further Reading

Keefe, J. T. "Review: *Horses Make a Landscape Look More Beautiful* by Alice Walker." *World Literature Today* 60, no. 1 (Winter 1986): 118.

## "Janie Crawford" (1991)

This poem was published in the collection *Her Blue Body Everything We Know*. Throughout her work, Alice Walker repeatedly affirms the centrality of ZORA NEALE HURSTON's novel *Their Eyes Were Watching God* to her own writing and life (Janie Crawford is the novel's protagonist). Walker is perhaps the person most responsible for rescuing Hurston's work from obscurity in the 1970s. The poem "Janie Crawford" is a tribute to the fictional figure who was so inspirational to her.

In the poem, Walker positions Hurston's protagonist Janie Crawford as a role model for healthy living. The poem highlights Janie's qualities of self-determination and endurance in the face of tribulation. What the narrator admires most about Janie Crawford is her independence of spirit, as embodied by her ability to leave "her husbands" because they did not allow her to fulfill her potential. Borrowing on Hurston's determination to assert that a woman, particularly a black woman, "is neither a mule / nor a queen / though she may suffer / and like a queen pace / the floor," Walker reinforces the novel's instructive qualities.

## *Once: Poems* (1968)

While a student at SARAH LAWRENCE COLLEGE in New York, Alice Walker was encouraged to express herself in writing. Her creative endeavors were mentored and developed by two women who would prove pivotal to her later success: HELEN LYND and MURIEL RUKEYSER. Walker took Lynd's philosophy course and credits her with making the works of the great philosophers accessible. In Rukeyser's class, Walker learned the craft of poetry, and Rukeyser also provided the young writer with access to avenues for publication. These were the positive and sustaining aspects of Walker's experience at Sarah Lawrence.

On the other end of the spectrum were her personal tribulations. While Walker was a student, she became pregnant. She agonized over her problem and felt that having an abortion was the best recourse for her in light of her circumstances. After the abortion, she plunged into a depression so bleak that she considered committing suicide. Rather than succumbing to self-destruction, she channeled her conflicted feelings into her writings. The book of poems that resulted, *Once*, eventually became her first book publication.

In addition to chronicling her personal problems, Walker's book of poetry examines the issues that surround the CIVIL RIGHTS MOVEMENT and the relationship between the antiracism activism that was occurring simultaneously in both the United States and in Africa. Walker had access to these comparisons as a result of her travel to Africa as a student in the early 1960s. Ultimately, the book and its poems are an affirmation of life yet present an honest examination of its struggles and hardships.

### Further Reading

Bloom, Harold, ed. *Alice Walker: Modern Critical Views*. New York: Chelsea House Publishers, 1989.

Christian, Barbara. "Alice Walker: The Black Woman Artist as Wayward." In *Black Women Writers (1950–1980)*, edited by Mari Evans, 457–477. New York: Anchor, 1984.

## "Poem at Thirty-Nine" (1984)

This poem was published in the collection *Horses Make a Landscape Look More Beautiful*. One of Alice Walker's fundamental assertions in her work is the primacy of the relationship between the living and the dead. When she turned 39, she became interested in the birthday as a kind of transition and used it as a springboard for reflection in this poem.

"Poem at Thirty-Nine" is a kind of elegy for Walker's father, Willie Lee Walker. She tries to enter into the particular experience of her father's life, mourning the fact that he was "so tired / when [she] was born." This exhaustion limited Walker's ability to access a multidimensional perspective of her father.

What the poem recalls are the details about her father that Walker uses to flesh out his humanity. It is the mundane and ordinary aspects of life that recall the man to her. "Writing deposit slips and checks / I think of him. / He taught me how." Of great significance to Walker is the information that she garnered from her father's example: "He taught me / that telling the truth / did not always mean / a beating; though many of my truths / must have grieved him / before the end." This stanza exposes the complexities of the lessons she derived from her father. Although they had great value to her, the lessons came with a price both for her and for him. Though his example taught his daughter to be honest, he was not always comfortable with the truths she found in her own life explorations.

In spite of these differences, Walker exclaims that she misses her father and wishes that he had had the opportunity to see and experience her present self. She finds echoes of her father in her own behavior. "Now I look and cook just like him: / my brain light; / tossing this and that / into the pot; seasoning none of my life / the same way twice; happy to feed / whoever strays my way."

Walker supposes that her father would "have grown / to admire / the woman I've become" and finds, through the poem, not only resolution of the angst of the past but resolution about aging and posthumous acceptance from her father.

## *Poem Traveled Down My Arm: Poems and Drawings, A* (2003)

*A Poem Traveled Down My Arm: Poems and Drawings* is a slim volume that employs a rather experimental form that Walker uses to express very brief observations about human experience and relationships. The book's content varies between simple language and drawings that express her belief in the power of connection to generate creativity and positivity.

According to the critic Gerri Bates, the idea for the short text came from Walker's experiences signing autographs. Rather than making the exercise a repetitive monotonous task, Walker chose to individualize the signatures with small, unique drawings. This experience led her to collect some of her drawings and expressions into a publication—an effort that became *A Poem Traveled Down My Arm: Poems and Drawings.*

### Further Reading

Bates, Gerri. *Alice Walker: A Critical Companion.* Santa Barbara, Calif.: Greenwood Press, 2006.

## "Revolutionary Petunias" (1973)

This poem was the title poem of its collection. One of the features that has made Walker's poetry consistently popular throughout her career is its accessibility, coupled with its insight into the lives of those individuals whose stories are not often the subject of literature. In "Revolutionary Petunias," Walker takes a woman's story that might have been simplistically interpreted and therefore misunderstood and turns it inside out. Her poetic rendering of the tale gives it a subtle nuance and subjectivity not experienced in other, more objective accounts. This poem is unusual for Walker in that it begins with a rhyme. Throughout, there are references to the ballad form. Walker seems to claim a kind of heroic stance for her protagonist.

Sammy Lou, the poem's central figure, has killed the man who murdered her husband. In the tradition of the ballad, this act of revenge would be justified; however, in the context of her life as a poor southern woman, Sammy Lou finds herself cast as a villain and a criminal. The narrator rewrites this reading of the woman's act through the title's invocation of the word *revolution.* For the narrator, Sammy Lou is a revolutionary in the vein of "a George, / a Martha / a Jackie and a Kennedy." By referencing these figures, the narrator enables reconsideration and rereading of the situation and circumstances of Sammy Lou, who, as she departs for the electric chair labeled as a danger to society, leaves the narrator with the lines,

"Don't yall forgit to *water* / my purple petunias." These lines reassures the reader that the impulse toward revolution will not end with this woman's execution and also makes self-evident the reasons why the struggle must continue.

## *Revolutionary Petunias & Other Poems* (1973)

Alice Walker published her second book of poetry, *Revolutionary Petunias & Other Poems,* in 1973. Much had happened in her life in the years between the publication of her first book of poetry, *Once,* in 1968 and *Revolutionary Petunias.* In the interval, Walker met and married her husband, MELVYN LEVENTHAL, and the couple spent most of the early years of their married life in Mississippi, battling racism, discrimination, and segregation in separate but overlapping ways. The couple also gave birth to their only child, REBECCA WALKER.

*Revolutionary Petunias* reflects the impact of these experiences. It is in this collection of poems that Walker most fully engages with the nuances and complexities of her southern roots. She also confronts some of the realities of what it means on a subjective level to embrace and fight for political and social change. Her literary efforts in her second poetry collection were rewarded with her receipt of the Lillian Smith Book Award in 1973.

### Further Reading

Barge, Laura. "Changing Forms of the Pastoral in Southern Poetry." *Southern Literary Journal* 26, no. 1 (Fall 1993): 30–41.

Oktenberg, Adrian. "Review: Revolutionary Contradictions." *Women's Review of Books* 9, no. 3 (December 1991): 24–25.

## "suicide" (1968)

This poem was published in *Once,* Walker's first book of poetry. She has said that these poems were in many ways a reflection of her experiences as she finished her undergraduate education at Sarah Lawrence College. During her final years there, Walker became pregnant, had an abortion, and subsequently considered suicide. Her poem "suicide" is a reflection of her experiences and yet is a repudiation of the act of suicide. It provides for the reader some insights as to why Walker ultimately decided that her life was worth living.

In the poem, the narrator provides instructions on how to write a suicide note. The poem's conceit is that the act of writing such a note, if completed according to the explicit instructions provided, will have the effect of changing the suicidal individual's mind and preventing him or her from carrying out the act.

The poem actually instructs the reader to engage in two fundamental tasks: to write and then to think. The verses presuppose that the act of writing is inherently powerful and can prevent despair and self-destruction. This is the assertion that begins the poem: "First, suicide notes should be / (not long) but written." With this opening, the poem casts a potential lifeline for one contemplating suicide and, at least, a mechanism for self-reflection and reconsideration.

The narrator proceeds with the suggestion that suicide notes "should be signed / in blood / by hand." This admonition invokes a level of commitment and also requires additional consideration of the ultimate act. The infliction of pain required to draw enough blood to write might cause the suicidal individual to reconsider the cost of additional agony. The connection between blood and the subjectivity of one's name also implies a kind of pact and can be read as a tacit affirmation of individuality and personhood.

There is a sudden turn in the poem when the narrator asserts that the point of suicide is "that there is none." The narrator has led the vulnerable individual toward reconsideration of the implications of suicide and overtly concludes that the act is meaningless.

Finally, the narrator suggests that the feelings that precipitate suicide are temporary and that conditions like emotional exhaustion can be survived by assuming a posture of laziness and also through the act of remembering the joys of one's life. The poem ends with another assertion of the power of writing, as the narrator suggests that the individual tell about his or her memories of joy. In so doing, creativity is once again invoked as a way to forestall, perhaps permanently, the possibility of suicide.

## "We Have a Beautiful Mother" (1991)

This poem was published in the collection *Her Blue Body Everything We Know*. It employs a poetic technique called anaphora, in which a poem repeats a phrase at the beginning of a stanza, lending the phrase particular emphasis and calling the reader's attention to the ideas, themes, symbols, or motifs it invokes. The phrase "We Have a Beautiful Mother" is here repeated throughout the poem.

The first word of the anaphoric phrase, *We*, draws the reader in a gesture of participatory inclusion into Walker's thesis. The message is that the reader is also part of the family and is invited to join in the narrator's celebration of the opportunities this relationship presents for appreciation.

The first two stanzas feature not only the repetition but also a reversal of images. In the first stanza, the complementary lines are "Her hills / are buffaloes / Her buffaloes / hills." In the second stanza, Walker couples two imagistic phrases, "Her oceans / are wombs / Her wombs / oceans." These pairings allow Walker to invoke the familiar and immediately recognizable entities of buffalo, hills, oceans, and wombs and to expand their connotative and denotative significances by asserting their inherent multiplicity. The buffalo is redefined as both buffalo and hill, an organic and besieged living creature with a finite existence, *and* a permanent and elemental feature of the landscape upon which it resides. The significance of the animal transcends its particularity, and the buffalo becomes at once a sign of the earth's mutability and permanence.

The linking of the oceans with the site of reproduction, the womb, couples the general associations of a larger body of water with a more particular and individualized generative and internal space. The vastness of the ocean and the intimate space of the womb coexist without contradiction and build on the narrator's personification of the earth.

Stanza three builds on that personification with the details of the physical elements of this collective mother. Walker uses traditional signifiers of female beauty, a woman's smile and her hair, and situates these markers in the natural world. "Her teeth / the white stones / at the edge / of the water / the summer / grasses / her plentiful / hair." These details help to support the extended metaphor that is the poem's premise.

The final stanza completes the sequence by implying that the earth's maternal characteristics provide a space of respite and comfort. From the physical and external characteristics that are associated with beauty, the poem moves to the invocation of the more intangible and relationship dimension of beauty—the warmth and comfort of nurturance. "Her green lap / immense / Her brown embrace / eternal." These closing images contain archetypal references to maternity and circle back to the central phrase. The final line adds to the power of these connotations in their subtle suggestion that this relationship is precious and vulnerable: "Her blue body / everything we know." The line implies that there is no replacement or substitute for this beautiful mother and that "we" must sustain this unique and precious relationship.

## "Why War Is Never a Good Idea" (2003)

This poem was published in the collection *Absolute Trust in the Goodness of the Earth*. In it, Walker personifies war as a monstrous and callous being that descends like a noxious cloud on various peaceful scenes.

In the opening stanza, frogs have gathered for their "pre-rainy-season convention" just as war approaches. Walker depicts war here as the "huge tires of a camouflaged vehicle about to squash them flat."

In another stanza, a boy is enjoying a warm day while, just above him, "something dark big as a car is dropping." One of the central features of Walker's characterization of war is her description of it as possessing cruel contradictions. These conflicts manifest so that war "has eyes of its own / & can see oil & gas / & mahogany trees / & every shining thing under the earth / when it comes to nursing mothers / it is blind."

In later observation, Walker notes that "Though War is old / it has not become wise." In her final characterization, Walker depicts war as having "bad manners." It "eats everything / in its path / & what it doesn't eat / it dribbles on." War "tastes terrible" and "smells bad" with "body odor."

In 2007, the poem was published as a children's book, featuring illustrations by Stefano Vitale. The cover of the book says that it is appropriate for "all ages."

# Nonfiction Collections and Selected Individual Essays

## *Alice Walker: Banned* (1996)

As an author and activist, Alice Walker is certainly no stranger to controversy, and most of her literary canon pushes various social and ideological hot buttons. As a result of her unflinching persistence in including all dimensions of human reality and experience in her writings, Walker's works are among the most frequently banned literary texts in the United States. Her 1996 publication *Alice Walker: Banned* examines this phenomenon and provides access to those of her writings and other documents that form the heart of the discussions.

The book consists of an introduction by Patricia Holt; two of Walker's short stories that have generated particular attention, "Roselily" and "Am I Blue"; and excerpts of some of the contested material from Walker's best-known work, *The Color Purple*. The book also includes materials that document the positions of those who fought to have Walker materials banned from use in various school districts. The book was issued by Aunt Lute Books, a publishing house that focuses on women writers of color.

### Further Reading

Neilen, Deirdre. "Review: *Alice Walker: Banned.*" *World Literature Today* 72, no. 1 (Winter 1998): 136–137.

Walker, Alice. *Alice Walker: Banned.* San Francisco: Aunt Lute Books, 1996.

## "Alice Walker on *Why War Is Never a Good Idea*"

Alice Walker has long been an activist for social justice, but the domestic and global upheaval of the post-9/11 attacks on the Pentagon and the World Trade Center deepened her belief in peace for the new millennium. In the 2001 essay collection *Sent by Earth: A Message from the Grandmother Spirit*, Walker articulates her perspectives on the contemporary political climate. Her fourth children's book, *Why War Is Never a Good Idea* (2007), is an antiwar story primarily geared toward children and the adults who shape them. The story is written in poetic form and features illustrations by Stefano Vitale.

At the time of the book's release, Walker wrote an essay explaining the book's genesis. In it, she says that "miniature rifles, tanks, and bombs" toys and "military print" clothing many parents purchase for babies and children inspired her to write the book. For Walker, "children who play 'war' long before they have any understanding of its meaning" are vulnerable and are the focus of her concerns. She is adamant that adults must play a more proactive role in questioning the notion that wars can be moral or justifiable.

Walker contends that war "isn't all right, and the adults of the world must say so." She provides a litany of war's effects, including the destruction of human, animal, and plant life as well as the quality of air and water. According to her argument, the effects of war are synonymous with an attack on "Life itself: everything that humans and other species hold sacred and dear. A war on a people anywhere is a war on the Life of the planet everywhere." Walker concludes that regardless of political differences, the natural features of the earth unite all of humanity. She views nonviolence as a teachable value that is the key to "maintaining a livable planet" and rejects the notion that a balanced argument about war is possible. "We are ultimately on the same side: the side of keeping our home, Earth, safe from attack."

### Further Reading

Walker, Alice. "Alice Walker on *Why War is Never a Good Idea.*" HarperCollins Publishers. Available online. URL: http://www.harpercollins.com/author/authorExtra.aspx?authorID=12848&isbn13=9780060753856&displayType=bookessay. Accessed January 2, 2010.

## "Alice Walker Reflects on Working Toward Peace"

In this essay, Alice Walker provides an autobiographical account of personal touchstones drawn from her five decades of social justice activism.

Walker recalls her occasional ambivalence toward the term *activist.* As a burgeoning activist, she felt that "given the magnitude of the task before us—the dismantling of American apartheid—our individual tasks were puny." Coupled with her concern that the task of transformation is Herculean, Walker expresses her concern that, as a young activist, she may not have been willing to subject herself to the personal costs involved in the fight for equality. She writes that "the most 'revolutionary' often ended up severely beaten, in prison, or dead." As a consequence of her experiences, Walker retrospectively finds not only the ability but the necessity to reconsider her understandings of the efficacy—as well as the vulnerability—of living an activist life.

Walker provides anecdotes to illustrate the philosophy derived from her musings. Among the examples she describes is her awakening during her time living in Mississippi from 1967 to 1974. While in Mississippi, Walker taught at two colleges, wrote essays, created teaching materials for local Head Start children, and also was in an interracial marriage. These commitments made her feel as if she were combating on a personal level the violence and destruction of those who opposed the movement toward an equality that she had devoted herself to serve. She recounts "the numbing assault" of the daily news during the era but says that she ultimately began to realize "that one's activism, however modest, fighting against this tide of death, provides at least the possibility of generating a different kind of 'news.' A 'news' that empowers rather than defeats."

During the course of her activism, Walker has come to include a range of responses in her dynamic definition of political engagement, including writing that is attuned to the daily struggles of living in modern society. Walker also highlights the importance of sacrificing personal comfort and safety for the sake of deeply held principles. Among the historical figures she cites as examples of that principle are "Martin Luther King Jr. at the mountaintop. Gandhi dying with the name of God on his lips. Sojourner Truth baring her breast at a women's rights convention in 1851. Harriet Tubman exposing her revolver to some of the slaves she had freed . . ."

These examples represent a model of activism to which Walker aspires, and they have catalyzed her personal engagements as well as her thinking about the subject. She questions the presumption that human beings are naturally, inevitably, evil, and she offers activism as the antidote to this presumption. According to Walker, activism creates a space where we experience "people at their best, reaching toward their fullness."

Walker concludes her account by pinpointing the two key lessons she has learned during her activist life. Notably, she is humbled by "the futility of expecting anyone, including oneself, to be perfect" and understands that "the awareness of having faults, . . . links us to everyone on Earth that opens us to courage and compassion."

### Further Reading

Walker, Alice. Introduction to *Anything We Love Can Be Saved: A Writer's Activism.* New York: Ballantine Books, 1997: xxi–xxv.

———. "Alice Walker Reflects on Working Toward Peace." The Markkula Center for Applied Ethics. Available online. URL: http://www.scu-edu/ethics/architects-of-peace/Walker/essay.html. Accessed September 3, 2010.

## "Alice Walker's Wise Counsel for Obama" (2008)

Barack Obama's election as U.S. president in November 2008 engendered immense hope in liberal and progressive circles in the United States and abroad. Many groups and individuals view Obama's election to the highest office in the nation, in spite of his identity as an African American, as a particular benchmark for racial progress. President Obama's political ascent elicited a warm response from Alice Walker in the form of a four-paragraph letter written for *The Nation.*

Walker begins the letter by describing the overwhelming pride Obama's election elicited in her as a black person born and raised in the southern United States. She raves that "seeing you deliver the torch so many others before you carried, year after year, decade after decade, century after century, only to be struck down before igniting the flame of justice and of law, is almost more than the heart can bear." Walker notes Obama's role as "a balm for the weary warriors of hope" as a result of his "wisdom, stamina and character." Walker also congratulates Obama for the optimism he has inspired in activist and justice communities.

Walker anchors her essay with two pieces of advice she offers to the newly elected president. The first is to "remember that you did not create the disaster that the world is experiencing, and you alone are not responsible for bringing the world back to balance." The second is "not to take on other people's enemies." She encourages the new president to continue to cultivate personal happiness, and to include "a schedule that permits sufficient time of rest and play with your gorgeous wife and lovely daughters." Walker suggests that this personal restoration is a component central to Obama's capacity to remain balanced and clear-eyed.

Walker responds to contemporary global hostilities and locates their source in deeply rooted historical conflicts. She sees these long-standing conflicts as a major source of contemporary political and military conflict. She asserts, "There must be no more crushing of whole communities, no more torture, no more dehumanizing as a means of ruling a people's spirit. This has already happened to people of color, poor people, women, children. We see where this leads, where it has led." She also offers the Dalai Lama's nuanced confrontations with the Chinese government regarding the Tibetan invasion as a model for working with enemies and preserving personal and spiritual integrity. In her estimation, the deterioration or loss of the soul disconnects humans from the very elements that sustain life. The weight of this potentiality makes it especially crucial for leaders to nurture their spirit. Walker concludes by reiterating to Barack Obama that phrase that resonated throughout his campaign: "We are the ones we have been waiting for."

### Further Reading

Walker, Alice. "Alice Walker's Wise Counsel for Obama." *The Nation* (November 2008). Available online. URL: http://www.commondreams.org/view/2008/11/13-1. Accessed January 2, 2010.

## Anything We Love Can Be Saved: A Writer's Activism (1997)

Alice Walker's *Anything We Love Can Be Saved: A Writer's Activism* is an eclectic collection of essays and observations about a wide variety of topics. Walker writes about nearly every aspect of her life and experiences. She frames these disparate pieces within her examination of the complex dynamics involved in constructing a life of activism. Walker asserts that writing—although, perhaps, less tangible than other forms of activism—is an essential way to work against oppression. She asserts that since her days as a participant in the CIVIL RIGHTS MOVEMENT, her activism has largely manifested as writing.

She contrasts her early optimism with the more pragmatic and less exacting expectations that she now holds for herself and for others who are engaged in trying to change the world. She reflects on her spiritual evolution and turn away from Christianity in order to consider the potential of having reverence for the world, other people, and the realm of spirits without the dictates and sexist oppressions of a formally defined way of believing. She also writes about her early experiences and of the resonances that these connections have for her as an adult.

Walker writes in separate essays about her mother and the various influences of her mother's life on her sense and definition of activism. She also writes about her brother and her daughter and tries to articulate what it means to be rooted in a traditional upbringing and to try to retain what was most effective about her role models and create the new versions of thought and activism that seem most appropriate for her own life and her life as a mother and partner.

In addition, Walker writes about activist models who came from beyond her family and early experiences. In this vein, she writes about her discovery and investigations of ZORA NEALE HURSTON, Winnie Mandela, CARL JUNG, FRIDA KAHLO, Salman Rushdie, and others. Through these essays, speeches, letters, poems, and other forms of expression, Walker articulates a loose definition of activism and personalizes what that engagement has meant for her after years of reflection on ways to confront, change, and improve the conditions of oppression in whatever forms they takes.

### Further Reading

Griffin, Farah Jasmine. "Review: *Anything We Love Can Be Saved:* The Courage of Her Convictions." *The Women's Review of Books* 15, no. 4 (January 1998): 23–24.

Walker, Alice. *Anything We Love Can Be Saved: A Writer's Activism.* New York: Random House, 1997.

## "Beauty: When the Other Dancer Is the Self" (1983)

"Beauty: When the Other Dancer Is the Self," which appeared in Alice Walker's collection *In Search of Our Mothers' Gardens,* depicts the emotional arc that Walker experienced in the transition from the time that she was a small child and considered "cute" through the injury to her left eye and her sense that she had become unattractive. The essay ends at the point in her life when she reclaims the joy of self-acceptance.

The essay opens in 1947, when Walker was two-and-a-half years old and a favorite of her father among her many siblings. A few years later, when she was six years old and dressed for Easter Sunday, neighbors at church commented on how lovely she looked, and Walker thought, "It is great fun being cute." She quickly adds: "But then one day, it ended."

At the age of eight, she was playing cowboys and Indians with her brothers when one of them accidentally shot a BB pellet into her left eye, which left her blinded in that eye. Many years later, as a middle-aged adult, she asked her mother and sister if she had changed after that accident. They said no, but Walker knows better.

From the day of the accident forward, Walker remembers, she no longer looked up at people. She did not want them to see the eye, which she describes as having a "glob" in it. She no longer felt cute. She became shy and was teased at a new school she attended. At 14, however, she began to make her way back to self-acceptance when an older brother brought her to a doctor who was able to modify the way her left eye looked, removing the glob.

Although the operation was a cosmetic procedure, and Walker remained blind in that eye, from then on, she started to lift her head again. She was not yet fully accepting, as her nervousness later in life about being photographed for a magazine cover testifies, but she could still see the world's beauty in her good eye, and this was a blessing, especially noted when she saw, for the first time, the beauty of a desert.

Her journey back to self-acceptance was completed when Walker was 27 and her three-year-old daughter, REBECCA WALKER, noticed that her mother's left eye looked different. Walker had worried about what to tell her daughter if the question came up, but Rebecca questioned her mother's appearance in a way that restored the older Walker's confidence. Rebecca, who watched a science program each day that featured the Earth as a big blue marble, asked: "Mommy, where did you get that world in your eye?" Walker loved this expansive image of her blind eye. That night, she dreamed she was dancing with someone to a Stevie Wonder song. She and this other person danced and kissed each other, both celebrating at having come through difficult times. The other person, she realized, was herself.

### CRITICAL COMMENTARY

Much of Alice Walker's work, particularly her nonfiction, is rooted in her examination of the realities and particulars of her own experiences. In many of her essays, she draws on occurrences that have had a profound effect on her perceptions of the world. Perhaps the most foundational event of Walker's young life was the incident where she was wounded in her eye and consequently lost her vision in it.

Walker's essay "Beauty: When the Other Dancer Is the Self" explores the significance of this trauma on Walker's understanding of the world; on her self-perceptions; on her relationships with others; and, most specifically, on her understanding of beauty and its attendant influence on her self-esteem.

Always considered bright and vivacious as a young child, Walker was encouraged by her family and teachers to pursue her creative impulses. She was particularly precocious, and at age four, earlier than most of her peers, she began a distinctive career as a student. She particularly loved to read and write, and she began to associate the acceptance and acclaim she experienced as not only as a consequence of her intelligence and creativity but as also rooted in her appearance.

Walker remembers herself as an outgoing and engaging child, but her sense of well-being in the world was forever altered at age eight as a result of the accident. She has maintained that it was a catalyst for her retreat into the world of books and to the less conspicuously expressive venue of writing, particularly of composing poetry. Walker's essay catalog the trauma of the event and the transformative impact it had on her sense of self. Where she had felt lovely and enviable, she now perceived herself as ugly and as someone worthy of scorn and derision.

As Walker has written, the other major trauma that derived from the accident was the fact that her brothers made her lie about it. As children afraid of getting in trouble, Walker's brothers made her tell their parents that the injury had been accidentally self-inflicted. Although her parents eventually learned the truth, this lie compounded the incident for Walker as she began to feel responsible for her impairment and pain. She also resented that she was the only one to suffer the consequences of her brothers' actions since she felt punished by the great pain caused by the incident and also did not feel that her brothers had to bear any responsibility for the irreparable harm they had caused. As noted in the essay, she began to feel alienated from her family and environs.

The rural world around Walker that had been interactive for her prior to the accident became solitary. This isolation—the psychological and emotional turn inward—encouraged her to become introspective and to use her intellect and creativity as solace and sanctuary. She also began to develop a writer's objective perspective, and her home became her first field of observation. This developing gaze also initiated a lifelong intimate engagement with the subtleties of the natural world.

It is difficult to overstate the centrality of Walker's cataract surgery at the age of 14, a critical juncture in her development and adult identity formation. The operation resulted in a dramatic improvement in her appearance and, consequently, her self-perception. With increased self-esteem, Walker began again to perform as a superlative and popular student and graduated from her high school as the valedictorian and the prom queen. She received a scholarship to attend SPELMAN COLLEGE.

As the essay reveals, even as an adult, Walker had not completely recovered from the schism in her self-esteem that occurred after her accident. It took the completely unfiltered observation of her then-infant daughter, Rebecca, for her to reconnect with the beauty of the natural world that she had so loved before the accident with her identity. With Rebecca's poetic assertion that Walker had a "world in her eye," Alice Walker was finally able to reclaim beauty in the most complete sense of the word.

## "Civil Rights Movement: What Good Was It, The" (1967)

"The Civil Rights Movement: What Good Was It" was Alice Walker's first published essay. It was chosen as the winner of an essay contest by *American Scholar* magazine in 1967. Walker won $300 for the publication of her essay. In it, she asserts that the CIVIL RIGHTS MOVEMENT will never be over as long as inequality for black Americans continues to be a reality.

The article casts the Civil Rights movement in personal terms as Walker describes the ways that the movement changed her psychological world—her self-perception and worldview. Walker speaks of her mother's infatuation with soap operas and relates the damage that watching these narratives (whose sagas did not include anyone who looked like her) did to Minnie Walker's self-esteem. In the essay, Walker describes seeing MARTIN LUTHER KING, JR., on the same television her mother watched her "stories" on, and she describes the ways in which his persona and message provided a crucial counternarrative to her mother's soap operas. She locates the value of the movement in its foregrounding of King as a moral leader, its presentation of an alternative to blind adoration of a racist and exclusionary culture, and its support of black people and black communities.

### Further Reading

Walker, Alice. "The Civil Rights Movement: What Good Was It?" *American Scholar* 36, no. 4 (Autumn 1967): 550–554.

## *I Love Myself When I Am Laughing . . . and Then Again When I Am Looking Mean and Impressive: A Zora Neale Hurston Reader* (1979)

Literary historians have frequently credited Alice Walker for reviving critical and historical interest in ZORA NEALE HURSTON's work. Walker has expressed particular admiration for the dialect and communalism Hurston (1891–1960) captured in *THEIR EYES WERE WATCHING GOD*. In 1973, Walker took a pilgrimage down to Hurston's gravesite in Fort Pierce, Florida. Upon seeing that Hurston's final resting place was unmarked, she became anxious about the historic erasure of Hurston and of artists generally. As a writer, Walker empathized with Hurston and feared sharing the author's fate. In a gesture of solidarity with her deceased compatriot, she purchased a headstone for Hurston. The stone reads "A Genius of the South" and features the caption "Novelist. Folklorist. Anthropologist."

Walker shared her interest in and admiration for Hurston in the essay "In Search of Zora Neale Hurston" published in Ms. magazine. She also paid homage to Hurston in her foreword to Robert Hemenway's study *Zora Neale Hurston: A Literary Biography* (1977) and in the 1979 collection of Hurston writings that she edited, *I Love Myself When I Am Laughing . . . and Then Again When I Am Looking Mean and Impressive: A Zora Neale Hurston Reader*. The collection contains 14 of Hurston's works, including essays, short stories, and excerpts from Hurston's longer works. Walker and the literary critic Mary Helen Washington provided commentary for this groundbreaking collection, which proved pivotal in the resurrection of Hurston's reputation and popularity.

### Further Reading

Hurston, Zora Neale. *I Love Myself When I Am Laughing . . . and Then Again When I Am Looking Mean and Impressive: A Zora Neale Hurston Reader.* Edited by Alice Walker. Old Westbury, N.Y.: Feminist Press, 1979.

Rushing, Andrea Benton. "Review: Jumping at the Sun, Reviewed Work: *I Love Myself When I Am Laughing . . . And Then Again When I Am Looking Mean and Impressive: A Zora Neale Hurston Reader.*" *Callaloo* 8/10 (February–October 1980): 228–230.

Skerrett, Joseph T., Jr. "Reviewed work(s): *I Love Myself When I Am Laughing: A Zora Neale Hurston Reader* by Alice Walker." *MELUS* 7, no. 3 (Autumn, 1980): 90–91.

## "In Search of Our Mothers' Gardens" (1974)

Written in 1974, the essay "In Search of Our Mothers' Gardens" begins by recounting how the African-American writer JEAN TOOMER (1894–1967) traveled south in the early 1920s and discovered what he felt was a suppressed artistic impulse in the black women there, suffering as they did at that time under the oppression of racial bigotry. Walker reflects on Toomer's observations and sees in those women the mothers and grandmothers of contemporary African-American women.

In addition to reflecting on Jean Toomer, Walker refers several times to VIRGINIA WOOLF and to her classic essay "A Room of One's Own." Although the subject matter of Woolf's essay was the suppression of the artistic spirit of white British women during the early 20th century, Walker makes the connection between Woolf's perspectives and the oppression of African-American women. She then asks the reader to "listen to the voices of Bessie Smith, Billie Holiday, Nina Simone, Roberta Flack, and Aretha Franklin, among others, and to imagine those voices muzzled for life." She also asks the reader to reflect on all the potential "Poets, Novelists, Essayists, and Short Story Writers (over a period of centuries), who died with their real gifts stifled within them."

As a particular example of one woman who was able to transcend her circumstances in order to express her creativity, Walker refers to PHILLIS WHEATLEY (ca. 1753–84). Wheatley was a slave who was the first African-American female poet to be published. Walker finds it unjust that black women should have to bear the burden of such epithets as "mule of the world," "Mean and Evil Bitches," "Superwomen," and "Castrators," when, in fact, they have always possessed and expressed a creative spirit that is common to all humanity. Her efforts in the essay document the ways that these women expressed that spirit through whatever means or media was at hand. As an example of that creative expression, Walker refers to a quilt "unlike any other in the world" that is made of worthless rags and now hangs in the Smithsonian Institution.

Walker also acknowledges the accomplishments of her own mother, who made an art form out of her gardens, adorning "with flowers whatever shabby house we were forced to live in." So beautiful were these gardens that strangers would come to see them. As her mother worked in her garden, Walker saw in her a creative radiance that she imagines her distant ancestors back in Africa must have possessed as they perhaps wove beautiful mats, painted daring decorations, and sang sweetly "in a voice like Roberta Flack" throughout the African villages.

## CRITICAL COMMENTARY

Arguably, "In Search of Our Mother's Gardens" is Alice Walker's most influential essay. The piece is one of her most reprinted and is included in many anthologies, including *The Norton Anthology of African American Literature.* The essay is considered to be foundational to a wide range of academic disciplines, including literary studies, women and gender studies, and African-American studies. One of the central points of the essay is that ordinary spaces became media for African-American women who did not have any other outlet for their artistic energies.

Through her crafting of this essay, Walker reimagines and reinterprets the garden as one of the few spaces where African-American women could cultivate their artistic and aesthetic proclivities in pragmatic and nonthreatening ways. She uses this conceit in its literal form to describe in glowing detail the productive artistry of women like her mother, but more influentially, she crafts this historical reality into a metaphor for the life of a creative artist. Walker not only draws on the immediate influences of her mother and the other women in her family, she also traces the "gardens" of the literary artists who preceded her and whom she counts as primary influences and models of how to live as an artist in a culture that does not support or take seriously the artistic endeavors of people of color.

One of the central influences Walker explores in her essay is the Harlem Renaissance writer Jean Toomer, whose 1920 book CANE Walker names as one of the most important books she has ever read. Toomer's creation of *Cane* derives from the historical realities of his time. African Americans were in the process of migrating from the South to the North in record numbers. The causes of that movement, known as the Great Migration, were complicated and various. Generally, African Americans left the South in search of economic opportunities; in an attempt to flee random and systematic racial violence; and in an effort to live in a place where segregation did not entirely control the ability to vote, to own land and property, and to attend schools.

With *Cane,* Toomer captured the violent, wistful, transient, poignant currents of this period in African-American history. The novel moves from the South to the North and returns to end in the South again. With that movement, Toomer captures the feeling of the transition from the rural South to the northern city and back again. This movement and the motif of the impact of physical, emotional, and psychological journeys form the subtextual core as well as the methodological model Walker asserts in her essay.

Several main themes recur in the essay. Of particular interest is Walker's personal quest to recover the overlooked history of black female artistic production. Centrally, she is concerned with the dearth of scholarly attention to black female authors such as Phillis Wheatley and ZORA NEALE HURSTON, among several others she claims as her literary foremothers. Hurston figures into many of Walker's discussions of the forgotten histories of African-American women. In the essay, Walker champions both Wheatley's and Hurston's array of complex depictions of African-American female subjectivity. An additional focus of "In Search of Our Mother's Gardens" is the important influence of a range of writers on the way Walker perceives literature and the craft of writing.

Walker also employs her childhood experiences, as well as stories of her mother's life and negotiations with and through black womanhood, as a reflection on the complicated relationship of African-American women to artistic production. Through the wide and disparate range of her examples, Walker acknowledges the complex array of the struggles black women have negotiated in order to reconcile development of culturally rich folk traditions and the impulse to create amidst the realities of white supremacy, oppression, and violence.

Walker employ multiple literary genres in the essay. In addition to her free-flowing prose, she includes several of her own poems as a kind of metanarrative to amplify and illustrate her points. Through these efforts, she created an essay that helped to redefine African-American literary study and provided new avenues through which to explore the complexities of black female subjectivity.

## *In Search of Our Mothers' Gardens: Womanist Prose* (1983)

The same year that she won the Pulitzer Prize, Walker published what is, arguably, her most important collection of essays, *In Search of Our Mother's Gardens,* spanning from 1967 to 1982. Walker divides her collection into four parts, and the anthology features 36 essays, letters, speeches, reviews, and previously unpublished pieces. Most of the collected works were previously published in trade magazines such as *Ms.* and *Redbook,* as well as scholarly journals including *The Black Scholar* prior to their collection in *In Search of Our Mothers' Gardens.*

The wide-ranging collection is best known for its opening pages, wherein Walker provides four definitions of her term *womanist,* variously defined as "a black feminist or feminist of color"; "a woman who loves other women, sexually and/or nonsexually"; a lover of music, dance, the moon and self, among other open-ended possibilities; and concluding with the statement that "Womanist is to feminist as purple to lavender."

According to Walker's definition of WOMANISM, FEMINISM becomes a term that is inappropriately narrow for African-American women, as well as for others who embrace an inclusive and humanist vision of the world. Although womanism shares commonalities with feminism, it represents an expansion beyond the traditional feminist critical and activist agendas.

The definitional introduction of the term *womanism* into the field of African-American women's writing has spawned a debate over its implications. Interdisciplinary critics who have embraced womanism as a foundational philosophy for their work include historians and theologians such as Darlene Clark Hines, Elsa Barkely Brown, and Katie Cannon. Womanism is an important literary critical movement that has influenced such scholars of African-American women's literature as Barbara Christian, Majorie Pryse, Hazel Carby, Valerie Smith, and others to analyze literature in womanist terms (that is, by relying on analyses of SELF-AFFIRMATION, tradition, matrilineal inheritance, and so on). Walker's definition transformed the field of black women's literary criticism.

Throughout, the collection builds on Walker's definition of *womanism.* Walker is highly attuned to intersections of race, class, gender, and sexuality and to the relevance of these spheres to social and political constructions and activism. She also invokes international struggles against racial supremacy and imperialism in her discussions of domestic oppressions.

Several core themes recur in the collection, particularly Walker's personal quest to recover the overlooked history of black female artistic production. Centrally, she is concerned with the dearth of scholarly attention to black female authors such as ZORA NEALE HURSTON, who Walker understands as a literary foremother. Hurston figures into many of Walker's discussions of the forgotten histories of African-American women. In the collection, Walker champions Hurston's array of complex depictions of African-American female subjectivity in essays that include "Zora Neale Hurston: A Cautionary Tale and a Partisan View," "Looking for Zora," and "If the Present Looks Like the Past What Does the Future Look Like?" Walker employs the trope of searching in her explorations of her literary models and of other female artists. An additional focus of her essays is the important influence of a range of writers on the way she perceives literature and her craft of writing, including Hurston, LANGSTON HUGHES, FLANNERY O'CONNOR, BESSIE HEAD, LEO TOLSTOY, and VIRGINIA WOOLF.

The enduring struggle of female authors to balance their creative work with their familial commitments and to command the critical respect that male authors regularly receive also permeates the collection. Walker maps out her gradual reconciliation of her identity as a mother and a writer, and she discusses her creative processes—for example, in the essay "Writing *The Color Purple*"—in addition to candidly reassessing the quality of some of her previously published work.

The Georgia-born Walker also frequently employs her childhood experiences, especially her pre- and postadolescent life and her adult experiences living with her then husband and daughter in Mississippi during the mid-1960s and early 1970s, as a reflection on the complicated relationship of African Americans to the South. Walker acknowledges the complex array of struggles blacks have negotiated to reconcile their development of their rich cultural traditions and the beauty of southern landscapes with the realities of white supremacy, oppression, and violence. In so doing, she also devotes considerable attention to the reasons African Americans have migrated to the northern United States and balanced with the region's failure to provide a space untroubled by racial discord.

Walker often translates her personal experiences into layered reflections on the execution and import of larger political issues, including the Civil Rights, antinuclear, and anti-imperialist movements. She applauds the accomplishments of the CIVIL RIGHTS MOVEMENT while acknowledging sexism within its ranks. Among her essays is a discussion of her experiences working as volunteer for the STUDENT NON-VIOLENT COORDINATING COMMITTEE in Mississippi ("But Yet and Still the Cotton Gin Kept on Working . . .") and a revealing interview with Coretta Scott King ("Coretta Scott King: Revisited"). She also questions the sexual politics of the Black Power movement and warns her readers against romanticizing revolutionary politics. Additionally, the collection represents her antinuclear politics and their racial implications by reprinting her 1982 review of Helen Caldecott's *Nuclear Madness: What You Can Do* and the essay "Only Justice Can Stop a Curse," which encourages ordinary citizens to question domestic and global involvement in nuclear proliferation.

*In Search of Our Mother's Gardens* also features Walker's perspective on a number of contemporary issues, including domestic abuse, FEMALE GENITAL MUTILATION, and the tendency toward homophobia and sexism in certain African-American communities. The cumulative effects of this literary sampler combine nearly seamlessly to establish the anthology as one of her most prescient, acclaimed, and enduring works.

### Further Reading


Baker, Houston A., Jr., and Patricia Redmond, eds. *Afro-American Literary Study in the 1990s*. Chicago: University of Chicago Press, 1989.

Byrd, Rudolph P. "Review: *In Search of Our Mothers' Gardens: Womanist Prose,* by Alice Walker." *Callaloo* 18 (Spring–Summer 1983): 123–129.

Hite, Molly. *The Other Side of the Story: Structures and Strategies of Contemporary Feminist Narrative*. Ithaca, N.Y.: Cornell University Press, 1989.

Joeres, Ruth-Ellen Boetcher, and Elizabeth Mittman, eds. *The Politics of the Essay: Feminist Perspectives*. Bloomington: Indiana University Press, 1993.

McDowell, Deborah. *"The Changing Same": Black Women's Literature, Criticism, and Theory*. Bloomington: Indiana University Press, 1995.

McMillan, Laurie: "Telling a Critical Story: Alice Walker's *In Search of Our Mothers' Gardens.*" *Journal of Modern Literature* 23, no. 1 (Fall 2004): 103–107.

Modleski, Tania. *Feminism without Women: Culture and Criticism in a "Postfeminist" Age*. New York: Routledge, 1991.

Morrison, Toni. "Memory, Creation, and Writing." *Thought* 59 (1984): 385–390.

Sadoff, Dianne F. "Black Matrilineage: The Case of Alice Walker and Zora Neale Hurston." *Signs* 11 (1985): 4–26.

Veeser, H. Aram. *Confessions of the Critics*. New York: Routledge, 1996.

Walker, Alice. *In Search of Our Mothers' Gardens: Womanist Prose*. San Diego: Harcourt Brace, 1983.

Warhol, Robyn R., and Diane Price Herndl, eds. *Feminisms: An Anthology of Literary Theory and Criticism*. Rev. ed. New Brunswick, N.J.: Rutgers University Press, 1997.

Williams, Jeffrey. "The New Belletrism." *Style* 33 (1999): 413–442.

Woolf, Virginia. *A Room of One's Own*. San Diego: Harcourt Brace, 1929.


## *Letters of Love and Hope: The Story of the Cuban Five* (Nancy Morejon, Alice Walker, and Leonard I. Weinglass) (2005)

In 1998, five men—Gerardo Hernández, Ramón Labañino Salazar, Rene González Sehwerert, Antonio Guerrero Rodríguez, and Fernando González Llort—were arrested and charged with conspiracy to spy against the U.S. government. For one respondent, Hernández, the charge was changed from conspiracy to murder. Hernández was implicated for providing the information that assisted the shootdown of an American plane that was flying in Cuban airspace.

The men, who came to be called the Cuban Five, were convicted and sentenced to prison. In the nearly three years between their arrest and conviction, they were not allowed to see their families, and for part of that time, they were held in solitary confinement. Their experience has been the subject of protests by various individuals and groups around the world. In 2009, the U.S. Supreme Court refused to hear an appeal. The men will be resentenced as a result of a lower court decision.

In 2005, Alice Walker edited and wrote the introduction for a collection of documents surrounding and describing the men's situation, including court documents and letters to and from the men to their families and other individuals. The book includes a detailed description of the human rights violations that many feel have been committed in this case by the United States.

### Further Reading


Brenner, Phillip, and Marguerita Jimenez. "U.S. Policy on Cuba beyond the Last Gasp." *NACLA Report on the Americas* 39, no. 4 (January/February 2006): 15–43.

Sweig, Julia E. "Fidel's Final Victory." *Foreign Affairs* 86, no. 1 (January/February 2007): 39–56.

Walker, Alice. "The Story of the Cuban Five." In *Letters of Love and Hope: The Story of the Cuban Five,* edited by Nancy Morejon, Alice Walker, and Leonard I. Weinglass. Melbourne: Ocean Press, 2005.

# "Letter to President Clinton, A" (1996)

In February 1996, Cuba shot down two civilian Cessna planes with U.S. passengers using air-to-air missiles. Cuban officials claimed the planes violated its airspace, whereas U.S. officials, including former president Bill Clinton and former secretary of state Madeleine Albright, viewed it as territorial aggression. The United Nations Security Council also officially condemned the shooting. Among the outcomes of this event was Clinton's advocacy for economic sanctions and his support of the Cuban Liberty and Democratic Solidarity Act (or the Helms-Burton Act), a bill sponsored by Senator Jesse Helms (R-N.C.) and Representative Dan Burton (R-Ind.) that tightened the U.S. embargo.

Alice Walker, who was invited but unable to attend a Clinton White House function in January 1996, responded to the situation and invitation in an open letter to the president. Walker's letter, written on March 13, 1996, questions the blockade, particularly its impact on Cuban children. The author begins by reflecting on her personal involvement in pro-Cuban activism, notably her attendance at her first protest, a 1962 "Hands Off Cuba" rally at the White House. Specifically, she recalls how an employee of the Kennedy administration brought out hot coffee to the protesters during the rally, which she viewed as a "compassionate gesture" that "humanized the president and the White House for me, and made it possible for me to feel a connection that I would not otherwise have felt."

Walker asserts that the humanitarian compassion she experienced from President Kennedy no longer exists. Her solidarity with Clinton is compromised by his support of the Helms-Burton Act. She calls the bill and the long-standing embargo wrong "because it punishes people, some of them unborn, for being who they are." Walker is particularly outraged that Clinton would collude with the Helms-sponsored bill since, for her, the Helms of 1996 is probably "the same Jesse Helms who caused my grandparents, my parents and my own generation profound suffering as we struggled against our enslavement under racist laws in the South." Walker questions the president, saying, "I voted for you," and she asks if he is compromising his integrity by "standing shoulder to shoulder with the Republicans and with Helms?"

Walker's perspective on the material needs of Cuban children and on U.S. distortions of Cuba are integral to her letter. Throughout, she notes the vulnerability of Cuban children and infants, susceptibilities that are compounded by economic penalties. Walker employs the following emotional appeal:

> Sometimes, when I don't know what to do, I imagine a little child standing beside my desk, or sometimes a small baby, kicking on my desk. There are Cuban children—as dear as any on earth, as dear as Chelsea, or my daughter Rebecca—standing beside your desk all the time now . . . One cannot justify starving them to death because their leader is a person of whom some people, themselves imperfect, human, disapprove.

In the letter's opening paragraphs, Walker says plainly, "I love Cuba and its people, including Fidel." Walker, who had previously met FIDEL CASTRO on several occasions and written about her experiences in Cuba, offers an alternative perspective to many characterizations of the former Cuban leader. She writes, "He is not the monster he has been portrayed," and she suggests to Clinton that "in all the study you have done of Cuba surely [it] is apparent to you that he has reason for being the leader he is. Nor am I saying he is without flaw. We are all substantially flawed, wounded, angry, hurt, here on Earth."

Walker invokes both biblical reasoning—"Do unto others . . . Love thy neighbor . . . all of it"—and a humanist approach—"I feel the suffering of each child as if it were my own," "Harmlessness now! Must be our peace cry"—to appeal to Clinton's conscience. She urges the president to move beyond the "poison of old patterns of punishment and despair" and notes that despite his support of the embargo and some questionable choices (for instance, his treatment of Lani Guinier and Jocelyn Elders), "I care about you, Hillary, and Chelsea, and wish you only good. I certainly would not deprive you of food in protest of anything you have done!"

### Further Reading

Walker, Alice. "A Letter to President Clinton." In *Anything We Love Can Be Saved: A Writer's Activism.* New York: Ballantine Books, 1997, 212–216.

## *Living by the Word: Selected Writings, 1973–1987* (1988)

Peppered with excerpts from Walker's own diary, this collection of essays explores the range of issues that concern her and that she feels should be central concerns not only of other Americans but of all humanity. However, many critics found the collection unsatisfactory, lacking in the substance and depth of her previous nonfiction collection *In Search of Our Mothers' Gardens* (1983). Walker herself provides some suggestions about the focus of her work in this collection with her titular phrase *Living by the Word.* As so often is the case with her work, she uses narrative to reframe a familiar situation or complexity, and that language becomes the avenue through which transformation becomes possible. For Walker, living by the word manifests in her attempt to convey a set of truths about her experiences.

Walker's collection begins with a 1984 journal entry in which she describes a dream that she has about a two-headed woman. In the dream, she asks the woman if the world will survive, and the woman tells her that the solution is to live by the word. The essays that follow seem to be Walker's effort to document that endeavor as it manifests in her subjectivity.

Each of the essays included in the collection function as a type of cautionary tale, a corrective to the grand narratives of the contemporary world. The essays articulate Walker's revelations—from her discovery that animals are as vulnerable to suffering as humans and her vow after that realization to abstain from eating meat to her reclamation of the tales Joel Chandler Harris appropriated from his slaves, reinvented, and published as his own—and as such, the volume is a wide-ranging exploration of issues of race, class, and gender from the perspective of an insider who values the perspective of those who do not often have the ability to use their own words in the effort to influence and inform others about their unique understandings and particularized attempts to live by the word.

Other lessons and themes that run through and connect these essays include the notion of the need to have familial compassion for those who are suffering and cannot help themselves; the necessity of regarding the artist with respect, irrespective of his or her human flaws and imperfections; the futility of attempts to repress and silence the truth in the form of the word; the way that the Great Wall of China and walls in general represent the misdirection of human energy and the waste of human spirit and creativity; the way that interraciality has always been a reality and fundamental component in the creation of the foundations of American life; the continuum of human sexuality; and the fact that the solution Walker had sought from the two-headed woman was one she knew all along—that there is a dynamic and interactive relationship between the universe and humanity that all humans have access to and that we can use to find the answers to survival and peaceful, nonhierarchical coexistence.

### Further Reading

Christian, Barbara. "Review: Conversations with the Universe." *Women's Review of Books* 6, no. 5 (February 1989): 9–10.

Walker, Alice. *Living by the Word: Selected Writings, 1973–1987.* San Diego: Harcourt Brace Jovanovich, 1988.

## *Overcoming Speechlessness: A Poet Encounters the Horror in Rwanda, Eastern Congo, and Palestine/Israel* (2010)

This new book is another in the Open Media Pamphlet Series. It contains Walker's reflections and insights about the social and political situations in

Rwanda, Congo, and Gaza. Walker's understandings of the conflicts that have occurred and are still going on in Africa and the Middle East as detailed in this publication derive from her experiences during two trips, one in 2006 and the other in 2009. Both trips were transformative for Walker, and she shares and analyzes these experiences from the position of witness.

Walker's act of witnessing begins with her trip to Rwanda, where she was able to observe the aftermath of the violent slaughter of the Tutsi by the Hutu. She locates the roots of this and of the other conflicts she outlines in the corruption and avarice of colonialism. Walker then moves to a discussion of the ongoing wars in eastern Congo, which, according to her, have cost 4 million Congolese lives. Walker personalizes the conflicts by moving behind the headlines to stories of unimaginable individual suffering and human brutality. She talks about the ways that these stories became a part of her. She finds that the horror of their suffering coupled with the ability of these individuals to survive and transcend their agonizing experiences make her realize that she can do something to help. She can pay homage to them by telling their stories.

One of the strengths of Walker's commentary is her ability to chronicle these terrible tales without segregating them. Although the collection is divided into 24 mini-chapters, the stories are not defined by national boundaries or by the divergent political situations that caused them. Walker weaves the stories of African suffering with her personal and first-hand experiences in the American Civil Rights movement, with thoughts about the Holocaust and the current situation in Gaza. While in Gaza, Walker joins in a spontaneous dance with the women there. The dance is a gesture of defiance and of hope that there is a way to transcend all of the sorrow and suffering to create a humane and livable situation that seems nearly unreachable at present.

Walker's personalization of these often inaccessibly large conflicts provides readers with a way into the nexus of these disputes, which she believes originates in the refusal to reconcile polarized positions and opinions. In the context of her trip to Gaza and the stories she hears there, Walker talks about her marriage to Melvyn Leventhal and the couple's radically divergent positions on the Israeli/Palestinian situation. Walker concludes with her thoughts about what must happen to resolve the Israeli/Palestinian situation and then suggests that the way to work through all of the acrimony is through testimony—by using narrative to achieve reconciliation and understanding.

### Further Reading

Walker, Alice. *Overcoming Speechlessness: A Poet Encounters the Horror in Rwanda, Eastern Congo, and Palestine/Israel.* New York: Open Media, 2010.

## *Same River Twice: Honoring the Difficult, The* (1996)

Alice Walker's *The Same River Twice: Honoring the Difficult* is a work about process more than anything else. Walker discloses the processes that went into the experience of the novel and the film version of *The Color Purple.* She chronicles her excitement at the production of her novel and then her consternation and dismay at some of the negative responses to the book, particularly those responses that were personal and that she felt were character assassinations rather than an engaged assessment of either the book or the movie.

Formally, the work is a montage of Walker's reflections, journal entries, letters sent and received, and a previously unpublished screenplay of *The Color Purple* that she wrote but was not used to create the STEVEN SPIELBERG film. Walker reveals her relationship with the principals on the set, including Spielberg, WHOOPI GOLDBERG, OPRAH WINFREY, Danny Glover, and others. She speaks of her time with these performers and artists in largely positive terms, although her creative tensions with Spielberg were one of the processes she had to undergo.

Walker is also candid about her relationship with her daughter, REBECCA WALKER, during the filming of the movie; she was proud of her daughter's involvement in the production. She also talks of her physical trials as she tried to combat a case of lyme disease. Walker also includes in *The Same River Twice* a discussion of the end of her relationship with Robert Allen, her partner at the time.

After reading the collection, most readers will find that the creation, release, and reinvention of *The Color Purple* as a film was a trying and painful process for Walker. In spite of the traumas associated with this experience, it seems reasonably certain that, while she is somewhat ambivalent, Walker feels that the processes around the various manifestations of *The Color Purple* were ultimately worthwhile and that in working through their intricacies, she became a stronger, more insightful human being.

### Further Reading

Davis, Bernadette Adams. "*The Color Purple* in Retrospect: Twenty Years after the Debut, The Film's Beauty Never Fades." *Black Issues Book Review* (November–December 2005).

Fitzsimmons, Kate. "Go Ask Alice: Alice Walker Talks about *The Color Purple* 10 Years Later." *San Francisco Review of Books* 21, no. 2 (March–April 1996): 20–23.

Templeton, David. "Review: Alice Walker's *The Same River Twice: Honoring the Difficult.*" *Sonoma Independent,* 15–21 February 1996.

Terry, Jill. "The Same River Twice: Signifying *The Color Purple.*" *Critical Survey* 12, no. 3 (2000): 59–76.

Walker, Alice. *The Same River Twice: Honoring the Difficult.* New York: Scribner, 1996.

## *Sent by Earth: A Message from the Grandmother Spirit after the Bombing of the World Trade Center and the Pentagon* (2001)

The small press Seven Stories publishes the Open Media Pamphlet Series. Many major figures have written for it, including HOWARD ZINN, Noam Chomsky, Arundhati Roy, Angela Y. Davis, Ariel Dorfman, and Ralph Nader. In 2001, as part of the series, Alice Walker published the title *Sent by Earth: A Message from the Grandmother Spirit after the Bombing of the World Trade Center and the Pentagon.* The writings in the very short text were extracted in part from a talk that she delivered to the Midwives Alliance of North America at Albuquerque, New Mexico, on September 22, 2001.

In *Sent by Earth,* Walker speaks about the process of altering the talk she had originally intended to present because of the events of 9/11. She proceeds to modify her original points and has a kind of thematic through line in the effort to connect the events of 9/11 with the other issues of global oppression. The issues she tackles and links with the terrorist attack include FEMALE GENITAL MUTILATION, the Iraqi children of war, and the impact of the Taliban. Walker suggests that forgiveness as well as resistance to the impulse to avenge is a possible alternative to violent reprisal. She makes the point that it is worth the investment of creative energy and effort to find healthier solutions for the crisis at hand, as well as for the other complex issues that confront humanity.

### Further Reading

Walker, Alice. *Sent by Earth: A Message from the Grandmother Spirit after the Bombing of the World Trade Center and the Pentagon.* New York: Open Media, 2001.

## *Warrior Marks: Female Genital Mutilation and the Sexual Blinding of Women* Alice Walker and Pratibha Parmar (1993)

This book is the print companion to the documentary of the same name produced by PRATIBHA PARMAR and Alice Walker. At the very beginning of *Warrior Marks,* there is a photograph of a little African girl. The book's dedication to the female children of Africa appears next to the photo. On the next page, Walker details her attraction to this child because of her own resemblance to the girl. These early textual references, the photograph, and Walker's accompanying explanation frame the book's discussion of FEMALE GENITAL MUTILATION. She draws on her own experience as a child victim of violence that occurred during the accident that blinded her eye. She writes that these experiences provide her access to understanding the global expression of violence against women.

The book employs the trope of the journey to detail the particulars of female genital mutilation. The book is divided into sections entitled "Alice's Journey," "Pratibha's Journey," and "Interviews"—titles that suggest the women's trajectories as they learn more about the facts, subjective realities, and impact of female genital mutilation. The titles also predict the potential experience of the reader who is willing to go on this painful journey with the authors.

"Alice's Journey" chronicles Walker's desire to expose more people to the truth about female genital mutilation, a desire that arose for her after writing her novel *Possessing the Secret of Joy*. The section consists of letters, journal entries, speeches, photographs, and excerpts from the text of the documentary itself. Through them, Walker chronicles her own experiences with the project and, more significantly, her growing awareness of the impact and consequences of female genital mutilation.

The second section begins with Parmar's biographical introduction and continues the framework established by Walker's contribution. This section of the text includes letters and reflections, as well as technical and production information and planning.

The book's final section consists of transcripts of the interviews Walker conducted with various individuals who compose part of the contemporary narratives that tell the story of female genital mutilation. All of the pieces in the volume expose the connections between the practice of genital mutilation and the general issues of female oppression. The reader gains valuable in-depth, subjective information about the experience, meanings, and activism that surround female genital mutilation.

## FILM SYNOPSIS

*Warrior Marks: Female Genital Mutilation and the Sexual Blinding of Women* is a documentary film that bears the same name as the book publication. The film, also by Pratibha Parmar and Walker, features a thematic repeating image of a dancing African woman who seems to represent a counterpoint, a hope for liberation and freedom from the practice of female genital mutilation for the millions of women throughout the world who have been subjected to this practice.

The video's main content consists of interviews with various individuals whose stories relate either directly or tangentially to the topic of female genital mutilation. Included is an interview with Walker herself as she tells the story of the childhood blinding of her eye and explains how that experience allowed her to understand and access the pain and trauma of mutilation. Walker's story also helps to illuminate the subtitle of the book and film, *the Sexual Blinding of Women*. The main title of the book and film also derive from this story. Walker explains that the permanent damage that injured individuals retain should be understood as triumphant markers of their survival—warrior marks. She then interviews various survivors of female genital mutilation, activists working to end the practice, and even purveyors of the practice. The video and the book publication provide access to the multiple narratives that surround this controversial issue and are Walker and Parmar's efforts to expose the specifics of the practice of female genital mutilation in all of its complexities so that audiences and readers can craft informed opinions and act accordingly.

### Further Reading

James, Stanlie. "Review: *Warrior Marks: Female Genital Mutilation and the Sexual Blinding of Women* by Pratibha Parmar and Alice Walker." *American Historical Review* 102, no. 2 (April 1997): 595–596.

———. "Shades of Othering: Reflections on Female Circumcision/Genital Mutilation." *Signs* 23, no. 4 (Summer 1998): 1,031–1,048.

King, Lovalerie. "Review: *Warrior Marks: Female Genital Mutilation and the Sexual Blinding of Women* by Alice Walker and Pratibha Parmar." *African American Review* 31, no. 3 (Autumn 1997): 542–545.

Levin, Tobe. "Review: *Warrior Marks: Female Genital Mutilation and the Sexual Blinding of Women* by Pratibha Parmar and Alice Walker." *NWSA Journal* 6, no. 3 (Autumn 1994): 511–514.

Perumal, Devina. "Review: Warriors and Tribunals, *Warrior Marks: Female Genital Mutilation and the Sexual Blinding of Women.*" *Agenda* 27 (1995): 115–118.

Walker, Alice. *Warrior Marks: Female Genital Mutilation and the Sexual Blinding of Women.* DVD. Directed by Pratibha Parmar. New York: Women Make Movies, 1993.

## *We Are the Ones We Have Been Waiting For* (2006)

In 1980, the poet June Jordan published "Poem for South African Women," which ends with the line "we are the ones we have been waiting for." This line became part of American popular vernacular after then presidential candidate Barack Obama used it in his political campaign.

The phrase has been used in a variety of situations, including as the title of Alice Walker's 2006 collection of essays. In Walker's *We Are the Ones We Have Been Waiting For,* she expounds on the tribulations of the moment, calling the modern period both the best and worst of times. The times, according to Walker, are the best because the adversity the natural and spiritual worlds have been subjected to provide humanity with the opportunity to redeem itself and to make right the wrongs it has committed. She makes this mission a personal responsibility and commits the remainder of the volume to demonstrating ways to make good on the responsibility to improve the world rather than relying on others to shoulder that burden.

Walker writes of the ordinary miracles of life, childbirth, and the corollary act of gardening, sharing with her reader the joy of showing her daughter a newly harvested potato she had grown in her garden. There are several graduation and occasional speeches in which Walker reflects on her various transitions, using her experiences as instructive tales. She writes of lessons discerned from her dog, Marley, and of the need to remember those who have been one's teachers. She makes peace with and pays homage to her teacher poet MURIEL RUKEYSER, with whom she became estranged prior to Rukeyser's death. She also recalls the funeral of Dr. MARTIN LUTHER KING, JR. *We Are the Ones We Have Been Waiting For* is also interspersed with various Walker poems. The volume is ultimately optimistic and encouraging of the human capacity to recover, to forgive, and to make amends. It was a *New York Times* best-seller.

## *World Has Changed: Conversations with Alice Walker, The* (2010)

The latest of Alice Walker's nonfiction collections, *The World Has Changed: Conversations with Alice Walker,* edited by Rudolph P. Byrd, is a compilation of interviews and conversations between Walker and notable intellectuals and artists, including Claudia Tate, Paula Giddings, Evelyn C. White, Pema Chödrön, Margo Jefferson, Amy Goodman, and Howard Zinn, from 1973 to 2006.

The opening work is a poem written by Walker in 2008 from which the collection takes its title. The poem encourages the reader to embrace the reality that life is about confronting and embracing the constant presence of change in human experience. The collection begins with a chronology of the major events in Walker's life, including the establishment in 2009 of the Emory University Alice Walker Archives, a collection from which *The World Has Changed* derives. Rudolph P. Byrd, a Walker scholar and friend of the artist, writes a detailed and thorough sketch of Walker's life that includes materials from the archives: an excerpt of a love letter between Walker and her former husband, Melvyn Levanthal; photographs from Walker's childhood, adult, and professional life; and a description of the quilt Walker created to alleviate writer's block while working on *The Color Purple.*

The interviews and conversations that constitute *The World Has Changed: Conversations with Alice Walker* are ordered chronologically. As a consequence, the discussions chart the transformation in Walker's thinking as well as in the political, economic, environmental, and social dynamics of the United States and of the world that transpired during Walker's coming of age and maturity.

Highlights of the collection include Walker's description in the first interview with John O'Brien of the intersection between her illegal abortion while in college and the birth of her identity as a writer. She says, "Writing poems is my way of celebrating with the world that I have not committed suicide the evening before." She also reveals that her poetry, like Langston Hughes's, comes from a place of sadness and grief rather than happiness. Walker's interview with Claudia Tate is a staple of African-American literary criticism and reveals Walker's processes for characterization and for storytelling generally.

The 1988 interview with Ellen Bring reveals the expansion of Walker's concerns about issues of animal rights. Walker tells Bring about her decision to become a vegetarian. In "Writing to Save My Life," Walker responds to questions about criticism of her work by dismissing it, saying that, "you can only be hurt by the criticism of the people you respect." She also alludes to the fundamental connections between her creative process and her "reading" of the natural world.

Walker's 1992 interview with Paula Giddings, originally published in *Essence* magazine, is a discussion of the creation of, and the issues surrounding, Walker's novel *Possessing the Secret of Joy* (1992). Walker's conversation with Isabel Allende and Jean Shinoda Bolen explores the authors' processes, particularly questions regarding the derivation of the plots, characters, and meanings of their works. Walker reveals, "what is painful is often understanding that what I'm writing about someone is actually living, millions of people. So that's really very painful."

The 1994 interview between Jody Hoy and Walker is an exploration of Walker's personal experiences. She talks autobiographically about her childhood, religion, patriarchy, her daughter, and, of course, her writing. The conversation with Tami Simon focuses on Walker's beliefs. Walker speaks about the lessons of childbirth and the frequent invisibility of suffering, particularly the suffering of women. Walker notes, "your true happiness, or my true happiness, is in a peaceful spirit. It's hard for me to think that there's anything else that matters."

One of the richest conversations in the book is the 1996 discussion between Walker and her longtime friend and mentor Howard Zinn. The two chat about the origins of their relationship when Zinn was Walker's professor at Spelman. Zinn's dismissal by the college was a major catalyst for Walker's transfer to Sarah Lawrence. The two discuss Walker's activism, including humanitarian trips to Cuba and Nicaragua. Zinn asks Walker about the personal impacts of *The Color Purple,* about her bisexuality and its effect on her family, and about her attempts to parse power and hierarchy.

One of the most extensive interviews is a 1996 conversation with Justine and Michael Toms. The discussion is mainly about Walker's writing and the centrality of stories to the human experience. She also talks about being a writer and about the complexities of finding time to write. She also expounds upon what gave her sustenance during the economic poverty of her childhood. The Toms also discuss with Walker her literary explorations of controversial topics, such as female genital mutilation.

The interview with Evelyn C. White begins with a discussion of *By the Light of My Father's Smile* (1998), particularly the issues of sexuality that the book involves. Walker also chronicles one of her trips to Cuba and relates other issues of social justice that she is committed to helping resolve. The moderated conversation between Pema Chödrön and Walker, which took place in 1998, engages questions about the relationship between suffering and joy, particularly in a Buddhist context.

The 1998 interview with William R. Ferris, entitled "I Know What the Earth Says," addresses some of the same issues and topics that circulate throughout the collection: the writer's life and motivation, influences, Walker's relationship to Zora Neale Hurston, her childhood and southern roots and identity, her involvement in civil rights issues and movements, and motherhood.

Walker's conversation with Margo Jefferson begins with Walker revealing that in her early life, she wrote primarily as an escape from her family. She discusses her mother's garden and the process of understanding metaphorically the work her mother did in it. The two writers also talk about *Uncle Tom's Cabin;* Walker's father's transition from a gentle, involved parent to a distant, sometimes brutalizing one; her choice of literary genres; female genital mutilation; her eye injury; and hair, among other topics. The interview concludes with a question-and-answer session.

The 2006 conversation with Amy Goodman begins with Walker discussing her arrest at the 2003 International Women's Day March. Walker explains that she and the other women were arrested while protesting the war in Iraq. She speaks about the experience and then proceeds with a more general conversation about the significance of social movements. Here again, Walker discusses her writing process and provides insights into the emergence of particular works. She also talks about the transformation of *The Color Purple* into a musical. The interview ends with Walker reading a letter she wrote to the *New York Times* in response to a negative review the newspaper had written about Toni Morrison's *The Bluest Eye.*

In a 2006 interview with George Galloway, Walker discusses her complex feelings about Fidel Castro and the Cuban revolution. A conversation in the same year with Marianne Schnall discusses Walker's book *We Are the Ones We Have Been Waiting For* (2006), feminism and womanism, Bill Cosby, God, the planet, and the future. Another 2006 interview, with David Swick, also responds to the publication of *We Are the Ones We Have Been Waiting For* in addition to discussions of other issues related to Buddhism and its tenets and practices. The interview also explores the role of spirituality and spiritual challenges generally as they involve the particular life experiences Walker has encountered.

The final interview of the book takes place with the editor of the volume, Rudolph P. Byrd. Byrd refocuses the reader with a set of questions that tie the volume together thematically. Walker reflects on the central question, How has the world changed? She responds with thoughts about Barack Obama, her travels on humanitarian missions, and spiritual quests. She discusses her current influences and the writing process. Walker talks about the creation of her Web site, Jung as an influence, and the transformations and long life of her creation *The Color Purple.* The interview ends with her talking about raising chickens at her home in northern California and how that experience has helped her to reconnect with her roots.

### Further Reading

Walker, Alice. *The World Has Changed: Conversations with Alice Walker.* New York: The New Press, 2010.

# Children's Books

## *Finding the Green Stone* (1991)

The central concept of this book is that each member of a "small community on the Earth" possesses a green stone that is a barometer of the person's thoughts and actions. It shimmers whenever the owner thinks and acts in a gracious manner; it grows dull from negative thoughts and actions.

The central characters in the story are a young brother and sister, Johnny and Katie. One day, Johnny loses his green stone, and his attempts to find it become the central action for the rest of the book. Without his stone, Johnny's mood darkens. He becomes jealous of his sister, who still has her green stone. Her sits under a tree in the town green, "fuming and casting mean looks at everybody who passed and sometimes muttering nasty things as well." Throughout his search, he must seek the help of people he has insulted, including his father, of whom, he said, he was ashamed because of his occupation, which is driving a pulpwood truck. But people forgive Johnny, and they even help him search for his green stone.

At one point, Johnny and Katie run into their mother, a doctor, who is usually too busy for them and about whom Johnny has also harbored negative thoughts. But in this moment, she slows down enough to offer words of wisdom in their search: "Listen, son, everybody has his or her own green stone. . . . Nobody can give it to you and nobody can take it away. Only you can misplace or lose it. If you've lost it, it's your own fault." Johnny is now sorry for his negative thoughts about his mother.

Now, everyone in the community joins in the search for Johnny's green stone—a teacher, minister, shoeshine man, paperboy, and even "a baby crawling after them." And although all these people cannot actually help him find it, Johnny's sister explains their presence in the search: "We wanted to be with you when you found it!" It is during this moment of community solidarity that a dull stone that Johnny is holding, and was ready to toss, starts to shimmer. He has found his green stone. The book ends with a series of three of CATHERINE DEETER's paintings, now without narration, viewing this community from above and pulling back to take in more of the surrounding terrain, ending with a view of the entire earth—painted in green.

## *Langston Hughes, American Poet* (1974)

Walker's *Langston Hughes: American Poet* is aimed at older children, with text written as short paragraphs. It is a straightforward narrative of the life of the African-American poet LANGSTON HUGHES (1902–67) from his childhood in the Midwest to his death while living in New York's Harlem. The story line covers many of the key points of Hughes's family life, including his visits to Mexico to see his father; his being raised first by his grandmother and then by his mother; and, at 17, his reunion with his father, whom he initially did not recognize.

Walker also chronicles Hughes's foundational experiences in this biography. She recounts his travels to Africa, where he felt he needed to declare his blackness to many of the Africans he met who thought he was white because he had lighter skin than they did. Throughout the book, Walker presents Hughes's observations about prejudice in America. While a young student, Hughes had in his classes fellow students who were immigrants. From them, young Langston learned that "African Americans were not the only people called bad names. He also learned that being called 'kike' or 'hunky' *hurt,* if you were Jewish or Hungarian, just as much as being called 'nigger' did if you were black." At the same time, Hughes also realized that his peers still were considered white and as such had advantages that he, as an African American, did not. Later in Hughes's life, after having trouble finding employment, he understood the refusal of white people to hire him as self-defeating.

Into this biography, Walker also weaves two of Hughes's poems written when he was a teenager, "When Susanna Jones Wears Red" and "The Negro Speaks of Rivers." The illustrations by CATHERINE DEETER have a textured look, as if painted on a fabric.

## *There Is a Flower at the Tip of My Nose Smelling Me* (2006)

According to Walker, *There Is a Flower at the Tip of My Nose Smelling Me* is a "thank you note" to nature and the world around her that she composed after she returned from a walk in a forest. As told in her author's note, as she hiked an old logging trail, she was struck by the beauty around her, and she was overcome by the thought of herself as part of all she was witnessing. The result was this children's book, listed as being for all ages. In it, Walker reverses the usual subjective reference to the world and instead turns the reader into the object, the viewer into the viewed. Thus, the narrator does not smell the flower, but the flower is smelling her. The narrator does not see the stars at night; rather, "There is a sky at the end of my eye seeing me" and, later, "There is a road at the bottom of my foot walking me." In this way, Walker moves through all the senses and through various activities: "There is a song deep in my body singing me" and "There is a dance that lives in my bones dancing me." She finishes her "thank you note" by saying, "There is a story at the end of my arms telling me." The book's brightly colored illustrations by Stefano Vitale are playful and attractive.

## *To Hell with Dying* (1988)

Originally published in 1981 as a short story, *To Hell with Dying* was reissued in 1988 as a children's book with illustrations by CATHERINE DEETER. It tells the story of a little girl and her brother whose love for an elderly neighbor seems able to bring him back from the brink of death. Told in the first person by the girl as an adult reflecting back, the story opens with a description of the old man, Mr. Sweet, as "a diabetic and an alcoholic and a guitar player . . . [who] lived down the road from us on a neglected cotton farm." Whenever Mr. Sweet is on his deathbed, the children's father—shouting, "To hell with dying, man . . . !"—brings his daughter and son to Mr. Sweet's bedside, where the two children kiss the old man, climb on him, and tickle him so that "he would laugh all down in his stomach." Each time the children visit him in this way, their elderly friend revives.

Much of the text is a profile of Mr. Sweet, an endearing man with a free spirit who, through his guitar playing, brings music and also gives gentle love to the children. But the visits cannot work forever. When the girl, now a doctoral student, learns that Mr. Sweet is ill, she returns home from her studies to see him at his bedside. Despite her efforts, Mr. Sweet, now 90, dies. The narrator inherits his guitar, and the story ends with her sadly playing the instrument and lamenting the loss of the man who had been her "first love."

## *Why War Is Never a Good Idea* (2007)

Illustrated by Stefano Vitale, Alice Walker's *Why War Is Never a Good Idea* is presented in a children's book format, though the dustcover says it is for "all ages." War, here, is depicted as a monstrous and callous being that descends like a noxious cloud upon various peaceful scenes of both humans and the earth.

In the opening episode, Walker and Vitale show an idyllic pond where frogs have gathered for their "pre-rainy-season convention" just as war approaches, depicted here as the "huge tires of a camouflaged vehicle about to squash them flat." In another scene, a Latino boy is sitting on a haystack and enjoying a warm day while, just above him and his donkey, "something dark big as a car is dropping." War is also presented as possessing cruel contradictions so that though it "has eyes of its own & can see oil & gas & mahogany trees & every shining thing under the earth[,] when it comes to nursing mothers it is blind." In an observation later on, Walker says that "Though War is old it has not become wise." Finally, war is depicted as having "bad manners." It "eats everything in its path & what it doesn't eat it dribbles on." It "tastes terrible" and "smells bad" with "body odor." Throughout Walker's story, Vitale illustrates the scenes of peace with bright colors, which are then contrasted with the dark shades of war.

# Selected Nonfiction Audio Recordings

## *Alice Walker in Conversation with Gloria Steinem at the 92nd Street Y* (2007)

Alice Walker joins her old friends GLORIA STEINEM and Wilma Mankiller in an engaging conversation about the contemporary world and the status of the feminist struggle. The conversation is wide-ranging, and each of the women discusses both their personal journeys and analyzes the ways in which those quests intersect with the progress in the fight for gender equality.

### Further Reading

*Alice Walker in Conversation with Gloria Steinem at the 92nd Street Y.* Audiocassette of Conversation with Gloria Steinem and Wilma Mankiller. New York: 92nd Street Young Men's and Young Women's Hebrew Association, 2007.

## *Gardening the Soul* (2000)

In this conversation, Walker borrows from her gardening metaphor, introduced in her collection of essays *In Search of Our Mothers' Gardens,* to discuss the complexities of life in the contemporary world. She posits that the secret to meeting the challenges presented by the rapid pace and disconnection of the present is to recognize and embrace the fundamental unity of human beings and to find solace in the lessons that are available in the natural world.

### Further Reading

Walker, Alice. *Gardening the Soul.* Two audiocassettes, with Michael Toms. Carlsbad, Calif.: Hay House Audio, 2000.

## *Giving Birth, Finding Form* (1993)

In this conversation with the feminist artists Isabel Allende and Jean Shinoda Bolen, Walker talks about her experiences in creating her works. The three share engaging banter about the creative process and the ways in which their personal experiences have informed and influenced their artistry.

### Further Reading

Walker, Alice. *Giving Birth, Finding Form.* Audiocassette, with Isabel Allende and Jean Shinoda Bolen. Boulder, Colo.: Sounds True Audio, 1993.

## *My Life as My Self* (1995)

In this audio narrative, Walker recounts the details of her life and her experiences as a creative artist. She is frank about the struggles she has had to face and provides listeners with some insights about the ways that she has learned to cope with tribulation. The cassette also includes Walker reading from her poetry. In the interview, she engages many of the central concerns of her life: global oppression, the subjugation of women, and the primacy of cultivating connections with the natural and spiritual worlds.

### Further Reading

Walker, Alice. *My Life as My Self.* Audiocassette. Boulder, Colo.: Sounds True Audio, 1995.

## *Pema Chödrön & Alice Walker in Conversation: On the Meaning of Suffering and the Mystery of Joy* (1998)

In this conversation between Alice Walker and PEMA CHÖDRÖN, the two women reveal their personal experiences with suffering and their quests to define and acquire a joyous outlook on life. They also speak about the development of their relationship and the ways in which Chödrön helped Walker to access a type of Buddhist meditation called TONGLEN.

Tonglen is a meditation practice found in Tibetan BUDDHISM. Translated as "giving and receiving," Tonglen is a visualization technique in which the practitioner takes on the suffering of another, or others, with each inhalation, and offers one's own happiness and peace to the other with each exhale. As such, Tonglen is meant to pursue and reinforce key teachings of Buddhism, including generating loving-kindness and decreasing self-attachment. It is not meant to increase one's own pain but to help break down the instinct of a self-protective ego. The practice can be directed toward a single individual, to a group, or to all across the world. Chödrön and Walker have found Tonglen to be a fundamental tool in their work to become more accepting and healthy.

### Further Reading

Chödrön, Pema, and Alice Walker. *Pema Chödrön & Alice Walker in Conversation: On the Meaning of Suffering and the Mystery of Joy.* CD. Boulder, Colo.: Sounds True Audio, 1998.

# PART III

# *Related People, Places, and Topics*

**Afra-American women's literary renaissance** The proliferation of writings by African-American women during the 1970s and 1980s—a literary profusion that the critic Joanne Braxton named the Afra-American renaissance—was in part catalyzed by the shortcomings and sexisms of the Black Power movement, the public and political demonization of black women, and the rise of the black feminist movement at the end of the 1960s. Generally speaking, the writings of the renaissance urge reconsideration and rearticulation of the particular experiences of African-American women. Many of the authors of the Afra-American renaissance—Alice Walker, Toni Cade Bambara, and Toni Morrison, among others—challenge dominant constructions of black womanhood through their rewriting and recasting stereotypes and flat portrayals of African-American women in literature.

By proposing and constructing a more complex black and female image, these texts challenge the fundamentally patriarchal and racist ideologies of American society, undermine pervasive and persistent negative stereotypes of black women, and reflect the currency and influence of black feminist thinking. Walker's definition of WOMANISM in her 1983 anthology *In Search of Our Mothers' Gardens* contributed a theoretical construct to this ongoing conversation.

### FURTHER READING

Braxton, Joanne, and Andree Nicola-McLaughlin. *Wild Women in the Whirlwind: Afra-American Culture and the Contemporary Literary Renaissance.* New Brunswick, N.J.: Rutgers University Press, 1990.

**African-American missionaries in Africa** In her novels *The Color Purple* and *Possessing the Secret of Joy*, Alice Walker uses her characters' experiences to explore the history of African-American missionaries in Africa. African Americans have been traveling to Africa as Christian missionaries since at least the early 19th century, although the history of their participation in American missionary work in Africa is not well-documented and is still the subject of continued inquiry by contemporary historians. According to historians such as William Seraile, Wilber Christian Harr, Miles Mark Frasier, and others, Lott Carey (1780–1828) was among the first, if not *the* first, missionary to Africa, traveling to Sierra Leone in 1821 as a part of the African Missionary Society, an organization he had helped to form in Richmond, Virginia, several years prior to his departure to West Africa.

In the same year that Carey left the United States to serve as a missionary in Sierra Leone, another African American, Daniel Coker (1780–1846) began 25 years of service in another location in Sierra Leone as a representative of the AFRICAN METHODIST EPISCOPAL CHURCH. After this documented beginning of African-American service as Christian missionaries to Africa, hundreds, and perhaps thousands of African Americans have served in this capacity.

During the eras of slavery and segregation, missionary work created an opportunity for African-American men and women to hold positions of authority and respect and to travel outside of the United States in ways that might not have been accomplished otherwise. The legacy of these missions is complex and not easily summarized. Some of the missionaries were supporters of various colonization efforts and embraced the pervasive beliefs of their congregations in the inherent inferiority of Africans. Others sought to work for the independence and autonomy of Africans, some expressing a pan-African sensibility that took as its foundation the belief that the destiny of Africans and Africans of the diaspora were permanently interconnected.

### FURTHER READING

Fisher, Miles Mark. "Lott Carey, the Colonizing Missionary." *Journal of Negro History* (October 1922): 381.

Harr, Wilber Christian. "The Negro as an American Protestant Missionary in Africa." Ph.D. diss., University of Chicago Divinity School, 1945.

Jacobs, S. M. *Black Americans and the Missionary Movement in Africa.* Westport, Conn.: Greenwood, 2004.

Sanneh, Lamin O. *Abolitionists Abroad: American Blacks and the Making of the Modern West Africa.* Cambridge, Mass.: Harvard University Press, 1999.

Walston, Vaughn J., and Robert J. Stevens, eds. *African-American Experience in World Mission: A Call Beyond Community.* Pasadena, Calif.: William Carey Library, 2002.

Williams, Walter L. *Black Americans and the Evangelization of Africa, 1887–1900.* Madison: University of Wisconsin Press, 1982.

**African-American quilting** Alice Walker references quilting in several of her works, most notably in the novel *The Color Purple* and in her short story "Everyday Use." Scholarship on African-American quilting has blossomed since the 1980s. African-American quilts are understood as functional, artistic, and even textual. Theories about the aesthetics, traditions, and practices of African-American quilting are widely disputed and are the subject of scholarly controversy. Some scholars maintain that traditional African quilting and textile production was a strong influence on early African-American quilt makers. At that time, although men were the major textile producers in West Africa, enslaved African-American women were the primary producers of quilts. Some scholars have noted patterns in early African-American quilts that suggest possible survivals from Africa that survived the Middle Passage and subsequent enslavement. There are observable patterns in these quilts that may connect them to some African aesthetic traditions. Some of those traditions include pattern improvisation, bright colors, asymmetrical design, and strip banding.

As African-American quilters incorporated European styles and designs into their quilts, African-American quilting, like so many other forms of African-American art, is a synthesis of many different cultures and traditions. For that reason, it is difficult to strictly define an African-American quilting tradition. Some scholars have posited that enslaved African Americans used quilts as texts, encoding in their various patterns messages, histories, and even maps of potential escape routes that they did not want their masters to be able to read or to understand. Others feel that such a thesis is unlikely.

Today, African Americans are actively involved in quilting as a hobby and as an art form. Modern African-American quilters produce traditional and experimental works using a variety of patterns, materials, and designs.

## FURTHER READING

Barry, A. "Quilting has African Roots, a New Exhibition Suggests." *New York Times,* 16 November 1989, p. B8.

Benberry, Cuesta. "African American Quilts: Paradigms of Black Diversity." *International Review of African American Art* 12 (1995): 30–37.

———. *Always There: The African American Presence in American Quilts.* Louisville: Kentucky Quilt Project, Inc., 1992.

Callahan, Nancy. *The Freedom Quilting Bee.* Tuscaloosa: University of Alabama Press, 1987.

Ferris, William. *Afro-American Folk Art and Crafts.* Jackson: University Press of Mississippi, 1983.

Fry, G. M. *Stitched from the Soul: Slave Quilts from the Ante-Bellum South.* New York: Dutton Books and the Museum of American Folk Art, 1990.

Grudin, Eva Ungar. *Stitching Memories: African American Story Quilts.* Williamstown, Mass.: Williams College Museum of Art, 1989.

Harrison, C., and Paul Wood, eds. *Art in Theory 1900–1990: An Anthology of Changing Ideas.* Oxford: Blackwell Publishers, 1995.

Jeffries, R. "African Retentions in African American Quilts and Artifacts." *International Review of African American Art* 11 (1994): 28–37.

Koplos, J. "Stitching Memories: African American Story Quilts, Who'd a Thought It: Improvisation in African American Quiltmaking." *Crafts, London Crafts Council* 103 (1990): 49.

Leon, Eli. *Models in the Mind: African Prototypes in American Patchwork.* Winston-Salem, N.C.: Winston-Salem State University, 1992.

———. *Who'd a Thought It: Improvisation in African American Quiltmaking.* San Francisco: San Francisco Craft and Folk Art Museum, 1987.

Lyles, C. Y. "Redefining Cultural Roots: Diversity in African American Quilts." *Surface Design Journal* 20 (Spring 1996): 13–14.

Picton, John, and John Mack. *African Textiles.* New York: Harper and Row, 1989.

Tobin, Jacqueline L., and Raymond G. Dobard. *Hidden in Plain View: The Secret Story of Quilts and the Underground Railroad.* New York: Doubleday, 1999.

Wahlman, M. S. "Religious Symbolism in African-American Quilts." *The Clarion* (Summer 1989): 36–44.

Watanabe, Y. "Afro-American Quilts." *Patchwork Quilt Tsushin* 25 (July 1988): 12–17.

**African Methodist Episcopal Church (A.M.E. Church)** The African Methodist Episcopal Church is a branch of the American Methodist Church, which emerged from the Methodist movement in England. In 1739, John Wesley began Methodism as a way of improving on Anglicanism. The movement gained strength and eventually became its own denomination. The founders of the Methodist Church realized that the future of the church was in the Americas, and so they began their expansion into the colonies. Methodists rapidly spread the new denomination across the country, and Methodism began to develop various branches. One of the main factions was the American Methodist Episcopal Church.

Although the American Methodist Church accepted African Americans as members and condemned slavery as an institution, African-American church members were not allowed to worship with whites. In 1787, this became unacceptable to a group of African Americans who were members of the St. George's Methodist Episcopal Church in Philadelphia, Pennsylvania. Refusing to endure the insult of segregated worship, a group of African Americans left the church and began the Free African Society, which eventually splintered into two entities, the Episcopalians and the Methodists. In 1816, the Methodist faction of the Free African Society formed the African Methodist Episcopal (A.M.E.) Church under the leadership of Richard Allen (1760–1831).

The newly established denomination grew rapidly as churches were established in Philadelphia; New York; Boston; Pittsburgh; Baltimore; Washington, D.C.; Cincinnati; Chicago; and Detroit—major urban areas with significant populations of free African Americans. With the outbreak of the Civil War, the church found a new outlet for the activism that had been such a pivotal element in its foundation. As the Confederacy began to collapse, A.M.E. ministers worked within the slave states to convert former slaves. As a result, church membership grew exponentially, and by 1880, it had reached a new high of approximately 400,000 members. Due largely to the activities of one of its prominent bishops, Henry McNeal Turner, the African Methodist Episcopal Church gained significant converts in Africa, particularly in the countries of Sierra Leone, Liberia, and South Africa. In the 21st century, the A.M.E. Church continues to be a vibrant African-American institution with an international membership of more than 2 million.

This sign from the Alice Walker Driving Tour provides information about Wards Chapel African Methodist Episcopal Church, the church Alice Walker and her family attended when she was a child. *(Photograph by Carmen Gillespie)*

As a child, Alice Walker attended and was baptized in Wards Chapel A.M.E. Church. She also refers extensively to the Church's missionary work in several of her novels, including *The Color Purple, The Temple of My Familiar,* and *Possessing the Secret of Joy.*

### FURTHER READING

Allen, Richard. *The Life Experience and Gospel Labors of the Rt. Rev. Richard Allen.* Nashville, Tenn.: Abingdon Press, 1960.

Broadway, Bill. "A Search for Meaning at AME Convocation." *Washington Post,* 22 August 1998. p. D7.

George, Carol V. R. *Segregated Sabbaths: Richard Allen and the Rise of Independent Black Churches, 1760–1840.* New York: Oxford University Press, 1973.

Klots, Steve. *Richard Allen.* New York: Chelsea House Publishers, 1991.

**Alice Walker Literary Society** Founded in 1997, the Alice Walker Literary Society is an author society of the American Literature Association. Its existence is grounded in a collaboration of Emory University's James Weldon Johnson Institute and SPELMAN COLLEGE's Women's Research and Resource Center. According to the objectives listed on its Web site, the society's mission is "to initiate, sponsor and encourage critical dialogue, scholarly publications, conferences, programs and research projects devoted to the study of the life and works of Alice Walker."

Rudolph P. Byrd, an American Studies professor at Emory and a Walker scholar, established the Alice Walker Literary Society with Walker's enthusiastic endorsement. In December 2007, Walker also designated Emory as the official home of her archives, now entitled *The Alice Walker Papers.* On April 24, 2009, the society cosponsored *A Keeping of Records: The Art and Life of Alice Walker: A Symposium* at Emory. The symposium celebrated the opening of Walker's archives with an exhibition of her drafts and various personal archival materials displayed in the Robert W. Woodruff Library's Schatten Gallery. Additionally, the daylong symposium featured four panels, including "Alice Walker and the Traditions of American and African-American Literature," with presentations by the literary scholars Beverly Guy-Sheftall, Michael Awkward, Cheryl Wall, and Deborah Plant; "Producing and Directing Alice Walker: *The Color Purple* from Peachtree Street to Broadway": "Be Nobody's Darling: Alice Walker as Activist and Feminist," featuring GLORIA STEINEM and HOWARD ZINN; and "Editing Alice Walker: the Life and Writings." The event concluded with Walker's public lecture, "Reflections on the Turning of the Wheel: Living a Life of Freedom and Choice," delivered at Emory's Glenn Memorial Auditorium. During the lecture, city representatives presented Walker with a plaque that officially declared April 24, 2009, as "Alice Walker Day" in Atlanta, Georgia.

Rudolph P. Byrd is the Goodrich C. White Professor of American Studies and founding director of the James Weldon Johnson Institute for Advanced Interdisciplinary Studies at Emory University in Atlanta, Georgia. He is an expert scholar on the life and writings of Alice Walker, codirector of the Alice Walker Literary Society, and curator of Emory University's exhibition *A Keeping of Records: The Art and Life of Alice Walker,* which was created in celebration of the opening of Emory University's Alice Walker Archives in April 2009. *(Photograph by Carmen Gillespie)*

The archives at Emory University are a major landmark in African-American women's studies. The Alice Walker Literary Society is open to laypeople and scholars who are interested in engaging in intellectual explorations of Walker's works.

### FURTHER READING

Alice Walker Literary Society. "Mission." Available online. URL: http://www.emory.edu/alicewalker/sub-mission.htm. Accessed February 28, 2009.

Emory University. "Alice Walker Archive Opens at Emory April 23." Available online. URL: http://www.emory.edu/home/news/releases/2009/04/alice-walker-archive-opens-at-emory-april-23.html. Accessed April 21, 2009.

**all-black towns** Although most all-black towns were established in the wake of the Civil War and the mass exodus of freed African Americans from the South, there were instances of African Americans forming towns that were inhabited primarily by other African Americans as early as the 1830s. There were hundreds of these towns scattered across the entire United States, including Alaska; however, most all-black towns were formed in the South, primarily in what is now the state of Oklahoma. At the time, the area was called the Indian Territory and was, according to treaty, in the possession of various Native American groups, at least for a short time. Often, the founders of these towns would obtain permission to settle land from Native Americans, and there were relationships between Native American enclaves and all-black towns, with intermarriage not uncommon. Although a few of them—such as Eatonville, Florida, the home of author ZORA NEALE HURSTON—survive today, most of these locales fell on hard times, and the towns disappeared.

Some of the most prominent all-black towns were Nicodemus in Kansas; Boley, Brooksville, Clearview, Grayson, Langston, Lima, Redbird, Rentiesville, Summit, Taft, Tatums, Tullahassee, and Vernon in Oklahoma; Dempsey, Alaska; Parting Ways, Massachusetts; and Coit Mountain, New Hampshire. The reasons for the creation of these towns varied. Some of them were formed by emancipated African Americans who sought the economic and social solidarity that could be achieved by pooling resources, skills, and strengths. Others did not believe that they would be accepted into American society and felt that their best chance for survival existed by cultivating autonomy and self-sufficiency. The conditions freed African Americans faced in the South were often perilous and life-threatening. For some, all-black towns may have represented sanctuary and a chance to escape the pervasive racism of the time in which they lived.

The establishment of these all-black towns was encouraged and supported by various individuals who were motivated by combinations of altruism and avarice. Men like Benjamin "Papa" Singleton advertised for African Americans who had been enslaved to leave the South and to relocate to Kansas and form towns there. Those who journeyed to Kansas were often referred to as Exodusters, so called from the Bible's book of Exodus, which tells the story of the Hebrew exodus from Egypt.

Of the hundreds of all-black towns that were formed in the United States, very few remain. The all-black towns that did not survive met their demise as a result of many different factors, including changes brought about by JIM CROW laws; internecine struggles; and deliberate, sometimes violent destruction by whites eager to have the land. Later factors such as integration and the loss of economic viability weakened the sustainability of many of these towns. Of those that survive, many are on the brink of extinction with declining populations, often in remote locations with few economic opportunities.

Alice Walker references all-black towns throughout her canon. Her connections with and promotion of Zora Neale Hurston's life and works are a highlight of her interest in this underexplored American historical reality.

### FURTHER READING

Crockett, Norman. *The Black Towns.* Lawrence: Regents Press of Kansas, 1979.

Hamilton, Kenneth M. *Black Towns and Profit: Promotion and Development in the Trans-Appalachian West, 1877–1915.* Urbana: University of Illinois Press, 1991.

Johnson, Hannibal B. *Acres of Aspiration: The All-Black Towns in Oklahoma.* Austin, Tex.: Eakin Press, 2002.

Katz, William Loren. *The Black West: A Documentary and Pictorial History of the African American Role in the Westward Expansion of the United States.* New York: Simon and Schuster, 1996.

Knight, T. *Sunset on Utopian Dreams: An Experiment of Black Separatism on the American Frontier.* Washington, D.C.: University Press of America, 1977.

Tolson, Arthur L. *The Black Oklahomans: A History, 1541–1972.* New Orleans: Edwards Printing Company, 1974.

Wickett, M. *Contested Territory: Whites, Native Americans, and African Americans in Oklahoma, 1865–1907.* Baton Rouge: Louisiana State University Press, 2000.

**Allen, Robert** (1942– ) Robert Lee Allen is a writer, scholar, teacher, and activist who was born in Atlanta, Georgia. He attended Morehouse College as an undergraduate student and first met Alice Walker in HOWARD ZINN's Russian history class. At the time the two met, Walker was a student at Morehouse's adjoining sister school, SPELMAN COLLEGE. In the 1970s, Allen began serving as the editor of the academic journal the *Black Scholar,* a position he still retains, coediting with Dr. Robert Chrisman.

In the late 1970s, while Allen was married and living in California, he and Walker began a bicoastal relationship. At the time, Walker was living in New York and was separated from her then husband, MELYVN LEVENTHAL. Eventually, she moved to San Francisco, and she and Allen began living together. They cofounded WILD TREES PRESS (1984–88), a book publishing company, with BELVIE ROOKS.

During the filming of *The Color Purple,* the relationship between Walker and Allen became strained, reportedly as a result of his feelings of neglect and envy. Subsequently, the couple separated.

Allen currently works at the University of California, Berkeley, in the African-American and Ethnic Studies department. He is the author of several books, including *Black Awakening in Capitalist America* (1969); *Reluctant Reformers: The Impact of Racism on Social Movement in the U.S.* (1983); and *Brotherman: The Odyssey of Black Men in America* (1995), an anthology he coedited with Herb Boyd. *Brotherman* was awarded an American Book Award. Some critics have found thinly disguised references to Walker's relationship with Allen in her collection of vignettes *The Way Forward Is with a Broken Heart.*

### FURTHER READING

Allen, Robert L. *Black Awakening in Capitalist America.* Trenton, N.J.: Africa World Press, Inc., 1990.

Lauret, Maria. *Alice Walker.* New York: Macmillan, 2000.

University of California Berkeley, Department of African-American Studies. "Robert L. Allen, Ph.D." Available online. URL: http://africam.berkeley.edu/faculty/allen.html. Accessed March 6, 2009.

White, Evelyn C. *Alice Walker: A Life.* New York: Norton, 2004.

Winchell, Donna Haisty. *Alice Walker.* New York: Twayne, 1992.

**antiapartheid movements** The term *apartheid* refers to the legalized system of segregation and discrimination practiced against blacks in South Africa from 1948 until 1994. Antiapartheid movements in South Africa, led most prominently by the African National Congress (ANC), formed the central oppositional voice to the system of apartheid. Although officially instituted in 1948, discrimination against black Africans had been a reality since the founding of the Union of South Africa in 1910. The organization that would come to be called the ANC was founded in 1912 and from that time worked and organized to question and protest discriminatory laws. The central denominator underlying its mission was the demand that South Africa establish laws and practices that would ensure access to freedom and equality for its black citizens.

Following the full assertion of legal apartheid in 1948, the South African government strengthened its original legal restrictions on its black citizens and instituted an even more comprehensive regulation of residential life, business, and politics. The system was structured to embrace and revivify notions of racial hierarchy and privilege. This institutionalized segregation stimulated the organization of various groups whose specific focus was the elimination of the unjust system.

In addition to the African National Congress, other antiapartheid groups engaged in various protest strategies. Some of these groups included the Federation of South African Women and the Pan Africanist Congress (PAC). The defiance campaigns and mass demonstrations drew international attention that, over time, motivated the South African government to declare the country an independent republic and to withdraw from the British Commonwealth in 1961.

Other pivotal events of the 1960s include the PAC's 10-day protest, which included arrests and attacks on marchers, and the 1963 arrest and life imprisonment of seven ANC members for sabotage, including the future South African president and movement icon lawyer Nelson Mandela.

The racial turbulence and oppression of the 1970s and 1980s brought increased international attention to apartheid and the activities of the South African government. The international community witnessed the development of the student-centered Black Consciousness movement, led in part by Steve Biko, who was murdered for his efforts in September 1977; the violent Soweto uprisings of 1976 and 1977; and the intensification of resistance by black South Africans, often in the form of guerrilla activity.

The international antiapartheid movement consisted of a complex array of public and private protests of the system of segregation. In the United States, the most important and arguably most effective form of protest was economic. Public pressure forced various major companies to divest themselves from their economic investments in South Africa. The cumulative impact of these economic losses combined with government economic sanctions were eventually effective and contributed to pressuring the South African government to end the system of apartheid.

The combination of an economy weakened by the United States's and the United Kingdom's economic sanctions and divestment carried out by various corporations, as well as the pressure of South Africa's increasing social and geopolitical isolation, eased the path to a new kind of leadership for the country. F. W. de Klerk's 1990 election as president ushered in a new era of reform. Under international pressure, de Klerk's agenda evolved to include the legalization and recognition of the ANC, the release of Nelson Mandela and other political prisoners, and the reformulation of the South African constitution.

On April 27, 1994, the country held its first free election, and Mandela, of the African National Congress political party, was elected president. In June 1994, apartheid officially ended in South Africa. Alice Walker and many other writers, intellectuals, and celebrities had contributed much time and money as well as their art to the efforts to end apartheid.

### FURTHER READING

Appiah, Kwame Anthony, and Henry Louis Gates Jr., eds. *The Dictionary of Global Culture.* New York: Alfred A. Knopf, 1997.

Falola, Toyin. *Key Events in African History: A Reference Guide.* Westport, Conn.: Greenwood Press, 2002.

Fieldhouse, Roger. *Anti-Apartheid: A History of the Movement in Britain; A Study in Pressure Groups Politics.* London: Merlin, 2005.

Gurney, C. "A Great Cause: The Origins of the Anti-Apartheid Movement, June 1959–March 1960." *Journal of South African Studies* 26, no. 1 (2000): 123–144.

Keck, Margaret E., and Kathryn Sikkink. *Activists beyond Borders: Advocacy Networks in International Politics.* Ithaca, N.Y.: Cornell University Press, 1998.

Plummer, B. G., ed. *Window on Freedom: Race, Civil Rights, and Foreign Affairs, 1945–1988.* Chapel Hill: University of North Carolina Press, 2003.

**antinuclear movement** Since the cold war era, American scientists, such as J. Robert Oppenheimer, who worked on the Manhattan Project, have articulated the importance of containing nuclear power in all of its manifestations and placing it under civilian rather than military control. These controversial efforts often led to professional marginalization for these individuals. Some scientific innovators were even labeled communist sympathizers as a result of their controversial positions about the use of nuclear weapons and power.

Beginning in the 1960s with the flourishing of the ecological and environmental movements, organized citizens' campaigns and research by public and private commissions have raised questions about the potential harmful effects of low-level radiation and pollution on the health of the general public. This increased awareness was the foundation of and catalyst for government action in the form of legislative and regulatory measures.

The energy crisis of 1973–74 was a particular benchmark for the emergence of a formal antinuclear movement. Among the key events of the period were the activism and public outcry of Ralph Nader, the Sierra Club, and Friends of the Earth. Efforts by these and other groups and individuals led to demands for a moratorium on nuclear power development and weapons proliferation. In 1974 and 1975, Nader organized two conferences under the title *Critical Mass.* These conferences significantly increased publicity about and support for antinuclear efforts.

There were other key moments of mobilization for the antinuclear movement. One of these widely publicized events was the suspicious and sudden death of labor advocate Karen Silkwood, whose unresolved demise in 1974 occurred as she attempted to expose some of the illegalities of the nuclear industry. Another important event was the Three Mile Island accident in 1979, when a nuclear power plant outside of Harrisburg, Pennsylvania, experienced a partial core meltdown. Negative publicity from the accident had a solidifying effect on public opinion regarding the use and safety of nuclear energy.

From the early 1970s through the early 1980s, a series of campaigns formed the core of the antinuclear movement. Today's antinuclear campaigning focuses on public articulation of the dangers of nuclear technology, stressing the need to search for energy alternatives, preserving the natural environment, and protecting citizens from the potential dangers of an accident or of exposure to radiation. Of particular concern is the safety of workers in various industries associated with nuclear energy and weaponry, as well as the preservation of a nontoxic environment in and around households in relatively close proximity to nuclear facilities.

Alice Walker has supported the antinuclear movement by lending her name, presence, and art to various campaigns throughout her tenure as a public figure. She has taken part in many public protests, and her fiction and nonfiction writings frequently have as their major themes the struggle against nuclear power and weaponry, which she sees as inevitably linked to the destruction of humanity and of the earth.

### FURTHER READING

Duffy, Robert J. *Nuclear Politics in America: A History and Theory of Government Regulation.* Lawrence: University of Kansas Press, 1997.

Entman, R. M., and A. Rojecki. "Freezing Out the Public: Elite and Media Framing of the U.S. Anti-Nuclear Movement." *Political Communication* 10, no. 2 (1993): 155–173.

Kitschelt, H. "Political Opportunity Structures and Political Protest: Anti-Nuclear Movements in Four Democracies." *British Journal of Political Science* 16 (1986): 57–85.

Ladd, A. E., T. C. Hood, and K. D. Van Liere. "Ideological Themes in the Antinuclear Movement: Consensus and Diversity." *Sociological Inquiry* 53, nos. 2–3 (2007): 252–269.

Opp, K. D. "Soft Incentives and Collective Action: Participation in the Anti-Nuclear Movement." *British Journal of Political Science* 16 (1986): 87–112.

Price, Jerome. *The Antinuclear Movement.* Boston: Twayne Publishers, 1982.

**Aquarius (astrological sign)** The sign of Aquarius is the astrological symbol designated for persons born between January 21 and February 19. Representing the 11th sign of the zodiac is the figure of a man pouring water from an amphora. Egyptians identified Aquarius with their god Hapi and viewed the rendering as the personification of the Nile River's fruitful floods, which nourished the country's agricultural and economic life.

Those who follow astrology read the sign as the representation of the process of dissolution and loosening. This opening and expansion, although potentially painful, is believed to be essential for personal and spiritual liberation and progress. Alice Walker is an Aquarian and is interested in discerning the relationships between the sign's astrological definitions and her life experiences, present and past. She references astrology throughout her writings and seems to give some credence to the information its ways of reading provide.

### FURTHER READING

Cirlot, J. E. *A Dictionary of Symbols.* Translated by Jack Sage. New York: Philosophical Library, 1962.

Culver, R. B., and P. A. Ianna. *The Gemini Syndrome: A Scientific Evaluation of Astrology.* Amherst, N.Y.: Prometheus Books, 1979.

Cumont, Franz. *Astrology and Religion.* New York: Dover Publications, 1960.

Kitson, Annabela, ed. *History and Astrology.* London: Mandala, 1989.

Lindsay, J. *Origins of Astrology.* London: Fredrick Muller, 1971.

MacNeice, Louis. *Astrology.* London: Aldus Books, 1964.

Shulman, Sandra. *The Encyclopedia of Astrology.* London and New York: Hamlyn, 1976.

West, J. A., and J. G. Toonder. *The Case for Astrology.* Baltimore, Md.: Penguin, 1973.

Whitefield, Peter. *Astrology: A History.* New York: Harry N. Abrams, Inc., 2001.

**Baartman, Sara (Saartjie Baartman, Sarah Baartman)** (1789–1815) Sara Baartman was an African woman who was brought to Europe in the early 19th century to be displayed in sideshows because of physical traits that Europeans considered to be unnaturally sexual—particularly, large breasts and buttocks and prominent labia. She was labeled the Hottentot Venus because members of the Khoikhoi tribe—of which Baartman was a member—were called Hottentots by whites.

A slave to an Afrikaner farmer in what is now South Africa, Baartman was brought to London where, in 1810, she began touring throughout Britain in shows that required her to dance in ways to show off her buttocks. She was later sold to a French animal trainer, who forced her into further sideshow tours, this time throughout France. She was subsequently treated as the subject of anthropological studies, especially by the renowned French naturalist Georges Cuvier. These studies often involved Baartman posing in the nude so that her image could be painted. When her novelty wore off in France, Baartman lost her source of income, and she spent her last years as a prostitute. She died at the age of 26.

Though Baartman's figure was exotic to Europeans, it was typical of Khoikhoi women—and men, to a lesser degree—and was considered a sign of beauty. The features were—and are—due to a genetic trait called steatopygia, which is a larger-than-typical accumulation of fat in the buttocks and often the front thighs and labia. Etchings and images made of Baartman exaggerated her features, but a cast made of her shows a figure that, while full-figured, would not attract attention today.

In her novel *Now Is the Time to Open Your Heart,* Walker uses Baartman as a GODDESS FIGURE who appears in spirit form to two women who are undergoing torture. Baartman's presence is a balm to the women. They find solace in her story and conjure up her image and presence when they are in the direst of circumstances. The women even begin to call each other Saartjie.

### FURTHER READING

Abrahams, Yvette. "Images of Sara Bartman: Sexuality, Race, and Gender in Early-Nineteenth-Century Britain." In *Nation, Empire, Colony: Historicizing Gender and Race,* edited by Ruth Roach Pierson and Nupur Chaudhuri, 220–236. Bloomington and Indianapolis: Indiana University Press, 1998.

Alexander, Elizabeth. *The Venus Hottentot.* Charlottesville: University Press of Virginia, 1990.

Brantley, Ben. "Of an Erotic Freak Show and the Lesson Therein" *New York Times,* 3 May 1996, p. C3.

Brantlinger, Patrick. "Victorians and Africans." *Critical Inquiry* 12 (1985): 166–203.

Chase-Riboud, Barbara. *Hottentot Venus.* New York: Doubleday, 2003.

Crais, Clifton, and Pamela Scully. *Sara Baartman and the Hottentot Venus: A Ghost Story and a Biography.* Princeton, N.J.: Princeton University Press, 2008.

Di Filippo, Paul. *The Steampunk Trilogy: Victoria, Hottentots, Walt and Emily.* New York: Four Walls Eight Windows, 1995.

Edwards, Paul, and James Walvin. *Black Personalities in the Era of the Slave Trade.* Baton Rouge: Louisiana State University Press, 1983.

Hobson, Janell. "The 'Batty' Politic: Toward an Aesthetic of the Black Female Body." *Hypatia* 18, no. 4 (October 2003): 87–105.

"The Hottentot Venus and the Grenvilles." *The Satirist, or, Monthly Meteor,* 1 November 1810, pp. 424–427.

Lindfors, Bernth, ed. *Africans on Stage: Studies in Ethnological Show Business.* Bloomington: Indiana University Press, 1998.

Magubane, Zine. "Which Bodies Matter? Feminism, Poststructuralism, Race, and the Curious Theoretical Odyssey of the 'Hottentot Venus.'" *Gender and Society* 15 (2001): 816–834.

Qureshi, Sadiah. "Displaying Sara Baartman." *History of Science* 42 (2004): 234–257.

Smith, Anna H. "Still More about the Hottentot Venus." *Africana Notes and News* 26 (September 1984): 95–98.

Terry, Jennifer, and Jacqueline Urla, eds. *Deviant Bodies: Critical Perspectives on Difference in Science and Popular Culture.* Bloomington and Indianapolis: Indiana University Press, 1995.

**Baldwin, James** (1924–1987) Born in Harlem, New York, to an impoverished family, James Baldwin developed into one of America's finest and most prolific writers. Alice Walker counts Baldwin as a particularly significant influence in the development of her early intellectual life. His work bridges generic boundaries. This flexibility may have originated with the coping skills Baldwin developed while young. His relatively unhappy childhood was relieved by his frequent forays into the imaginative world of books. Later in life, he credited reading and writing, both of which he learned at a very early age, with providing him options that allowed him to transcend, empathize with, share, and escape from the world into which he had been born. During his life, he produced novels, essays, children's books, and short stories. Generally, Baldwin's work is concerned with the complexities of human interaction, particularly as those encounters are informed by the artificial, yet all-encompassing, categories of identity definition such as race, class, gender, nationality, religious affiliation, and sexual orientation.

Each of Baldwin's novels—from his landmark and defining first novel, *Go Tell It on the Mountain* (1953), to his final work on the Atlanta child murders, *The Evidence of Things Not Seen* (1985)—offers his readers an unflinching examination of difficult and uncomfortable issues that reside in the heart of the conflict between American ideals and its realities. *Go Tell It on the Mountain,* perhaps Baldwin's most autobiographical novel, details the coming-of-age of a young African-American boy and the difficult negotiations he faces as the result of pressure from the various, sometimes conflicting, elements of his universe.

Baldwin was one of the first African-American writers to deal with homosexuality explicitly in fiction. His second novel, *Giovanni's Room* (1966), is an explicit investigation into the life of a homosexual white European man. Disturbed by American racism and racial violence, Baldwin relocated to Europe, where he spent much time for the remainder of his life. Although he seemed to find life in Europe preferable to living in the United States, he was not naive about the exoticism and racism African Americans were experiencing in Europe. His essays often investigate the questions raised by oppression and inequity and their possible solutions.

Baldwin was the recipient of many awards during his career, including a Eugene F. Saxon Fellowship, a Rosenwald Fellowship, Guggenheim Fellowship, the MacDowell Colony Fellowship, and the French Legion of Honor. He also received several honorary degrees from several universities, including City University of New York and University of Massachusetts. Baldwin lost a long battle with stomach cancer when he died in France at age 63.

### FURTHER READING

Baldwin, James. *The Amen Corner.* New York: Dial, 1968.

———. *Another Country.* New York: Dial, 1962.

———. *Blues for Mr. Charlie.* New York: Dial, 1964.

———. *A Dialogue: James Baldwin and Nikki Giovanni.* Philadelphia: Lippincott, 1973.

———. *Evidence of Things Not Seen.* New York: Holt, Rinehart and Winston, 1985.

———. *The Fire Next Time.* New York: Dial, 1963.
———. *Giovanni's Room.* New York: Dial, 1956.
———. *Going to Meet the Man.* New York: Dial, 1965.
———. *Go Tell It on the Mountain.* New York: Knopf, 1953.
———. *If Beale Street Could Talk.* New York: Dial, 1974.
———. *Jimmy's Blues: Selected Poems.* London: Joseph, 1983.
———. *Nobody Knows My Name: More Notes of a Native Son.* New York: Dial, 1961.
———. *Notes of a Native Son.* Boston: Beacon, 1955.
———. *Tell Me How Long the Train's Been Gone.* New York: Dial, 1968.
Burt, Nancy V., and Fred L. Standley, eds. *Critical Essays on James Baldwin.* Boston: G. K. Hall, 1988.
Campbell, James. *Talking at the Gates; A Life of James Baldwin.* New York: Penguin Books, 1991.
Eckman, Fern M. *The Furious Passage of James Baldwin.* New York: M. Evans, 1966.
Harris, Trudier. *Black Women in the Fiction of James Baldwin.* Knoxville: University of Tennessee Press, 1985.
Hatch, James V., and Ted Shine, eds. *Black Theatre U.S.A.: Plays by African Americans 1847 to Today.* New York: Free Press, 1996.
Kinnamon, Kenneth. *James Baldwin; A Collection of Critical Essays.* Englewood Cliffs, N.J.: Prentice-Hall, 1974.
Leeming, David A. *James Baldwin: A Biography.* New York: Knopf, 1994.
Macebuh, Stanley. *James Baldwin; A Critical Study.* New York: Third Press, 1973.

**Bantu** Alice Walker refers to the Bantu occasionally throughout her writings. The word *Bantu* refers both to an extremely large group of disparate people who are located throughout central and southern Africa and to the foundation for many languages that derive from a common source known as Bantu. This language relationship is the primary commonality of the groups of people who are called Bantu.

Bantu-speaking people originated in West Africa, south of the Congo River, and produced deeply innovative cultures that utilized Africa's natural resources and were central to artistic and intellectual development on the continent. The Bantu are sometimes referred to as Iron Age farmers in recognition of their formidable iron-working skills, which are associated with a host of agricultural innovations. These particular skills made their eastward and southern migrations across the African continent integral to the successful habitation of many locations that had not had previously been occupied by humans.

The Bantu language family includes the Niger-Congo language group spanning most of sub-Saharan Africa and is the root source for approximately 450 derivative languages. The combination of agricultural expertise, advanced iron craft, and the development of various forms of social and political organizations within village structures are among the primary contributions of the Bantu peoples. A large percentage of the individuals who were captured in Africa and shipped off as human cargo to become slaves in North and South America and the Caribbean were part of the Bantu group.

## FURTHER READING

Falola, Toyin. *Key Events in African History: A Reference Guide.* Westport, Conn.: Greenwood Press, 2002.
Holloway, Joseph E., ed. *Africanisms in American Culture.* 2d ed. Bloomington: Indiana University Press, 2005.
Sundkler, Bengt. *Bantu Prophets in South Africa.* London: Oxford University Press, 1961.
Tempels, Placide. *Bantu Philosophy.* Paris: Présence Africaine, 1959.
Vass, Winifred Kellersberger. *The Bantu Speaking Heritage of the United States.* Los Angeles: Center for Afro-American Studies, 1979.

**Baptists** Although Alice Walker's family belonged to another denomination, the African Methodist Episcopal Church, she references black Baptists throughout her canon. The Baptist denomination of Protestantism gained footing in the United States between the years 1780 until approximately 1830. By the late 19th century, Baptists were the nation's third-largest denomination and by the early 20th century, their numbers were second only to practicing Catholics.

The Baptist and Methodist faiths were widely adopted by free and enslaved blacks. Religious historians note that a certain degree of autonomy and informality in the worshipping rituals of these both groups made them culturally appealing to African Americans. Religious gatherings of African Americans led to their churches becoming centers of black cultural development and subsequently centers for both social and political organization.

During the mid-1800s, independent black churches began to emerge in the United States. Among the milestones in the development of black Baptists in the United States were the 1840 formation of the American Baptist Missionary Convention and the 1895 founding of the National Baptist Convention, United States of America. Both organizations formed in response to exclusion from white Baptist organizations.

Performing missionary work in Africa was a main objective for black Baptists, especially after the Civil War. Political activism was a central outgrowth of the black Baptist tradition, most notably during the Civil Rights era of the 1950s and 1960s. Today, there are more than 10 million black Baptists in the United States.

### FURTHER READING

Ahlstrom, Sydney E. *A Religious History of the American People.* 2d edition. New Haven: Yale University Press, 2004.

Ammerman, Nancy Tatom. *Baptist Battles: Social Change and Religious Conflict in the Southern Baptist Convention.* New Brunswick, N.J.: Rutgers University Press, 1990.

Fitts, Leroy. *A History of Black Baptists.* Nashville, Tenn.: Broadman, 1985.

Gaustad, Edwin S., and Leigh E. Schmidt. *The Religious History of America.* Rev. ed. San Francisco: Harper San Francisco, 2002.

Harding, S. F. "Convicted by the Holy Spirit: The Rhetoric of Fundamental Baptist Conversion." *American Ethnologist* 14, no. 1 (2004): 167–181.

Harvey, Paul. *Redeeming the South: Religious Cultures and Racial Identities among Southern Baptists, 1865–1925.* Chapel Hill: University of North Carolina Press, 1997.

Raboteau, Albert J. "The Black Experience in American Evangelicalism: The Meaning of Slavery." In *African-American Religion: Interpretive Essays in History and Culture,* edited by Timothy E. Fulop and Albert J. Raboteau, 90–106. New York: Routledge, 1997.

Sobel, Mechal. *Trabelin' On: The Slave Journey to an Afro-Baptist Faith.* Princeton, N.J.: Princeton University Press, 1988.

Washington, James Melvin. *Frustrated Fellowship: The Black Baptist Quest for Social Power.* Macon, Ga.: Mercer University Press, 2004.

Wills, David W. "The Central Themes of American Religious History." In *African-American Religion: Interpretive Essays in History and Culture,* edited by Timothy E. Fulop and Albert J. Raboteau, 6–20. New York: Routledge, 1997.

**Black Aesthetic** In his 1968 article "The Black Arts Movement," Larry Neal articulated his version of the foundational principles of the Black Aesthetic. According to Neal, the function of black art is to conflate ethics and aesthetics, political action and artistic creation. In literary terms, the Black Aesthetic was one of the central artistic objectives of the writings produced during the BLACK ARTS MOVEMENT. The Black Aesthetic was defined by several architects, including Houston Baker, Larry Neal, Hoyt Fuller, and Addison Gayle. Although there are many different components of the various definitions of Black Aesthetic, fundamentally the Black Aesthetic of the 1960s asserted that art produced by African Americans should, in addition to artistic concerns, address and help to transform the political, social, and economic problems faced by African-American communities.

According to the precepts of the Black Aesthetic, the value of art can be measured by the extent to which it expresses the realities of African-American communities and helps those communities to advance. The writers articulating Black Aesthetic principles also felt that there were particular characteristics that could be assigned to blackness, and therefore a work deserved merit to the extent to which it could be described as black.

An important aspect of the Black Aesthetic was the reclamation of definitions of blackness. For centuries, blackness had been associated with negative ideas such as ugliness, dishonor, and evil. Neal, Fuller, and others attempted to reclaim the word and redefine *black* as beautiful. This redefinition of blackness included a reexamination of the history of African Americans and Africans and an affirmation of what that history represents. There was a sense of mission among the Black Aestheticians. They believed there was a truth, an essential quality of blackness and black people that had been lost and could be recaptured by art that understood and valued the essential quality that had been erased by the legacy of slavery and racism.

The Black Aesthetic insists on affirming the connection between a black present and past through art. This connection would catalyze a revolution in thought that would lead to a revolution in action. The revolution would itself usher in a world of black power and control over the destiny of black people. Black Aesthetic theory, even as expressed by the artists themselves, did not necessarily contain or confine the literature produced in its name. Although not limited to the philosophies of the Black Aesthetic, Alice Walker and other writers of the AFRA-AMERICAN WOMEN'S LITERARY RENAISSANCE were influenced by its dictates, particularly by its attempts to use literature to reclaim and redefine oppressive language.

## FURTHER READING

Baker, Houston A., Jr. *Afro-American Poetics, Revisions of Harlem and the Black Aesthetic.* Madison: University of Wisconsin Press, 1988.

———. *Blues, Ideology, and Afro-American Literature: A Vernacular Theory.* Chicago: University of Chicago Press, 1984.

Cruse, Harold. *The Crisis of the Negro Intellectual.* New York: Morrow, 1967.

———. "Rebellion or Revolution?" *Liberator* 4, no. 1 (1964): 14–16.

Fuller, Hoyt. "Towards a Black Aesthetic." In *The Black Aesthetic,* edited by Addison Gayle. Garden City: N.Y.: Doubleday, 1971, 3–12.

Gayle, Addison. *The Black Aesthetic.* Garden City, N.Y.: Doubleday Publishers, 1971.

Henderson, Stephen. *Understanding the New Black Poetry: Black Speech and Black Music as Poetic References.* New York: William Morrow, 1973.

Jones, LeRoi. Black Art. Newark, N.J.: Jihad Productions, 1967.

Neal, Larry. "Any Day Now: Black Art and Black Liberation." *Ebony* 24 (1969): 54–58.

———. "The Black Arts Movement." *The Drama Review* 12, no. 4 (1968): 29–39.

———. "The Black Writer's Role." *Liberator* 6, no. 6 (1966): 7–9.

———. "The Cultural Front." *Liberator* 5, no. 6 (1965): 26–27.

———. *Visions of a Liberated Future.* St. Paul, Minn.: Thunder's Mouth Press, 1989.

Scot-Heron, Gil. "The Revolution Will Not Be Televised." *The Revolution Will Not Be Televised.* New York: BMG Music, 1988.

**Black Arts Movement** Along with many other members of the AFRA-AMERICAN WOMEN'S LITERARY RENAISSANCE, Alice Walker was influenced by the principles and artists of the Black Arts Movement and BLACK AESTHETIC. In literary terms, the Black Arts Movement consists of the writings produced approximately between the years of 1965 and 1972 that affirmed many of the precepts of the Black Aesthetic. The artists of the Black Arts Movement, generally speaking, embraced the Black Power movement and produced works that attempted to catalyze both collective affirmation and political action.

The phrase *Black Power* was popularized during the CIVIL RIGHTS MOVEMENT when, in 1966, Stokely Carmichael (who later renamed himself Kwame Ture), as chair of the STUDENT NON-VIOLENT COORDINATING COMMITTEE (SNCC), began to advocate for Black Power rather than nonviolent direct action as a strategy to achieve equality. This shift caused a rift between the SNCC and other organizations, such as the Southern Christian Leadership Conference (SCLC), involved in the Civil Rights struggle. As advocated by Carmichael and SNCC, Black Power called for self-defense, affirmation of black people's rights, and eradication of white domination.

LeRoi Jones, who changed his name to Amiri Baraka in 1967, is often named as the artistic founder of the Black Arts Movement. In 1965, in the wake of the assassination of MALCOLM X, Jones founded the Black Arts Repertory Theatre in Harlem. The theater became a haven for young writers eager to use drama as an accessible means of social statement and transformation. The Black Arts Repertory Theatre, along with other organizations, began to produce poetry and plays that were primarily performed with the intention of reaching people in the community who might not otherwise be attracted to literature.

In addition to Baraka, other important voices in the articulation of Black Arts Movement theory were Askia Toure, Larry Neal, Hoyt Fuller, and Maulana Karenga. Some of the writers associated with the movement were Ed Bullins, Gwendolyn Brooks, Eldridge Cleaver, Jayne Cortez, Harold Cruse, Mari Evans, Hoyt Fuller, Nikki Giovanni, Lorraine Hansberry, Gil-Scott Heron, Maulana Ron Karenga, Etheridge Knight, Adrienne Kennedy, Haki R. Madhubuti, Larry Neal, Dudley Randall, Ishmael Reed, Sonia Sanchez, Ntozake Shange, Quincy Troupe, and John Alfred Williams. They found a public voice for their work in new publications venues created and designated for black writers, such as the *Journal of Black Poetry, Black Scholar, Negro Digest, Lotus Press, Broadside Press,* and *Third World Press.* Another important vehicle for the dissemination of Black Arts Movement writers were anthologies. Some of the most significant collections were *Black Fire* (1968), *New Black Voices* (1972), *The Black Woman* (1970), and *Understanding the New Black Poetry* (1970).

Despite its rhetorical commitment to the production of art inseparably connected to the elimination of oppression experienced by black people, the gender oppression of black women was not acknowledged by the founders of the Black Arts Movement as germane to their struggle. The movement has also been considered by some as homophobic and racially exclusive. By the mid-1970s, African-American writers associated with the Black Arts Movement began to work in other directions and to experiment with other forms, but the lasting impact of the movement remains, especially in terms of the integration of African-American studies into the academic field and African-American literature into mainstream publishing.

### FURTHER READING

Chapman, Abraham, ed. *New Black Voices.* New York: New American Library, 1972.

Frost, Elisabeth A. "'a fo / real / revolu / shun': Sonia Sanchez and the Black Arts Movement." In *The Feminist Avant-Garde in American Poetry.* Iowa City: University of Iowa Press, 2003.

Fuller, Charles H. "Black Writing is Socio-Creative Art." *Liberator* 7, no. 4 (1967): 8–10.

———. "Black Writing: Release from Object." *Liberator* 7, no. 9 (1967): 17.

Henderson, Stephen. *Understanding the New Black Poetry: Black Speech and Black Music as Poetic References.* New York: William Morrow, 1973.

Henderson, Stephen E., and Mercer Cook. *The Militant Black Writer in Africa and the United States.* Madison: University of Wisconsin Press, 1969.

Jones, LeRoi. "The Black Arts Repertory Theatre School." *Liberator* 5, no. 4 (1965): 21.

Jones, LeRoi, and Larry Neal. *Black Fire: An Anthology of Afro-American Writing.* New York: Morrow, 1968.

Neal, Larry. "Any Day Now: Black Art and Black Liberation." *Ebony* 24 (1969): 54–58.

———. "The Black Arts Movement." *The Drama Review* 12, no. 4 (1968): 29–39.

———. "The Black Writer's Role." *Liberator* 6, no. 6 (1966): 7–9.

———. "The Cultural Front." *Liberator* 5, no. 6 (1965): 26–27.

———. *Visions of a Liberated Future: Black Arts Movement Writings.* New York: Thunder's Mouth Press, 1989.

Smith, David Lionel. "The Black Arts Movement and Its Critics." *American Literary History* 3 (Spring 1991): 98–110.

Thompson, Julius E. *Dudley Randall, Broadside Press, and the Black Arts Movement in Detroit 1960–1995.* New York: McFarland and Company, Inc., 1998.

Toure, Askia Muhammad. "Black Magic!" *Journal of Black Poetry* 1 (Fall 1968): 63–64.

Ya Salaam, Kalamu. *Magic of Juju: An Appreciation of the Black Arts Movement.* Chicago: Third World Press, 2001.

**Black Elk** (1863–1950) Black Elk was an Oglala Lakota (Sioux) medicine man whose birth in 1863 coincided with a period of conflict and decimation for his people. Although the lands where he was born had been designated as permanent possessions in treaties with the U.S. government, over time the treaties were broken, instigating conflicts between the government and the Lakota. These conflicts culminated in the creation of reservations, including the Great Sioux Reservation, coupled with the demand that all native peoples submit to life on the reservation or be considered criminals. This dictate led to the Indian Wars of the 1860s and 1870s. These events provided the context for Black Elk's early life as he witnessed the destruction of the native rebels, including his cousin Crazy Horse.

A vision at the age of nine ultimately led Black Elk to become a medicine man, a profession of great significance and prestige within his community. As a result of his travels overseas with Buffalo Bill's Wild West Show and his experiences with Western culture, Black Elk eventually converted to Catholicism and, in later years, wrote his autobiography with the writer John Neidhart. Black Elk's autobiography, *Black Elk Speaks* (1932), remains a classic work of Native American literature.

In the preface to her novel *Meridian,* Alice Walker includes a well-known quotation about Wounded Knee from *Black Elk Speaks.*

> I did not know then how much was ended. When I look back now . . . I can still see the butchered women and children lying heaped and scattered all along the crooked gulch as plain as when I saw them with eyes still young. And I can see that something else died there in the bloody mud, and was buried in the blizzard. A people's dream died there. It was a beautiful dream . . . the nation's hoop is broken and shattered. There is no center any longer, and the sacred tree is dead.

Black Elk articulates a philosophy in which SELF-AFFIRMATION is connected to the well-being of the entire community. In his narrative, chaos is associated with disunity. Like African Americans, the Oglala Lakota experienced a deterioration of common meaning and purpose due to oppressive external circumstances. Early in his autobiography, Black Elk is given the power to restore harmony to his people through a mystical vision. The character Meridian functions in Walker's novel of the same name in much the same capacity. As such, self-affirmation as developed in *Meridian* takes place within Walker's protagonist but also has the potential for revolution and reunification not only for African Americans but for the entire human community.

### FURTHER READING


Black Elk and John Neihardt. *Black Elk Speaks.* Lincoln: University of Nebraska Press, 1932.

DeMallie, Raymond J., ed. *The Sixth Grandfather.* Lincoln: University of Nebraska Press, 1984.

Lazarus, Edward. *Black Hills, White Justice.* New York: HarperCollins, 1989.

Steltenkamp, Michael F. *Black Elk: Holy Man of the Lakota.* Norman: University of Oklahoma Press, 1993.


**Black Madonna** The Black Madonna is an icon that the literary scholar Małgorzata Oleszkiewicz-Peralba has defined as "a fluid syncretic blend of the Virgin Mary and ancient Mother Goddesses from Eurasian, Native American and African cultures" worshipped around the world. Scholarship documents the existence of more than 450 images of the Black Madonna worldwide. Historically and contemporarily, the icon is featured in visual, literary, and musical compositions.

Scholarly discourses about the Black Madonna often suggest that Eurocentric art critics, historians, and religious practitioners have neglected the complex history of black pre-Christian female divinity figures. Various groups, including California vineyard workers, Mexico's Zapatista movement, and the Nicaraguan Sandinista movement, commonly employ Black Madonnas as icons of hope and liberation.

Many African-American women writers have used the notion of the black female divine as suggested by the figure of the Black Madonna in the writings of the AFRA-AMERICAN WOMEN'S LITERARY RENAISSANCE. Alice Walker employs the trope of black female divinity and references the Black Madonna throughout her work. For example, in her novel *The Temple of My Familiar,* the character Miss Lissie, a polyandrous GODDESS FIGURE, writes a letter in invisible ink that discusses the historical erasure of female goddess worship and references the Black Madonna. In a moment of textual self-reflexivity, Miss Lissie not only refers to the Black Madonna but positions herself as a manifestation of the icon.

### FURTHER READING

Birnbaum, Lucia Chiavola. *Black Madonnas: Feminism, Religion, and Politics in Italy.* Boston: Northeastern University Press, 1993.

Gustafson, Fred. *The Black Madonna.* Boston: Sigo Press, 1990.

Kaiser, L. "The Black Madonna: Notions of True Womanhood from Jacobs to Hurston." *South Atlantic Review* 60 (1995): 97–109.

Lauret, Maria. *Alice Walker.* New York: St. Martin's Press, 2000.

Oleszkiewicz-Peralba, Małgorzata. *The Black Madonna in Latin American and Europe: Tradition and Transformation.* Albuquerque: University of New Mexico Press, 2007.

Smith, Felipe. *American Body Politics: Race, Gender, and Black Literary Renaissance.* Athens: University of Georgia Press, 1998.

Van Sertima, Ivan. *Black Women in Antiquity.* New Brunswick, N.J.: Transaction Books, 1984.

**blues, the** The music known as the blues was originally an African-American art form that expressed the joys and heartbreaks of a wide range of experiences. Although there are a number of forms, the primary classic form of the blues is the 12-bar structure in which the first two lines of each stanza are the same and then the third is a response to the first two. The structure of the blues is thought to derive from the African and African-American practice of communication and exchange between audience and performer known as call and response. This structure contributed to the originality and the improvisation of the blues as a form of expression. Ironically, singing the blues is supposed to have the effect of lifting the singer's mood and relieving his or her sadness. Although the blues is primarily sung, there are blues instrumentalists as well, especially musicians of the piano, drums, harmonica, and guitar.

Most scholars agree that the blues began as an art form after the Civil War. The form is thought to be a hybrid of African-American work song and the spiritual. The blues are thought to originate in the Mississippi Delta region of the southern United States, but also to have deep roots in Georgia and Texas. One of the first singers popularly associated with the blues was Huddy Ledbelly, who was one of the first 19th-century celebrities of the genre. One of the first popular blues songs was W. C. Handy's "Memphis Blues."

In the 1920s, the first blues recordings appeared by such luminaries as Ma Rainey, BESSIE SMITH, Mamie Smith, and Ida Cox. The blues is said to have moved north with African Americans in the Great Migration, and by the 1930s and 1940s, the heart of the blues was in the urban North, particularly in the midwestern mecca of Chicago.

The blues has been highly influential in the development of contemporary popular music, from rock to JAZZ. Many of the most popular rock musicians, including the Beatles and the Rolling Stones, name the blues and blues musicians as their primary source of inspiration.

Alice Walker references the blues throughout her canon. One example of her use of the form is as a primary expression of the musicians who perform in Harpo's JUKE JOINT in *The Color Purple.*

### FURTHER READING

Charters, Samuel B. *The Bluesmakers.* New York: Da Capo Press, 1991.

———. *The Roots of the Blues.* Salem, N.H.: Marion Boyars, 1981.

Cohn, Lawrence, et al. *Nothing but the Blues: The Music and the Musicians.* New York: Abbeville Press, 1993.

Davis, Angela Yvonne. *Blues Legacies and Black Feminism: Gertrude "Ma" Rainey, Bessie Smith, and Billie Holiday.* New York: Pantheon Books, 1998.

Davis, Francis. *The History of the Blues.* New York: Hyperion, 1995.

Epstein, Dana. *Sinful Tunes and Spirituals: Black Folk Music to the Civil War.* Urbana: University of Illinois Press, 1977.

Erlewine, Michael, ed. *All Music Guide to the Blues.* San Francisco: Miller Freeman, 1996.

Harrison, Daphne Duval. *Black Pearls: Blues Queens of the 1920s.* New Brunswick, N.J.: Rutgers University Press, 1988.

Herzhaft, Gerand. *Encyclopedia of the Blues.* Fayetteville: University of Arkansas Press, 1992.

Jones, Leroi. *Blues People: Negro Music in White America.* New York: W. Morrow, 1963.

Keil, Charles. *Urban Blues.* Chicago: University of Chicago Press, 1966.

Leadbitter, Mike, ed. *Nothing but the Blues: An Illustrated Documentary.* New York: Hanover Books, 1971.

Lomax, Alan. *The Land Where the Blues Began.* New York: Pantheon Books, 1993.

McKee, Margaret, and Fred Chisenhall. *Beale Black and Blue: Life and Music on Black America's Main Street.* New Orleans: Louisiana State University Press, 1981.

Oliver, Paul. *Blues Fell This Morning: Meaning in the Blues.* Cambridge: Cambridge University Press, 1990.

Palmer, Robert. *Deep Blues.* New York: Penguin, 1981.

Sackheim, Eric, ed. *The Blues Line: A Collection of Blues Lyrics.* New York: Ecco Press, 1993.

Santelli, Robert. *The Best of the Blues: The 101 Essential Albums.* New York: Penguin, 1997.

Southern, Eileen. *Music of Black Americans: A History.* 3d ed. New York: W. W. Norton, 1997.

Welding, Pete, and Toby Byron. *Bluesland.* New York: Dutton, 1991.

Woods, Clyde Adrian. *Development Arrested: The Blues and Plantation Power in the Mississippi Delta.* London: Verso, 1998.

**Buddhism** Although she has said that she does not consider herself to be a strict Buddhist, Alice Walker maintains that she is influenced and guided by the principles of Buddhism. She has written and worked with the Buddhist scholar and teacher PEMA CHÖDRÖN and is an admirer of the Buddhist monk Thich Nhat Hanh.

Buddha, which means "Awakened" or "Enlightened One," is a title given to Siddhartha Gautama. Gautama (563–483 B.C.E.) was born in Lumbini, Nepal, into a royal family. After marrying and having a child, he embarked on a search for an enlightened state that he termed *nirvana.* Gautama's experiences while living with Hindu ascetics led him toward the Middle Way, a luminal space that exists between affluence and sparseness.

The three major streams of Buddhist thought are Theravāda, Mahāyāna, and Vajrayāna. Central to Buddhist philosophy is the doctrine of the Four Noble Truths, the tenets of which articulate the inevitability of suffering. Following the stages of what is known as the Noble Eightfold Path—adopting the right views, aspirations, speech, conduct, livelihood, effort, mindfulness and contemplation—is the antidote for ending suffering and provides access to nirvana.

Alice Walker making a *namaste* gesture, a greeting associated with Buddhism *(Photograph by Carmen Gillespie)*

Buddhism has been the dominant religion in many Asian cultures for centuries and attracted adherents in the West in the late 19th century. American interest in Buddhism emerged as a phenomenon in the 1960s as a result of young adults traveling abroad on a quest for spiritual alternatives. Today there are thousands of Buddhist centers for training and worship in the United States.

### FURTHER READING

Appiah, Kwame Anthony, and Henry Louis Gates, Jr., eds. *The Dictionary of Global Culture.* New York: Alfred A. Knopf, 1997.

Bowker, John, ed. *The Cambridge Illustrated History of Religions.* Cambridge: Cambridge University Press, 2002.

Breuilly, Elizabeth, Joanne O' Brien, and Martin Palmer. *Religions of the World: The Illustrated Guide to Origins, Beliefs, Traditions, and Festivals.* New York: Facts On File, 1997.

Chödron, Pema. *Awakening Loving-Kindness.* Boston: Shambhala, 1996.

———. *Comfortable with Uncertainty: 108 Teachings.* Boston: Shambhala, 2002.

———. *From Fear to Fearlessness: Teachings on the Four Great Catalysts of Awakening.* Louisville, Colo.: Sounds True, 2002.

———. *Getting Unstuck: Breaking Your Habitual Patterns and Encountering Naked Reality.* Louisville, Colorado: Sounds True, 2004.

———. *The Places that Scare You: A Guide to Fearlessness in Difficult Times.* Boston: Shambhala, 2002.

———. *Pure Meditation: The Tibetan Buddhist Practice of Inner Peace.* Louisville, Colo.: Sounds True, 2000.

———. *Start Where You Are: A Guide to Compassionate Living.* Boston: Shambhala, 2001.

———. *When Things Fall Apart: Heart Advice for Difficult Times.* Boston: Shambhala, 2000.

———. *The Wisdom of No Escape: And the Path of Loving Kindness.* Boston: Shambhala, 2001.

Conze, Edward. *Buddhism: A Short History.* Oxford, Eng.: Oneworld, 2000.

Prebish, Charles S. *American Buddhism.* North Scituate, Mass.: Duxbury Press, 1979.

Seager, Richard Hughes. *Buddhism in America.* New York: Columbia University Press, 1999.

Suzuki, Daisetz Jeyaraja. *An Introduction to Zen Buddhism.* New York: Grove Press, 2004.

Tambiah, Stanley Jeyaraja. *Buddhism and the Spirit Cults in North-East Thailand.* Cambridge: Cambridge University Press, 1970.

Thomas, E. J. *The History of Buddhist Thought.* Mineola, N.Y.: Dover Publications, 2002.


**Buffalo Soldiers** Black soldiers who served in the 9th and 10th Cavalry of the U.S. Army and four infantry units—the 38th, 39th, 40th, and 41st (later amalgamated into the 24th and 25th Infantry)—were nicknamed Buffalo Soldiers by their Native American adversaries. Congress originally formed the units in 1866 during a period of westward expansion. The soldiers played a major role in the Indian Wars of the post–Civil War era. In Walker's novel *The Temple of My Familiar,* one of the major characters, Suwelo, calls one of his wife Fanny's spiritual lovers a Buffalo Soldier.


### FURTHER READING

Leckie, W. H., and S. A. Leckie. *The Buffalo Soldiers: A Narrative of the Black Cavalry in the West.* Norman: University of Oklahoma Press, 2006.

Schubert. Frank N. *Black Valor: Buffalo Soldiers and the Medal of Honor, 1870–1898.* Wilmington, Del.: S. R. Books, 1997.

———, ed. *Voices of the Buffalo Soldier: Records, Reports, and Recollections of Military Life and Service in the West.* Albuquerque: University of New Mexico Press, 2003.

Schubert, Frank N., and Irene Schubert, eds. *On the Trail of the Buffalo Soldier II: New and Revised Biographies of African Americans in the U.S. Army, 1866–1917.* Lanham, Md.: Scarecrow Press, 2004.


**Camus, Albert** (1913–1960) Albert Camus was a social philosopher, novelist, essayist, and dramatist. Camus was born in 1913 in Algiers and is one of the intellectuals commonly associated with absurdism and existentialism. Unlike many existentialists, Camus found that, although the universe may essentially be meaningless, there is still purpose in existence, and the fundamental conundrum of the human condition is the attempt to grapple with this seeming contradiction. One of the most important outlines of Camus's philosophical tenets can be found in his seminal essay *Le mythe de Sisyphe* (The Myth of Sisyphus), which appeared in 1942 and elaborates on the understanding Camus had of the human condition, perhaps best summarized in his definition of the absurd. Camus won the 1957 Nobel Prize in literature and is best known for his 1942 novel *The Stranger.*

Alice Walker was first exposed to Camus's writing through HELEN LYND, her faculty adviser at

SARAH LAWRENCE COLLEGE. Walker credits Lynd's class for making Western philosophy accessible to her for the first time. Several critics have noted Camus's influence on Walker's writing, particularly on her construction of rebellion in her 1976 novel *Meridian*.

### FURTHER READING

Camus, Albert. *A Happy Death*. New York: Knopf, 1972.

———. *The Myth of Sisyphus*. Harmondsworth, Eng.: Penguin Books, 1975.

———. *The Plague*. New York: A. A. Knopf, 1948.

———. *The Rebel*. Harmondsworth, Eng.: Penguin Books, 1971.

———. *Resistance, Rebellion, and Death*. New York: Knopf, 1961.

———. *The Stranger*. New York: A. A. Knopf, 1996.

Cruickshank, John. *Albert Camus and the Literature of Revolt*. Westport, Conn.: Greenwood, 1978.

Lottman, Herbert R. *Albert Camus: A Biography*. London: Axix Publications, 1997.

Thody, Philip Malcolm. *Albert Camus, 1913–1960*. New York: Macmillan, 1962.

Todd, Olivier. *Albert Camus: A Life*. New York: Alfred A. Knopf, 1997.

White, Evelyn C. *Alice Walker: A Life*. New York: W. W. Norton and Company, 2004.

***Cane* (Jean Toomer)** (1923) Many literary critics believe that the publication of *Cane* marks the beginning of what is known as the HARLEM RENAISSANCE, when African-American writers such as Claude McKay, ZORA NEALE HURSTON, LANGSTON HUGHES, and many others produced a number of significant American literary works. The Harlem Renaissance was also a period in which African-American artists in other genres, such as art, music, and theater, produced a great number of landmark works.

*Cane* follows a thematic circle that takes the reader through the experience of African-American migration from the rural South to the urban North and back. During the time JEAN TOOMER (1894–1967) wrote *Cane*, African Americans were migrating from the South to the North in record numbers. The causes of that movement, known as the Great Migration, were complicated and various. Generally, African Americans left the South to find economic opportunities; to flee random and systematic racial violence; and to live in a place where segregation did not entirely control their ability to vote, own land and property, and attend schools.

Jean Toomer captured the violent, wistful, transient, poignant feeling of this period in African-American history with *Cane*. The novel moves from the South to the North and returns to end in the South again. With that movement, Toomer evokes the feeling of the transition from rural south to city and the relationship between the two. The location of the urban section of Toomer's narrative is Washington, D.C., the city Toomer was from, but also, and perhaps more importantly, it is the symbolic and ideological center of the country.

The book's move to Washington represents the hopefulness of the individuals relocating to the very site where they had, less than a century before, been granted citizenship and the rights therein with the ratification of the Thirteenth, Fourteenth, and Fifteenth Amendments to the Constitution. The failure of the narrator's return south in "Kabnis," the final section of *Cane*, is a wistful reminder that such a return is neither literally or figuratively possible.

*Cane* represents the inauguration of the contemporary period of African-American literature, and Alice Walker mentions the novel frequently as a major influence on her work. Toomer's novel shares many of the characteristics of texts that are considered works of American modernism, such as ambiguity, fragmentation, experimentation with form, and themes of alienation and, to some extent, hopelessness. *Cane* functions as a multigenre text in that it is at once poetry, drama, and fiction.

Alice Walker counts Jean Toomer as one of her primary influences and has stated that *Cane* is one of the most important books she has ever read. She has also said that she used *Cane* as a model for her second novel, *Meridian*.

### FURTHER READING

Bontemps, Arna. Introduction to *Cane*, by Jean Toomer. New York: Harper & Row, 1969.

Brinkmeyer, Robert H., Jr. "Wasted Talent, Wasted Art: The Literary Career of Jean Toomer." *The Southern Quarterly* 20, no. 1 (1981): 75–84.

Bush, Ann Marie, and Louis D. Mitchell. "Jean Toomer: A Cubist Poet." *Black American Literature Forum* 17, no. 3 (1983): 106–108.

Duncan, Bowie. "Jean Toomer's *Cane:* A Modern Black Oracle." *CLA Journal* 15 (1972): 223–233.

Frank, Waldo. *Our America.* 1919. New York: AMS, 1972.

Goede, William J. "Jean Toomer's Ralph Kabnis: Portrait of the Negro Artist as a Young Man." *Phylon* 30 (1969): 73–85.

Golding, Alan. "Jean Toomer's *Cane:* The Search for Identity through Form." *Arizona Quarterly* 39 (1983): 197–214.

Kerman, Cynthia Earl, and Richard Eldridge. *The Lives of Jean Toomer: A Hunger for Wholeness.* Baton Rouge: Louisiana State University Press, 1987.

Larson, Charles R. "*Cane* by Jean Toomer." *New Republic* 19 (June 1976): 30–32.

Toomer, Jean. *Cane.* New York: Boni and Liveright, 1923.

**cassava** Cassava is a starchy root of South American origin that is commonly grown in tropical environments. Cassava, also known as manioc, is a staple source of carbohydrates for many economically depressed communities, including tropical areas of Africa. In Nettie's letters to Celie in Walker's novel *The Color Purple,* she frequently refers to the ways the Olinka tribe grows and consumes cassava. The food is a centerpiece of life for the fictional village.

### FURTHER READING

Agboola, S. A. "The Introduction and Spread of Cassava in Western Nigeria." *Nigerian Journal of Economic Social Studies* 3 (1968): 369–385.

Armstrong, Joseph E. "Cassava—*Manihot esculenta,* a Low-Protein, Starchy Staple." Available online. URL: http://www.bio.ilstu.edu/Armstrong/syllabi/cassava/cassava.htm. Accessed April 2, 2009.

Babaleye, Taye. "Cassava, Africa's Food Security Crop." Available online. URL: www.worldbank.org/html/cgiar/newsletter/Mar96/4cas2.htm. Accessed April 2, 2009.

Blain, D. "A Farming System for Women: The Case of Cassava Production in Zaire." *Ceres: FAO* 18, no. 3 (1985): 43.

Edwards, Bryan. *The History Civil and Commercial, of the British Colonies in the West Indies.* 3 vols. London: John Stockdale, 1807.

Newbury, M. Catharine. "Ebutumwa Bw'Emiogo: The Tyranny of Cassava, a Women's Tax Revolt in Eastern Zaire." *Canadian J. of African Studies* 18, no. 1 (1984): 35–54.

Odigboh, E. U. *Cassava: Production, Processing and Utilization Handbook of Tropical Foods.* New York: Marcel Dekker, 1983.

**Castro, Fidel** (1926– ) Fidel Castro served as the leader of the Caribbean island nation of Cuba from 1959 until he stepped down from the position in 2008 due to ill health. Castro's reign as the dictator of the country since the Cuban Revolution was dominated by adherence to a political and social philosophy rooted in his particularized version of communism.

Castro's leadership of Cuba and his complete control of the country's affairs have in many ways been defined by his opposition to the United States. An overtly communist nation existing in such close proximity to a firmly democratic one has engendered enduring tensions between the two countries. The United States has responded to Castro's leadership and Cuba's status as a communist country by maintaining a trade embargo and restricting U.S. citizens from traveling to the country. Reportedly, the CIA has also instigated many failed assassination attempts on Castro's life.

Castro was born into a wealthy family, was educated in law, and began working as an attorney in 1950. He was ideologically opposed to Fulgencio Batista's corrupt and inequitable regime and played a part in an organized rebellion against the then president, which led to Castro's 1953 imprisonment. In 1955, upon his released from prison, Castro left Cuba for Mexico, where he began a revolutionary movement with the assistance of the young Argentinean CHE GUEVARA and others. After a botched 1956 effort to take over the Criente Province in Cuba, he and his supporters regrouped in the Cuban mountains and, after several years, successfully staged a coup in Havana in 1959.

Photograph of Alice Walker with Fidel Castro during her 1995 visit to Cuba. The photograph was on display at the 2009 exhibition, *A Keeping of Records: The Art and Life of Alice Walker,* which was held in celebration of the public opening of Walker's archives at Emory University in Atlanta, Georgia, in April 2009. The photograph is from Walker's personal collection. The original photographer is unknown. *(Photograph of exhibit by Carmen Gillespie, courtesy of the Emory University Alice Walker Archives Exhibition, April 24, 2009)*

The initially liberal government that formed in the years following the revolution invigorated the Cuban civil sector but ultimately transitioned into a more unilaterally controlled and regulated system. As prime minister, Castro took firmer control over civic institutions and the country's private industries, which he nationalized. In 1961, he merged his forces with the Cuban Communist Party, after which he supported curtailing many of the Cuban people's civil liberties. This restriction of personal autonomy coupled with the end of capitalism on the island led many citizens to seek asylum in the United States and elsewhere.

The United States has routinely sought to overthrow Castro's regime, most famously during the 1962 Bay of Pigs invasion. Nonetheless, his control of Cuba has outlasted every attempt to undermine his authority, and although he is no longer the country's political leader, he still wields influence. Castro's brother, Raúl Castro, was elected Cuba's president in 2008 and continues to serve in that capacity.

Alice Walker's participation in the 1962 World Festival of Youth and Students sparked her interest in Castro and the Cuban Revolution. She read Castro's 1953 legal defense *History Will Absolve Me* in an attempt to gain insight into the Cuban Revolution and Marxism, and she traveled to Cuba with a group of black artists in the late 1970s. During her visit, she inquired about cultural taboos regarding homosexuality and issues of racial pride among black Cubans. Walker has visited the country on several occasions, including a 1995 visit to Havana, and has declared that she feels a sense of affinity with Castro.

## FURTHER READING

Baggins, Brian. *Fidel Castro History Archive.* Available online. URL: http://www.marxists.org/history/cuba/archive/castro/index.htm. Accessed February 28, 2009.

Bunck, Julie Marie. *Fidel Castro and the Quest for a Revolutionary Culture in Cuba.* University Park: University of Pennsylvania Press, 1994.

Castro, Fidel. *Cuba at the Crossroads.* Melbourne, Australia: Ocean Press, 1996.

———. *Fidel Castro: My Life, a Spoken Autobiography.* Penguin: London, 2008.

———. *History Will Absolve Me: The Moncada Trial Defense Speech, Santiago de Cuba, October 16th, 1953.* London: Came, 1968.

———. *Tomorrow Is Too Late: Development and the Environmental Crisis in the Third World.* Melbourne, Australia: Ocean Press, 1993.

DuBois, Jules. *Fidel Castro: Rebel, Liberator or Dictator?* Indianapolis: Bobbs-Merrill, 1988.

Halperin, Maurice. *The Rise and Decline of Fidel Castro: An Essay in Contemporary History.* Berkeley: University of California Press, 1974.

Skierka, Volker. *Fidel Castro: A Biography.* Cambridge: Polity, 2004.

White, Evelyn C. *Alice Walker: A Life.* New York: W. W. Norton and Company, 2004.

**Chapman, Tracy** (1964– ) Since her 1988 debut album entitled *Tracy Chapman,* Tracy Chapman has been one of the country's most acclaimed and popular folk artists. Heavily influenced by Odetta, Joan Baez, and Joan Armatrading, she has a spare vocal style and a penchant for topical themes that involve explorations of the questions of social injustice.

Born in Cleveland, Ohio, Chapman was raised by a single mother. While a student at Tufts University, the self-taught guitar player became a fixture in Boston area music venues. After a time, she was discovered by a classmate who recommended her to his father, a prominent record executive. Her eponymous debut album, recorded for Elektra Records, was critically acclaimed and commercially embraced. In addition to topping *Billboard* magazine's album chart, it featured the hit single "Fast Car" and won her three Grammy Awards. Subsequent albums met with more moderate success until the release of her 1995 album *New Beginning,* which, propelled by the popular BLUES ballad "Give Me One Reason," reinvigorated her career.

Chapman periodically releases albums to her devoted fan base, remains an outspoken activist, and is a regular concert performer. Her austere visual style and discreet private life have inspired considerable speculation regarding her sexual orientation. Alice Walker has publicly acknowledged that she and Chapman had an intimate and sexual relationship during the mid-1990s.

### FURTHER READING

All Music Guide. "Tracy Chapman." Available online. URL: http://www.allmusic.com/cg/amg.dll?p=amg&sql=11:hifuxqw5ldfe. Accessed February 20, 2009.

Chapman, Tracy. *Collection.* New York: Elektra, 2001.

———. *Crossroads.* New York: Elektra, 1989.

———. *Let it Rain.* New York: Elektra, 2002.

———. *Matters of the Heart.* New York: Elektra, 1992.

———. *New Beginning.* New York: Elektra, 1995.

———. *Our Bright Future.* New York: Atlantic, 2008.

———. *Telling Stories.* New York: Elektra, 2000.

———. *Tracy Chapman.* New York: Elektra, 1988.

———. *Where You Live.* New York: Elektra, 2005.

Gaar, G. G. *She's a Rebel: The History of Women in Rock and Roll.* New York: Seal Press, 2002.

George-Warren, Holly, and Patricia Romanowski, eds. *The Rolling Stone Encyclopedia of Rock and Roll.* 3d ed. New York: Fireside, 2001.

Wajid, Sara. "No Retreat: Writer and Feminist Alice Walker Talks to Sara Wajid about Growing Older, Her Affair with Tracy Chapman and the Connection between the Niqab and High Heels." *Guardian,* 15 December 2006. Available online. URL: http://www.guardian.co.uk/books/2006/dec/15/gender.world. Accessed February 24, 2009.

White, Evelyn C. *Alice Walker: A Life.* New York: W. W. Norton and Company, 2004.

**Chödrön, Pema** (1936– ) Pema Chödrön is a renowned, ordained Buddhist nun and director of Gampo Abbey, the first Tibetan monastery for Westerners, which is located in Cape Breton, Nova Scotia. Born Deidre Blonfield-Brown in New York City, Chödrön began studying BUDDHISM in 1974. Her first two books on Buddhism, *The Wisdom of No Escape* (1991) and *Start Where You Are* (1994), gained her international attention and acclaim. Chödrön's teachings first introduced Alice Walker to the Tibetan Buddhist breathing technique called TONGLEN. In 2005, Walker and Chödrön released an audio recording on Tonglen, *Pema Chödrön and Alice Walker in Conversation: On the Meaning of Suffering and the Mystery of Joy.*

### FURTHER READING

Chödrön, Pema. *Awakening Loving-Kindness.* Boston: Shambhala, 1996.

———. *Comfortable with Uncertainty: 108 Teachings.* Boston: Shambhala, 2002.

———. *From Fear to Fearlessness: Teachings on the Four Great Catalysts of Awakening.* Louisville, Colo.: Sounds True, 2002.

———. *Getting Unstuck: Breaking Your Habitual Patterns and Encountering Naked Reality.* Louisville, Colo.: Sounds True, 2004.

———. *The Places That Scare You: A Guide to Fearlessness in Difficult Times.* Boston: Shambhala, 2002.

———. *Pure Meditation: The Tibetan Buddhist Practice of Inner Peace.* Louisville, Colo.: Sounds True, 2000.

———. *Start Where You Are: A Guide to Compassionate Living.* Boston: Shambhala, 2001.

———. *When Things Fall Apart: Heart Advice for Difficult Times.* Boston: Shambhala, 2000.

———. *The Wisdom of No Escape: And the Path of Loving Kindness.* Boston: Shambhala, 2001.

Friedman, Lenore. *Meetings with Remarkable Women: Buddhist Teachers in America.* Boston: Shambhala, 2000.

Pema Chödrön: Biography. Available online. URL: www.shambhala.org/teachers/pema/biography.php. Accessed February 28, 2009.

**Civil Rights movement** The Civil Rights movement in the United States was the struggle for African Americans to achieve the same rights provided to white males in the Constitution. Throughout African-American history, there have been two major strains of thought regarding the nature of what the African-American struggle for equality comprised, how that battle was to be waged, and what the ultimate objective should be. These two major intellectual and political beliefs, known generally by the labels integrationism and nationalism, were held by individuals who, for the most part, adhered to the notions that the solutions to African-American problems could be achieved either through fighting for the right to assimilate and integrate into American society or through strengthening African-American communities from within and developing them as separate communities, largely independent from American society as a whole.

The Civil Rights movement of the late 1950s and early-to-mid-1960s was largely based on the integrationist school of thought elaborated by men and women such as Frederick Douglas, Anna Julia Cooper, Frances Ellen Watkins Harper, W. E. B. DuBois, Walter White, Septima Clark, Diane Nash, and Martin Luther King, Jr.

From times of slavery and up through the first half of the 20th century, the black church was the stronghold and organizing center of the African-American community. Although formally initiated by various experts within African-American political organizations such as the National Association for the Advancement of Colored People in the early decades of the 20th century, the Civil Rights movement of the 1950s and 60s came about largely through the actions and support of black Christian churches. The main strategy of the Civil Rights movement was to confront racist and segregationist laws and practices with nonviolent direct action. This strategy took the form of boycotts, sit-ins, and other nonviolent protests that forced confrontation and examination of the practice of Jim Crow segregation in public life, housing, schooling, and voting practices.

In the mid-to-late 1960s, there occurred a major schism in the movement between those who favored integration and those younger people who had abandoned the principles of the early movement in favor of nationalism, separatism, communism, socialism—in other words, for a multiplicity of ideologies. These ideological divisions in the intellectual and activist community marked the beginning of the disintegration of integrationism and nonviolent direct action as the movement's dominant strategic tool. The actions of the individuals involved in the movement brought about the 1954 Supreme Court decision in *Brown v. Board of Education of Topeka* that ruled segregated schooling to be illegal and, subsequently, various voting rights acts, the 1961 Interstate Commerce Commission's ban on segregation in pubic transportation, and the Civil Rights Act of 1964.

Alice Walker was deeply involved in the Civil Rights movement as an activist. The philosophies of her writings are grounded in the principles and strategies that guided the movement. Her novel *Meridian* is explicitly about the movement's struggles and the toll that activism took on those who dedicated their energies, and sometimes their lives, to moving the country toward social justice. Walker remains committed to the fight for human equality and views her craft as a conduit for that struggle.

## FURTHER READING

Anderson, Carol. *Eyes off the Prize: The United Nations and the African-American Struggle for Human Rights,*

*1944–1955.* Cambridge: Cambridge University Press, 2003.

Berger, Dan. *Outlaws of America: The Weather Underground and the Politics of Solidarity.* Oakland: Arkansas Press, 2006.

Blake, John. *Children of the Movement.* Chicago: Lawrence Hill Books, 2004.

Bloom, Jack M. *Class, Race, and the Civil Rights Movement.* Bloomington: Indiana University Press, 1987.

Blumberg, Rhoda Lois. *Civil Rights: The 1960s Freedom Struggle.* Boston: Twayne Publishers, 1984.

———. "White Mothers as Civil Rights Activists." In *Women and Social Protest,* edited by Guida West and Rhoda Lois Blumberg. New York: Oxford University Press, 1990.

Borden, Philip. "Review of *CORE, a Study in the Civil Rights Movement, 1942–1968,* by August Meier and Elliot Rudwick." *The History Teacher* 7 (February 1974): 319–320.

Borstelmann, Thomas. *The Cold War and the Color Line: American Race Relations in the Global Arena.* Cambridge, Mass.: Harvard University Press, 2003.

Branch, Taylor. *Parting the Waters: America in the King Years, 1954–1963.* New York: Simon and Schuster, 1988.

———. *Pillar of Fire: America in the King Years, 1963–1965.* New York: Simon and Schuster, 1998.

Campbell, Clarice. *Civil Rights Chronicle: Letters from the South.* Oxford: University Press of Mississippi, 1997.

Carmichael, Stokely. *Black Power: The Politics of Liberation in America.* New York: Random House, 1967.

———. *Stokely Speaks: Black Power Back to Pan-Africanism.* New York: Random House, 1971.

Carson, Clayborne, et al. *The Eyes on the Prize Civil Rights Reader: Documents, Speeches, and Firsthand Accounts from the Black Freedom Struggle.* New York: Penguin Books, 1991.

Chafe, William Henfy. *Civilities and Civil Rights: Greensboro, N.C. and the Struggle for Freedom.* Oxford: Oxford University Press, 1990.

Crawford, Vicki, et al., eds. *Women in the Civil Rights Movements: Trailblazers and Torchbearers, 1941–1965.* Brooklyn, N.Y.: Carlson Publishing, 1990.

Curry, Constance. *Deep in Our Hearts: Nine White Women in the Freedom Movement.* Athens: University of Georgia Press, 2000.

Davis, Townsend. *Weary Feet, Rested Souls: A Guided History of the Civil Rights Movement.* New York: W. W. and Norton Company, 1998.

Dierenffield, Bruce J. *The Civil Rights Movement.* White Plains, N.Y.: Longman, 2004.

Dudziak, Mary L. *Cold War Civil Rights: Race and the Image of American Democracy.* Princeton, N.J.: Princeton University Press, 2002.

Eskew, Glenn T. *But for Birmingham: The Local and National Movements in the Civil Rights Struggle.* Chapel Hill: University of North Carolina Press, 1997.

Eubanks, W. Ralph. *Ever Is a Long Time: A Journey into Mississippi's Dark Past: A Memoir.* New York: Basic Books, 2003.

Evans, Sara. *Personal Politics: The Roots of Women's Liberation in the Civil Rights Movement and the New Left.* New York: Vintage Books, 1980.

Fendrich, James M. "Keeping the Faith or Pursuing the Good Life: A Study of the Consequences of Participation in the Civil Rights Movement." *American Sociological Review* 42 (February 1977): 144–157.

Friedland, Michael B. *Lift Up Your Voice Like a Trumpet: White Clergy and the Civil Rights and Antiwar Movements, 1954–1973.* Chapel Hill: University of North Carolina Press, 1998.

Gaillard, Frye. *Cradle of Freedom: Alabama and the Movement That Changed America.* Tuscaloosa: University of Alabama Press, 2004.

Garner, Roberta, and John Tenuto. *Social Movement Theory and Research: An Annotated Bibliographical Guide.* Lanham, Md.: Scarecrow Press; Pasadena, Calif.: Salem Press, 1997.

Garrow, David. *Bearing the Cross: Martin Luther King and the Southern Christian Leadership Conference, 1955–1968.* New York: William Morrow, 1986.

Genovese, Eugene D. *Roll, Jordan, Roll: The World the Slaves Made.* New York: Pantheon Books: 1974.

Goldberg, Robert A. *Grassroots Resistance: Social Movements in Twentieth Century America.* Belmont, Calif.: Wadsworth; Philadelphia: Temple University Press, 1991.

Gosse, Van. *The Movements of the New Left, 1950–1975: A Brief History with Documents.* New York: Palgrave Macmillan, 2005.

Grant, Joanne. *Ella Baker: Freedom Bound.* Hoboken, N.J.: John Wiley and Sons, 1998.

Greenberg, Cheryl Lynn, ed. *A Circle of Trust: Remembering SNCC.* New Brunswick, N.J.: Rutgers University Press, 1998.

Greene, Christina. "'We'll Take Our Stand': Race, Class, and Gender in the Southern Student Organizing Committee, 1964–1969." In *Hidden Histories of Women in the New South,* edited by Virginia Bernhard et al., 191. Columbia: University of Missouri Press, 1994.

Haines, Herbert H. *Black Radicals and the Civil Rights Mainstream, 1954–1970.* Knoxville: University of Tennessee Press, 1988.

Halberstam, David. *The Children.* New York: Random House, 1998.

Hampton, Henry, and Steve Fayer. *Voices of Freedom: An Oral History of the Civil Rights Movement from the 1950s through the 1980s.* New York: Bantam Books, 1990.

Hansen, Drew D. *Dream: Martin Luther King, Jr. and the Speech That Inspired a Nation.* New York: HarperCollins, 2003.

Higham, John. *Civil Rights and Social Wrongs: Black-White Relations since World War II.* University Park: Pennsylvania State University Press, 1997.

Hill, Lance. *Deacons for Defense: Armed Resistance and the Civil Rights Movement.* Chapel Hill: University of North Carolina Press, 2004.

Honigsberg, Peter. *Crossing Border Street: A Civil Rights Memoir.* Berkeley: University of California Press, 2000.

Huckaby, Elizabeth. *Crisis at Central High, Little Rock, 1957–58.* Baton Rouge: Louisiana State University Press, 1980.

Laue, James H. *Direct Action and Desegregation, 1960–1962: Toward a Theory of the Rationalization of Protest.* Brooklyn, N.Y.: Carlson Publishing, 1989.

Lawson, Steven. "Freedom Then, Freedom Now: The Historiography of the Civil Rights Movement." *American Historical Review* 96 (April 1991): 456–471.

Lawson, Steven, and Charles Payne. *Debating the Civil Rights Movement: 1945–1968.* New York: Roman and Littlefield, 1998.

Lazerow, Jama, and Yohuru Williams, eds. *In Search of the Black Panther Party: New Perspectives on a Revolutionary Movement.* Durham, N.C.: Duke University Press, 2006.

Lee, Chana Kai. *For Freedom's Sake: The Life of Fannie Lou Hamer.* Champagne: University of Illinois Press, 2000.

Levy, Peter. *Civil War on Race Street: The Civil Rights Movement in Cambridge, Maryland.* Gainesville: University Press of Florida, 2003.

———. *Documentary History of the Modern Civil Rights Movement.* New York: Greenwood Press, 1992.

———, ed. *Let Freedom Ring: A Documentary History of the Modern Civil Rights Movement.* New York: Praeger, 1992.

Lewis, John, with Michael D'Orso. *Walking with the Wind: A Memoir of the Movement.* New York: Simon and Schuster, 1998.

Litwack, Leon F. *Trouble in Mind: Black Southerners in the Age of Jim Crow.* New York: Alfred A. Knopf, 1998.

Manis, Andrew Michael. *A Fire You Can't Put Out: The Civil Rights Life of Birmingham's Reverend Fred Shuttlesworth.* Tuscaloosa: University of Alabama Press, 1999.

Marwell, Gerald, Michael T. Aiken, and N. J. Demerath III. "The Persistence of Political Attitudes Among 1960s Civil Rights Activists." *Public Opinion Quarterly* 51 (Autumn 1987): 359–375.

Matthews, Glenna. "Review of *Throwing Off the Cloak of Privilege: White Southern Women Activists in the Civil Rights Era,* by Gail S. Murray." *American Historical Review* 111 (October 2006): 1,222–1,223.

Irons, Jenny. "The Shaping of Activist Recruitment and Participation: A Study of Women in the Mississippi Civil Rights Movement." *Gender and Society* 12, no. 6 (December 1998): 692–709.

Jacobs, Paul, and Saul Landau. *The New Radicals: A Report with Documents.* New York: Random House, 1966.

Jenkins, J. Craig. *The Politics of Insurgency: The Farm Worker Movement and the Politics of the 1960s.* New York: Columbia University Press, 1985.

Jennings, James. *The Politics of Black Empowerment: The Transformation of Black Activism in Urban America.* Detroit: Wayne State University Press, 1992.

Joseph, Peniel E., ed. *The Black Power Movement: Rethinking the Civil Rights–Black Power Era.* New York: Routledge, 2006.

Katz, Judith H. *White Awareness: Handbook for Antiracism Training.* Norman: University of Oklahoma Press, 2003.

Kincaid, John. "Beyond the Voting Rights Act: White Responses to Black Political Power in Tchula, Mississippi." *Publius* 16 (Autumn 1986): 155–172.

King, Mary. *Freedom Song: A Personal History of the 1960's Civil Rights Movement.* New York: William Morrow, 1987.

Macedo, Stephen, ed. *Reassessing the Sixties: Debating the Political and Cultural Legacy.* New York: W. W. Norton & Company, 1997.

Marable, Manning. *Race, Reform, and Rebellion: The Second Reconstruction in Black America, 1945–1982.* Jackson: University Press of Mississippi, 1991.

McAdam, Doug. "The Biographical Consequences of Activism." *American Sociological Review* 54 (1989): 744–760.

McKnight, Gerald D. *The Last Crusade: Martin Luther King, Jr., the F.B.I., and the People's Campaign.* Boulder, Colo.: Westview Press, 1998.

McWhoter, Dianne. *A Dream of Freedom: The Civil Rights Movement from 1954 to 1968.* New York: Scholastic, 2004.

Minkoff, Debra C. *Organizing for Equality: The Evolution of Women's and Racial-ethnic Organizations in America, 1955–1985.* New Brunswick, N.J.: Rutgers University Press, 1995.

Moody, Anne. *Coming of Age in Mississippi.* New York: Dell Publishing, 1975.

Morgan, Edward P. *The 60s Experience: Hard Lessons about Modern America.* Philadelphia: Temple University Press, 1991.

Morris, Aldon D. *The Origins of the Civil Rights Movement: Black Communities Organizing for Change.* New York: Free Press, 1984.

Olson, Lynne. *Freedom's Daughters: The Unsung Heroines of the Civil Rights Movement from 1830–1970.* New York: Simon and Schuster, 2001.

Palmer, Phyllis. "Review of A *Promise and a Way of Life: White Antiracist Activism,* by Becky Thompson, and *Deep in Our Hearts: Nine White Women in the Freedom Movement,* edited by Emmie S. Adams." *NWSA Journal* 15 (Summer 2003): 168–172.

Parsons, Sara Mitchell. *From Southern Wrongs to Civil Rights: The Memoir of a White Civil Rights Activist.* Tuscaloosa: University of Alabama Press, 2000.

Postgrove, Carol. *Divided Minds: Intellectuals and the Civil Rights Movement.* New York: Norton, 2001.

Poussaint, Alvin. "The Stresses of the White Female Workers in the Civil Rights Movement in the South." *American Journal of Psychiatry* 123 (October 1966): 401–407.

Ransby, Barbara. *Ella Baker and the Black Freedom Movement: A Radical Democratic Vision.* Chapel Hill: University of North Carolina Press, 2003.

Riches, William Terence Martin. *The Civil Rights Movement: Struggle and Resistance.* New York: Palgrave Macmillan, 2004.

Robinson, Armstead L., and Patricia Sullivan, eds. *New Directions in Civil Rights Studies* Charlottesville: University Press of Virginia, 1991.

Shakoor, Jordana Y. *Civil Rights Childhood.* Oxford: University Press of Mississippi, 1999.

Webb, Clive. *Fight against Fear: Southern Jews and Black Civil Rights.* Athens: University of Georgia Press, 2001.

Weisbrot, Robert. *Freedom Bound: A History of America's Civil Rights Movement.* New York: Plume, 1990.

Wexler, Sanford. *An Eyewitness History of the Civil Rights Movement.* New York: Facts On File, 1999.

Williams, Juan. *Eyes on the Prize: America's Civil Rights Years, 1954–65.* New York: Viking Press, 1987.

Young, Andrew. *An Easy Burden.* New York: HarperCollins, 1996.

**Colette (Sidonie-Gabrielle Colette)** (1873–1954) Colette is the pen name for the French novelist and short story writer Sidonie-Gabrielle Colette. The central concerns of Colette's writing generally involve the delineation of women's struggles in love and relationships. Her work was highly autobiographical and boldly integrated female sexuality. She is best known for the novels *Chéri* (1920), which later became a play and movie, and 1944's *Gigi,* which was later adapted for Broadway and for a 1948 feature film. The story had another incarnation in the form of the popular 1958 film musical directed by Vincent Minnelli. Colette was honored as the first woman elected to the office of president of the Concourt Academy. In 1953, she became the second woman named as a grand officer in the Legion of Honor.

In her anthology *In Search of Our Mothers' Gardens,* Alice Walker lists Colette as part of the canon of womanist writers alongside ZORA NEALE

HURSTON, JEAN TOOMER, VIRGINIA WOOLF, Anaïs Nin, and Tillie Olsen.

### FURTHER READING

Boatright, Robert G. *The Intersecting Realities and Fictions of Virginia Woolf and Colette.* Columbus: Ohio State University Press, 2004.

Crosland, Margaret. *Colette: The Difficulty of Loving.* Indianapolis: Bobbs-Merrill, 1973.

———. *Madame Colette: A Provincial in Paris.* London: Peter Owen, 1953.

Cummins, Laurel. *Colette and the Conquest of Self.* Birmingham: Summa Publications, 2005.

Goudeket, Maurice. *Close to Colette: An Intimate Portrait of a Woman of Genius.* New York: Farrar, Straus and Cudahy, 1957.

Huffer, Lynne. *Another Colette: The Question of Gendered Writing.* Ann Arbor: University of Michigan Press, 1993.

Jouve, Nicole Ward. *Colette: Critical Essay.* Bloomington: Indiana University Press, 1987.

Ladimer, Bethany. *Colette, Beauvoir, and Duras: Age and Women Writers.* Gainesville: University Press of Florida, 1999.

Le Hardouin, Maria. *Colette.* London: Staples, 1958.

Lottman, Herbert R. *Colette: A Life.* New York: Little Brown and Company, 1991.

Lucey, Michael. *Never Say I: Sexuality and the First Person in Colette, Gide, and Proust.* Durham, N.C.: Duke University Press, 2006.

Massie, Allan. *Colette.* New York: Penguin Books, 1986.

Mitchell, Yvonne. *Colette: A Taste for Life.* London: Weidenfeld and Nicolson, 1975.

Norell, Donna M. *Colette: An Annotated Primary and Secondary Bibliography.* New York: Garland, 1993.

Peebles, Catherine M. *The Psyche of Feminism: Sand, Colette, Sarraute.* Lafayette, Ind.: Purdue University Press, 2004.

Richardson, Joanna. *Colette.* Essex, Mass.: Methuen, 1983.

Strand, Dana. *Colette: A Study of the Short Fiction.* New York: Twayne, 1995.

Thurman, Judith. *Secrets of the Flesh: A Life of Colette.* London: Bloomsbury, 1999.

**Congress of Racial Equality (CORE)** The Congress of Racial Equality (CORE) was an early Civil Rights organization founded at the University of Chicago in 1942. The work of CORE was particularly influential for Walker, and the experiences of the Freedom Riders were a catalyst for her activism. In the beginning, the membership of the organization was mostly white and middle class. Several of the original members of CORE were also members of an older civil rights organization, the Fellowship of Reconciliation (FOR). The organization was always integrated and was formed with the objective of implementing civil disobedience as modeled and defined by Henry David Thoreau and Mahatma Gandhi as a strategy for combating the inequalities experienced by African Americans in the United States. Members of CORE, including Bayard Rustin, George Houser, Anna Murray, and James Farmer, became major figures in the CIVIL RIGHTS MOVEMENT of the 1950s and 1960s.

One of CORE's early important actions, implemented in spring 1947, five years after the organization's founding, was called the Journey of Reconciliation. The members of CORE wanted to push the federal government to acknowledge that segregation in interstate travel was unconstitutional even though it was the practice throughout the southern United States. In order to accomplish this task, black and white members of CORE assembled to travel together through the South, defying the segregation rules in the states they would pass through: Virginia, North Carolina, Tennessee, and Kentucky.

During the Journey of Reconciliation, CORE members faced physical violence and arrest. The most productive result of the journey was the national and international focus it brought to the injustices of segregation. The Journey of Reconciliation was the first of many of CORE's protests through nonviolent civil disobedience. These actions included more attempts to defy segregation in interstate transportation, voter registration drives, and sit-ins.

The fight against segregation in interstate transportation reached a climax with a series of actions called the Freedom Rides. Riders of different races traveled together through the states that were most resistant to desegregation—Georgia, Alabama, Louisiana, and Mississippi—where they met with violence, resistance, and arrest. The Freedom Rides continued until 1961, when the federal government was forced to intervene and to declare segregation in interstate travel illegal.

CORE was one of the organizations that were responsible for organizing and implementing the 1963 March on Washington. Although Bayard Rustin's participation was relegated to behind-the-scenes status because he was a gay man and therefore, at the time, thought to be a potential liability, many participants and historians have asserted that the march would not have happened without his efforts.

CORE worked with the STUDENT NON-VIOLENT COORDINATING COMMITTEE, the Southern Christian Leadership Conference, and the National Association for the Advancement of Colored People to plan a voter registration drive and to encourage the growth of grassroots activism in Mississippi during the summer of 1964. This collaborative effort, known as Freedom Summer, focused its efforts on registering black people to vote and establishing freedom schools to provide education generally and teach organizing techniques. The summer drew the participation of local residents, as well as that of volunteers from other states. During the summer, three young men involved in the work of Freedom Summer, James Chaney, Andrew Goodman, and Michael Schwener, were kidnapped and killed by local whites. Again, the publicity the event attracted to the conditions of life for blacks in the South brought pressure on the federal government to pass legislation to support the efforts of CORE and the other groups working in the struggle for civil rights. The most significant of these measures was the Voting Rights Act, passed in 1965. The act was designed to ensure that all American citizens, including African Americans, were guaranteed that they would not be discriminated against at the state or local level when they attempted to exercise their right to vote.

CORE continued throughout the 1960s and works into the present day to advocate for racial equality. The organization has programs that continue to support its founding principles of the establishment of equality for all of the citizens of the United States and the world, irrespective of color.

## FURTHER READING

Arsenault, Raymond. *Freedom Riders: 1961 and the Struggle for Racial Justice.* Oxford: Oxford University Press, 2006.

Congress of Racial Equality Web site. Available online. URL: www.core-online.org. Accessed on February 17, 2010.

Fairclough, Adam. *Better Day Coming: Blacks and Equality, 1890–2000.* New York: Penguin, 2002.

Farmer, James. *Lay Bare the Heart: An Autobiography of the Civil Rights Movement.* New York: Arbor House Publishing Company, 1985.

Houser, George M. *CORE: A Brief History.* Chicago: Congress of Racial Equality, 1949.

*Interviews with Civil Rights Workers from the Congress of Racial Equality.* Microfilm; Stanford University Project South Oral History Collection. Glen Rock, N.J.: Microfilming Corp. of America, 1975.

Meier, August, and Elliot Rudwick. *CORE: A Study in the Civil Rights Movement, 1942–1968.* Chicago: University of Illinois Press, 1973.

*The Papers of the Congress of Racial Equality.* Microfilm. Glen Rock, N.J.: Microfilming Corp. of America, 1982.

Wink, Walter. *Peace Is the Way: Writings on Nonviolence from the Fellowship of Reconciliation.* New York: Orbis Books, 2000.

**conjure woman** When enslaved Africans arrived in the United States, the Caribbean, and South America, they brought with them religious customs and traditions that they were often prohibited from practicing openly. Consequently, many African religious philosophies and practices were combined with Christian religions, particularly Catholicism, and created new systems of belief such as Voodun and Santeria. On the surface, these new religions resembled the religions of the slaveholders and therefore allowed those who were enslaved to retain some of the elements of West African traditional religious practice.

In the belief systems that evolved in slave communities, there were frequently individuals to whom special powers were attributed. These individual men and women were said to be conjurers, and purportedly they were able to use supernatural powers and incantations to shift the dynamic of power from the slaveholder to the slave. Conjure men and women were often revered and sometimes feared. Other slaves would go to them seeking solutions to problems and difficulties.

When African Americans began to publish their writings, the conjure woman became an important literary figure, most notably in the fiction of Charles Chestnutt. Like their real-life progenitors, literary conjure women frequently use knowledge, cunning, and community solidarity to subvert the power of an oppressor. The conjure woman as a literary trope enjoyed a renaissance with the proliferation of contemporary African-American women's writing. Critics have called many of Alice Walker's characters conjure women, including Miss Lissie, Sofia, and Tashi.

#### FURTHER READING

Ammons, Elizabeth, and Annette White-Parks. *Tricksterism in Turn-of-the-Century American Literature: A Multicultural Perspective.* Hanover and London: University Press of New England, 1994.

Tucker, Lindsey. "Recovering the Conjure Woman: Texts and Contexts in Gloria Naylor's *Mama Day.*" *African American Review* 28, no. 2 (1994): 173–188.

**Cooper, Jane** (1924–2007) Jane Cooper was a prolific and well-respected poet, essayist, and teacher. Among her works were the collections of poetry *The Weather of Six Mornings* (1969), which received the Lamont Award of the Academy of American Poets; *Scaffolding: New and Selected Poems* (1984); and *Green Notebook, Winter Road* (1994). Cooper taught at SARAH LAWRENCE COLLEGE from 1950 to 1987 and worked closely with Alice Walker on her writing during Walker's undergraduate years. She was an advocate for Walker's work from the time Walker was a student.

Cooper consistently praised the freshness and clarity of Walker's prose and in 1972 recommended her for a writing fellowship grant at Harvard University's Radcliffe Institute. Walker dedicated her anthology of short stories *In Love and Trouble: Stories of Black Women* (1973) to Cooper and others. Cooper retired from teaching in 1987. In 1995, she served as the state poet of New York. She and Walker remained friends until Cooper's death in Newtown, Pennsylvania, on October 26, 2007.

#### FURTHER READING

Cooper, Jane. *Calling Me from Sleep: New and Selected Poems, 1961–1973.* Bronxville, N.Y.: Sarah Lawrence College. 1974.

———. *Green Notebook, Winter Road.* Gardiner, Maine: Tilbury House, Publishers, 1994.

———. *Maps and Windows: Poems.* New York: Macmillan, 1974.

———. *Scaffolding: New and Selected Poems.* London: Anvil Press Poetry Ltd., 1984.

———. *Scaffolding: Selected Poems.* Gardiner, Maine: Tilbury House, Publishers, 1993.

———. *Threads: Rosa Luxemburg from Prison.* New York: Flamingo Press, 1978.

———. *The Weather of Six Mornings: Poems.* New York: Macmillan, 1969.

New York State Writers Institute, State University of New York. "Jane Cooper: State Poet 1995." Available online. URL: http://www.albany.edu/writers-inst/webpages4/archives/coopersp.html. Accessed March 6, 2009.

White, Evelyn C. *Alice Walker: A Life.* New York: W. W. Norton and Company, 2004.

**Deeter, Catherine** (1959– ) Catherine Deeter is a designer, artist, and illustrator who has worked for a wide range of commercial projects, including publishing. She has illustrated books by several publishing houses and individual authors, including three by Alice Walker: *To Hell with Dying, Finding the Green Stone,* and *Langston Hughes, American Poet.* Deeter has also published her own children's book, entitled *Seymour Blue,* which features a cat as the main character who guides grade-school children through an exploration of the artistic process.

#### FURTHER READING

Catherine Deeter Web site. Available online. URL: http://www.catherinedeeter.com/. Accessed January 11, 2010.

Deeter, Catherine. *Seymour Blue.* New York: Simon & Schuster Children's Publishing, 1998.

**Dostoyevsky, Fyodor** (1821–1867) The Russian author Fyodor Dostoyevsky, one of the most influential and respected 19th-century novelists and the son of a physician, was born into a professional family who valued education. He showed promise as a writer even from adolescence and published his first novel, *Poor Folk* (1846), when he was 25. Dostoyevsky became involved with a socialist group that was perceived as seditious, and as a result, he was sentenced to imprisonment until 1858. After he was released, he began writing in earnest and wrote perpetually. His most notable works, including *Crime and Punishment* (1866) and *The Brothers Karamazov* (1880), were written during this time. Dostoyevsky also experienced personal tragedy including periodic epileptic seizures, and the death of his brother and his first wife. In spite of these traumas, he continued to write.

By the time of his death in 1867, Dostoyevsky was a literary and cultural hero. His work is notable for its investigation of the complexities of human psychology. In many ways, he laid a foundation for the form the novel genre would take in the 20th century. Many authors, including Alice Walker, count Dostoyevsky as a profound influence on their work.

### FURTHER READING

Frank, Joseph. *Dostoyevsky: The Miraculous Years, 1865–1871.* Princeton, N.J.: Princeton University Press, 1995.

Holquist, Michael. *Dostoyevsky and the Novel.* Princeton, N.J.: Princeton University Press, 1977.

Kjetsaa, Geir. *Fyodor Dostoyevsky, A Writer's Life.* New York: Viking, 1987.

Leatherbarrow, William J. *Fedor Dostoyevsky: A Reference Guide.* Boston: G. K. Hall, 1990.

Murav, Harriet. *Holy Foolishness: Dostoyevsky's Novels and the Poetics of Cultural Critique.* Stanford, Calif.: Stanford University Press, 1992.

Simmons, Ernest Joseph. *Feodor Dostoyevsky.* New York: Columbia University Press, 1969

**double consciousness** Double consciousness is the construct set forth by W. E. B. DuBois in his classic 1903 work *The Souls of Black Folk,* which articulates his understanding of the racial struggle of African Americans. DuBois felt that as a result of racism, discrimination, and exclusion, African Americans perpetually face the dilemma of trying to reconcile the contradictions of their identity. By defining double consciousness, DuBois articulated the conflict inherent in being an American and yet not fully participating in the rights and privileges of that national designation because of the racial caste system. His metaphor continues to resonate today and is still used as a way of describing and theorizing the African-American condition.

At the turn of the last century, W. E. B. DuBois prophesied that the problem of the 20th century would be the problem of the color line. Narratives and histories of the 20th century reveal the power of the color line to fracture and polarize, to murder and destroy. Consider DuBois's task as he sat down to articulate a narrative of African Americans in *The Souls of Black Folk.* Without hesitation, he appropriated the role of storyteller and interpreter of his people's story. Although the solutions he presents in the text for the rise of post–Civil War African Americans were hotly contested, his insightful analysis, particularly his definition of double consciousness, is still highly regarded today.

As with many African-American writers, Alice Walker explores the dilemmas of double consciousness throughout her canon.

### FURTHER READING

DuBois, W. E. B. *The Conservation of Races.* Washington, D.C.: American Negro Academy, 1897.

———. *Darkwater: Voices from Within the Veil. The Oxford W.E.B. DuBois Reader.* Edited by Eric J. Sundquist. New York and Oxford: Oxford University Press, 1996.

———. *Dusk of Dawn: An Essay toward an Autobiography of a Race Concept.* New Brunswick, N.J., and London: Transaction Books, 1984.

———. *The Souls of Black Folk.* 1903. Reprint, New York: Signet, 1969.

———. *Writings by W. E. B. DuBois in Periodicals Edited by Others.* Edited by Herbert Aptheker. Millwood, N.Y.: Kraus-Thomson Organization Limited, 1982.

———. *Writings in Periodicals Edited by W. E. B. Du Bois: Selections from the Crisis.* Vol. 1. Edited by

Herbert Aptheker. Millwood, N.Y.: Kraus-Thomson Organization Limited, 1983.

Fox, Frank W. "Washington, DuBois, and the Problem of Negro Two-ness." *Markham Review* 7 (1978): 21–25.

Jones, D. Marvin. "A Darkness Made Visible: Law, Metaphor, and the Racial Self." In *Critical White Studies: Looking behind the Mirror*, edited by Richard Delgado and Jean Stefancic, 66–84. Philadelphia: Temple University Press, 1997.

**DuBois, W. E. B. (William Edward Burghardt DuBois)** (1868–1963) W. E. B. DuBois was the influential editor of the *Crisis* from 1910 to 1934. He was also one of the most important cultural critics and political activists of the 20th century. DuBois was a New Englander born into a black upper middle-class family. He excelled at school and entered Fisk University early. After graduation, he pursued graduate school at the University of Berlin and continued at Harvard. When DuBois graduated from Harvard in 1895, he was the first African American to earn a Ph.D. from that institution.

DuBois worked as an academic, serving on the faculty of Wilberforce University, the University of Pennsylvania, and Atlanta University. DuBois was also centrally concerned with the precarious situation African Americans found themselves at the turn of the century in the wake of the failures of Reconstruction. DuBois began to organize other politically minded, socially conscious intellectuals. One of the organizational meetings led to the formation of the Niagara Movement, which was a multiracial coalition of activists dedicated to the achievement of civil rights.

The Niagara Movement was the root organization that led to the formation of the most important American civil rights organization, the National Association for the Advancement of Colored People (NAACP). The NAACP's journal the *Crisis* provided DuBois with a forum for expressing his political opinions, beliefs, and strategies for change.

In addition to his work with the NAACP, DuBois continued to write important scholarly works and novels. His activism and scholarship led to unwarrantable charges by the U.S. government. Although he was acquitted of the crimes against the state that he had been accused of, this indictment laid the groundwork for his belief that racial equality would never be achieved in the United States. As a result, in 1961, DuBois moved to Ghana, where he would live out the remainder of his life. He also embraced communism as a political philosophy.

DuBois grew to believe that African-American people could not achieve social equality by emulating white ideals and that equality could be achieved only by teaching black racial pride with an emphasis on an African cultural heritage. One of many of Alice Walker's allusions to DuBois occurs in *The Color Purple* when Nettie writes to Celie and mentions his life and works.

## FURTHER READING

Andrews, William L. *Critical Essays on W.E.B. DuBois.* Boston: G. K. Hall, 1985.

Bell, Bernard W., Emily Grosholz, and James B. Stewart, eds. *W. E. B. DuBois on Race and Culture: Philosophy, Politics, and Poetics.* New York: Routledge, 1996.

Broderick, Francis L. *W.E.B. DuBois: Negro Leader in a Time of Crisis.* 1959.

Foner, Philip S., ed. *W. E. B. DuBois Speaks: Speeches and Addresses, 1890–1919.* New York: Pathfinder Press, 1966

Holloway, Jonathan S. "The Soul of W. E. B. DuBois." *American Quarterly* 49, no. 3 (September 1997): 603–615.

Lewis, David L. *W.E.B. DuBois: Biography of a Race, 1868–1919.* New York: H. Holt, 1993.

Marable, Manning. *W.E.B. DuBois: Black Radical Democrat.* Boston: Twayne, 1986.

Rampersad, Arnold. *The Art and Imagination of W. E. B. DuBois.* Cambridge: Harvard University Press, 1976.

———. "W. E. B. DuBois as a Man of Literature." *American Literature* 51 (1979): 50–68.

Rudwick, Elliott M. *W. E. B. DuBois, Voice of the Black Protest Movement.* Urbana: University of Illinois Press, 1982.

Sundquist, Eric J., ed. *The Oxford W. E. B. DuBois Reader.* New York: Oxford University Press, 1996.

**Eatonton, Georgia** Alice Walker was born in Eatonton, Georgia, on February 9, 1944, to Willie Lee and Minnie Lou (Tallulah) Grant Walker. Founded in 1808, Eatonton is located in Putnam County, about an hour and a half drive southwest from Atlanta. In 2008, there were approximately 6,300 residents living in the town. The Walker family's roots in the area extend at least to the early 19th century.

Her origins in Eatonton have played a prominent role in Walker's writing career. In her 1981 speech "The Dummy in the Window: Joel Chandler Harris and the Invention of Uncle Remus," delivered to the Atlanta Historical Society, she denounced the town's most celebrated resident, JOEL CHANDLER HARRIS. She accused Harris, who first published *UNCLE REMUS* stories, of stealing and distorting African folk culture.

Later, after the publication of her Pulitzer Prize–winning novel *The Color Purple,* the film version of the book premiered at the Pex Theater in Eatonton on January 18, 1986. Walker's older sister, Ruth Walker Hood, was the main organizer for the event. The proceeds from the Eatonton premiere went to The Color Purple Scholarship Fund for high school students involved in the arts.

Visitors to Eatonton can take "The Alice Walker Driving Tour" to sites that were important locations in her childhood, including Wards Chapel AFRICAN METHODIST EPISCOPAL CHURCH and the site of her childhood home. Interestingly, FLANNERY O'CONNOR's hometown of Milledgeville,

The Eatonton/Putnam County Courthouse, constructed between 1905 and 1906 in Eatonton, Georgia, the hometown of both Alice Walker and Joel Chandler Harris *(Photograph by Carmen Gillespie)*

Georgia, is only a little over a 30-minute drive from Eatonton.

### FURTHER READING

"Eatonton." *New Georgia Encyclopedia.* Available online. URL: http://www.georgiaencyclopedia.org/nge/Article.jsp?id=h-2249. Accessed February 12, 2009.

Little, Windee Allienor. *Reminiscent: A Pictorial History of Eatonton/Putnam County, Georgia.* Virginia Beach, Va.: Donning, 1999.

White, Evelyn C. *Alice Walker: A Life.* New York: W. W. Norton and Company, 2004.

**Ellington, Duke (Edward Kennedy)** (1899–1974) The man who would ultimately be known as the world-famous musician Duke Ellington was born into a middle-class African-American family in Washington, D.C., at the turn of the 20th century. Ellington had a wide exposure to the arts and culture and received a fine arts education at the Armstrong Manual Training School. Finding himself more interested in playing the piano, he left high school to pursue a career in music. He began by starting a band, which became popular, a favorite for parties and social engagements, and developed an audience through radio engagements. After a time, Ellington relocated in order to have greater access to the more extensive music venues of New York. Once there, he and his band gained a national and, eventually, international audience. Recording contracts followed as Ellington became known not only as a musician and bandleader but also as a composer.

By the time of his death in 1974, Ellington had become one of the most popular, respected, and innovative musicians of the 20th century. Alice Walker has written about the profound stimulus Ellington's works have had on her creative energies.

### FURTHER READING

Ellington, Duke. *Music Is My Mistress.* New York: Doubleday, 1973.

Hasse, John Edward. *Beyond Category: The Life and Genius of Duke Ellington.* New York: Simon and Schuster, 1993.

Montgomery, Elizabeth R., and Paul Frame. *Duke Ellington: King of Jazz.* New York: Garrard, 1972.

Tucker, Mark, ed. *The Duke Ellington Reader.* New York: Oxford University Press, 1993.

Yanow, Scott. *Duke Ellington.* New York: Friedman/Fairfax, 1999.

**Evers, Medgar** (1925–1963) Born in Decatur, Mississippi, Medgar Evers was a vigilant figure in the struggle for civil rights in Mississippi who became one of the first tragic figures of the era after being assassinated on June 12, 1963, by Byron De La Beckwith. In 1954, Evers became the state's first field secretary of the NATIONAL ASSOCIATION FOR THE ADVANCEMENT OF COLORED PEOPLE (NAACP). In spite of overt threats on his life, he opened the NAACP office in Jackson, and some of his key achievements included vigorous efforts to investigate racial violence, boycott discriminatory merchants, and advocate for James Meredith's admission to the University of Mississippi in 1962.

Evers was assassinated in the driveway of his home by a single shot fired by Byron De La Beckwith. De La Beckwith was acquitted by all-white juries in 1964 and 1965 trials but was finally convicted and sentenced to life in 1994; he died in prison in 2001.

Evers's widow, Myrlie Evers-Williams, is an activist and author who persisted in seeking justice for Evers's death and continues to fight for social justice.

Medgar Evers figures in Walker's novel *Meridian.*

### FURTHER READING

Brown, Jennie. *Medgar Evers.* Los Angeles: Melrose Square Publishing Co., 1994.

Massengill, Reed. *Portrait of a Racist: The Man Who Killed Medgar Evers?* New York: St. Martin's Press, 1994.

Nossiter, Adam. *Of Long Memory: Mississippi and the Murder of Medgar Evers.* Reading, Mass.: Addison-Wesley, 1994.

Padgett, John B. "Medgar Evers." *The Mississippi Writers Page.* Available online. URL: http://www.olemiss.edu/mwp/dir/evers_medgar/index.html. Accessed February 28, 2009.

Salter, John R. *Jackson, Mississippi: An American Chronicle of Struggle and Schism.* Hicksville, N.Y.: Exposition Press, 1979.

Scott, R. W. *Glory in Conflict: A Saga of Byron De La Beckwith.* Camden, Ark.: Camark Press, 1991.

Vollers, Maryanne. *Ghosts of Mississippi: The Murder of Medgar Evers, The Trials of Byron De La Beckwith, and the Haunting of the New South.* Boston: Little, Brown, 1995.

**familiar** The familiar is a concept common to many disparate cultures. A familiar is most often understood to be a supernatural entity that serves as a connection, sometimes a conduit, between human beings and the spirit world. In some lore, familiars are household guardians. In other traditions, the familiar takes the form of an animal who acts as a kind of agent for its owner. A contemporary iconic survival of this notion lies in the depiction of an evil witch with her cat who serves her and performs malevolent acts at the witch's command.

The concept of the familiar is a critical tool that Alice Walker uses as a central controlling metaphor in her novel *The Temple of My Familiar.* Walker employs various aspects of the history of narratives surrounding the familiar in order to explore the relationship between the corporeal and spirit worlds.

### FURTHER READING

Golden, Richard, ed. *Encyclopedia of Witchcraft: The Western Tradition.* Santa Barbara, Calif.: ABC-Clio, 2006

Sanders, Andrew. *A Deed without a Name: The Witch in Society and History.* Oxford and Washington, D.C.: Berg, 1995.

Willis, Deborah. *Malevolent Nurture: Witch-Hunting and Maternal Power in Early Modern England.* Ithaca, N.Y., and London: Cornell University Press, 1995.

**female genital mutilation (female circumcision, clitoridectomy)** The custom of female genital mutilation, sometimes referred to as female circumcision or clitoridectomy, is practiced in Africa, the Far East, and the Middle East. Although there are locally specific variations in the procedure, in general female genital mutilation involves the excision of the clitoris and other parts of the female genitalia.

The procedure has become a subject of concern and activism for various writers, intellectuals, and public figures. Protest against it comes both from within and without the cultures that practice this tradition. Critics of the practice generally express concern about the impact of the ritual on female sexual enjoyment and health.

The Egyptian writer, physician, and activist Nawal El Saadawi and the Ghanaian writer Ama Ata Aidoo are among those who have questioned the politics surrounding African female sexuality and the practice of clitoridectomy. Among the health risks associated with the procedure are hemorrhage, HIV transmission, increased vulnerability to infection, and emotional and psychological trauma.

Alice Walker first learned of female genital mutilation during a trip to Eastern Africa in the summer of 1965. Her interest in becoming a public spokesperson against the practice began with her interactions with a Kenyan actress who worked on the film adaptation of *The Color Purple.* Walker directly addressed the toll that the ritual has on individuals through the creation of the character Tashi in her 1992 novel *Possessing the Secret of Joy.* She and the filmmaker PRATIBHA PARMAR also generated global attention about the issues surrounding female genital mutilation through their 1993 documentary and companion book *Warrior Marks: Female Genital Mutilation and the Sexual Blinding of Women.*

Walker's role in presenting the procedure as an issue of relevance for Western feminists led to considerable controversy in the mid- to late 1990s. While many book reviewers praised her novel *Possessing the Secret of Joy* and its explicit treatment of female genital mutilation as a groundbreaking examination of a relatively unexplored social issue, some questioned Walker's ability to accurately represent African female subjectivity in both the novel and the documentary, directed by Parmar. Other critics felt that Walker's position as a prominent Westerner obscured the voices of the non-Western activists whose protests had preceded hers. She also was accused of writing without sufficiently differentiating the various ways the procedure is practiced in different countries or discussing the relationships between the ritual and colonialism, racism, sexism, and violence.

### FURTHER READING

El-Defrawi, M. H., et al. "Female Genital Mutilation and Its Psychosexual Impact." *Journal of Sex and Marital Therapy* 27, no. 5 (2001): 465–473.

Lane S. D., and R. A. Rubinstein. "Judging the Other: Responding to Traditional Female Genital Surgeries." *Hastings Centre Report* 26, no. 3 (1996): 31–40.

Toubia, Nahid. *Female Genital Mutilation: A Call for Global Action.* Rainbo: New York, 1993.

Toubia, Nahid, and Susan Izett. *Female Genital Mutilation: An Overview.* Geneva: World Health Organization, 1998.

Toubia, Nahid, and Anika Rahman. *Female Genital Mutilation: A Guide to Laws and Policies Worldwide.* London: Zed, 2000.

Walker, Alice, and Pratibah Parmar. *Warrior Marks: Female Genital Mutilation and the Sexual Blinding of Women.* New York: Harcourt Brace, 1993.

White, Evelyn C. *Alice Walker: A Life.* New York: W. W. Norton and Company, 2004.

**feminism** *Feminism* is a complicated and controversial term. At its most basic level, *feminism* refers to the struggle for social, political, and economic equality for women. In the history of that struggle, there has never been a single unified movement for women's equality. Feminism in the United States is generally defined by its historical chronology.

The so-called first wave of feminism in the United States occurred during the early to mid-19th century and emerged largely from women's activism in the antislavery/abolitionist movements. Most historians point to the 1848 Seneca Falls Convention as a starting point for the first wave of American feminism. At that gathering, women including Elizabeth Cady Stanton and others drafted and endorsed a document called the Declaration of Sentiments, which pointed to the fundamental contradictions in the U.S. Constitution. Most fundamentally, women, although citizens of the country, were not allowed to vote and did not have the same legal rights and status as men.

The demand for voting rights for women was complicated by issues of race. Although the Seneca Falls Convention included the concerns of African-American women and the need to abolish the institution of slavery, the objectives of the first-wave feminists (who did not call themselves that) were divided when, with the abolition of slavery, African-American men were granted the right to vote but white and black women were not. Many analyses of the period by historians mark this division as a turning point when the struggle for white middle- and upper-class women's rights became divided from the struggle for civil and human rights.

From the late 19th century to the early 20th century in the United States, women worked to acquire the vote, and the first wave of feminism, after the abolition of slavery, was largely concerned with this effort. In 1920, the Nineteenth Amendment to the Constitution legalized the vote for women. However, this change materialized in reality for only a small segment of female citizens as working class and minority women were often excluded from the opportunity to exercise this most fundamental right.

The second wave of American feminism, as it emerged in the 1950s and 1960s, was largely concerned with addressing the political, social, and economic interests of white, middle-class, heterosexual women. The beginning of the second-wave movement is associated with women's changing role in American life during World War II. With the male labor force largely involved in the military, women, particularly white middle-class women, worked in jobs from which they had previously been excluded. As a result, some women began to challenge the limitations that traditionally had been placed on them.

The second wave of feminist activism began for the most part as an intellectual movement and resulted in books such as Simone de Beauvoir's *The Second Sex* (1948), Betty Friedan's *The Feminine Mystique* (1963), and Erica Jong's *Fear of Flying* (1972). Although different in focus, each book was an important influence on generations of women who recognized within the texts truths about the inequalities women experience and how that lack of equality affected and, often, limited the possibilities of their lives.

Important issues that were central to the second wave of American feminism were the acknowledgement and resolution of pay inequities, gaining access to birth control, legalizing abortion, and ending violence against and domestic abuse and sexual harassment of women. During the second wave of feminism, important institutions developed that had as their goals advancing the fight for women's equality. Some of those organizations were the National Organization for Women (NOW), which was founded in 1966, and MS. MAGAZINE, which was cofounded by Walker's close friend GLORIA STEINEM.

A major objective for many of those involved in the second wave of feminism was passage of the Equal Rights Amendment. Second-wave feminists also confronted issues of women's sexuality and tried to amend restrictive gender-specific cultural practices through awareness, education, and legislation. Women's Studies programs developed in American colleges and universities as a result of efforts by feminists, and feminist theoretical inquiry became a common tool for intellectual analysis.

The second wave of feminism, like the third later, was forced to confront issues of class and race. Minority and poor women complained that the major voices in the feminist movement did not address their concerns and that they remained invisible and voiceless in the struggle for women's equality. This belief led to the formation of feminist groups that were identity-specific, such as the National Black Feminist Organization, which was founded in 1973. The failure of the Equal Rights Amendment to be ratified by a sufficient number of states is a significant event signaling, perhaps, the ending phase of the second wave of feminism.

The third wave of feminism has been characterized by a reaction against the purportedly narrow definitions of women's desires and aspirations that were central to the actions and foci of the second wave. The third-wave feminists, such as Alice Walker's daughter, REBECCA WALKER, have suggested that their concerns are more complicated than those articulated by previous generations of feminists and that they want to both retain their right to equality and make choices about what it means to live their lives as women. Third-wave feminists have expressed their concerns about the limitations of identity constructions in all their configurations and demand to be considered in terms of the entirety of their selfhood, not just understood in terms of gender.

Alice Walker was a central figure in the generation of second-wave feminists and was particularly involved in articulating the schism between black and white feminists. In her collection *In Search of Our Mothers' Gardens,* she expanded and recast feminism by introducing what she called WOMANISM, a term borrowing from African-American vernacular. Walker defined *womanism* as "A black feminist or feminist of color," "A woman who loves other women, sexually and/or nonsexually. Appreciates and prefers women's culture . . . ," "Loves music. Loves dance, Loves the moon, Loves the *Spirit,*" and concluded: "Womanist is to feminist as purple to lavender." Walker's integration of women of color, sexual plurality, sensuality, and spirituality into public understandings of the female experience was widely embraced as a framework that destigmatized women's liberation for many by integrating women's race, class, and gender struggles. Literary critics, historians, and religious philosophers have employed womanism to examine African-American female experience in a variety of areas. For more information and an extensive outline of the development of this critical paradigm, see the entry on *womanism* and the accompanying bibliography.

## FURTHER READING

Acholonu, Catherine Obianuju. *Motherism: The Afrocentric Alternative to Feminism.* Owerri, Nigeria: Afa Publications, 1995.

Barkley Brown, Elsa. "Womanist Consciousness: Maggie Lena Walker and the Independent Order of Saint Luke." In *Black Women in America: Social Science Perspectives,* edited by Micheline R. Malson, Elisabeth Mudimbe-Boyi, Jean F. O'Barr and Mary Wyer, 175–196. Chicago: University of Chicago Press, 1988.

Beauvoir, Simone de. *The Second Sex*. Translated by H. M. Parshley. London: Vintage, 1949.

Belsey, Catherine, and Jane Moore, eds. *The Feminist Reader: Essays in Gender and the Politics of Literary Criticism*. New York: B. Blackwell, 1989.

Butler, Judith. "Feminism in Any Other Name." *Differences* 6 (March 1992): 30.

———. *Gender Trouble: Feminism and the Subversion of Identity*. New York: Routledge, 1999.

Christian, Barbara. "Alice Walker: The Black Woman Artist as Wayward." In *Black Women Writers (1950–1980): A Critical Evaluation*, edited by Mari Evans, 457–477. Garden City, N.Y.: Anchor-Doubleday, 1984.

Echols, Alice. *Daring to Be Bad: Radical Feminism in America, 1967–1975*. Minneapolis: University of Minnesota Press, 1989.

Faludi, Susan. *Backlash: The Undeclared War against Women*. London: Vintage, 1992.

Freedman, Estelle B. *No Turning Back: The History of Feminism and the Future of Women*. New York: Ballantine Books, 2003.

Freeman, Jo. *The Politics of Women's Liberation: A Case Study of an Emerging Social Movement and Its Relation to the Policy Process*. New York: McKay, 1975.

Friedan, Betty. *Feminine Mystique*. New York: W. W. Norton, 1963.

Gillis, Stacy, Gillian Howie, and Rebecca Munford. *Third Wave Feminism: A Critical Exploration*. Basingstoke, Eng.: Palgrave Macmillan, 2007.

Godard, Barbara, comp. *Bibliography of Feminist Criticism*. Toronto: ECW Press, 1987.

Henry, Astrid. *Not My Mother's Sister: Generational Conflict and Third-Wave Feminism*. Bloomington: Indiana University Press, 2004.

hooks, bell. *Feminist Theory: From Margin to Center*. Cambridge, Mass.: South End Press, 2000.

Humm, Maggie. *Modern Feminisms: Political, Literary, Cultural*. New York: Columbia University Press, 1992.

Krolokke, Charlotte, and Anne Scott Sorensen. "Three Waves of Feminism: From Suffragettes to Grrls." In *Gender Communication Theories and Analyses: From Silence to Performance*. Thousand Oaks, Calif.: Sage Publications, 2006, pp. 1–24.

Laurent, Maria. *Alice Walker*. New York: St. Martin's Press, 2000.

Leslie, Heywood, and Jennifer Drake. *Third Wave Agenda: Being Feminist, Doing Feminism*. Minneapolis: University of Minnesota Press, 1997.

Mitchell, Juliet. "Women: The Longest Revolution." *New Left Review* (November–December 1966): 26.

Moleskin, Tania. *Feminism without Women: Culture and Criticism in a "Postfeminist" Age*. New York: Routledge, 1991.

Ogunyemi, Chikwenye Okonjo. "Womanism: The Dynamics of the Contemporary Black Female Novel in English." *Signs* 11, no. 1 (Autumn 1985): 63–80.

Phillips, Melanie. *The Ascent of Woman: A History of the Suffragette Movement and the Ideas Behind It*. London: Abacus, 2004.

Pollitt, Katha. *Reasonable Creatures: Essays on Women and Feminism*. New York: Vintage Books, 1995.

Rosen, Ruth. *The World Split Open: How the Modern Women's Movement Changed America*. New York: Penguin, 2001.

Sellers, Susan, ed. *Feminist Criticism: Theory and Practice*. Toronto: University of Toronto Press, 1991.

Showalter, Elaine. *The New Feminist Criticism: Essays on Women, Literature, and Theory*. New York: Pantheon, 1985.

———. *Sister's Choice: Traditions and Change in American Women's Writing*. Gloucestershire, Eng.: Clarendon Press, 1991.

Walker, Alice. *In Search of Our Mothers' Gardens: Womanist Prose*. San Diego: Harcourt Brace Jovanovich, 1983.

Walker, Rebecca. "Becoming the Third Wave." Ms (January/February 1992): 39–41.

———. *To Be Real: Telling the Truth and Changing the Face of Feminism*. New York: Anchor Books, 1995.

Warhol, Robyn R., and Diane Price Herndl, eds. *Feminisms Redux: An Anthology of Literary Theory and Criticism*. New Brunswick, N.J.: Rutgers University Press, 2009.

Whelehan, Imelda. *Modern Feminist Thought: From the Second Wave to "Post-Feminism."* Edinburgh: Edinburgh University Press, 1995.

White, Evelyn C. *Alice Walker: A Life*. New York: W. W. Norton and Company, 2004.

Zajko, Vanda, and Miriam Leonard, eds. *Laughing with Medusa: Classical Myth and Feminist Thought*. Oxford and New York: Oxford University Press, 2006.

Zinn, Maxine Baca, and Bonnie Dill Thornton. *Women of Color in U.S. Society.* Philadelphia: Temple University Press, 1994.

**Freedom Riders** In summer 1961, the CONGRESS OF RACIAL EQUALITY (CORE) organized a series of Freedom Rides—bus rides featuring black and white volunteers who came to be called Freedom Riders. Their objective was to test and challenge the enforcement of desegregated interstate travel in the South. The rides occurred in response to the 1960 Supreme Court decision *Boynton v. Virginia,* which forbade segregated facilities in association with interstate commerce. The rides were modeled after CORE and the Fellowship of Reconciliation's 1947 "Journey of Reconciliation," a 16-person test of the 1946 Supreme Court ruling in *Morgan v. Commonwealth of Virginia.*

The Freedom Rides began in May 1961 and featured riders on the Greyhound and Trailways bus lines traveling from Washington, D.C., to various southern states. The trips were initially uneventful, but during a mid-May trip, Freedom Riders traveling through Anniston, Birmingham, and Montgomery in Alabama faced sabotage, bombings, and beatings from angry local residents. During the final leg of the trip in Mississippi, the Riders were arrested and imprisoned. In September 1961, the Interstate Commerce Commission tightened laws against segregated bus terminals, and most southern states complied. By 1962, CORE, led by James Farmer, declared that segregated interstate travel had virtually ended.

Learning about the Freedom Rides was a catalyst to Walker's involvement in the Civil Rights Movement.

## FURTHER READING

Arsenault, Raymond. *Freedom Riders: 1961 and the Struggle for Racial Justice.* Oxford: Oxford University Press, 2006.

Brakke, Crystal. "Freedom Rides in Southern States." In *Grassroots Social Action: Lessons in People Power Movements,* edited by Charles V. Willie, Steven P. Ridini, and David A. Willard, 117–127. Lanham, Md.: Rowman and Littlefield, 2008.

Loory, S. H. "Freedom Riders in Montgomery." In *Black Protest: History, Documents and Analyses, 1619 to the Present.* Fawcett: New York, 1995.

Viorst, Milton. *Fire in the Streets: America in the 1960s.* New York: Simon and Schuster, 1979.

Zinn, H. "Abolitionists, Freedom-Riders, and the Tactics of Agitation." In *The Antislavery Vanguard.* Princeton, N.J.: Princeton University Press, 1965.

**Gaines, Ernest** (1933– ) Ernest Gaines is one of the most acclaimed fiction writers of the post–World War II era. Gaines specializes in rich depictions of African-American life in the southern United States, especially Louisiana. His most acclaimed works are the novels *The Autobiography of Miss Jane Pittman* (1971) and *A Lesson Before Dying* (1993). Both works have been made into films that attracted large audiences.

Ernest Gaines was born on January 15, 1933, in the Pointe Coupee Parish of Oscar, Louisiana. After serving in the military, he graduated from San Francisco State College in 1957. He has received various honors for his writing, including a National Endowment for the Arts grant (1967), a Guggenheim Fellowship (1971), and a MacArthur Foundation grant (1993). Gaines currently teaches as a Writer-in-Residence at the University of Louisiana, Lafayette, a position he has held since 1983.

Gaines has been a mentor to Alice Walker, particularly when she was an emerging writer. He and Walker corresponded during her drafting of her first novel, *The Third Life of Grange Copeland,* published in 1970.

## FURTHER READING

Babb, Valerie M. *Ernest Gaines.* Boston: Twayne, 1991.

Beavers, Herman. *Wrestling Angels into Song: The Fictions of Ernest J. Gaines and James Alan McPherson.* Philadelphia: University of Pennsylvania Press, 1995.

Clark, Keith. *Black Manhood in James Baldwin, Ernest J. Gaines, and August Wilson.* Bloomington: University of Illinois Press. 2002.

Estes, David C. *Critical Reflections on the Fiction of Ernest J. Gaines.* Athens: University of Georgia Press, 1994.

Gaines, Ernest J. *The Autobiography of Miss Jane Pittman.* New York: Dial Press, 1971.
———. *A Gathering of Old Men.* New York: Alfred A. Knopf, 1984.
———. *In My Father's House.* New York: Alfred A. Knopf, 1978.
———. *A Lesson Before Dying.* New York: Alfred A. Knopf, 1993.
———. *A Long Day in November.* New York: Random House, 1971.
———. *Of Love and Dust.* New York: Dial Press, 1967.
Gaudet, Marcia, and Carl Wooton. *Porch Talk with Ernest Gaines.* Baton Rouge: Louisiana State University Press, 1990.
Lowe, John, ed. *Conversations with Ernest Gaines.* Jackson: University Press of Mississippi, 1995.
Simpson, Anne K. *A Gathering of Gaines: The Man and the Writer.* Lafayette: Center for Louisiana Studies, University of Southwestern Louisiana, 1991.

**Gnostic Gospels** According to leading scholars on the Gnostic Gospels, particularly Elaine Pagels, an Egyptian man named Muhammad Ali al-Samman and several of his brothers were digging for fertilizer in the desert during the winter of 1945 when they discovered an earthen jar buried in the soil. According to Ali al-Samman's own testimony, he and his brothers broke open the jar and found within 13 ancient books written on papyrus. Not realizing what he had discovered, he brought them home and several of them were burned as firewood. Ultimately, the majority of the remaining texts became the possession of the Egyptian government. One of the volumes, however, found its way to Europe and gained the attention of the religious scholar Gilles Quispel. Quispel discovered that the volume contained several controversial and excluded biblical gospels, such as the Gospels of Thomas, Phillip, Truth, Egyptians, and James. These books revealed different and sometimes divergent portraits of Jesus and his messages. All in all, the collection contained approximately 52 writings from the early Christian church, some that challenge some of the fundamental premises of the Old and New Testament.

Some literary critics have speculated that Sofia, a primary character in Alice Walker's novel *The Color Purple,* may be an allusion to a figure from the Gnostic Gospels, the deity SOPHIA.

### FURTHER READING

Hoeller, Stephan A. *Gnosticism: New Light on the Ancient Tradition of Inner Knowing.* New York: Quest Books, 2002.
Holroyd, Stuart. *The Elements of Gnosticism.* Rockport, Mass.: Element Books, 1994.
Meyer, Marvin. *The Gospel of Thomas: The Hidden Sayings of Jesus.* San Francisco: Harper, 1992.
Pagels, Elaine. *Beyond Belief: The Secret Gospel of Thomas.* New York: Random House, 2003.
———. *The Gnostic Gospels.* New York: Random House, 1978.
Seymor-Smith, Marvin. *Gnosticism: The Path of Inner Knowledge.* San Francisco: Harper, 1996.

**goddess figures (in literature by African-American women)** The contemporary goddess figure in fiction written by African-American women emerges not only from social and literary histories but also from diasporic cultural roots. In addition to having a symbolic connection with the religious iconography of parts of West Africa, the goddess figure functions in many African-American women's novels as a correlation to the successful struggle to achieve selfhood in a racist, sexist, and classist society. As these characters refuse to comply with the oppressor's limitations, they open new possibilities for black womanhood.

Through their goddess figures, many of the writers of the AFRA-AMERICAN WOMEN'S LITERARY RENAISSANCE examine the complexities of "authentic," if mythological, black womanhood, the need for rethinking of imposed understandings of the black female self, and the possibilities and implications of personal and communal liberation for African-American women and their communities. By creating a mythology rife with images of goddess figures, some contemporary African-American women writers transcend the limitations of traditional stereotypes by rewriting and recreating black womanhood. Rather than impeding the creative energies of African-American women writers, these goddess figures mark an important paradigm shift. Like many mythological deities, Afra-American goddess figures are powerful in their creative abilities and yet grounded in their humanity. The presence of goddess figures in contemporary African-American women's fiction represents a literary inversion of the traditional denigration of black women in American society.

The emergence in contemporary fiction of a specifically African-American female iconography reflects an attempt to reclaim power by regaining control over images and representations. These fictional goddesses metaphorize the histories, humanity, power, pain, complexity, and creativity of black womanhood. Arguably, Alice Walker employs the literary figure of the goddess, a divine wise woman, in many of her works, particularly *The Color Purple* and *The Temple of My Familiar*.

*See also* BLACK MADONNA; SOPHIA.

### FURTHER READING

Badejo, Diedre L. "The Goddess Osun as a Paradigm for Feminist Criticism." *SAGE* 7 (Summer 1989): 27–32.

Engelsman, Sabrina. *The Feminine Dimension of the Divine*. Oxford: Oxford University Press, 1993.

Harris, Trudier. "This Disease Called Strength: Some Observations on the Compensating Construction of Black Female Character." *Callaloo* 23 (May 1996): 14–38.

**Goldberg, Whoopi (Caryn Elaine Johnson)** (1955– ) The actress, comedian, and director known to the world as Whoopi Goldberg was born on November 13, 1955, to Emma and Robert Johnson, who named their baby girl Caryn Elaine. The family was residing in Manhattan when Goldberg's mother became solely responsible for her two children after Robert Johnson left the family. According to Goldberg's autobiography, she was an outgoing and much-loved child whose mother was demanding and smart. Goldberg was always interested and involved in performing and left school early to take minor roles in Broadway musicals. She suffered from drug addiction for a time as a young adult, recovered, and traveled to California to find work.

Before leaving for California, Goldberg married and subsequently divorced her drug counselor, Alvin Martin, with whom she had a daughter named Alexandrea. It was in California that Caryn Johnson changed her name to Whoopi Goldberg. The reasons for the choice of Goldberg as a last name are a matter of some controversy, with various accounts about how she chose that name. Consistently, she has said that the name Whoopi came from the comic stage prop, the whoopee cushion.

In California, Goldberg began performing and working on her one-woman show, which consisted of a series of comic and dramatic monologues. Discovered by the director Mike Nichols, she returned to New York to develop her act into the Broadway show *Whoopi Goldberg*.

STEVEN SPIELBERG saw Goldberg's Broadway performance while he was in the midst of casting the movie *The Color Purple*. After her inspired and convincing role as Celie in the film version of the novel, Goldberg was nominated for a Best Actress Academy Award and won a Golden Globe for her performance.

After her triumph in *The Color Purple*, Whoopi Goldberg became a household name and a popular performer. The movie roles available to her as a black actress were limited, although she made a reputation of generating appealing characters from weak material. Her best-known and respected movie roles include *Jumpin' Jack Flash* (1986); *Clara's Heart* (1988); *The Long Walk Home* (1990); *Ghost* (1990), for which she won an Academy Award; *Sister Act* (1992); *Made in America* (1993); and *Corinna, Corinna* (1994). Goldberg has also worked as a television personality and actor in the programs and specials *Comic Relief; Baghdad Café; Star Trek: The Next Generation; The Whoopi Goldberg Show;* the annual Oscar telecast as host in 1994, 1996, 1999, and 2002; *Whoopi;* and *The View*.

### FURTHER READING

Caper, William. *Whoopi Goldberg: Comedian and Movie Star*. Springfield, N.J.: Enslow Publishers, 1999.

Gaines, Ann. *Whoopi Goldberg*. Philadelphia: Chelsea House, 1999.

Goldberg, Whoopi. *Book*. New York: R. Weisbach Books, 1997.

Parish, James Robert. *Whoopi Goldberg: Her Journey from Poverty to Megastardom.* Secaucus, N.J.: Carol Publishing Group, 1997.

**Gold Dust Twins** The Gold Dust Twins were twin racist trademark symbols, "pickaninnies" named "Goldy" and "Dusty" who were created by the cartoonist E. W. Kemble in 1884 for N. K. Fairbanks Company's Gold Dust Washing Powder. The twins emerged during a late 19th-century shift toward marketing through "human interest" trademarks. The Gold Dust Twins exemplified the company's slogan "Let the Gold Dust Twins Do Your Work." In 1925, white impersonators even performed as the twins on national radio advertisements. As a result of diminished sales for the powder in the 1930s, the icons disappeared. The twins figure in Walker's first novel, *The Third Life of Grange Copeland.*

### FURTHER READING

Baker, M., C. Motley, and G. Henderson. "From Despicable to Collectible: The Evolution of Collective Memories for and the Value of Black Advertising Memorabilia." *Journal of Advertising* 33, no. 3 (2004): 37–51.

Goings, Kenneth W. *Mammy and Uncle Mose: Black Collectibles and American Stereotyping.* Bloomington: Indiana University Press, 1994.

Kern-Foxworth, M. *Aunt Jemima, Uncle Ben, and Rastus: Blacks in Advertising, Yesterday, Today, and Tomorrow.* Westport, Conn.: Greenwood Press, 1994.

Strausbaugh, John. *Black Like You: Blackface, Whiteface, Insult and Imitation in American Popular Culture.* New York: Jeremy P. Tarcher/Penguin, 2007.

**griot** The term *griot* derives from West Africa, probably from the cultures of ancient Mali. The term refers to an individual, usually a man but sometimes a woman, who functions as the historical collective voice of a family or community by memorizing and occasionally reciting the history of the group. Griots are performers who provide a critical and revered function in the cultures in which they are found. They are often perceived as intercessors between the living and their ancestors. Griots often have a rich musical tradition and become repositories for the arts of a community.

The griot figure appears frequently in the literature of the African diaspora. Alice Walker has written about the role of the griot and employs the historical figure of the griot as a model for several of her characters, particularly Lizzie of *The Temple of My Familiar.* Griots are also sometimes referred to as *djeli* or *jeli.*

### FURTHER READING

Badejo, Deidre. "The Yoruba and Afro-American Trickster: A Contextual Comparison." *Presence Africaine* 147 (1988): 3–17.

Diallo, Yaya, and Mitchell Hall. *The Healing Drum: African Wisdom Teachings.* Rochester, Vt.: Destiny Books, 1989.

Foley, John M. *Oral Tradition in Literature.* Columbia: University of Missouri Press, 1986.

Gleason, Judith, ed. *Leaf and Bone: African Praise-Poems.* New York: Penguin, 1994.

Hale, Thomas A. *Scribe, Griot, and Novelist: Narrative Interpreters of the Songhay Empire, Followed by the Epic of Askia Mohammed Recounted by Nouhou Malio.* Gainesville: University of Florida Press Center for African Studies, 1990.

Jackson-Jones, Patricia. *When Roots Die: Endangered Traditions on the Sea Islands.* Athens: University of Georgia Press, 1987.

Johnson, John William, Thomas A. Hale, and Stephen Belcher, eds. *Oral Epics from Africa: Vibrant Voices from a Vast Continent.* Bloomington: Indiana University Press, 1997.

Jones, Eldred Durosimi, Eustace Palmer, and Marjorie Jones, eds. *Orature in African Literature Today: A Review.* Trenton, N.J.: Africa World Press, 1992.

Mbiti, John S. *Introduction to African Religion.* 2d ed. Portsmouth, N.H.: Heinemann, 1991.

Mutere, Malaika. "Introduction to African History and Cultural Life." Available online. URL: http://artsedge.kennedy-center.org/aoi/history/ao-guide.html. Accessed July 20, 2009.

Nketia, J. H. Kwabena. *The Music of Africa.* London: Victor Gollancz Ltd., 1979.

Ogede, Ode S. "Oral Performance as Instruction: Aesthetic Strategies in Children's Play Songs from a

Nigerian Community." *Children's Literature Association Quarterly* 14, no. 3 (1994): 113–117.
Ong, Walter J. *Orality and Literacy: The Technologizing of the Word.* London: Routledge, 1982.
Schmidt, Nancy. "Nigerian Fiction and the African Oral Tradition." *Journal of the New African Literature and the Arts* 5, no. 6 (1968): 10–19.
Soyinka, Wole. *Myth, Literature and the African World.* 1978. Reprint, Cambridge and New York: Cambridge University Press, 1990.
Ugorji, Okechukwu K. *The Adventures of Torti: Tales from West Africa.* Trenton, N.J.: African World Press, 1991.

**Guevara, Che (Ernesto Guevara)** (1928–1966) Although he is most often associated with the Cuban Revolution, Che Guevara was an Argentinean by birth. As a young man, he trained to become a physician. Even while he was in school, Guevara was involved in political activism and participated in protests against the administration of Juan Perón.

Disillusioned with Argentine politics, Guevara left his home country, relocating to several Central and South American countries. While living in Guatemala, he began to study Marxism and became acquainted with several Cubans who advocated the overthrow of oppressive regimes. He was forced to flee Guatemala when the government he supported fell.

In 1954, Guevara left Guatemala for Mexico. While there, he met FIDEL CASTRO, and together, they planned to overthrow the Batista government. In November 1955, Castro, Guevara, and their followers boarded the legendary boat *Granma* and invaded Cuba. By 1959, the revolution had succeeded, and Castro and Guevara's forces gained control of the island.

After serving for several years in the government that Castro established in Cuba, Guevara decided to leave in 1966. After traveling to Africa and leading a Cuban force in a conflict in the Congo, he entered Bolivia under disguise in order to aid a revolutionary movement there. He was discovered and executed in 1967.

Che Guevara remains an international symbol of the fight for justice and human rights. Alice Walker references Che explicitly in her novel *The Temple of My Familiar.*

### FURTHER READING

Casey, Michael. *Che's Afterlife: The Legacy of an Image.* New York: Vintage Books, 2009.
Guevara, Ernesto Che. *The African Dream: The Diaries of the Revolutionary War in the Congo.* New York: Grove Press, 2001.
———. *Che Guevara on Global Justice.* London: Ocean Press, 2002.
———. *Che Guevara Reader: Writings on Guerrilla Strategy, Politics and Revolution.* 2d ed. Edited by David Deutschmann. London: Ocean Press, 2003.
———. *Che: Self Portrait.* London: Ocean Press, 2003.
———. *Guerrilla Warfare.* Lincoln: University of Nebraska, 1998.
———. *The Motorcycle Diaries: Notes on a Latin American Journey.* London: Ocean Press, 2003.
———. *Reminiscences of the Cuban Revolutionary War: The Authorized and Revised Edition.* London: Ocean Press, 2005.

**Harlem Renaissance** New York City was the most frequent destination of those African Americans fleeing the South in the exodus known as the Great Migration. This surge in the African-American population and concentration specifically in Harlem generated the artistic flourishing known as the Harlem Renaissance, a period of creative expression during the 1920s and '30s.

Although most often associated with literary production, the artistry of the Harlem Renaissance also included the genres of film, music, theater, journalism, and politics. In each of these fields, various artists contributed unique and innovative creations. The Renaissance catalyzed the writings of men such as W. E. B. DUBOIS, James Weldon Johnson, Claude McKay, and Alain Locke.

The Harlem Renaissance brought to the forefront of American culture and awareness the mores of African-American life and culture. Some of its literary themes and motifs include the concept of DOUBLE CONSCIOUSNESS, the theme of alienation, the condition of marginalization, the notion of Africa as ancestral homeland, questions about identity, the river as a symbol, the BLUES as metaphor, the role of the marginalized artist in American society, the construction of beauty ideals, and the role of race in personal relationships.

Frequently, Renaissance artists focused on the ideal of Africa as a mythical homeland in their work. Another central concept was the idea of the New Negro as articulated by Alain Locke. The era of the New Negro was to inaugurate a new sensibility and definition of negro—black—identity. Marcus Garvey's activism and ideology, particularly his focus on self-sufficiency, was also important to some of the artists of the Renaissance. The foundation of affirmation of black selfhood would reemerge in the BLACK ARTS MOVEMENT, which reached fruition in the 1960s.

The stock market crash of 1929 and the Great Depression were devastating to many of the artists of the Renaissance and to Harlem itself. The Renaissance, which began to disintegrate by the final years of the 1930s, is recognized today as one of the most prolific and important artistic periods in American history. Alice Walker has written about the Harlem Renaissance and particularly admires the Renaissance writers ZORA NEALE HURSTON and LANGSTON HUGHES.

### FURTHER READING


Anderson, Jervis. *This Was Harlem.* New York: Scriber, 1974.

Andrews, William. *Classic Fiction of the Harlem Renaissance.* New York: Oxford University Press, 1994.

Baker, Houston. *Modernism and the Harlem Renaissance.* Chicago: University of Chicago Press, 1987.

Bloom, Harold, ed. *Langston Hughes.* New York: Chelsea House, 1989.

Brown, Sterling Allen. *The Collected Poems.* New York: Harper and Row, 1980.

Cullen, Countee. *Caroling Dusk: An Anthology of Verse by Negro Poets.* New York: Harper and Row, 1955.

———. *Color.* New York: Harper and Brothers, 1925.

———. *My Soul's High Song.* New York: Doubleday, 1991.

DuBois, W. E. B. *The Souls of Black Folk.* Millwood, N.Y.: Kraus-Thomson Organization, 1973.

Fauset, Jessie Redmon. *Plum Bun: A Novel without a Moral.* Boston: Beacon Press, 1990.

———. *There Is Confusion.* Boston: Northeastern University Press, 1989.

Honey, Maureen. *Shadowed Dreams: Women's Poetry of the Harlem Renaissance.* New Brunswick, N.J.: Rutgers University Press, 1989.

Huggins, Nathaniel. *Harlem Renaissance.* New York: Oxford University Press, 1976.

Hughes, Langston. *Selected Poems.* New York: Vintage Books, 1987.

———. *The Weary Blues.* New York: Knopf, 1926.

Hull, Gloria T. *Color, Sex, and Poetry: Three Women Writers of the Harlem Renaissance.* Bloomington: Indiana University Press, 1987.

Johnson, James Weldon. *The Autobiography of an Ex-Colored Man.* New York: Vintage Books, 1989.

———. *The Book of American Negro Poetry.* San Diego: Harcourt Brace Jovanovich, 1983.

———. *God's Trombones: Seven Negro Sermons in Verse.* New York: Viking Press, 1980.

Kellner, Bruce, ed. *The Harlem Renaissance: A Historical Dictionary for the Era.* Westport, Conn.: Greenwood Press, 1986.

Larsen, Nella. *Quicksand; and Passing.* New Brunswick, N.J.: Rutgers University Press, 1986.

Lewis, David. *When Harlem Was in Vogue.* New York: Knopf, 1981.

Locke, Alain. *The New Negro: An Interpretation.* New York: Johnson Reprint Corp., 1968.

McKay, Claude. *Home to Harlem.* Chatham, N.J.: Chatham Bookseller, 1973.

Toomer, Jean. *Cane.* New York: Boni and Liveright, 1923.

Van Vechten, Carl. *Nigger Heaven.* New York: A. Knopf, 1926.

Wintz, Cary D. *Black Culture and the Harlem Renaissance.* Houston: Rice University Press, 1988.


**Harris, Joel Chandler** (1845 or 1848–1904) Joel Chandler Harris was an American journalist and fiction writer best known for his UNCLE REMUS tales, a collection of stories for children based mostly on the oral narratives of African Americans in the South. Born in EATONTON, GEORGIA, Harris apprenticed as a printing compositor for a plantation owner who ran a small newspaper. It was on this plantation that Harris heard most of the tales he would later use in his Uncle Remus books.

The Eatonton, Georgia, farm of Joel Chandler Harris, a writer famous for the Uncle Remus tales. The Chandler farm is within easy walking distance of Alice Walker's family homestead. *(Photograph by Carmen Gillespie)*

For most of his adult years, Harris worked as a journalist, primarily on the *Atlanta Constitution.* Writing under his journalistic pen name Joe Harris, he promoted reconciliation not only between North and South but between black and white. The character of Uncle Remus, an elderly slave and ostensible narrator of the stories, first appeared in one of Harris's columns. Remus became very popular with the *Constitution*'s readers, and the first collection of Remus tales in book form was published in 1881 under the title *Uncle Remus: His Songs and Sayings.* The central character of the action is Br'er Rabbit—Brother Rabbit—a traditional trickster figure from the folk traditions of both the African Yoruba tribe and the American Cherokee tribe, both of which contributed to Harris's collections. One of the most famous stories is "Tar Baby," which pits Br'er Rabbit against his nemesis, Br'er Fox. In this tale, Br'er Fox dresses up a pile of tar to look like a person, and Br'er Rabbit, because of his curiosity and anger, becomes stuck to it. Before Br'er Fox can eat him, however, Br'er Rabbit escapes by using his wits, as is typical in the trickster tales. Br'er Rabbit pleads with Br'er Fox not to throw him into a briar patch, which the fox, succumbing to reverse psychology, then does. Once in the familiar briar patch, Br'er Rabbit escapes because Br'er Fox is unable to follow.

All in all, there were eight Uncle Remus books, containing a total of 185 tales. The last book—*Told by Uncle Remus: New Stories of the Old Plantation*—was published in 1905. Praised during Harris's lifetime for their supposed recreation of "negro-slave" dialect, the Uncle Remus tales revolutionized children's literature by using an American idiom and creating an ongoing, open-ended series of tales using the same characters. Starting in the second half of the 20th century, however, Harris's reputation declined for many commentators, who accused him of stealing the tales from those African Americans who had told them, without sharing full credit. Also, though Harris had considered himself a folklorist and insisted that his stories and the dialects were documented and accurate, starting in the late 20th century, his critics viewed the dialects as inaccurate and demeaning to African Americans, as was the use of Uncle Remus himself, a stereotype of the contented old slave.

In 1946, the Walt Disney studio produced a mixed live-action and animated feature based on the Uncle Remus tales called *Song of the South,* but the company has yet to release a full version on DVD because of elements that they say might be considered insensitive to African Americans.

Throughout her career, Alice Walker has challenged the idyllic portrait of southern black life Harris depicted in his stories. In her 1981 speech to the Atlanta Historical Society, "The Dummy in the Window: Joel Chandler Harris and the Invention of Uncle Remus"—also printed in her collection of essays, *Living by the Word*—she denounced Harris for stealing and distorting African folk culture. Walker's assertions about the African origins of the tales surface in her novel *The Color Purple* when Nettie describes how Celie's daughter, Olivia, who is on a missionary trip, learns that the "Uncle Remus" stories were actually derived from African sources. Olivia acquires this information from an Olinkan girl named Tashi. Walker has also noted how various themes and characters from African folktales pervade Cherokee folk literature.

Coincidentally, Joel Chandler Harris was also from Alice Walker's hometown of Eatonton, Georgia and lived a few short miles from where Walker grew up, although the two were separated chronologically by a century.

## FURTHER READING


Armistead, Samuel G. "Two Br'er Rabbit Stories from the Eastern Shore of Maryland." *Journal of American Folklore* 84 (1971): 442–444.

Bergainnier, Earl F. "The Myth of Moonlight and Magnolias." *Louisiana Studies* 15 (1976): 5–20.

Birnbaum, Michele. "Dark Dialects: Scientific and Literary Realism in Joel Chandler Harris's Uncle Remus Series." *New Orleans Review* 18, no. 1 (1991): 6–45.

Brestensky, Dennis F. "Uncle Remus: Mere Buffoon or Admirable Man of Stature?" *West Virginia University Philological Papers.* Morgantown 22 (1975): 51–58.

Cousins, Paul M. *Joel Chandler Harris: A Biography.* Baton Rouge: Louisiana State University Press, 1968.

David, Beverly R. "Visions of the South: Joel Chandler Harris and His Illustrators." *American Literary Realism* 9 (1976): 189–206.

English, Thomas H. "The Other Uncle Remus." *Georgia Review* 21 (1967): 210–217.

Flusche, Michael. "Underlying Despair in the Fiction of Joel Chandler Harris." *Mississippi Quarterly: The Journal of Southern Culture* 29 (1976): 91–103.

Griska, Joseph M., Jr. "Joel Chandler Harris: 'Accidental Author' or 'Aggressive Businessman.'" *Atlanta Historical Journal* 30, nos. 3–4 (Fall–Winter 1986–87): 71–78.

———. "Uncle Remus Correspondence: The Development and Reception of Joel Chandler Harris' Writing." *American Literary Realism* 14, no. 1 (Spring 1981): 26–37.

Hedin, Raymond. "Uncle Remus: Puttin' on Ole Massa's Son." *Southern Literary Journal* 15, no. 1 (Fall 1982): 83–90.

Keenan, Hugh T., ed. "Joel Chandler Harris: The Writer in His Time and Ours." *Atlanta Historical Journal* 30, nos. 3–4 (Fall–Winter 1986–87): 5–7.

———. "Twisted Tales: Propaganda in the Tar-Baby Stories." *Southern Quarterly: A Journal of the Arts in the South* 22, no. 2 (Winter 1984): 54–69.

Kelly, Karen M. "The Early Days of the Uncle Remus Memorial Association." *Atlanta Historical Journal* 30 (Fall–Winter 1986–87): 3–4, 113–127.

MacKethan, Lucinda H. "A 'Deluge of Simplicity': Contradictions in the Life and Work of Joel Chandler Harris." *Southern Literary Journal* 11, no. 2 (1979): 87–96.

Mikkelsen, Nina. "When the Animals Talked—A Hundred Years of Uncle Remus." *Children's Literature Association Quarterly* 8, no. 1 (Spring 1983): 3–5, 31.

Montenyohl, Eric L. "Joel Chandler Harris's Revision of Uncle Remus: The First Version of 'A Story of the War.'" *American Literary Realism* 19, no. 1 (Fall 1986): 65–72.

———. "The Origins of Uncle Remus." *Folklore Forum* 18, no. 2 (Spring 1986): 136–167.

Peterson, Lee. "Language in the Uncle Remus Tales." *Modern Philology: A Journal Devoted to Research in Medieval and Modern Literature* 82, no. 3 (February 1985): 292–298.

———. "Rewriting Dialect Literature: 'The Wonderful Tar-Baby Story.'" *Atlanta Historical Journal* 30, nos. 3–4 (Fall–Winter 1986–87): 57–70.

Piacentino, Edward J. "Another Chapter in the Literary Relationship of Mark Twain and Joel Chandler Harris." *Mississippi Quarterly: The Journal of Southern Culture* 38, no. 1 (Winter 1984–85): 73–85.

Rubin, Louis D., Jr. "Uncle Remus and the Ubiquitous Rabbit." *Southern Review* 10 (1974): 787–804.

Thomas, Kenneth H., Jr. "Roots and Environment: The Family Background of Joel Chandler Harris." *Atlanta Historical Journal* 30, nos. 3–4 (Fall–Winter 1986–97): 37–56.

Turner, Darwin T. "Daddy Joel Harris and His Old-Time Darkies." *Southern Literary Journal* 1, no. 1 (1968): 20–41.

Walton, David A. "Joel Chandler Harris as Folklorist: A Reassessment." *Keystone Folklore* 11 (1966): 21–26.

**Head, Bessie** (1937–1986) Bessie Head was a South African writer whose work includes the acclaimed novels *Maru* (1971) and *A Question of Power* (1973). Alice Walker has praised Head's use of fantasy, myth, and mystery that extends beyond the traditional confines of realist writing. Head spent most of her adult life in Botswana, and her work negotiates the complexities of exile, postcolonialism, poverty, and exploitation.

Walker dedicated the poem "Having Eaten Two Pillows," published in her 1979 poetry collection *Goodnight Willie Lee, I'll See You in the Morning,* to Head. Literary critics particularly note Head's surrealist influence on postmodern literature and its impact on Walker's work, seen especially in Walker's novel *The Temple of My Familiar* (1989), a work within which Head appears as a character.

### FURTHER READING

Bazin, Nancy Topping. "Feminist Perspectives in African Fiction: Bessie Head and Buchi Emecheta." *Black Scholar* 17, no. 2 (1986): 34–40.

Beard, Linda Susan. "Bessie Head's Syncretic Fictions: The Reconceptualization of Power and the Recovery of the Ordinary." *MFS: Modern Fiction Studies* 37, no. 3 (1991): 575–589.

BHead Heritage Trust. "Bessie Amelia Head, 1937–2007." Available online. URL: http://www.bessiehead.org/index.html. Accessed February 28, 2009.

Driver, Dorothy. "Reconstructing the Past, Shaping the Future: Bessie Head and the Question of Feminism in a New South Africa." In *Black Women's Writing,* edited by Gina Wisker, 160–187. New York: St. Martin's Press, 1993.

Head, Bessie. *The Collector of Treasures and Other Botswana Village Tales.* London: Heinemann, 1977.

———. *Maru.* New York: McCall, 1971.

———. *A Question of Power.* New York: Pantheon, 1973.

———. *Serowe: Village of the Rain Wind.* Cape Town: David Philip, 1981.

———. *When Rain Clouds Gather.* New York: Simon and Schuster, 1968.

Head, Bessie, and Craig Mackenzie, eds. *A Woman Alone: Autobiographical Writings.* Oxford: Heinemann, 1990.

Ibrahim, Huma. *Bessie Head: Subversive Identities in Exile.* Charlottesville: University Press of Virginia, 1996.

Lorenz, Paul H. "Colonization and the Feminine in Bessie Head's *A Question of Power.*" *MFS: Modern Fiction Studies* 37, no. 3 (1991): 591–605.

Sarvan, Charles Ponnwthuai. "Bessie Head: *A Question of Power* and Identity." *African Literature Today* 15 (1987): 82–88.

White, Evelyn C. *Alice Walker: A Life.* New York: W. W. Norton and Company, 2004.

**hot comb** According to scholars, metal combs intended for straightening curly hair were invented in France in the mid-19th century. The combs became popular with women of African descent throughout the diaspora. To straighten African-American hair with a hot comb, the hair is first thoroughly washed and dried. Oil is then applied to the hair to protect it from the potentially damaging effects of the heat. Traditionally, the metal comb was heated on a stove. Later, electric heaters were used, and today hot combs are often electric. The heated comb is run through the hair, and the back of the comb is used to pull and straighten the hair with heat.

The practice of straightening hair with a hot comb became routine in the United States during the early 20th century. The practice was discontinued with the introduction and improvement of chemical straightening products. In *The Color Purple,* Celie stops straightening her hair after she meets and begins a relationship with Shug. Alice Walker also makes negative comments about the practice in an essay with a pun in its title. The essay, which originally was a speech delivered at SPELMAN COLLEGE is entitled "Oppressed Hair Puts a Ceiling on the Brain."

### FURTHER READING

Byrd, Ayana D., and Lori L. Tharps. *Hair Story: Untangling the Roots of Black Hair in America.* New York: St. Martin's Press, 2002.

Morrow, Willie L. *The Art of Barbering: African American Hair.* San Diego, Calif.: Morrow's Unlimited, 1993.

Radcliff-Darden. Bessie. *Hair Matters: African Ancestry.* Dubuque, Iowa: Kendall/Hunt Publishing Company, 1996.

Rooks, Noliwe. *Hair Raising: Beauty, Culture, and African American Women.* New Brunswick, N.J.: Rutgers University Press, 1996.

Sagay, Esi. *African Hairstyles: Styles of Yesterday and Today.* Oxford: Heinemann International Literature and Textbooks, 1983.

Sieber, Roy, and Frank Herreman, eds. *Hair in African Art and Culture.* New York: Museum for African Art, 2000.

Simon, Diane. *Hair: Public, Political, Extremely Personal.* New York: St. Martin's Press, 2000.

White, Shane, and Graham White. *Stylin': African American Expressive Culture from Its Beginnings to the Zoot Suit.* Ithaca, N.Y.: Cornell University Press, 1998.

**Hughes, Langston** (1902–1967) Langston Hughes is one of the preeminent voices in American literature and theater. Hughes gained national attention during the HARLEM RENAISSANCE for his distinctly rhythmic writing style, detailed attention to black lower- and working-class experience, and fresh critical voice.

Born in Joplin, Missouri, Hughes briefly attended Columbia University before dropping out in 1922 to become a full-time writer. He became a Harlem fixture and befriended some of the most prominent New York–based writers, particularly those of the Harlem Renaissance, including ZORA NEALE HURSTON, Countee Cullen, Alain Locke, Claude McKay, and Wallace Thurman. Together, these writers cofounded the groundbreaking magazine *Fire!!*

In the early 1920s, Hughes traveled through Europe before returning to the United States and enrolling at Lincoln University, where, in 1929, he completed his undergraduate degree. In 1926, he published his first poetry book, *The Weary Blues,* and the classic essay "The Negro Writer and the Racial Mountain." Other significant poetry collections include *Fine Clothes to the Jew* (1927), *Shakespeare in Harlem* (1942), and *Montage of a Dream Deferred* (1951). Hughes also published two autobiographies, 1940's *The Big Sea* and 1956's *I Wonder as I Wander;* several prose collections, including *The Ways of White Folks* (1934) and *Simple Speaks His Mind* (1950); and multiple plays, including *Mulatto* (1935) and *Black Nativity* (1961).

Within the theater community, Hughes founded black drama groups. The most successful groups were located in Harlem, New York, and in Los Angeles, California. Hughes even wrote librettos. Additionally, many songwriters have adapted his poetry to music, including Nina Simone, who in 1967 recorded a musical version of Hughes's "Backlash Blues."

Langston Hughes has been immensely influential. His work resonates across the artificial divides of genre, race, and time. Even though he has such widespread cross-cultural influence, elements of his style are particularly evident among prominent African-American writers ranging from JAMES BALDWIN to Toni Morrison.

Alice Walker's first published work was the short story "To Hell with Dying," originally published in 1967's *The Best Short Stories by Negro Writers,* edited by Hughes, who enthusiastically endorsed her story and became a mentor and friend. In tribute to his legacy, Walker wrote the 1974 children's book *Langston Hughes: American Poet,* in which she referred to Hughes as her "literary father." Hughes also appears as a character in her collection of vignettes *The Way Forward Is with a Broken Heart.*

## FURTHER READING

Bloom, Harold, ed. *Langston Hughes.* New York: Chelsea House, 1989.

Gates, Henry Louis, Jr., and Kwame Anthony Appiah, eds. *Langston Hughes: Critical Perspectives Past and Present.* New York: Amistad; Dist. by Penguin USA, 1993.

Haskins, James. *Always Movin' On: The Life of Langston Hughes.* Trenton, N.J.: Africa World Press, 1993.

Hughes, Langston. *Ask Your Mama: 12 Moods for Jazz.* New York: Knopf, 1961.

———. *The Ballad of the Brown King.* Libretto by Hughes, music by Margaret Bonds. New York: Sam Fox, 1961.

———. *The Big Sea: An Autobiography.* New York: Thunder's Mouth Press, 1986.

———. *Black Magic: A Pictorial History of the Negro in American Entertainment.* New York: Prentice-Hall, 1967.

———. *The Block: Poems.* New York: Viking, 1995.

———. *Carol of the Brown King: Poems.* New York: Athenaeum Books, 1997.

———. *The Collected Poems of Langston Hughes.* Edited by Arnold Rampersad and D. E. Roessel. New York: Knopf, 2004.

———. *The Collected Works of Langston Hughes.* Columbia: University of Missouri Press, 2001.

———. *Dear Lovely Death.* Amenia, N.Y.: Troutbeck Press, 1931.

———. *The Dream Keeper and Other Poems.* New York: Knopf, 1932.

———. *Fields of Wonder.* New York: Knopf, 1947.

———. *Fight for Freedom: The Story of the NAACP.* New York: Norton, 1962.

———. *Fine Clothes to the Jew.* New York: Knopf, 1927.

———. *Five Plays by Langston Hughes.* Edited by Webster Smalley. Bloomington: Indiana University Press, 1963.

———. *Freedom's Plow.* New York: Musette Publishers, 1943.

———. *Good Morning Revolution: Uncollected Social Protest Writings by Langston Hughes.* Edited by Faith Berry. New York and Westport, Conn.: Lawrence Hill, 1973.

———. *I Wonder as I Wander: An Autobiographical Journey.* New York: Thunder's Mouth Press, 1986.

———. *Jim Crow's Last Stand.* Atlanta: Negro Publication Society of America, 1943.

———. *The Langston Hughes Reader.* New York: Braziller, 1958.

———. *Laughing to Keep from Crying.* New York: Holt, 1952.

———. *Montage of a Dream Deferred.* New York: Holt, 1951.

———. *A Negro Looks at Soviet Central Asia.* Moscow and Leningrad: Co-operative Publishing Society of Foreign Workers in the U.S.S.R., 1934.

———. *The Negro Mother and Other Dramatic Recitations.* New York: Golden Stair Press, 1931.

———. *A New Song.* New York: International Working Order, 1938.

———. *Not Without Laughter.* New York: Macmillan, 1986.

———. *One-Way Ticket.* New York: Knopf, 1949.

———. *The Panther and the Lash: Poems of Our Times.* New York: Vintage Books, 1992.

———. *The Pasteboard Bandit.* New York: Oxford University Press, 1997.

———. *A Pictorial History of the Negro in America.* New York: Crown, 1956.

———. *The Return of Simple.* New York: Hill and Wang, 1994.

———. *Scottsboro Limited: Four Poems and a Play.* New York: Golden Stair Press, 1932.

———. *Shakespeare in Harlem.* New York: Knopf, 1942.

———. *Short Stories of Langston Hughes.* New York: Hill and Wang, 1996.

———. *Simple Speaks His Mind.* New York: Simon & Schuster, 1950.

———. *Simple Stakes a Claim.* New York: Rinehart, 1957.
———. *Simple's Uncle Sam.* New York: Hill and Wang, 1965.
———. *Simple Takes a Wife.* New York: Simon and Schuster, 1953.
———. *Simply Heavenly.* Book and lyrics by Hughes, music by David Martin. New York: Dramatists Play Service, 1959.
———. *Something in Common and Other Stories.* New York: Hill and Wang, 1963.
———. *The Sweet Flypaper of Life.* Washington, D.C.: Howard University Press, 1984.
———. *Tambourines to Glory.* New York: Harlem Moon, 2006.
———. *The Ways of White Folks.* New York: Random House, 1971.
———. *The Weary Blues.* New York: Knopf, 1926.

**Hurston, Zora Neale** (1891–1960) Zora Neale Hurston was a preeminent female writer of the HARLEM RENAISSANCE and one of the pivotal voices in integrating black southern folklore into American popular culture. Hurston was born in Notasulga, Alabama, but was raised primarily in the all-black town of Eatonville, Florida, where her family moved when she was five. While attending Howard University, she met Alain Locke, who would soon join her as one of the key architects of the Harlem Renaissance. In 1925, Hurston moved to New York to become a writer and studied anthropology at Barnard College under Franz Boas. As part of her studies, she went to Florida to collect African-American folklore. The richness of her findings culminated in the 1935 publication of *Mules and Men.*

Hurston began publishing short stories and writing plays in the 1920s, but her writing career soared after the release of 1937's *THEIR EYES WERE WATCHING GOD.* The novel's depiction of the character Janie Crawford was a seminal portrait of a southern black woman's emotional and psychological progression toward personal autonomy. Initially attacked in some critical circles for being overly lyrical and romantic rather than polemical, the novel has gained canonical status as ranking among the finest American novels.

Hurston's other novels include *Jonah's Gourd Vine* (1934); *Tell My Horse* (1938); and *Moses, Man of the Mountain* (1939). She also published the autobiography *Dust Tracks on a Road* (1942) and continued to write short stories, essays, and plays. Her career took a downward turn in the late 1940s and 1950s. During that time, her writing was more sporadic, and she took on a series of odd jobs, as a librarian and substitute teacher, to support herself. After suffering a stroke in 1959, Hurston died in 1960 in relative obscurity and poverty. At the time of her death, her books were out of print.

Literary historians have frequently credited Alice Walker for reviving critical and historical interest in Hurston's work. Walker has expressed particular admiration for the dialect and communalism Hurston captured in *Their Eyes Were Watching God.* In 1973, she took a pilgrimage down to Fort Pierce, Florida, to Hurston's gravesite. Upon seeing that it was unmarked, she became anxious about the historical erasure of Hurston and of artists generally. As a writer, Walker empathized with Hurston and feared sharing the author's fate. In a gesture of solidarity with her deceased compatriot,

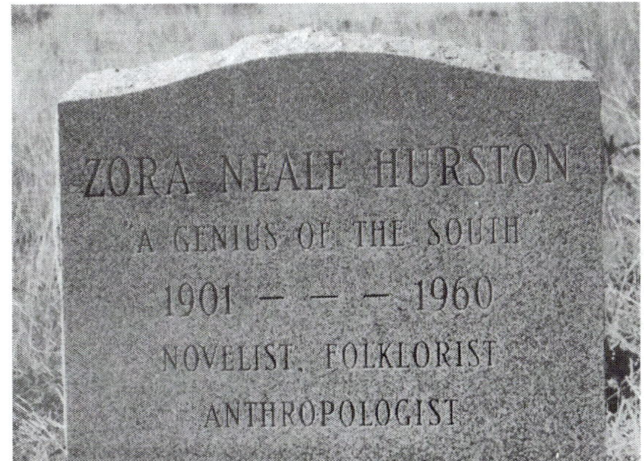


The tombstone Alice Walker placed in the Fort Pierce, Florida, cemetery where it is believed writer and ethnographer Zora Neale Hurston is buried. Until Walker placed this stone, which incorrectly notes Hurston's birth year, in the cemetery, Hurston's grave was unmarked. Walker was instrumental in rescuing the works of Hurston and in reestablishing Hurston's reputation as a major American writer. *(Photograph by Carmen Gillespie)*

she purchased a headstone for Hurston. The stone, which incorrectly ascribes Hurston's birth year as 1901, reads "A Genius of the South" and features the caption "Novelist. Folklorist. Anthropologist."

Walker shared her interest in and admiration for Hurston in the essay "In Search of Zora Neale Hurston," published in *Ms.* magazine. She also paid homage to Hurston in her foreword to Robert Hemenway's study *Zora Neale Hurston: A Literary Biography* (1977) and in the collection of Hurston writings that she edited, *I Love Myself When I Am Laughing . . . and then Again When I Am Looking Mean and Impressive: A Zora Neale Hurston Reader* (1979).

## FURTHER READING

Bloom, H. *Zora Neale Hurston.* New York: Chelsea House, 1986.

Gates, Henry Lewis, Jr., and Kwame Anthony Appiah, eds. *Zora Neale Hurston: Critical Perspectives Past and Present.* New York: Amistad; Distributed by Penguin USA, 1993.

Holloway, Karla F. C. *The Character of the Word: The Texts of Zora Neale Hurston.* New York: Greenwood Press, 1987.

hooks, bell. "Saving Black Folk Culture: Zora Neale Hurston as Anthropologist and Writer." In *Yearning: Race, Gender, and Cultural Politics,* 148–165. Boston: South End Press, 1990.

Howard, L. P. *Alice Walker and Zora Neale Hurston: The Common Bond.* Westport, Conn.: Greenwood Press, 1993.

Hurston, Zora Neale. *Dust Tracks on the Road.* New York: HarperCollins, 1994.

———. *Jonah's Gourd Vine: A Novel.* San Bernadino, Calif.: Borgo Press, 1992.

———. *Moses, Man of the Mountain.* Urbana: University of Illinois Press, 1984.

———. *Novels and Stories.* New York: Library of America, 1995.

———. *Seraph on the Suwanee: A Novel.* New York: HarperPerennial, 1991.

———. *Their Eyes Were Watching God.* New York: Perennial Library, 1990.

Jones, Sharon L. *Rereading the Harlem Renaissance: Race, Class, and Gender in the Fiction of Jessie Fauset, Zora Neale Hurston, and Dorothy West.* Westport, Conn.: Greenwood Press, 2002.

Jordan, June. "On Richard Wright and Zora Neale Hurston: Notes toward a Balancing of Love and Hatred." *Black World* 23 (August 1974): 6.

McKay, Nellie Y. "'Crayon Enlargements of Life': Zora Neale Hurston's *Their Eyes Were Watching God* as Autobiography." In *New Essays on* Their Eyes Were Watching God, edited by Michael Awkward, 51–70. Cambridge: Cambridge University Press, 1990.

Miles, Diana. *Women, Violence, and Testimony in the Works of Zora Neale Hurston.* New York: Peter Lang, 2003.

Official Zora Neale Hurston Web site. Available online. URL: http://www.zoranealehurston.com/chronology.html. Accessed February 28, 2009.

Peters, Pearlie. "'Ah Got the Law in My Mouth': Black Women and Assertive Voice in Hurston's Fiction and Folklore." *CLA Journal* 37, no. 3 (1994): 293–302.

Plant, D. G. *Every Tub Must Sit on Its Own Bottom: The Philosophy and Politics of Zora Neale Hurston.* Urbana: University of Illinois Press.

Walker, Alice. "In Search of Zora Neale Hurston." *Ms.* 3, no. 9 (March 1975): 74–89.

White, Evelyn C. *Alice Walker: A Life.* New York: W. W. Norton and Company, 2004.

***I Ching*** The *I Ching* is a classic Chinese book of mythology and moral guidance that is central to Confucianism and Chinese literature. It is thought to have been written near the end of the Zhou period (1027–256 B.C.E.) of Chinese history. Alice Walker has mentioned the *I Ching* (also known as the *Yi Ching,* or *The Book of Changes*) as an important source of spiritual guidance in her life.

## FURTHER READING

Hacker, Edward. *The I Ching Handbook. A Practical Guide to Logical and Personal Perspectives from the Ancient Chinese Book of Changes.* Brookline, Mass.: Paradigm, 1993.

Hacker, Edward, Steve Moore, and Lorraine Patsco. *I Ching: An Annotated Bibliography.* New York: Routledge, 2002.

Karcher, Stephen. *The Elements of the I Ching.* Rockport, Mass.: Element, 1995.

Legge, James, trans. *I Ching Book of Changes.* New York: Bantam Books, 1969.

Sorrell, Roderic, and Amy Max Sorrell, *The I Ching Made Easy.* San Francisco, Calif.: Harper, 1994.

**Jackson, Rebecca** (1795–1871) Rebecca Jackson was born a free black woman in 1795. In 1857, she founded a Shaker sisterhood in Philadelphia. Jean McMahon Humez collected and edited her autobiographical writings in 1981's *Gifts of Power: The Writings of Rebecca Jackson, Black Visionary, Shaker Eldress.* Among Jackson's most compelling accounts was her story of acquiring literacy through divine intervention.

Walker reviewed *Gifts of Power* in a 1981 essay in *Black Scholar,* a piece she later included as an essay in her collection *In Search of Our Mothers' Gardens.* In the review, Walker questioned Humez's observation that Jackson, who left her husband and traveled with a female companion for more than 30 years, could not live openly as a lesbian. Walker ponders the issue of whether the word *lesbian* had the flexibility and open-endedness to encompass the complexities of Jackson's situation.

The literary critic and scholar Henry Louis Gates, Jr., has written about the parallels he has found between Jackson's acquisition of literacy through what she believed was divine access to God and Walker's depiction of her character Celie's struggle for identity and voice in *The Color Purple.*

### FURTHER READING

Braxton, Joanne M. *Black Women Writing Autobiography: A Tradition within a Tradition.* Philadelphia: Temple University Press, 1989.

Commire, Anne, ed. *Women in World History: A Biographical Encyclopedia.* Waterford, Conn.: Yorkin Publications, 2000.

Douglass-Chin, Richard J. *Preacher Woman Sings the Blues: The Autobiographies of Nineteenth-Century African American Evangelists.* Columbia: University of Missouri Press, 2001.

Evans, James H. *Spiritual Empowerment in Afro-American Literature: Frederick Douglass, Rebecca Jackson, Booker T. Washington, Richard Wright, Toni Morrison.* Lewiston, N.Y.: Edgar Mellen Press, 1987.

Gates, Henry Louis, Jr. "Color Me Zora." In *Alice Walker: Critical Perspectives Past and Present,* edited by Henry Louis Gates, Jr., and Kwame Anthony Appiah, 239–260. New York: Amistad, 1993.

Hine, Darlene Clark, ed. *Black Women in America: An Historical Encyclopedia.* Brooklyn, N.Y.: Carlson Publishing, 1993.

Jackson, Rebecca Cox. *Gifts of Power: The Writings of Rebecca Jackson, Black Visionary, Shaker Eldress.* Edited by Jean McMahon Humez. Amherst: University of Massachusetts Press, 1981.

Smith, Jessie Carney. *Notable Black American Women.* Detroit: Gale Research, 1992.

Walker, Alice. "Gifts of Power: The Writings of Rebecca Jackson." *Black Scholar* 12, no. 5 (September–October 1981): 64–67.

Williams, Richard E. *Called and Chosen: The Story of Mother Rebecca Jackson and the Philadelphia Shakers.* Metuchen, N.J.: Scarecrow Press, 1981.

Winchell, Donna Haisty. *Alice Walker.* New York: Twayne Publishers, 1992.

Woods, Naurice Frank, Jr. *Picturing a People: A History of African Americans from 1619–1900.* Dubuque, Iowa: Kendall/Hunt Publishing Co., 1997.

**jazz** Jazz is a musical form that arose in the African-American community, combining African rhythms brought over by slaves with European harmonic structures. A major component of jazz is the musicians' spontaneous, improvisational playing over set chord changes.

The beginnings of jazz can be traced to the second half of the 19th century and various musical forms current in the black community: black work songs, field shouts, sorrow songs, hymns, and SPIRITUALS. As a new and recognizable art form, jazz first gained prominence in New Orleans. Subsequently. it spread to northern cities such as Chicago, Kansas City, and New York City, and to the West Coast, with each location producing its own unique sound and experimentation.

Now recognized as one of the greatest artistic contributions to emerge from the United States, jazz originally was not accepted by the wider white community because of its association with black culture. White audiences and some black audiences considered jazz lower class and suggestive of loose morals. It was not until the 1930s, when Benny Goodman, a white clarinetist and bandleader, performed jazz with black musicians—especially in his concerts at Carnegie Hall—that jazz started to become more "respectable" to white audiences.

The sound of jazz can vary greatly, but a few generalities can be made. First, a key influence in jazz is the BLUES—a 12-bar music form based on the tonic, dominant, and subdominant chords. Jazz also emphasizes syncopations, where the rhythmic emphasis does not fall on the downbeat. In the melody line, jazz uses the "blue" notes—flattened thirds and sevenths in a chord. Throughout, a key feature of jazz is improvisation. It is through improvisation that jazz musicians express themselves most personally and, in this way, hold an equal footing with the composer.

The resulting sound of jazz can be tragic, playful, dark, intellectual, upbeat, mournful—indeed, it can express the whole range of human emotion. This emotional content has been presented in a great variety of ways, depending on the time period and the artist. Through the decades, different categories of jazz emerged as the art form developed.

Ragtime is a piano style that emphasizes syncopation and polyrhythms; Dixieland, or New Orleans jazz, is played with small brass bands emphasizing counterpoint above a steady beat. Swing uses a small wind orchestration. Bop revolts against traditional harmony, melody, and rhythm and is characterized by the flatted fifth and an emphasis of harmony over melody. Progressive jazz emphasizes more laid-back harmonies. Hard bop sounds more explosive in its rhythms and harmonies.

There are far more varieties and sounds of jazz. Often, composers and musicians blend, or "fuse" jazz with other musical traditions, such as classical music, rock, Latin, Afro-beat, and so forth. Often jazz is purely instrumental. Other times it is sung, and many of America's greatest songs are songs inspired by jazz.

Within a hundred years, jazz has emerged from being a grassroots folk music to an established art form to holding an enshrined position at the Lincoln Center for the Performing Arts. Jazz is a feature throughout Alice Walker's canon, notably as a fixture in Harpo's JUKE JOINT in *The Color Purple.*

## FURTHER READING


Arnaud, Gerald, and Jacques Chesnel. *Masters of Jazz.* Edinburgh: W and R Chambers Ltd 1991.

Barlow, William. *Looking Up at Down: The Emergence of the Blues Culture.* Philadelphia: Temple University Press, 1989.

Bergreen, Laurence. *Louis Armstrong: An Extravagant Life.* New York: Broadway Books, 1997.

Charters, Samuel Barclay IV. *Jazz: New Orleans 1885–1963: An Index to the Negro Musicians of New Orleans.* New York: Oak Publications.

Collier, James Lincoln. *The Making of Jazz: A Comprehensive History.* Boston: Houghton Mifflin Company 1978.

Cook, Richard, and Brian Morton. *The Penguin Guide to Jazz on CD, LP and Cassette.* London: Penguin Books, 1992.

Dufty, William, and Billy Holiday. *The Lady Sings the Blues.* New York: Lancer Books, 1965.

Epstein, Dean J. *Sinful Tunes and Spirituals: Black Folk Music to the Civil War.* Urbana: University of Illinois Press, 1977.

Feather, Leonard. *The Encyclopedia of Jazz.* New York: Da Capo Press, 1960.

———. *The Jazz Years: Earwitness to an Era.* New York: Da Capo Press, 1987.

Fordham, John. *Jazz.* London: Dorling Kindersley, 1993.

Haskins, James. *Black Music in America: A History through Its People.* New York: Harper Trophy, 1987.

Hodier, Andre. *Toward Jazz.* New York: Grove Press, 1962.

Jones, Leroi. *Black Music.* New York: William Morrow and Company, 1967.

Morgenstern, Dan. *Jazz People.* New York: Da Capo Press, 1993.

Porter, Lewis. *John Coltrane: His Life and Music.* Ann Arbor: University of Michigan Press, 1998.

Rosenthal, David. *Hard Bop: Jazz and Black Music 1955–1965.* New York: Oxford University Press, 1992.

Stearns, Marshall. *The Story of Jazz.* New York: Oxford University Press, 1956.

Ulanov, Barry. *A Handbook of Jazz.* New York: Viking Press, 1960.

Ward, Geoffrey C., and Ken Burns. *Jazz: A History of America's Music.* New York: Alfred A. Knopf, 2000.

Wexler, Jerry. *Rhythm and the Blues: A Life in American Music.* New York: St. Martin's Press 1993.

**Jim Crow** The term *Jim Crow* refers to both the laws that enforced racial segregation in the American South between 1877 and the 1950s and the resulting attitudes and lifestyle in the South, in which African Americans and whites could not mingle in most public arenas, forcing blacks into degrading and insulting social roles.

The name "Jim Crow" was derived from a stereotypical black character in a minstrel show. The segregation laws under Jim Crow were a reaction by southern whites against Reconstruction, which was introduced into the South after the Civil War. Many southern whites were angered and frightened by the freedoms granted to African Americans—almost all of them ex-slaves—under Reconstruction. Unable to live in a society where blacks were their equals, the southern state legislatures began to pass laws that forced the two races apart and took back from blacks many of their rights as U.S. citizens. This meant blacks and whites had to be kept separate in such public spaces as streetcars, restaurants, schools, hospitals, public toilets, boardinghouses, theaters, public parks, and so forth. Even sidewalks were often included in Jim Crow laws. In some municipalities, blacks had to step aside to let whites pass. The separate facilities designated for African Americans were typically inferior to those for whites.

Because the message of Jim Crow was that whites were somehow superior to blacks, many whites felt free to insult and take advantage of African Americans. Black women could be raped by white men without legal recourse, black sharecroppers could be cheated of their money by white landlords, and even black shoppers could be publicly insulted by a white shopkeeper. At its worst, Jim Crow victimized blacks with white mob violence and LYNCHINGs.

A Supreme Court case that helped entrench Jim Crow was *Plessy v. Ferguson*. In 1892, Homer Plessy challenged the segregation laws on the southern railroads by intentionally sitting in a whites-only car. His case was brought to the Supreme Court, which ruled that separate facilities for whites and blacks were constitutional.

It was not until after World War II that the constitutionality of Jim Crow laws was seriously challenged. In 1950, the Supreme Court ruled that the University of Texas had to admit a black man to the law school on the grounds that the state did not provide equal education for him. In 1954, the Supreme Court ruled in *Brown v. Board of Education of Topeka, Kansas,* that separate facilities by race were unconstitutional. During the CIVIL RIGHTS MOVEMENT, African Americans and their white allies used boycotts, sit-ins, and court challenges to fight Jim Crow. In 1963, a march on Washington, D.C., against segregation drew more than 200,000 people.

Southern whites often responded with violence to the gains made by blacks, and the federal government had to send in troops to preserve order and protect blacks. Notable examples were at Little Rock, Arkansas, in 1957; Oxford, Mississippi, in 1962; and Selma, Alabama, in 1965.

The legal support for Jim Crow finally ended with a several pieces of legislation: the Civil Rights Act of 1964, the Voting Rights Act of 1965, and the Fair Housing Act of 1968. Alice Walker's novel *Meridian* deals explicitly with the impacts of Jim Crow segregation and the personal costs of the struggle to end this system of oppression.

### FURTHER READING

Chafe, William H., et al. *Remembering Jim Crow: African Americans Tell about Life in the Segregated South.* New York: New Press, 2001.

Chappell, David L. A *Stone of Hope. Prophetic Religion and the Death of Jim Crow.* Chapel Hill: University of North Carolina Press, 2003.

Conrad, Earl. *Jim Crow America.* New York: Duel, Sloan, and Pearce, 1947.

Dailey, Jane, et al. *Jumpin' Jim Crow: Southern Politics from Civil War to Civil Rights.* Princeton, N.J.: Princeton University Press, 2000

Finkelman, Paul, ed. *The Age of Jim Crow: Segregation from the End of Reconstruction to the Great Depression.* New York: Garland Publishing, 1992.

Gellman, David Nathaniel. *Jim Crow New York: A Documentary History of Race and Citizenship, 1777–1877.* New York: New York University Press, 2003.

George, Charles. *Life under Jim Crow Laws.* San Diego, Calif.: Lucent Books, 2000.

Gilpin, Patrick J., and Charles S. Johnson. *Leadership beyond the Veil in the Age of Jim Crow.* Albany: State University of New York Press, 2003.

Kennedy, Stetson. *Jim Crow Guide to the U.S.A.: The Way It Was.* Boca Raton: Florida Atlantic University Press, 1990.

Klarman, Michael J. *From Jim Crow to Civil Rights: The Supreme Court and the Struggle for Racial Equality.* New York: Oxford University Press, 2004.

Litwack, Leon F. *Trouble in Mind: Black Southerners in the Age of Jim Crow.* New York: Knopf, 1999.

Packard, Jerrold M. *American Nightmare: The History of Jim Crow.* New York: St. Martin's Press, 2002.

Payne, Charles M. *Time Longer than Rope: A Century of African American Activism.* New York: New York University Press, 2003.

Raper, Arthur Franklin. *The Tragedy of Lynching.* New York: Arno Press, 1969.

Smith, J. Douglas. *Managing White Supremacy: Race, Politics, and Citizenship in Jim Crow Virginia.* Chapel Hill: University of North Carolina Press, 2002.

Williams, Donnie, and Wayne Greenhaw. *The Thunder of Angels: The Montgomery Bus Boycott and the People Who Broke the Back of Jim Crow.* Chicago: Chicago Review Press, 2005.

Woodward, C. Vann. *The Strange Career of Jim Crow.* New York: Oxford University Press, 1955.

Wormser, Richard. *The Rise and Fall of Jim Crow.* New York: St. Martin's Press, 2003.

**Jones, Quincy** (1933– ) Quincy Jones is an iconic record producer and music industry figure who has worked with a vast spectrum of artists ranging from Count Basie to Michael Jackson. Jones was born in Chicago on March 14, 1933. During the early years of his career, he worked as an arranger for Ray Charles, jazz bassist Oscar Pettiford, and others. After arranging and conducting music in Paris and throughout Europe during the 1950s, in 1961 Mercury Records appointed Jones as their vice president. Subsequently, Jones returned to the United States to accept this position.

Jones spent the transitional musical decade of the 1960s arranging and producing for such recording artists as Lesley Gore, Frank Sinatra, and Sarah Vaughan, and he also composed soundtracks for various films and television programs. From the 1970s to the 1990s, he released multiple solo albums, produced many popular recordings (such as Michael Jackson's *Thriller*), and ventured into television and film production. In 1985, he coproduced STEVEN SPIELBERG's film adaptation of Alice Walker's novel *The Color Purple,* and he received Academy Award nominations for cocomposing its score and the song "Miss Celie's Blues (Sister)."

### FURTHER READING

George-Warren, Holly, and Patricia Romanowski, eds. *The Rolling Stone Encyclopedia of Rock and Roll.* 3d ed. New York: Fireside, 2001.

Jones, Quincy. *Q: The Autobiography of Quincy Jones.* New York: Doubleday, 2001.

Ross, Courtney, ed. *Listen Up: The Lives of Quincy Jones.* New York: Warner Books. 1990.

Jones, Quincy, and Tamia. *Q's Jook Joint.* Burbank, Calif.: Qwest/Warner Bros, 1995.

"Quincy Jones." All Music Guide. Available online. URL: http://www.allmusic.com/cg/amg.dll. Accessed February 20, 2009.

**juke joint (jook joint)** Juke joints are post–Reconstruction era African-American gathering places that originated in black southern rural areas in the United States. Traditionally, juke joints featured a mixture of eating, drinking, gambling, musical performances, and dancing. The joints derive their name from the term *jook,* a term for wickedness and or dancing that is believed to be of West African origin.

Juke joints were black-owned and -operated businesses that attracted a lower- and working-class constituency who regularly ate, dance, gambled, and sang along to BLUES-oriented music. From the 1920s through the 1950s, much of the music, visual style, and dances of these ethnic venues was appropriated and integrated into mainstream American entertainment. Many historians and cultural anthropologists have come to view them as benchmarks in the formation of a black public sphere. The juke joint was particularly important in the creation of the network of black performance venues known in popular vernacular as the "chitlin' circuit."

Juke joints inspired other variations, including more urbane and jazz-oriented honky-tonks and after-hours clubs in the northern United States. There is also a connection between the juke joint and the phenomenon of the rent party, which was particularly popular in Harlem, New York. Literary and cinematic depictions of early-to-mid-20th century African-American life frequently feature scenes set in juke joints.

In Alice Walker's novel *The Color Purple,* Harpo, who is Albert's son and Celie's stepson, opens a juke joint after his wife, Sofia, leaves him. Harpo names his juke joint "Harpos of _____ Plantation." He manages and co-owns it with his friend Swain. The juke joint gradually builds an audience and begins to be extremely popular once Shug Avery returns to town and begins singing there.

### FURTHER READING

Carr, M. H. *Denying Hegemony: The Function and Place of Florida's Jook Joints during the Twentieth Century's First Fifty Years.* Ph.D. diss., Florida State University, 2002.

Hazzard-Gordon, Katrina. *Jookin': The Rise of Social Dance Formations in African-American Culture.* Philadelphia: Temple University Press, 1990.

Neal, M. A. *What the Music Said: Black Popular Music and Black Popular Culture.* New York: Routledge, 1999.

Ogren, Kathy J. *The Jazz Revolution: Twenties America and the Meaning of Jazz.* New York: Oxford University Press, 1989.

Oliver, Paul. *Blues off the Record: Thirty Years of Blues Commentary.* New York: Da Capo Press, 1984.

Wald, Elijah. *Escaping the Delta: Robert Johnson and the Invention of the Blues.* New York: HarperCollins, 2004.

**Jung, Carl Gustav** (1875–1961) Carl Jung was a Swiss psychiatrist best known for his integration of what he called the collective unconscious into the understanding of human nature and treatment of psychiatric patients. A concept in analytic psychology—a field founded by Jung—the collective unconscious refers to the shared built-in response to the world of every person (or every member of a given species). This is distinguished from the personal unconscious, which refers to the experiences and responses of a given individual. Jung believed that this collective unconscious could be explored through cultural expressions in the forms of myths, religion, and philosophy, and through individual expressions in the form of dreams. In a break with his mentor, Sigmund Freud, Jung believed that the central goal for psychological well-being rested with the individual's need to balance his or her individual nature with the collective unconscious. This could lead to harmony and autonomy for the individual in a process Jung called individualization.

Alice Walker creates a character in her novel *Possessing the Secret of Joy,* named Mzee, who is a composite of Jung. He is a therapist and is responsible for helping the novel's main protagonist, Tashi, discover the source of her anguish. Walker has spoken extensively about her embrace of aspects of Jungian psychology and is particularly enamored of Jung's understanding of the role of dreams in accessing answers about individual and collective truth.

### FURTHER READING

Bair, Deidre. *Jung: A Biography.* Boston: Little Brown and Company, 2003.

Dourley, John P. *Paul Tillich, Carl Jung and the Recovery of Religion.* New York: Routledge, 2008.

Hayman, Ronald. *A Life of Jung.* New York: W. W. Norton, 2001.

Jung, Carl G. *Analytic Psychology: Its Theory and Practice.* New York: Random House, 1968.

———. *The Basic Writings of C. G. Jung.* New York: Modern Library, 1959.

———. *The Collected Works of Carl G. Jung.* Princeton: Princeton University Press, 1978.

———. *Man and His Symbols.* New York: Dell, 1968.

Jung, Carl G., with Aniela Jaffé. *Memories, Dreams, Reflections.* New York: Vintage, 1965.

McLynn, Frank. *Carl Gustav Jung: A Biography.* New York: St. Martin's Press, 1997.

Nagy, Marilyn. *Philosophical Issues in the Psychology of C. G. Jung.* New York: State University of New York Press, 1991.

Schultz, Duane P. *Intimate Friends, Dangerous Rivals: The Turbulent Relationship between Freud and Jung.* Los Angeles: Jeremy P. Tarcher, 1990.

Wehr, Gerhard. *Jung: A Biography.* Boston: Shambhala, 1987.

**Kahlo, Frida** (1907–1954) Frida Kahlo was one of the most influential painters in modern art, notable for her often surreal self-portraits and still-life paintings. Kahlo was born in Coyoacán, Mexico, to parents of mixed ethnic and religious heritage. She survived a childhood bout with polio and was a bright and precocious teenager. When she was 18, her life was violently disrupted by a severe bus accident, in which she suffered injuries so traumatic that she was not expected to live. Demonstrating her characteristic tenacity, she was released from the hospital in about a month and endured a long and excruciating recovery, during which she began to paint.

From the beginning, Kahlo's work was experimental and self-referential. In 1929, she married the Mexican painter Diego Rivera, who influenced her painting and political perspective. Kahlo met Rivera when she was a young student and he had come to her school when he was commissioned to paint a mural on a wall of the building.

During the late 1920s and 1930s, Kahlo grew into her art, and she had her first solo exhibit in 1938 in New York at the Julien Levy Gallery. In 1939, she and Rivera divorced, only to remarry the next year. The relationship between the two was always turbulent and remained so for the rest of Kahlo's life. An example of the unusual nature of their relationship occurred when Leon Trotsky and his wife, Natalia, stayed at the couple's home and had an affair with Frida. Shortly after he left their home, he was assassinated.

Kahlo's career flourished during the 1940s. In 1954, during her final illness, she either succumbed to complications from her accident or committed suicide. What actually happened has never been determined, and no autopsy was performed.

In the last decades of the 20th century, the rise of both the Neomexicanismo (or NeoMexican) artistic and the feminist movements revived interest in Kahlo's life and career. Various filmmakers have iconized Kahlo's legacy as an artistic and political influence. There have been two notable feature films, including Paul Leduc's *Frida, naturaleza viva* (1986) and Julie Taymor's *Frida* (2002), as well as several documentaries and various commercial reproductions.

Alice Walker has honored Kahlo several times in her writings, including in "Frida, the Perfect Familiar," an essay in her 1998 collection *Anything We Love Can Be Saved.* Walker has also written about Kahlo in poetry. Her poem "Dream of Frida Kahlo" is one of the poems in her 2004 collection *Absolute Trust in the Goodness of the Earth: New Poems.*

## FURTHER READING

Darbyshire, P. "Understanding the Life of Illness: Learning through the Art of Frida Kahlo." *Esthetics and the Art of Nursing* 17, no. 1 (1994): 51–59.

Frida Kahlo Corporation. Available online. URL: http://www.fkahlo.com/. Accessed March 28, 2009.

Herrera, Hayden. *Frida: A Biography of Frida Kahlo.* New York: Perennial, 2002.

Kahlo, Frida. *The Diary of Frida Kahlo: An Intimate Self-portrait.* New York: H. N. Abrams, 1995.

Kettenmann, Andrea. *Frida Kahlo, 1907–1954: Pain and Passion.* Köln: Benedikt Taschen, 1993.

Lowe, Sarah M. *Frida Kahlo.* New York: Universe, 1991.

Zamora, Martha. *Frida Kahlo: The Brush of Anguish.* San Francisco: Chronicle Books, 1990.

**King, Martin Luther, Jr.** (1929–1968) As a civil rights activist, Alice Walker has written extensively about Martin Luther King, Jr., and his philosophies are a major influence on both her fiction and nonfiction prose. King was the most prominent civil rights leader in the United States during the 1950s and 1960s. As a major figure in the movement to end racial segregation after World War II, King believed this could best be done through nonviolence. Much of the success of the CIVIL RIGHTS MOVEMENT is credited to his nonviolent protests and marches.

Born in Atlanta, Georgia, King was the son and grandson of Baptist ministers and attended segregated schools in the Jim Crow South of Georgia. He was himself ordained in the ministry in 1954, becoming pastor of a church in Montgomery, Alabama. The following year, he received his doctorate in theology from Boston University. It was at Boston that he met and married Coretta Scott, who was to become his ally in the fight for civil rights.

One of King's first efforts to win civil rights for African Americans was leading a boycott to end Montgomery's racial segregation on public transportation. This boycott began in December 1955, when Rosa Parks refused to give up her seat to a white man on the bus. During this boycott, tensions became so high that King's house was firebombed, but the protest ended with a Supreme Court decision declaring that segregation was unconstitutional.

In 1957, King became president of the Southern Christian Leadership Conference, which furthered the use of nonviolence to achieve civil rights for African Americans. A great influence on his organization, as well as on King himself, was the civil-disobedience tactics of Mahatma Gandhi in that leader's successful movement to push British colonizers out of India.

In 1960, King became copastor with his father of Ebenezer Baptist Church in Atlanta, Georgia. In that city, he was jailed for protesting against racial segregation at a lunch counter. John F. Kennedy, then a candidate for president, obtained his release.

In 1963, while again jailed—this time for his protests in Birmingham, Alabama—King wrote his "Letter from a Birmingham Jail," which was a response to white Alabama clergymen who said that the struggle for civil rights should be fought solely in the courts, not in the streets. King responded that civil rights for African Americans would not occur without the highly public civil disobedience that he espoused. As Gandhi believed before him, civil disobedience was justified when confronting unjust laws. King also explained in his letter that African Americans should not be expected to wait any longer for their civil rights.

In 1963, King helped organize the March on Washington, which drew more than 200,000 people to protest segregation and became a major influence on the Civil Rights Act of 1964 and Voting Rights Act of 1965. It was at this march that he delivered his famous "I Have a Dream" speech, which spoke to his vision of an America free of bigotry, where people "will not be judged by the color of their skin but by the content of their character."

In 1964, King won the Nobel Peace Prize; at 35, he was the prize's youngest recipient. Soon after, his protest actions included not just African Americans but all people who were disenfranchised. He also began to speak out against the Vietnam War. King was in Memphis, Tennessee, to support a strike by sanitation workers when he was assassinated. He is the only non-president of the United States to have his birthday celebrated as a national holiday.

### FURTHER READING

Garrow, David J. *Bearing the Cross: Martin Luther King, Jr., and the Southern Leadership Conference.* New York: Morrow, 1986.

King, Coretta Scott. *My Life with Martin Luther King, Jr.* New York: Holt, Rinehart and Winston, 1969.

King, Martin Luther, Jr. *Stride toward Freedom: The Montgomery Story.* New York: Perennial Library, Harper, 1958.

———. *A Testament of Hope: The Essential Writings of Martin Luther King, Jr.* Edited by James Melvin Washington. San Francisco: Harper, 1986.

———. *The Trumpet of Conscience.* New York: Harper and Row, 1967.

———. *Why We Can't Wait.* New York: Harper and Row, 1963.

Lewis, David L. *King, a Critical Biography.* Urbana: University of Illinois Press, 1978.

Lokos, Lionel. *House Divided; The Life and Legacy of Martin Luther King.* New Rochelle, N.Y.: Arlington House, 1968.

Oates, Stephen B. *Let the Trumpet Sound.* New York: Harper and Row, 1982.

**Ku Klux Klan** The Ku Klux Klan is a group of loosely linked organizations that promotes racism, anti-Semitism, anti-immigration, and (in past decades) anti-Catholicism in order to create an American society that is ruled by the concept of white supremacy.

The Ku Klux Klan has had two incarnations. It was founded in 1866 after the Civil War in Pulaski, Tennessee, in a reactionary and violent response to Reconstruction. Originally intended as a social club for six ex-Confederate officers, the organization quickly transformed into a terrorist organization. Feeling threatened by newly freed African Americans, the Klan's members started intimidating, shooting, and LYNCHING black Americans in an attempt to restore the social hierarchy in which whites were superior to blacks. The Klan also targeted "carpetbaggers" from the North and local Republicans, murdering thousands, but its main goals, most of which were successful at the time, were to restrict or eliminate black education, economic advancement, voting rights, and their right to bear arms. As part of their terrorism, the Klan's members dressed in sheets and pointed hoods to cover their bodies and faces. The organization went into decline partly because some southern politicians and other influential leaders abandoned the group, but it was eventually destroyed in the early 1870s by President Ulysses S. Grant's aggressive use of the Civil Rights Act of 1871.

The Ku Klux Klan reappeared in 1915 with no formal connection to its earlier namesake but with the same goals. Its rebirth was spurred by a number of factors, including the influx of immigrants into the United States; the lynching of Leo Frank, a Jewish man accused of the rape and murder of a white girl, and, most dramatically, by the film *The Birth of a Nation* (1915), which glorified the earlier Klan and whose factual content was endorsed by President Woodrow Wilson, who said of the film, "It is like writing history with lightning, and my only regret is that it is all so terribly true." The new Ku Klux Klan preached racism, anti-Semitism, anti-Catholicism, and nativism. Many local chapters of the Klan participated in the same terrorist activities of shootings and lynchings as did its earlier namesake. At its height, in the 1920s, the Klan had almost 5 million members in both the South and the North.

Over the decades, the Klan lost influence and members, first due to a scandal in which a Grand Dragon of the Klan was convicted of the bizarre rape and murder of a woman in the 1930s and, later, by the Klan's association with Nazi sympathizers during World War II. Finally, with the expansion of the CIVIL RIGHTS MOVEMENT after the war, in which civil rights organizations actively took on the Klan, the total membership of loosely knit Klan groups shrank to a couple of thousand, which is its current approximate total. The Klan is an oppressive force in several of Walker's novels, most particularly in *Meridian*.

### FURTHER READING


Alexander, Charles. *The Ku Klux Klan in the Southwest.* Norman: University of Oklahoma Press, 1995.

Goldberg, David. *Disconnected America: The U.S. in the 1920.* Baltimore: Johns Hopkins University Press, 1999.

Jackson, Kenneth. *The Ku Klux Klan in the City.* New York: Oxford University Press, 1957.

Mecklin, John. *The Ku Klux Klan: A Study of the American Mind.* New York: Harcourt, Brace and Co., 1923.


**land-grant colleges** A land-grant college is a U.S. institution of higher learning created from federal grants, starting in the 19th century. Congress's goal was to create institutions throughout the United States that focused on agriculture, the mechanic arts, and military tactics but that would also provide a traditional education in higher learning to more Americans, especially in the working class. Called the Land Grant College Act of 1862—or the Morrill Act, after the Vermont congressman who sponsored it—the act granted each state 30,000 acres of federal land for each of that state's congressional seats. The states were free to use the money in whatever way they wished to further the goal of Congress, which meant they could create new schools or contribute to schools they already had.

The Second Morrill Act, in 1890, provided additional endowments for the land-grant colleges, but it prohibited giving the money to states that used race in their admissions policy, thus denying blacks access to the colleges. In a compromise, however, the act did allow states to provide a separate land-grant institution to African Americans. The land-grant institutions that were designated for blacks in the then-segregated South came to be called the 1890 land-grants. A similar compromise in the act existed for Native Americans, and the 29 tribal colleges are sometimes called the 1994 land-grants. SPELMAN COLLEGE, where Alice Walker began her undergraduate career, is a land-grant college.

### FURTHER READING

Christy, Ralph D., and Lionel Williamson, eds. *A Century of Service: Land-Grant Colleges and Universities, 1890–1990.* New Brunswick, N.J.: Transaction Publishers, 1992.

Ohles, John F., and Shirley M. Ohles. *Public Colleges and Universities.* Westport, Conn.: Greenwood Press, 1986.

**Lenox Avenue** Lenox Avenue, located in New York City's Harlem neighborhood, has become synonymous with African-American cultural life. That association was particularly the case during the years of the Harlem Renaissance, when the neighborhood became a magnet for African-American artistry. This aspect of Lenox Avenue's identity applies especially to its well-respected and vibrant jazz scene. Lenox Avenue has become an important symbol in African-American literary texts.

### FURTHER READING

Boyd, Herb, ed. *The Harlem Reader: A Celebration of New York's Most Famous Neighborhood, from the Renaissance Years to the Twenty-First Century.* New York: Three Rivers, 2003.

Gaines, Ann G. *The Harlem Renaissance in American History.* Berkeley Heights, N.J.: Enslow Publishers, 2002.

Osofsky, Gilbert. *Harlem: The Making of a Ghetto. Negro New York, 1890–1930.* Chicago: Ivan R. Dee, 1996.

———. "Symbols of the Jazz Age: The New Negro and Harlem Discovered." *American Quarterly* 17, no. 2 (1965): 229.

Wintz, Cary D., and Paul Finkelman. "Lenox Avenue." In *Encyclopedia of the Harlem Renaissance.* New York: Routledge, 2004.

**Leopold II** (1835–1909) Léopold-Louis-Philippe-Marie-Victor, better known as King Leopold II (king of the Belgians), was a Belgian ruler who annexed territories in central Africa and created the Congo Free State as a private enterprise in 1885. The colonization process was infamous for brutal slave labor practices. The Congo struggled to reach independence from Belgium, which it finally achieved in 1960 after decades of activist struggle.

### FURTHER READING

Anstey, R. *King Leopold's Legacy: The Congo under Belgian Rule, 1908–1960.* London: Oxford University Press, 1966.

Ascherson, N. *The King Incorporated: Leopold the Second and the Congo.* London: Granta, 1999.

Edgerton, R. B. *The Troubled Heart of Africa: A History of the Congo.* New York: St. Martin's Press, 2002.

Falola, Toyin. *Key Events in African History: A Reference Guide.* Westport, Conn.: Greenwood Press, 2002.

Hochschild, A. *King Leopold's Ghost: A Story of Greed, Terror, and Heroism in Colonial Africa.* London: Pan, 2002.

**Leventhal, Melvyn** (1943– ) Melvyn (Mel) Rosenman Leventhal and Alice Walker were married from 1967 to 1976 and have one child, a daughter named Rebecca Grant Leventhal, now known as REBECCA WALKER. Leventhal was born to a Jewish family in Brooklyn, New York, in 1943. His father abandoned the family when Mel was a boy, a pivotal experience for Leventhal, who sometimes felt like an abused outcast, which he has connected to his strong sense of empathy and consequent involvement in the CIVIL RIGHTS MOVEMENT. While completing his studies in law at New York University, he worked periodically for various civil rights organizations in the South.

After interning with the Student's Civil Rights Research Council during summer 1965, Leventhal interned in summer 1966 for the NAACP Legal Defense Fund (LDF). During an assignment in Greenwood, Mississippi, he met Alice Walker, and the pair worked together to interview poor and disenfranchised black residents. In Greenwood, both Walker and Leventhal were subjected to overt and threatening harassment, and Walker has stated that they bonded over their shared vulnerability.

As the two deepened their connection, Walker began sharing her writing with Leventhal and introduced him to her family. They married in New York City on March 17, 1967. In the "summer of love," they bought a house in Jackson, Mississippi, where Marian Wright Edelman hired Leventhal as a staff attorney to the NAACP.

Living in Mississippi eventually created tensions between the couple. Their interracial marriage was controversial to their families, and Leventhal's visibility as an increasingly prominent civil rights lawyer led to security concerns. In addition to experiencing various levels of harassment from racist whites, some African Americans questioned Walker's racial solidarity. The stress the couple experienced may have been a factor in Walker's miscarriage of their first child shortly after the assassination of MARTIN LUTHER KING, JR., in April 1968. Walker was able to conceive another child shortly thereafter, and on November 17, 1969, Rebecca was born.

Despite external pressures, Walker was very productive during her marriage to Leventhal. In 1967, she published her first work of nonfiction, the essay "The Civil Rights Movement: What Good Was It?" (first published in *American Scholar* and later collected in her anthology *In Search of Our Mothers' Gardens*). This essay was followed by her first book of poetry, *Once: Poems* (1968), and her first novel, *The Third Life of Grange Copeland* (1970). She also won a writing fellowship to the Radcliffe Institute at Harvard. Walker flourished as a fellow at the institute. In 1973, at Walker's insistence, the family left Mississippi and the South and moved to New York City.

Eventually, in the face of irreconcilable differences, Walker and Leventhal separated. In 1976, the couple filed for divorce and agreed to share custody of Rebecca, who, while coming of age, lived with her parents for alternating two-year intervals, a situation she would later write about critically.

According to Walker's biographer, Evelyn C. White, Leventhal believes that the marriage failed in part because Walker felt pressure from various African Americans to reject her relationship with a white man.

In 1978, following his divorce from Walker, Leventhal married Judith Goldsmith, with whom he has two children and to whom he remains married.

### FURTHER READING


Lauret, Maria. *Alice Walker.* Macmillan: New York, 2000.

Walker, Alice. *The Way Forward Is with a Broken Heart.* New York: Ballantine Books, 2001.

White, Evelyn C. *Alice Walker: A Life.* New York: Norton, 2004.

Winchell, Donna H. *Alice Walker.* New York: Twayne, 1992.


**Livingstone, David** (1813–1873) David Livingstone was a prominent Scotsman who worked for the LONDON MISSIONARY SOCIETY and conducted his evangelical work in Central Africa. Livingstone believed that Christianity was a positive "civilizing" force and worked in Africa from 1841 until his death in 1873 to spread his doctrine.

In a letter to Celie in *The Color Purple,* Nettie references several pictures of white men that are prominently displayed in the Missionary Society of New York's office. Among those are representations of Livingstone and of the explorer Henry Morton Stanley.

### FURTHER READING


De Gruchy, John, ed. *The London Missionary Society in Southern Africa*: Historical Essays in Celebration of the Bicentenary of the LMS in Southern Africa, 1799–1999. Athens: Ohio University Press, 2000.

Livingstone, David, and Christopher Hibbert. *The Life and African Explorations of Dr. David Livingstone.* New York: Cooper Square Press, 2002.

———. *Missionary Travels and Researches in South Africa.* London: Murray, 1857.

———. *Narrative of an Expedition to the Zambezi and Its Tributaries.* London: Murray, 1865.

Ross, Andrew. *David Livingstone: Mission and Empire.* London: Continuum, 2006.

Royer, Galen B. "David Livingstone: Africa's Great Missionary and Explorer." Available online. URL: http://www.wholesomewords.org/missions/bliving2.html. Accessed March 25, 2009.

**London Missionary Society** The London Missionary Society is a nondenominational missionary organization originally founded in 1795 in London by a group of individuals from different churches. These people founded the society with the intention of evangelizing in parts of the South Pacific and Africa. The group provided linguistic training to its members and translated scriptures into native languages in order to be able to converse with local populations to bring about conversion.

In 1966, the London Missionary Society merged its efforts and endeavors with another proselytizing organization, the Commonwealth Missionary Society. The Council for World Mission is the organization that emerged from the consolidation, and therefore the work of the London Missionary Society continues today.

Walker references the work of missionary societies and their interactions with peoples of color, particularly with Africans throughout her canon.

### FURTHER READING

Council for World Mission: A Global Community of Churches. "History of the London Missionary Society." Available online. URL: http://www.cwmission.org/history/history-of-the-london-missionary-society. Accessed March 25, 2009.

De Gruchy, John, ed. *The London Missionary Society in Southern Africa: Historical Essays in Celebration of the Bicentenary of the LMS in Southern Africa, 1799–1999.* Athens: Ohio University Press, 2000.

Lovett, Richard. *History of the London Missionary Society: 1795–1895.* London: Oxford University Press, 1899.

Northcott, Cecil. *Glorious Company: 150 Years Life and Work of the London Missionary Society: 1795–1945.* London: Livingstone Press, 1945.

O'Sullivan, Leona. "The London Missionary Society: A Written Record of Missionaries and Printing Presses in the Straits Settlements 1815–1847." *Journal of the Malayan Branch of the Royal Asiatic Society* 57, no. 2 (1984): 61–104.

**Lumumba, Patrice** (1925–1961) Patrice Lumumba was a nationalist leader who worked for the independence of the Congo—then called the Belgian Congo—from Belgium, becoming the first prime minister of the newly independent Democratic Republic of the Congo. A member of the small Batetela tribe, Lumumba was a passionate anticolonialist and an equally avid pan-Africanist all his life due to his bitterness over the cruel treatment the Congolese people received under Belgian rule. Soon after Lumumba took office, however, the new nation broke out in violence from conflicting powers. The army in particular was dissatisfied with Lumumba. Rank-and-file soldiers felt bypassed when he raised the pay for other branches of government. Ten weeks after his election, as the nation descended into violent chaos—sending European residents fleeing the country—he was deposed in a coup led by Joseph Mobutu. Lumumba was later taken from his imprisonment and driven to a remote spot, where he was killed by firing squad.

Both the Belgian and U.S. governments tried to assassinate Lumumba, and it was suspected that they were involved in his death. The United States accused him of being a communist, particularly since he took the Soviet Union as an ally, but Lumumba denied this accusation, explaining that he sided with the Soviets only because he needed a powerful ally against the Western powers. His official international position was to be neutral in the conflicts between East and West.

Lumumba's legacy has been mixed. He has been blamed for the breakdown of government in the new nation—which, in turn, led to decades of war and strong-arm rule from other dictators—but he is also remembered as a powerful leader who helped free the Congolese people from European colonialism.

As a result of his political and social philosophies, his accomplishments, and the circumstances of his death, Patrice Lumumba remains an international icon of colonial resistance. Walker's novel *Meridian* features an untitled chapter that includes the names of slain activist figures from the 1960s, including MALCOLM X, CHE GUEVARA, and Lumumba.

### FURTHER READING

De Witte, Ludo. *The Assassination of Lumumba.* Translated by Ann Wright and Renee Fenby. London and New York: Verso, 2001.

Kanza, Thomas R. *The Rise and Fall of Patrice Lumumba: Conflict in the Congo.* Boston: G. K. Hall, 1979.

Lumumba, Patrice. *Congo, My Country.* New York: Praeger, 1962.

———. *Lumumba Speaks: The Speeches and Writings of Patrice Lumumba, 1958–1961.* Translated by Helen R. Lane. Edited by Jean Van Lierde. Little, Brown and Company, 1972.

McKown, Robin. *Lumumba: A Biography.* New York: Doubleday, 1969.

**lynching** Lynching is defined as the violent injury or murder of an individual at the hands of a group of antagonists operating outside the law. Some historians have speculated that the word derives from Charles Lynch, a legal administrator who lived in Virginia in the 1700s and was known for his unduly harsh sentences. In the United States, the term historically has been associated with a particular form of white mob violence toward black men and women that includes brutal beatings, rape, castration, burning, mutilation, and hanging. In spite of this association, white abolitionists were the primary targets of lynching from the 1830s to the 1850s. In subsequent decades, tensions resulting from Reconstruction-era reforms intended to foster greater legal and social access for blacks were often cited as the motivation for vigilante justice leveled at African Americans. The formation of the KU KLUX KLAN in 1867 in Pulaski, Tennessee, was a signal for the rise of organized and systemic violence against black people and communities.

In the face of black political activism during the Reconstruction era, southern white supremacist groups arose, leading to a particularly intense period of antiblack violence, and more than 10,000 lynchings occurred in the years between 1865 and 1895, primarily in Mississippi, Alabama, Georgia, and Louisiana. White fears of racial revolts and black supremacist movements were often used to justify lynching activity, but the most potent and enduring myth rationalizing violence against blacks was the characterization of black men as sexual threats to white womanhood. Thousands of black men were beaten and hanged in the United States as a result of unsubstantiated accusations of their having raped or attacked white women. Black women and men were also murdered as a result of gratuitous or unfounded accusations of public insubordination, theft, and other violations of the social codes that segregated whites and blacks.

In the face of pervasive violence and lack of legal recourse, an antilynching movement began, prompted by the activism of such figures as Ida B. Wells and Frederick Douglass, and later by women including Mary Talbert and Jessie Daniel Ames. Organizations such as the National Organization for the Advancement of Colored People (NAACP), the Woman's Loyal Union, the National Association of Colored Women, the Anti-Lynching Crusade, and the Association of Southern Women for the Prevention of Lynching were involved in the campaign to raise awareness about and end the practice of lynching.

In spite of these efforts, lynching endured as a common form of antiblack violence well into the 20th century, although by the 1950s, incidents of lynching were far less frequent. There were isolated incidents of racially motivated lynchings reported even at the end of the 20th century. Two of the best-known incidents were the murders of Michael Donald in 1981 and James Byrd in 1998. In 2005, the U.S. Senate passed a resolution acknowledging their past inaction and issuing an apology to surviving relatives of the victims of lynching.

The legacy of lynching spawned an array of literary, musical, and visual responses, most famously jazz singer Billie Holiday's 1939 recording of "Strange Fruit." Alice Walker refers to lynching in many of her novels and short stories, including *Meridian* and *The Color Purple.*

## FURTHER READING

Brundage, W. Fitzhugh. *Lynching in the New South: Georgia and Virginia, 1880–1930.* Urbana: University of Illinois Press, 1993.

Cutler, James E. *Lynch-law: An Investigation into the History of Lynching in the United States.* Montclair, N.J.: Petterson Smith, 1969.

Davis, Angela. *Women, Race, and Class.* New York: Vintage Books, 1981.

Dray, Philip. *At the Hands of Persons Unknown: The Lynching of Black America.* New York: Random House, 2002.

Franklin, John Hope, and Alfred A. Moss, Jr. *From Slavery to Freedom: A History of African Americans.* Boston: McGraw-Hill, 2000.

Harris, Trudier. *Exorcising Blackness: Historical and Literary Lynching and Burning Rituals.* Bloomington: Indiana University Press, 1985.

Perkins, Kathy A. "The Impact of Lynching on the Art of African American Women." In *Strange Fruit: Plays on Lynching by American Women,* edited by Kathy A. Perkins and Judith L. Stephens. Bloomington: Indiana University Press, 1998.

Tolnay, Stewart Emory, and E. M. Beck. *A Festival of Violence: An Analysis of Southern Lynchings, 1882–1930.* Urbana: University of Illinois Press, 1995.

Tolnay, Stewart Emory, G. Deane, and E. M. Beck. "Vicarious Violence: Spatial Effects on Southern Lynchings, 1890–1919." *American Journal of Sociology* 102, no. 3 (1996): 788–815.

**Lynd, Helen** (1896–1982) Helen Lynd was a social philosopher most famous for her groundbreaking 1929 study of social class in America, *Middletown: A Study in Contemporary American Culture,* cowritten with her husband, Robert Lynd. Based on a recommendation from her son, the historian STAUGHTON LYND, who taught Alice Walker at SPELMAN COLLEGE, she arranged for Walker's transfer to SARAH LAWRENCE COLLEGE on a full scholarship. According to Walker, in addition to serving as a her faculty adviser, Lynd played a pivotal role in making Western philosophy accessible to her, particularly the works of ALBERT CAMUS and Friedrich Nietzsche, among others.

### FURTHER READING

Lynd, Robert S., and Helen Lynd. *Middletown: A Study in Contemporary American Culture.* New York: Harcourt, Brace, and Company, 1929.

———. *Middletown in Transition: A Study in Cultural Conflicts.* New York: Harcourt, Brace, and Company, 1937.

White, Evelyn C. *Alice Walker: A Life.* New York: W. W. Norton and Company, 2004.

**Lynd, Staughton** (1929– ) Staughton Lynd is a historian who was educated at Columbia University and taught at SPELMAN COLLEGE and Yale University. During the summer of 1964, he was responsible for leading the Freedom Schools in Mississippi. Lynd was impressed by Walker's writing. Like his friend HOWARD ZINN, he met Walker when she was an undergraduate student in his class at Spelman College. Lynd recommended that Walker transfer to SARAH LAWRENCE COLLEGE, where his mother, HELEN LYND, was a social activist and professor. Helen Lynd helped Walker to secure a full scholarship to Sarah Lawrence and served as her faculty adviser while she attended the college. Walker has remained close friends with Staughton Lynd and his wife, Alice, who continue their activism in the Youngstown, Ohio, area.

### FURTHER READING

"Staughton and Alice Lynd Collection." University Archives, Kent State University. Available online. URL: http://www.speccoll.library.kent.edu/labor/lynd.html. Accessed February 28, 2009.

White, Evelyn C. *Alice Walker: A Life.* New York: W. W. Norton and Company, 2004.

**Malcolm X (Malcolm Little)** (1925–1965) Malcolm X was a Black Muslim leader in the United States who, for much of his career, advocated black pride and separation of the races. A year before his assassination, he made a pilgrimage to Mecca, which transformed his thinking to a belief that all races shared a common brotherhood.

Malcolm X was born Malcolm Little in Omaha, Nebraska, where his father was a Baptist minister who spoke out against racism and was an avid supporter of the Black Nationalist leader Marcus Garvey. The family had to move several times to avoid threats from white racists. In Michigan, the family's house was burned down by the Ku Klux Klan. Two years later, Malcolm X's father, Earl, was found dead on some trolley tracks. The police ruled it an accident, but the family was certain that members of a racist organization had murdered him. Several years later, Malcolm's mother, Louise, suffered an emotional breakdown and was committed to a mental hospital. Her eight children were then split up and sent to various foster homes and orphanages.

As a young man, Malcolm X became involved in narcotics, prostitution, and gambling. In 1946, he was sent to prison for burglary. He used his time there to pursue his education and, at the behest of his brother, read up on the Nation of Islam, led by Elijah Muhammad, who taught that white society worked to keep African Americans from attaining political and economic success. According to the Nation of Islam, the solution was a separate state for blacks. By 1952, when he was paroled, Malcolm had converted to the Black Muslim faith and changed his last name to X to reject his "slave name."

As a member of the Nation of Islam, Malcolm X proved himself to be a brilliant organizer and became that sect's major spokesman. His speeches drew a huge number of converts. In keeping with the teachings of Elijah Muhammad, he spoke out against the white exploitation of blacks and against much of the CIVIL RIGHTS MOVEMENT, which emphasized integration. He called for black separatism and the use of violence for self-protection.

In 1964, however, Malcolm X left the Nation of Islam when he learned that Elijah Muhammad was having affairs with six women, some of whom had had his children. Elijah Muhammad asked him to use his skills to help him cover up the potential scandals, but Malcolm X refused. That same year, he made a pilgrimage to Mecca, which led him to convert to orthodox Islam and to consider the possibility that the races could live together in peace. Rival Black Muslims threatened his life, and he was shot to death at a rally in Harlem. Some scholars have speculated that the federal government was involved in Malcolm X's assassination. Alice Walker references Malcolm X in both her fiction and nonfiction work.

### FURTHER READING


Breitman, George, ed. *By Any Means Necessary: Speeches, Interviews, and a Letter by Malcolm X.* New York: Pathfinder Press, 1970.

———. *Malcolm X Speaks.* New York: Pathfinder Press, 1965.

Clark, Steve, ed. *February 1965: The Final Speeches.* New York: Pathfinder Press, 1992.

Cone, John H. *Martin and Malcolm and America: A Dream or a Nightmare.* Maryknoll, N.Y.: Orbis Books, 1991.

DeCaro, Louis A., Jr. *Malcolm and the Cross: The Nation of Islam, Malcolm X, and Christianity.* New York: New York University Press, 1998.

———. *On the Side of My People: A Religious Life of Malcolm X.* New York: New York University Press, 1996.

Dyson, Michael Eric. *Making Malcolm: The Myth and Meaning of Malcolm X.* Oxford: Oxford University Press, 1995.

Epps, Archie, ed. *Malcolm X and the American Negro Revolution: The Speeches of Malcolm X.* London: Peter Owen, 1968.

Karim, Benjamin, ed. *The End of White World Supremacy: Four Speeches by Malcolm X.* New York: Little, Brown, 1971.

Lee, Martha F. *The Nation of Islam: An American Millenarian Movement.* Lewiston, N.Y.: Edwin Mellen, 1988.

Lincoln, C. Eric. *The Black Muslims in America.* 3d ed. Grand Rapids, Mich.: William B. Eerdmans Publishing, 1994.

Malcolm X, and Alex Haley. *The Autobiography of Malcolm X.* New York: Grove Press, 1965.

Perry, Bruce. *Malcolm: A Life of the Man Who Changed Black America.* Barrytown, N.Y.: Station Hill Press, 1990.

Wolfenstein, Eugene Victor. *The Victims of Democracy: Malcolm X and the Black Revolution.* New York: Guilford, 1993.

Wood, Joe, ed. *Malcolm X: In Our Own Image.* New York: Anchor Books, 1992.


**mammy stereotype** Even before her generally unwilling arrival on American shores, the African woman was beset with negative and pernicious rhetoric regarding the nature of her character. The African-American woman has suffered from societal representations as alternately bestial, primitive, hypersexual, and emotional. This depiction continues into the 20th century and has been the cornerstone of characterizations of African-American women as depicted in various media. These depictions center on the issue of sexuality. The sexualized black woman generally appears in American films as victimized and powerless, an antecedent to the literary tragic mulatto or as hypersexual and out of control, fulfilling the persistent image of the wild and unrestrained black woman.

Perhaps one of the most famous lines from the film *Gone With the Wind* (1939) is Mammy's reprimand of Scarlett O'Hara when Scarlett insists that she will go to Atlanta to meet Ashley as he visits his wife Melanie on his furlough from the war. Mammy angrily tells Scarlett that she will "be sitting there jes lak a *spider*." Despite Mammy's advice and to the horror of Atlanta Confederate society, Scarlett journeys to Atlanta to be by Ashley's side. What this iconographic moment in film history reveals are the classic representations of the mammy stereotype. The scene from *Gone With the Wind* illustrates the role cinematic mammies often play as the moral guardians of their white female charges.

In many Hollywood films, the mammy character frequently functions as a moral arbiter and barometer for the white woman protagonist. One of Mammy's most frequently repeated reprimands of Scarlett in *Gone With the Wind* is, "'taint fittin.' It just ain't fittin.'" Throughout the film, Mammy chastises Scarlett with this refrain when Scarlett's behavior transgresses the boundaries of Mammy's superior moral code. Hattie McDaniel's powerful performance in *Gone With the Wind* helped to establish Mammy's primary characteristics in the public consciousness.

Like the several cosmetic changes Proctor & Gamble has made in the appearance of its trademark pancake symbol Aunt Jemima, the mammy stereotype has undergone a similar and equally superficial evolution. By excavating the roots of the mammy stereotype, the source of many contemporary depictions of African-American women becomes evident. African-American women writers such as Toni Morrison counter the mammy stereotype in their work by presenting female characters who have dimension and complexity. Alice Walker rewrites and gives multidimensionality to the stereotype of the mammy by creating African-American female characters who are nurturing but have other characteristics and qualities as well. Sofia in *The Color Purple* may be an example of such a character.

### FURTHER READING


Alexander, Elizabeth. *Black Interior: Essays.* Saint Paul, Minn.: Graywolf Press, 2004.

Brody, Jennifer DeVere. *Impossible Purities: Blackness, Femininity, and Victorian Culture.* Durham, N.C.: Duke University Press, 1998.

Campbell, Cathy. "A Battered Woman Rises: Aunt Jemima's Corporate Makeover." *Village Voice* 7 (November 1989): 45–46.

Cleage, Pearl. "Hairpiece." *African American Review* 27 (1993): 37–41.

Collins, Patricia Hill. "Get Your Freak On: Sex, Babies, and Images of Black Femininity." In *Black Sexual Politics: African Americans, Gender and the New Racism.* New York: Routledge, 2004, 119–148.

Craig, Maxine Leeds. *Ain't I a Beauty Queen?: Black Women, Beauty, and the Politics of Race.* New York: Oxford University Press, 2002.

Gilman, Sander. "Black Bodies, White Bodies: Toward an Iconography of Female Sexuality in Late Nineteenth-Century Art, Medicine, and Literature." In *Race, Writing, and Difference,* edited by Henry Louis Gates, Jr. Chicago: University of Chicago Press, 1985.

Haug, Kate. "Myth and Matriarchy: An Analysis of the Mammy Stereotype." In *Dirt and Domesticity: Constructions of the Feminine.* New York: Whitney Museum of American Art, 1992.

hooks, bell. *Black Looks: Race and Representation.* Boston: South End Press, 1992.

———. *Yearning: Race, Gender, and Cultural Politics.* Boston: South End Press, 1990.

Jones, Lisa. *Bulletproof Diva: Tales of Race, Sex and Hair.* New York: Doubleday, 1994.

Mitchell, Margaret. *Gone with the Wind.* New York: Macmillan, 1939.

Rose, Tricia. "Black Texts/Black Contexts." In *Black Popular Culture: A Project by Michele Wallace,* edited by Gina Dent. Seattle: Bay Press, 1992.


**Mbeles** Alice Walker invented a warrior tribe called the *mbeles* in her novel *The Color Purple.* The fictional tribe is comprised of many other smaller groups. The literary critic Linda Selzer has argued that the Mbeles' connection, manifesting as they do through racial rather than biological ties, reveals the power of a bond grounded in a shared sense of oppression rather than by blood. The common denominator that binds the Mbeles is their unified resistance to white missionary work and colonization. The Mbeles also appear in Walker's novel *Possessing the Secret of Joy*.

### FURTHER READING

Selzer, Linda. "Race and Domesticity in *The Color Purple*." *African American Review* 29, no. 1 (Spring 1995): 67–82.

**medium** A medium—also called a psychic or spirit medium—is reputed to be an intermediary between this world and the spirits of the dead. Virtually all cultures have mediums, some of whom play a central role in certain religious traditions, such as voodoo, Umbanda, and various other forms of African and African diasporic traditions. In these and other traditional—or animist—societies, including Native American tribes, the role of medium was often undertaken by a shaman. The reputed skills of mediums are less accepted in current Western and industrialized societies, but mediumship gained particular popularity in the United States during the 19th century in a movement known as Spiritualism. Much of this tradition employed séances, a ritual in which a generally small group of people engaged a medium to help them contact the spirits of dead relatives and friends. Séances are still conducted today, but for many people who are uncertain about the validity of contact between the living and spirit worlds, mediums more often provide a form of popular entertainment—some, on occasion, even hosting their own television programs.

Alice Walker employs many mediums as characters throughout her canon, including Irene from her novel *By the Light of My Father's Smile* (1998).

*See also* BLACK ELK.

### FURTHER READING

Boa, Frantz. *The Way of the Dream: Conversations on Jungian Dream Interpretation with Marie-Louise von Franz*. Boston: Shambala, 1994.

Black Elk. *Black Elk Speaks: Being the Life Story of a Holy Man of the Oglala Sioux*. New York: Bison Books Corporation, 2000.

Blakemore, Colin. *Mechanics of the Mind*. Cambridge: Cambridge University Press, 1977.

Capra, Frito. *The Tao of Physics*. Toronto: Bantam Books, 1988.

Chewing, Tom. *Dictionary of Symbols*. London: Torsions, 1982.

Cleary, T., trans. *The Taoist I Ching*. Boston: Shambala, 1982.

Drury, Nevill. *The Elements of Human Potential*. Longmead, Dorset, Eng.: Element Books, 1989.

Evans, Hilary. *Alternate States of Consciousness: Unself, Overself, and Superself*. Wellingborough, Northamptonshire, Eng.: Aquarian Press, 1989.

Faraday, Ann. *Dream Power—The Use of Dreams in Everyday Life*. London: Pan, 1972.

Gackenbach, Jayne. *Control Your Dreams*. New York: HarperCollins, 1989.

Garfield, Patricia. *Creative Dreaming: A Revolutionary Approach to Increased Self-Awareness*. Aylesbury, Eng.: Futura Publications, 1976.

Garrett, Eileen J. *Many Voices*. New York: Putnams, 1968.

Jung, Carl Gustave. *Man and His Symbols*. Garden City, N.Y.: Doubleday, 1964.

Kelzer, Kenneth. *The Sun and the Shadow: My Experiment with Lucid Dreaming*. New York: A.R.E. Press, 1987.

Laberge, Stephen. *Lucid Dreaming*. New York: Ballantine Books, 1998.

Lilly, John C. *The Centre of the Cyclone: An Autobiography of Inner Space*. New York: Julian Press, 1985.

Mansfield, Victor. *Synchronicity, Science and Soul-Making*. Chicago: Open Court Publishing 1985.

Moss, Robert. *Conscious Dreaming: A Spiritual Path for Everyday Life*. New York: Crown Pub., 1996.

Opie, Iona. *Oxford Dictionary of Superstitions*. Oxford: Oxford University Press, 1989.

Taylor, Jeremy. *Where People Fly and Water Runs Uphill: Using Dreams to Tap the Wisdom of the Unconscious*. New York: Warner Books, 1993.

Tillich, Paul. *The Courage to Be*. New Haven, Conn.: Yale University Press, 2000.

———. *Morality and Beyond*. Westminster: John Knox Press, 1995.

Wilhelm, Hellmut. *The I Ching or Book of Changes*. London: Routledge and Kegan Paul Ltd., 1951.

**Medusa** In Greek mythology, Medusa is a female Gorgon, a deadly monster who, along with her two sisters, Euryale and Stheno, is feared for her ability to turn onlookers to stone. The sisters are isolated on an island, and Medusa is the only mortal Gorgon.

The common Greek myth is that Perseus yearned for an appropriate gift to celebrate the wedding of his mother to Polydectes. He decided that killing and beheading a Gorgon would be a noble gift for Polydectes and embarked on a lengthy journey to obtain proper tools for killing one. Through the god Hermes and the goddess Athena's guidance and with the assistance of Nymphs, he obtained winged sandals, a magic wallet (kibsis), and a magic cap (of Hades) that would protect him. After arriving at the island, he cut Medusa's throat, seized her head, and placed it in the wallet; the Gorgons awoke and attempted to catch him, but he was invisible.

Among the variations on the Medusa myth are interpretations that she was a cursed beauty killed for comparing herself to greater beauties; an African queen who stood up to Perseus and was murdered; and the Gorgons' protector whose appearances masked a plethora of unique female secrets. These narratives have enabled Medusa to endure as a symbol of female power and resistance. One feminist take on the myth posits that the Gorgons were a tribe of black Amazons ridiculed by the Greeks. These more recent interpretations of the myth are thought to have partially informed Alice Walker's incorporation of Medusa into *The Temple of My Familiar.*

### FURTHER READING

DuBois, Paige. *Sewing the Body: Psychoanalysis and Ancient Representations of Women.* Chicago: University of Chicago Press, 1988.

Garber, Marjorie, and Nancy J. Vickers, eds. *The Medusa Reader.* New York: Routledge, 2000.

Goodrich, Norma Lorne. *Priestesses.* New York: Harper Perennial, 1989.

Hamilton, Edith. *Mythology: Timeless Tales of Gods and Heroes.* New York: Meridian, 1989.

Reeder, Ellen D. *Pandora: Women in Classical Greece.* Princeton, N.J.: Princeton University Press, 1995.

Wilk, Stephan R. *Medusa: Solving the Mystery of the Gorgon.* New York: Oxford University Press, 1999.

**Meyjes, Menno** (1954– ) Menno Meyjes is a screenwriter and director who was born in the Netherlands and immigrated to the United States with his parents in 1972. After studying at the Art Institute of California, Meyjes embarked upon a career as a writer, and he spent some time working in television. His breakthrough writing project was his screenplay adaptation of Alice Walker's novel *The Color Purple.* The screenplay earned Meyjes an Academy Award nomination and launched his career as a screenplay writer. Among his other credits are the screenplays for two other STEVEN SPIELBERG films, *Empire of the Sun* (1987) and *Indiana Jones and the Last Crusade* (1989). Meyjes also wrote the screenplay for the hit film *Lionheart* (1989).

Currently, Meyjes works as a writer/director.

### FURTHER READING

Bobo, Jacqueline. "The Color Purple: Black Women as Cultural Readers." In *Female Spectators: Looking at Film and Television,* edited by Deidre Pribram: 90–109. London: Verso, 1988.

———. "Reading through the Text: The Black Woman as Audience." In *Black American Cinema,* edited by Manthia Diawara, 272–287. New York: Routledge, 1993.

———. "Sifting through the Controversy: Reading *The Color Purple.*" *Callaloo: A Journal of African-American and African Arts and Letters* 2 (Spring 1989): 332–342.

Butler, C. B. "The *Color Purple* Controversy—Black Woman Spectatorship." *Wide Angle: A Quarterly Journal of Film History Theory And Criticism* 13 (1999): 62–69.

Collins, Glenn. "*The Color Purple.*" *New York Times,* 15 December 1985, T1.

Digby, Joan. "From Walker to Spielberg: Transformations of *The Color Purple.*" In *Novel Images: Literature in Performance,* edited by Peter Reynolds, 157–174. London: Routledge, 1993.

Dole, Carol M. "The Return of the Father in Spielberg's *The Color Purple.*" *Literature-Film Quarterly* 24 (January 1996): 12–17.

Fitzsimmons, Kate. "Go Ask Alice: Alice Walker Talks about *The Color Purple* 10 Years Later." *San Francisco Review of Books* 21 (March–April 1996).

Gilliam, Dorothy. "*The Color Purple* Not as Simple as Black or White." *Washington Post,* 23 December, 1985, p. B3.

"Menno Meyjes." Internet Movie Database. Available online. URL: http://www.imdb.com/name/nm0583675/. Accessed October 15, 2009.

Milloy, Courtland. "A 'Purple' Rage over a Rip-off," *Washington Post,* 24 December 1985, B3.

Shipp, E. R. "Blacks in Heated Debate over *The Color Purple.*" *New York Times,* 27 January 1986, pp. A11, A13.

Walker, Alice. "*The Color Purple.*" Ms. 15 (November 1986): 32–25.

———. *The Same River Twice: Honoring the Difficult: A Meditation on Life, Spirit, Art, and the Making of the Film, The Color Purple, Ten Years Later.* New York: Scribner, 1996.

**Monrovia, Liberia** Monrovia is the capital of the West African nation of Liberia. A port city on the Atlantic Ocean, Monrovia was founded in 1822 and named after the American president James Monroe, who helped promote the repatriation of African Americans to Africa—including emancipated slaves and those had not been born into slavery. At this time, slavery was still part of the economic system in the American South. An organization called the American Colonization Society was created by whites, and particularly supported by white southerners, who feared a violent revolt by a population of freed slaves within the United States. The area designated for Monrovia was already inhabited by African tribes, predominantly the Krus. Today these indigenous people are citizens of Liberia, but the descendants of the original African-American population dominate the city's politics and businesses.

Monrovia, and the whole nation of Liberia, was rent by a civil war, the first phase from 1989 to 1996, the second phase from 1999 to 2003. Resulting in hundreds of thousands of deaths, the conflicts were due partly to tribal conflicts and partly to a struggle for democracy. A siege of the city in 2003 left thousands of people homeless and otherwise displaced. Today, the city, and the nation, are rebuilding under a democratic government.

In *The Color Purple* the character Nettie writes a letter to Celie informing her of a missionary stop in Monrovia and noting that Liberia is an African country founded by ex-slaves.

## FURTHER READING

Barnes, Kenneth. *Journey of Hope: The Back-to-Africa Movement in Arkansas in the Late 1800s* Chapel Hill: University of North Carolina Press, 2004.

Burin, Eric. *Slavery and the Peculiar Solution: A History of the American Colonization Society.* Gainesville: University Press of Florida, 2005.

Campbell, Penelope. *Maryland in Liberia: The Maryland State Colonization Society, 1831–1857.* Urbana: University of Illinois Press, 1971.

Cassell, C. Abayomi. *Liberia: History of the First African Republic.* New York: Irvington, 1983.

Clegg, Claude A. III. *The Price of Liberty: African Americans and the Making of Liberia.* Chapel Hill: University of North Carolina Press, 2004.

Ellis, Stephen. "Liberia 1989–1994, A Study of Ethnic and Spiritual Violence." *African Affairs* 94 (1995): 165–197.

Hall, Richard. *On Afric's Shore: A History of Maryland in Liberia, 1834–1857.* Baltimore: Maryland Historical Society, 2003.

Huffman, Alan. *Mississippi in Africa: The Saga of the Slaves of Prospect Hill Plantation and their Legacy in Liberia Today.* New York: Gotham Books, 2004.

Shick, Tom. *Behold the Promised Land: A History of Afro-American Settler Society in Nineteenth-Century Liberia.* Baltimore: Johns Hopkins University Press, 1980.

Staudenraus, Phillip. *The African Colonization Movement, 1816–1865.* New York: Columbia University Press, 1961.

**Moors** Alice Walker refers to the Moors and their influences throughout her work. The term *Moors* refers to various peoples who have traditionally inhabited northern Africa, up to and including much of the Mediterranean coast. The term does not refer to a singular ethnic group but to a collection of peoples who still inhabit this region. These ethnic groups include Berbers, Arabs, and black Africans. The group predates Islam, but the Moors were converted and became Muslims in the seventh century. In turn, they spread Islam across North Africa and in 711, they crossed the Strait of Gibraltar to conquer the Iberian Peninsula. They later crossed the Pyrenees into France, but in 732, they were defeated by Charles Martel at the Battle of Poitiers.

Nonetheless, they remained rulers in Spain and Portugal, establishing a caliphate under the Umayyad dynasty at Cordoba, which was superseded by the Almoravids in the 11th century. They, in turn, were defeated by the Almohads. These were all Muslim caliphates, but control of the Iberian Peninsula by Muslims was never total, and Christian forces began making significant returns as early as 1085 with the recovery of Toledo by Alfonso VI.

Over the next few centuries, Moorish kingdoms fell to Christian forces, with the process of re-Christianization of Spain and Portugal largely completed in 1492, when King Ferdinand and Queen Isabella recovered Granada. Spain suffered a cultural decline after the expulsion of the Moors, but their legacy in Iberia remained. During their rule, the Moors made Spain and Portugal the center of philosophy, science, medicine, art, and architecture. Because of an open atmosphere to new ideas, their universities became important centers of learning not only for Muslims but also for Christian and Jewish thinkers. Spain and Portugal have recently made a more concerted effort to acknowledge their Moorish inheritance, which can be seen most dramatically in much surviving Islamic architecture found in the once-Moorish regions of the Iberian Peninsula.

### FURTHER READING

Banjoko, Adisa Sebaku. "Moor Reflections." *4080* 2, no. 2 (February 1994): 44–45.

Brunson, James E., and Runoko Rashidi. "The Moors in Antiquity." In *Golden Age of the Moor,* edited by Ivan Van Sertima, 27–84. New Brunswick, N.J.: Transaction Press, 1992.

Fletcher, Richard. *Moorish Spain.* New York: Henry Holt, 1992.

Jackson, John G. "The Empire of the Moors." In *Golden Age of the Moor,* edited by Ivan Van Sertima, 85–92. New Brunswick, N.J.: Transaction Press, 1992.

Pimienta-Bey, Jose V. "Moorish Spain: Academic Source and Foundation for the Rise and Success of Western European Universities in the Middle Ages." In *Golden Age of the Moor,* edited by Ivan Van Sertima, 182–247. New Brunswick, N.J.: Transaction Press, 1992.

Rashidi, Runoko. "The Expulsion from Spain and the Dispersal of the Moors." *The Knowledge Broker* (January 1995): 2.

———. "The Moorish Conquest of Europe." *The Knowledge Broker* (November 1995): 2, 6.

Ravell, James. "An Annotated Bibliography of the Moors: 711–1492 A.D." In *Golden Age of the Moor,* edited by Ivan Van Sertima, 407–454. New Brunswick, N.J.: Transaction Press, 1992.

Read, Jan. *The Moors in Spain and Portugal.* London: Faber and Faber, 1974.

Reynolds, Dana. "The African Heritage and Ethnology of the Moors: Background to the Emergence of Early Berber and Arab Peoples, from Prehistory to the Islamic Dynasties." In *Golden Age of the Moor,* edited by Ivan Van Sertima, 93–150. New Brunswick, N.J.: Transaction Press, 1992.

Van Sertima, Ivan. "The African Presence in Early Europe: The Definitional Problem." In *African Presence in Early Europe,* edited by Ivan Van Sertima, 134–143. New Brunswick, N.J.: Transaction Press, 1985.

———, ed. *Golden Age of the Moor.* New Brunswick, N.J.: Transaction Press, 1992.

———. "The Moor in Africa and Europe: Origins and Definitions." In *Golden Age of the Moor,* edited by Ivan Van Sertima, 1–8. New Brunswick, N.J.: Transaction Press, 1992.

**Motherpeace tarot deck** After her marriage to MELVYN LEVENTHAL ended, Alice Walker reevaluated her spirituality and studied meditation and various spiritual practices, including tarot cards. Tarot cards date back at least to 14th-century medieval Europe. While Walker was a fellow at the Radcliffe Institute during the 1970s, the poet Fanny Howe became her tarot card reader.

Walker's interest in tarot cards was reinvigorated when she discovered the Motherpeace tarot deck, a version created by the renegade feminists and scholars Karen Vogel and Vicki Noble. Since her first experience with the Motherpeace deck, struck by its originality, beauty, and power, Walker has used them as a source for her own readings as well as the readings she gives. During the filming of *The Color Purple,* Walker provided Motherpeace tarot card readings for the cast and crew during breaks in shooting.

### FURTHER READING

Kaplan, Stuart R. *The Encyclopedia of Tarot.* New York: U.S. Games Systems, 1978.

*Motherpeace Tarot.* Available online. URL: http://www.motherpeace.com. Accessed February 28, 2009.

Noble, Vicki. *Motherpeace.* New York: Harper and Row, 1983.

———. *Rituals and Practices with the Motherpeace Tarot.* Rochester, Vt.: Bear and Co., 2003.

Schnall, Marianne. "Conversation with Alice Walker." Available online. URL: http://www.feminist.com/resources/artspeech/interviews/alicewalker.html. Accessed February 28, 2009.

Walker, Barbara G. *The Secrets of the Tarot.* New York: Harper and Row, 1984.

White, Evelyn C. *Alice Walker: A Life.* New York: W. W. Norton and Company, 2004.

***Ms.* magazine** *Ms.* was the first U.S.-based magazine fully devoted to contemporary issues pertaining to women, including abortion access, legislative reform, and gender-based oppression. Through its publication, *Ms.* has increased public awareness of issues such as domestic violence, sexual harassment, and exploitation.

Originally a monthly magazine, *Ms.* has been published quarterly since 1988. It has been published by the Feminist Majority Foundation since 2001.

*Ms.* was cofounded by feminist activists GLORIA STEINEM and Joanne Edgar and originally appeared as an insert in a 1971 issue of *New York* magazine. In July 1972, the first issue of *Ms.* was published. Despite media skepticism, *Ms.* was an instant commercial success, with sales and subscription orders exceeding initial expectations.

Alice Walker's writing caught Joanne Edgar's attention, and *Ms.* published her short story "Roselily" in its August 1972 issue. In 1974, after Walker and her husband MELVYN LEVENTHAL moved to New York City, Steinem offered Walker a contributing editor position. Walker first appeared on its masthead in December 1974. As a contributing editor, Walker routinely pointed readers toward under-recognized authors, including Florence Anthony (later known as Ai), Margaret Atwood, Mary Gordon, Ntozage Shange, and Ann Allen Shockley. Among Walker's personal triumphs at the magazine were the articles "In Search of Zora Neale Hurston," about her pilgrimage to ZORA NEALE HURSTON's gravesite, and Steinem's June 1982 cover story "Do You Know This Woman? She Knows You: A Profile of Alice Walker."

### FURTHER READING

Bean, Kellie. *Post-Backlash Feminism: Women and the Media since Reagan-Bush.* Jefferson, N.C.: McFarland and Company, 2007.

Caroli, Betty Boyd. *First Ladies.* New York: Oxford University Press, 1987.

Delsman, Mary A. *Everything You Need to Know about ERA.* Riverside, Calif.: Meranza Press, 1975.

Faludi, Susan. *Backlash: The Undeclared War against American Women.* New York: Crown Publishers, 1991.

Farrell, Amy Erdman. *Yours in Sisterhood:* Ms. *Magazine and the Promise of Popular Feminism.* Chapel Hill: University of North Carolina Press, 1998.

Friedan, Betty. *It Changed My Life: Writings on the Women's Movement.* New York: Random House, 1976.

Hymowitz, Carol, and Michaele Weissman. *A History of Women in America.* New York: Bantam Books, 1978.

Levine, Suzanne, and Harriet, Lyons. *The Decade of Women: A* Ms. *History of the Seventies in Words and Pictures.* New York: Putnam, 1980.

Mills, Kay. *A Place in the News: From the Women's Pages to the Front Page.* Dodd Mead and Co., 1988.

Ms. Magazine. "Her Story: 1971–Present." Available online. URL: http://www.msmagazine.com/about.asp. Accessed February 28, 2009.

O'Neill, Lois Decker. *The Women's Book of World Records and Achievements.* New York: DeCapo Press, 1983.

Robertson, Nan. *The Girls in the Balcony: Women, Men and the New York Times.* New York: Random House, 1992.

Thom, Mary. *Inside* Ms.*: 25 Years of the Magazine and the Feminist Movement.* New York: Henry Holt, 1997.

White, Evelyn C. *Alice Walker: A Life.* New York: W. W. Norton and Company, 2004.

**mudra** A mudra, which can be translated as "symbol," is one of many gestures in Hindu and Buddhist dance, meditation, and ritual. Mudras can involve the entire body but focus mostly on the hands and fingers. These gestures symbolize a comprehensive range of concepts in the spiritual quest, including those of emotion, social obligation, and religious practice. Specific examples include gestures of peace, kindness, meditation, enlightenment, charity, compassion, veneration, touching the earth, and moments from the Buddha's life, but the number of mudras in the various traditions extends into the hundreds. The gestures, however, go beyond the purely symbolic in that they are intended to produce, in conjunction with a practice such as yoga or mantra recitation, positive energies that help the practitioner achieve greater health, calm, and spiritual growth.

Alice Walker makes use of mudras in her spiritual practices and writings.

### FURTHER READING

Arun Kumar, Anjani. *Compositions for Bharathanatyam: A Soulful Worship of the Divine.* Bombay: Bharatiya Vidya Bhavan, 1992.

Bhavnani, Enakshi. *The Dance in India.* Bombay: Taraporevala Sons and Co., 1965.

Bunce, Fredrick W. *Mudras in Buddhist and Hindu Practices: An Iconographic Consideration.* London: D. K. Printworld, 2009.

Samson, Leela. *Rhythm in Joy: Classical Indian Dance Traditions.* New Delhi: Lustre Print Madia Pvt. Ltd., 1987.

**National Association for the Advancement of Colored People (NAACP)** The National Association for the Advancement of Colored People (NAACP) is the oldest and largest civil rights organization in the United States. It was founded in 1909 by a large group of activists, including W. E. B. DuBois, Ida Wells Barnett, Henry Moskowitz, Mary White Ovington, and William English Walling. The organization was—and is—dedicated to securing political, educational, social, and economic parity for African Americans. Its list of accomplishments throughout the decades is long and is only touched upon here.

Much of the motivation for starting the organization was the Jim Crow laws of the South, which legalized racial discrimination. In its first years, these were the laws that NAACP first tackled, bringing suits in court to overturn legislation that promoted racial segregation.

The NAACP also organized opposition to President Woodrow Wilson's introduction of racial segregation in federal policy, and it helped win the right of African Americans to serve as officers in World War I. As a result, hundreds of African Americans were commissioned as officers, and 700,000 African Americans registered for the draft. Shortly after, the NAACP organized a nationwide protest against D. W. Griffith's *Birth of a Nation,* a film that justified the Ku Klux Klan.

After the World War I, the NAACP targeted the lynching of African Americans, and in 1919, the organization also investigated the Elaine Race Riot in which up to 200 black tenant farmers were killed by white vigilantes and federal troops. The killings had been the response after a white man was killed in a sheriff's interruption of a sharecroppers' union meeting.

After World War II, the NAACP continued in its efforts against segregation. In the late 1940s, it pressed for desegregation of the armed forces, which they accomplished by 1948, and in 1954, it sued for school desegregation in *Brown v. Board of Education of Topeka, Kansas.*

One of the NAACP's general counsels in the 1950s and 1960s was Thurgood Marshall, who went on to become, in 1967, the U.S. Supreme Court's first African-American justice. The NAACP is a prominent feature in Alice Walker's nonfiction and fiction, most notably in her novel *Meridian.*

*See also* Civil Rights movement.

### FURTHER READING

Finch, Minnie. *The NAACP: Its Fight for Justice.* Lanham, Md.: Scarecrow Press, 1981.

Harris, Jacqueline L. *History and Achievements of the NAACP.* The African American Experience. New York: F. Watts, 1992.

NAACP Legal Defense and Educational Fund. *It's Not the Distance, "It's the Niggers."* New York: NAACP Legal Defense and Educational Fund, Division of Legal Information and Community Service, 1972.

St. James, Warren D. *NAACP: Triumphs of a Pressure Group, Nineteen Hundred and Nine thru Nineteen Hundred and Eighty.* New York: Exposition Press, 1980.

Zangrando, Robert L. *The NAACP Crusade against Lynching, 1909–1950.* Philadelphia: Temple University Press, 1980.

**Norman, Marsha (Marsha Williams)** (1947– ) Marsha Norman is an American playwright, novelist, and screenwriter, perhaps best known for her 1983 Pulitzer Prize–winning play *'night, Mother.* She also wrote lyrics for *The Secret Garden,* for which she won a Tony Award and a Drama Desk Award, and *The Red Shoes,* plus the book for the musical adaptation of Alice Walker's *The Color Purple.* Originally staged at Atlanta's Alliance Theatre in 2004, Norman's adaptation of the Walker novel premiered on Broadway in 2005. It was directed by Gary Griffin and coproduced by OPRAH WINFREY, QUINCY JONES, and SCOTT SANDERS. Music and lyrics were written by Brenda Russell, Allee Willis, and Stephen Bray. Donald Byrd did the choreography. The musical earned 11 2006 Tony Award nominations—including one for Norman's book—and closed on Broadway in 2008 after a profitable run.

### FURTHER READING

Ginter-Brown, Linda. *Marsha Norman: A Casebook.* New York: Garland Publishers, 1996.

Norman, Marsha. *'night, Mother: A Play.* New York: Hill and Wang, 1983.

———. *Third and Oak: The Laundromat: A Play in One Act.* New York: Dramatist Play Service, 1980.

**Nzinga Mbande (Queen Nzinga, Queen Anne)** (ca. 1582–1663) Nzinga Mbande, or Queen Nzinga (queen of Ndongo and Matamba), was an African ruler during the 17th century, known today for having challenged the Portuguese slave trade in what is now Angola. She ruled over two kingdoms, Ndongo and Matamba, both of which were of the Mbundu people. Allying herself with the Dutch as part of her strategy to counter the Portuguese, Nzinga succeeded for 30 years in keeping the Portuguese from invading her kingdoms and pursuing the slave trade. Aside from her alliance with the Dutch, she used various other methods to challenge the Portuguese, such as organizing a resistance army, often leading them herself into battle; encouraging slaves to revolt; and, eventually, engaging in diplomacy, but from a position of power. In 1648, the Portuguese had gained enough ground to force Nzinga into negotiations, which she stretched out to six years. They eventually reached a compromise, but it was not until her death at the age of 82 that the Portuguese were able to fully press their advantages. Though they were finally able to invade the kingdoms and open the region to the capture of slaves, Nzinga's legacy is that of a critical figure in Africa's resistance to the slave trade.

Alice Walker refers to Nzinga in several of her novels but is most explicit in her reference to her in *Possessing the Secret of Joy.*

### FURTHER READING

Clark, John Henrick. "African Warrior Queens." In *Black Women in Antiquity,* edited by Ivan Van Sertima. New Brunswick, N.J.: Transaction Books, 1988.

Heywood, Linda, and John K. Thornton. *Central Africans, Atlantic Creoles, and the Making of the Americas, 1580–1660.* Cambridge: Cambridge University Press, 2007.

Mazrui, Elizabeth Orchardson. *Nzinga, the Warrior Queen.* Nairobi, Kenya: Jomo Kenyatta Foundation, 2006.

McKissack, Patricia. *Nzingha: Warrior Queen of Matamba, Angola, Africa, 1595.* New York: Scholastic, 2000.

Van Sertima, Ivan, ed. *Black Women in Antiquity.* New Brunswick, N.J.: Transaction Books, 1990.

**O'Connor, Flannery** (1925–1964) Born in Savannah, Georgia, the quintessential southern writer Flannery O'Connor is best known for her often grotesque and comic depictions of the South. Literary critics and historians frequently list O'Connor among the most accomplished American writers of southern life, alongside William Faulkner, ZORA NEALE HURSTON, Carson McCullers, and Eudora Welty.

O'Connor graduated from Georgia State College for Women and studied creative writing at the University of Iowa. Her published work includes the short story collections *A Good Man Is Hard to Find* (1955) and *Everything That Rises Must Converge* (1965) and the novels *Wise Blood* (1952) and *The Violent Bear It Away* (1960). O'Connor died prematurely after a bout with lupus in 1964.

Alice Walker frequently cites O'Connor as a significant influence on her writing. She has praised O'Connor's economical diction, critical view of southern sentimentality, and ability to write fully developed black characters. In the 1975 MS. MAGAZINE essay "Beyond the Peacock: The Reconstruction of Flannery O'Connor," Walker also addressed the ways in which O'Connor's racial and economic status influenced her literary success. Several critics link Walker's writing directly to O'Connor's and describe both women as essential components of the United States's rich southern literary heritage.

### FURTHER READING

Cash, Jean W. *Flannery O'Connor: A Life.* Knoxville: University of Tennessee Press, 2002.

Farmer, David. *Flannery O'Connor: A Descriptive Bibliography.* New York: Garland, 1981.

Johansen, Ruthann K. *The Narrative Secret of Flannery O'Connor: The Trickster as Interpreter.* Tuscaloosa: University of Alabama Press, 1995.

O'Brien, John. "Alice Walker: An Interview." In *Alice Walker: Critical Perspectives Past and Present,* edited by Henry Louis Gates, Jr., and Kwame Anthony Appiah, 326–346. New York: Amistad, 1993.

O'Connor, Flannery. *Collected Works.* New York: Viking Press, 1988.

———. *The Complete Stories.* New York: Farrar, Straus and Giroux, 1971.

———. *Everything That Rises Must Converge.* New York: Farrar, Straus and Cudahy, 1965.

———. *A Good Man Is Hard to Find, and Other Stories.* New York: Harcourt, 1955.

———. *The Habit of Being.* New York: Farrar, Straus and Giroux, 1979.

———. *Mystery and Manners: Occasional Prose.* New York: Farrar, Straus and Giroux, 1969.

———. *The Presence of Grace, and Other Book Reviews.* Athens: University of Georgia Press, 1983.

———. *The Violent Bear It Away.* New York: Farrar, Straus and Giroux, 1960.

———. *Wise Blood.* New York: Harcourt, 1952.

Orvell, Miles. *Flannery O'Connor: An Introduction.* Jackson: University Press of Mississippi, 1991.

Scott, R. Neil. *Flannery O'Connor: An Annotated Reference Guide to Criticism.* Milledgeville, Ga.: Timberlane, 2002.

Whitt, Margaret E. *Flannery O'Connor.* Columbia: University of South Carolina Press, 1997.

**Parmar, Pratibha** (1955– ) London-based Pratibha Parmar is a well-known filmmaker and producer and the author of various political documentaries, music videos, and essays on cinema. Parmar's primary themes include issues facing women, minorities, gays, and lesbians. She has many award-winning films to her credit, starting with her debut in 1983 with the documentary short *Emergence.* In 1993, Parmar collaborated with Alice Walker on *Warrior Marks: Female Genital Mutilation and the Sexual Blinding of Women,* a 1993 documentary about the ritualistic mutilation of the female genitals in various parts of the world, primarily in Africa and the Middle East (*see* FEMALE GENITAL MUTILATION. In addition to coproducing the film, the two coauthored a companion book to the film.

Born in Nairobi, Kenya, to parents of East Indian heritage, Parmar and her family moved to England in 1967, but she has retained a particular interest in the issues facing women of South Asian heritage. Throughout her life, she has been an activist for social causes not only through her films but through her work as editor and publisher of works by Asian and African-Caribbean women.

### FURTHER READING

Foster, Gwendolyn Audrey. *Women Filmmakers of the African and Asian Diaspora.* Carbondale: Southern Illinois University Press, 1997.

Internet Movie Database. "Pratibha Parmar." Available online. URL: http://www.imdb.com/name/nm0663101/. Accessed February 28, 2009.

Kaplan, Ann. "'Can One Know the Other?': The Ambivalence of Post Colonialism in *Chocolat, Warrior Marks* and *Mississippi Masala*." In *Looking for the Other: Feminism, Film and the Imperial Gaze.* New York: Routledge, 1997.

Lauret, Maria. *Alice Walker.* New York: St. Martin's Press, 2000.

Parmar, Pratibha. "Asian Women—Race, Class and Culture." In *The Empire Strikes Back: Race and Racism in 70s Britain.* London: Hutchinson, 1982.

———. "Challenging Imperial Feminism with Valerie Amos." In *Feminism and Race.* Oxford: Oxford University Press, 2000.

———. "Perverse Politics." *Feminist Review,* no. 34 (1991).

———. *The Politics of Articulation in Identity: Community, Culture, Difference.* Lawrence and Wishart, 1990.

Walker, Alice, and Pratibha Parmar. *Warrior Marks: Female Genital Mutilation and the Sexual Blinding of Women.* New York: Harcourt Brace, 1993.

White, Evelyn C. *Alice Walker: A Life.* New York: W. W. Norton and Company, 2004.

**Pippin, Horace** (1888–1946) Horace Pippin is a famous African-American folk painter who gained national attention in the late 1930s for his remarkable painting technique and for his vivid depictions of African Americans. The self-taught artist was born in West Chester, Pennsylvania, and began painting after serving in World War I. After an arm injury, Pippin returned to the United States and began experimenting with wood-carving techniques and oil painting. While displaying his work in various Pennsylvania exhibitions in the late 1930s, he aroused the interest and attention of various patrons, and his work gained prominence and acceptance in some national galleries. Among his most notable works are *The Domino Players, Christmas Morning, Breakfast,* and *The End of the War: Starting Home.* Walker refers to Pippin throughout her writing, particularly in *Possessing the Secret of Joy.*

### FURTHER READING

Bearden, Romare. *Horace Pippin: The Phillips Collection.* Washington: Phillips Collection, 1976.

ExplorePAhistory.com. "Horace Pippin." Available online. URL: http://www.explorepahistory.com/hmarker.php?markerId=618. Accessed February 22, 2009.

National Gallery of Art Classroom. "Horace Pippin." Available online. URL: http://www.nga.gov/education/classroom/counting_on_art/bio_pippin.shtm. Accessed February 22, 2009.

Rodman, Selden, and Carole Cleaver. *Horace Pippin; The Artist as a Black American.* Garden City, N.Y.: Doubleday, 1972.

Stein, Judith. *I Tell My Heart: The Art of Horace Pippin.* New York: Pennsylvania Academy of the Fine Arts, 1993.

West, Cornel. "Horace Pippin's Challenge to Art Criticism." In *The Cornel West Reader,* 55–66. New York: Basic Civitas Books, 1999.

**Presley, Elvis** (1935–1977) Historically regarded as the "King of Rock and Roll," Elvis Presley was the most commercially successful solo singer of the post–World War II era. Born on January 8, 1935, in Tupelo, Mississippi, he grew up playing the guitar and was influenced by gospel, country, and BLUES music. From 1953 to 1956, he recorded for Memphis's Sun Records, but signing with RCA Records in 1956 catapulted him to national and international stardom as a singer, television performer, and film actor.

The novelty of a white singer who successfully fused diverse strands of American popular music made Presley a teenage icon. He initially faced critical resistance from adults because many felt he had an overly sexualized image, but with his rise in popularity, opposition to Presley gradually subsided.

In 1958, Presley entered into army service, returning to civilian life in 1960. Throughout the next decade, he focused his energies on film roles and soundtrack recordings. A popular 1968 television special was a particular triumph, and by 1969 Presley had become a Las Vegas headliner. During the 1970s, his struggles with weight, drugs, and financial issues made him a tabloid fixture. He died on August 16, 1977, and remains an enduring icon through popular musical compilations and books. Each year, thousands of tourists make the pilgrimage to visit his former home in Memphis, Tennessee, the estate called Graceland.

Alice Walker alludes to Presley's exploitation of African-American music in the short story "Nineteen Fifty-Five," featured in the 1982 collection *You Can't Keep a Good Woman Down: Short Stories.*

### FURTHER READING


All Music Guide. "Elvis Presley." Available online. URL: http://www.allmusic.com/cg/amg.dll. Accessed February 20, 2009.

Bret, David. *Elvis: The Hollywood Years.* London: Robson Books, 2004.

George-Warren, Holly, and Patricia Romanowski, eds. *The Rolling Stone Encyclopedia of Rock and Roll.* 3d ed. New York: Fireside, 2001.

Goldman, Albert Harry. *Elvis.* New York: McGraw-Hill Book Company. 1984.

Guralnick, Peter. *Careless Love: The Unmaking of Elvis Presley.* London: Abacus, 2000.

———. *Last Train to Memphis: The Rise of Elvis Presley.* London: Abacus, 1995.

Keogh, Pamela C. *Elvis Presley: The Man. The Life. The Legend.* London: Simon and Schuster, 2004.


**quilting** *See* AFRICAN-AMERICAN WOMEN'S QUILTING.

**Rogers, J. A.** (1883–1966) In Alice Walker's novel *The Color Purple,* Nettie writes a letter to Celie describing her tour of the Anti-Slavery Missionary Society in England. She specifically describes the African artifacts collected in an English museum and states how she learned about Africa's advanced precolonial civilization from reading the works of J. A. Rogers.

Born in Negril, Jamaica, Joel Augustus Rogers immigrated to the United States in 1906. He subsequently became a prolific historian whose deeply influential writings on Africa and people of the African diaspora challenged racism, particularly white supremacy. Rogers's works share the common denominator of questioning Eurocentric historiography and illuminating African achievements.

### FURTHER READING


Asukile, Thabiti. "J. A. Rogers: The Scholarship of an Organic Intellectual." *The Black Scholar* 36, nos. 2–3 (Summer–Fall 2006).

Rashidi, Runoko. "J. A. Rogers (1883–1966)." In *African-American Historian Reference Guide.* 3d ed. Available online. URL: http://www.cwo.com/~lucumi/rogers-ref.html. Accessed February 28, 2009.

Rogers, J. A. *As Nature Leads: An Informal Discussion of the Reason Why Negro and Caucasian Are Mixing in Spite of Opposition.* Baltimore: Black Classic Press, 1987.

———. *Five Negro Presidents.* New York: Helga Rogers, 1965.

———. *From Superman to Man.* New York: Buccaneer Books, 1987.

———. *Ku Klux Spirit.* New York: Helga Rogers, 1980.

———. *Nature Knows No Color-Line: Research into the Negro Ancestry in the White Race.* New York: Helga Rogers, 1980.

———. *Sex and Race.* New York: Helga Rogers, 1972.

———. *World's Greatest Men of Color.* New York: Collier Macmillan Publishers, 1972.


**Rooks, Belvie** (1946– ) In her essay "My Big Brother Bill," about her filial relationship with the Native American activist Bill Wahpepah, Alice Walker acknowledges that her relationship with Wahpepah began as a result of their mutual friendship with Belvie Rooks. Rooks is an activist, educator, writer, and producer who partnered with ROBERT ALLEN and Alice Walker to form their book publishing company WILD TREES PRESS, in 1984. Rooks and Walker share many common interests, and their lives overlap in significant ways. Both women are originally from Georgia and came of age working as activists in the CIVIL RIGHTS MOVEMENT of the 1960s. Rooks won an American Book Award in 1993 for *Paris Connections: African American Artists in Paris,* coedited with Asake Bomani. She has published articles in many anthologies and wrote a play called *Who's Gonna Be There* (1997) for Danny Glover and Roy Scheider. She continues to work for Glover as the vice president of project development for Carrie Productions, his production company.

### FURTHER READING

Bell-Scott, Patricia. *Double Stitch: Black Women Write about Mothers and Daughters.* HarperCollins, 1992.

Bomani, Asake, and Belvie Rooks, eds. *Paris Connections: African American Artists in Paris.* Curated by Raymond Saunders. New York: Q.E.D. Press, 1992.

Rooks, Belvie. "Hey, Listen Up!" In *YES Magazine: A Journal of Positive Futures; Sacred Poems and Prayers in Praise of Life,* edited by Mary-Ford Grabowsky, 23–46. New York: Doubleday, 1998.

———. "Holding on and Remembering." In *Life Notes: Personal Writings by Contemporary Black Women,* edited by Patricia Bell-Scott, 255–270. New York: Norton, 1994.

———. "How to Turn a Brownfield into a Flower Garden: Socially and Ecologically Relevant Teaching Practices." *Journal of Race, Poverty and the Environment* (Spring 2001): 36–49.

———. "Revelation by Grace." In *My Soul Is a Witness: African-American Women's Spirituality,* edited by Gloria Wade Gayles, 105–108. New York: Beacon Press, 1996.

Walker, Alice. *The Same River Twice: Honoring the Difficult by Alice Walker.* New York: Scribner, 1996.

**root woman** *See* CONJURE WOMAN.

**Rukeyser, Muriel** (1913–1980) Poet, novelist, essayist, and creative writing teacher Muriel Rukeyser mentored Alice Walker at SARAH LAWRENCE COLLEGE. Rukeyser was also an early champion of Walker and circulated to publishers the manuscript of what became Walker's first published poetry collection, *Once: Poems* (1968). She sent Walker's essay "To Hell with Dying" to LANGSTON HUGHES, who enthusiastically included it in a short story collection he was editing.

Walker dedicated her 1979 essay "One Child of One's Own" to Rukeyser. As she gained prominence as a writer, the relationship between the two women was strained by several incidents, including Walker's leaving her first literary agent, Monica McCall. Rukeyser had helped Walker acquire McCall as an agent and was personally offended by this dismissal of her friend. She saw Walker's actions as evidence of a cavalier dismissal of her support. She also felt that Walker lacked gratitude to those who had helped her gain access to publishing venues. Walker has questioned what she has viewed as Rukeyser's constant need for gratitude and recognition.

### FURTHER READING

Daniels, Kate, and Richard Jones. *Poetry East: A Special Double Issue on Muriel Rukeyser* 16–17 (Spring–Summer 1985).

Gardinier, Suzanne. "'A World That Will Hold All the People': On Muriel Rukeyser." *Kenyon Review* 14, no. 3 (1992): 88–105.

Kertesz, Louise. *The Poetic Vision of Muriel Rukeyser.* Baton Rouge: Louisiana State University Press, 1980.

Lauret, Maria. *Alice Walker.* New York: St. Martin's Press, 2000.

McDaniel, Judith. "A Conversation with Muriel Rukeyser." *New Women's Times Feminist Review* (April 25–May 8, 1980).

Poets.org, Academy of American Poets. "Muriel Rukeyser." Available online. URL: http://www.poets.org/poet.php/prmPID/100. Accessed March 6, 2009.

Rukeyser, Muriel. *The Collected Poems of Muriel Rukeyser.* New York: McGraw-Hill, 1978.

———. *A Muriel Rukeyser Reader.* Edited by Jan Heller Levi. New York: Norton, 1994.

———. *Out of Silence: Selected Poems.* Edited by Kate Daniels. Evanston, Ill.: TriQuarterly, 1992.

White, Evelyn C. *Alice Walker: A Life.* New York: W. W. Norton and Company, 2004.

Winchell, Donna Haisty. *Alice Walker.* New York: Twayne Publishers, 1992.

**runes** Although the system of runes may be one of the oldest systems of writing in the world, knowledge about their exact origins and applications is uncertain. Runes constitute one of the most highly developed ancient Western alphabets. They also are believed by some to possess metaphysical content and are thought to reveal some aspect of the inner soul. Most rune users employ a set of 24 runes and interpret them through the most widespread runic system, the Common Germanic Futhark, or the Elder Futhark.

Walker often refers to runes in her works, most particularly in her novel *The Temple of My Familiar*. One of the characters in the novel, Suwelo, is named after the rune for wholeness.

### FURTHER READING


Elliott, Ralph W. V. *Runes: An Introduction*. New York: Philosophical Library, 1959.

Page, R. I. *An Introduction to English Runes*. London: Methuen, 1973.

———. *Runes and Runic Inscriptions: Collected Essays on Anglo-Saxon and Viking Runes*. Rochester, N.Y.: Boydell Press, 1995.

Pennick, Nigel. *Rune Magic: The History and Practice of Ancient Runic Traditions*. London: Aquarian Press, 1992.


**Sanders, Scott** (1957– ) Scott Sanders is an American television and theatrical producer best known for his stage productions, among them the musical adaptation of Alice Walker's novel *The Color Purple*. Walker was at first resistant to the idea of the adaptation, but Sanders convinced her that her novel was good material for a musical. *The Color Purple* premiered in Atlanta in 2004 and opened on Broadway in 2005. A year later, Alice Walker dedicated her collection of essays *We Are the Ones We Have Been Waiting For* to Scott Sanders, among others, and in 2008, ordained by Universal Ministries, she officiated at the marriage ceremony between Sanders and Brad D. Lamm. Other of Sanders's credits include the 2002 Broadway production of *Elaine Stritch: At Liberty*; gala events for President Bill Clinton; and, early in his career, stage productions at Radio City Music Hall for performing artists including Liberace, Sting, the Grateful Dead, and Diana Ross. Such acts are credited for helping to bring Radio City back from bankruptcy.

### FURTHER READING


Rohan, Preston. "Getting 'Purple' Onstage and On Tour; Show Producer Scott Sanders Opens Up about the Back Story of *The Color Purple*." *Star Tribune*, 15 March 2009.

Scott Sanders Productions. Web site. Available online. URL: http://www.scottsandersproductions.com/. Accessed January 5, 2010.


**Sarah Lawrence College** Sarah Lawrence College is a liberal arts college renowned for progressive education and located in the village of Bronxville, New York. Sarah Lawrence College was founded in 1926 by William Van Duzer Lawrence as a women's college; he named the college after his wife, Sarah, who was an advocate of women's suffrage and educational equality.

Sarah Lawrence College began admitting male students during the 1940s as veterans returned from the war. The institution became fully coeducational in 1968. A Sarah Lawrence College education has become synonymous with a highly individualized curriculum, strong support for student activism, and serious commitment to cultural diversity on its campus.

After two years of attending SPELMAN COLLEGE, in 1963 Alice Walker transferred to Sarah Lawrence College on a scholarship. She spent her junior year studying abroad in Africa. The sociologist HELEN LYND and the poets JANE COOPER and MURIEL RUKEYSER were among her primary mentors at Sarah Lawrence. Walker completed a B.A. in 1966.

### FURTHER READING


Kaplan, Barbara. "History of the College: Becoming Sarah Lawrence." Available online. URL: http://www.slc.edu/about/History_of_the_College.php. Accessed February 28, 2009.

White, Evelyn C. *Alice Walker: A Life*. New York: W. W. Norton & Company, 2004.


**scarification** As with human communities throughout the world, many cultural groups in Africa traditionally mark the transition from youth to adulthood with various religiously rooted rituals. Sometimes those rites are memorialized with a permanent mark or scar, a procedure called scarification. There is much cultural variation in the timing, role, and specificity of these rituals. These transitional ceremonies often correlate with the occasions of birth, maturation, marriage, entry into elder status, and sometimes death. The scarification sometimes associated with these events can occur anywhere on the skin, particularly on the face or upper torso. The methodology used to create these body markings frequently involves tattooing or cicatrization (scar formation).

Alice Walker confronts the complexities of these cultural practices in several of her novels, including *The Color Purple*, *The Temple of My Familiar*, and *Possessing the Secret of Joy*.

### FURTHER READING


Ajisafe, Ajayi Kolawole. *The Laws and Customs of the Yoruba People*. Lagos, Nigeria: Kash and Klare Bookshop, 1946.

Akiga. "The Origin of the Tiv Tribe, and Some of the Tribal Customs." In *Akiga's Story: the Tiv Tribe as Seen by One of its Members*. Translated by Rupert East. Ibadan, Nigeria: Caltop Publications Ltd., 2003. 12–53.

Bohannan, Paul. "Beauty and Scarification amongst the Tiv." In *Marks of Civilization: Artistic Transformations of the Human Body*, edited by Arnold Rubin, 77–82. Los Angeles: Museum of Cultural History, University of California, 1988.

Brain, Robert. "The Scarred Body." In *The Decorated Body*, 68–81. London: Hutchison, 1979.

Burton, John W. "Him and Her: Initiation of the Body." In *Culture and the Human Body: An Anthropological Perspective*. Prospect Heights, Ill.: Waveland Press, Inc., 2001, 82–85, 87.

Drewal, Henry John. "Art or Accident: Yoruba Body Artists and Their Deity Ogun." In *Africa's Ogun: Old World and New*, 2d ed., edited by Sandra T. Barnes, 235–260. Indianapolis and Bloomington: Indiana University Press, 1997.

———. "Beauty and Being: Aesthetics and Ontology in Yoruba Body Art." In *Marks of Civilization: Artistic Transformations of the Human Body*, edited by Arnold Rubin, 83–96. Los Angeles: Museum of Cultural History, University of California, 1988.

Eicher, Joanne B., Sandra Lee Evenson, and Hazel A. Lutz, eds. *The Visible Self: Global Perspectives on Dress, Culture, and Society*. New York: Fair Child Publications, 2000.

Falola, Toyin. *Key Events in African History: A Reference Guide*. Westport, Conn.: Greenwood Press, 2002.

Favazza, A. R. *Bodies under Siege: Self-Mutilation and Body Modification in Culture and Psychiatry*. Baltimore: Johns Hopkins University Press, 1996.

Lincoln, Bruce. "The Religious Significance of Women's Scarification among the Tiv." *Africa* 45, no. 3 (1975): 316–326.

Mascia-Lees, Frances E., and Patricia Sharpe, eds. *Tattoo, Torture, Mutilation, and Adornment: The Denaturalization of the Body in Culture and Text*. Albany: State University of New York Press, 1992.

Rush, John A. *Spiritual Tattoo: A Cultural History of Tattooing, Piercing, Scarification, Branding, and Implants*. Berkeley, Calif.: Frog, Ltd., 2005.


**Schweitzer, Albert** (1875–1965) Albert Schweitzer was a Christian theologian, medical physician, and classical musician, best known for his "Reverence for Life" philosophy. Born in Alsace, Germany, he studied medicine at the University of Strasbourg, and in 1913, he founded a hospital in Labaréné, Gabon, in French Equatorial Africa. Over the course of his life, he maintained his dedication to providing medical care for Africans and expanded the hospital he founded. Schweitzer was a prolific author and a highly regarded musician. In 1952, he was awarded the Nobel Peace Prize for his scholarly and humanitarian work. Alice Walker mentions Albert Schweitzer in *The Color Purple*.

### FURTHER READING


*Albert Schweitzer: Life and Thought*. Available online. URL: http://www.albertschweitzer.info/life_thought.html. Accessed March 28, 2009.

Brabazon, James. *Albert Schweitzer*. New York: G. P. Putnam's Sons, 1975.

Ice, Jackson Lee. *Prophet of Radical Theology*. Philadelphia: Westminster Press, 1971.

Marshall, George, and David Poling. *Schweitzer: A Biography*. New York: Doubleday, 1975.

Nobelprize.org. Albert Schweitzer. Available online. URL: http://nobelprize.org/nobel_prizes/peace/laureates/1952/schweitzer-bio.html. Accessed March 28, 2009.

Schweitzer, Albert. *Albert Schweitzer: Essential Writings*. Selected by James Brabazon. Maryknoll, N.Y.: Orbis Books, 2005.

**self-affirmation** Alice Walker creates a unique, radical, and untraditional theology throughout her writing. She reveals the foundation of her revolutionary sense of spirituality in the epistolary short story "Letter of the Times, or Should This Sado-Masochism Be Saved," which is included in her collection of short stories *You Can't Keep a Good Woman Down*. Walker's narrator writes that her subject is:

> . . . God. That is, the inner spirit, the inner voice; the human compulsion when deeply distressed to seek healing counsel within ourselves, and the capacity within ourselves to both create this counsel and to receive it.
>
> (It had always amused me that the God who spoke to Harriet Tubman and Sojourner Truth told them exactly what they needed to hear, no less than the God of the Old Testament constantly reassured the ancient Jews.)
>
> Indeed, as I read the narratives of black people who were captured and set to slaving away their lives in America, I saw that this inner spirit, this inner capacity for self-comforting, this ability to locate God within that they expressed, demonstrated something marvelous about human beings. . . .
>
> It was as if these women found a twin self who saved them from their abused consciousness and chronic physical loneliness; and that twin self is in all of us waiting only to be summoned.

Within this definition of God and of spiritual experience, individuals are inherently divine, and there is no demarcation between that which is holy and that which is human. According to this theological premise, the only act necessary for the acquisition of divinity is recognition and acknowledgment of what is inherent in one's self. Walker suggests that divinity is equivalent to reunification of the split self through self-affirmation.

### FURTHER READING

Bell-Scott, Patricia. *Life Notes: Personal Writing by Contemporary Black Women*. New York: W. W. Norton, 1993.

Butler, Judith, and J. Scott. *Feminists Theorize the Political*. New York: Routledge, 1992.

Collins, Patricia. "The Sexual Politics of Black Womanhood." In *Violence against Women: The Bloody Footprints*, edited by Pauline B. Bart and Eileen Gell Moran, 85–104. Newbury Park, Calif.: Sage Publications, 1993.

Dugger, K. "Social Location and Gender Role Attitudes: A Comparison on Black and White Women." In *The Social Construction of Gender*, edited by Judith Lober and Susan A. Farrell, 38–59. Newbury Park, Calif.: Sage Publications, 1991.

Gay, Geneva and Willie L. Baber, eds. *Expressively Black: The Cultural Basis of Ethnic Identity*. New York: Praeger Publishers, 1987.

Gergen, M. and K. Gergen. "Narratives of the Gendered Body in Popular Autobiography." In *The Narrative Study of Lives*, vol. 1, edited by R. Josselson and A. Lieblich, 191–218. Newbury Park, Calif.: Sage Publications, 1993.

Hall, Christine C. Iijima, Brenda J. Evans, and Stephanie Salice, eds. *Black Females in the United States: A Bibliography from 1967 to 1987*. Washington, D.C.: PsycINFO, American Psychological Association, 1989.

Stoller, Robert. "The Sense of Femaleness." In *Essential Papers on the Psychology of Women*, edited by Claudia Zanardi, 278–289. New York: New York University Press, 1990.

Wallace, Michelle. *Black Macho and the Myth of the Superwoman*. New York: Verso, 1979.

Ward, Janie Victoria. "Racial Identity Formation and Transformation." In *Making Connections: The Relational Worlds of Adolescent Girls at Emma Willard School*, edited by Carol Gilligan, Nona P. Lyons, and Trudy J. Hammer, 215–232. Cambridge: Harvard University Press, 1990.

Whitehead, T. and B. Reid. eds. *Gender Constructs and Special Issues*. Urbana: University of Illinois Press, 1992.

**sharecropping** Sharecropping was a system of farming where the sharecropper lived on and worked land owned by someone else. The sharecropper contributed his labor, and the owner, or landlord, provided the animals, equipment, seed, tools, and living quarters. The institution arose in the United States at the end of the Civil War.

It grew out of the plantation system, whereby the newly freed slaves became sharecroppers on plantations because they had few other options. The ex-slave owners, and other planters, had land but little money for wages. In this way, the white landowners were able to keep ex-slaves in a subordinate position, and the cultivation of cotton continued. The system eventually included poor white farmers.

The sharecropping system was abusive. The landlord kept the accounts, marketed the crops, and often cheated the sharecropper out of his rightful share, which were usually half the profits. The landowner also gave the sharecropper advanced credit to meet living expenses, but the interest rates were often so high that the sharecropper's portion of the profits went directly toward reducing his debt to the landlord. In this way, the sharecropper was tied to both the land and the landlord.

The system can still be found in various parts of the world and includes other cash crops besides cotton, but in the United States, sharecropping largely faded when mechanization supplanted much of the manual work on farms, and fewer acres were devoted to cotton. Many of Alice Walker's characters suffer under the exploitative system of sharecropping. Walker depicts this reality of life in the JIM CROW South in her novels *The Color Purple* and *The Third Life of Grange Copeland.*

### FURTHER READING


Byres, T. J., ed. *Sharecropping and Sharecroppers.* London and Totowa, N.J.: F. Cass, 1983.

Cohen, William. *At Freedom's Edge: Black Mobility and the Southern White Quest for Racial Control, 1861–1915.* Baton Rouge: Louisiana State University Press, 1991.

Daniel, Pete. *Breaking the Land: The Transformation of Cotton, Tobacco, and Rice Cultures since 1880.* Urbana: University of Illinois Press, 1985.

Davis, Ronald L. F. *Good and Faithful Labor: From Slavery to Sharecropping in the Natchez District, 1860–1890.* Westport, Conn.: Greenwood Press, 1982.

Harris, William H. *The Harder We Run: Black Workers since the Civil War.* New York: Oxford University Press, 1982.

Higgs, Robert. *Competition and Coercion: Blacks in the American Economy, 1865–1914.* Cambridge: Cambridge University Press, 1977.

Jaynes, Gerald D. *Branches without Roots: Genesis of the Black Working Class in the American South, 1862–1882.* New York: Oxford University Press, 1986.

Jones, Jacqueline. *The Dispossessed: America's Underclasses from the Civil War to the Present.* New York: Basic Books, Harper and Collins, 1992.

———. *Labor of Love, Labor of Sorrow: Black Women, Work, and the Family from Slavery to the Present.* New York: Basic Books, 1985.

Litwack, Leon F. *Been in the Storm So Long: The Aftermath of Slavery.* New York: Knopf, 1979.

Mandle, Jay R. *Not Slave, Not Free: The African American Economic Experience since the Civil War.* Durham, N.C.: Duke University Press, 1992.

———. *The Roots of Black Poverty: The Southern Plantation Economy after the Civil War.* Durham, N.C.: Duke University Press, 1978.

McGlynn, Frank, and Seymour Drescher. *The Meaning of Freedom: Economics, Politics, and Culture after Slavery.* Pittsburgh: University of Pittsburgh Press, 1992.

Nieman, Donald G., ed. *From Slavery to Sharecropping: White Land and Black Labor in the Rural South, 1865–1900.* New York: Garland, 1994.

Otto, John S. *Southern Agriculture during the Civil War Era, 1860–1880.* Westport, Conn.: Greenwood Press, 1994.

Royce, Edward C. *The Origins of Southern Sharecropping.* Philadelphia: Temple University Press, 1993.

Stokes, Melvyn, and Rick Halpern, eds. *Race and Class in the American South since 1890.* Oxford: Berg Publishing, 1994.

Woodman, Harold D. *New South? New Law: The Legal Foundations of Credit and Labor Relations in the Postbellum Agricultural South.* Baton Rouge: Louisiana State University Press, 1995.

Wright, Gavin. *Old South, New South: Revolutions in the Southern Economy since the Civil War.* New York: Basic Books, 1986.


**slave narratives** These are first-person accounts by enslaved individuals, describing their experiences. In the case of African-American slave narratives, they were written both before and after emancipation. The texts have become critically important historical documents about life in the American South—and, to some degree, in the North—as well as the basis of treatises about freedom and the nature of the United States and other countries that participated in the African slave trade.

American slave narratives date back to Briton Hammon, who wrote *A Narrative of the Uncommon Sufferings and Surprising Deliverance of Briton Hammon, a Negro Man* (1760). There is some debate over whether Hammon was an indentured servant or a slave, but his writing is considered the first African-American prose in North America.

Another slave narrative from the 18th century was *An Interesting Narrative of the Life of Olaudah Equiano* (1789). Equiano became one of the most widely read authors of African descent in the English-speaking world, and he is often credited with being among the most influential creators of the slave narrative.

The most famous of the slave narratives were written by such 19th-century writers as Nat Turner, Frederick Douglass, William Wells Brown, and Harriet Jacobs. Their writings not only describe their personal experiences trying to survive and attempts at freedom, but they are a commentary on the hypocrisy of a nation that allowed slavery and yet insisted, as Thomas Jefferson wrote, that "all men are created equal." Jefferson himself owned slaves. These first-person accounts of the cruelty and humiliation of slavery helped strengthen the abolitionist cause.

At the turn of the 20th century, the most widely read slave narrative was *Up from Slavery*, by Booker T. Washington. It described the rise of Washington from slavery to a position of leadership in the African-American community but also outlined his vision of how black Americans could eventually become fully accepted citizens of the United States through their labor.

An important source of slave narratives in the 20th century occurred between 1936 and 1938, during the Great Depression, when the Works Progress Administration financed writers to interview more than 2,300 former slaves. Mostly born toward the end of slavery, these men and women described their experiences on plantations and in the cities. In these remarkable interviews, the former slaves discussed the lives they led, the nature of slavery, the relationships between masters and slaves, the role of religion in their lives, the slavery system, and their struggles for freedom. Some literary critics have noted that some of Walker's novels, particularly *The Color Purple*, resonate with the traditions and conventions of slave narratives.

## FURTHER READING

Andrews, William L. *To Tell a Free Story: The First Century of Afro-American Autobiography, 1760–1865.* Urbana: University of Illinois Press, 1986.

Andrews, William L., and Henry Louis Gates, Jr., eds. *Six Women's Slave Narratives.* New York: Oxford University Press, 1988.

———, eds. *Slave Narratives.* New York: Library of America, 2000.

Bennett, Michael. "Anti-Pastoralism, Frederick Douglass, and the Nature of Slavery." In *Beyond Nature Writing: Expanding the Boundaries of Ecocriticism*, edited by Karla Armbruster and Kathleen R. Wallace, 195–210. Charlottesville: University of Virginia Press, 2001.

Berlin, Ira, Marc Favreau, and Steven F. Miller, eds. *Remembering Slavery: African Americans Talk about Their Personal Experiences of Slavery and Emancipation.* New York: New Press, 1998.

Blassingame, John W., ed. *Slave Testimony: Two Centuries of Letters, Speeches, Interviews, and Autobiographies.* Baton Rouge: Louisiana State University Press, 1977.

Botkin, B. A., ed. *Lay My Burden Down: A Folk History of Slavery.* New York: Delta, 1994.

Braxton, Joanne M. *Black Women Writing Autobiography: A Tradition within a Tradition.* Philadelphia: Temple University Press, 1989.

Bromell, Nicholas Knowles. *By the Sweat of the Brow: Literature and Labor in Antebellum America.* Chicago: University of Chicago Press, 1993.

Costanzo, Angelo. *Surprising Narrative: Olaudah Equiano and the Beginnings of Black Autobiography.* New York: Greenwood Press, 1987.

Cugoano, Ottobah. *Thoughts and Sentiments on the Evil of Slavery and Other Writings.* Edited by Vincent Carretta. New York: Penguin Books, 1990.

Curtin, Philip D., ed. *Africa Remembered: Narratives by West Africans from the Era of the Slave Trade.* Madison: University of Wisconsin Press, 1967.

Davis, Charles T., and Henry Louis Gates, Jr., eds. *The Slave's Narrative.* Oxford: Oxford University Press, 1985.

Douglass, Frederick. *Autobiographies: Narrative of the Life; My Bondage and My Freedom; Life and Times.* New York: Library of America, 1994.

Equiano, Olaudah. *The Interesting Narrative of the Life of Olaudah Equiano.* 2d ed. Edited by Robert J. Allison. New York: Bedford/St. Martin's, 2006.

Ferguson, Moira, ed. *The History of Mary Prince: A West Indian Slave—Related by Herself.* Ann Arbor: University of Michigan Press, 1997.

Foster, Frances Smith. *Witnessing Slavery: The Development of Ante-Bellum Slave Narratives.* Madison: University of Wisconsin Press, 1994.

Gronniosaw, James Albert Ukawsaw. *Narrative of the Most Remarkable Particulars in the Life of James Albert Ukawsaw Gronniosaw, an African Prince, as Related by Himself.* Leeds: Davies and Booth, 1841.

Hopkins, Dwight N. *Cut Loose Your Stammering Tongue: Black Theology in the Slave Narratives.* Maryknoll, N.Y.: Orbis Books, 1991.

Jacobs, Harriet. *Incidents in the Life of a Slave Girl, Written by Herself.* Cambridge, Mass.: Harvard University Press, 1987.

Judy, Ronald A. T. *(Dis)forming the American Canon: African-Arabic Slave Narratives and the Vernacular.* Minneapolis: University of Minnesota Press, 1993.

Mellon, James, ed. *Bullwhip Days: The Slaves Remember.* New York: Weidenfeld and Nicolson, 1988.

Meltzer, Milton. *The Black Americans: A History in Their Own Words, 1619–1983.* New York: Harper and Row, 1984.

Osofsky, Gilbert, ed. *Puttin' On Ole Massa. The Slave Narratives of Henry Bibb, William Wells Brown and Solomon Northup.* New York: Harper and Row, 1969.

Perdue, Charles L., Jr., Thomas E. Barden, and Robert K. Phillips, eds. *Weevils in the Wheat: Interviews with Virginia Ex-Slaves.* Charlottesville: University of Virginia Press, 1992.

Porter, Dorothy, ed. *Early Negro Writing 1760–1837.* Baltimore: Black Classic Press, 1994.

Russell, Sandi. *Render Me My Song: African-American Women Writers from Slavery to the Present.* New York: St. Martin's Press, 1990.

Sekora, John, and Darwin T. Turner, eds. *The Art of Slave Narrative: Original Essays in Criticism and Theory.* Macomb: Western Illinois University Press, 1982.

Smith, Valerie. *Self-Discovery and Authority in Afro-American Narrative.* Cambridge, Mass.: Harvard University Press, 1987

Starling, Marion Wilson. *The Slave Narrative: Its Place in American History.* 2d ed. Washington, D.C.: Howard University Press, 1988.

Taylor, Yuval, ed. *I Was Born a Slave: An Anthology of Classic Slave Narratives.* Chicago: Lawrence Hill Books, 1999.

Washington, Booker T. *Up from Slavery.* New York: Penguin, 1986.

Winter, Kari J. *Subjects of Slavery, Agents of Change: Women and Power in Gothic Novels and Slave Narratives, 1790–1865.* Athens: University of Georgia Press, 1992.

Yetman, Norman R., ed. *Voices from Slavery: 100 Authentic Slave Narratives.* Mineola, N.Y.: Dover Publications, 2000.

**Smith, Bessie** (1894?–1937) Bessie Smith was one of the great BLUES singers of the 1920s and early 1930s. During her career, she became the most prominent black performer in the country as well as a great influence on both singers and instrumentalists in both the blues and JAZZ.

Born in Chattanooga, Tennessee, Smith began as a street musician. She later went on the road with Ma Rainey's traveling show, the Rabbit Foot Minstrels, and eventually ended up in the vaudeville circuit, where she became one of the most in-demand blues singers. Her first recording, "Down-Hearted Blues," released in 1923, was a hit, selling more than 2 million copies in its first year. From then on, she continued to make recordings and tour the country, becoming the highest-paid black entertainer of the time. She recorded with many of the jazz greats of her day, including Louis Armstrong, Fletcher Henderson, Charlie Green, and James P. Johnson. Her voice was rough and earthy, able to convey a great range of emotion, but it was also strong and clear, often soaring.

Smith's career faltered somewhat in the 1930s. In 1937, she was in a car accident and was driven to a hospital for African Americans. Her arm was amputated, but she never regained consciousness and died from her injuries. In *The Color Purple,* Shug Avery is said to count Bessie Smith as one of her acquaintances. Alice Walker also references Smith in several of her other books.

### FURTHER READING

Davis, Angela Yvonne. *Blues Legacies and Black Feminism: Gertrude 'Ma' Rainey, Bessie Smith, and Billie Holiday.* New York: Pantheon, 1998.

Fraher, James. *The Blues Is a Feeling: Voices and Visions of African-American Blues Musicians.* Mount Horeb, Wisc.: Midwest Traditions, 1998.

Grimes, Sara. *Backwater Blues: In Search of Bessie Smith.* Amherst, Mass.: Rose Island Pub., 2000.

Manera, Alexandria. *Bessie Smith.* Chicago: Raintree, 2003.

Welding, Pete. *Bluesland: Portraits of Twelve Major American Blues Masters.* New York: E. P. Dutton, 1992.

**Smith-Robinson, Ruby Doris** (1942–1967) Smith-Robinson was a civil rights leader whose major work was within the STUDENT NON-VIOLENT COORDINATING COMMITTEE (SNCC). A southern-based civil rights organization that began in 1960 and lasted until the mid-1970s, SNCC participated in many of the major civil rights demonstrations of the 1960s, including sit-ins, freedom rides, the 1963 March on Washington, and Freedom Summer in 1964. Smith-Robinson was active in the field, engaged in such activities as picketing and organizing voter registration drives, and she also served as SNCC's executive secretary, the only woman to do so. Smith-Robinson died prematurely of a sudden onset of cancer. Many of her friends and colleagues in the movement believe that it was her fierce engagement with the activist work of the movement that was the source of her demise.

Alice Walker has said that the central character in her novel *Meridian* is based loosely on Ruby Doris Smith-Robinson. Walker and Smith-Robinson crossed paths during her years at SPELMAN COLLEGE.

### FURTHER READING

Fleming, Cynthia. *Soon We Will Not Cry: The Liberation of Ruby Doris Smith Robinson.* New York: Rowman and Littlefield Publishers, 1998.

**Sophia** A version of the contemporary GODDESS FIGURE in African-American women's fiction exists in the spiritual and metaphorical death and reawakening of the Gnostic goddess Sophia. According to the GNOSTIC GOSPELS, Sophia is the personification of wisdom.

Sophia is the daughter and replication of the mother goddess, Mother Sophia. According to the Gnostic Gospels, Sophia is the creator of the earth. Her narrative tells the tale of her alienation from the divine, a tale in which she loses her way and incidentally creates the earth. During her perilous journey through symbolic darkness, Sophia is unable to return to the light, heaven, and to her mother. Mother Sophia sends Christ to rescue his sister, Sophia, and he helps her to return to the way of enlightenment.

Examples of Sophia goddesses in African-American women's fiction are numerous. Sofia in *The Color Purple* mirrors the Gnostic goddess Sophia's descent into the realm of darkness and reemergence into light: Sofia loses her family and community and suffers years of incarceration and near-enslavement as the mayor's wife's maid, before reemerging as a central and self-assured character. This journey places Sofia in a communal context and parallels the archetype Sophia's reassertion of divinity.

### FURTHER READING

Dames, Michael. *The Silbury Treasure: The Great Goddess Rediscovered.* London: Thames and Hudson, 1976.

Engelsman, Sabrina. *The Feminine Dimension of the Divine.* Oxford: Oxford University Press, 1993.

Harding, M. Esther. *Woman's Mysteries, Ancient and Modern: A Psychological Interpretation of the Feminine Principle as Portrayed in Myth, Story, and Dreams.* New York: Harper and Row, 1971.

Morgan, Elaine. *The Descent of Woman.* New York: Bantam, 1971.

Pagels, Elaine. *The Gnostic Gospels.* New York: Random House, 1979.

Preston, James J., ed. *Mother Worship: Theme and Variations.* Chapel Hill: University of North Carolina, 1982.
Reed, Evelyn. *Woman's Evolution from Matriarchal Clan to Patriarchal Family.* New York: Pathfinder Press, 1975.
Showerman, G. *The Great Mother of the Gods.* Chicago: University of Chicago Press, 1969.
Sjoo, Monica, and Barbara Mor. *The Great Cosmic Mother: Rediscovering the Religion of the Earth.* San Francisco: Harper, 1991.
Stone, Merlin. *When God Was a Woman.* New York: Dial Press, 1976.

**Speke, John Hanning** (1827–1864) Born in May 1827, John Speke became an important figure in the British military in his earliest years and then became an explorer working with Richard Burton (1821–90) to try to discover the source of the Nile River.

The two men began their quest in late 1856 and originally set off in search of a body of water called Lake Nyassa, which was believed at the time to be the great river's source. While on their journey, the two men were the first non-Africans to reach another large body of water known as Lake Tanganyika. Burton fell ill during the expedition, and Speke proceeded on his own, eventually becoming the first non-African to see and document the existence of an enormous body of water he named Lake Victoria.

In 1862, Speke continued the original quest for the origins of the Nile without Burton, with whom he had severed ties after an acrimonious feud. While on this voyage, Speke was able to locate Rippon Falls, a point he claimed to be the source of the Nile. He died two years later under mysterious circumstance during a hunting accident. Since the incident, there has been much speculation about whether Speke's death was accidental or intentional.

Alice Walker interrogates the history of African exploration in many of her writings and specifically references Speke in her novel *The Color Purple.*

### FURTHER READING

Bridges, Roy C. "John Hanning Speke: Negotiating a Way to the Nile." In *Africa and Its Explorers,* edited by Robert I. Rotberg. 95–137. Cambridge, Mass.: Harvard University Press, 1970.
———. "John Speke and the Royal Geographical Society." *Uganda Journal* 26 (1962): 23–43.
Burton, John Hill. "Captain Speke's Journal." *Blackwood's Magazine* 45 (January 1864): 1–24.
Burton, Sir Richard Francis Burton. *First Footsteps in East Africa.* London: Longman, Brown, Green, and Longman, 1856.
Casada, James A. "British Exploration in East Africa: A Bibliography with Commentary." *Africana Journal* 5 (Fall 1974): 195–239.
Faris, John T. *Real Stories of the Geography Makers.* New York: Ginn and Company, 1925.
Garstin, William. *Fifty Years of Nile Exploration, and Some of Its Results.* London: Royal Geographical Society, 1909.
Geddie, John. *The Lake Regions of Central Africa—a Record of Discovery.* London, Edinburgh, and New York: T. Nelson and Sons, 1892.
Ingham, Kenneth. "John Hanning Speke: A Victorian and His Inspiration." *Tanzanya Notes and Queries* 49 (1957): 247–255.
Loftus, Ernest Achey. *Speke and the Nile Source.* Edinburgh: T. Nelson, 1954.
Maitland, Alexander. *Speke and the Discovery of the Source of the Nile.* London: Constable, 1971.
Moorehead, Alan. *The White Nile.* New York: Harper and Brothers, 1960.
Speke, John Hanning. *Early Maps and Expedition Reports from the East Africa Expedition.* Gotha: Justus Perthes, 1859.
———. *My Second Expedition to Eastern Intertropical Africa.* Cape Town: Privately printed by Saul Solomon and Co., 1860.

**Spelman College** Established in 1881 as the Atlanta Female Baptist Seminary, Spelman College is a historically black women's liberal arts college located in Atlanta, Georgia. Sophia B. Packard and Harriet E. Giles were the college's founders. In 1883, John D. Rockefeller donated $6,700, which allowed the college to improve its facilities and stature. In 1884, the seminary was renamed Spelman Seminary in honor of the family of Laura Spelman, Rockefeller's wife. Spelman's family had been staunch advocates of and activists in the abolitionist movement. In 1924, the seminary became Spelman College.

Since 1929, Spelman has been a sister college to the all-male Morehouse College. It is highly regarded as one of the premier institutions of higher education for African-American women and regularly ranks among the finest liberal arts colleges in the nation. Spelman has a notable history of activist involvement in the Civil Rights, feminist, and antiapartheid movements. In 1987, the college appointed its first female college president, Johnetta Betsch Cole, who served until 1997.

Alice Walker attended Spelman College from 1961 to 1963 with the assistance of a scholarship. At Spelman, she developed an interest in civil rights activism and forged friendships with the historians HOWARD ZINN and STAUGHTON LYND, both of whom nurtured and supported her intellectual interests and encouraged her to continue her education in a more progressive and expansive environment. Walker ultimately found Spelman's environment politically and culturally conservative. As a result, in 1964, with the assistance of Lynd and his mother, HELEN LYND, she transferred to SARAH LAWRENCE COLLEGE, where Helen Lynd was a professor. Walker has returned to Spelman throughout the years as a guest lecturer.

### FURTHER READING


Guy-Sheftall, Beverly. "Black Women and Higher Education: Spelman and Bennett Colleges Revisited." *Journal of Negro Education* 51, no. 3 (Summer 1982): 278–287.

Lefever, Harry G. *Undaunted by the Fight: Spelman College and the Civil Rights Movement, 1957–1967.* Macon, Ga.: Mercer University Press, 2005.

Read, Florence M. *The Story of Spelman College.* Princeton, N.J.: Princeton University Press, 1961.

Spelman College. Facts: History in Brief. Available online. URL: http://www.spelman.edu/about_us/facts/. Accessed February 28, 2009.

White, Evelyn C. *Alice Walker: A Life.* New York: W. W. Norton and Company, 2004.


**Spielberg, Steven** (1946– ) Steven Spielberg is the most commercially successful film director in the history of American cinema. Born on December 18, 1946, in Cincinnati, Ohio, Spielberg is notable for ushering in an era of Hollywood blockbusters. The blockbuster phenomenon began with the colossal commercial success of his 1975 film *Jaws.* The director's canon has become synonymous with sentimental fare, including family dramas such as *E.T.: The Extra Terrestrial* (1982), action-adventure films such as *Raiders of the Lost Ark* (1981), and fantasy epics such as *Hook* (1991). In the 1990s, Spielberg received multiple Oscars for his 1993 Holocaust-themed film *Schindler's List* and the 1998 World War II drama *Saving Private Ryan.* He continues to direct, produce, and write screenplays for popular and critically respected films and TV programming. His films all have narrative accessibility and high production values in common.

Over the course of his career, Spielberg has tackled increasingly complex dramatic narratives, including his 1985 adaptation of Alice Walker's novel *The Color Purple,* a film that received 11 Academy Award nominations. The mainstream press uniformly praised the film, but some critics questioned its often harsh depictions of African-American men. Walker has written extensively about her professional relationship with Spielberg, particularly in her 1996 nonfiction work *The Same River Twice: Honoring the Difficult: A Meditation on the Life, Spirit, Art, and the Making of the Film* The Color Purple *Ten Years Later.*

### FURTHER READING


All Movie Guide. "Steven Spielberg: Biography." Available online. URL: http://www.allmovie.com/artist/steven-spielberg-112325. Accessed February 20, 2009.

Buckland, Warren. *Directed by Steven Spielberg: Poetics of the Contemporary Hollywood Blockbuster.* New York: Continuum, 2006.

Jackson, Kathi. *Steven Spielberg: A Biography.* Westport, Conn.: Greenwood Press, 2007.

Silet, Charles L. P. *The Films of Steven Spielberg: Critical Essays.* Lanham, Md.: Scarecrow Press, 2002.

Spielberg, Steven, Kathleen Kennedy, et al. *The Color Purple.* DVD. Burbank, Calif.: Warner Home Video, 2003.

Taylor, Philip M. *Steven Spielberg: The Man, His Movies, and Their Meaning.* New York: Continuum, 1992.

**spirituals** In the United States, spirituals are songs or hymns that are sung in church. Though its usage has varied from one culture or region to another, the term *spiritual* is most often associated with the traditions of African-American services originating in southern congregations.

Early in U.S. history, African-American spirituals were adapted from hymns sung in white churches. The lyrics were usually related to biblical passages. Of particular interest to black congregations were texts taken from the Old Testament that spoke of the Israelite struggles for freedom. In this way, American slaves were able to express their own yearnings to be free.

Musically, black congregations added African musical forms to the spiritual. As sung in black churches, the spiritual became an outwardly emotional, often melancholic song characterized by syncopation and polyrhythms. Another African influence is the call-and-response and freer improvisations during singing. The more joyous spirituals have been an influence on gospel music. In *The Color Purple,* we learn that Shug Avery learned how to sing by singing spirituals.

### FURTHER READING

Epstein, Dena J. *Sinful Tunes and Spirituals: Black Folk Music to the Civil War.* Urbana: University of Illinois Press, 1977.

Jones, Art. *Wade in the Water: The Wisdom of the Spirituals.* Maryknoll, N.Y.: Orbis Books, 1993.

Katz, Bernard, ed. *The Social Implications of Early Negro Music in the United States.* New York: Arno Press and the *New York Times,* 1969.

Levine, Lawrence. *Black Culture and Black Consciousness: Afro-American Folk Thought from Slavery to Freedom.* New York: Oxford University Press, 1977.

Reagon, Bernice Johnson. *If You Don't Go, Don't Hinder Me: The African American Sacred Song Tradition.* Lincoln: University of Nebraska Press, 2001.

**Stanley, Henry Morton** (1841–1904) Henry Morton Stanley was a journalist whose writing was central to Belgium's colonization of the Congo. In 1869, the *New York Herald* sponsored the Welsh-born Stanley, who was employed at the time as a special correspondent, to embark on a search to find the missionary DAVID LIVINGSTONE, whom he located and met in 1871. Subsequently, Stanley traveled throughout central Africa, and he documented these forays in his 1878 book *Through the Dark Continent.* In 1879, under the sponsorship of Belgium's notorious King Leopold II, Stanley supervised efforts to colonize the Lower Congo. His controversial work, which relied on slave labor, significantly contributed to Leopold's eventual private ownership of the Congo Free State in 1885.

In a letter to Celie in Alice Walker's *The Color Purple,* Nettie references several pictures of white men prominently displayed in the Missionary Society of New York's office, including photographs of Henry Stanley and David Livingstone.

### FURTHER READING

BBC. "Historic Figures: Henry Stanley (1841–1904)." Available online. URL: http://www.bbc.co.uk/history/historic_figures/stanley_sir_henry_morton.shtml. Accessed March 28, 2009.

Farwell, Byron. *The Man Who Presumed: A Biography of Stanley.* New York: Henry Holt and Company, 1957.

Gallop, Alan. *Mr. Stanley, I Presume? The Life and Explorations of Henry Morton Stanley.* Stroud, Eng.: Sutton Publishing, 2004.

Jeal, Tim. *Stanley: The Impossible Life of Africa's Greatest Explorer.* New Haven, Conn.: Yale University Press, 2007.

Liebowitz, Daniel, and Charles Pearson. *The Last Expedition: Stanley's Mad Journey through the Congo.* New York: Norton, 2005.

McLynn, Frank J. *Stanley: Dark Genius of African Exploration.* London: Pimlico, 2004.

Newman, James L. *Imperial Footprints: Henry Morton Stanley's African Journeys.* Washington, D.C.: Brassey's, 2004.

Stanley, H. M., and D. Stanley. *The Autobiography of Sir Henry Morton Stanley: The Making of a 19th Century Explorer.* Santa Barbara, Calif.: Narrative Press, 2001.

Stanley, Henry Morton. *How I Found Livingstone in Central Africa.* Mineola, N.Y.: Dover Publications, 2002.

———. *In Darkest Africa: Or the Quest, Rescue, and Retreat of Emin Governor of Equatoria.* Crabtree, Oreg.: The Narrative Press, 2001.

———. *Through the Dark Continent: or, The Sources of the Nile around the Great Lakes of Equatorial Africa and down the Livingstone River to the Atlantic Ocean.* 2 vols. Mineola, N.Y.: Dover Publications, 1988.

**Steinem, Gloria** (1934– ) Steinem, a friend of Alice Walker's, is an American feminist and writer. In the 1960s, she was one of the leading founders of the second-wave FEMINISM movement, which addressed many issues of inequality facing American women, such as those in the workplace, law, and reproductive rights. Along with other feminist leaders, including Betty Friedan, Shirley Chisholm, and Bella Abzug, among others, Steinem helped found the National Women's Political Caucus, an organization that promotes the participation of women as political candidates. In the early 1970s, she was among several women who founded Ms. magazine, which continues to be perhaps the most prominent feminist publication.

As a journalist, Steinem gained national recognition in the early 1960s when she secretly posed as a Playboy bunny to write an exposé on the workplace treatment of the "bunnies." Over the years, she has been not only an advocate for women but a supporter of black civil rights; an antiwar critic during the Vietnam and Gulf Wars; an advocate for children; and an activist on national presidential campaigns, including supporting George McGovern in 1968 and Shirley Chisholm in 1972, speaking against the reelection of George W. Bush in 2004, and supporting the presidential bid of Hillary Rodham Clinton in 2008. She has authored several books, including *Revolution from Within: A Book of Self-Esteem* (1992), *Outrageous Acts and Everyday Rebellions* (1983), and *Marilyn: Norma Jean* (1986). In 1998, Steinem was inducted into the American Society of Magazine Editors Hall of Fame along with, among others, Hugh Hefner of *Playboy.* Steinem and Walker remain very close and often appear together at public events.

Gloria Steinem is one of the best-known activists of the contemporary feminist movement and one of Alice Walker's oldest and closest friends. Steinem is also an author and the cofounder of *Ms.* magazine. *(Photograph by Carmen Gillespie)*

## FURTHER READING

Bright, Susan, ed. *Foundations for a Compassionate Society. Feminist Family Values Forum: Mililani Trask, Gloria Steinem, Angela Davis, Maria Jimenez.* Austin, Tex.: Plain View Press, 1996.

Heilbrun, Carolyn G. *The Education of a Woman: The Life of Gloria Steinem.* New York: Dial Press. 1995.

Marcello, Patricia Cronin. *Gloria Steinem: A Biography.* Westport, Conn.: Greenwood Press, 2004.

Steinem, Gloria. "1971: The Birth of Ms." *New York* (April 19, 1993): 134.

———. "Codifying Indifference and Exclusion." *Los Angeles Times,* 26 June 1994, p. 5.

———. "Gloria Steinem Spends a Day with Saul Bellow." In *Conversations with Saul Bellow,* edited by

Gloria L. Cronin and Ben Siegel Cronin, 49–57. Jackson: University Press of Mississippi, 1994.
———. "Humanism and the Second Wave of Feminism: A Four-Point Plan to Carry Humanism and Feminism into the Next Century." *The Humanist* 47 (May/June 1987): 11–15.
———. "Let's Get Real about Feminism: The Backlash, the Myths, the Movement." *Ms.* 4, no. 2 (September/October): 34–43.
———. *Marilyn.* New York: Henry Holt, 1986.
———. *Moving beyond Words.* New York: Simon and Schuster, 1994.
———. *Outrageous Acts and Everyday Rebellions.* 2d ed. New York: Henry Holt, 1995.
———. *Revolution from Within: A Book of Self-Esteem.* Boston: Little, Brown and Co., 1992.
———. "Seeking Out the Invisible Woman." *New York Times,* 13 March 1992, p. C1.
———. "Sex, Lies and Advertising." *Ms.* 8, no. 2 (July/August 1990): 18–21.
———. "Six Great Ideas That Television Is Missing." In *Television as a Social Issue,* edited by Stuart Oskamp, 18–29. Beverly Hills, Calif.: Sage Publications, 1988.
———. "Voting as Rebellion." *Ms.* 7, no. 2 (March/April 1997): 54–61.
———. "Womb Envy, Testyria, and Breast Castration Anxiety." *Ms.* 4, no. 5 (March/April 1994): 48–56.
———. "Words and Change." *Ms.* 6, no. 2 (September/October 1996): 93–95.
———. "Would You Send This Memo?" *Washington Post,* 28 March 1993, p. H1.
Stern, Sydney Ladensohn. *Gloria Steinem: Her Passions, Politics, and Mystique.* Secaucus, N.J.: Carol Publishing Group. 1997.

**Student Non-Violent Coordinating Committee (SNCC)** The Student Non-Violent Coordinating Committee (SNCC) was a Mississippi-based, youth-centered civil rights organization. SNCC developed from an April 1960 meeting at Shaw University between Ella Baker, executive secretary of the Southern Christian Leadership Conference (SCLC), and college students with histories of activist involvement. SNCC—sometimes referred to as "snick"—advocated nonviolent direct-action strategies. In 1961, they participated in the Freedom Rides across the South organized by the CONGRESS OF RACIAL EQUALITY (CORE), which sought and finally achieved the desegregation of interstate travel. SNCC was also heavily involved in voter registration efforts in Mississippi, notably during the Mississippi Freedom Summer of 1964.

The organization's prominence made it vulnerable to attack. For example, three of the SNCC's Mississippi Summer Project volunteers—James Earl Chaney, Andrew Goodman, and Michael Schwerner—disappeared in 1964 and were later found to have been murdered by eight KU KLUX KLAN (KKK) members. During the mid-1960s, the group questioned its original interracial composition and integrationist aims and adopted a more radical perspective. In 1966, when Stokely Carmichael became chairman, SNCC aligned itself with the Black Power movement. SNCC became the Student Nationalist Coordinating Committee under H. Rap Brown's leadership and gradually dissolved.

Alice Walker worked for SNCC during the summer of 1964. SNCC's activism informed the themes Walker depicted in *Meridian.* She loosely based the novel's central character on activist RUBY DORIS SMITH-ROBINSON, who died in 1967, to highlight the internal conflicts that occurred within civil rights organizations of the 1960s.

*See also* FREEDOM RIDERS.

### FURTHER READING

Barbour, Floyd B., ed. *Black Power Revolt: A Collection of Essays.* Boston: Sargent, 1968.
Barlow, William, and Peter Shapiro. *An End to Silence: The San Francisco State College Student Movement in the '60s.* New York: Pegasus, 1971.
Barnes, Paula. Review of *Throwing Off the Cloak of Privilege: White Southern Women Activists in the Civil Rights Era,* edited by Gail S. Murray. *Arkansas Historical Quarterly* 64 (Summer 2005): 225–227.
Belfrage, Sally. *Freedom Summer.* New York: Viking Press, 1965.
Burner, Eric R. *And Gently He Shall Lead Them: Robert Parris Moses and Civil Rights in Mississippi.* New York: New York University Press, 1994.
Carson, Clayborne. *In Struggle: SNCC and the Black Awakening of the 1960's.* Cambridge, Mass.: Harvard University Press, 1995.

———, ed. *The Student Voice, 1960–1965: Periodical of the Student Nonviolent Coordinating Committee.* Compiled by the staff of the Martin Luther King, Jr., Papers Project. Westport, Conn.: Meckler, 1990.

Carson, Clayborne, Jr. "Toward Freedom and Community: The Evolution of Ideas in the Student Nonviolent Coordinating Committee, 1960–1966." Thesis, University of California, Los Angeles, 1975. Ann Arbor, Mich.: Xerox University Microfilms, 1976.

Chafe, William H. *Civilities and Civil Rights: Greensboro, North Carolina and the Black Struggle for Freedom.* New York: Oxford University Press, 1980.

Chalmers, David. "Committed, Proud, and Distrustful: The Mississippi Freedom Volunteers 20 Years Later." *USA Today,* September 1984, 36–39.

Chappell, David L. *Inside Agitators: White Southerners in the Civil Rights Movement.* Baltimore: Johns Hopkins University Press, 1994.

Chilcoat, George W., and Jerry A. Ligon. "'Helping to Make Democracy a Living Reality': The Curriculum Conference of the Mississippi Freedom Schools." *Journal of Curriculum and Supervision* 15 (Fall 1999): 43–68.

———. "Theatre as an Emancipatory Tool: Classroom Drama in the Mississippi Freedom Schools." *Journal of Curriculum Studies 3* (1998): 518.

Cobb, Charles. "Organizing the Freedom Schools." In *Freedom Is a Constant Struggle: An Anthology of the Mississippi Civil Rights Movement,* edited by Susan Erenrich. Montgomery, Ala.: Black Belt Press, 1999, 136–154.

Congress, Senate, Committee on the Judiciary. *Testimony of Stokely Carmichael.* United States Senate, 91st Congress, 2d Session, March 25, 1970. Washington, D.C.: Government Printing Office, 1970.

Dittmer, John. *Local People: The Struggle for Civil Rights in Mississippi.* Urbana: University of Illinois Press, 1994.

———. "The Politics of the Mississippi Movement." In *The Civil Rights Movement in America,* edited by Charles Eagles, 65–93. Jackson: University Press of Mississippi, 1986.

Holt, Len. *The Summer That Didn't End: The Story of the Mississippi Civil Rights Project of 1964.* New York: Da Capo Press, 1965.

Lewis, John. *Walking with the Wind: A Memoir of the Movement.* New York: Simon and Schuster, 1998.

McAdam, Doug. *Freedom Summer.* New York: Oxford University Press, 1988.

———. "Gender as a Mediator of the Activist Experience: The Case of Freedom Summer." *American Journal of Sociology* 97, no. 5 (1991): 1,211–1,240.

McEvoy, James. *Black Power and Student Rebellion.* Belmont, Calif.: Wadsworth Pub. Co., 1969.

McFadden, Grace Jordan. "Septima P. Clark and the Struggle for Human Rights." In *Women in the Civil Rights Movement: Trailblazers and Torchbearers 1941–1965,* edited by Vicki L. Crawford, Jacqueline Anne Rouse, and Barbara Woods, 85–97. Bloomington: Indiana University Press, 1993.

Meier, August, and Elliott Rudwick. *CORE: A Study in the Civil Rights Movement, 1942–1968.* Urbana: University of Illinois Press, 1975.

Murphree, Vanessa D. "Black Power: Public Relations and Social Change in the 1960s." *American Journalism* 21 (2004): 13–32.

Murray, Gail S., ed. *Throwing off the Cloak of Privilege: White Southern Women Activists in the Civil Rights Era.* Gainesville: University Press of Florida, 2004.

Newman, Mark. *The Civil Rights Movement.* Westport, Conn.: Praeger, 2004.

Nordhaus, Edward. "S.N.C.C. and the Civil Rights Movement in Mississippi, 1963–64: A Time of Change." *The History Teacher* 17 (November 1983): 95–102.

Oberschall, Anthony. *Social Movements: Ideologies, Interests, and Identities.* New Brunswick, N.J.: Transaction, 1993.

Ogbar, Jeffrey Ogbonna. *Black Power: Radical Politics and African American Identity.* Baltimore, Md.: Johns Hopkins University Press, 2004.

Olson, Lynne. *Freedom's Daughters: The Unsung Heroines of the Civil Rights Movement from 1830–1970.* New York: Simon and Schuster, 2001.

Oppenheimer, Martin. *The Sit-In Movement of 1960.* Brooklyn, N.Y.: Carlson, 1989.

Palmer, Phyllis. Review of *A Promise and a Way of Life: White Antiracist Activism,* by Becky Thompson, and *Deep in Our Hearts: Nine White Women in the Freedom Movement,* edited by Emmie S. Adams. *NWSA Journal* 15 (Summer 2003): 168–172.

Parsons, Sara Mitchell. *From Southern Wrongs to Civil Rights: The Memoir of a White Civil Rights Activist.* Tuscaloosa: University of Alabama Press, 2000.

Payne, Charles M. *I've Got the Light of Freedom: The Organizing Tradition and the Mississippi Freedom Struggle.* Berkeley: University of California Press, 1995.

Pearlstein, Daniel. "Teaching Freedom: SNCC and the Creation of the Mississippi Freedom Schools." *History of Education Quarterly* 30 (Fall 1990): 297–324.

Peterson, Rachel. "The White Problem: Class and Racial Divisions within the Student Nonviolent Coordinating Committee." *Proteus* 15 (1998): 13–19.

Rothschild, Mary Aickin. *Case of Black and White: Northern Volunteers and the Southern Freedom Summers, 1964–1965.* Westport, Conn.: Greenwood Press, 1982.

———. "The Volunteers and the Freedom Schools: Education for Social Change in Mississippi." *History of Education Quarterly* 22 (Winter 1982): 401–420.

———. "White Women Volunteers in the Freedom Summers: Their Life and Work in a Movement for Social Change." *Feminist Studies* 5, no. 3 (1979): 466–495.

Salomon, Larry R. *Roots of Justice: Stories of Organizing in Communities of Color.* Berkeley, Calif.: Chardon Press, 1998.

Schultz, Debra L. *Going South: Jewish Women in the Civil Rights Movement.* New York: New York University Press, 2001.

Sinsheimer, Joseph A. "The Freedom Vote of 1963: New Strategies of Racial Protest in Mississippi." *Journal of Southern History* 55 (May 1989): 217–244.

Stephens, Julie. *Anti-Disciplinary Protest: Sixties Radicalism and Postmodernism.* Cambridge and New York: Cambridge University Press, 1998.

Stoper, Emily. *The Student Nonviolent Coordinating Committee: The Growth of Radicalism in a Civil Rights Organization.* Brooklyn, N.Y.: Carlson Publishing, 1989.

Sugarman, Tracy. *Stranger at the Gates: A Summer in Mississippi.* New York: Hill and Wang, 1967.

Sutherland, Elizabeth, ed. *Letters from Mississippi.* New York: McGraw-Hill, 1965.

Terry, Robert W. *For Whites Only.* Grand Rapids, Mich.: W. B. Eerdmans Pub. Co., 1970.

Thompson, Becky. *A Promise and a Way of Life: White Antiracist Activism.* Minneapolis: University of Minnesota Press, 2001.

Thompson, Cooper, Emmet Schaefer, and Harry Brod, eds. *White Men Challenging Racism: 35 Personal Stories.* Durham, N.C.: Duke University Press, 2003.

Umoja, Akinyele O. "1964: The Beginning of the End of Nonviolence in the Mississippi Freedom Movement." *Radical History Review* (Winter 2003): 201–226.

———. "The Ballot and the Bullet: A Comparative Analysis of Armed Resistance in the Civil Rights Movement." *Journal of Black Studies* 29 (March 1999): 558–578.

Useem, Michael. Review of *Dynamics of Idealism: White Activists in a Black Movement,* by N. J. Demerath III, Gerald Marwell, and Michael T. Aiken. *American Journal of Sociology* 81 (May 1976): 1,526–1,528.

Wagstaff, Thomas. *Black Power: The Radical Response to White America.* Beverly Hills, Calif.: Glencoe Press, 1969.

Wigginton, Eliot, ed. *Refuse to Stand Silently By: An Oral History of Grass Roots Social Activism in America, 1921–1964.* New York: Doubleday, 1991.

Williamson, Joy Ann. *Black Power on Campus: The University of Illinois, 1965–75.* Urbana: University of Illinois Press, 2003.

**sugartit** *Sugartit* is a vernacular term that refers to a piece of cloth filled with sugar in the shape of a ball or nipple that is employed as a pacifier for babies. In a passage in *The Third Life of Grange Copeland,* Walker writes how Brownfield's mother, Margaret, "left him each morning with a hasty hug and a sugartit, on which he sucked . . ."

### FURTHER READING

Howard, Philip. *A Dictionary of the Verbs of the Slave Language.* Ottawa: Northern Social Research Division, Department of Northern and Indian Affairs, 1977.

———. *A Dictionary of the Verbs of Southern Slavery.* Yellowknife: Department of Culture and Communication, Government of the Northwest Territories, 1990.

———. "A Preliminary Presentation of Slavery Phonemes." *University of California Publications in Linguistics* 29 (1963): 42–47.

Mufwene, Salikoko S., et al., eds. *African American English: Structure, History and Use.* London: Routledge, 1998.

Rickford, John R. *African American Vernacular English: Features and Use, Evolution, and Educational Implications.* Oxford: Blackwell, 1999.

Rickford, John R., with Russell J. Rickford. *Spoken Soul: The Story of Black English.* New York: John Wiley, 2000.

Rickford, John R., with Suzanne Romaine. *Creole Genesis, Attitudes and Discourse: Studies Celebrating Charlene Sato.* Amsterdam: John Benjamins, 1999.

**tarot cards** *See* MOTHERPEACE TAROT DECK.

***Their Eyes Were Watching God*** In her 1937 novel *Their Eyes Were Watching God,* ZORA NEALE HURSTON employs the actions and development of her protagonist, Janie Crawford Killicks Starks Woods, to develop a theology akin to that often articulated by Alice Walker. Walker has repeatedly affirmed the centrality of Hurston's novel to her writing and life and was one of the primary individuals responsible for Hurston's resurrection from literary obscurity in the 1970s.

In *Their Eyes Were Watching God,* Hurston develops a unique mythology that establishes not only Janie's role as a spiritual model but the inherent, if often undiscovered, merits of all humanity. Hurston was a student of anthropology, and consequently her work is full of both biblical and mythological references. Rather than resurrecting an ancient archetype to serve as a foundation for her novel, she created a contemporary heroine who goes on a quest to rescue herself.

The novel begins at the story's chronological end. From the very first page, Hurston presents the reader with evidence of Janie's strength and purposefulness, traits to which she can lay claim as a consequence of her successful quest. The novel's third paragraph begins with the sentence "So the beginning of this was woman and she had come back from burying the dead" (9). This sentence recalls the opening words of Genesis, yet by specifying that the "beginning of this was woman," Hurston eliminates patriarchal notions of God and creation and introduces the possibility of female authority and self-determination, specifically Janie's spiritual potential.

From the novel's beginning, the reader is made aware of Hurston's conflation of biblical mythology and folklore and of her revelation of the divinity of everyday humanity. In this beginning, Hurston lays the groundwork for tracing the process of her heroine's acquisition of SELF-AFFIRMATION. Hurston establishes that Janie is the figure throughout the book whom all are watching. Even the "sudden dead" watch Janie with "their eyes flung open in judgment" (9). The dead are not the only ones who watch her. Throughout the book, there are references to Janie being observed, watched by various individuals and groups.

As the book begins, Janie is returning to her hometown after a long absence. On the pages that describe Janie's arrival, Hurston's sentence structure reinforces Janie's position as the observed subject. Hurston uses the simple "They *verb*[ed]" sentence structure seven times in order to emphasize the townspeople's reaction to Janie's return. This normally vociferous group is, in fact, silenced upon her arrival: "The porch couldn't talk for looking. . . . Nobody moved, nobody spoke, nobody even thought to swallow spit until after the gate slammed behind her" (11). Indeed, the eyes of the town are watching Janie, who, upon her return to Eatonville, has recognized and claimed her own power and autonomy through self-affirmation. Before achieving her understanding and awareness, however, Janie has undergone a long journey, and so, after this establishing scene, the novel proceeds to unveil this process of discovery.

After Janie walks past and silences the townspeople, she is joined by her friend Phoeby, who welcomes her back from her journey and eventually becomes the recipient of Janie's story. Significantly, the name Phoeby (Phoebe) recalls the biblical character of the same name. The significance of the biblical Phoebe is as "helper" or "deaconess." In his letter to the Romans, Paul writes, "I commend to you our sister Phoebe, who is a servant of the church . . . that you receive her in the church in a manner worthy of the saints, and that you help her in whatever matter she may have need of now, for she herself has also been a helper of many" (Rom. 16:1–2). As a result of her name, Phoeby of *Their Eyes Were Watching God* can be understood as a deaconess who will aid in the community's gaining awareness of Janie's spiritual understanding and insight. She is the conduit through which Janie's mysterious faith and understanding can be passed on to the larger community. As Phoeby herself says to Janie, "If you so desire, Ah'll tell 'em what you tell me to tell 'em" (17). Phoeby's role in the tale is as a deaconess of the spirituality personified by Janie.

Throughout the chapter, Janie speaks of her desire to wash her feet. Significantly, Phoeby does not wash Janie's feet; Janie washes them herself. By performing this act herself, Janie establishes that her newfound confidence and self-assurance does not depend on the understanding or adulation of others. Her journey is a personal unfolding of truth and something Janie must recognize and nurture in herself. The example that Hurston's novel presents for the possibilities of repurposing the quest becomes a primary source for Alice Walker throughout her life and canon. Walker has said that *Their Eyes Were Watching God* is the most important book she has ever read.

## FURTHER READING

Ashe, Bertram D. "'Why Don't He Like My Hair?': Constructing African-American Standards of Beauty in Toni Morrison's *Song of Solomon* and Zora Neale Hurston's *Their Eyes Were Watching God.*" *African American Review* 29, no. 4 (Winter 1995): 579–593.

Brogan, Jacqueline Vaught. "The Hurston/Walker/Vaughn Connection: Feminist Strategies in American Fiction." *Women's Studies* 28, no. 2 (1999): 185–201.

Crabtree, Claire. "The Confluence of Folklore, Feminism and Black Self-Determination in Zora Neale Hurston's *Their Eyes Were Watching God.*" *Southern Literary Journal* 17, no. 2 (Spring 1985): 54–66.

Davis, Rose Parkman. *Zora Neale Hurston: An Annotated Bibliography and Reference Guide.* Westport, Conn.: Greenwood Press, 1997.

duCille, Ann. "Stoning the Romance: Passion, Patriarchy, and the Modern Marriage Plot." In *The Coupling Convention: Sex, Text and Tradition in Black Women's Fiction.* New York: Oxford University Press, 1993, 110–142.

Hattenhauer, Darryl. "Hurston's *Their Eyes Were Watching God.*" *Explicator* 50, no. 2 (Winter 1992): 111–113.

Gates, Henry Louis, Jr. "Zora Neale Hurston and the Speakerly Text." In *The Signifying Monkey: A Theory of Afro-American Literary Criticism.* New York: Oxford University Press, 1988, 170–214.

Hurston, Zora Neale. *Their Eyes Were Watching God.* New York: Harper and Row, 1937.

Hubbard, Dolan. "'. . . Ah Said Ah'd Save De Text for You': Recontextualizing the Sermon to Tell (Her) story in Zora Neale Hurston's *Their Eyes Were Watching God.*" *African American Review* 27, no. 2 (Summer 1993): 167–179.

Johnson, Maria. "'The World in a Jug and the Stopper in [Her] Hand': Their Eyes as Blues Performance." *African American Review* 32, no. 3 (Fall 1998): 401–415.

King, Sigrid. "Naming and Power in Zora Neale Hurston's *Their Eyes Were Watching God.*" *Black American Literature Forum* 24, no. 4 (Winter 1990): 683–697.

Kodat, Catherine Gunther. "Biting the Hand That Writes You: Southern African-American Folk Narrative and the Place of Women in *Their Eyes Were Watching God.*" In *Haunted Bodies: Gender and Southern Texts,* edited by Anne Goodwyn Jones and Susan V. Donaldson, 319–342. Charlottesville: University Press of Virginia, 1997.

Lowe, John. "Laughin' up a World: *Their Eyes Were Watching* God and the (Wo)Man of Words." In *Jump at the Sun: Zora Neale Hurston's Cosmic Comedy.* Chicago: University of Illinois Press, 1994, 156–204.

McGowan, Todd. "Liberation and Domination: *Their Eyes Were Watching God* and the Evolution of Capitalism." *MELUS* 24, no. 1 (Spring 1999): 109–129.

Racine, Maria J. "Voice and Interiority in Zora Neale Hurston's *Their Eyes Were Watching God.*" *African American Review* 28, no. 2 (Summer 1994): 283–293.

Sheppard, David M. "Living by Comparisons: Janie and her Discontents." *English Language Notes* 30, no. 2 (December 1992): 63–76.

Trombold, John. "The Minstrel Show Goes to the Great War: Zora Neale Hurston's Mass Cultural Other." *MELUS* 24, no. 1 (Spring 1999): 85–108.

Walker, Alice. "Looking for Zora." In *In Search of Our Mothers' Gardens: Womanist Prose*. New York: Harcourt Brace Jovanovich, 1983, 93–116.

**Tolstoy, Leo** (1828–1910) Leo Tolstoy was a prolific Russian-born fiction writer and social critic most famous for his novels *War and Peace* (1865–69) and *Anna Karenina* (1875–77). Tolstoy also wrote three autobiographies. After an immersion in philosophical and religious works, his writings, such as the 1899 text *The Resurrection*, became increasingly critical of capitalism. Tolstoy's ideological shift alienated his family and led to his excommunication from the Russian Orthodox Church.

During her sophomore year in college, Alice Walker became deeply engaged in reading Russian writers including, FYODOR DOSTOYEVSKY, Nikolai Gogol, and Tolstoy. She has cited Tolstoy's short stories and his novels *The Resurrection* and *The Kruetzer Sonata* (1899) as teaching her the importance of fully developing characters regardless of the politics or social issues they represent.

### FURTHER READING

Greenwood, Edward Baker. *Tolstoy: The Comprehensive Vision*. New York: St. Martin's Press, 1975.

Gustafson, Richard F. *Leo Tolstoy: Resident and Stranger*. Princeton, N.J.: Princeton University Press, 1986.

O'Brien, John. "Alice Walker: An Interview." In *Alice Walker: Critical Perspectives Past and Present*, edited by Henry Louis Gates, Jr., and Kwame Anthony Appiah, 326–346. New York: Amistad, 1993.

Redfearn, David. *Tolstoy: Principles for a New World Order*. London: Shepheard-Walwyn, 1992.

Wilson, A. N. *Tolstoy*. New York: Norton, 2001.

**Tonglen** Tonglen is a meditation practice found in Tibetan BUDDHISM. Translated as "giving and receiving," Tonglen is a visualization technique in which the practitioner takes on the suffering of another, or others, with each inhalation and offers one's own happiness and peace to the other with each exhalation. As such, Tonglen is meant to pursue and reinforce key teachings of Buddhism, including generating loving kindness and decreasing self-attachment. It is not meant to increase one's own pain but to help break down the instinct of a self-protective ego. The practice can be directed toward a single individual, to many, or to all across the world. The suffering being addressed may take any form: emotional, physical, or spiritual. It can be the pain of those terminally ill or even of those who have died. It may be a specific pain or one poorly understood. Tonglen may be conducted in formal sitting meditation, or it may be conducted as a spontaneous response to the witnessing of another's pain. In each case, the practice of Tonglen creates positive karma and provides a path toward enlightenment.

Alice Walker learned the practice of Tonglen through the teachings of an ordained Buddhist Nun, PEMA CHÖDRÖN. Chödrön and Walker also coreleased the 2005 audio recording on Tonglen, *Pema Chödrön and Alice Walker in Conversation: On the Meaning of Suffering and the Mystery of Joy*.

### FURTHER READING

Chödrön Pema, and Alice Walker. *Pema Chödrön and Alice Walker in Conversation: On the Meaning of Suffering and the Mystery of Joy*. Louisville, Colo.: Sounds True, 1999.

Chödrön, Pema, and Tingdzin Otro. *Tonglen: The Path of Transformation*. Halifax, Nova Scotia: Vajradhatu Publications, 2001.

Kamalashila. *Meditation: The Buddhist Art of Tranquility and Insight*. Birmingham: Windhorse Publications, 1996.

Schnall, Marianne. "Conversation with Alice Walker." Available online. URL: www.feminist.com/resources/artspeech/interviews/alicewalker.html. Accessed February 28, 2009.

Trungpa, Chogyam. *Training the Mind and Cultivating Loving-Kindness*. Boston: Shambhala Classics, 1993.

**Toomer, Jean** (1894–1967) The poet and novelist Jean Toomer was a leading figure in the HARLEM RENAISSANCE and an important influence on Alice Walker. His maternal grandfather was P. B. S. Pinchback, the first African American elected as lieutenant governor and then acting governor of the state of Louisiana. Pinchback was born free. His daughter, Nina Pinchback, was Jean Toomer's mother. Jean was born Nathan Pinchback Toomer on December 26, 1894. His father abandoned the family, and Jean and his mother lived with P. B. S. Pinchback, who had relocated to Washington, D.C. As a boy, Toomer was frequently ill, a circumstance that seems to have colored his experience and perceptions of the world. When his mother died in 1909, he remained with his grandparents for the remainder of his childhood.

Following his graduation from Dunbar High School in Washington, D.C., Jean Toomer attended many institutions of high education, but he never graduated from any of them. He published CANE in 1923, and the text was well received. Many literary critics note the publication of *Cane* as the beginning of the Harlem Renaissance, the literary time period, roughly between World War I and World War II, when African-American writers such as Claude McKay, ZORA NEALE HURSTON, LANGSTON HUGHES, and many others produced a number of significant American literary works. It was also a period in which African-American artists in other genres, such as art, music, and theater, produced a great number of significant works.

Although Toomer has an extensive canon of other works, his literary reputation remains primarily linked to *Cane*. Today, Toomer is considered one of the most important American writers of the early 20th century.

### FURTHER READING

Benson, Brian J., and Mabel M. Dillard. *Jean Toomer.* Boston: Twayne Press, 1980.

Byrd, Rudolph P. *Jean Toomer's Years with Gurdjieff: Portrait of an Artist, 1923–1936.* Athens: University of Georgia Press, 1990.

Jones, Robert B. *Jean Toomer and the Prison-House of Thought: A Phenomenology of the Spirit.* Amherst: University of Massachusetts Press, 1993.

Kerman, Cynthia E., and Richard Eldridge. *The Lives of Jean Toomer: A Hunger for Wholeness.* Baton Rouge: Louisiana State University Press, 1987.

Larson, Charles R. *Invisible Darkness: Jean Toomer and Nella Larsen.* Iowa City: University of Iowa Press, 1993.

McKay, Nellie Y. *Jean Toomer, Artist: A Study of His Literary Life and Work, 1894–1936.* Chapel Hill: University of North Carolina Press, 1984.

O'Daniel, Therman B., ed. *Jean Toomer: A Critical Evaluation.* Washington, D.C.: Howard University Press, 1988.

Scruggs, Charles W. *Jean Toomer and the Terrors of American History.* Philadelphia: University of Pennsylvania Press, 1998.

Toomer, Jean. *Cane.* New York: Liveright Publishing, 1997.

———. *The Collected Poems of Jean Toomer.* Edited by Robert B. Jones and Margery Toomer Latimer. Chapel Hill: University of North Carolina Press, 1988.

———. *Jean Toomer: Selected Essays and Literary Criticism.* Edited by Robert B. Jones. Knoxville: University of Tennessee Press, 1997.

Turner, Darwin T., ed. *In a Minor Chord: Three Afro-American Writers and Their Search for Identity: Toomer, Cullen, Hurston.* Carbondale, Ill.: Southern Illinois University Press, 1971.

———. *The Wayward and the Seeking: A Collection of Writings by Jean Toomer.* Washington, D.C.: Howard University Press, 1980.

**Transcendental Meditation** The meditative spiritual practice of Transcendental Meditation fuses various Indian spiritual traditions and was pioneered by Marishi Mahesh Yogi. The maharishi had studied physics and brought the technique of Transcendental Meditation to the United States. Some of his most famous students included celebrities such as the Beatles and Mia Farrow.

Transcendental Meditation aims to nurture natural wisdom through meditation centered on mantra repetition. Transcendental Meditation has been documented to create brain waves that are not the same as those produced during sleep or full wakefulness. Through scientific study, the practice has been shown to have tangible effects on health and well-being.

Walker became a practitioner of Transcendental Meditation after her divorce from MELVYN LEV-

ENTHAL, and she continues to incorporate it into her spiritual life.

### FURTHER READING


Fox, D. *Meditation and Reality: A Critical Review.* Atlanta, Ga.: John Knox, 1986.

Mason, Paul. *The Maharishi: The Biography of the Man Who Gave Transcendental Meditation to the World.* Lyndhurst, Eng.: Evolution Publishing, 2005.

Squier, S. M. "Meditation, Disability, and Identity." *Literature and Medicine* 23, no. 1 (2004): 23–45.

White, Evelyn C. *Alice Walker: A Life.* New York: W. W. Norton and Company, 2004.

Yogi, Maharishi Mahesh. *Transcendental Meditation: Science of Being and Art of Living.* New York: Signet Books, 1988.


**Truth, Sojourner (Isabella Baumfree)** (ca. 1797–1883) In her novel *Meridian,* Walker has a tree that is called the Sojourner. The name of the tree is probably an allusion to Sojourner Truth, an American evangelist and social reformer. As a self-taught speaker, she provided white audiences with a compelling voice for the cause of abolition directly from someone who had been a slave. She also spoke out for the rights of women.

Born Isabella Baumfree to slave parents in a Dutch settlement in Ulster County, New York, Truth spoke only Dutch until the age of 11, when she was sold from her family to an English-speaking slaveholder. She was sold several times and experienced several cruel slave masters until 1827, when New York outlawed slavery.

In the initial period of her life as a free woman, Baumfree made her living as a domestic servant. Then she began preaching on street corners, adopting the name Sojourner Truth. She left New York for the Midwest to preach not only religion but in behalf of abolition and women's rights. Using scripture to make her points, Sojourner Truth drew large crowds, which were moved by her oratory. She spoke firsthand of the cruelties of slavery. In 1851, at the Ohio Women's Rights Convention in Akron, she gave her most famous speech, "Ain't I a Woman?"

When the American Civil War began, Truth helped gather supplies for African-American volunteers for the Northern army. In 1864, she helped integrate streetcars in Washington, D.C., where she also met President Abraham Lincoln. After the war ended, Truth worked in the National Freedman's Relief Association, an organization dedicated to creating better conditions for the newly freed slaves. Despite increasing health problems, she remained active into old age. She died in a sanitarium in Battle Creek, Michigan.

### FURTHER READING


Bernard, Jacqueline. *Journey toward Freedom: The Story of Sojourner Truth.* New York: Norton, 1967.

Fitch, Suzanne P., and Roseanne M. Medium. *Sojourner Truth as Orator: Wit, Story and Song.* Westport, Conn.: Greenwood Press, 1997.

Mabee, Carleton, and Susan M. Newhouse. *Sojourner Truth—Slave, Prophet, Legend.* New York: New York University Press, 1993.

Painter, Nell I. *Sojourner Truth: A Life, a Symbol.* New York: W. W. Norton, 1996.

Stetson, Erlene, and Linda David. *Glorying in Tribulation: The Lifework of Sojourner Truth.* East Lansing: Michigan State University Press, 1994.

Truth, Sojourner. *Narrative of Sojourner Truth.* Salem, N.H.: Ayer Co., 1988.


**Tucker, Sophie** (1884–1966) Tucker was a vaudeville-era performer best known for brassy performances of songs like "I'm the Last of the Red Hot Mamas" and "Some of These Days." She began her vaudeville career in 1906, joined the Ziegfeld Follies in 1909, and performed in blackface until 1911. From the 1920s to the 1940s, she was a successful singer and actress. Sophie Tucker died on February 9, 1966, in New York City.

In *The Color Purple,* Celie describes Shug Avery's burgeoning singing career by describing her vast repertoire, which includes the music of Sophie Tucker, Duke Ellington, and various lesser-known singers.

### FURTHER READING


All Music Guide. "Sophie Tucker." Available online. URL: http://www.allmusic.com/cg/amg.dll. Accessed February 20, 2009.

Cullen, Frank, with Florence Hackman and Donald McNeilly. *Vaudeville, Old and New: An Encyclopedia of Variety Performers in America.* New York: Routledge, 2007.

Freedland, Michael. *Sophie: The Sophie Tucker Story.* London: Woburn Press, 1978.

Gilbert, Douglas. *American Vaudeville: Its Life and Times.* New York: Dover, 1963.

Tucker, Sophie. *Some of These Days: The Autobiography of Sophie Tucker.* Garden City, N.Y.: Doubleday, Doran and Co., 1945.

**Uncle Remus** Uncle Remus was a fictional slave narrator featured in several popular anthologies of African folktales collected by writer JOEL CHANDLER HARRIS (1848–1908). Harris first heard the tales as a child living on a plantation in EATONTON, GEORGIA. Cultural critics have continually noted how Chandler's stories present a troublingly romantic, idealized portrait of life of contented blacks living in the South during the slave era. In 1946, Walt Disney used the tales as a foundation for the film *Song of the South.*

Throughout her career, Alice Walker has challenged the idyllic portrait of southern black life Harris depicted in his stories. In her 1981 speech to the Atlanta Historical Society, "The Dummy in the Window: Joel Chandler Harris and the Invention of Uncle Remus" (reprinted in *Living by the Word*), she denounced Harris for stealing and distorting African folk culture. The African origins of the tales surface in *The Color Purple* when Nettie describes how Celie's daughter, Olivia, who is on a missionary trip, learns that "Uncle Remus" stories were actually African from an Olinkan girl named Tashi. Walker has also noted how various themes and characters from African folktales pervade Cherokee folk literature. Interestingly, Joel Chandler Harris was also from Alice Walker's hometown of Eatonton, Georgia.

### FURTHER READING

Bickley, R. Bruce, Jr., and Hugh T. Keenan, eds. *Joel Chandler Harris: An Annotated Bibliography of Criticism, 1977–1996; with Supplement, 1892–1976.* Westport, Conn.: Greenwood Press, 1997.

Harris, Joel Chandler. *Tar Baby: Tales of Br'er Rabbit.* London: Creation Books, 2000.

Howell, Marcella. "Will the Authentic 'Hare' Please Stand Up: An Analysis of Joel Chandler Harris' Uncle Remus Tales." *Selected Proceedings of the 3rd Annual Conference on Minority Studies* 4 (April 1975): 23–30.

Montenyohl, Eric L. "Joel Chandler Harris and American Folklore." *Atlanta Historical Journal* 30, nos. 3–4 (Fall–Winter 1986–87): 79–88.

———. "The Origins of Uncle Remus." *Folklore-Forum* 18, no. 2 (Spring 1986): 136–167.

White, Evelyn C. *Alice Walker: A Life.* New York: W. W. Norton and Company, 2004.

**Walker, Rebecca Grant (Rebecca Grant Leventhal)** (1969– ) Rebecca Grant Walker is the only child of Alice Walker and MELVYN LEVENTHAL. She was born on November 17, 1969, in Jackson, Mississippi. After graduating from Yale University in 1992, she established herself as an author, lecturer, activist, and writing consultant.

In her 2001 memoir *Black White and Jewish: Autobiography of a Shifting Self,* Walker details her struggles growing up biracial and discusses the challenges of being the daughter of two prominent figures. After her parents divorced, Rebecca divided her time between them, spending two-year intervals with each. She also discusses various challenges in her life, including becoming pregnant at 14 and having an abortion.

In her memoir, Rebecca Walker chronicles the differences between her experiences with her father and his wife, whom she characterizes as having a white and suburban lifestyle, with her time living in California with her mother, whose world she characterizes as Afra-feminist and artistic. Her eventual feelings of alienation from her father's white, Jewish culture motivated her to adopt her mother's maiden name as her last name. In spite of this symbolic embrace of her mother, Rebecca has characterized Alice Walker as negligently focused on her own needs and inattentive to those of her daughter.

Rebecca Walker's reputation as a public persona emerged from her writings about third-wave FEMINISM. In 1997, she cofounded the Third Wave Foundation, devoted to feminist activism. She has also edited a number of collections that address changing notions of feminism, masculinity and family structures, and has written various articles for mainstream publications.

Walker, who is bisexual, was in a relationship with the singer Me'Shell N'degeocello for several years and is a coparent to N'degeocello's son, Solomon. In her 2007 book *Baby Love,* she addressed the importance of young feminists to embrace motherhood rather than viewing it as a deterrent from their professional and political ambitions. Her belief and public assertion that raising a biological child differs emotionally from raising a stepchild or nonbiological child engendered mild controversy. Currently, she is raising her own biological son, Tenzin (born 2004), with the baby's father, Choyin Rangdrol, with whom she lives in Maui, Hawaii. Walker uses the pseudonym Glen for Rangdrol in her writings.

Rebecca and Alice Walker are currently estranged. Rebecca Walker has written publicly that her mother was absent and unsupportive during her childhood and young adulthood. She has said that the break with her mother happened after she told her mother that she was pregnant and her mother was not happy with her decision to have a child. Rebecca has also written about what she has called her mother's jealousy about her literary successes. She has speculated that she has been written out of her mother's will and has written that her mother "resigned" from the job of being her mother. Alice Walker has commented that she was initially hurt by some of her daughter's observations but has since made peace with them.

### FURTHER READING

Driscoll, Margarette. "The Day Feminist Icon Alice Walker Resigned as My Mother: *The Color Purple* Brought Alice Walker Global Fame, But Her Strident Views Led to an Irreconcilable Rift, Her Daughter Tells." *Sunday Times,* 4 May 2008, p. 3.

Rebecca Walker Web site. Available online. URL: http://www.rebeccawalker.com/. Accessed February 28, 2009.

Rosenbloom, Stephanie. "Evolution of a Feminist Daughter." *New York Times,* 17 March 2007. Available online. URL: http://www.nytimes.com/2007/03/18/fashion/18walker.html?pagewanted=1&_r=1. Accessed February 28, 2009.

Third Wave Foundation. "Our History." Available online. URL: http://www.thirdwavefoundation.org/about/growth. Accessed February 28, 2009.

Walker, Alice. "The Two of Us." *Essence* 26.1 (May 1995): 172–181.

Walker, Rebecca. *Baby Love: Choosing Motherhood after a Lifetime of Ambivalence.* New York: Riverhead Books, 2007.

———. *Black White and Jewish: Autobiography of a Shifting Self.* New York: Riverhead Books, 2001.

———, ed. *One Big Happy Family: 18 Writers Talk about Polyandry, Open Adoption, Mixed Marriage, Househusbandry, Single Motherhood, and Other Realities of Truly Modern Love.* New York: Riverhead Books, 2009.

———. *To Be Real: Telling the Truth and Changing the Face of Feminism.* New York: Anchor Books, 1995.

———. *What Makes a Man: 22 Writings Imagine the Future.* New York: Riverhead Books, 2005.

White, Evelyn C. *Alice Walker: A Life.* New York: W. W. Norton and Company, 2004.

Winchell, D. H. *Alice Walker.* Twayne: New York, 1992.

**Wheatley, Phillis** (ca. 1753–1784) In 1773, Phillis Wheatley became the first African American to publish a book of poetry. Before she was allowed to submit her volume, she had to undergo a trial to prove her competence and demonstrate that she was capable of writing her own poems.

The act of public testimony has always been a precarious, high-stakes endeavor for black women. Always, though, black women have refused to accept silence as an option.

Born in Gambia, West Africa, Wheatley was kidnapped at the age of eight and brought to Boston, where she was bought by John Wheatley. Her first name came from the slave ship, the *Phillis.* It was in the Wheatley home that she learned to speak and write English. Her great intelligence was obvious to the Wheatleys, and they encouraged her to study theology and the classics.

As a young teenager, Wheatley published her first poem, *On Messrs. Hussey and Coffin* (1767). Several years later, in 1773, she published a poetry collection, *Poems on Various Subjects.* She was freed that same year.

Her poetry was recognized widely, and Wheatley traveled to London to speak and to promote her book. Political figures of the day, such as George

Washington and Voltaire, sought to talk with her. The influences on her poetry were diverse, including both the oral traditions of African-American slaves as well as her knowledge of classic Latin.

Wheatley's life ended in poverty. A second volume of her poetry did not find a publisher, and the manuscript was lost. Walker writes poignantly about Wheatley in an essay on the poet in her collection of essays *In Search of Our Mothers' Gardens.*

### FURTHER READING


Flanzbaum, Hilene. "Unprecedented Liberties: Rereading Phillis Wheatley." *MELUS* 18, no. 3 (Fall 1993): 71.

Kendrick, Robert. "Re-membering America: Phillis Wheatley's Intertextual Epic." *African American Review* 30, no. 1 (Spring 1996): 71–89.

Levernier, James A. "Phillis Wheatley and the New England Clergy." *Early American Literature* 26, no. 1 (1991): 21–38.

Mason, Julian. *Poems of Phillis Wheatley.* Chapel Hill: University of North Carolina Press, 1966.

Nott, Walt. "From 'Uncultivated Barbarian' to 'Poetical Genius': The Public Presence of Phillis Wheatley." *MELUS* 18, no. 3 (Fall 1993): 21.

Ogude, S. E. "Slavery and the African Imagination: A Critical Perspective." *World Literature Today: A Literary Quarterly of the University of Oklahoma* 55, no. 1 (1981): 21–25.

O'Neale, Sondra. "A Slave's Subtle War: Phyllis Wheatley's Use of Biblical Myth and Symbol." *Early American Literature* 21, no. 2 (1986): 144–165.

Richards, Phillip M. "Phillis Wheatley and Literary Americanization." *American Quarterly* 44, no. 2 (1992): 163–191.

Robinson, William H. *Phillis Wheatley: A Bio-Bibliography.* Boston: G. K. Hall, 1981.

Scruggs, Charles. "Phillis Wheatley and the Poetical Legacy of Eighteenth-Century England." *Studies in Eighteenth-Century Culture* 10 (1981): 279–295.

Shields, John C. "Phillis Wheatley's Use of Classicism." *American Literature* 52 (1980): 97–111.

Sistrunk, Albertha. "The Influence of Alexander Pope on the Writing Style of Phillis Wheatley." In *Critical Essays on Phillis Wheatley,* edited by William H. Robinson, 175–188. Boston: G. K. Hall, 1982.

Steele, Thomas J. S. J. "The Figure of Columbia: Phillis Wheatley Plus George Washington." *New England Quarterly* 54, no. 2 (1981): 264–266.

Watson, Marsha. "A Classic Case: Phillis Wheatley and Her Poetry." *Early American Literature* 31, no. 2 (1996): 103–132.

Wheatley, Phillis. *An Elegiac Poem, on the Death of that Celebrated Divine, and Eminent Servant of Jesus Christ, the Late Reverend, and Pious George Whitefield, Chaplain to the Right Honourable the Countess of Huntingdon.* Boston: Ezekiel Russell, 1770.

———. *Poems on Various Subjects, Religious and Moral.* London: Printed for A. Bell, 1773.


**Wild Trees Press** (1984–1988) Wild Trees Press was an independent publishing company that Alice Walker, her then partner, ROBERT L. ALLEN, and her friend BELVIE ROOKS cofounded in 1984 in Anderson Valley, California. Wild Trees focused on publishing works with a feminist perspective. The press's published titles include J. California Cooper's 1984 short story collection *A Piece of Mine;* JoAnne Brasil's *Escape from Billy's Bar-B-Que* (1985); the 1986 memoir *Ready from Within: Septima Clark and the Civil Rights Movement,* by Septima Poinsette Clark (edited by Cynthia Stokes Brown), which won an American Book Award; Charlotte Méndez's *Condor and Hummingbird* (1986); Henry Crowder's *As Wonderful as All That?: Henry Crowder's Memoir of His Affair with Nancy Cunard, 1928–1935* (1987); and Madi Kertonegoro's *The Spirit Journey: Stories and Paintings of Bali* (1988). The trio decided in 1988 to end publishing operations as the work had become overwhelming and had exceeded their original commitment to and vision of the project.

### FURTHER READING


Brasil, JoAnne. *Escape from Billy's Bar-B-Que.* Navarro, Calif.: Wild Trees Press, 1985.

Clark, Septima. *Ready from Within: Septima Clark and the Civil Rights Movement.* Edited by Cynthia Stokes Brown. Navarro, Calif.: Wild Trees Press, 1986.

Cooper, J. California. *A Piece of Mine.* Foreword by Alice Walker. Navarro, Calif.: Wild Trees Press, 1984.

Crowder, Henry, with the assistance of Hugo Speck. *As Wonderful as All That?: Henry Crowder's Memoir of his Affair with Nancy Cunard, 1928–1935.* Navarro, Calif.: Wild Trees Press, 1987.

Joyce, Donald F. *Black Book Publishers in the United States: A Historical Dictionary of the Presses, 1817–1990.* New York: Greenwood Press, 1991.

Kertonegoro, Madi. *The Spirit Journey: Stories and Paintings of Bali.* Navarro, Calif.: Wild Trees Press, 1988.

Méndez, Charlotte. *Condor and Hummingbird.* Navarro, Calif.: Wild Trees Press, 1986.

White, Evelyn C. *Alice Walker: A Life.* New York: W. W. Norton and Company, 2004.

**Winfrey, Oprah** (1954– ) Oprah Winfrey is a talk show host, magazine publisher, film producer, and actress. The popularity of her television show and other business enterprises has made her one of the first African-American women to become a billionaire.

Born in Kosciusko, Mississippi, to poor, unmarried teenage parents, Winfrey was raised first by her grandmother, Hattie Mae Lee, on a farm. At six, she moved to Milwaukee to live with her mother, Vernita Lee. After experiencing the trauma of sexual molestation, she ran away from home at age 13. Eventually she found herself living with her father, Vernon Winfrey, in Nashville, Tennessee.

From her earliest forays into the professional world, Winfrey was interested in and pursued journalism. She earned her undergraduate degree in speech communications and performing arts at Tennessee State University, then began to work in radio stations in Nashville as a student. She then moved on to positions at various television stations, working as a reporter and, eventually, as a news anchor. After a stint as a television anchor in Baltimore, in 1984 Winfrey moved to Chicago, where she helped raise the ratings of a local television talk show that became *The Oprah Winfrey Show,* which was first broadcast nationally in 1986.

The format of Winfrey's hourlong program, which is still on the air in 2010, generally entails Winfrey interviewing people from all walks of life—housewives, doctors, writers, and so forth—although the show has traditionally placed an emphasis on personal interviews with celebrities. The subject matter of Winfrey's interviews usually derives from the national or international headlines or is prompted by an artist or celebrity promotional tour.

Winfrey was a cast member of the film *The Color Purple.* As legend has it, shortly before Winfrey began broadcasting nationally, QUINCY JONES, a coproducer of the project, was in Chicago on business and was watching television in his hotel when he saw her then local talk show. He felt immediately that she would be the perfect person to cast as Sofia, one of the novel's major characters. Although Winfrey says that she had wanted always to be an actress, she had little experience before she was selected for this part by Jones and director STEVEN SPIELBERG.

Winfrey was a natural for the part of Sofia. Having grown up in the rural South, she was able to identify with Walker's characters on a personal level, and she brought realism and authenticity to her portrayal of the much-maligned character of Sofia. She has said that her experiences making the film catapulted her to another level of understanding and awareness—one that allowed her to make her show the unexpectedly exponential success that it has become. As a result of her role as Sofia, Winfrey was nominated for both a Golden Globe and an Academy Award. She has also appeared as an actress in the films *Native Son* (1986) and *Beloved* (1998) and the made-for-television movies *The Women of Brewster Place* (1989), *There Are No Children Here* (1993), and *Before Women Had Wings* (1997).

Winfrey is considered to be among the most influential of all celebrities. In the late 1990s, her program unveiled a new segment entitled "Oprah's Book Club." Each month, Winfrey chose a book—a novel, history, work of philosophy, etc.—interviewed the writer, and encouraged her readers to purchase and read the book. Whether the book was by a famous or obscure writer, it became an instant best-seller.

Through her production company Harpo, Winfrey has produced television movies and films. In 1998, she produced and starred in the film version of Toni Morrison's Pulitzer Prize–winning novel *Beloved*. She has also produced the television movies *Tuesdays with Morrie* (1999), based on the best-selling book by Mitch Albom; *David and Lisa* (1998), a remake of a 1962 film; THEIR EYES WERE WATCHING GOD (2005), based on the ZORA NEALE HURSTON novel of the same name; and the film *Precious* (2009), based on the novel *Push*, by Sapphire. Winfrey was also the producer of the Broadway production of the musical version of *The Color Purple* (2005).

### FURTHER READING

Adler, Bill. *The Uncommon Wisdom of Oprah Winfrey: A Portrait in Her Own Words.* New York: W. Morrow, 1997.

Bly, Nellie. *Oprah! Up Close and Down Home.* New York: Kensington Publishing, 1993.

Farr, Cecilia Konchar. *Reading Oprah: How Oprah's Book Club Changed the Way America Reads.* Albany, N.Y.: State University of New York Press, 2005.

Garson, Helen S. *Oprah Winfrey: A Biography.* Westport, Conn.: Greenwood Press, 2004.

Harris, Jennifer, and Elwood Watson, eds. *The Oprah Phenomenon.* Louisville: University Press of Kentucky, 2007.

Illouz, Eva. *Oprah Winfrey and the Glamour of Misery: An Essay on Popular Culture.* New York: Columbia University Press. 2003.

King, Norman. *Everybody Loves Oprah! Her Remarkable Life Story.* New York: W. Morrow, 1987.

Lawrence, Ken. *The World According to Oprah: An Unauthorized Portrait in Her Own Words.* New York: Andrews McMeel Publishing, 2005.

Lowe, Janet. *Oprah Winfrey Speaks: Insights from the World's Most Influential Voice.* New York: John Wiley and Sons, 2001.

Mair, George. *Oprah Winfrey: The Real Story.* New York: Kensington Publishing, 1994.

Nelson, Marcia Z. *The Gospel According to Oprah.* Westminster: John Knox Press, 2005.

Oprah.com. Available online. URL: http://www2.oprah.com/index.jhtml. Accessed September 22, 2006.

Rooney, Kathleen. *Reading with Oprah: The Book Club That Changed America.* Fayetteville: University of Arkansas Press, 2008.

Waldron, Robert. *Oprah!* New York: St. Martin's Press, 1987.

Woods, Geraldine. *The Oprah Winfrey Story: Speaking Her Mind: An Authorized Biography.* Minneapolis, Minn.: Dillon Press, 1992.

**womanism** In 1983, the same year that she won the Pulitzer Prize, Alice Walker published what is, arguably, her most important collection of essays and short works, *In Search of Our Mothers' Gardens.* This is an anthology of Walker's nonfiction writing, spanning from 1967 to 1982 and featuring 36 essays, letters, speeches, reviews, and previously unpublished pieces. She divides her collection into four parts. Most of the collected works were previously published in trade magazines such as MS. and *Redbook*, as well as scholarly journals such as *The Black Scholar.* The wide-ranging collection is best known for its opening pages, wherein Walker provides the definition of her term *womanist:* variously defined as "a black feminist or feminist of color"; "a woman who loves other women, sexually and/or nonsexually"; and a lover of music, dance, the moon, and self, among other open-ended possibilities. She concludes with the statement that "Womanist is to feminist as purple to lavender" (xi–xii).

According to Walker's definition of womanism, FEMINISM becomes a term that is inappropriately narrow for African-American women, as well as for others who embrace an inclusive and humanist vision of the world. Although womanism shares commonalities with feminism, it represents an expansion beyond the traditional feminist critical and activist agendas.

The introduction of the term *womanism* into the field of African-American women's writing spawned a debate over its implications. Interdisciplinary critics who have embraced womanism as a foundational philosophy for their work include historians and theologians such as Darlene Clark Hines, Elsa Barkely Brown, and Katie Cannon. Womanism is an important literary critical movement that has influenced scholars of African-American women's literature such as Barbara Christian, Majorie Pryse, Hazel Carby, Valerie Smith, and others to analyze literature in womanist terms (that is, by relying on analyses of SELF-AFFIRMATION, tradition, matrilineal inheritance, etc.). Walker's introduction and definition of womanism transformed the field of black women's literary criticism.

## FURTHER READING

The following is an extensive listing of articles on Africana feminism, black feminism, and womanism.


Acholonu, Catherine Obianuju. *Motherism: The Afrocentric Alternative to Feminism.* Owerri, Nigeria: Afa Publishers, 1995.

Alexander, Jacqui. "Remembering *This Bridge,* Remembering Ourselves: Yearning Memory, and Desire." In *This Bridge We Call Home: Radical Visions for Transformation,* edited by Gloria E. Anzaldua and Analouise Keating, 81–103. New York: Routledge, 2002.

Anderson, Lisa M. *Black Feminism in Contemporary Drama.* Urbana: University of Illinois Press, 2008.

Athey, Stephanie. "Reproductive Health, Race and Technology: Political Fictions and Black Feminist Critiques 1970s–1990s." *Sage Race Relations Abstracts* 22, no. 1 (February 1997): 3–27.

———, ed. *Sharpened Edge: Women of Color, Resistance, and Writing.* Westport, Conn.: Praeger, 2003.

Awkward, Michael. "A Black Man's Place(s) in Black Feminist Criticism." In *Who Can Speak? Authority and Critical Identity,* edited by Judith Roof and Robyn Wiegman. Urbana: University of Illinois Press, 1995.

———. *Negotiating Difference: Race, Gender, and the Politics of Postionality.* Chicago: University of Chicago Press, 1995.

———. "Race, Gender, and the Politics of Reading." *Black American Literature Forum* 22, no. 1 (1988): 5–27.

Baca Zinn, Maxine, and Bonnie Thorton Dill, eds. *Women of Color in U.S. Society.* Philadelphia: Temple University Press, 1994.

Baker, Houston A. *Workings of the Spirit: The Poetics of Afro-American Women's Writings.* Chicago: University of Chicago Press, 1991.

Bassard, Katherine Clay. "Gender and Genre: Black Women's Autobiography and the Ideology of Literacy." *African American Review* 26, no. 1 (1992): 119–129.

Beal, Frances M. "Slave of a Slave No More: Black Women in Struggle." *Black Scholar* 6, no. 6 (1975): 2–10.

Beaulieu, Elizabeth Ann. *Black Women Writers and the American Neo-Slave Narrative: Femininity Unfettered.* Westport, Conn.: Greenwood Press, 1999.

Bell, Roseann P., Bettye J. Parker, and Beverly Guy-Sheftall, eds. *Sturdy Black Bridges: Visions of Black Women in Literature.* New York: Doubleday, 1979.

Bell-Scott, Patricia, ed. *Life Notes: Personal Writings by Contemporary Black Women.* New York: Norton, 1994.

Bell-Scott, Patricia, et al. *Double Stitch: Black Women Write about Mothers and Daughters.* Boston: Beacon Press, 1991.

Bennett, Michael, and Vanessa D. Dickerson, eds. *Recovering the Black Female Body: Self Representations by African American Women.* New Brunswick, N.J.: Rutgers University Press, 2001.

Berlant, Lauren. "Cultural Struggle and Literary History: African-American Women's Writing." *Modern Philology* 88, no. 1 (August 1990): 57–65.

———. "Race, Gender, and Nation in *The Color Purple.*" In *Alice Walker: Critical Perspectives Past and Present,* edited by Henry Louis Gates, Jr., and Kwame Anthony Appiah, 831–859. New York: Amistad Press, 1993.

Blackburn, Regina. "In Search of the Black Female Self: African-American Women's Autobiographies and Ethnicity." In *Women's Autobiography: Essays in Criticism,* edited by Estelle C. Jelinek, 133–148. Bloomington: Indiana University Press, 1980.

Blanchard, Mary Loving. "Poets, Lovers, and the Master's Tools: A Conversation with Audre Lorde." In *This Bridge We Call Home: Radical Visions for Transformation,* edited by Gloria E. Anzaldua and Analouise Keating. New York: Routledge, 2002.

Booth, Alison. "Feminist Criticism at the English Track Meet." *Callaloo* 17, no. 2 (1994): 1,559–1,563.

Bowles, Gloria, M. Giulia Fabi, and Arlene R. Keizer, eds. *New Black Feminist Criticism, 1985–2000.* Urbana: University of Illinois Press, 2007.

Braxton, JoAnne. "Ancestral Presence: The Outraged Mother Figure in Contemporary Afra-American Writing." *Barnard Occasional Papers on Women's Issues* 3, no. 2 (1988): 1–42.

———. *Black Women Writing Autobiography: A Tradition within a Tradition.* Philadelphia: Temple University Press, 1989.

Braxton, Joanne M., and Andree Nicola McLaughlin, eds. *Wild Women in the Whirlwind. Afra-American Culture and the Contemporary Literary Renaissance.* New Brunswick, N.J.: Rutgers University Press, 1990.

Brown, Elsa Barkley. "Womanist Consciousness: Maggie Lena Walker and the Independent Order of Saint Luke." *Signs* 14 (1989): 610–633.

———. "Words Whispered over Voids: A Context for Black Women's Rebellious Voices in the Novel of the African Diaspora." In *Black Feminist Criticism and Critical Theory,* edited by Joe Weixlmann and Houston A. Baker, Jr. Greenwood, Fla.: Penkevill, 1988.

Busia, Abena P. A. "Performance, Transcription and the Languages of Self: Interrogating Identity as a 'Post-Colonial' Poet." In *Theorizing Black Feminisms: The Visionary Pragmatism of Black Women,* edited by Stanlie M. James and Abena P. A. Busia, 203–213. New York: Routledge, 1993.

Cade, Toni. *The Black Woman: An Anthology.* New York: Signet, 1970.

Cannon, Katie G. *Black Womanist Ethics.* Atlanta: Scholars Press, 1988.

———. *Katie's Cannon: Womanism and the Soul of the Black Community.* New York: Continuum, 1996.

Carby, Hazel V. "'Hear My Voice, Ye Careless Daughters': Narrative of Slave and Free Women before Emancipation." In *African American Autobiography: A Collection of Critical Essays,* edited by William L. Andrews. Englewood Cliffs, N.J.: Prentice Hall, 1993.

———. "It Jus Be's Dat Way Sometime: The Sexual Politics of Women's Blues." *Radical America* 20, no. 4 (1987): 9–22.

———. "'On the Threshold of Woman's Era': Lynching, Empire, and Sexuality in Black Feminist Theory." *Critical Inquiry* 12, no. 1 (1985): 262–277.

———. "The Politics of Fiction, Anthropology, and the Folk: Zora Neale Hurston in African American Culture." In *New Essays on Their Eyes Were Watching God,* edited by Michael Awkward, 28–44. Cambridge: Cambridge University Press, 1990.

———. *Reconstructing Womanhood: The Emergence of the Afro-American Woman Novelist.* New York: Oxford University Press, 1987.

———. "Reinventing History/Imagining the Future." *African American Review* 23 (1989): 381–387.

Chang, Robert S., and Adrienne D. Davis. "The Adventure(s) of Blackness in Western Culture: An Epistolary Exchange on Old and New Identity Wars." *U.C. Davis Law Review* 39 (2005–06): 1,189–1,210.

Chay, Deborah. "Rereading Barbara Smith: Black Feminist Criticism and the Category of Experience." *New Literary History: A Journal of Theory and Interpretation* 24, no. 3 (1993): 635–652.

Christian, Barbara. *Alice Walker's* The Color Purple *and Other Works: A Critical Commentary.* New York: Simon and Schuster, 1987.

———. "Being the Subject and the Object: Reading African-American Women's Novels." In *Changing Subjects: The Making of Feminist Literary Criticism,* edited by Gayle Greene and Coppelia Kahn, 195–200. London: Routledge, 1993.

———. *Black Feminist Criticism: Perspectives on Black Women Writers.* New York: Pergamon, 1985.

———. "Black Women Artist as Wayward." In *Alice Walker,* edited by Harold Bloom, 457–477. New York: Chelsea House Publishers, 1989.

———. *Black Women Novelists: The Development of a Tradition, 1892–1976.* Westport, Conn.: Greenwood Press, 1980.

———. "But What Do We Think We're Doing Anyway: The State of Black Feminist Criticism(s) or My Version of a Little Bit of History." In *Changing Our Own Words: Essays on Criticism, Theory, and Writing by Black Women,* edited by Cheryl A. Wall, 58–74. New Brunswick, N.J.: Rutgers University Press, 1989.

———. "Contrary Women of Alice Walker: A Study of *In Love and Trouble.*" *The Black Scholar* 12, no. 2 (March–April 1981): 21–30.

———. "The Highs and Lows of Black Feminist Criticism." In *Feminisms: An Anthology of Literary Theory and Criticism,* edited by Robyn R. Warhol and Diane Price Herndl, 44–51. New Brunswick, N.J.: Rutgers University Press, 1997.

———. *New Black Feminist Criticism, 1985–2000.* Edited by Gloria Bowles, M. Giulia Fabi, and

Arlene R. Keizer. Urbana: University of Illinois Press, 2007.

———. "No More Buried Lives: The Theme of Lesbianism in Lorde, Naylor, Shange, Walker." *Feminist Issues* 5, no. 1 (1985): 3–20.

———. "Novels for Everyday Use." In *Alice Walker: Critical Perspectives Past and Present,* edited by Henry Louis Gates, Jr. and Kwame Anthony Appiah, 50–104. New York: Amistad, 1993.

———. "The Race for Theory." *Cultural Critique* 6 (Spring 1987): 51–63.

———. "A Rough Terrain: The Case of Shaping an Anthology of Caribbean Women Writers." In *The Ethnic Canon: Histories, Institutions, and Interventions,* edited by David Palumbo Liu, 241–259. Minneapolis: University of Minnesota Press, 1995.

———. "Shadows Uplifted." In *Feminist Criticism and Social Change: Sex, Class, and Race in Literature and Culture,* edited by Judith Newton and Deborah Rosenfelt, 181–215. New York: Methuen Press, 1985.

———. "Trajectories of Self-Definition: Placing Contemporary Afro-American Women's Fiction." In *Conjuring: Black Women, Fiction, and Literary Tradition,* edited by Marjorie Pryse and Hortense J. Spillers, 233–248. Bloomington: Indiana University Press, 1985.

———. "What Celie Knows That You Should Know." In *Anatomy of Racism,* edited by David Theo Goldberg, 295–331. Minneapolis: University of Minnesota Press, 1990.

Christian, Barbara, et al. "Conference Call." *Differences: A Journal of Feminist Cultural Studies* 2, no. 3 (1990): 52–108.

Christian, Barbara, and Gwin Minrose. "A Theory of Black Women's Text and White Women's Readings: Or . . . the Necessity of Being Other." *NWSA Journal* 1, no. 1 (1988): 21–36.

Clarke, Cheryl. "Black Feminist Communalism: Ntozake Shange's *For Colored Girls Who Have Considered Suicide When the Rainbow is Enuf.*" In *After Mecca: Women Poets and the Black Arts Movement.* New Brunswick, N.J.: Rutgers University Press, 2005, 94–120.

———. "Knowing the Danger and Going There Anyway." *Sojourner: The Women's Forum* 16, no. 1 (1990): 14–15.

Clarke, Cheryl, Jewell Gomez, Evelyn Hammonds, Bonnie Johnson, and Linda Powell. "Conversations and Questions: Black Women on Black Women Writers: Conversations and Questions." *Conditions Nine* 3, no. 3 (1983): 88.

Cleaver, Kathleen Neal. "Sister Act." *Transition* 60 (1993): 84–100.

Cliff, Michele. *Claiming an Identity They Taught Me to Despise.* Watertown, Mass.: Persephone Press, 1982.

Combahee River Collective. "The Combahee River Collective Statement." In *Home Girls, a Black Feminist Anthology,* edited by Barbara Smith, 264–274. New York: Kitchen Table Women of Color Press, 1983.

Comfort, Juanita Rogers. "Becoming a Writerly Self: College Writers Engaging Black Feminist Essays." *Journal of the Conference on College Composition and Communication* 51, no. 4 (June 2000): 540–559.

Cotera, Maria Eugenia. "'De nigger woman is de mule uh de world': Storytelling and the Black Feminist Tradition." In *Native Speakers: Ella Deloria, Zora Neale Hurston, Jovita Gonzalez, and the Poetics of Culture,* 171–198. Austin: University of Texas Press, 2008.

Davies, Carol Boyce. "Black Woman's Journey into Self: A Womanist Reading of Paule Marshall's *Praisesong for the Widow.*" *Matatu* 1, no. 1 (1987): 19–34.

———. *Black Women, Writing and Identity: Migrations of the Subject.* New York: Routledge, 1996.

———. "Mothering and Healing in Recent Black Women's Fiction." *Sage: A Scholarly Journal on Black Women* 2, no. 1 (1985): 41–43.

———. "Wrapping One's Self in Mother's Akatado-Cloths: Mother-Daughter Relationships in the Words of African Women Writers." *Sage: A Scholarly Journal on Black Women* 4, no. 2 (1987): 11–19.

Davis, Kathleen. "Zora Neale Hurston's Poetics of Embalmment: Articulating the Rage of Black Women and Narrative Self Defense." *African American Review* 26, no. 1 (1992): 147–159.

Davis, Olga Idriss. "A Black Woman as Rhetorical Critic: Validating Self and Violating the Space of Otherness." *Women's Studies in Communication* 21, no. 1 (1998): 77–89.

Davis, Thadious. "Alice Walker's Celebration of Self in Southern Generations." In *"Everyday Use,"* by Alice Walker, edited by Barbara Christian. New Brunswick, N.J.: Rutgers University Press, 1994.

———. "Poetry as Preface to Fiction: Alice Walker's Recurrent Apprenticeship." *Mississippi Quarterly* 44, no. 2 (1991): 133–142.

———. "Women's Art and Authorship in the Southern Region: Connections." In *The Female Tradition in Southern Literature,* edited by Carol S. Manning, 15–36. Urbana: University of Illinois Press, 1993.

Delrosso, Jeana. "Catholicism's Other(ed) Holy Trinity: Race, Class, and Gender in Black Catholic Girl School Narratives." *Signs* 12, no. 1 (Spring 2000): 24–43.

Dickerson, Glenda. "The Cult of True Womanhood: Toward a Womanist Attitude in African-American Theatre." In *Performing Feminisms: Feminist Critical Theory and Theatre,* edited by Sue-Ellen Case, 109–118. Baltimore: Johns Hopkins University Press, 1990.

Doyle, Laura. *Bordering on the Body: The Racial Matrix of Modern Fiction and Culture.* New York: Oxford University Press, 1994.

Dubey, Madhu. *Black Women Novelists and the National Aesthetic.* Bloomington: Indiana University Press, 1994.

duCille, Ann. *The Coupling Convention: Sex Text, and Tradition in Black Women's Fiction.* New York: Oxford University Press, 1993.

———. "The Occult of True Black Womanhood: Critical Demeanor and Black Feminist Studies." *Signs: Journal of Women in Culture and Society* 19, no. 3 (1994): 591–629.

———. "Phallus(ies) of Interpretation: Toward Engendering the Black Critical 'I'." *Callaloo* 16, no. 3 (1993): 559.

———. "Postcoloniality and Afrocentricity: Discourse and Dat Course." In *Black Columbiad: Defining Moments in African American Literature and Culture,* edited by Werner Sollors and Maria Deidrich, 28–41. Cambridge, Mass.: Harvard University Press, 1994.

Elie, Nada. *Trances, Dances, and Vociferations.* New York: Garland Publishing, 2001.

Evans, Mari, ed. *Black Women Writers (1950–1980): A Critical Evaluation.* New York: Anchor, 1984.

Exum, Pat Crutchfield, ed. *Keeping the Faith.* Greenwich, Conn.: Fawcett, 1974.

Ferguson, Roderick A. "Something Else to Be: *Sula,* the Moynihan Report, and the Negations of Black Lesbian Feminism." In *Aberrations in Black: Toward a Queer of Color Critique,* 110–137. Minneapolis: University of Minnesota Press, 2004.

Ferreira, Patricia. "What's Wrong with Miss Anne: Whiteness, Women, and Power in *Meridian* and *Dessa Rose.*" *Sage: A Scholarly Journal on Black Women* 8, no. 1 (1991): 15–20.

Foster, Frances Smith. "Between the Sides: Afro-American Women Writers as Mediators." *Nineteenth Century Studies* 3 (1989): 53–64.

———. *Literary Production by African American Women, 1746–1892.* Bloomington: Indiana University Press, 1993.

———. "Parents and Children in Autobiography by Southern Afro-American Women." In *Home Ground: Southern Autobiography,* edited by Bill J. Berry, 98–109. Columbia: University of Missouri Press, 1991.

Freeman, Alma. "Zora Neale Hurston and Alice Walker: A Spiritual Kinship." *Sage: A Scholarly Journal on Black Women* 2, no. 1 (1985): 37–40.

Fulton, DoVeanna S. *Speaking Truth to Power: Black Feminist Orality in Women's Narratives of Slavery.* New York: State University of New York Press, 2006.

Gates, Henry Louis, Jr., ed. *Reading Black, Reading Feminist: A Critical Anthology.* New York: Meridian, 1990.

Gilkes, Cheryl Townsend. "'A Conscious Connection to 'All That Is': *The Color Purple* as Subversive and Critical Ethnography." In *Embracing the Spirit: Womanist Perspectives on Hope, Salvation, and Transformation,* edited by Emilie Maureen Townes, 175–191. Maryknoll, N.Y.: Orbis Books, 1997.

Gomez, Jewell. "A Cultural Legacy Denied and Discovered: Black Lesbians in Fiction by Women." In *Home Girls: A Black Feminist Anthology,* edited by Barbara Smith, 110–125. New York: Kitchen Table: Women of Color Press, 1983.

———. "Speculative Fiction and Black Lesbians." *Signs: Journal of Women in Culture and Society* 18, no. 4 (1993): 948–955.

———. "To Grandmother's House I Go." *Journal of Lesbian Studies* 4, no. 4 (2000): 71–77.

Grant, Jacquelyn, ed. In *Perspectives on Womanist Theology*. Atlanta: ITC Press, 1995.

Grayson, Sandra M. "Black Women and American Slavery: Forms of Resistance." In *Sharpened Edge: Women of Color, Resistance and Writing,* edited by Stephanie Athey, 71–77. Westport, Conn.: Praeger, 2003.

Griffin, Farah Jasmine. "Textual Healing: Claiming Black Women's Bodies, the Erotic and Resistance in Contemporary Novels of Slavery." *Callaloo* 19, no. 2 (1996): 519–536.

———. "That the Mothers May Soar and the Daughters May Know Their Names: A Retrospective of Black Feminist Literary Criticism." *Signs: Journal of Women in Culture and Society* 32, no. 2 (2007): 483–507.

Gwin, Minrose C. "Green-Eyed Monsters of the Slavocracy: Jealous Mistresses in Two Slave Narratives." In *Conjuring: Black Women, Fiction, and Literary Tradition,* edited by Marjorie Pryse and Hortense J. Spillers, 39–52. Bloomington: Indiana University Press, 1985.

Hamlet, Janice D. "Assessing Womanist Thought: The Rhetoric of Susan L. Taylor." *Communication Quarterly* 48, no. 4 (Fall 2000): 420–437.

Hankins, Rebecca. "Uncovering Black Feminist Writers 1963–90: An Evaluation of Their Coverage in Research Tools." *Reference and User Services Quarterly* 48, no. 3 (2009): 270–286.

Hardman-Cromwell. "Living in the Intersection of Womanism and Afrocentrism: Black Women Writers." In *Living in the Intersection: Womanism and Afrocentrism in Theology,* edited by Cheryl Anne Sanders, 105–120. Minneapolis: Fortress Press, 1995.

Harris, Trudier. "The Color Purple: Revisions and Redefinitions." *Sage: A Scholarly Journal on Black Women* 2, no. 1 (1985): 14–18.

———. "From Exile to Asylum: Religion and Community in the Writings of Contemporary Black Women." In *Women's Writing in Exile,* edited by Mary Lynn Broe and Angela Ingram. Chapel Hill: University of North Carolina Press, 1989.

———. *From Mammies to Militants: Domestics in Black American Literature.* Philadelphia: Temple University Press, 1982.

———. "On *The Color Purple,* Stereotypes, and Silence." *Black American Literature Forum* 18, no. 4 (1984): 155–161.

———. *Saints, Sinners, and Saviors: Strong Black Women in African American Literature.* New York: Palgrave, 2001.

———. "This Disease Called Strength: Some Observations on the Compensating Construction of Black Female Character." *Literature and Medicine* 14, no. 1 (Spring 1995): 109–126.

———. "Three Black Women Writers and Humanism: A Folk Perspective." In *Black American Literature and Humanism,* edited by R. Baxter Miller, 50–74. Lexington: University Press of Kentucky, 1981.

———. "What Women? What Canon? African American Women and the Canon." In *Speaking the Other Self: American Women Writers,* edited by Jeanne Campbell Reesman, 90–95. Athens: University of Georgia Press, 1997.

Henderson, Mae G. "The Color Purple: Revisions and Redefinitions." In *Alice Walker,* edited by Harold Bloom, 67–80. New York: Chelsea House Publishers, 1989.

———. "Speaking in Tongues: Dialogics, Dialectics, and the Black Woman's Literary Tradition." In *Feminists Theorize the Political,* edited by Judith Butler and Joan W. Scott, 343–351. New York: Routledge, 1992.

———. "(W)riting the Work and Working the Rites." *Black American Literature Forum* 23, no. 4 (1989): 631–660.

Henderson, Mae Gwendolyn, ed. Introduction in *Borders Boundaries, and Frames.* New York: Routledge, 1995, 1–30.

Hernton, Calvin. *The Sexual Mountain and Black Women Writers.* New York: Anchor, 1987.

Hickman, Mark S. "Feminism: Black Women on the Edge." *Women and Language* 12, no. 1 (1989): 5–14.

Holland, Sharon P. "On *Waiting to Exhale:* Or What to Do When You're Feeling Black and Blue. A Review of Recent Black Feminist Criticism." *Feminist Studies* 12, no. 1 (Spring 2000): 101–112.

———. "'Which Me Will Survive': Audre Lorde and the Development of a Black Feminist Ideology." *Critical Matrix: The Princeton Journal of Women, Gender, and Culture* 31 (March 1988): 1.

Holloway, Karla F. C. "The Body Politic." In *Subjects and Citizens: Nation, Race, and Gender from "Oroonoko" to Anita Hill,* edited by Michael Moon and Cathy Davidson, 481–482. Durham, N.C.: Duke University Press, 1995.

———. *The Character of the Word: The Texts of Zora Neale Hurston.* New York: Greenwood Press, 1987.

———. *Codes of Conduct: Race, Ethics and the Color of Our Character.* New Brunswick, N.J.: Rutgers University Press, 1995.

———. *Moorings and Metaphors: Figures of Culture and Gender in Black Women's Literature.* New Brunswick, N.J.: Rutgers University Press, 1992.

hooks, bell. *Ain't I a Woman?: Black Women and Feminism.* Boston: South End Press, 1981.

———. "Black Women Writing: Creating More Space." *Sage: A Scholarly Journal on Black Women* 2, no. 1 (1985): 44–46.

———. "Giving Ourselves Words: Dissident Black Woman Speech." *Zeta Magazine* (January 1989): 39–42.

———. "Reading and Resistance: *The Color Purple.*" In *Alice Walker: Critical Perspectives Past and Present,* edited by Henry Louis Gates, Jr., and Kwame Anthony Appiah, 284–295. New York: Amistad Press, 1993.

———. *Talking Back, Thinking Feminist, Thinking Black.* Boston: South End Press, 1989.

———. "Writing the Subject: Reading *The Color Purple.*" In *Critical Essays on Toni Morrison,* edited by Nellie McKay, 68–76. Boston: G. K. Hall, 1988.

Houston, Marsha. "The Politics of Difference: Race, Class, and Women's Communication." In *Women Making Meaning: New Feminist Directions in Communication,* edited by Lana F. Raklow, 45–59. New York: Routledge, 1992.

Houston, Marsha, and Olga Idriss Davis, eds. *Centering Ourselves: African American Feminist and Womanist Studies of Discourse.* Cresskill, N.J.: Hampton Press, 2002.

Hubbard, Dolan. *Recovered Writers/Recovered Texts: Race, Class and Gender in Black Women's Literature.* Knoxville: University of Tennessee Press, 1997.

Hudson-Weems, Clenora. *Africana Womanism: Reclaiming Ourselves* Troy, Mich.: Bedford Publishers, 1993.

———. *Africana Womanist Literary Theory.* Trenton, N.V.:Africa World Press, 2004.

Hull, Gloria T. "Afro-American Women Poets: A Bio-Critical Survey." In *Shakespeare's Sisters: Feminist Essays on Women Poets,* edited by Sandra M. Gilbert and Susan Gubar, 165–182. Bloomington: Indiana University Press, 1979.

———. "Black Women Poets from Wheatley to Walker." In *Sturdy Black Bridges: Visions of Black Women in Literature,* edited by Roseann P. Bell, Bettye J. Parker, and Beverly Guy-Sheftall, 91–96. Garden City, N.Y.: Anchor Books, 1979.

———. "Black Woman Writers and the Diaspora." *The Black Scholar* 17, no. 2 (1986): 2–4.

———. *Color, Sex and Poetry: Three Women Writers of the Harlem Renaissance.* Bloomington: Indiana University Press, 1987.

———. "History/My History." In *Changing the Subjects: The Making of Feminist Literary Criticism,* edited by Gayle Greene and Coppelia Kahn, 48–63. London: Routledge, 1993.

———. "Rewriting Afro-American Literature: A Case for Black Women Writers." *The Radical Teacher* 6 (May 1977): 10–14.

Hull, Gloria, Patricia Bell Scott, and Barbara Smith, eds. *All the Women Are White, All the Blacks Are Men, but Some of Us Are Brave.* Old Westbury, N.Y.: Feminist Press, 1982.

Ikard, David. *Breaking the Silence: Toward a Black Male Feminist Criticism.* Baton Rouge: Louisiana State University, 2007.

Johnson, Cheryl Lynn. "A Womanist Way of Speaking: An Analysis of Language in Alice Walker's *The Color Purple,* Toni Morrison's *Tar Baby* and Gloria Naylor's *The Women of Brewster Place.*" In *Critical Perspectives to Gloria Naylor,* edited by Sharon Felton and Michelle C. Loris, 23–26. Westport, Conn.: Greenwood Press, 1997.

Kamitsuka, Margaret D. "Reading the Raced and Sexed Body in *The Color Purple:* Patterning White Feminist and Womanist Theological Hermeneutics." *Journal of Feminist Studies in Religion* 19, no. 2 (Fall 2003): 45–66.

Kaplan, Sara Clarke. "Love and Violence/Maternity and Death: Black Feminism and the Politics of Reading (Un)representability." *Black Women, Gender, and Families* 1, no. 1 (Spring 2007): 94–124.

King, Deborah. "Multiple Jeopardy, Multiple Consciousnesses: The Context of Black Feminist Ideology." *Signs* 14 (1988): 42–72.

King, Lovalerie. "African American Womanism: From Zora Neale Hurston to Alice Walker." In *The African American Novel,* edited by Maryemma Graham, 232–252. New York: Cambridge University Press, 2004.

Kolawole, Mary Ebun Modupe. *Womanism and African Consciousness.* Trenton, N.J.: Africa World Press, 1997.

Korenman, Joan S. "African-American Women Writers, Black Nationalism and the Matrilineal Heritage." *CLA Journal* 38, no. 2 (1994): 143–161.

Kubitschek, Missy Dehn. *Claiming the Heritage: African-American Women Novelists and History.* Jackson: University Press of Missouri, 1991.

———. "Subjugated Knowledge: Toward a Feminist Exploration of Rape in Afro-American Fiction." In *Black Feminist Criticism and Critical Theory,* edited by Joe Weixlmann and Houston A. Baker, Jr., 43–56. Greenwood, Fla.: Penkevill, 1988.

Kuenz, Diane J. "*The Bluest Eye:* Notes on History, Community, and Black Female Subjectivity." *African American Review* 27, no. 3 (1993): 421–431.

Langley, April. "Lucy Terry Prince: The Cultural and Literary Legacy of Africana Womanism." *Western Journal of Black Studies* 25, no. 3 (Fall 2001): 153–164.

Logan, Shirley. *We Are Coming: The Persuasive Discourse of Nineteenth-Century Black Women.* Carbondale: Southern Illinois University Press, 1999.

———. "'When and Where I Enter': Race, Gender and Composition Studies." In *Feminism and Composition Studies: In Other Words,* edited by Susan C. Jarratt and Lynn Worsham, 45–57. New York: Modern Language Association, 1998.

Lorde, Audre. "Above the Wind: An Interview with Audre Lorde." *Callaloo* 14, no. 1 (1991): 83–95.

———. "Sharing Our True Color." *Callaloo* 14, no. 1 (1991): 67–71.

———. *Sister Outsider: Essays and Speeches.* Trumansburg, N.Y.: Crossing Press, 1984.

Marshall, Carmen Rose. *Black Professional Women in Recent American Fiction.* Jefferson, N.C.: McFarland, 2004.

McCluskey, Audrey T., ed. *Women of Color: Perspectives on Feminism and Identity.* Bloomington: Women's Studies Program, Indiana University, 1985.

McCray, Donald. "Womanist Theology and Its Efficacy for the Writing Classroom." *Journal of the Conference on College Composition and Communication* 52, no. 4 (June 2001): 521–552.

McDowell, Deborah. "Boundaries: Or, Distant Relations and Close Kin." In *Afro-American Literary Study in the 1990s,* edited by Houston A. Baker, Jr., and Patricia Redmond, 51–70. Chicago: University of Chicago Press, 1989.

———. *The Changing Same: Black Women's Literature, Criticism, and Theory.* Bloomington: Indiana University Press, 1995.

———. "New Directions for Black Feminist Criticism." *Black American Literature Forum* 14 (Winter 1980): 153–159.

———. "Pecs and Reps: Muscling in on Race and the Subject of Masculinities." In *Race and the Subject of Masculinities,* edited by Harry Stecopoulos and Michael Uebel, 361–366. Durham, N.C.: Duke University Press, 1997.

———. "Reading Family Matters." In *Haunted Bodies: Gender and Southern Texts,* edited by Anne Goodwyn Jones and Susan V. Donaldson, 389–415. Charlottesville: University Press of Virginia, 1997.

———. "Recycling: Race, Gender, and the Practice of Theory." In *Feminisms: An Anthology of Literary Theory and Criticism,* edited by Robyn R. Warhol and Diane Price Herndl, 231–247. New Brunswick, N.J.: Rutgers University Press, 1997.

———. "The Self in Bloom: Alice Walker's *Meridian.*" *CLA Journal* 24 (March 981): 262–275.

McKay, Nellie Y. "Alice Walker's 'Advancing Luna—and Ida B. Wells': A Struggle toward Sisterhood." In *Rape and Representation,* edited by Lynn Higgins and Brenda Silver. New York: Columbia University Press, 1991.

———. "Black Women's Literary Scholarship: Reclaiming an Intellectual Tradition." *Sage: A Scholarly Journal on Black Women* 6, no. 1 (1989): 89–91.

———. "Literature and Politics: Black Feminist Scholars Reshaping Literary Education in the White University, 1970–1986." In *Left Politics and the Literary Profession,* edited by Lennard J.

Davis and M. Bella Mirabella, 84–102. New York: Columbia University Press, 1990.

———. "Reflections on Black Women Writers: Revising the Literary Canon." In *Feminisms: An Anthology of Literary Theory and Criticism*, edited by Robyn R. Warhol and Diane Price Herndl, 151–164. New Brunswick, N.J.: Rutgers University Press, 1997.

———. "Response to 'The Philosophical Bases of Feminist Literary Criticism.'" *New Literary History* 19, no. 1 (1987): 164.

———. "W. E. B. DuBois: The Black Woman in His Writings: Selected Fictional and Autobiographical Portraits." In *Critical Essays on W. E. B. DuBois*, edited by William L. Andrews. Boston: G. K. Hall, 1985.

———. "'What Were They Saying?' Black Women Playwrights of the Harlem Renaissance." In *The Harlem Renaissance Re-Examined*, edited by Victor A. Kramer, 151–166. New York: AMS Press, 1987.

McLendon, Jacquelyn Y. "A Position of Kinship." *Women's Review of Books* (February 1991): 19.

McShine, Lilly. "Black Feminist Language." *Kinesis* (February 2000): 9.

Mitchell, Angelyn. *The Freedom to Remember: Narrative, Slavery, and Gender in Contemporary Black Women's Fiction.* New Brunswick, N.J.: Rutgers University Press, 2002.

Mittlefehldt, Pamela Klass. "A Weaponry of Choice: Black American Women Writers and the Essay." In *The Politics of the Essay: Feminist Perspectives*, edited by Ruth-Ellen Boetcher Joeres and Elizabeth Mittman, 196–208. Bloomington: Indiana University Press, 1993.

Montelaro, Janet J. *Producing a Womanist Text: The Maternal as Signifier in Alice Walker's* The Color Purple. Victoria, B.C., Canada: University of Victoria, 1996.

Mossell, Mrs. N. F. *The Work of the Afro-American Woman.* Philadelphia: Geo S. Ferguson, 1908.

Ogunyemi, Chikwenye Okonojo. "Womanism: The Dynamics of the Contemporary Black Female Novel in English." *Signs: Journal of Women in Culture and Society* 11, no. 11 (1985): 63–80.

O'Neale, Sondra. "Inhibiting Midwives, Usurping Creators: The Struggling Emergence of Black Women in American Fiction." In *Feminist Studies, Critical Studies*, edited by Teresa de Lauretis, 139–156. Bloomington: Indiana University Press, 1986.

Peterson, Carla L. *Doers of the Word: African American Women Speakers and Writers in the North (1830–1880).* New Brunswick, N.J.: Rutgers University Press, 1995.

———. "Subject to Speculation: Assessing the Lives of African-American Women in the Nineteenth Century." In *Women's Studies in Transition: The Pursuit of Interdisciplinarity*, edited by Kate Conway-Turner, et al. Newark: University of Delaware Press, 1998.

Peterson, Elizabeth A. *African American Women: A Study of Will and Success.* Jefferson, N.C.: McFarland and Company, Inc., 1992.

Pettis, Joyce. "Difficult Survival: Mothers and Daughters in *The Bluest Eye.*" *Sage: A Scholarly Journal on Black Women* 4, no. 2 (1987): 26–29.

Phillips, Layli. *The Womanist Reader.* New York: Taylor & Francis, 2006.

Pough, Gwendolyn D. "Girls in the Hood and Other Ghetto Dramas: Representing Black Womanhood in Hip-Hop Cinema and Novels." In *Check It While I Wreck It: Black Womanhood, Hip-Hop Culture, and the Public Sphere.* Boston: Northeastern University Press, 2004, 127–162.

———. "My Cipher Keeps Movin' Like a Rollin' Stone: Black Women's Expressive Cultures and Black Feminist Legacies." In *Check It While I Wreck It: Black Womanhood, Hip Hop Culture, and the Public Sphere.* Boston: Northeastern University Press, 2004, 41–74.

Reed, Pamela Yaa Asantewaa. "Africana Womanism and African Feminism: A Philosophical, Literary, and Cosmological Dialectic on Family." *Western Journal of Black Studies* 25, no. 3 (Fall 2001): 168–176.

Roberts, Diane. *The Myth of Aunt Jemima: Representations of Race and Region.* New York: Routledge, 1994.

Rushing, Andrea Benton. "Comparative Study of the Idea of Mother in Contemporary African and African-American Poetry." *Colby Library Quarterly* 14 (1979): 275–288.

———. "God's Divas: Women Singers in African-American Poetry." In *Women in Africa and the African Diaspora: A Reader*, edited by Rosalyn Terborg-Penn and Andrea Benton Rushing, 193–203. Washington, D.C.: Howard University Press, 1996.

———. "Images of Black Women in Afro-American Poetry." In *The Afro-American Woman: Struggles and Images,* edited by Sharon Harley and Rosalyn Terborg-Penn, 73–83. Baltimore: Back Classic Press, 1997.

———. "On Becoming a Feminist: Learning from Africa." In *Women in Africa and the African Diaspora: A Reader,* edited by Rosalyn Terborg-Penn and Andrea Benton Rushing, 121–134. Washington, D.C.: Howard University Press, 1996.

Sadoff, Dianne F. "Black Matrilineage: The Case of Alice Walker and Zora Neale Hurston." *Signs: Journal of Women in Culture and Society* 11, no. 1 (1985): 4–26.

Sanchez-Eppler, Karen. "Bodily Bonds: The Intersecting Rhetorics of Feminism and Abolition." *Representations* 24 (Fall 1988): 28–59.

Shockley, Ann Allen. "The Black Lesbian in American Literature: An Overview." *Conditions Five* 2, no. 1 (1979): 133–142.

Showalter, Elaine. "A Criticism of Our Own: Autonomy and Assimilation in Afro-American and Feminist Literary Theory." In *The Future of Literary Theory,* edited by Ralph Cohen, 213–234. New York: Routledge, 1989.

Smith, Barbara. "A Press of Our Own: Kitchen Table Women of Color Press." *Frontiers: A Journal of Women's Studies* 10, no. 3 (1989): 11–13.

———. "Teaching about Black Women Writers." *Women's Studies Quarterly* 25, nos. 1–2 (1997): 100–102.

———. "Toward a Black Feminist Criticism." *Conditions Two* 1, no. 2 (1977): 27–28.

———. "The Truth That Never Hurts: Black Lesbians in Fiction in the 1980s." In *Third World Women and the Politics of Feminism,* edited by C. T. Mohanty. Bloomington: Indiana University Press, 1991.

———. "Whose American History?: Gays, Lesbians, and American History." *Gay Community News* 20, no. 4 (1995): 9–12.

———. "Women of Color: Our Stories." *New Statesman,* 8 June 1984, pp. 23–24.

Smith, Barbara, and Beverly Smith. "Across the Kitchen Table: A Sister-to-Sister Dialogue." In *This Bridge Called My Back: Writings by Radical Women of Color,* edited by Cherrie Moraga and Gloria Anzaldua. Watertown, Mass.: Persephone Press, 123–140.

Smith, Pamela A. "Green Lap, Brown Embrace, Blue Body: The Ecospirituality of Alice Walker." *Cross Currents* 48, no. 4 (Winter 1998): 471.

Smith, Valerie. "Black Feminist Theory and the Representation of the 'Other.'" In *Changing Our Own Words: Essays on Criticism, Theory, and Writing by Black Women,* edited by Cheryl A. Wall, 38–57. New Brunswick, N.J.: Rutgers University Press, 1989.

———. "Convergences: 4/29/92." In *Not Just Race, Not Just Gender.* New York: Routledge, 1998, 123–140.

———. "Gender and Afro-Americanist Literary Theory and Criticism." In *Within the Circle: An Anthology of African American Criticism from the Harlem Renaissance to the Present,* edited by Angelyn Mitchell, 482–498. Durham: Duke University Press, 1994.

———. "Reading the Intersection of Race and Gender in Narratives of Passing." *Diacritics* 24, nos. 2–3 (1994): 43–57.

———. "Split Affinities: The Case of Interracial Rape." In *Theorizing Feminism: Parallel Trends in the Humanities and Social Sciences,* edited by Anne C. Hermann and Abigail J. Stewart, 155–170. Boulder, Colo.: Westview Press, 1994.

Smith-Wright, Geraldine. "Revision as Collaboration: Zora Neale Hurston's *Their Eyes Were Watching God* as Source for Alice Walker's *The Color Purple.*" *Sage: A Scholarly Journal on Black Women* 4, no. 2 (1987): 20–24.

Spillers, Hortense. "'All the Things You Could Be by Now If Sigmund Freud's Wife Was Your Mother': Psychoanalysis and Race." *Critical Inquiry* 22, no. 4 (1996): 726–751.

———. "Changing the Letter: The Yokes, the Jokes of Discourse: Or, Mrs. Stowe, Mr. Reed." In *Slavery and the Literary Imagination,* edited by Deborah McDowell and Arnold Rampersad, 178–202. Baltimore: Johns Hopkins University Press, 1989.

———. "*Chosen Place, Timeless People:* Some Figurations on the New World." In *Conjuring: Black Women, Fiction, and Literary Tradition,* edited by

Marjorie Pryse and Hortense Spillers, 151–175. Bloomington: Indiana University Press, 1985.

———. *Comparative American Identities: Race, Sex, and Nationality in the Modern Text.* New York: Routledge, 1991.

———. "*The Crisis of the Negro Intellectual:* A Post-Date." *Boundary* 221, no. 3 (1994): 65–116.

———. "Cross-Currents, Discontinuities: Black Women's Fiction." In *Conjuring: Black Women, Fiction, and Literary Tradition,* edited by Marjorie Pryse and Hortense J. Spillers, 249–261. Bloomington: Indiana University Press, 1985.

———. "Interstices: A Small Drama of Words." In *Pleasure and Danger: Exploring Female Sexuality,* edited by Carol A. Vance, 152–175. London: Pandora, 1992.

———. "Kinship and Remembrances: Women on Women." *Feminist Studies* 11, no. 1 (1985): 111–125.

———. "Mama's Baby, Papa's Maybe: An American Grammar Book." *Diacritics* 17, no. 2 (1987): 65–85.

Splawn, P. Jane. "Recent Developments in Black Feminist Literary Scholarship: A Selective Annotated Bibliography." *Modern Fiction Studies* 39, 3–4 (Fall–Winter 1993): 819–834.

Stephens, Ronald J., Maureen Keaveny, and Venetta K. Patton. "Come Colour My Rainbow: Themes of Africana Womanism in the Poetic Vision of Audrey Kathryn Bullett." *Journal of Black Studies* 32, no. 4 (March 2002): 464–479.

Tate, Claudia. *Black Women Writers at Work.* New York: Continuum, 1983.

———. "On Black Literary Women and the Evolution of Critical Discourse." *Tulsa Studies in Women's Literature* 5, no. 1 (1986): 111–123.

———. "Reshuffling the Deck; Or, (Re) Reading Race and Gender in Black Women's Writing." *Tulsa Studies in Women's Literature* 7, no. 1 (1988): 119–132.

Thompson, Betty Taylor. "Common Bonds from Africa to the U.S.: Africana Womanist Literary Analysis." *Western Journal of Black Studies* 25, no. 3 (Fall 2001): 177–184.

Trace, Jacqueline. "Dark Goddess: Black Feminist Theology in Morrison's *Beloved.*" *Obsidian II* 6, no. 3 (1991): 14–30.

Verge, Shane Trudell. "Revolutionary Vision: Black Women Writers, Black Nationalist Ideology, and Interracial Sexuality." *Meridians: Feminism, Race, and Transnationalism* 2, no. 2 (2002): 101–125.

Wade-Gayles, Gloria. "Anti-Sexist Celebration of Black Women in Literature: *The Sexual Mountain and Black Women Writers* and a Conversation with Calvin Hernton." *Sage: A Scholarly Journal on Black Women* 6, no. 1 (1989): 45–48.

———. "Black, Southern, Womanist: The Genius of Alice Walker." In *Southern Women Writers: The New Generation,* edited by Tonette Bond Inge, 301–323. Tuscaloosa: University of Alabama Press, 1990.

———. *No Crystal Stair: Visions of Race and Sex in Black Women's Fiction.* New York: Pilgrim Press, 1984.

———. "The Truths of Our Mothers Lives: Mother-Daughter Relationships in Black Women's Fiction." *Sage: A Scholarly Journal on Black Women* 1, no. 2 (Fall 1984): 8–12.

Walker, Alice. *In Search of Our Mothers' Gardens.* New York: Harcourt Brace Jovanovich, 1983.

Wall, Cheryl. *Changing Our Own Words: Essays on Criticism, Theory, and Writing by Black Women.* New Brunswick, N.J.: Rutgers University Press, 1989.

———. *Worrying the Line: Black Women Writers, Lineage, and Literary Tradition.* Chapel Hill: University of North Carolina Press, 2005.

Wallace, Michele. "Variations on Negation and the Heresy of Black Feminist Creativity." *Heresies: A Feminist Publication on Art and Politics* 6, no. 4 (1989).

———. "Who Dat Say Who Dat When I Say Who Dat? Zora Neale Hurston Then and Now." *Voice Literary Supplement* (April 1988): 18–21.

Washington, Mary Helen. "Anna Julia Cooper: The Black Feminist Voice of the 1890s." *Legacy: A Journal of American Women Writers* 4, no. 2 (1987): 3–15.

———. "Black Women Image Makers: Their Fiction Becomes Our Reality." *Black World* 23, no. 10 (1974): 10–18.

———. "'The Darkened Eye Restored': Notes for a Literary History of Black Women." In *Within the Circle: An Anthology of African American Literary Criticism from the Harlem Renaissance to Present,* edited by Angelyn Mitchell. Durham, N.C.: Duke University Press, 1994.

———. "An Essay on Alice Walker." In *Sturdy Black Bridges: Visions of Black Women in Literature,* edited by Roseann P. Bell, Bettye J. Parker, and Beverly Guy-Sheftall, 133–149. Garden City, N.Y.: Anchor Books, 1979.

———, ed. *Invented Lives: Narratives of Black Women 1860–1960.* New York: Anchor Press Book, 1987.

———. "New Lives and New Letters: Black Women Writers at the End of the Seventies." *College English* 43 (Summer 1983): 293–322.

———. "Teaching Black-Eyed Susans: An Approach to the Study of Black Women Writers." *Black American Literature Forum* 11 (1977): 20–24.

———. "These Self-Invented Women: A Theoretical Framework for a Literary History of Black Women." In *Politics of Education: Essays from Radical Teacher,* edited by Susan Gushee O'Malley, Robert C. Rosen, and Leonard Vogt. Albany: State University of New York Press, 1990.

Washington, Teresa. "Power of the Word/Power of the Works: The Signifying Soul of Africana Women's Literature." *Femspec* 1 (June 30, 2005): 58.

Waxman, Barbara Frey. "Canonicity and Black American Literature: A Feminist View." *MELUS: The Journal of the Society for the Study Multiethnic Literature of the United States* 14, no. 2 (1987): 87–93.

Weems, Renita. "'Artists without Art Form': A Look at One Black Woman's World of Unrevered Black Women." *Conditions 5: The Black Women's Issue* 2, no. 2 (1979): 48–58.

Wilentz, Cheryl. *Binding Cultures: Black Women Writers and the African Diaspora.* Bloomington: Indiana University Press, 1992.

Wilkerson, Margaret B. "Lorraine Hansberry: The Complete Feminist." *Freedomways* 19, no. 4 (1979): 235–245.

Williams, Bettye J. "Nella Larsen: Early Twentieth-Century Novelist of Afrocentric Feminist Thought." *CLA Journal* 39, no. 2 (December 1995): 165.

Williams, Sherley Anne. *Give Birth to Brightness: A Thematic Study in Neo-Black Literature.* New York: Dial Press, 1972.

———. "Some Implications of Womanist Theory." *Callaloo: A Journal of African American Arts and Letters* 9, no. 2 (1986): 303–308.

Willis, Susan. *Specifying: Black Women Writing the American Experience.* Madison: University of Wisconsin, 1987.

**Woolf, Virginia** (1882–1941) London-based novelist, essayist, and publisher Virginia Woolf's vivid depictions of psychological interiority made her an innovative fiction writer. Her public lectures and essays on the female experience have also deeply shaped modern feminist consciousness and activism.

Born Adeline Virginia Stephan in London, Woolf began publishing essays in 1912 and published her first novel, *The Voyage Out,* in 1915. She married the writer Leonard Woolf, and in 1917, they cofounded the Hogarth Press, an independent publishing house specializing in avant-garde writers such as E. M. Forster and T. S. Eliot. Woolf herself wrote short stories, children's books, essays, and novels. Among her most celebrated fictional works are *Jacob's Room* (1922), *Mrs. Dalloway* (1925), *To the Lighthouse* (1927), and her most popular work, *Orlando: A Biography* (1928). Her essay collections *A Room of One's Own* (1929) and *Three Guineas* (1938) are particularly influential for their incisive observations about living as a female artist and citizen in a patriarchal society. Allusions to lesbianism and gender subversion litter Woolf's work, and she is believed to have had a bisexual or lesbian orientation. Woolf, who struggled with mental health issues throughout her life, drowned herself in 1941.

Though Alice Walker's experience of race and social class were quite different from Woolf's, she has cited her predecessor as an influence. For example, Walker included Woolf's work in the black women writers' class she taught at Wellesley College in 1972 because she wrote about human experience from a female perspective. She has also noted the Hogarth Press as an influence on her cofounding of the specialty publisher WILD TREES PRESS with ROBERT L. ALLEN and BELVIE ROOKS. The scholar Maria Lauret has drawn various parallels between Walker and Woolf, including their vast formal range, critiques of social power, and employment of family drama to expose social taboos. Walker has reflected on the female writing tradition, including Woolf's legacy, in the essay "Saving the Life That Is Your Own: The Importance of Models in the Artist's Life," and she invoked Woolf's metaphor in the essay "One Child of One's Own" (both featured *In Search of Our Mothers' Gardens.*)

### FURTHER READING

Benzel, K. N. *Trespassing Boundaries: Virginia Woolf's Short Fiction.* London: Palgrave Macmillan, 2004.

Briggs, Julia. *Virginia Woolf: An Inner Life.* Orlando, Fla.: Harcourt, 2005.

Goldman, J. *The Feminist Aesthetics of Virginia Woolf: Modernism, Post-Impressionism, and the Politics of the Visual.* Cambridge: Cambridge University Press, 1998.

King, J. *Virginia Woolf.* New York: W. W. Norton, 1995.

Lauret, Maria. *Alice Walker.* New York: St. Martin's Press, 2000.

McNees, E., ed. *Virginia Woolf: Critical Assessments.* London: Helm Information, 1994.

O'Brien, John. "Alice Walker: An Interview." In *Alice Walker: Critical Perspectives Past and Present,* edited by Henry Louis Gates, Jr., and Kwame Anthony Appiah, 326–346. New York: Amistad, 1993.

Peach, L. *Virginia Woolf.* London: Palgrave Macmillan, 2000.

Roe, S., and S. Sellers, eds. *The Cambridge Companion to Virginia Woolf.* Cambridge: Cambridge University Press, 2000.

White, Evelyn C. *Alice Walker: A Life.* New York: W. W. Norton & Company, 2004.

Woolf, Virginia. *Between the Acts.* London: Hogarth Press, 1941.

———. *The Captain's Death Bed, and Other Essays.* London: Hogarth Press, 1950.

———. *The Common Reader.* London: Hogarth Press, 1925.

———. *The Common Reader: Second Series.* London: Hogarth Press, 1932.

———. *The Death of the Moth, and Other Essays.* London: Hogarth Press, 1942.

———. *Flush: A Biography.* London: Hogarth Press, 1933.

———. *A Haunted House, and Other Short Stories.* London: Hogarth Press, 1944.

———. *Jacob's Room.* Richmond: Hogarth Press, 1922.

———. *Kew Gardens.* Richmond: Hogarth Press, 1919.

———. *A Letter to a Young Poet.* London: Hogarth Press, 1932.

———. *The Mark on the Wall.* Richmond: Hogarth Press, 1917.

———. *The Moment, and Other Essays.* London: Hogarth Press, 1947.

———. *Monday or Tuesday.* Richmond: Hogarth Press, 1921.

———. *Mr. Bennett and Mrs. Brown.* London: Hogarth Press, 1924.

———. *Mrs. Dalloway.* London: Hogarth Press, 1925.

———. *Night and Day.* London: Duckworth, 1919.

———. *On Being Ill.* London: Hogarth Press, 1930.

———. *Orlando: A Biography.* London: Hogarth Press, 1928.

———. *Roger Fry: A Biography.* London: Hogarth Press, 1940.

———. *A Room of One's Own.* London: Hogarth Press, 1929.

———. *Three Guineas.* London: Hogarth Press, 1938.

———. *The Voyage Out.* London: Duckworth, 1915.

———. *To the Lighthouse.* London: Hogarth Press, 1927.

———. *The Waves.* London: Hogarth Press; New York: Harcourt Brace, 1931.

———. *The Years.* London: Hogarth Press, 1937.

**Wright, Richard** (1908–1960) Richard Wright's politically charged, naturalist writing style was pivotal to translating the often gritty and harrowing experiences of the black underclass onto America's literary landscape. Wright's gripping realism is particularly evident in his 1940 novel *Native Son,* the 1941 essay "12 Million Black Voices," and his 1945 autobiography *Black Boy.* In his later years, Wright wrote existentialist novels, political travelogues, and haikus, but his polemical writings from the 1940s greatly influenced ongoing debates about the proper role of politics in black literary production. Critics have connected Walker's emphasis on socially marginal figures to Wright, though her often surrealist, lyrical style contrasts with his writing style.

### FURTHER READING


Bloom, Harold, ed. *Richard Wright: Modern Critical Views*. New York: Chelsea House, 1987.

Gates, Henry Louis, Jr., and Kwame Anthony Appiah, *Richard Wright: Critical Perspectives Past and Present*. New York: Amistad, 1993.

Kinnamon, Keith, comp. *A Richard Wright Bibliography: Fifty Years of Criticism and Commentary, 1932–1982*. New York: Greenwood, 1988.

Kinnamon, Keith, and Michel Fabre, eds. *Conversations with Richard Wright*. Jackson: University Press of Mississippi, 1993.

Levy, Debbie. *Richard Wright: A Biography*. Minneapolis: Twenty-First Century Books, 2007.

Wright, Richard. *American Hunger*. New York: Harper and Row, 1975.

———. *Black Boy: A Recollection of Childhood and Youth*. New York: Harper, 1945.

———. *Black Power: A Record of Reactions in a Land of Pathos*. New York: Harper, 1954.

———. *The Color Curtain: A Report on the Bandung Conference*. New York: World, 1958.

———. *Eight Men*. New York: World, 1961.

———. *A Father's Law*. London: Harper Perennial, 2008.

———. *Lawd Today!* New York: Walker, 1963.

———. *The Long Dream*. New York: Doubleday, 1958.

———. *Native Son*. New York: Harper, 1940.

———. *The Outsider*. New York: Harper, 1953.

———. *Pagan Spain*. New York: Harper, 1957.

———. *Rite of Passage*. New York: HarperCollins, 1994.

———. *Savage Holiday*. New York: Avon, 1954.

———. *Twelve Million Black Voices: A Folk History of the Negro in the United States*. New York: Viking, 1941.

———. *Uncle Tom's Children: Five Long Stories*. New York: Harper, 1938.

———. *White Man, Listen!* New York: Doubleday, 1957.


**yage** In Alice Walker's novel *Now Is the Time to Open Your Heart*, the novel's protagonist, Kate, is engaged in a search for selfhood that takes her to the jungles of the Amazon. Kate takes something called yage. The word *yage* is used by the peoples who reside in the northernmost reaches of the Amazon River to describe a substance that they use to instigate spiritual access. Yage is associated with the work of shamans and is purported to enable access to the spiritual world for those who take it, working with a trained practitioner who is familiar with the associated necessary rituals to accompany the journey. Yage is also sometimes called ayahuasca.

### FURTHER READING


Cowan, T. *Shamanism as a Spiritual Practice for Daily Life*. Freedom, Calif.: Crossing Press, 1996.

Davis, Wade. *One River: Explorations and Discoveries in the Amazon Rain Forest*. New York: Simon and Schuster, 1996.

Dobkin de Rios, Marlene. *Amazon Healer: The Life and Times of an Urban Shaman*. London: Prism Press, 1992.

Eliade, Mircea. *Shamanism: Archaic Techniques of Ecstasy*. Translated by Willard Trask. Princeton, N.J.: Princeton University Press, 1964.

Harner, M. J., ed. *Hallucinogens and Shamanism*. Oxford: Oxford University Press, 1973.

Harvey, G. *Shamanism: A Reader*. London: Routledge, 2003.

McKenna, T. *Food of the Gods: The Search for the Original Tree of Knowledge*. San Francisco: Harper, 1992.

Narby, J. and F. Huxley, eds. *Shamans through Time: 500 Years on the Path to Knowledge*. New York: Putnam, 2001.

Schultes, R. E., and R. Raffauf. *The Healing Forest: Medicinal and Toxic Plants of the Northwest Amazonia*. Portland, Oreg.: Dioscorides Press, 1990.


**Zinn, Howard** (1922–2010) Historian, professor, activist, and playwright, Howard Zinn is most famous for his best-selling history text *A People's History of the United States*. Zinn was born in Brooklyn, New York, in 1922, and after serving in World War II, he completed a B.A. at New York University and an M.A. and Ph.D. in history from Columbia University.

Zinn began his teaching career as the chair in the departments of history and social science at Atlanta, Georgia's SPELMAN COLLEGE. He was an

Howard Zinn, a noted historian and professor at Boston University, was a close friend and mentor of Alice Walker before his death in 2010. *(Photograph by Carmen Gillespie)*

advocate for students' right at the socially conservative Spelman and also heavily involved in civil rights activism. Alice Walker and Marian Wright Edelman are among the Spelman students he mentored. In June 1963, the tenured Zinn was fired from Spelman for what many felt were political reasons. After leaving Spelman, he taught at Boston University from 1964 to 1988, where he remained professor emeritus until his death in January 2010. He had also been a visiting professor at the University of Paris and the University of Bologna. Zinn remained active throughout his life as an author, essayist, and political activist.

Alice Walker first met Zinn in 1961 and has referred to him as the first white man she was ever able to have a real conversation with because he took her seriously as a thinker and human being. In autumn 1962, his Russian history course "Revolution and Response" introduced Walker to Russian writers, including Nikolai Gogol and LEO TOLSTOY, and inspired her also to explore Russian female writers. Zinn was very impressed by Walker's work and was among the Spelman faculty members who encouraged her to become a writer. After Zinn's dismissal, Walker corresponded with him privately and wrote a letter of protest to the college's newspaper, *The Spotlight.*

Walker dedicated her 1968 poetry collection *Once* to Zinn. She also appeared in the 2004 biographical documentary *Howard Zinn: You Can't Be Neutral on a Moving Train.*

## FURTHER READING

HowardZinn.org. Available online. URL: http://howardzinn.org/default/index.php?option=com_frontpage&Itemid=1. Accessed March 12, 2009.

White, Evelyn C. *Alice Walker: A Life.* New York: W. W. Norton & Company, 2004.

Zinn, Howard. *Declarations of Independence: Cross-Examining American Ideology.* New York: HarperCollins, 1990.

———. *Disobedience and Democracy: Nine Fallacies on Law and Order.* Cambridge, Mass.: South End Press, 2002.

———. *Emma: A Play in Two Acts about Emma Goldman, American Anarchist.* Cambridge, Mass.: South End Press, 2002.

———. *Failure to Quit: Reflections of an Optimistic Historian.* Cambridge, Mass.: South End Press, 2002.

———. *The Future of History: Interviews with David Barsamian.* Monroe, Maine: Common Courage Press, 1999.

———. *Justice?: Eyewitness Accounts.* Boston: Beacon Press, 1977.

———, ed. *Justice in Everyday Life: The Way It Really Works.* 1974. Cambridge, Mass.: South End Press, 2002.

———. *LaGuardia in Congress.* Ithaca, N.Y.: Cornell University Press, 1959.

———. *Marx in Soho: A Play on History.* Cambridge, Mass.: South End Press, 1999.

———. *New Deal Thought.* Indianapolis: Bobbs-Merrill, 1966.

———. *A People's History of the United States: 1492–Present.* New ed. New York: HarperCollins, 2003.

———. *The People Speak: American Voices, Some Famous, Some Little Known.* New York: Perennial, 2004.

———. *The Politics of History.* 2d ed. Boston: Beacon Press, 1990.

———. *Postwar America: 1945–1971.* Indianapolis: Bobbs-Merrill, 1973.

———. *A Power Governments Cannot Suppress.* San Francisco: City Lights, 2007.

———. *SNCC: The New Abolitionists.* Cambridge, Mass.: South End Press, 2002.

———. *The Southern Mystique.* Cambridge, Mass: South End Press, 2002.

———. *The Unraveling of the Bush Presidency.* New York: Seven Stories Press, 2007.

———. *Vietnam: The Logic of Withdrawal.* Boston: Beacon Press, 1967.

———. *You Can't Be Neutral on a Moving Train: A Personal History of Our Times.* Boston: Beacon Press, 2002.

Zinn, Howard, and Anthony Arnove. *Terrorism and War.* New York: Seven Stories Press, 2002.

Zinn, Howard, with Donaldo Machedo. *Howard Zinn on Democratic Education.* Boulder, Colo.: Paradigm Publishers, 2005.

# PART IV

# *Appendixes*

# Chronology of Alice Walker's Life

**1793?–1918?**

According to Walker family history, Walker's great-great-great grandmother, May Poole, walked from Virginia to Georgia as a part of a slave coffle. Poole is said to have died at the age of 125.

**1907**

Alice Walker's father, William Lee Walker, is born on August 7.

**1912**

Alice Walker's mother, Minnie Lou (Tallulah) Grant, is born on December 2.

**1944**

Alice Malsenior Walker is born to Minnie Lou Grant Walker and Willie Lee Walker on February 9, in EATONTON, GEORGIA.

**1952**

Walker loses the sight in her right eye as a result of an accident with BB gun. Her brothers Curtis and Bobby are the unintentional perpetrators.

**1958**

Walker has scar tissue removed from her injured eye. Her older brother, Bill, provides financial resources for the operation.

**1961**

Honored as class valedictorian and prom queen, Walker graduates from Butler-Baker High School in Eatonton, Georgia.

Walker receives a scholarship to attend SPELMAN COLLEGE in Atlanta, Georgia.

**1962**

As an honor for her academic accomplishments, Walker is invited to the home of Coretta Scott and MARTIN LUTHER KING, JR.

Walker is selected to attend the Youth World Peace Festival in Helsinki, Finland.

**1963**

In August, Walker attends the March on Washington.

With the help of STAUGHTON LYND and his mother, HELEN LYND, Walker receives a scholarship and transfers to SARAH LAWRENCE COLLEGE in New York.

**1966**

Walker graduates from Sarah Lawrence and works briefly for the Welfare Office in New York City.

Walker moves to Jackson, Mississippi, where she works for the NAACP's Legal Defense Fund.

Walker meets a young Jewish civil rights lawyer, MELVYN LEVENTHAL, while working in Mississippi.

**1967**

Leventhal and Walker marry in March.

The short story "To Hell with Dying" is Walker's first published fictional work; it is included in *The Best Short Stories by Negro Writers,* edited by LANGSTON HUGHES.

*American Scholar* publishes Walker's essay "The Civil Rights Movement: What Good Was It?" and awards her $300 for winning its national annual essay contest.

**1968**

*Once,* Walker's first book of poetry, is published.

Walker is named writer-in-residence at Jackson State College in Mississippi.

**1969**

Rebecca Grant Leventhal (later REBECCA WALKER) is born to Walker and Mel Leventhal on November 17.

**1970**

Walker publishes her first novel, *The Third Life of Grange Copeland.*

Tougaloo College appoints Walker to a writer-in-residence position.

**1971**

Walker leaves Mississippi to accept a fellowship at Radcliffe College of Harvard University.

**1972**

Walker is awarded a lectureship at the University of Massachusetts, Boston, and at Wellesley College. At Wellesley, she teaches one of the first courses on African-American women writers.

**1973**

Walker publishes her second poetry book, *Revolutionary Petunias and Other Poems.*

*In Love and in Trouble,* Walker's first short story collection, is also published.

Willie Lee Walker, Alice Walker's father, dies.

Walker places a tombstone on ZORA NEALE HURSTON's previously unmarked Florida grave.

**1974**

Walker, Leventhal, and Rebecca move back to New York.

Walker accepts an appointment from MS. founder, GLORIA STEINEM, to serve as an editor.

Walker salutes her friend and mentor, Langston Hughes, by publishing her first children's book, *Langston Hughes: American Poet.*

**1976**

Mel Leventhal and Alice Walker divorce.

Walker publishes *Meridian,* her second novel.

**1978**

Walker moves to northern California and begins a 13-year relationship with Robert Allen.

Rebecca Walker spends alternate two-year periods with one parent, then the other.

**1979**

Walker publishes her third poetry book, *Good Night, Willie Lee, I'll See You in the Morning.* The title comes from a phrase she heard her mother whisper to her father's coffin shortly before he was buried.

Walker's tribute to the HARLEM RENAISSANCE writer Zora Neale Hurston, "Looking for Zora," is a featured essay in her edited collection *I Love Myself When I Am Laughing . . . and Then Again When I Am Looking Mean and Impressive: A Zora Neale Hurston Reader.*

**1981**

Walker publishes *You Can't Keep a Good Woman Down,* a short story collection.

Walker's mother, Minnie Grant Walker, has a severe stroke; she will spend the rest of her life immobilized.

**1982**

Walker publishes her most acclaimed work, the novel *The Color Purple.*

**1983**

Walker is awarded the Pulitzer Prize in fiction, the first awarded to an African-American woman, and also receives the National Book Award, among other honors.

Walker publishes *In Search of Our Mothers' Gardens,* an anthology of essays and unpublished material written between 1967 and 1982. The collection is particularly notable for Walker's influential definition of the term WOMANISM. Womanism becomes an important theoretical approach for the study of African-American women's fiction.

**1984**

Walker publishes the poetry collection *Horses Make a Landscape Look More Beautiful.*

Walker cofounds the independent publishing company WILD TREES PRESS.

Walker's daughter, Rebecca, legally changes her name from Rebecca Grant Leventhal to Rebecca Grant Walker.

**1985**

Director STEVEN SPIELBERG helms the film adaptation of *The Color Purple,* starring WHOOPI GOLDBERG, OPRAH WINFREY, Margaret Avery, Danny Glover, and Adolph Caesar. The film is well-reviewed, although controversial, and is the recipient of numerous honors, including 11 Academy Award nominations. Several scholars and critics challenge the film's depictions of African-American men, which becomes a controversy Walker addresses in her future writings.

**1988**

Walker publishes *To Hell with Dying,* a children's book featuring illustrations by CATHERINE DEETER.

Walker also publishes *Living by the Word,* an essay collection featuring reflections on crafting *The Color Purple* and other contemporary themes.

Walker, Robert Allen, and Belvie Rook decide to end publishing operations of Wild Trees Press as the work had become overwhelming and had exceeded their original commitment to and vision of the project.

**1989**

Walker publishes her fourth novel, the epic *The Temple of My Familiar.*

**1990**

Walker ends her romantic relationship with Robert Allen, with whom she remains friends.

**1991**

Walker publishes her third children's book, *Finding the Green Stone,* and her fifth poetry collection, *Her Blue Body Everything We Know.*

**1992**

Walker Publishes the novel *Possessing the Secret of Joy,* which is, in part, the tale of a central character's struggle with FEMALE GENITAL MUTILATION. After her research on the topic, she becomes an activist in and advocate for the movement to end the practice of female genital mutilation as a worldwide phenomenon.

**1993**

Walker and the British-Indian filmmaker PRATIBHA PARMAR produce *Warrior Masks,* a documentary on female genital mutilation.

Walker's mother, Minnie Grant Walker, dies on September 10.

**1994**

Walker releases *Alice Walker: The Complete Stories,* an anthology of all of Walker's previously published short fiction.

In celebration of the life of her maternal grandmother, Walker changes her middle name to Tallulah-Kate.

**1996**

Walker publishes *The Same River Twice: Honoring the Difficult,* her first nonfiction essay collection in nearly a decade. Controversies surrounding the novel and film versions of *The Color Purple* are the book's focus.

*Alice Walker Banned* is published. The collection addresses issues of censorship as they relate to Walker's work.

**1997**

*Anything We Love Can Be Saved,* a highly personal collection of essays, letters, and reflections on political activism, is published.

The Alice Walker Literary Society is founded.

**1998**

Walker publishes the novel *By the Light of My Father's Smile.*

**2000**

Walker publishes a new collection of short stories, *The Way Forward Is with a Broken Heart.*

**2001**

Walker's examinations of the national and global impact of the September 11, 2001, World Trade Center and Pentagon attacks appear in her short book *Sent by Earth: A Message from the Grandmother Spirit.*

Rebecca Walker publishes her memoir *Black White and Jewish.* In it, she is critical of both of her parents and tries to articulate her racial and cultural conflicts.

2003

Walker publishes two new poetry collections, *Absolute Trust in the Goodness of the Earth* and *A Poem Traveled down My Arm.*

2004

Walker publishes her first novel of the new millennium, *Now Is the Time to Open Your Heart.*

The musical adaptation of *The Color Purple* premiers at Atlanta's Alliance Theater.

In December, Alice Walker's only grandchild, Rebecca's son, Tenzin, is born to Rebecca and Choyin Rangdrol.

2005

In December, *The Color Purple: The Musical* debuts on Broadway at the Broadway Theatre, with Oprah Winfrey as the producer.

Walker and the Buddhist nun PEMA CHÖDRÖN coauthor the audio recording *Pema Chödrön and Alice Walker in Conversation: On the Meaning of Suffering and the Mystery of Joy.*

2006

Walker publishes the essay collection *We Are the Ones We Have Been Waiting For,* which features tributes to revolutionaries of the past, such as Dr. Martin Luther King, Jr., and FIDEL CASTRO, and suggests the need for contemporary activist strategies.

Walker publishes the children's book *There Is a Flower at the End of My Nose.*

2007

Walker publishes the children's book *Why War Is Never a Good Idea.*

In December, Walker designates Emory University as the official home of her archive *The Alice Walker Papers.*

Chicago, Illinois, hosts the premiere of the touring-company version of *The Color Purple, The Musical.*

Walker's daughter, Rebecca, publishes an account of her experiences with pregnancy and motherhood in a book called *Baby Love: Choosing Motherhood after a Lifetime of Ambivalence.* In it, Rebecca Walker challenges what she calls the feminist premise that autonomy and selfhood are antithetical to motherhood. She elaborates on the details of her estrangement from her mother.

2008

Alice Walker begins the Web site *Alice Walker's Garden.* She has a blog on the site that allows her to access a new avenue for her writing and through which to share her perceptions, travels, and activism.

In December, Alice Walker's sister, Ruth Walker Hood, dies.

2009

On April 24, the Alice Walker Literary Society cosponsors *A Keeping of Records: The Art and Life of Alice Walker: A Symposium* at Emory University. In addition to celebrating the opening of Walker's archives, the symposium features an exhibition of Walker's writings and various personal archival materials in a display at the university's Robert W. Woodruff Library Schatten Gallery.

2010

Walker releases several publications in 2010, including the short volume *Overcoming Speechlessness: A Poet Encounters the Horror in Rwanda, Eastern Congo, and Palestine/Israel;* a poetry collection, *Hard Times Require Furious Dancing;* and a collection of interviews entitled *The World Has Changed: Conversations with Alice Walker,* edited by Rudolph P. Byrd.

As of 2010, there is talk of producing *The Color Purple, The Musical* as a movie.

# Selected Awards and Recognitions

Bread Loaf Writers' Conference Scholar, 1966
Charles Merrill Fellowship, 1966
MacDowell Colony Residency, 1967
The Radcliffe Institute Fellowship, 1971
Lillian Smith Book Award, *Revolutionary Petunias and Other Poems,* 1973
National Institute of Arts and Letters award, *In Love and Trouble,* 1974
Yaddo Fellowship, 1975
Guggenheim Fellowship, 1977
Pulitzer Prize for Fiction, *The Color Purple,* 1983
National Book Award, *The Color Purple,* 1983
The Townsend Prize, 1984
O. Henry Award, short story "Kindred Spirits," 1986
California Governor's Award for Literature, 1994
The American Humanist Association "Humanist of the Year," 1997
Georgia Writers Hall of Fame, 2001
California Hall of Fame, 2006

# Bibliography of Walker's Works


*Absolute Trust in the Goodness of the Earth: New Poems.* New York: Random House, 2003.

*Alice Walker: Banned.* San Francisco: Aunt Lute Books, 1996.

*Anything We Love Can Be Saved: A Writer's Activism.* New York: Random House, 1997.

*By the Light of My Father's Smile.* New York: Random House, 1998.

*The Color Purple: A Novel.* New York: Pocket Books, 1982.

*The Complete Stories.* London: Phoenix, 2005.

*Finding the Green Stone.* Illustrated by Catherine Deeter. New York: Harcourt Brace, 1991.

*Five Poems.* Highland Park, Mich.: Broadside Press, 1972.

*Gardening the Soul.* Carlsbad, Calif.: Hay House Audio Books, 2000.

*Giving Birth: Finding Form.* With Isabel Allende. Boulder, Colo.: Sounds True, Inc., 1993.

*Good Night, Willie Lee, I'll See You in the Morning.* New York: Harcourt Brace, 1979.

*Hard Times Require Furious Dancing.* Novato, Calif.: New World Library, 2010.

*Her Blue Body Everything We Know: Earthling Poems 1965–1990 Complete.* New York: Harvest Poems, 1991.

*Horses Make a Landscape Look More Beautiful.* New York: Harcourt Brace, 1984.

*In Love and Trouble: Stories of Black Women.* New York: Harcourt Brace, 1973.

*In Search of Our Mothers' Gardens: A Womanist Prose.* New York: Harcourt Brace, 1983.

*Langston Hughes: American Poet.* Illustrated by Don Miller. New York: Amistad, 2002.

*Living by the Word: Selected Writings, 1973–1987.* San Diego: Harcourt Brace, 1988.

*Meridian.* New York: Pocket Books, 1976.

*Now Is the Time to Open Your Heart.* New York: Random House, 2004.

*Once: Poems.* New York: Harcourt Brace, 1968.

*Overcoming Speechlessness: A Poet Encounters the Horror in Rwanda, Eastern Congo, and Palestine/Israel.* New York: Open Media, 2010.

*A Poem Traveled down My Arm: Poems and Drawings.* New York: Random House, 2003.

*Possessing the Secret of Joy.* New York: Washington Square Press, 1992.

*Revolutionary Petunias and Other Poems.* New York: Harcourt Brace, 1973.

*The Same River Twice: Honoring the Difficult. Meditations on Life, Spirit, Art, and the Making of* The Color Purple. New York: Scribner, 1996.

*Sent by Earth: A Message from the Grandmother Spirit after the Bombing of the World Trade Center and the Pentagon.* New York: Open Media, 2001.

*The Temple of My Familiar.* New York: Washington Square Press, 1989.

*There Is a Flower at the Tip of My Nose Smelling Me.* Illustrated by Stefano Vitale. New York: HarperCollins, 2006.

*The Third Life of Grange Copeland.* New York: Pocket Books, 1970.

*To Hell with Dying.* Illustrated by Catherine Deeter. New York: Voyager Book, 1988.

*The Way Forward Is with a Broken Heart.* New York: Ballantine, 2000.

*We Are the Ones We Have Been Waiting For: Inner Light in a Time of Darkness.* New York: New Press, 2006.

*The World Has Changed: Conversations with Alice Walker.* New York: New Press, 2010.

*You Can't Keep a Good Woman Down.* New York: Harcourt Brace, 1981.

## Coauthored and Edited Works

Morejon, Nancy. *Letters of Love and Hope: The Story of the Cuban Five.* Edited by Alice Walker. Melbourne, Australia: Ocean Press, 2005.

Walker, Alice, ed. *I Love Myself When I Am Laughing . . . and Then Again When I Am Looking Mean and Impressive: A Zora Neale Hurston Reader.* Old Westbury, N.Y.: Feminist Press, 1979.

Walker, Alice, and Pema Chödrön. *Pema Chödrön and Alice Walker in Conversation on the Meaning of Suffering and the Mystery of Joy.* Audio recording. Louisville, Colo.: Sounds True, Inc., 2005.

Walker, Alice, and Pratibha Parmar. *Warrior Marks: Female Genital Mutilation and the Sexual Blinding of Women.* New York: Harcourt Brace, 1996.

# Bibliography of Secondary Sources


Abbandonato, Linda. "'A View from Elsewhere': Subversive Sexuality and the Rewriting of the Heroine's Story in *The Color Purple*." *PMLA: Publications of the Modern Language Association of America* 106, no. 5 (October 1991): 1,106–1,115.

Abend-David, Dror. "The Occupational Hazard: The Loss of Historical Context in Twentieth-Century Feminist Readings, and a New Reading of the Heroine's Story in Alice Walker's *The Color Purple*." In *Critical Essays on Alice Walker,* edited by Ikenna Dieke, 13–20. Westport, Conn.: Greenwood, 1999.

Abernathy, Jeff. *To Hell and Back: Race and Betrayal in the Southern Novel.* Athens: University of Georgia Press, 2003.

Adisa, Opal Palmer. "A Writer/Healer: Literature, A Blueprint for Healing." In *Healing Culture: Art and Religion as Curative Practices in the Caribbean and Its Diaspora,* edited by Margarite Fernández-Olmos and Lizabeth Paravisini-Gebert, 179–194. New York: Palgrave, 2001.

Ahokas, Pirjo. "Constructing Hybrid Ethnic Female Identities: Alice Walker's *Meridian* and Louise Erdrich's *Love Medicine*." In *Literature on the Move: Comparing Diasporic Ethnicities in Europe and the Americas,* edited by Dominique Marais, Mark Niemeyer, Bernard Vincent, and Cathy Waegner, 199–207. Heidelberg: Carl Winter Universititsverlag, 2002.

———. "Hybridized Black Female Identity in Alice Walker's *Meridian*." In *America Today: Highways and Labyrinths,* edited by Gigliola Nocera, 481–488. Siracusa, Italy: Grafi, 2003.

Allan, Tuzyline Jita. "A Voice of One's Own: Implications of Impersonality in the Essays of Virginia Woolf and Alice Walker." In *The Politics of the Essay: Feminist Perspectives,* edited by Ruth-Ellen Boetcher Joeres and Elizabeth Mittman, 131–148. Bloomington: Indiana University Press, 1993.

———. "Womanism Revisited: Women and the (Abuse of Power in *The Color Purple*." In *Feminist Nightmares: Women at Odds: Feminism and the Problem of Sisterhood,* edited by Susan Ostrov Weisser and Jennifer Fleischner, 88–105. New York: New York University Press, 1994.

Alps, Sandra. "Concepts of Self-Hood in *Their Eyes Were Watching God* and *The Color Purple*." *Pacific Review* 4 (Spring 1986): 106–112.

Anderson, Jace. "Re-Writing Race: Subverting Language in Anne Moody's *Coming of Age in Mississippi* and Alice Walker's *Meridian*." *A/B: Auto/Biography Studies* 8, no. 1 (Spring 1993): 33–50.

Applegate, Nancy. "Feminine Sexuality in Alice Walker's *Possessing the Secret of Joy*." *Notes on Contemporary Literature* 24, no. 4 (September 1994): 11.

Ash, Susan. "Aid Work, Travel and Representation: Inez Baranay's *Rascal Rain* and Alice Walker's *Warrior Marks*." *LiNQ* 24, no. 2 (October 1997): 44–54.

Awkward, Michael. *Inspiriting Influences: Tradition, Revision, and Afro-America Women's Novels.* New York: Columbia University Press, 1991.

Ayres-Ricker, Brenda. "The Huntress of Soft Touches: The Strumpet in Alice Walker's *The Third Life of Grange Copeland*." *MAWA Review* 6, no. 2 (December 1991): 28–30.

Babb, Valerie. "*The Color Purple:* Writing to Undo What Writing Has Done." *Phylon: A Review of Race and Culture* 47, no. 2 (June 1986): 107–116.

———. "Women and Words: Articulating the Self in *Their Eyes Were Watching God* and *The Color*

*Purple*." In *Alice Walker and Zora Neale Hurston: The Common Bond*, edited by Lillie P. Howard, 83–93. Westport, Conn.: Greenwood, 1993.

Baker, Houston A., Jr. "Patches: Quilts and Community in Alice Walker's 'Everyday Use.'" *The Southern Review* 21, no. 3 (Summer 1985): 706–720.

Banks, Erma Davis, and Keith Eldon Byerman. *Alice Walker: An Annotated Bibliography 1968–1986*. New York: Garland, 1989.

Barker, Deborah E. "Visual Markers: Art and Mass Media in Alice Walker's *Meridian*." *African American Review* 31, no. 3 (Fall 1997): 463–479.

Barker, E. Ellen. "Creating Generations: The Relationship between Celie and Shug in Alice Walker's *The Color Purple*." In *Critical Essays on Alice Walker*, edited by Ikenna Dieke, 55–65. Westport, Conn.: Greenwood, 1999.

Barksdale, Richard K. "Castration Symbolism in Recent Black American Fiction." *CLA Journal* 29, no. 4 (June 1986): 400–413.

Barnes, Paula C. "Alice Walker (1944– )." In *African American Autobiographers: A Sourcebook*, edited by Emmanuel S. Nelson, 360–364. Westport, Conn.: Greenwood, 2002.

Barnett, Pamela E. "'Miscegenation,' Rape, and 'Race' in Alice Walker's *Meridian*." *Southern Quarterly: A Journal of the Arts in the South* 39, no. 3 (Spring 2001): 65–81.

Bass, Carole, and Paul Bass. "Censorship American-Style." *Index on Censorship* 14, no. 3 (June 1985): 6–7.

Bass, Margaret Kent. "Alice's Secret." *CLA Journal* 28, no. 1 (September 1994): 1–10.

Bauer, Margaret D. "Alice Walker: Another Southern Writer Criticizing Codes Not Put to 'Everyday Use.'" *Studies in Short Fiction* 29, no. 2 (Spring 1992): 143–151.

———. "When a Convent Seems the Only Viable Choice: Questionable Callings in Stories by Alice Dunbar-Nelson, Alice Walker, and Louise Erdrich." In *Critical Essays on Alice Walker*, edited by Ikenna Dieke, 45–54. Westport, Conn.: Greenwood, 1999.

Bean, Annemarie. "Disclosures, Silences, Agency: African Female Genital Circumcision." *Women and Performance: A Journal of Feminist Theory* 7–8, nos. 2(14)–1(15) (1995): 324–338.

Bekers, Elisabeth. "Daughters of Africa W/Riting Change: Female Genital Excision in Two African Short-Stories and in Alice Walker's *Possessing the Secret of Joy*." *Thamyris: Mythmaking from Past to Present* 6, no. 2 (Autumn 1999): 255–271.

Benston, Kimberly W. "Facing Tradition: Revisionary Scenes in African American Literature." *PMLA: Publications of the Modern Language Association of America* 105, no. 1 (January 1990): 98–109.

Berlant, Lauren. "Race, Gender, and Nation in *The Color Purple*." *Critical Inquiry* 14, no. 4 (Summer 1988): 831–859.

Birkerts, Sven. *Reading Life: Books for the Ages*. St. Paul, Minn.: Graywolf, 2007.

Bloom, Harold, ed. *Alice Walker*. New York: Chelsea House, 1989.

Bloxham, Laura J. "Alice (Malsenior) Walker (1944– )." In *Contemporary Fiction Writers of the South: A Bio-Bibliographical Sourcebook*, edited by Joseph M. Flora and Robert Bain, 457–467. Westport, Conn.: Greenwood, 1993.

Bobo, Jacqueline. "*The Color Purple*: Black Women as Cultural Readers." In *Female Spectators: Looking at Film and Television*, edited by Deidre E. Pribram, 90–109. London: Verso, 1988.

———. "Sifting through the Controversy: Reading *The Color Purple*." *Callaloo: A Journal of African American and African Arts and Letters* 12, no. 2 (Spring 1989): 332–342.

Bochman, Andrew A. "The Inscription of Violence and Historical Recovery." In *The Image of Violence in Literature, the Media, and Society*, edited by Will Wright and Steven Kaplan, 13–45. Pueblo, Colo.: Society for the Interdisciplinary Study of Social Imagery, University of Southern Colorado, 1995.

Bockting, Ineke. "Betrayal, Guilt, and 'Unreality' in Southern Civil Rights Novels." In *Twelfth International Conference on Literature and Psychoanalysis*, edited by Frederico Pereira, 133–144. Lisbon: Instituto Superior de Psicologia Aplicada, 1996.

Boesenberg, Eva. *Gender-Voice-Vernacular: The Formation of Female Subjectivity in Zora Neale Hurston, Toni Morrison and Alice Walker*. Heidelberg: Carl Winter Universititsverlag, 1999.

Bomarito, Jessica, Jeffrey Hunter, and Amy Hudock, eds. *Feminism in Literature: A Gale Critical Companion*. Detroit: Thomson Gale, 2004.

Borgmeier, Raimund. "Alice Walker: Everyday Use (1973)." In *The African American Short Story 1970–1990*, edited by Wolfgang Karrer and Barbara Puschmann-Nalenz, 59–73. Trier: Wissenschaftlicher, 1993.

Boyd, Valerie. "In Search of Alice Walker; Or, Alice Doesn't Live Here Anymore." *Creative Nonfiction* 12 (1999): 128–146.

Braendlin, Bonnie. "Alice Walker's *The Temple of My Familiar* as a Pastiche." *American Literature: A Journal of Literary History, Criticism, and Bibliography* 68, no. 1 (March 1996): 47–67.

Bröck, Sabine, and Anne Koenen. "Alice Walker in Search of Zora Neale Hurston: Rediscovering a Black Female Tradition." In *History and Tradition in Afro-American Culture,* edited by Günter H. Lenz, 167–180. Frankfurt: Campus, 1984.

Broome, Lillie Jones. "Sex, Violence, and History: Images of Black Men in the Selected Fiction of Gayl Jones, Alice Walker, and Toni Morrison." *Dissertation Abstracts International* 52, no. 3 (September 1991): 913A.

Brown, Joseph A. "'All Saints Should Walk Away': The Mystical Pilgrimage of *Meridian.*" *Callaloo: A Journal of African American and African Arts and Letters* 12, no. 2 (39) (Spring 1989): 310–320.

Bruck, Sabine. "The Urbency of Petunias: Womanism as Cultural Intervention." In *The Sixties Revisited: Culture-Society-Politics,* edited by Jurgen Heideking, Jorg Helbig, and Anke Ortlepp, 399–412. Heidelberg: Universititsverlag Winter, 2001.

Buckman, Alyson R. "The Body as a Site of Colonization: Alice Walker's *Possessing the Secret of Joy.*" *Journal of American Culture* 18, no. 2 (Summer 1995): 89–94.

Buncombe, Marie H. "Androgyny as Metaphor in Alice Walker's Novels." *CLA Journal* 30, no. 4 (June 1987): 419–427.

Butler, Cheryl B. "*The Color Purple* Controversy: Black Woman Spectatorship." *Wide Angle: A Film Quarterly of Theory, Criticism, and Practice* 13, nos. 3–4 (1991): 62–69.

Butler, Robert. "Alice Walker's Vision of the South in *The Third Life of Grange Copeland.*" *African American Review* 27, no. 2 (Summer 1993): 195–204.

———. "Making a Way Out of No Way: The Open Journey in Alice Walker's *The Third Life of Grange Copeland.*" *Black American Literature Forum* 22, no. 1 (Spring 1988): 65–79.

———. "Visions of Southern Life and Religion in O'Connor's *Wise Blood* and Walker's *The Third Life of Grange Copeland.*" *College Language Association Journal* 36, no. 4 (June 1993): 349–370.

Butler-Evans, Elliott. *Race, Gender, and Desire: Narrative Strategies in the Fiction of Toni Cade Bambara, Toni Morrison, and Alice Walker.* Philadelphia: Temple University Press, 1989.

Byerman, Keith. "Desire and Alice Walker: The Quest for a Womanist Narrative." *Callaloo: A Journal of African American and African Arts and Letters* 12, no. 2 (Spring 1989): 321–331.

———. "Gender and Justice: Alice Walker and the Sexual Politics of Civil Rights." In *The World Is Our Culture: Society and Culture in Contemporary Southern Writing,* edited by Jeffrey J. Folks and Nancy Summers Folks, 93–106. Lexington: University Press of Kentucky, 2000.

———. "Walker's Blues." In *Modern Critical Views: Alice Walker,* edited by Harold Bloom, 59–66. New York: Chelsea House, 1989.

Byerman, Keith, and Erma Banks. "Alice Walker: A Selected Bibliography, 1968–1988." *Callaloo: A Journal of African American and African Arts and Letters* 12, no. 2 (Spring 1989): 343–345.

Byrd, Rudolph P. "Shared Orientation and Narrative Acts in *Cane, Their Eyes Were Watching God,* and *Meridian.*" *MELUS* 17, no. 4 (Winter 1991–92): 41–56.

Byrne, Mary Ellen. "Welty's 'A Worn Path' and Walker's 'Everyday Use': Companion Pieces." *Teaching English in the Two-Year College* 16, no. 2 (May 1989): 129–133.

Callahan, John F. "The Hoop of Language: Politics and the Restoration of Voice in *Meridian.*" In *Modern Critical Views: Alice Walker,* edited by Harold Bloom, 153–184. New York: Chelsea House, 1989.

Campbell, Jennifer. "Teaching Class: A Pedagogy and Politics for Working-Class Writing." *College Literature* 23, no. 2 (June 1996): 116–130.

Carroll, Rachel. "Invisible Men: Reading Africa-American Masculinity." In *Masculinities in Text and Teaching,* edited by Ben Knights, 141–154. New York: Palgrave Macmillan, 2008.

Carter, Nancy Corson. "Claiming the Bittersweet Matrix: Alice Walker, Sandra Cisneros, and Adrienne Rich." *Critique: Studies in Contemporary Fiction* 35, no. 4 (Summer 1994): 195–204.

Chambers, Kimberly R. "Right on Time: History and Religion in Alice Walker's *The Color Purple.*" *CLA Journal* 31, no. 1 (September 1987): 44–62.

Chang, Ya-Hui Irenna. "Food, Food Consumption and the Troubled Self in Kingston's *The Woman Warrior,* Walker's *The Color Purple,* Tan's *The Joy Luck Club,* and Erdrich's *Love Medicine.*" In *You Are What You Eat: Literary Probes into the Palate,* edited by Annette Magid, 345–366. Newcastle upon Tyne, Eng.: Cambridge Scholars, 2008.

Cheung, King-Kok. "'Don't Tell': Imposed Silences in *The Color Purple* and *The Woman Warrior.*" *PMLA: Publications of the Modern Language Association of America* 103, no. 2 (March 1988): 162–174.

Christian, Barbara T. "Alice Walker." In *Afro-American Fiction Writers after 1955,* edited by Thadious M. Davis and Trudier Harris, 258–271. Detroit: Gale, 1984.

———. "Alice Walker: The Black Woman Artist as Wayward." In *Black Women Writers (1950–1980): A Critical Evaluation,* edited by Mari Evans, 457–477. Garden City, N.Y.: Anchor-Doubleday, 1984.

———, ed. *Alice Walker: "Everyday Use."* New Brunswick, N.J.: Rutgers University Press, 1994.

Christophe, Marc-A. "*The Color Purple:* An Existential Novel." *College Language Association Journal* 36, no. 3 (March 1993): 280–290.

Cochran, Kate. "'When the Lessons Hurt': *The Third Life of Grange Copeland* as Joban Allegory." *Southern Literary Journal* 34, no. 1 (Fall 2001): 79–100.

Coleman, Jeffrey Lamar. "Revolutionary Stanzas: The Civil and Human Rights Poetry of Alice Walker." In *Critical Essays on Alice Walker,* edited by Ikenna Dieke, 83–100. Westport, Conn.: Greenwood, 1999.

Coleman, Viralene J. "Miss Celie's Song." *Publications of the Arkansas Philological Association* 11, no. 1 (Spring 1985): 27–34.

Collins, Gina Michelle. "*The Color Purple:* What Feminism Can Learn from a Southern Tradition." In *Southern Literature and Literary Theory,* edited by Jefferson Humphries, 75–87. Athens: University of Georgia Press, 1990.

Collins, Janelle. "'Like a Collage': Personal and Political Subjectivity in Alice Walker's *Meridian.*" *CLA Journal* 44, no. 2 (December 2000): 161–188.

Colton, Catherine A. "Alice Walker's Womanist Magic: The Conjure Woman as Rhetor." In *Critical Essays on Alice Walker,* edited by Ikenna Dieke, 33–44. Westport, Conn.: Greenwood, 1999.

Cornwell, JoAnne. "Searching for Zora in Alice's Garden: Rites of Passage in Hurston's *Their Eyes Were Watching God* and Walker's *The Third Life of Grange Copeland.*" In *Alice Walker and Zora Neale Hurston: The Common Bond,* edited by Lillie P. Howard, 97–107. Westport, Conn.: Greenwood, 1993.

Courington, Chella. "Virginia Woolf and Alice Walker: Family as Metaphor in the Personal Essay." In *Virginia Woolf: Emerging Perspectives,* edited by Mark Hussey and Vara Neverow, 239–245. New York: Pace University Press, 1994.

Cowart, David. "Heritage and Deracination in Alice Walker's 'Everyday Use.'" *Studies in Short Fiction* 33, no. 2 (Spring 1996): 171–184.

Crosland, Andy. "Alice Walker's 'Nineteen Fifty-Five': Fiction and Fact." *English Language Notes* 34, no. 2 (December 1996): 59–63.

Cutter, Martha J. "Philomela Speaks: Alice Walker's Revisioning of Rape Archetypes in *The Color Purple.*" *MELUS* 25, nos. 3–4 (Fall–Winter 2000): 161–180.

Daly, Brenda O. "Teaching Alice Walker's *Meridian:* Civil Rights According to Mothers." In *Narrating Mothers: Theorizing Maternal Subjectivities,* edited by Brenda O. Daly and Maureen T. Reddy, 239–257. Knoxville: University of Tennessee Press, 1991.

Danielson, Susan. "Alice Walker's *Meridian,* Feminism, and the 'Movement.'" *Women's Studies: An Interdisciplinary Journal* 16, nos. 3–4 (1989): 317–330.

Davis, Amanda J. "To Build a Nation: Black Women Writers, Black Nationalism, and the Violent Reduction of Wholeness." *Frontiers: A Journal of Women Studies* 26, no. 3 (2005): 24–53.

Davis, Jane. "*The Color Purple:* A Spiritual Descendant of Hurston's *Their Eyes Were Watching God.*" *Griot: Official Journal of the Southern Conference of Afro-American Studies* 6, no. 2 (Summer 1987): 79–96.

Davis, Lisa. "An Invitation to Understanding among Poor Women of the Americas: *The Color Purple* and *Hasta no verte Jesús mío.*" In *Reinventing the Americas: Comparative Studies of Literature of the United States and Spanish America,* edited by Bell Gale Chevigny and Gari LaGuardia, 224–242. New York: Cambridge University Press, 1986.

Davis, Thadious M. "Alice Walker." In *American Novelists since World War II,* edited by James E. Kibler, Jr., 350–358. Detroit: Gale, 1980.

———. "Alice Walker's Celebration of Self in Southern Generations." *Southern Quarterly: A Journal of the Arts in the South* 21, no. 4 (Summer 1983): 39–53.

———. "Poetry as Preface to Fiction: Alice Walker's Recurrent Apprenticeship." *Mississippi Quarterly: The Journal of Southern Culture* 44, no. 2 (Spring 1991): 133–142.

Dawson, Emma J. Waters. "Images of the Afro-American Female Character in Jean Toomer's *Cane,* Zora Neale Hurston's *Their Eyes Were*

*Watching God,* and Alice Walker's *The Color Purple.*" *Dissertation Abstracts International* 48, no. 10 (April 1988): 2,627A.

———. "Redemption through Redemption of the Self in *Their Eyes Were Watching God* and *The Color Purple.*" In *Alice Walker and Zora Neale Hurston: The Common Bond,* edited by Lillie P. Howard, 69–82. Westport, Conn.: Greenwood, 1993.

De Lancey, Frenzella Elaine. "Squaring the Afrocentric Circle: Womanism and Humanism in Alice Walker's *Meridian.*" *MAWA Review* 7, no. 2 (December 1992): 94–101.

Demirterk, E. Lyle. "The Black Woman's Selfhood in Alice Walker's *Possessing the Secret of Joy.*" *Journal of American Studies of Turkey* 2 (Fall 1995): 33–36.

Dieke, Ikenna. "Alice Walker: Poesy and the Earthling Psyche." In *Critical Essays on Alice Walker,* edited by Ikenna Dieke, 197–208. Westport, Conn.: Greenwood, 1999.

———. *Critical Essays on Alice Walker.* Westport, Conn.: Greenwood, 1999.

———. "From Fractured Ego to Transcendent Self: A Reading of Alice Walker's *Possessing the Secret of Joy.*" *Literary Griot: International Journal of Black Expressive Cultural Studies* 11, no. 1 (Spring 1999): 48–68.

———. "Toward a Monastic Idealism: The Thematics of Alice Walker's *The Temple of My Familiar.*" *African American Review* 26, no. 3 (Fall 1992): 507–514.

———. "Walker's *The Temple of My Familiar:* Womanist as Monistic Idealist." In *Critical Essays on Alice Walker,* edited by Ikenna Dieke, 127–140. Westport, Conn.: Greenwood, 1999.

Digby, Joan. "From Walker to Spielberg: Transformations of *The Color Purple.*" In *Novel Images: Literature in Performance,* edited by Peter Reynolds, 157–174. London: Routledge, 1993.

Dole, Carol M. "The Return of the Father in Spielberg's *The Color Purple.*" *Literature/Film Quarterly* 24, no. 1 (1996): 12–16.

Downey, Anne M. "'A Broken and Bloody Hoop': The Intertextuality of *Black Elk Speaks* and Alice Walker's *Meridian.*" *MELUS* 19, no. 3 (Fall 1994): 37–45.

Dozier, Judy. "Who You Callin a Lady?: Resisting Sexual Definition in *The Color Purple.*" *Griot: Official Journal of the Southern Conference on Afro-American Studies, Inc.* 21, no. 2 (Fall 2002): 8–16.

Duck, Leigh Anee. "Rethinking Community: Post-Plantation in Literatures in Postmodernity." *Mississippi Quarterly: The Journal of Southern Cultures* 56, no. 4 (Fall 2003): 511–519.

Duckworth, Victoria. "The Redemptive Impulse: *Wise Blood* and *The Color Purple.*" *Flannery O'Connor Bulletin* 15 (1986): 51–56.

Durso, Patricia Keefe. "Private Narrative as Public (Ex)Change: 'Intimate Intervention' in Alice Walker's *The Temple of My Familiar.*" *In Process: A Journal of African American and African Diasporan Literature and Culture* 2 (Spring 2000): 137–154.

Early, Gerald. "*The Color Purple* as Everybody's Protest Art." *Antioch Review* 44, no. 3 (Summer 1986): 261–275.

Eddy, Charmaine. "Marking the Body: The Material Dislocation of Gender in Alice Walker's *The Color Purple.*" *ARIEL: A Review of International English Literature* 34, nos. 2–3 (April–July 2003): 37–70.

———. "Material Difference and the Supplementary Body in Alice Walker's *The Color Purple.*" In *Body Matters: Feminism, Textuality, Corporeality,* edited by Avril Horner and Angela Keane, 97–108. Manchester, Eng.: Manchester University Press, 2000.

Elliott, Emory. "History and Will in *Dog Soldiers, Sabbatical,* and *The Color Purple.*" *Arizona Quarterly: A Journal of American Literature, Culture, and Theory* 43, no. 3 (Autumn 1987): 197–217.

Ellis, Deborah S. "*The Color Purple* and the Patient Griselda." *College English* 49, no. 2 (February 1987): 188–201.

Ellis, R. J. "Out from under the Cucumber: *The Color Purple*'s Discursive Critique of Postmodern Deferral." In *Liminal Postmodernisms: The Postmodern, the (Post-) Colonial, and the (Post-) Feminist,* edited by Theo D'haen and Hans Bertens, 275–299. Amsterdam: Rodopi, 1994.

El Saffar, Ruth. "Alice Walker's *The Color Purple.*" *International Fiction Review* 12, no. 1 (Winter 1985): 11–17.

Elsey, Judy. "Laughter as Feminine Power in *The Color Purple* and 'A Question of Silence.'" In *New Perspectives on Women and Comedy,* edited by Regina Barreca, 193–199. Philadelphia: Gordon and Breach, 1992.

———. "'Nothing Can Be Sole or Whole That Has Not Been Rent': Fragmentation in the Quilt and *The Color Purple.*" *Weber Studies: An Interdisciplinary Humanities Journal* 9, no. 2 (Spring–Summer 1992): 71–81.

Ensslen, Klaus. "Collective Experience and Individual Responsibility: Alice Walker's *The Third Life of*

*Grange Copeland.*" In *The Afro-American Novel Since 1960,* edited by Peter Bruck and Wolfgang Karrer, 189–218. Amsterdam: Grüner, 1982.

———. "History and Fiction in Alice Walker's *The Third Life of Grange Copeland* and Ernest Gaines' *The Autobiography of Miss Jane Pittman.*" In *History and Tradition in Afro-American Culture,* edited by Gonter H. Lenz, 147–163. Frankfurt: Campus, 1984.

Erickson, Peter. "'Cast Out Alone/To Heal/And Re-Create/Ourselves': Family-Based Identity in the Work of Alice Walker." *College Language Association Journal* 23 (1979): 71–94.

Estes, David C. "Alice Walker's 'Strong Horse Tea': Folk Cures for the Dispossessed." *Southern Folklore* 50, no. 3 (1993): 213–229.

Estes-Hicks, Onita. "The Way We Were: Precious Memories of the Black Segregated South." *African American Review* 27, no. 1 (Spring 1993): 9–18.

Fabi, M. Giulia. "Sexual Violence and the Black Atlantic: On Alice Walker's *Possessing the Secret of Joy.*" In *Black Imagination and the Middle Passage,* edited by Maria Diedrich; Henry Louis Gates, Jr.; and Carl Pedersen, 228–239. Oxford: Oxford University Press, 1999.

Fabre, Genevieve. "Genealogical Archaeology or the Quest for Legacy in Toni Morrison's *Song of Solomon.*" In *Critical Essays on Toni Morrison,* edited by Nellie Y. McKay. Boston: Hall, 1988.

Fannin, Alice. "A Sense of Wonder: The Pattern for Psychic Survival in *Their Eyes Were Watching God* and *The Color Purple.*" *Zora Neale Hurston Forum* 1, no. 1 (Fall 1986): 1–11.

Farrell, Susan. "Fight vs. Flight: A Re-Evaluation of Dee in Alice Walker's 'Everyday Use.'" *Studies in Short Fiction* 35, no. 2 (Spring 1998): 179–186.

Fernald, Anne. "A Room, a Child, a Mind of One's Own: Virginia Woolf, Alice Walker and Feminist Personal Criticism." In *Virginia Woolf: Emerging Perspectives,* edited by Mark Hussey and Vara Neverow, 245–251. New York: Pace University Press, 1994.

Fifer, Elizabeth. "Alice Walker: The Dialect and Letters of *The Color Purple.*" In *Contemporary American Women Writers: Narrative Strategies,* edited by Catherine Rainwater and William J. Scheick, 155–165. Lexington: University Press of Kentucky, 1985.

Fike, Matthew A. "Jean Toomer and Okot p'Bitek in Alice Walker's *In Search of Our Mothers' Gardens.*" *MELUS* 25, nos. 3–4 (Fall–Winter 2000): 141–160.

Fisher, Berenice. "Wandering in the Wilderness: The Search for Women Role Models." *Signs* 13, no. 2 (Winter 1988): 211–233.

Fishman, Charles. "Naming Names: Three Recent Novels by Women." *Names: A Journal of Onomastics* 32, no. 1 (March 1984): 33–44.

Fitzgerald, Stephanie. *Alice Walker: Author and Social Activist.* Minneapolis: Compass Point Books, 2008.

Fitzsimmons, Kate. "Go Ask Alice: Alice Walker Talks about *The Color Purple* 10 Years Later." *San Francisco Review of Books* 21, no. 2 (March–April 1996): 20–23.

Fontenot, Chester J. "Alice Walker: 'The Diary of an African Nun' and DuBois' Double Consciousness." *Journal of Afro-American Issues* 5 (1977): 192–196.

Fraile-Marcos, Ana Maria. "'as Purple to Lavender': Alice Walker's Womanist Representation of Lesbianism." In *Literature and Homosexuality,* edited by Michael J. Meyer, 1–34. Amsterdam: Rodopi, 2000.

Freeman, Alma S. "Zora Neale Hurston and Alice Walker: A Spiritual Kinship." *SAGE: A Scholarly Journal on Black Women* 2, no. 1 (Spring 1985): 37–40.

Frias, Maria. "The Walker-Spielberg Tandem and Lesbianism in *The Color Purple:* '[Spielberg] Don't Like It Dirty.'" *BELLS: Barcelona English Language and Literature Studies* 9 (1998): 49–56.

Friedman, Sandra, and Alec Irwin. "Christian Feminism, Eros, and Power in Right Relation." *Cross Currents* 40, no. 3 (Fall 1990): 387–405.

Friedman, Susan Stanford. "Migration, Encounter, and Indigenisation: New Ways of Thinking about Intertextuality in Women's Writing." In *European Intertexts: Women's Writing in English in a European Context,* edited by Patsy Stoneham, Ana María Sánchez-Arce, and Angela Leighton, 215–272. Bern, Switzerland: Peter Lang, 2005.

Froula, Christina. "The Daughter's Seduction: Sexual Violence and Literary History." *Signs* 11, no. 4 (Summer 1986): 621–644.

Gaard, Greta. "Strategies for a Cross-Cultural Ecofeminist Ethics: Interrogating Tradition, Preserving Nature." *Bucknell Review: A Scholarly Journal of Letters, Arts and Sciences* 44, no. 1 (2000): 82–101.

Gardiner, Judith Kegan. "Empathetic Ways of Reading: Narcissism, Cultural Politics, and Russ's *Female Man.*" *Feminist Studies* 20, no. 1 (Spring 1994): 87–111.

Gaston, Karen C. "Women in the Lives of Grange Copeland." *College Language Association Journal* 24, no. 3 (March 1981): 276–286.

Gates, Henry Louis, Jr. "Color Me Zora: Alice Walker's (Re)Writing of the Speakerly Text." In *Intertextuality and Contemporary American Fiction,* edited by Patrick O'Donnell and Robert Con Davis, 144–170. Baltimore: Johns Hopkins University Press, 1989.

George, Olakunle. "Alice Walker's Africa: Globalization and the Province of Fiction." *Comparative Literature* 53, no. 4 (Fall 2001): 354–372.

Gerhardt, Christine. "The Greening of African-American Landscapes: Where Ecocriticism Meets Post-Colonial Theory." *Mississippi Quarterly: The Journal of Southern Cultures* 55, no. 4 (Fall 2002): 515–533.

Gerstenberger, Donna. "Revisioning Cultural Norms: The Fiction of Margaret Atwood and Alice Walker." In *Cross-Cultural Studies: American, Canadian and European Literatures: 1945–1985,* edited by Mirko Jurak, 47–51. Ljubljana: English Department of Filozofska Fakulteta, 1988.

Gilyard, Keith. "Genopsycholinguisticide and the Language Theme in African-American Fiction." *College English* 52, no. 7 (November 1990): 776–786.

Gourdine, Angeletta K. *The Difference Place Makes: Gender, Sexuality and Diaspora Identity.* Columbus: Ohio State University Press, 2003.

———. "Postmodern Ethnography and the Womanist Mission: Postcolonial Sensibilities in *Possessing the Secret of Joy.*" *African American Review* 30, no. 2 (Summer 1996): 237–244.

Grewal, Inderpal, and Caren Kaplan. "*Warrior Marks:* Global Womanism's Neo-Colonial Discourse in a Multicultural Context." *Camera Obscura: A Journal of Feminism, Culture, and Media Studies* 39 (September 1996): 4–33.

Grimes, Dorothy. "Mariama Bao's *So Long a Letter* and Alice Walker's *In Search of Our Mothers' Gardens:* A Senegalese and an African American Perspective on 'Womanism.'" In *Global Perspectives on Teaching Literature: Shared Visions and Distinctive Visions,* edited by Sandra Ward Lott, et al., 65–76. Urbana, Ill.: National Council of Teachers of English, 1993.

———. "'Womanist Prose' and the Quest for Community in American Culture." *Journal of American Culture* 15, no. 2 (Summer 1992): 19–24.

Gruesser, John Cullen. *Confluences: Postcolonialism, African-American Literary Studies, and the Black Atlantic.* Athens: University of Georgia Press, 2005.

———. "Walker's 'Everyday Use.'" *Explicator* 61, no. 3 (Spring 2003): 183–185.

Hadella, Charlotte. "From Passive Flower to Goddess: The Evolution of Women in Alice Walker's Fiction." *MAWA Review* 6, no. 2 (December 1991): 23–27.

Hall, Christine. "Art, Action and the Ancestors: Alice Walker's *Meridian* in Its Context." In *Black Women's Writing,* edited by Gina Wisker, 96–110. New York: St. Martin's, 1993.

Hall, James C. "Towards a Map of Mis(sed) Reading: The Presence of Absence in *The Color Purple.*" *African American Review* 26, no. 1 (Spring 1992): 89–97.

Hankinson, Stacie Lynn. "From Monotheism to Pantheism: Liberation from Patriarchy in Alice Walker's *The Color Purple.*" *Midwest Quarterly: A Journal of Contemporary Thought* 38, no. 3 (Spring 1997): 320–328.

Harris, Trudier. "Folklore in the Fiction of Alice Walker: A Perpetuation of Historical and Literary Traditions." *Black American Literature Forum* 11, no. 1 (Spring 1977): 308.

———. "From Victimization to Free Enterprise: Alice Walker's *The Color Purple.*" *Studies in American Fiction* 14, no. 1 (Spring 1986): 1–17.

———. "Our People, Our People." In *Alice Walker and Zora Neale Hurston: The Common Bond,* edited by Lillie P. Howard, 31–42. Westport, Conn.: Greenwood, 1993.

———. "Three Black Women Writers and Humanism: A Folk Perspective." In *Black American Literature and Humanism,* edited by R. Baxter Miller, 50–74. Lexington: University of Press of Kentucky, 1981.

———. "Tiptoeing through Taboo: Incest in 'The Child Who Favored Daughter.'" *MFS: Modern Fiction Studies* 28, no. 3 (Autumn 1982): 495–505.

———. "Violence in *The Third Life of Grange Copeland.*" *College Language Association Journal* 19 (1975): 238–247.

Hart, Kylo-Patrick R., and Metasebia Woldemariam. "Oprah Winfrey as Melodramatic Actress: Contributions of Winfrey's Feature-Film Performance to the Authenticity of Her Star Persona." *Quarterly Review of Film and Video* 25, no. 3 (2008): 183–195.

Hayes, Elizabeth T. "'Like Seeing You Buried': Persephone in *The Bluest Eye, Their Eyes Were Watching God,* and *The Color Purple.*" In *Images of Persephone: Feminist Readings in Western Literature,* edited by Elizabeth T. Hayes, 170–194. Gainesville: University Press of Florida, 1994.

Hedges, Elaine. "The Needle or the Pen: The Literary Rediscovery of Women's Textile Work." In *Tradition and the Talents of Women,* edited by Florence Howe, 338–364. Urbana: University of Illinois Press, 1991.

Heglar, Charles J. "Named and Namelessness: Alice Walker's Pattern of Surnames in *The Color Purple.*" *ANQ: A Quarterly Journal of Short Articles, Notes, and Reviews* 13, no. 1 (Winter 2000): 39–41.

Hellenbrand, Harold. "Speech, after Silence: Alice Walker's *The Third Life of Grange Copeland.*" *Black American Literature Forum* 20, nos. 1–2 (Spring–Summer 1986): 113–128.

Hemenway, Robert E. *Zora Neale Hurston: A Literary Biography.* Urbana: University of Illinois, 1977.

Henderson, Mae G. "*The Color Purple:* Revisions and Redefinitions." In *Modern Critical Views: Alice Walker,* edited by Harold Bloom, 67–80. New York: Chelsea House, 1989.

Hendrickson, Robert M. "Remembering the Dream: Alice Walker, *Meridian* and the Civil Rights Movement." *MELUS* 24, no. 3 (Fall 1999): 111–128.

Henke, Suzette. "Women's Life-Writing and the Minority Voice: Maya Angelou, Maxine Hong Kingston, and Alice Walker." In *Traditions, Voices, and Dreams: The American Novel since the 1960s,* edited by Melvin J. Friedman and Ben Siegel, 210–233. Newark: University of Delaware Press, 1995.

Hiers, John T. "Creation Theology in Alice Walker's *The Color Purple.*" *Notes on Contemporary Literature* 14, no. 4 (September 1984): 2–3.

Hines, Maude. "Body Language: Corporeal Semiotics, Literary Resistance." In *Body Politics and the Fictional Double,* edited by Debra Walker King, 38–55. Bloomington: Indiana University Press, 2000.

Hirsch, Marianne. "Clytemnestra's Children: Writing (Out) the Mother's Anger." In *Modern Critical Views: Alice Walker,* edited by Harold Bloom, 195–213. New York: Chelsea House, 1989.

Hite, Molly. *The Other Side of the Story: Structures and Strategies of Contemporary Feminist Narratives.* Ithaca, N.Y.: Cornell University Press, 1989.

———. "Romance, Marginality, Matrilineage: Alice Walker's *The Color Purple* and Zora Neale Hurston's *Their Eyes Were Watching God.*" *Novel: A Forum on Fiction* 22, no. 3 (Spring 1989) 257–273.

Hoel, Helga. "Personal Names and Heritage: Alice Walker's 'Everyday Use.'" *American Studies in Scandinavia* 31, no. 1 (1999): 34–42.

Hogue, W. Lawrence. "Discourse of the Other: *The Third Life of Grange Copeland.*" In *Modern Critical Views: Alice Walker,* edited by Harold Bloom, 97–114. New York: Chelsea House, 1989.

———. "History, the Feminist Discourse, and Alice Walker's *The Third Life of Grange Copeland.*" *MELUS* 12, no. 2 (Summer 1985): 45–62.

Hollenberg, Donna Krolik. "Teaching Alice Walker's *Meridian:* From Self-Defense to Mutual Discovery." *MELUS* 17, no. 4 (Winter 1991–92): 81–89.

Hollister, Michael. "Tradition in Alice Walker's 'To Hell with Dying.'" *Studies in Short Fiction* 26, no. 1 (Winter 1989): 90–94.

Holt, Sandra Waters. "A Rhetorical Analysis of Three Feminist Themes Found in the Novels of Toni Morrison, Alice Walker, and Gloria Naylor." *Dissertation Abstracts International* 50, no. 10 (April 1990): 3,224A.

Homans, Margaret. "'Her Very Own Howl': The Ambiguities of Representation in Recent Women's Fiction." *Signs* 9, no. 2 (Winter 1983): 186–205.

Hooker, Deborah Anne. "Reanimating the Trope of the Talking Book in Alice Walker's 'Strong Horse Tea.'" *Southern Literary Journal* 37, no. 2 (Spring 2005): 81–102.

hooks, bell. "Writing the Subject: Reading *The Color Purple.*" In *Modern Critical Views: Alice Walker,* edited by Harold Bloom, 215–228. New York: Chelsea House, 1989.

Houser, Catherine. "Missing in Action: Alienation in the Fiction of Award-Winning Women Writers." *Mid-American Review* 14, no. 2 (1994): 33–39.

Hoving, Isabel. "Three Local Cases of Cross-Atlantic Reading." In *The Practice of Cultural Analysis: Exposing Interdisciplinary Interpretation,* edited by Mieke Bal, 203–218. Stanford, Calif.: Stanford University Press, 1999.

Howard, Lillie P., ed. *Alice Walker and Zora Neale Hurston: The Common Bond.* Westport, Conn.: Greenwood Press, 1993.

———. "Benediction: A Few Words about *The Temple of My Familiar, Variously Experienced,* and *Possessing the Secret of Joy.*" In *Alice Walker and Zora Neale Hurston: The Common Bond,* edited by Lillie P. Howard, 139–146. Westport, Conn.: Greenwood, 1993.

Hubbard, Dolan. "Society and Self in Alice Walker's *In Love and Trouble.*" In *American Women Short*

*Story Writers: A Collection of Critical Essays,* edited by Julie Brown, 209–233. New York: Garland, 1995.

Hubert, Linda. "To Alice Walker: Carson McCullers' Legacy of Love." *Pembroke Magazine* 20 (1988): 89–95.

Iannone, Carol. "A Turning of the Critical Tide?" *Commentary* 88, no. 5 (November 1989): 57–59.

Ingman, Heather. *Women's Spirituality in the Twentieth Century: An Exploration through Fiction.* Oxford: Peter Lang, 2004.

Irwin, Edward E. "Freedoms as Value in Three Popular Southern Novels." *Proteus: A Journal of Ideas* 6, no. 1 (Spring 1989): 37–41.

Jablon, Madelyn. "Rememory, Dream History, and Revision in Toni Morrison's *Beloved* and Alice Walker's *The Temple of My Familiar.*" *College Language Association Journal* 37, no. 2 (December 1993): 136–144.

Jackson, Kathy Dunn. "The Epistolary Text: A Voice of Affirmation and Liberation in So Long a Letter and *The Color Purple.*" *The Griot* 12, no. 2 (Fall 1993): 13–20.

Jackson, Tommie L. "Orphanage in Simone Schwarz-Bart's *The Bridge of Beyond* and Alice Walker's *The Third Life of Grange Copeland.*" *Griot: Official Journal of the Southern Conference on Afro-American Studies* 15, no. 2 (Fall 1996): 7–13.

James, Stanlie M. "Shades of Othering: Reflections on Female Circumcision/Genital Mutilation." *Signs* 23, no. 4 (Summer 1998): 1,031–1,048.

Jamison-Hall, Angelene. "She's Just Too Womanish for Them: Alice Walker and *The Color Purple.*" In *Censored Books: Critical Viewpoints,* edited by Nicholas J. Karolides, Lee Burress, and John M. Kean, 192–200. Metuchen, N.J.: Scarecrow, 1993.

Jenkins, Candice M. "Queering Black Patriarchy: The Salvific Wish and Masculine Possibility in Alice Walker's *The Color Purple.*" *MFS: Modern Fiction Studies* 48, no. 4 (Winter 2002): 969–1,000.

Johnson, Cheryl Lynn. "A Womanist Way of Speaking: An Analysis of Language in Alice Walker's *The Color Purple,* Toni Morrison's *Tar Baby,* and Gloria Naylor's *Women of Brewster Place.*" In *The Critical Response to Gloria Naylor,* edited by Sharon Felton and Michelle C. Loris, 23–26. Westport, Conn.: Greenwood Press, 1997.

Johnson, Maria V. "'You Just Can't Keep a Good Woman Down': Alice Walker Sings the Blues." *African American Review* 30, no. 2 (Summer 1996): 221–236.

Johnson, Yvonne. *The Voices of African American Women: The Use of Narrative and Authorial Voice in the Works of Harriet Jacobs, Zora Neale Hurston, and Alice Walker.* New York: Peter Lang, 1998.

Jones, Suzanne W. "Dismantling Stereotypes: Interracial Friendships in *Meridian* and *A Mother and Two Daughters.*" In *The Female Tradition in Southern Literature,* edited by Carol S. Manning, 140–158. Urbana: University of Illinois Press, 1993.

Juncker, Clara. "Black Magic: Woman(Ist) as Artist in Alice Walker's *The Temple of My Familiar.*" *American Studies in Scandinavia* 24, no. 1 (1992): 37–49.

———. "Womanizing Theory." *American Studies in Scandinavia* 30, no. 2 (1998): 43–49.

Juneja, Om P. "The Purple Colour of Walker Women: Their Journey from Slavery to Liberation." *The Literary Criterion* 25, no. 3 (1990): 66–76.

Kane, Patricia. "The Prodigal Daughter in Alice Walker's 'Everyday Use.'" *Notes on Contemporary Literature* 15, no. 2 (March 1985): 7.

Kanneh, Kadiatu. "'Africa' and Cultural Translation: Reading Difference." In *Cultural Readings of Imperialism: Edward Said and the Gravity of History,* edited by Keith Ansell-Perason, Benita Parry, and Judith Squires, 267–289. New York: St. Martin's, 1997.

Karanja, Ayana. "Zora Neal Hurston and Alice Walker: A Transcendent Relationship-*Jonah's Gourd Vine* and *The Color Purple.*" In *Alice Walker and Zora Neale Hurston: The Common Bond,* edited by Lillie P. Howard, 121–137. Westport, Conn.: Greenwood Press, 1993.

Karrer, Wolfgang. "Nostalgia, Amnesia, and Grandmothers: The Uses of Memory in Albert Murray, Sabine Ulibarri, Paula Gunn Allen, and Alice Walker." In *Memory, Narrative, and Identity: New Essays in Ethnic American Literatures,* edited by Amritjit Singh, Joseph T. Skerrett, Jr., and Robert E. Hogan, 128–144. Boston: Northeastern University Press, 1994.

Katz, Tamar. "'Show Me How to *Do* Like You': Didacticism and Epistolary Form in *The Color Purple.*" In *Modern Critical Views: Alice Walker,* edited by Harold Bloom, 185–193. New York: Chelsea House, 1989.

Keating, Gail. "Alice Walker: In Praise of Maternal Heritage." *Literary Griot: International Journal of Black Expressive Cultural Studies* 6, no. 1 (Spring 1994): 26–37.

Kelley, Margot Anne. "Sisters' Choices: Quilting Aesthetics in Contemporary African-American Women's Fiction." In *Alice Walker: "Everyday Use,"* edited by Barbara T. Christian, 167–194. New Brunswick, N.J.: Rutgers University Press, 1994.

Kelly, Erna. "A Matter of Focus: Men in the Margins of Alice Walker's Fiction." In *Critical Essays on Alice Walker,* edited by Ikenna Dieke, 171–183. Westport, Conn.: Greenwood Press, 1999.

Kelly, Ernece B. "Paths to Liberation in Alice Walker's *The Color Purple* (1982)." In *Women in Literature: Reading through the Lens of Gender,* edited by Jerilyn Fisher and Ellen S. Silber, 75–78. Westport, Conn.: Greenwood Press, 2003.

Kelly, Lori Duin. "Theology and Androgyny: The Role of Religion in *The Color Purple.*" *Notes on Contemporary Literature* 18, no. 2 (March 1988): 7–8.

Kenyon, Olga. "Alice Walker and Buchi Emecheta Rewrite the Myth of Motherhood." In *Forked Tongues?: Comparing Twentieth-Century British and American Literature,* edited by Ann Massa and Alistair Stead, 310–341. London: Longman, 1994.

Kester, Gunilla T. "The Blues, Healing, and Cultural Representation in Contemporary African American Women's Literature." In *Women Healers and Physicians: Climbing a Long Hill,* edited by Lilian R. Furst, 114–130. Lexington: University Press of Kentucky, 1997.

Kieti, Nwikali. "Homesick and Eurocentric? Alice Walker's Africa." In *Of Dreams Deferred, Dead or Alive: African Perspectives on African-American Writers,* edited by Femi Ojo-Ade, 157–170. Westport, Conn.: Greenwood Press, 1996.

Kim, Min-Jung. "'Creative Mistranslation?': Adaptation as Violence." *Feminist Studies in English Literature* 9, no. 2 (Winter 2002): 49–76.

———. "The Subversiveness of the Letters from Africa: Alice Walker's *The Color Purple.*" *Feminist Studies in English Literature* 8, no. 2 (Winter 2001): 105–129.

King, Lovalerie. "African American Womanism: From Zora Neale Hurston to Alice Walker." In *The Cambridge Companion to the African American Novel,* edited by Maryemma Graham, 233–252. Cambridge: Cambridge University Press, 2004.

Kirschner, Susan. "Alice Walker's Nonfictional Prose: A Checklist, 1966–1984." *Black American Literature Forum* 18, no. 4 (Winter 1984): 162–163.

Korenman, Joan S. "African-American Women Writers, Black Nationalism, and the Matrilineal Heritage." *CLA Journal* 38. 2 (December 1994): 143–161.

Krauth, Leland. "Mark Twain, Alice Walker, and the Aesthetics of Joy." *Proteus: A Journal of Ideas* 1, no. 2 (Fall 1984): 9–14.

Kubitschek, Missy Dehn. "Subjugated Knowledge: Toward a Feminist Exploration of Rape in Afro-American Fiction." In *Black Feminist Criticism and Critical Theory,* edited by Joe Weixlmann and Houston A. Baker, Jr. Greenwood, Fla.: Penkevill, 1988.

Kuhlmann, Deborah J. "Alice Walker's *Secret of Joy:* The Role of the Artist." *Griot: Official Journal of the Southern Conference on Afro-American Studies* 14, no. 2 (Fall 1995): 24–27.

Kuhne, Dave. "Alice Walker's African Connection." *Conference of College Teachers of English Studies* 63 (September 1998): 69–76.

Kunishiro, Tadao. "'So Much of Life in Its Meshes!': Alice Walker's *The Color Purple* and Zora Neale Hurston's *Their Eyes Were Watching God.*" *Marjorie Kinnan Rawlings Journal of Florida Literature* 7 (1996): 67–83.

Kusalik, Sheila Davis. "Making Connections: The Uses and Meaning of Needle Arts in *The Color Purple* and *The Mountain and the Valley.*" *Atlantis: A Women's Studies Journal/Revue d'Etudes Sur La Femme* 18, nos. 1–2 (Fall 1992–93): 212–216.

Kusunose, Keiko. "Bessie Head and Pan-Africanism." In *Migrating Words and Worlds: Pan-Africanism Updated,* edited by Anthony E. Hurley, Renée Larrier, and Joseph McLaren, 233–245. Trenton, N.J.: Africa World, 1999.

Lauret, Maria. *Alice Walker.* New York: St. Martin's, 1999.

———. "'I've Got a Right to Sing the Blues': Alice Walker's Aesthetic." In *Dixie Debates: Perspectives on Southern Culture,* edited by Richard H. King and Helen Taylor, 51–66. New York: New York University Press, 1996.

Leder, Priscilla. "Alice Walker's American Quilt: *The Color Purple* and American Literary Tradition." *JASAT (Journal of the American Studies Association of Texas)* 20 (October 1989): 79–93.

———. "In the Sight of God: Religious Illumination in Short Stories by Flannery O'Connor, Philip Roth, and Alice Walker." *Louisiana English Journal, New Series* 1, no. 2 (Spring 1994): 76–79.

Lee, Kyung Soon. "Black Feminism: *Sula* and *Meridian.*" *Journal of English Language and Literature* 38, no. 3 (Fall 1992): 585–599.

Lenhart, Georgann. "Inspired Purple?" *Notes on Contemporary Literature* 14, no. 3 (May 1984): 2–3.

Lester, Neal A. "'Not my mother, not my sister, but it's me, O Lord, standing . . .' : Alice Walker's 'The Child Who Favored Daughter' as Neo-Slave Narrative." *Studies in Short Fiction* 34, no. 3 (Summer 1997): 289–305.

Levin, Amy K. *Africanism and Authenticity in African-American Women's Novels.* Gainesville: University Press of Florida, 2003.

Levin, Tobe, and Freifrau von Gleichen. "Alice Walker, Activist: Matron of FORWARD." In *Black Imagination and the Middle Passage,* edited by Maria Diedrich, Henry Louis Gates, Jr., and Carl Pedersen, 240–254. Oxford: Oxford University Press, 1999.

Lewis, Catherine E. "Serving, Quilting, Knitting: Handicraft and Freedom in *The Color Purple* and 'A Women's Story.'" *Literature/Film Quarterly* 29, no. 3 (2001): 236–245.

Lewis, T. W. "Moral Mapping and Spiritual Guidance in *The Color Purple.*" *Soundings: An Interdisciplinary Journal* 73, nos. 2–3 (Summer–Fall 1990): 483–491.

Light, Alison. "Fear of the Happy Ending: *The Color Purple,* Reading and Racism." *Essays and Studies* 40 (1987): 103–117.

Lindberg-Seyersted, Brita. "Who is Nettie? and What is She Doing in Alice Walker's *The Color Purple.*" *American Studies in Scandinavia* 24, no. 2 (1992): 83–96.

Lioi, Anthony. "An End to Cosmic Loneliness: Alice Walker's Essays as Abolitionist Enchantment." *Isle: Interdisciplinary Studies in Literature and Environment* 15, no. 1 (Winter 2008): 11–37.

Loeb, Monica. "Walker's 'The Flowers.'" *Explicator* 55, no. 1 (Fall 1996): 60–62.

Lupton, Mary Jane. "Clothes and Closure in Three Novels by Black Women." *Black American Literature Forum* 20, no. 4 (Winter 1986): 409–421.

Lysik, Marta. "'You have seen how a [Wo]Man was made a Slave; You Shall See how a Slave was made a [Wo]Man': Alice Walker's *The Color Purple* as a Neo-Slave Narrative." *American Studies* 21 (2004): 17–34.

Mainino, Wirba Ibrahim. "The Problem of Language in Modern Feminist Fiction by Black Women: Alice Walker and Calix the Beyala." *New Literatures Review* 37 (Summer 2000): 59–74.

Manora, Yolanda M. "'Us': Southern Black Communal Subjectivity and Male Emergence in Alice Walker's *The Color Purple.*" *Southern Studies: An Interdisciplinary Journal of the South* 13, nos. 3–4 (Fall–Winter 2006): 77–99.

Manvi, Meera. "The Second Reconstruction and the Southern Writer: Alice Walker and William Kelley." In *Literature and Politics in Twentieth Century America,* edited by J. L. Plakkoottam and Prashant K. Sinha, 92–98. Hyderabad: American Studies Research Centre, 1993.

Manzulli, Mia. "Edith Wharton's Gardens as a Legacy to Alice Walker." *Edith Wharton Review* 11, no. 2 (Fall 1994): 9–12.

Marvin, Thomas F. "'Preachin' the Blues': Bessie Smith's Secular Religion and Alice Walker's *The Color Purple.*" *African American Review* 28, no. 3 (Fall 1994): 411–421.

Mason, Theodore O., Jr. "Alice Walker's *The Third Life of Grange Copeland:* The Dynamics of Enclosure." *Callaloo: A Journal of African American and African Arts and Letters* 12, no. 2 (Spring 1989): 297–309.

Mays, Jackie Douglas. "'Nineteen Fifty-Five': A Second Opinion." *Journal of College Writing* 4, no. 1 (2001): 103–106.

McDowell, Deborah E. "'The Changing Same': Generational Connections and Black Women Novelists." *New Literary History: A Journal of Theory and Interpretation* 18, no. 2 (Winter 1987): 281–302.

———. "The Self in Bloom: Alice Walker's *Meridian.*" *College Language Association Journal* 24, no. 3 (March 1981): 262–275.

McDowell, Margaret B. "The Black Woman as Artist and Critic: Four Versions." *Kentucky Review* 7, no. 1 (Spring 1987): 19–41.

McGowan, Martha J. "Atonement and Release in Alice Walker's *Meridian.*" *Critique: Studies in Contemporary Fiction* 23, no. 1 (1981): 25–36.

McKay, Nellie Y. "Alice Walker's 'Advancing Luna—and Ida B. Wells': A Struggle toward Sisterhood." In *Rape and Representation,* edited by Lynn A. Higgins and Brenda R. Silver, 248–262. New York: Columbia University Press, 1991.

McKenzie, Tammie. "*The Color Purple*'s Celie: A Journey of Selfhood." *College Teachers of English Studies* 51 (September 1986): 50–58.

McMillan, Laurie. "Telling a Critical Story: Alice Walker's *In Search of Our Mothers' Gardens.*" *Journal of Modern Literature* 28, no. 1 (Fall 2004): 107–123.

Menke, Pamela Glenn. "'Hard Glass Mirrors' and Soul Memory: Vision Imagery and Gender in Ellison, Baldwin, Morrison, and Walker." *West Virginia University Philological Papers* 38 (1992): 163–170.

Michlin, Monica. "Narrative as Empowerment: *Push* and the Signifying on Prior African-American Novels on Incest." *Études Anglaises: Grande-Bretagne, États-Unis* 59, no. 2 (April–June 2006): 170–185.

Mickelsen, David J. "'You Ain't Never Caught a Rabbit': Covering and Signifyin' in Alice Walker's 'Nineteen Fifty-Five.'" *Southern Quarterly: A Journal of the Arts in the South* 42, no. 3 (Spring 2004): 5–20.

Mogu, Francis Ibe. "The African Response to American Feminism: A Reading of Flora Nwapa and Alice Walker." In *Black Women Writers across Cultures: An Analysis of Their Contributions*, edited by Valentine Udoh James, et al., 89–102. Lanham, Md.: International Scholars, 2000.

Montelaro, Janet J. *Producing a Womanist Text: The Maternal as Signifier in Alice Walker's* The Color Purple. Victoria, B.C., Canada: University of Victoria, 1996.

Moore, Geneva Cobb. "Archetypal Symbolism in Alice Walker's *Possessing the Secret of Joy.*" *Southern Literary Journal* 33, no. 1 (Fall 2000): 111–121.

Morgan, Elizabeth. "Writing Our Way Out: The Cross-Cultural Dynamics of African Woman's Novels." *World Literature Written in English* 37, nos. 1–2 (1998): 102–113.

Morgan, Winifred. "Alice Walker: *The Color Purple* as Allegory." In *Southern Writers at Century's End*, edited by Jeffrey J. Folks and James A. Perkins, 177–184. Lexington: University Press of Kentucky, 1997.

Munro, C. Lynn. "In Search of Our Mothers' Gardens." *Black American Literature Forum* 18, no. 4 (Winter 1984): 161.

Nadel, Alan. "Reading the Body: Alice Walker's *Meridian* and the Archeology of Self." *MFS: Modern Fiction Studies* 34, no. 1 (Spring 1988): 55–68.

Nako, Nontasa. "Possessing the Voice of the Other: African Women and the Crisis of Representation in Alice Walker's *Possessing the Secret of Joy.*" *JENDA: A Journal of Culture and African Women Studies* 1, no. 2 (2001). Available online. URL: http://www.jendajournal.com/vol1.2nako.html. Accessed September 10, 2010.

Navarro, Mary L., and Mary H. Sims. "Settling the Dust: Tracking Zora through Alice Walker's 'The Revenge of Hannah Kemhuff.'" In *Alice Walker and Zora Neale Hurston: The Common Bond*, edited by Lillie P. Howard, 21–29. Westport, Conn.: Greenwood Press, 1993.

Nazareth, Peter. "Nineteen Fifty-Five: Alice, Elvis, and the Black Matrix." *JALA: Journal of the African Literature Association* 1, no. 2 (Summer–Fall 2007): 148–160.

Nedelhaft, Ruth. "Domestic Violence in Literature: A Preliminary Study." *Mosaic: A Journal of the Interdisciplinary Study of Literature* 17, no. 2 (Spring 1984): 242–259.

Newman, Georgia A. "Censorship and the Classroom." In *Ethics, Literature, Theory: An Introductory Reader*, edited by Stephen George, 329–338. Lanham, Md.: Rowman and Littlefield, 2005.

Niemi, Minna. "Challenging Pyschoanalysis: A Black Woman's Experience of Race, Class and Gender in Alice Walker's *Meridian.*" In *Close Encounters of an Other Kind: New Perspectives on Race, Ethnicity, and American Studies*, edited by Roy Goldblatt, Jopi Nyman, and John A. Stotesbury, 85–94. Joensuu, Finland: University of Joensuu, 2005.

Noe, Marcia, and Michael Jaynes. "Teaching Alice Walker's 'Everyday Use': Employing Race, Class, and Gender, with an Annotated Bibliography." *Eureka Studies in Teaching Short Fiction* 5, no. 1 (Fall 2004): 123–136.

Norman, Brian. *The American Protest Essay and National Belonging: Addressing Division.* Albany, N.Y.: State University of New York Press, 2007.

Nowik, Nan. "Mixing Art and Politics: The Writings of Adrienne Rich, Marge Piercy, and Alice Walker." *Centennial Review* 30, no. 2 (Spring 1986): 208–218.

O'Brien, John. *Interviews with Black Writers.* New York: Liveright, 1973.

———. "Interview with Alice Walker." In *Alice Walker: "Everyday Use,"* edited by Barbara T. Christian, 55–81. New Brunswick, N.J.: Rutgers University Press, 1994.

O'Connor, Mary. "Subject, Voice, and Women in Some Contemporary Black American Women's Writing." In *Feminism, Bakhtin, and the Dialogic*, edited by Dale M. Bauer and Susan Jaret McKinstry, 199–218. Albany: State University of New York Press, 1991.

Orkin, Joan, and Frank Rumboll. "*Fried Green Tomatoes* and the Colour Purple." *CRUX: A Journal on the Teaching of English* 28, no. 1 (February 1994): 37–40.

Oyewumi, Oyeronle. "Alice in Motherland: Reading Alice Walker on Africa and Screening the Colour 'Black.'" *JENDA: A Journal of Culture and African Women Studies* 1, no. 2 (2001). Available online. URL:

http://www.jendajournal.com/vol1.2/oyewumi.html. Accessed September 10, 2010.

Palumbo-Liu, David. "The Politics of Memory: Remembering History in Alice Walker and Joy Kogawa." In *Memory and Cultural Politics: New Approaches to American Ethnic Literatures,* edited by Amritjit Singh and Joseph T. Skerrett, Jr., 211–226. Boston: Northeastern University Press, 1996.

Panda, Prasanta Kumar. "Strategies of Intertextuality in Alice Walker's *The Temple of My Familiar.*" *New Quest* 124 (July–August 1997): 226–230.

Parmar, Pratibha. "Interview from Warrior Marks." In *Feminist Theory and the Body: A Reader,* edited by Janet Price and Margrit Shildrick, 302–307. New York: Routledge, 1999.

Payant, Katherine B. "Female Friendship in Contemporary Bildungsroman." In *Communication and Women's Friendships: Parallels and Intersections in Literature and Life,* edited by Janet Doubler Ward and JoAnna Stephens Mink, 151–163. Bowling Green, Ky.: Popular Press, 1993.

Petry, Alice Hall. "Alice Walker: The Achievement of the Short Fiction." *Modern Language Studies* 19, no. 1 (Winter 1989): 12–27.

Pezzulich, Evelyn. "Shifting Paradigms: The Reemergence of Literary Texts in Composition Classrooms." In *Teaching Composition/Teaching Literature: Cross Great Divides,* edited by Michelle M. Tokarcyzk and Irene Papoulis, 26–40. New York: Peter Lang, 2003.

Phillips, Rebecca. "The Thousand and First Face of the Hero." *Bulletin of the West Virginia Association of College English Teacher* 13, no. 2 (Fall 1991): 91–102.

Piacentino, Ed. "Reconciliation with Family in Alice Walker's 'Kindred Spirits.'" *Southern Quarterly: A Journal of the Arts in the South* 46 (Fall 2008): 91–99.

Pifer, Lynn. "Coming to Voice in Alice Walker's *Meridian:* Speaking Out for the Revolution." *African American Review* 26, no. 1 (Spring 1992): 77–88.

Pifer, Lynn, and Tricia Slusser. "'Looking at the Back of Your Head': Mirroring Scenes in Alice Walker's *The Color Purple* and *Possessing the Secret of Joy.*" *MELUS* 23, no. 4 (Winter 1998): 47–57.

Pollock, Kimberly Joyce. "A Continuum of Pain: A Woman's Legacy in Alice Walker's *Possessing the Secret of Joy.*" In *Women of Color: Mother-Daughter Relationships in 20th-Century Literature,* edited by Elizabeth Brown-Guillory, 38–56. Austin, Tex.: University of Texas Press, 1996.

Porter, Nancy. "Women's Interracial Friendships and Visions of Community in *Meridian, The Salt Eaters, Civil Wars,* and *Dessa Rose.*" In *Tradition and the Talents of Women,* edited by Florence Howe, 251–267. Urbana: University of Illinois Press, 1991.

Powers, Peter Kerry. "'Pa Is Not Our Pa': Sacred History and Political Imagination in *The Color Purple.*" *South Atlantic Review* 60, no. 2 (May 1995): 69–72.

———. *Recalling Religions: Resistance, Memory, and Cultural Revision in Ethnic Women's Literature.* Knoxville: University of Tennessee Press, 2001.

Pratt, Louis H. "Alice Walker's Men: Profiles in the Quest for Love and Personal Values." *Studies in Popular Culture* 12, no. 1 (1989): 42–57.

Preble-Niemi, Oralia. "Magical Realism and the Great Goddess in Two Novels by Alejo Carpentier and Alice Walker." *The Comparatist: Journal of the Southern Comparative Literature Association* 16 (May 1992): 101–114.

Premo, Cassie. "Lessons for Life in *Meridian* and *The Color Purple.*" *North Carolina Humanities* (Spring 1993): 35–45.

Proudfit, Charles. "Celie's Search for Identity: A Psychoanalytic Developmental Reading of Alice Walker's *The Color Purple.*" *Contemporary Literature* 32, no. 1 (Spring 1991): 12–37.

———. "A Century of Change: A Look at Contemporary Psychoanalytic Ego Psychology from the Perspectives of George Vaillant's *The Wisdom of the Ego* and Alice Walker's *The Color Purple.*" *Journal of Evolutionary Psychology* 19, nos. 1–2 (March 1998): 61–69.

Pu, Ruoqian. "On the Lesbian Love of Celie and Shug in Alice Walker's *The Color Purple.*" In *Re-Reading America: Changes and Challenges,* edited by Weihe Zhong and Rui Han, 372–376. Cheltenham, Eng.: Reardon, 2004.

Quashie, Kevin Everod. "Morrison's *Sula* and Alice Walker's *The Color Purple.*" *Meridians: Feminism, Race, Transnationalism* 2, no. 1 (2001): 187–217.

———. "The Other Dance as Self: Girlfriend Selfhood in Toni Morrison's *Sula* and Alice Walker's *The Color Purple.*" *Meridians: Feminism, Race, Transnationalism* 2, no. 1 (2001): 187–217.

Ray, Arunima. "The Quest for 'Home' and 'Wholeness' in *Sula* and *Meridian:* Afro-American Identity in Toni Morrison and Alice Walker." *Indian Journal of American Studies* 23, no. 2 (Summer 1993): 59–65.

Reckley, Ralph, Sr. "His/tory: The Black Male in Alice Walker's *The Temple of My Familiar.*" *MAWA Review* 6, no. 2 (December 1991): 19–22.

Reddy, Maureen T. "Maternal Reading: Lazarre and Walker." In *Narrating Mothers: Theorizing Maternal Subjectivities*, edited by Brenda O. Daly and Maureen T. Reddy, 222–238. Knoxville: University of Tennessee Press, 1991.

Restuccia, Frances L. "Literary Representations of Battered Women: Spectacular Domestic Punishment." In *Bodies of Writing, Bodies in Performance: New York*, edited by Thomas Foster, Carol Siegel, and Ellen E. Berry, 103–128. New York: New York University Press, 1996.

Richards, Constance S. *On the Winds and Waves of Imagination: Transnational Feminism and Literature.* New York: Garland, 2000.

Ridley, Chauncey. "Animism and Testimony in Alice Walker's *The Color Purple.*" *MAWA Review* 4, no. 2 (December 1989): 32–36.

Riley, Patricia. "Wrapped in the Serpent's Tail: Alice Walker's African-Native American Subjectivity." In *When Brer Rabbit Meets Coyote: African-Native American Literature*, edited by Jonathan Brennan, 241–256. Urbana: University of Illinois Press, 2003.

Robinson, Daniel. "Problems in Form: Alice Walker's *The Color Purple.*" *Notes on Contemporary Literature* 16, no. 1 (January 1986): 2.

Roden, Molly. "Alice Walker (1944– )." In *Contemporary African American Novelists: A Bio-Bibliographical Critical Sourcebook*, edited by Emmanuel S. Nelson and Deborah G. Plant, 458–468. Westport, Conn.: Greenwood Press, 1999.

Roemer, Astrid H., and Wanda Boeke. "Astrid H. Roemer Meets Alice Walker in Amsterdam." *Callaloo: A Journal of African American and African Arts and Letters* 12, no. 2 (Spring 1995): 242–243.

Ross, Daniel W. "Celie in the Looking Glass: The Desire for Selfhood in *The Color Purple.*" *MFS: Modern Fiction Studies* 34, no. 1 (Spring 1988): 69–84.

———. "The Making of Celie in Alice Walker's *The Color Purple.*" In *Teaching American Ethnic Literatures: Nineteen Essays*, edited by John R. Maitino and David R. Peck, 159–174. Albuquerque: University of New Mexico Press, 1996.

Royster, Philip M. "In Search of Our Fathers' Arms: Alice Walker's Persona of the Alienated Darling." *Black American Literature Forum* 20, no. 4 (Winter 1986): 347–370.

Sadoff, Dianne F. "Black Matrilineage: The Case of Alice Walker and Zora Neale Hurston." *Signs* 11, no. 1 (Fall 1985): 4–26.

Sample, Maxine. "Psychic Journeys and the Fragmented Self: Navigating Bessie Head's *A Question of Power* and Alice Walker's *Possessing the Secret of Joy.*" In *Fissions and Fusions*, edited by Lesley Marx, Loes Nas, and Lara Dunwell. Bellville, S. Africa: University of the Western Cape, 1997.

———. "Walker's *Possessing the Secret of Joy.*" *Explicator* 58, no. 3 (Spring 2000): 169–172.

Sanae, Tokziane. "Letters, Diaspora, and Home in *The Color Purple.*" In *Seeking the Self—Encountering the Other: Diasporic Narrative and the Ethics of Representation*, edited by Tuomas Huttunen, Jane Korkka, and Elina Valovirta, 276–290. Newcastle upon Tyne, Eng.: Cambridge Scholars, 2008.

Sauer, Hans. "The American Black English of Alice Walker's Novel *The Color Purple:* Its Structure and Status." *Poetica: An International Journal of Linguistic-Literary Studies* 42 (1994): 123–150.

Saunders, James Robert. "Womanism as the Key to Understanding Zora Neale Hurston's *Their Eyes Were Watching God* and Alice Walker's *The Color Purple.*" *The Hollins Critic* 25, no. 4 (October 1988): 1–11.

Scholl, Diane Gabrielsen. "With Ears to Hear and Eyes to See: Alice Walker's Parable *The Color Purple.*" *Christianity and Literature* 40, no. 3 (Spring 1991): 255–266.

Schomburg, Connie R. "Southern Women Writers in a Changing Landscape." In *The History of Southern Women's Literature*, edited by Carolyn Perry and Mary-Louise Weaks, 478–490. Baton Rouge: Louisiana State University Press, 2002.

Schwenk, Katrin. "Lynching and Rape: Border Cases in African American History and Fiction." In *The Black Columbiad: Defining Moments in African American Literature and Culture*, edited by Werner Sollors and Maria Diedrich, 312–324. Cambridge, Mass.: Harvard University Press, 1994.

Segrest, Mab. "Rebirths of a U.S. Nation: Race and Gendering of the Nation State." *Mississippi Quarterly: The Journal of Southern Cultures* 57, no. 1 (Winter 2003–04): 27–40.

Seidel, Kathryn Lee. "The Lilith Figure in Toni Morrison's *Sula* and Alice Walker's *The Color Purple.*" *Weber Studies: An Interdisciplinary Humanities Journal* 10, no. 2 (Spring–Summer 1993): 85–94.

Selzer, Linda. "Race and Domesticity in *The Color Purple.*" *African American Review* 29, no. 1 (Spring 1995): 67–82.

Sengupta, Ashis. "Search for Black Womanhood in Alice Walker's *Meridian.*" *New Quest* 106 (July–August 1994): 221–224.

Sevillano, Lilia Maria. "The Treatment of Women in Toni Morrison's *Song of Solomon* and Alice Walker's *The Color Purple:* A Feminist Reading." *Likha* 16, no. 1 (1995–96): 89–104.

Shattuc, Jane. "Having a Good Cry over *The Color Purple:* The Problem of Affect and Imperialism in Feminist Theory." In *Melodrama: Stage Picture Screen,* edited by Jacky Bratton, Jim Cook, and Christine Gledhill, 147–156. London: British Film Institute, 1994.

Showalter, Elaine. "Common Threads." In *Alice Walker: "Everyday Use,"* edited by Barbara T. Christian, 169–194. New Brunswick, N.J.: Rutgers University Press, 1994.

Sievers, Stefanie. "From 'Text as Quilt' to 'Quilt as Text': Alice Walker's Rewriting of *The Color Purple* as Film Script." In *Entwicklungslinien: 120 Jahre Anglistik in Halle,* edited by Wolf Kindermann, 130–143. Münster, Germany: LIT, 1997.

Sikorski, Grace. "Stepping into the Same River Twice: The Tragic Sexual Mulatto and Subversion of the Inside/Outside Dialectic in the Novels of E. Lynn Harris and Alice Walker." In *Straight Writ Queer: Non-Normative Expressions of Heterosexuality in Literature,* edited by Richard Fantina, 183–195. Jefferson, N.C.: McFarland, 2006.

Simcikova, Karla. "Life and Its Survival: Walker's New Religion in 'Now Is the Time to Open Your Heart.'" *Cuadernos De Literatura Inglesa y Norteamericana* 9, nos. 1–2 (May–November 2006): 37–46.

Smith, Barbara. "The Truth That Never Hurts: Black Lesbians in Fiction in the 1980s." In *Feminisms: An Anthology of Literary Theory and Criticism,* edited by Robyn R. Warhol and Diane Price Herndl, 784–806. New Brunswick, N.J.: Rutgers University Press, 1997.

Smith, Felipe. "Alice Walker's Redemptive Art." *African American Review* 26, no. 3 (Fall 1992): 437–451.

Smith, Pamela A. "Green Lap, Brown Embrace, Blue Body: The Ecospirituality of Alice Walker." *Cross Currents: The Journal of the Association for Religion and Intellectual Life* 48, no. 4 (Winter 1998–99): 471–487.

Smith-Wright, Geraldine. "Revision as Collaboration: Zora Neale Hurston's *Their Eyes Were Watching God* as Source for Alice Walker's *The Color Purple.*" *SAGE: A Scholarly Journal on Black Women* 4, no. 2 (Fall 1987): 20–25.

Sol, Adam. "Questions of Mastery in Alice Walker's *The Temple of My Familiar.*" *Critique: Studies in Contemporary Fiction* 43, no. 4 (Summer 2002): 393–404.

Souris, Stephen. "Multiperspectival Consensus: Alice Walker's *Possessing the Secret of Joy,* the Multiple Narrator Novel, and the Practice of 'Female Circumcision.'" *CLA Journal* 40, no. 4 (June 1997): 405–431.

Spencer, Helen Benjamin. "The Aristotelian Tradition in the Novels of Alice Walker: A Contemporary Application of the Five Canons." *Dissertation Abstracts International* 51, no. 3 (September 1990): 847A–848B.

Spillers, Hortense J. "'The Permanent Obliquity of an in(Pha)Llibly Straight': In the Time of the Daughters and the Fathers." In *Changing Our Own Words: Essays on Criticism, Theory, and Writing by Black Women,* edited by Cheryl A. Wall, 230–250. New Brunswick, N.J.: Rutgers University Press, 1989.

Stade, George. "Womanist Fiction and Male Characters." *Partisan Review* 52, no. 3 (1985): 264–270.

Stanford, Ann Folwell. "Dynamics of Change: Men and Co-Feeling in the Fiction of Zora Neale Hurston and Alice Walker." In *Alice Walker and Zora Neale Hurston: The Common Bond,* edited by Lillie P. Howard, 109–120. Westport, Conn.: Greenwood Press, 1993.

Stein, Karen F. "*Meridian:* Alice Walker's Critique of Revolution." *Black American Literature Forum* 20, nos. 1–2 (Spring–Summer 1986): 129–141.

Tally, Justine. "Black Women's Studies in the 1980s: An Interview with Beverly Guy-Sheftall." *Revista Canaria de Estudios Ingleses* 10 (April 1985): 195–204.

———. "Personal Development in the Fictional Women of Alice Walker." *Revista Canaria de Estudios Ingleses* 13–14 (April 1987): 181–196.

Tapia, Elena. "Symmetry as Conceptual Metaphor in Walker's *The Color Purple.*" *International Journal of English Studies* 3, no. 1 (2003): 29–44.

Tate, Claudia. "Alice Walker." In *Black Women Writers at Work,* edited by Claudia Tate, 175–187. New York: Continuum, 1983.

Tavormina, M. Teresa. "Dressing the Spirit: Clothworking and Language in *The Color Purple.*" *Journal of Narrative Technique* 16, no. 3 (Fall 1986): 220–230.

Terry, Jill. "The Same River Twice: Signifying *The Color Purple*." *Critical Survey* 12, no. 3 (2000): 59–76.

Tharp, Julie. "Ideology and Eros: An Approach to Writing by Women of Color." *West Virginia University Philological Papers* 38 (1992): 236–245.

Thielmann, Pia. "Alice Walker and the 'Man Question.'" In *Critical Essays on Alice Walker,* edited by Ikenna Dieke, 67–82. Westport, Conn.: Greenwood Press, 1999.

Thomas, H. Nigel. "Alice Walker's Grange Copeland as a Trickster Figure." *Obsidian II: Black Literature in Review* 6, no. 1 (Spring 1991): 60–72.

Thomas, Jackie. "Reverend Samuel: The Missionary Minister in *The Color Purple*." *Griot: Official Journal of the Southern Conference of Afro-American Studies* 16, no. 2 (Fall 1997): 15–18.

Thyreen, Jeannine. "Alice Walker's *The Color Purple:* Redefining God and (Re)Claiming the Spirit Within." *Christianity and Literature* 49, no. 1 (Autumn 1999): 49–66.

Toombs, Veronica M. "Deconstructing Violence against Women: William Faulkner's *Sanctuary* and Alice Walker's *Possessing the Secret of Joy*." In *The Image of Violence in Literature, the Media, and Society,* edited by Will Wright and Steven Kaplan, 212–217. Pueblo: University of Southern Colorado, 1995.

Torsney, Cheryl B. "'Everyday Use': My Sojourn at Parchman Farm." In *The Intimate Critique: Autobiographical Literary Criticism,* edited by Diane P. Freedman, Olivia Frey, and Frances Murphy Zauhar, 67–74. Durham, N.C.: Duke University Press, 1993.

Tucker, Lindsey. "Alice Walker's *The Color Purple:* Emergent Woman, Emergent Text." *Black American Literature Forum* 22, no. 1 (Spring 1988): 81–95.

Turner, Daniel E. "Cherokee and Afro-American Interbreeding in *The Color Purple*." *Notes on Contemporary Literature* 21, no. 5 (November 1991): 10–11.

Turner, Darwin. "A Spectrum of Blackness." *Parnassus: Poetry in Review* 4, no. 2 (1976): 202–218.

Tuten, Nancy. "Alice Walker's 'Everyday Use.'" *Explicator* 51, no. 2 (Winter 1993): 125–128.

Ulman, H. Lewis. "Seeing, Believing, Being, and Acting: Ethics and Self-Representation in Ecocriticism and Nature Writing." In *Reading the Earth: New Directions in the Study of Literature and Environment,* edited by Michael P. Branch, et al., 225–233. Moscow: University of Idaho Press, 1998.

Uwakweh, Pauline Ada. "Female Choices: The Militant Option in Buchi Emecheta's Destination Biafra and Alice Walker's *Meridian*." *Bulletin: A Publication of the African Literature Association* 23, no. 1 (Winter 1997): 47–59.

Vega, Susana. "Surviving the Weight of Tradition: Alice Walker's *Possessing the Secret of Joy*." *Journal of American Studies of Turkey* 5 (Spring 1997): 19–26.

Viswanathan, Meera, and Evangelina Mancikam. "Is Black Woman to White as Female is to Male? Restoring Alice Walker's Womanist Prose to the Heart of Feminist Literary Criticism." *Indian Journal of American Studies* 28, nos. 1–2 (Winter–Summer 1998): 15–20.

Wade-Gayles, Gloria. "Black, Southern, Womanist: The Genius of Alice Walker." In *Southern Women Writers: The New Generation,* edited by Tonette Bond Inge, 301–323. Tuscaloosa: University of Alabama Press, 1990.

Wainwright, Mary Katherine. "'Through Different Eyes': The Aesthetics of Community in the Texts of Zora Neale Hurston, Toni Morrison, and Alice Walker." *Dissertation Abstracts International* 30, no. 9 (March 1990): 2,901A.

Walker, Alice, and Clarissa Pinkola Estes. "Ungovernable Women: A Conversation between Alice Walker and Clarrisa Pinkola Estes, Speaking of Their Ancestors, Raising Children and Writing, and What Matters about the Broken Heart." *Bloomsbury Review* 21, no. 6 (November–December 2001): 17–19.

Walker, Charlotte Zoë. "A Saintly Reading of Nature's Text." *Bucknell Review: A Scholarly Journal of Letters, Arts and Sciences* 44, no. 1 (2000): 43–55.

Walker, Robbie Jean, et al. "Implications for Survival: Coping Strategies of the Women in Alice Walker's Novels." *Explorations in Ethnic Studies: The Journal of the National Association for Ethnic Studies* 10, no. 1 (January 1987): 9–24.

Wall, Cheryl A. *Worrying the Line: Black Women Writers, Lineage, and Literary Tradition.* Chapel Hill: University of North Carolina Press, 2005.

Wall, Wendy. "Lettered Bodies and Corporeal Texts in *The Color Purple*." *Studies in American Fiction* 16, no. 1 (Spring 1988): 83–97.

———. "Poetry as Preface to Fiction: Alice Walker's Recurrent Apprenticeship." *Mississippi Quarterly: The Journal of Southern Culture* 44, no. 2 (Spring 1991): 133–142.

Walsh, Margaret. "The Enchanted World of *The Color Purple.*" *Southern Quarterly: A Journal of the Arts in the South* 25, no. 2 (Winter 1987): 89–101.

Walter, Roland. "The Dialectics between the Act of Writing and the Act of Reading in Alice Walker's *The Temple of My Familiar,* Gloria Naylor's *Mama Day* and Toni Morrison's *Jazz.*" *Southern Quarterly: A Journal of the Arts in the South* 35, no. 3 (Spring 1997): 55–66.

Walton, Priscilla L. "'What She Got to Sing About?': Comedy and *The Color Purple.*" *ARIEL: A Review of International English Literature* 21, no. 2 (April 1990): 59–74.

Ward, Cynthia. "Reading African Women Readers." *Research in African Literatures* 27, no. 3 (Fall 1996): 78–86.

Warhol, Robyn R. "How Narration Produces Gender: Femininity as Affect and Effect in Alice Walker's *The Color Purple.*" *Narrative* 9, no. 2 (May 2001): 182–187.

Warren, Nagueyalti. "Resistant Mothers in Alice Walker's *Meridian* and Tina McElroy Ansa's *Ugly Ways.*" In *Southern Mothers: Fact and Fictions in Southern Women's Writing,* edited by Nagueyalti Warren and Sally Wolff, 182–203. Baton Rouge: Louisiana State University Press, 1999.

Warren, Nagueyalti, and Sally Wolff. "'Like the Pupil of an Eye': Sexual Blinding of Women in Alice Walker's Works." *Southern Literary Journal* 31, no. 1 (Fall 1998): 1–16.

Washington, J. Charles. "Positive Black Male Images in Alice Walker's Fiction." *Obsidian II: Black Literature in Review* 3, no. 1 (Spring 1988): 23–48.

Washington, Mary Helen. "Black Women Image Makers." *Black World* 23, no. 10 (1974): 10–18.

———. "An Essay on Alice Walker." In *Sturdy Black Bridges: Vision of Black Women in Literature,* edited by Roseann P. Bell, Bettye J. Parker, and Beverly Guy-Sheftall, 85–104. Garden City, N.Y.: Doubleday (Anchor), 1979.

———. "I Sign My Mother's Name: Alice Walker, Dorothy West, Paule Marshall." In *Mothering the Mind: Twelve Studies of Writers and Their Silent Partners,* edited by Ruth Perry and Martine Watson Brownley, 142–163. New York: Holmes and Meier, 1984.

Washington, Teresa N. "Power of the Word/Power of the Works: The Signifying Soul of Africana Women's Literature." *FEMSPEC: An Interdisciplinary Feminist Journal Dedicated to Critical and Creative Work in the Realms of Science Fiction, Fantasy, Magical Realism, Surrealism, Myth, Folklore, and Other Supernatural Genres* 6, no. 1 (2005): 58–70.

Wasserman, Jerry. "Queen Bee, King Bee: *The Color Purple* and the Blues." *Canadian Review of American Studies/Revue Canadienne d'Etudes Americaines* 30, no. 2 (2000): 301–316.

Waters-Dawson, Emma. "From Victim to Victor: Walker's Women in *The Color Purple.*" In *The Aching Hearth: Family Violence in Life and Literature,* edited by Sara Munson Deats and Lagretta Tallent Lenker, 255–268. New York: Plenum, 1991.

Watson, Reginald. "Negative Male Imagery in Zora Neale Hurston's *Their Eyes Watching God* and Alice Walker's *The Third Life of Grange Copeland.*" *MAWA Review* 14, no. 1 (June 1999): 9–23.

———. "The Power of the 'Milk' and Motherhood: Images of Deconstruction in Toni Morrison's *Beloved* and Alice Walker's *The Third Life of Grange Copeland.*" *CLA Journal* 48, no. 2 (December 2004): 156–182.

Waxman, Barbara Frey. "Dancing out of Form, Dancing into Self: Genre and Metaphor in Marshall, Shange, and Walker." *MELUS* 19, no. 3 (Fall 1994): 91–106.

Weisenburger, Steven C. "Errant Narrative and *The Color Purple.*" *Journal of Narrative Technique* 19, no. 3 (Fall 1989): 257–275.

Weston, Ruth D. "Inversion of Patriarchal Mantle Images in Alice Walker's *Meridian.*" *Southern Quarterly: A Journal of the Arts in the South* 25, no. 2 (Winter 1987): 102–107.

———. "Who Touches This Touches a Woman: The Naked Self in Alice Walker." *Weber Studies: An Interdisciplinary Humanities Journal* 9, no. 2 (Spring–Summer 1992): 49–60.

White, Evelyn C. "Alice Walker's Compassionate Crusade." *Sojourner: The Women's Forum* 19, no. 7 (March 1994): 1H–2H.

———. *Alice Walker: A Life.* New York: Norton, 2004.

White, Vernessa C. *Afro-American and East German Fiction.* New York: Lang, 1983.

Whitsitt, Sam. "In Spite of It All: A Reading of Alice Walker's 'Everyday Use.'" *African American Review* 34, no. 3 (Fall 2000): 443–459.

Whitt, Jan. "What Happened to Celie and Idgie? 'Apparitional Lesbians' in American Film." *Studies in Popular Culture* 27, no. 3 (April 2005): 43–57.

Williams, Carolyn. "'Trying to Do without God': The Revision of Epistolary Address in *The Color Purple.*" In *Writing the Female Voice: Essays on*

*Epistolary Literature,* edited by Elizabeth Goldsmith, 273–285. Boston: Northeastern University Press, 1989.

Williams, Delores S. "Black Women's Literature and the Task of Feminist Theology." In *Immaculate and Powerful: The Female in Sacred Image and Social Reality,* edited by Clarissa W. Atkinson, Constance H. Buchanan, and Margaret R. Miles, 88–110. Boston: Beacon, 1985.

Willis, Susan. "Alice Walker's Women." *New Orleans Review* 12, no. 1 (Spring 1985): 33–41.

Wilson, Charles E. "'Everyday Use' and Incidents in the Life of a Slave Girl: Escaping Antebellum Confinement." In *Southern Mothers: Fact and Fictions in Southern Women's Writing,* edited by Nagueyalti Warren and Sally Wolff, 169–181. Baton Rouge: Louisiana State University Press, 1999.

Wilson, Mary Ann. "That Which the Soul Lives By': Spirituality in the Works of Zora Neale Hurston and Alice Walker." In *Alice Walker and Zora Neale Hurston: The Common Bond,* edited by Lillie P. Howard, 57–68. Westport, Conn.: Greenwood Press, 1993.

Wilson, Sharon. "A Conversation with Alice Walker." *Kalliope: Journal of Women's Art* 6, no. 2 (1984): 37–45.

Winchell, Donna Haisty. "Alice Walker." In *American Novelists since World War II: Third Series,* edited by James R. Giles and Wanda H. Giles, 277–294. Detroit: Gale, 1994.

Winchell, Mark Royden. "Fetching the Doctor: Shamanistic House Calls in Alice Walker's 'Strong Horse Tea.'" *Mississippi Folk Register* 15, no. 2 (Fall 1981): 97–101.

Wisker, Gina. "'Disremembered and Unaccounted For': Reading Toni Morrison's *Beloved* and Alice Walker's *The Temple of My Familiar.*" In *Black Women's Writing,* edited by Gina Wisker, 78–95. New York: St. Martin's, 1993.

Woll, Allen. "*The Color Purple:* Translating the African American Novel for Hollywood." In *Twentieth-Century American Fiction on Screen,* edited by R. Barton Palmer, 191–201. Cambridge: Cambridge University Press, 2007.

Woods, Paula L. "Writing, Activism, and Coming-of-Age Tales." *High Plains Literary Review* 12, no. 2 (Fall 1997): 119–124.

Worsham, Fabian Clements. "The Poetics of Matrilineage: Mothers and Daughters in the Poetry of African American Women, 1965–1985." In *Women of Color: Mother-Daughter Relationships in 20th Century Literature,* edited by Elizabeth Brown-Guillory, 117–131. Austin: University of Texas Press, 1996.

Wurst, Gayle. "Cultural Stereotypes and the Language of Identity: Margaret Atwood's *Lady Oracle,* Maxine Hong Kingston's *The Woman Warrior,* and Alice Walker's *The Color Purple.*" In *Cross-Cultural Studies: American, Canadian and European Literatures: 1945–1985,* edited by Mirko Jurak, 53–64. Ljubljana, Slovenia: English Department of Filozofska Fakulteta, 1988.

Yeo, Jae-Hyu. "Alice Walker: Community, Quilting and Sewing." *Studies in Modern Fiction* 8, no. 2 (Winter 2001): 111–135.

Yoon, Seongho. "Gendering the Movement: Black Womanhood, SNCC, and Post–Civil Rights Anxieties in Alice Walker's *Meridian.*" *Feminist Studies in English Literature* 14, no. 2 (Winter 2006): 179–207.

Zinn, Howard. "Howard Zinn Talks with Alice Walker." *Brick* 53 (Winter 1996): 14–21.

# INDEX

**Boldface** entries and page numbers indicate major treatment of a topic. *Italic* page numbers denote photos or illustrations.

## A

## D



## E



## F

## G

## M

## N

## O



## P

## Q



## R